SENTENCE PROCESSING:
Psycholinguistic Studies
Presented to Merrill Garrett

SENTENCE PROCESSING:
Psycholinguistic Studies
Presented to Merrill Garrett

EDITED BY
WILLIAM E. COOPER
Harvard University

EDWARD C. T. WALKER
Massachusetts Institute of Technology

 LAWRENCE ERLBAUM ASSOCIATES, PUBLISHERS
1979   Hillsdale, New Jersey

DISTRIBUTED BY THE HALSTED PRESS DIVISION OF
JOHN WILEY & SONS
New York   Toronto   London   Sydney

Lawrence Erlbaum Associates, Inc., Publishers
365 Broadway
Hillsdale, New Jersey 07642

Distributed solely by Halsted Press Division
John Wiley & Sons, Inc., New York

Library of Congress Cataloging in Publication Data

Main entry under title:

Sentence processing.

Includes indexes.
1. Speech perception. 2. Human information
processing. I. Garrett, Merrill F. II. Cooper,
William E. III. Walker, Edward C. T.
BF455.S43   153   79-12024
ISBN 0-470-26731-3

Printed in the United States of America

Contents

Preface

Merrill Garrett's published work reveals an abiding interest in the mental states and processes that underlie sentence perception and production. The diversity of his collaborators in this work demonstates not only the scope of his scientific interest, but also the scrupulous integrity with which he has given intellectual credit in his scholarly undertakings.

What the published record does not reveal directly is the profound personal and scientific impact of Merrill's work and collaboration on those who are engaged in the study of language. The authors of this book hope that by dedicating this collection of papers to him, they will have begun to acknowledge Merrill's influence at a time when he persists in having it.

The book begins and ends with theoretical discussion, and it encompasses an extensive and varied body of experiments and observations dealing with all aspects of sentence processing. In this, the authors had only to observe the principle that their writings reflect Merrill's own scientific stance. We hope, however, that in addition to demonstrating the extent and pervasiveness of his scientific influence, we will have marked in print our deep appreciation of the difference Merrill Garrett has made to us—as colleague, teacher, and friend—throughout his career.

WILLIAM E. COOPER
EDWARD C. T. WALKER

SENTENCE PROCESSING:
Psycholinguistic Studies
Presented to Merrill Garrett

1 The Wherefores and Therefores of the Competence–Performance Distinction

Virginia Valian
CUNY Graduate Center

INTRODUCTION

How has it happened that the competence–performance distinction has come to be seen as invalid, or if valid, irrelevant, or if relevant, actually harmful to psycholinguistic research? This paper suggests three reasons for the present obloquy of the competence–performance distinction. (a) The grammar of a language does not have an automatic performance interpretation. That is, a model of competence does not contain a specification of a model of performance and does not entail a particular model of performance. (b) Candidate grammars keep changing. (c) In response to these two difficulties, psycholinguists have attempted to specify performance independently of competence. To the extent that they have been successful, they have suggested that the distinction between competence and performance is unnecessary and that competence itself is not a useful notion.

This paper begins with some definitions and then presents a sociohistorical review of the competence–performance distinction. Two conclusions can be drawn. First, since the competence–performance distinction is a logical one, all psycholinguistic theories observe it, although they differ in what they take the content of competence to be. Second, most arguments about whether there is a distinction between competence and performance have been over other issues.

Chomsky (1965) has equated competence with knowledge and performance with use. Stated in that general form, the distinction is applicable to any area of psychology where it is assumed that the person has knowledge *of* something or *that* something. In the case of syntax, a person has knowledge of

1

a language; the knowledge consists, by hypothesis, of rules which, in various combinations, predict the syntactic properties and relations of sentences and parts of sentences. In the case of logic, to take another example, knowledge may consist of rules of inference predicting certain logical relations that hold among statements. Even more generally, people know facts that they use in solving problems, making decisions, answering questions, and so on. I refer to the distinction between knowledge and use as the *general* distinction.

As Chomsky (1977a) points out, all psychologists observe the general distinction. It could not be otherwise, because the distinction is not an empirical matter, but a logical one. No data could be brought to bear on the *general* distinction, any more than data could be brought to bear on the distinction between knowledge by acquaintance (i.e., knowledge through direct experience) and knowledge by description (i.e., knowledge at second-hand, see Russell, 1912).

What is an empirical matter is the character of the knowledge (if any), and the character of the device that accesses and uses the knowledge. (Similarly, it is largely an empirical matter which knowledge is by acquaintance, which by description, and which is perhaps from another source.) With respect to syntax and logic, it is a question of empirical fact whether people's syntactic knowledge takes the form specified in the syntactic component of a transformational grammar, and a matter of empirical fact whether a predicate calculus characterizes a portion of people's logical knowledge.

A transformational grammar is a particular hypothesis about what form linguistic knowledge takes. Many particular hypotheses are possible. For example, transformational grammars in which the semantic component interprets the syntactic component claim that a syntactic level exists called *deep structure*; generative semantics theories claim that there is no such level. That dispute is a dispute over how competence should be characterized, not a dispute over whether there is such a thing as competence. A similar dispute is over whether a grammar should include information about sex of the speaker or other "social" generalizations that interact with sentence acceptability. The dispute in such cases is over *how* to draw the competence–performance distinction not over *whether* to draw it. The class of theories including the standard theory, the extended standard theory, the revised extended theory, and so on draws the competence–performance distinction in a *particular* way in that all the theories in the class label some generalizations extralinguistic, and, within linguistic generalizations, label some syntactic, some semantic, and some phonological. I refer to the distinction between knowledge and use as characterized by most transformational grammars as the *particular* distinction.

To summarize, the general distinction between competence and performance is a conceptual one and impervious to data. The particular distinction is a question of theory and evidence. Disagreements about how to draw the distinction do not bear on the existence of the general distinction.

If competence refers to knowledge and a linguistic theory is one claim about the nature of that knowledge, what does performance refer to? Performance refers to how knowledge is used. In the psycholinguistic literature it is common to restrict performance to behavior on particular tasks, such as speed to detect a phoneme within different sentence structures (Foss & Lynch, 1969), or accuracy in detecting a nonspeech noise in sentences as a function of distance from constituent boundaries (Fodor & Bever, 1965; Garrett, 1965). If a particular linguistic rule or structure is functional in such an experiment, psycholinguists call it *psychologically real.* Put another way, if a linguistic entity must be referred to to explicate an aspect of behavior, it is called *psychologically real* and held to be relevant to performance.

Within Chomsky's definition (Chomsky, 1965, 1975, 1977a), however, it is incorrect to limit the term *psychologically real* to a narrow class of performance tasks; the notion of performance must include any and all forms of possible performance, including the act of having intuitions. A linguistic entity is psychologically real if it is part of knowledge. It would be strange if knowledge were never put to use, but it is logically possible, because the relevant situation might never arise. (For example, I know the meaning of the word *ruching,* but I may never be called upon to perform a task making use of that knowledge.) By Chomsky's definition, the correct linguistic theory characterizes knowledge. Because knowledge is mental or psychological, the correct linguistic theory is also a psychological theory.[1] Linguistic entities are psychologically real if they correctly characterize competence. I henceforth avoid the term *psychological reality* and use the term *performance,* or *use,* to include any and all performance data that require reference to linguistic entities for their explanation (so as to distinguish them from nonspeech performances like bicycle riding).

Thus far, competence and performance are each unproblematic, as is the distinction between them. I suggest that the difficulties involved in constructing a psycholinguistic theory have led some to the invalid conclusion that the distinction is problematic. As mentioned earlier, there have been two main difficulties in constructing a performance model. The first is that a theory of knowledge does not entail a particular theory of use. Essentially this point was made by Fodor and Garrett (1966). Transformational grammar entails the dismissal of some use theories; e.g., a theory stating that people have stored thousands of sentences and pick the one they need for each speaking occasion. Knowledge imposes constraints on use. Within the constraints imposed by knowledge, however, is an extremely large range of

---

[1]A separate question is whether a grammar should be taken to be, as Chomsky proposes, a specification of competence, in addition to being a theory of a language. Katz (1978), for example, puts forward a Platonist view of grammar, in which a grammar is only a theory of a language. Another theory will characterize competence or knowledge of grammar. Even on a Platonist view, knowledge is distinct from use.

use theories. There is no automatic performance interpretation for a model of competence.

The second difficulty compounds the first. The candidate transformational grammar of English changed dramatically from 1957 to 1965, and since 1965 there have been many candidate transformational grammars. A use theory must be compatible with the correct knowledge theory; it must make room for the entities that a correct knowledge theory posits. For a psycholinguist the difficulty is extreme uncertainty about what linguistic structures and rules to accommodate within a use theory.

Both difficulties are inherent in any applied science. In response to the difficulties, psycholinguists have tried to constrain use and knowledge theories from the use end. By finding out more facts about performance, the reasoning goes, we can constrain what a performance model should look like. The projected performance model, the reasoning continues, will be also compatible with only some linguistic entities and will therefore constrain what a competence model should look like.

The reasoning is correct and is a good research strategy. Adopting it is not logically tantamount to dismissing the competence–performance distinction, but one unfortunate by-product of its application has been the dismissal of the distinction and the dismissal of transformational grammar as a model of competence. It also has a built-in danger. If performance is construed narrowly, to include only a subset of linguistic behaviors, the wrong projection will be made to a competence model as well as to a performance model.

DERIVATIONAL THEORY OF COMPLEXITY, PRO AND CON

Early psycholinguistic theory (Miller, 1962) proposed a close, direct connection between a model of competence and a model of sentence perception, one component of a model of performance. The theory came to be called the *derivational theory of complexity* (DTC). Every grammatical transformation between deep and surface structure represented a computation that listeners made in reverse in order to uncover the deep structure of a sentence. The computations were presumed to occur serially, so that total computation time would be some function of the individual computations.

The theoretical advantage of DTC lay both in its simplicity and in the fact that it provided a principle for a performance interpretation of the grammar: every grammatical operation corresponded to a real-time psychological operation. A further point is that the proposal was plausible in that it assumed that important listening operations, such as semantic analysis, were calculated over deep structure. Since the grammar relates deep and surface structure by transformations, a reasonable first hypothesis was that the processing mechanism did also.

If DTC is incorrect, it is incorrect as a model of performance. From the falsity of DTC nothing would follow about whether a particular linguistic entity is or is not a feature of a model of competence. Nothing even follows about whether that entity is a feature of a correct model of performance. Transformations, for example, might properly play a role in a model of performance; the falsity of DTC would show it could not be *that* model.

The history of DTC has been reviewed in many places (e.g., Fodor, Bever, & Garrett, 1974), so only a brief summary is presented here. The initial experiments that tested DTC were confirmatory (Mehler, 1963; Miller, 1962; Miller & McKean, 1964; Savin & Perchonock, 1965; Slobin, 1963), although later work has failed to replicate some of the earlier studies (Matthews, 1968) or has suggested alternative nonsyntactic explanations for the effects (Epstein, 1969; Glucksberg & Danks, 1969). It should be noted, however, that no experiment "disproved" DTC, and as a first approximation DTC may be correct.

More important than the experimental results was the change in the type of transformational grammar proposed for English. DTC had been based on the 1957 grammar, in which negatives, questions, and passives were derived from active affirmative declarative strings. The theoretical changes resulting in the 1965 grammar meant that DTC was still a possible theory, but for a different set of sentences than those to which it was originally applied. What had previously appeared to be a homogeneous set of sentences (homogeneous in that they were all transformationally related to the same deep structure) was now a mixed collection. There was still a theory, and still a set of results, but the theory (updated to accommodate the 1965 grammar) was no longer applicable to the results.[2]

Fodor and Garrett (1966) make two important arguments about DTC and its implications for psycholinguistic theories. They suggest that a more abstract relation exists between a model of competence and a model of performance than DTC proposes and that structural descriptions are psychologically real, but transformations are not. They support their claim for the psychological reality of structural descriptions (by which they mean the deep and surface structure pair) by noting that listeners must have access to

---

[2]Fodor, Bever, and Garrett (1974) point out that DTC, properly applied, would not even have predicted the obtained results with a 1957 grammar. For example, in converting a passive (P) to a passive question (PQ), only one transformation is required; but in converting a question (Q) to a PQ, three transformations are required. This is because the passive transformation must occur before the question transformation. Thus, a P can be directly converted to a PQ, but a Q must first be converted to a declarative, then to a P, then to a PQ. The obtained results do not show conversion of a Q to a PQ to be three times as hard as conversion of a P to a PQ nor was that asymmetry predicted, but it should have been.

structural descriptions in order to judge the ambiguity, grammaticality, and so on, of word strings. They support their claim for the nonreality of transformations by noting that not all examples of apparent greater transformational complexity are paralleled by greater perceptual complexity.[3]

Fodor and Garrett also note that there is no reason to expect isomorphism between the linguistic steps of generating a sentence and the steps of the listener's processing mechanism. The listener could use different rules to represent the same information that the grammar represents by using phrase structure rules and transformations.[4]

Fodor and Garrett's (1966) claim that transformations are not psychologically real only holds if psychological reality is equated with performance on a small set of tasks. Because that equation is not justified neither is the claim that transformations are not psychologically real. The justifiable claim is, at most, that people can perform many linguistic tasks without (implicitly) referring to transformations or intermediate phrase structures, i.e., without constructing a full derivation of the sentence being responded to.

Fodor and Garrett (1966) correctly infer that a performance model requiring that people always generate a full derivation of a sentence, no matter what the linguistic task, will be incorrect. (Since DTC was not spelled out thoroughly, it is not clear if it made such a claim about talker–listeners.) An "abstract" relation between competence and performance then means, simply, that a performance model is not a device that, in producing speech, always generates sentences from an initial S symbol nor one that, in understanding speech, always generates derivations from a surface string. It does not mean that a competence model is not "incorporated" in a performance model; it means that not all aspects of a competence model are used in every example of performance.

---

[3]Some of the "negative" experiments Fodor and Garrett (1966) cite (e.g., the ease of short over full passives, of adjectives over relatives) are no longer relevant, because the putative derivations of the sentences involved have changed. (For example, short passives are not derived from full passives, so that they would not have more transformations, and, therefore, DTC would not predict them to be more difficult psychologically.) Modifications in transformational grammar have frequently had the effect of eliminating the psychologically negative cases, although that was not their aim.

[4]Both Fodor and Garrett (1966) and Bever (1970) split structural descriptions and grammatical "operations" as if structural descriptions were not themselves the output of grammatical operations or rules. In addition to proposing rules or strategies to replace transformations as a means of arriving at deep structure from a surface string, they must also propose rules to replace the phrase structure rules that determine constituent structure. In trace theory, the surface phrase marker provides all the information needed by the semantic and phonological components. It does so, however, because traces of all transformations that deform structure in ways that are relevant to semantic interpretations remain as clues to grammatical relations. It is not clear what consequences trace theory would have for Fodor and Garrett's attempted split between rules and structures.

Yet, Fodor and Garrett (1966) conclude that a performance model need not incorporate a competence model; what is left out of the performance model, in their view, is transformations. Their conclusion, however, would follow only if transformations were *never* exploited in a linguistic task. The existence of intuitions indicates that transformations are sometimes exploited, and in the concluding section I discuss other tasks that implicate transformations. Only under one interpretation of "abstract" is the relation between competence and performance, as Fodor and Garrett claimed, abstract: people do not construct a full derivation of a sentence in all linguistic tasks.

Fodor and Garrett (1966) can be interpreted as pointing out the first difficulty mentioned in the introduction, that there is no automatic performance interpretation of the grammar. Although Fodor and Garrett may have construed the concepts of psychological reality and performance too narrowly, such that some of their conclusions do not follow, their primary point holds. There is an abstract (i.e., indirect) relation between competence and performance.

WATT

Watt (1970), like Fodor and Garrett, also concludes that a performance model should not be thought to be isomorphic to a transformational grammar, but he goes on to propose a different relation between grammar and performance. Watt takes the lack of correspondence between transformational grammar and psychological operations to be an argument for the postulation of two grammars, one of which is an abstract linguistic grammar, taking a transformational form, the other a mental grammar, to which psychological operations would correspond.

Watt (1970) proposes that a linguistic grammar not be identified with a mental grammar because of the same sorts of evidence that Fodor and Garrett considered.[5] Whereas the evidence led Fodor and Garrett to argue for an abstract relation between grammar and performance, it leads Watt to propose a direct relation between a mental grammar and performance and nonidentity between a mental grammar and a linguistic grammar. Watt accepts what Fodor and Garrett specifically reject, that there should be a direct correspondence between grammar and performance. Since the evidence and need for a linguistic grammar are so strong, and therefore a linguistic grammar cannot be eliminated, the only way out is to conclude that there are two grammars, one mental and one abstract, such that a mental

---

[5]Watt notes that many unexplored variations of DTC might be successful, although he does not discuss the variations. One of them, that basic operations may be relevant in performance, is explored by Foss and Fay (1975), Fay (1974), Mayer, Erreich, and Valian (1978); and Valian, Erreich, and Mayer (1978). Their research is discussed later.

grammar does not take the form of a transformational grammar. The mental grammar is that body of knowledge which a performance mechanism utilizes, where performance is narrowly construed. The mental grammar, like the abstract grammar, supplies derivations for sentences, but supplies different ones. According to Watt, for example, the linguistic grammar derives the truncated passive from the full passive,[6] but the mental grammar does not.

Watt (1970) rejects Fodor and Garrett's (1966) proposal for two reasons. First, he argues that "no plausible performance factor actually seemed capable of accounting for all discrepancies [p. 192]" between competence and performance. Second, Fodor and Garrett's assumption of an identity between a mental grammar and a linguistic grammar had no "a priori warrant." Both his arguments could be true without damaging Fodor and Garrett's primary point that competence and performance are indirectly related. First, the lack of sufficient performance principles to explain the apparent "discrepancies" between performance and competence could represent present lack of knowledge or could mean that the correct relation is even more indirect than Fodor and Garrett first supposed.

Second, although there may be no a priori reason to assume that a mental and linguistic grammar are identical,[7] there is also no a priori reason to suppose that a performance mechanism should directly interpret a mental grammar, even if a mental grammar is nonidentical to a linguistic grammar. Watt can be correct in supposing that the two grammars are distinct, but Fodor and Garrett's (1966) basic position that there is no reason to expect a competence model also to serve as a performance model can be correct, too.[8] Whether the grammar that is serving as a competence model is a mental grammar or a linguistic grammar is irrelevant. Watt does not challenge Fodor and Garrett's basic argument. He conflates two issues (Watt, 1970, 1974). Whether a linguistic grammar is a mental grammar is a different question from whether a mental grammar has a direct performance interpretation. Watt seems to assume that if a linguistic grammar is not a model of competence, then the actual competence model will have a direct performance interpretation. That does not follow.

Watt (1970) supposes, in addition, that the mental grammar's contents will be determined solely by investigations of on-line processing; a predictable problem results. Watt recognizes that people can make more generalizations

---

[6]The example is no longer relevant since "short" passives are no longer considered to be truncated forms of full passives, but are independently generated (Culicover, 1976).

[7]There is at least a historical reason to assume that a mental and linguistic grammar are identical, because Chomsky's (1965) theory explicitly proposed that.

[8]If Watt's suggestion of a separation between a mental grammar and a linguistic grammar is correct, then, it is so independently of the arguments he gives for it. See Katz (1978) for discussion of this topic.

and grammatical judgments than would be possible on the basis of a mental grammar built to mediate on-line processing alone. To solve the problem, Watt suggests that the performance mechanism has access to the mental grammar plus an "archival faculty."[9] The two together comprise the "linguistic faculty." The archival faculty seems to include that portion of the linguistic grammar that was left out of the mental grammar because it did not directly relate to performance. Watt has reinvented the competence–performance distinction. Knowledge is distinct from use; use involves more than on-line processing; knowledge does not entail a particular theory of use.

One historical consequence of Fodor and Garrett's paper (1966) proposing an abstract relation between competence and performance was to make people think that there were no empirical constraints on a model of competence. Any deviation from what the grammar supposedly predicted could now be brushed away as the result of "performance factors," or so Watt (1974), Derwing (1973), and others have mistakenly concluded. The point, however, is that the grammar does not make predictions about performance; it makes predictions about grammatical properties and relations. Fodor and Garrett may have misstated a true claim, but the claim is true. The claim is that knowledge does not carry with it a blueprint for how it is going to be used. Fodor and Garrett's misstatement was that the performance model does not incorporate a competence model, as if incorporation required "direct" implementation of the grammar à la DTC.

From the true version of Fodor and Garrett's (1966) claim, nothing follows about whether empirical results constrain competence models. The view that Watt, Derwing, and others appear to take is that only some kinds of data count as empirical results. Watt (1974), for example, states that although intuitions "may warrant the psychological reality of the *language*, [they are] patently inadequate as guarantors of psychological reality for the rules of a *grammar* [p. 363, Watt's italics]." It is unclear what Watt might mean by this claim (which he attributes to Bever). All data, whether intuitional or "experimental," are subject to error and do not guarantee anything. If Watt's supposition that the mental and linguistic grammars are different is correct, one would, if anything, suppose that intuitions would reveal mental, rather than linguistic, structures.

Perhaps Watt (1974) means that intuitional data alone are insufficient to confirm a grammar. Just as it is a mistake to limit performance to a few aspects of on-line processing, it would be a mistake to limit it to the act of having intuitions. But saying intuitions should not be the only source of evidence is different from saying that they should not be a source of evidence at all. A theory that uses intuitions as data can be an empirical theory.

---

[9]In a later discussion of the archival faculty, Watt (1974) abandoned it.

BEVER

In an extremely influential article, Bever (1970) suggested that the distinction between competence and performance was "artificial."[10] Bever's article has incorrectly been viewed as proof that competence and performance cannot be separated, that grammars are suspect because intuitions are subject to error, and that (as some psychologists and linguists had already believed) the competence–performance distinction removed the study of grammar from an empirical realm.

Two aspects of Bever's (1970) paper are particularly important. The first is the range of "nonlinguistic" principles, or strategies, that he proposes to mediate surface strings and meanings, replacing transformations. The second is his proposal that nonlinguistic structures and processes will determine which of the possible languages specified by universal grammar can be learned, and, of those that can be learned, which rules within them will be exploited. The second proposal has usually been referred to as proposing that performance affects competence. My analysis of Bever's proposals will claim that many of the "nonlinguistic" strategies may be linguistically derived, but that even if they are purely perceptual, their behavioral importance is irrelevant to the competence–performance distinction.

Bever's (1970) suggestion that perceptual and cognitive structures and processes constrain what languages can be learned is, at a general level, a suggestion that you can only learn what you can learn. That has to be true, because it is a tautology. On a Chomskian view (Chomsky, 1977b), linguistic theory specifies all the possible natural languages, of which the learnable ones are a subset. There is no more reason for linguistic theory to specify only the learnable languages than there is for a particular grammar to specify only the understandable sentences. (See Wexler, Culicover, and Hamburger [1976] for an opposing approach in which linguistic theory does specify only the learnable languages.) What picks out the learnable subset is other mental structures and processes that together compose a simplicity metric. (For example, some possible languages might be learnable if people lived longer, or communicated via pencil and paper.) Universal grammar specifies *potential* competence; other mental structures select what will become *actual* competence. Depending on the nature of the mental machinery in which universal grammar is embedded, different particular grammars will result.

---

[10]In later papers, Bever (1971, 1972, 1974a, 1974b, 1975; Bever, Carroll, & Hurtig, 1976b; Bever & Langendoen, 1971) clarifies and develops his 1970 views. For example, the distinction is indeterminate rather than artificial, and his remarks are to be taken as concerning candidate, rather than true, grammars. Only the 1970 paper is discussed in the text because it had the maximal historical impact.

Similarly, the mental machinery of language users will determine how frequently various rules will be used and under what circumstances. Just as it is not the task of linguistic theory to determine why some rules are used more than others, it is not the job of linguistic theory to determine what languages are learned. Bever (1971) makes a similar point.

Within the context of a Chomskian linguistic theory, Bever's general form of the proposal is not a challenge;[11] it does not call the competence–performance distinction into question. Performance features affect the selection of a competence system that will be learned and the selection of forms within a competence system that will be used in performance. But what is learned is still distinct from how what is learned is used, and from the principles that determine what will be learned and how it will be used.

Bever's (1970) specific proposals, in which particular strategies are claimed to exert a particular effect on what is learned, are not tautologous and are, therefore, of more interest. Even if the strategies have the effect Bever claims, however, they still do not call the competence–performance distinction into question. They at most demonstrate properties of the performance system that select which of the potential languages will actually be learned, just as they may select which rules get the most use.

A separate question concerning the strategies Bever proposes is whether they work. They must work at two levels. First, they must be nonlinguistic, rather than being derived from linguistic rules or principles; second, they must select the to-be-learned grammar and the to-be-used forms within a grammar. Using two examples, I claim that the strategies have not been shown successful at either level.

As an example of a nonlinguistic strategy influencing the form of the (learned) grammar, Bever (1970) proposes that children interpret initial noun–verb (NV) sequences as starting the main (or only) clause of a sentence. He suggests that this is responsible for the fact that initial subordinate clauses are marked as such with a subordinating conjunction (such as *while, because*). Such marking insures the proper implementation of the nonlinguistic strategy. The child and the adult can use this strategy without fear of error, because a subordinate clause will always be marked as such by a conjunction if it is the first clause of a sentence. If there is no such marking, the listener can correctly interpret the first clause as the independent clause. Thus, Bever suggests, the existence of a main clause strategy is an explanation for the fact that initial subordinate clauses are clearly marked and that the (learned) grammar will not generate a sentence with an initial subordinate clause unless it is marked.

---

[11]What would challenge a Chomskian linguistic theory is the demonstration that nonlinguistic mental structures specify what is a possible natural language, as opposed to a learnable one.

There are other kinds of strategies, however, that do not have the result of constraining the (learned) grammar. For example, children of a certain age and adults on certain occasions tend to interpret an NVN sequence as corresponding to an actor–action–acted upon (or object) relation. As a result, children at one age (3½ to 4 years) misinterpret passive sentences as actives, and adults are unable to find a meaning for, or unable to recognize as grammatical, sentences like (1), where there is a reduced relative clause.

(1) The horse raced past the barn fell.

It is interpreted as a sentence with an extra word, *fell,* tacked on at the end.

What is not clear in Bever's (1970) examples is why some strategies lead to the grammar's not generating certain strings (as in the main clause strategy), whereas others (as in the NVN strategy) do not affect the grammar. What are the properties of the main clause strategy such that the form of the grammar is influenced? What are the properties of the NVN strategy such that the grammar is not influenced? Bever does not address this question nor the possibility that the influence could be directed in the opposite direction, from the grammar to the strategies. The main clause strategy, for example, could be derived from the grammar, rather than the reverse.

The NVN strategy, however, could not be interpreted in this way. It operates strongly for adults with sentences like (1), but there are many other sentential constructions that violate this strategy and yet are easy to process, such as (2), (3), and (4).

(2) The horse was kicked by the cow.
(3) The army suffered defeat.
(4) The statue interested John.

Thus, not only does the (learned) grammar allow such sentences, but the NVN strategy seems to be bypassed in their interpretation. Children have trouble with at least some of these sentences, but adults do not. Sentence (2) is a typical "reversible" passive in which either noun phrase (NP) could logically be the actor. In (3) and (4) there is no correspondence between the nouns and the roles of actor and object.

The NVN strategy is not stated very precisely by Bever (1970), so that later formalization could eliminate some of the examples given above from consideration. With respect to the strategy's present form, examples (2), (3), and (4) suggest that the strategy is too broadly formulated or else that it admits of too many counter-examples. It seems clear that the initial development of the strategy comes through the statistical preponderance of certain sentence types (where NVN does correspond to actor–action–object) over others. This is only a partially successful explanation, however, because it does not account for why the strategy should be abandoned for a large number of cases and reserved for a few such as (1). It could be the case that there are particular grammatical properties to those cases where it is in force.

From these two examples of strategies, it can be seen that when a strategy selects a grammar cannot be predicted and that in the case where the grammar is constrained in a particular way[12] it can be argued that the grammar's constraint selected the strategy, rather than the reverse.

Yet another argument that Bever (1970) uses to call the competence–performance distinction into question is that linguists' intuitions are fallible and are themselves the product, in part, of a performance system. His conclusion here is a non sequitur, because it can only apply to candidate grammars, not true grammars. In his 1974b paper Bever makes clear that he is talking about candidate grammars, not true grammars, whereas in his 1970 paper he does not specify that it is a candidate grammar that will be affected by the fallibility of intuitions. Although any actual candidate grammar may be subject to the properties of those who are constructing it, it does not follow that the actual candidate grammar is a correct grammar or that a correct grammar will be subject to such considerations. The validity of the competence–performance distinction is independent of what model of competence linguists propose. It assumes that there is a correct model but not that we can necessarily discover it. If Bever's reasoning is correct, it may be difficult to construct a "true" grammar, but this does not alter the theoretical status of the distinction between competence and performance.

The fallibility of intuitions is irrelevant to the status of the true grammar. It would also undermine current methods of grammar construction only if there were some other source of data which was infallible, or if there were a less fallible source of data. Intuitions are not, however, provably more fallible than any other source of data. Further, they have contributed to a systematic theory of language, which no other data source has. I am not arguing that other data sources should be ignored but that intuitions should not be ignored, either. Also see Bever (1971, 1974a) for discussion.

In a related discussion, Bever (1970) suggests that there may be no reflection of competence in performance, outside of the having of intuitions: "I have argued that a proper understanding of the behavioral and phenomenological nature of "basic linguistic intuitions" forces us to reject the claim that a linguistic grammar is in any sense internal to such linguistic performances as talking and listening [p. 344]." Then he proposes that the relation between grammar and performance may be not abstract, but nonexistent. Thus, Bever distinguishes two kinds of psycholinguistic behavior, both of which probably involve nonlinguistic determinants, one of

---

[12]English's use of direct quotation may be a counter-example (see Fodor, Bever, and Garrett [1974] for discussion of this point).

which may have no linguistic determinants at all. One behavior is having intuitions, the other behavior is normal talking and listening. A grammar may be psychologically real in the sense of contributing to intuitions without being psychologically real in the sense of contributing to normal talking and listening.

A problem with this part of Bever's analysis is pointed out by Elizabeth Sharpless (personal communication, 1975). If there is a sharp division between intuitions and comprehension–production, such that the grammar partially accounts for intuitions but may account not at all for comprehension–production, there is no reason for properties of the comprehension–production system to affect intuitions and, thus, no reason for them to affect the form that the grammar will take. Further, the developing child's nonlinguistic strategies should not affect the form of the grammar, because, on Bever's view, the child is not acquiring a grammar for any purpose other than to systematize its intuitions; it is not acquiring a grammar as a base for talking and listening, but is acquiring some other system for that purpose. Thus, as in the case of adult performance principles, by Bever's own argument that intuitions and on-line processing are to be separated, there is no reason for the grammar, which deals with linguistic facts, to be constrained by performance. Sharpless's argument is compelling.

In summary, Bever's 1970 paper neither casts doubt on the competence–performance distinction nor on the validity of linguists' enterprise. Bever proposed the existence of strategies instead of transformations. Investigation of strategies was a way of finding out about a performance model and, in turn, seemed to be a way of specifying not only what was part of knowledge but what could be part of knowledge.

CLARK AND HAVILAND

Clark and Haviland (1974) make the most direct attack on the competence–performance distinction. As seen in the following discussion, their arguments are irrelevant to the *general* distinction and do not succeed in showing that the *particular* distinction (as drawn by Chomsky, 1965) is incorrectly drawn. Clark and Haviland are a paradigm case of incorrectly thinking that arguments about how to draw the distinction bear on whether the distinction should be drawn. Their paper represents a culmination of the attempt to have a theory of performance constrain and determine a theory of competence.

First, Clark and Haviland (1974) try to show, using four different examples, that many linguistic phenomena are better handled by "process" rather than "structure" theories. That is, appeals to the structures of the sentences in question do not suffice to determine people's interpretations of them. For example, the sentence sequence "See those two people over there?

He has rabies" will be considered unacceptable if both people are men (or women), but acceptable if one of the two people is a woman. Since there is just one sentence sequence, with just one structure, structure is insufficient to explain people's interpretation. That is true. Two possibilities are then open: (a) explain the facts outside of grammar, leaving grammar alone; (b) explain the facts within grammar, changing the grammar as necessary. In Clark and Haviland's example, as in the others they offer, they apparently assume that whatever contributes in an orderly, rule-determined way to acceptability judgements should be handled within grammar. But that assumption is illicit. The claim requires justification outside of the theory that assumes it to be true.

Presumably, some cases of unacceptability should clearly not be handled within grammar. For example, if someone utters obscenities in a religious ceremony, the utterance will be unacceptable, but to try to account for the unacceptability within grammar would be absurd.[13] Some argument must then be made for new cases, to see whether they are like swearing, where the *utterance* is unacceptable relative to the context in which it occurs, or like saying, "she been has running," where the *sentence* is ungrammatical, relative to the rule system of English. But Clark and Haviland (1974) provide no argument for supposing that their examples fall with cases of sentence nongrammaticality rather than with cases of utterance inappropriateness. Hence, their demonstration that appeal to structural factors alone is insufficient in explaining people's interpretation of some sentences is irrelevant. What is needed is not a demonstration that the disputed cases require process explanations, but a demonstration that *no* cases require only structure explanations. Linguists who claim that the disputed cases do not fall within grammar will be quite happy to hear that there is a performance explanation of them; that is what they would predict.

Clark and Haviland's (1974) examples, then, challenge neither the particular nor the general competence–performance distinction. To challenge the particular distinction, Clark and Haviland would have to show that no linguistic phenomena can be satisfactorily handled with just a structure explanation. They do not attempt to do that. To challenge the general distinction, Clark and Haviland would have to show, on logical and conceptual grounds, that the distinction was unmotivated. They do not attempt that, either.

---

[13]If Clark and Haviland (1974) do not consider that absurd, everything is within grammar. We then have to divide the domain of grammar into subcomponents, because it would be unwieldy otherwise. The same dispute about how to handle certain phenomena, such as those discussed in the text, would still occur, but with a different terminology. See Chomsky (1972) for a similar reply to G Lakoff.

I turn now to the second relevant aspect of Clark and Haviland's (1974) paper in which they first doubt that the grammar will be a component of a performance model. They next argue that by specifying a performance model in complete detail, cognitive psychologists will be able to account for all grammaticality judgments and all judgments about grammatical properties and relations; grammatical phenomena will be a by-product of the performance model. They further explicitly assume that people have a variety of kinds of knowledge available to them, including linguistic, that will be divided into the usual subcomponents. There is an internal contradiction here. If a grammar is not a component of a performance model, then what are Clark and Haviland calling the linguistic knowledge that *is* part of a performance model? It is inconsistent to speak of grammatical phenomena as being a by-product of a performance model when a necessary ingredient for their explanation, a grammar, has been built into the performance model.

The remaining problem to discuss is Clark and Haviland's (1974) contention that even if grammar and performance are conceptually separable, they cannot be studied separately. In discussing their contention, I use arguments similar to those made by Dretske (1974) and Katz (1977), the latter of whose arguments are made on behalf of a Platonist conception of grammar. Their arguments are adapted to show that similar reasoning will work for a Chomskian conception of grammar.

One aspect of Clark and Haviland's (1974) contention is definitely true. Our explicit, scientific knowledge of grammar comes via intuitions, which are a form of performance. In Katz's (1977) terminology, the *source* of information about grammatical properties and relations is people's judgments, which are the output of performance. Similarly, physical properties and relations are investigated by using, among other things, people's judgments about meter-readings. In the nonempirical realm, mathematical properties and relations are investigated by using people's mathematical judgments.

Yet, although the *source* of information is people's judgments, the *import* of the information is, as the case may be, a linguistic theory, a physical theory, a mathematical theory. The implication of Clark and Haviland's (1974) contention is that grammar should only be arrived at through a model of how people process sentences; grammar, on their view, will be a by-product of a performance model. Imagine telling a physicist that physical theory should only be arrived at through a model of how bridges, rocket ships, and so on, are built. Or imagine telling a mathematician that mathematical truths will be a by-product of a model of how people add and subtract, have mathematical intuitions, and so on.

The physicist or mathematician would properly reply that that would be a strange way to do physics or mathematics, although a reasonable way to study how people put physics or mathematics to use. The reason it would be a strange way to do physics or mathematics is that you would have to put into the performance model the very facts you wanted to get out as a by-product.

My counter-argument to Clark and Haviland (1974) does not imply that study of, for example, what contributes to intuitions is useless for linguists (it is, of course, interesting in itself as a part of performance). It would allow linguists to check their intuitions in new ways. Linguists already perform mini-experiments to check their intuitions. For example, they try out sentences with different lexical items to see if the phenomenon is general across all words, whether it is an artifact of particular words, or whether it holds for one class of words but not for another. In other words, linguists already do experiments aimed at verifying and pinning down their intuitions. The psychological study of the act of having intuitions could help linguists do even better "experiments." In particular, the study of intuitions might help explain why unclear cases are unclear, why, for example, it is hard to decide whether "That slipped me by" (instead of "That slipped by me") is ungrammatical.

My counter-argument also does not imply that psychologists should forego trying to constrain performance models by investigating properties of performance that cut across the material used in performance. For example, facts about memory may be important to a performance model of language, even if the memory facts come from experiments on the memory of digits. Such experiments provide an important source of hypotheses for perform-ance theorists.

What my arguments do imply is that: (a) there is no problem with the general competence–performance distinction; (b) although there may be a problem with the particular distinction, Clark and Haviland (1974) have failed to demonstrate that; (c) performance models cannot supplant competence models because they must assume, as one component, the information they want to explain as a by-product; and (d) a truism: both competence and performance models are needed.

ARTIFICIAL INTELLIGENCE

The artificial intelligence (AI) literature provides a potentially serious kind of complaint about the particular form of the competence–performance dis-tinction, though not about the general distinction, because the AI research presupposes a distinction between knowledge and use. For example, Winograd (1972) suggests that a transformational grammar is inadequate as the linguistic knowledge component in a program built to respond appropriately (within a limited world) to English sentences. If he is correct, there is then empirical evidence that a transformational model of competence is not a component of a model of performance, at least for computers operating within an extremely limited domain.

The demonstration of the inadequacy of transformational grammar would not bear on the general distinction between knowledge and use, but it would show that knowledge has been incorrectly characterized. Notice that in Winograd's programs, as with the performance (augmented transition network) model developed by Wanner and Maratsos (1974), linguistic (and other) knowledge is explicitly made a component of the model. In principle the different types of knowledge are separable, even though they are accessed in parallel (or semi-parallel) by the user. Although programs are procedural, the procedures operate on knowledge. The question is how to characterize the knowledge. Hence, my discussion here focuses on the particular competence-performance distinction.

Dresher and Hornstein (1976) argue that Winograd (1972) was too quick to reject transformational grammar as a model of the knowledge component. Halliday's Systemic Grammar, which Winograd incorporated in his program, accounts for the necessary syntactic facts, but so does transformational grammar. Systemic Grammar, however, was apparently more directly interpretable within a performance model than was transformational grammar, and, therefore, was easier to work with. The first difficulty mentioned in the introduction, that transformational grammar has no automatic performance interpretation, is relevant here. As a performance model for a computer in a restricted world, transformational grammar did not work as well as Systemic Grammar apparently did. In addition to the question of how many of the problems that arise with computers might be expected to arise with humans is the question of the importance of direct incorporability.

As Dresher and Hornstein (1976) point out, a performance model that accessed a transformational grammar in an indirect manner might also work, because the same information is also represented in a transformational grammar. It cannot be concluded that something is wrong with transformational grammar because one performance model incorporating it is incorrect. Their argument is similar to Fodor and Garrett's (1966) argument that an indirect relation exists between a competence model and a performance model. A transformational grammar is not a set of temporal instructions.

Tyler and Marslen-Wilson (1977) make a similar error to that made by many AI researchers. They assume that, because one performance model incorporating transformational grammar is incorrect, no performance model incorporating a transformational grammar could be correct. This is like assuming that if the Brooklyn Bridge falls down, physical theory should be scrapped.

Tyler and Marslen-Wilson (1977) demonstrate that listeners use semantic information within a clause to select one of two syntactic parsings; thus

Fodor, Bever, and Garrett's (1974) claim that semantic processing proceeds clause-by-clause is false. So far so good. Tyler and Marslen-Wilson (1977) go on, however, to conclude that their results:

> cast doubt upon the viability of using a transformational generative grammar...as a basis for a psycholinguistic processing theory. According to the conventional interpretation of the implications of such a grammar for a performance system, the syntactic structure of an entire clause or sentence must be computed before a semantic representation can be assigned [p. 690].

The conclusion about the relevance of transformational grammar for a processing model is a non sequitur. The theory being tested in Tyler and Marslen-Wilson's (1977) experiment is not the theory of transformational grammar, it is a psycholinguistic theory about how people process sentences. Their evidence shows that the psycholinguistic theory offered by Fodor et al. (1974) is incorrect in one of its main claims. For their evidence to bear on transformational grammar's suitability for incorporation in a performance model, they would also have to show that there is no performance interpretation of a transformational grammar possible other than the "conventional" one they describe. That, however, they have not shown. Like the AI researchers, Tyler and Marslen-Wilson fail to support the claim that a transformational grammar cannot serve as a model of knowledge or competence.

For the purposes of assessing the compentence–performance distinction, two facts from the AI and related Augmented Transition Network (ATN) literature are important. Syntactic, semantic, and "phonological" information must all be incorporated; also, the various kinds of linguistic information are kept distinct, even though they are interwoven in performance. Although the programs focus on procedures, and on interactions among the components, the components exist. The general distinction is thus honored, and the particular distinction has also largely been observed.

EXPERIMENTS AND INTUITIONS

The main conclusion about psycholinguistic theory and research that comes out of this historical review is that it is important to look at the widest range of different kinds of performance phenomena in trying to specify the role of competence in performance. Performance tasks vary in what kinds of linguistic knowledge they exploit. Therefore, concern with too narrow a range leads to mistakes about the nature of the competence underlying performance. No given performance task, with its special knowledge requirements, can fully reflect the entire range of underlying competence. It is like judging the contents of a library by looking at how frequently borrowers take out best sellers.

In the data I have reviewed so far, the intuitional data have seemed to stand alone as evidence of the psychological existence of transformations. There are at least two other tasks, however, that have important properties in common with intuitions, and, as would be predicted, they too yield performance which can be explained by assuming that transformations are a feature of competence. Syntactic intuitions are usually the outcome of asking whether a particular structure is permissible given the rules of the language. Having the intuition is preliminary to determining what rule has been violated or obeyed. A series of structures is submitted to intuitions to determine the domain of the rule in question. Hence, the having of intuitions is directly concerned with underlying rules (Bever, 1974). Two other tasks that also involve access to or creation of systematized knowledge are (a) successful behavior in a What? situation and (b) language learning.

Valian and Wales (1976) and Valian and Caplan (1978) have investigated adults' and children's behavior in a laboratory analogue of a What? situation. A What? situation is a common occurrence in noisy environments: The speaker says something the listener has failed to hear and understand. The listener queries the speaker by asking "What?" The speaker must then decide how, if at all, to modify the original utterance. For talkers to succeed in a What? situation (i.e., for talkers to make their utterance easier to hear and understand), they must have access to a wide variety of types of knowledge. Although the original utterance was grammatical, they must still evaluate it and determine whether it can be improved in any way. Unlike intuitions, the task does not require determining whether a rule has been violated, but like intuitions, it does require access to potential rule outputs. Otherwise, the talker will be making blind guesses about how to improve the utterance.

Two different formalizations of a What? situation were invented. In the procedure used for adults, sentences exemplifying different linguistic constructions were created and typed one to a card. Within each construction all the sentences were fully grammatical, but half of them had slightly more clearly displayed sentential relations than the other half. For example, complement sentences either had the complementizer *that* present (clear version) or absent (distorted version). The adult read each card and was usually queried with a What? by an experimenter in an adjoining room. Subjects were told to respond as they naturally would had they uttered the original sentence; they could repeat it verbatim or change it in any way they wished.

In the procedure for children, two experimenters were used. The first read the child a sentence and asked the child to repeat it verbatim (to insure that the child could encode the sentence properly). The second, sitting at the other end of the room, queried the child with a What?

Although adults and children often decide to limit themselves to pronunciation changes, even 6 year olds showed that they can coordinate their knowledge of syntax, semantics, and listeners' processing systems to produce a rapid, often elegant, response to a What? The children and adults showed that they are sensitive to subtle syntactic properties of the sentences they utter. For example, missing complementizers are reinserted more often than existing ones are omitted; verb–NP–particle constructions are reconstituted as verb–particle–NP constructions more often than verb–particle–NP constructions are changed to verb–NP–particle constructions. In both cases, transformational grammar postulates a transformation: in the case of complementizers the transformation is deletion; in the case of particle, the transformation is permutation.

Speakers do not always, however, "undo" putative optional transformations in a What? situation. For example, speakers never change "it surprised them that she was late" to "that she was late surprised them." (Such a change may not be transformational; see Chomsky, 1973.) One reason they may not is that such center-embedded sentences are, as we know independently, hard to process. Speakers show their knowledge of how listeners' processing systems work by changing center-embedded constructions to right-branching ones or coordinate-structure ones, and by changing two-clause sentences to one-clause sentences. In some cases, then, "undoing" an optional transformation may result in a sentence that is hard to understand for extra-linguistic reasons, and, therefore, it will not be an exploited option. More work needs to be done on setting up such conflicts to determine when transformations will be undone and whether there are equally plausible alternative explanations for those cases where speakers do show transformational sensitivity.

Speakers also make semantic changes. For example, they show their knowledge of converse verbs (Katz, 1972): adults and children often change a sentence like "the salesman sold a football to Jerry" to "Jerry bought a football (from the salesman)."

Although there are clearly many differences between responding to a What? and having intuitions, there is the similarity that producing or understanding the sentence is not enough. In the case of intuitions, one reflects on the sentence for the purpose of understanding something about it. In the case of responses to a What?, one reflects on the sentence for the purpose of determining how to improve it. Both behaviors lead to a focus on rules. Delis and Slater (1977) showed that subjects who speak about cellular energy to an uninformed audience use fewer reduction transformations than subjects who write about it to an informed audience. Here, too, the task demands paying attention to the form of the communication.

Another behavioral area where rules should be important is in language learning, as Chomsky (1965), Katz (1966), and others have long proposed. Syntactic knowledge is acquired in the form of rules (I leave aside for the moment the question of what the content of the rules is), and rule learning requires systematication. Children cannot just talk and listen; they must systematize what they hear and say to form rules. In a series of papers, my colleagues and I (Mayer, Erreich, & Valian, 1978; Erreich, Valian, & Mayer, in press; Valian, Erreich, & Mayer, 1978; Valian, Mayer, & Erreich, in press) have proposed that transformations are among the rules that children learn and that learning takes place by projecting hypotheses about what basic operations compose transformations and about what the structural description and structural change of a transformation are.

To take a simple example, among the incorrect hypotheses a child could have about a movement transformation is the hypothesis that the transformation consists only of copying or only of deletion, because those are the two basic operations that compose movement (Chomsky, 1965). In the case of particle movement, an incorrect hypothesis that analyzed movement as copying alone would produce a sentence such as "the barber cut off his hair off" instead of "the barber cut his hair off" (Menyuk, 1969). We predict that child speech will contain errors due to the projection of incorrect hypotheses about the form of the rules the child is in the process of learning. Many of the predicted errors have been observed; some have not.

Fay (Fay, 1974, 1977; Foss & Fay, 1975) has suggested a similar transformational analysis of speech errors made by children and adults, but attributes the children's errors to performance limitations rather than, as we have, to competence limitations. Work on speech errors cannot be assimilated to the cases suggested so far in which production or comprehension of an utterance is not the processor's main concern. Yet, to account for syntactic speech errors, it seems necessary to posit that transformations are, in Foss and Fay's terms, "mental operations."

Thus, although tasks that require reflection show the relevance of linguistic rules to performance, so do some aspects of ordinary talking. Speech errors in adults presumably reflect stress points within the production system where there is too much overload for completely accurate functioning. When the system breaks down, it does so along the divisions that mark how it is put together. Hence, errors are a rich source of information; errors vary in kind and substance, requiring analyses that must meet a number of constraints.

What about the second difficulty mentioned in the introduction, that the candidate grammars keep changing and multiplying? I suggest that this is not as much of a difficulty as it seems. To set the stage, I first review some of the differences between intuitions and formal experiments/observations. (I refer from now on only to formal experiments, but I intend that to refer to formal observations as well.)

There has been much criticism of the method of intuitions, particularly, that they are subject to performance variables and are unreliable. Yet, intuitions are the data that have led to a systematic linguistic theory. (Chomsky [1977a] makes a similar point.) In contrast, although there has been much criticism of individual experiments, no one has criticized the method of formal experimentation and observation. Yet experimental data have not led to a systematic psycholinguistic theory or a systematic linguistic theory, and experimental results are also unreliable. The person who is sketical about intuitions should, by parity of argument, be just as skeptical, if not more so, about formal experimentation. I conclude that since we should obviously keep the formal experimental method, we should also obviously keep intuitions.

Both sources of data are valuable, and intuitions have had the edge as far as building linguistic theory is concerned. It is not difficult to see why. Even though performance factors enter into the having of intuitions, limited time is not one of them nor is limited materials. Linguists can spend weeks, months, thinking over a set of sentences, adding new sentences, altering lexical items within sentences, seeing if they all passivize the same way, pseudocleft the same way, and so on. A final feature is that the point of the whole procedure is to come up with a grammar.

The intuition situation contrasts dramatically with formal experiments. Decisions here are usually speeded: they typically take less than 1 sec, and almost never take more than 10 sec. Significant time differences between experimental conditions are often between 25 and 65 msec (Cairns & Kamerman, 1975; Foss & Jenkins, 1973; Holmes & Forster, 1970; Tyler & Marslen-Wilson, 1977).

The materials in experiments are limited, because they have to meet many constraints. The sentences of one set cannot be longer than the sentences of a matching set, because subjects might respond in terms of length; the words of one set cannot be more frequent than the words of the matching set, because subjects might respond in terms of frequency, and so on. Because one must control for many irrelevant properties that might covary with the property being tested, one cannot use a wide range of materials.[14]

The conclusion of this discussion about intuitions vs. formal experiments is that formal experiments, by their nature, are more involved with performance features than are intuitions. Psycholinguistic experiments primarily test aspects of the performance model, and only indirectly test the grammar, even if the experiment was explicitly designed to test the grammar. Our knowledge about speech performance is relatively meager, and our experimental methods are relatively crude. For any experimental outcome it will be as easy to construct an alternate processing model with the same grammar as it will be to construct an alternate grammar with the same processing model. If all the data (intuitional and formal experimental) superficially converged on the

---

[14]The requirement of using items as well as subjects as the random effect in statistical tests of significance only guarantees generalizability across all items within the same population as the test items. When items have been chosen to meet various constraints, that population *may* have funny characteristics.

same linguistic theory and the same psycholinguistic theory, there would be no problem, but the data do not superficially converge.

The conclusion that experiments only indirectly test the grammar suggests that it would be a mistake to try to test subtle aspects of the formalism. To take an example, adults and children in a What? situation consistently change "Lonely?" to "Are you lonely?" and almost never change "Are you lonely?" to "Lonely?" Current transformational grammar derives the two questions from two different deep structure representations: "Lonely?" has more empty nodes in its deep structure than "Are you lonely?" does. In other words, the two are not transformationally related. A different grammar might co-derive the two questions, designating the lexical items *be* and *you* as deletable. The What? results cannot choose between the two linguistic formulations; the results are compatible with both. The results show only that talkers in a What? situation prefer the full form over the short form and know how to construct the full form given the short form. Both grammars mark a difference between the two forms, and in both grammars the full form provides more specific information, namely, what the subject is.

It is not just the methodological properties of formal experimentation that limit it to indirect tests of a grammar. Exactly because there is no automatic performance interpretation of a grammar, it is impossible to use an experiment to decide on the correct form of a particular rule of condition. Since knowledge may be used in many ways, or not used except under rare conditions, all conclusions about the form of knowledge based on results on use must be highly tentative.

The research strategy suggested by this discussion is one which does not try to choose between two hypotheses about how a rule or condition should be formulated, since the precise statements of rules or conditions are what is most unstable in the grammar and what an experiment is least likely to be able to test directly. Thus, one should concentrate either on more stable aspects of the grammar or on aspects that an experimenter will be likely to test directly. The latter half of the research strategy is the same as that already discussed in the introduction; the only change is that here you do not throw competence away just because the focus is on performance.

ACKNOWLEDGMENTS

For their helpful criticisms, suggestions and discussions I am indebted to an embarrassingly large number of people, of whom the most important are: J. J. Katz, D. T. Langendoen, N. Chomsky, and F. Katz.

REFERENCES

Bever, T. G. The cognitive basis for linguistic structures. In J. R. Hayes (Ed.), *Cognition and the development of language.* New York: Wiley, 1970.

Bever, T. G. The integrated study of language behavior. In J. Morton (Ed.), *Biological and social factors in psycholinguistics*. London: Logos Press Limited, 1971.

Bever, T. G. The limits of intuition. *Foundations of Language*, 1972, *8*, 411.

Bever, T. G. The ascent of the specious. In D. Cohen (Ed.), *Explaining linguistic phenomena*. Washington, D.C.: Hemisphere Press, 1974. (a)

Bever, T. G. The interaction of perception and linguistic structures: A preliminary investigation of neo-functionalism. In T. E. Sebeok (Ed.), *Current trends in linguistics* (Vol. 12). The Hague: Mouton, 1974. (b)

Bever, T. G. Psychologically real grammar emerges because of its role in language acquisition. In D. Dato (Ed.), *Developmental psycholinguistics: Theory and applications*. Washington, D.C.: Georgetown University Press, 1975.

Bever, T. G., Carroll, J. M., & Hurtig, R. Analogy. In T. G. Bever, J. J. Katz, & D. T. Langendoen (Eds.), *An integrated theory of linguistic ability*. New York: Crowell, 1976.

Bever, T. G., & Langendoen, D. T. A dynamic model of the evolution of language. *Linguistic Inquiry*, 1971, *2*, 433-463.

Cairns, H. S., & Kamerman, J. Lexical information processing during sentence comprehension. *Journal of Verbal Learning and Verbal Behavior*, 1975, *14*, 170-179.

Chomsky, N. *Aspects of the theory of syntax*. Cambridge: MIT Press, 1965.

Chomsky, N. *Studies on semantics in generative grammar*. The Hague: Mouton, 1972.

Chomsky, N. Conditions on transformations. In S. Anderson & P. Kiparsky (Eds.), *A Festschrift for Morris Halle*. New York: Holt, Rinehart, & Winston, 1973.

Chomsky, N. *Reflections on language*. New York: Pantheon, 1975.

Chomsky, N. On the biological basis of language capacities. In R. W. Rieber (Ed.), *The neuropsychology of language*. New York: Plenum Press, 1977. (a)

Chomsky, N. Comment made during a conference on Language and Learnability (R. May, organizer), MIT, 1977. (b)

Clark, H., & Haviland, S. Psychological processes as linguistic explanation. In D. Cohen (Ed.), *Explaining linguistic phenomena*. Washington, D.C.: Hemisphere Press, 1974.

Culicover, P. W. *Syntax*. New York: Academic Press, 1976.

Delis, D., & Slater, A. S. Toward a functional theory of reduction transformations. *Cognition*, 1977, *5*, 119-132.

Derwing, B. L. *Transformational grammar as a theory of language acquisition*. Cambridge: Cambridge University Press, 1973.

Dresher, B. E., & Hornstein, N. On some supposed contributions of artificial intelligence to the scientific study of language. *Cognition*, 1976, *4*, 321-398.

Dretske, F. I. Explanation in linguistics. In D. Cohen (Ed.), *Explaining linguistic phenomena*. Washington, D.C.: Hemisphere Press, 1974.

Epstein, W. Recall of word lists following learning of sentences and of anomalous and random strings. *Journal of Verbal Learning and Verbal Behavior*, 1969, *8*, 20-25.

Erreich, A., Valian, V. V., & Mayer, J. W. Aspects of a theory of language acquisition. *Journal of Child Language*, in press.

Fay, D. *Simplification in children's speech and the formulation of movement rules*. Paper presented at the summer meeting of the Linguistic Society of America, Amherst, 1974.

Fay, D. *Transformational errors*. Paper presented at the Twelfth International Congress of Linguists, Vienna, 1977.

Fodor, J. A., & Bever, T. The psychological reality of linguistic segments. *Journal of Verbal Learning and Verbal Behavior*, 1965, *4*, 414-420.

Fodor, J. A., Bever, T. G., & Garrett, M. F. *The psychology of language*. New York: McGraw-Hill, 1974.

Fodor, J. A., & Garrett, M. F. Some reflections on competence and performance. In J. Lyons & R. J. Wales (Eds.), *Psycholinguistic papers*. Edinburgh: Edinburgh University Press, 1966.

Foss, D., & Fay, D. Linguistic theory and performance models. In J. Wirth & D. Cohen (Eds.), *Testing linguistic hypotheses*. New York: Hemisphere Press, 1975.

Foss, D. J., & Jenkins, C. M. Some effects of context on the comprehension of ambiguous sentences. *Journal of Verbal Learning and Verbal Behavior*, 1973, *12*, 577–589.

Foss, D. J., & Lynch, R. H., Jr. Decision processes during sentence comprehension: Effects of surface structure on decision times. *Perception & Psychophysics*, 1969, *5*, 145–148.

Garrett, M. F. *Syntactic structures and judgments of auditory events.* Unpublished doctoral dissertation, University of Illinois, 1965.

Glucksberg, S., & Danks, J. H. Grammatical structure and recall: A function of the space in immediate memory or of recall delay? *Perception & Psychophysics*, 1969, *6*, 113–117.

Holmes, V. M., & Forster, K. I. Detection of extraneous signals during sentence recognition. *Perception & Psychophysics*, 1970, *7*, 297–301.

Katz, J. J. *The philosophy of language.* New York: Harper & Row, 1966.

Katz, J. J. *Semantic theory.* New York: Harper & Row, 1972.

Katz, J. J. The real status of semantic representations. *Linguistic Inquiry*, 1977, *8*, 559–584.

Katz, J. J. *Language and other abstract objects: What a grammar is a theory of.* Unpublished manuscript, CUNY Graduate Center, 1978.

Matthews, W. A. Transformational complexity and short-term recall. *Language and Speech*, 1968, *11*, 120–128.

Mayer, J. W., Erreich, A., & Valian, V. Transformations, basic operations and language acquisition. *Cognition*, 1978, *6*, 1–13.

Mehler, J. Some effects of grammatical transformations on the recall of English sentences. *Journal of Verbal Learning and Verbal Behavior*, 1963, *2*, 346–351.

Menyuk, P. *Sentences children use.* Cambridge: MIT Press, 1969.

Miller, G. A. Some psychological studies of grammar. *American Psychologist*, 1962, *17*, 748–762.

Miller, G. A., & McKean, K. A chronometric study of some relations between sentences. *Quarterly Journal of Experimental Psychology*, 1964, *16*, 297–308.

Russell, B. *The problems of philosophy.* London: Oxford University Press, 1912.

Savin, H., & Perchonock, E. Grammatical structure and the immediate recall of English sentences. *Journal of Verbal Learning and Verbal Behavior*, 1965, *4*, 348–353.

Slobin, D. I. *Grammatical transformations in childhood and adulthood.* Unpublished doctoral dissertation, Harvard University, 1963.

Tyler, L., & Marslen-Wilson, W. The on-line effects of semantic context on syntactic processing. *Journal of Verbal Learning and Verbal Behavior*, 1977, *16*, 683–692.

Valian, V. V., & Caplan, J. *What children say when asked "What?": A study of the use of syntactic knowledge.* Unpublished manuscript, CUNY Graduate Center, 1978.

Valian, V. V., Erreich, A., Mayer, J. W. *From where do speech errors come from?* Unpublished manuscript, CUNY Graduate Center, 1978.

Valian, V. V., Mayer, J. W., & Erreich, A. A little-linguist model of syntax learning. In S. Tavakolian (Ed.), *Language acquisition and linguistic theory.* Cambridge: MIT Press, in press.

Valian, V. V., & Wales, R. What's what: Talkers help listeners hear and understand by clarifying sentential relations. *Cognition*, 1976, *4*, 155–176.

Wanner, E., & Maratsos, M. *An augmented transition network model of relative clause comprehension.* Unpublished manuscript, Harvard University, 1974.

Watt, W. C. On two hypotheses concerning psycholinguistics. In J. R. Hayes (Ed.), *Cognition and the development of language.* New York: Wiley, 1970.

Watt, W. C. Competing economy criteria. In F. Bresson & J. Mehler (Eds.), *Current problems in psycholinguistics.* Paris: Editions du Centre National de la Recherche Scientifique, 1974.

Wexler, K., Culicover, P. W., & Hamburger, H. Learning-theoretic foundations of linguistic universals. *Theoretical Linguistics*, 1976, *2*, 213–253.

Winograd, T. Understanding natural language. *Cognitive Psychology*, 1972, *3*, 1–191.

2 Levels of Processing and the Structure of the Language Processor

K. I. Forster
Monash University

The past 10 years of research in psycholinguistics has produced a dramatic increase in the range and sophistication of experimental techniques that can be focused on the problem of analyzing the structure and function of the human language processor. Unfortunately, this phenomenon has not led to a corresponding increase in our confidence that we are actually gaining ground in the struggle to make sense of the experimental observations. In my view, it is becoming increasingly clear that we need to develop a more general theory that incorporates general assumptions about the information-processing characteristics of the experimental tasks themselves. In fact, I would go so far as to claim that for any given hypothesis about the nature of the language processor, there is at least one task that will apparently produce clear evidence in favor of that hypothesis and at least one that will seem to equally clearly disconfirm it.

The purpose of this paper is to sketch the preliminary outlines of a theory of the language processor that is embedded in a theory of information processing. The theory is extremely vague in places and quite incomplete in others. However, it is hoped that a discussion of the issues involved may serve some heuristic purpose for future research.

The type of experiment that has now become the vogue can be referred to as a *speeded classification task*. In such a task, the subject of the experiment is presented with some item of linguistic input, which must be classified according to some experimenter-defined criterion as rapidly as possible. The criterion is designed so that the classification cannot be made until the subject has successfully completed some particular type of linguistic processing that is of interest in the experiment. For example, the subject may have to classify the input according to whether it contains a particular phonetic element, or whether it constitutes a grammatically well-formed sequence, or whether it contains a familiar lexical item. Each of these criteria would be designed to tap a different level of processing. The datum of such an experiment is the time required by the subject to make the correct classification reliably, and this is assumed to reflect the time taken for the necessary processing to be completed.

In analyzing the results of experiments of this type, one finds a number of fairly general assumptions that play a critical role. Because these are not always shared, it is perhaps useful to state them explicitly, as follows:

1. Language processing can usefully be regarded as a sequence of operations, each of which transforms a mental representation of a linguistic stimulus into a mental representation of a different form (usually more abstract in the case of perception). Corresponding to each type of mental representation in such a sequence, there is a distinct *level of processing,* and a given operation belongs to Level X just in case it is directly involved in computing a mental representation of Type X.

2. In most speeded classification tasks, it is possible that several *different* processing systems may have sufficient computational power to provide the information required for the decision. Depending on the circumstances, the subject's decision may be based on the output of any one of these systems.

3. All other things being equal, the decision will be based on the output of the processing system that finishes first. This assumption is usually referred to as a *race model* assumption (Meyer & Ellis, 1970). However, the fastest processor will not always control the decision; this will depend on at least two additional factors. First, because we would naturally assume that the system that makes the decision and selects the appropriate response is quite separate from the language processor, the question of the relative *accessibility* of outputs to the decision-maker arises. That is, information from each of the levels of the language processor must be transmitted to the decision-maker, and there is no a priori reason to assume that the information transfer rates are all equally fast. What is important is not the time at which a given processor completes the analysis, but the time at which the results of this analysis arrive at the decision-maker.

The second factor that must be taken into account is the time required by the decision maker to infer the correct response for this item. Some types of representations of the input may give rise to very rapid decisions in one kind of task, but relatively slow decisions in others. Thus, even if the output from one level reaches the decision-maker before another, it is still possible for the second output to "overtake" the first, because it enables the decision to be made more rapidly.

Needless to say, this greatly complicates the race model and increases alarmingly the degree of flexibility of any given theory. Whether it makes the task of selecting the correct theory entirely unmanageable remains to be seen.

As a concrete example of the type of problem that we are faced with, consider the results of an experiment comparing naming time and lexical decision time (Forster & Chambers, 1973). In this experiment, subjects were presented with letter sequences that were either words or orthographically legal nonwords, e.g., *thamon*. Subjects in one group were required to pronounce these items as rapidly as possible, and the naming time was defined as the time between the presentation of the stimulus and the onset of vocalization. Subjects in a second group were required to say "yes" or "no" depending on whether or not the item was a familiar word. The vocalization onset time in this case constituted the lexical decision time.

The purpose of this experiment was to determine whether the (probable) pronounciation of a word needs to be determined before it can be recognized as a word (the presumption being that some kind of phonologically organized access system might be involved in word recognition). The results showed that for both the naming task and the lexical decision task, high-frequency words produced faster responses than nonwords. From the fact that words can be pronounced faster than equally pronounceable nonwords, it follows that some lexical representation of a word must be located before overt pronounciation begins. From this it might be deduced that lexical decision times should be substantially shorter than naming times, because as soon as a lexical representation has been found, the "yes" response in the lexical decision task can be initiated.

But this was certainly not the case. For high-frequency words, the mean lexical decision time was 608 msec, whereas the mean naming time for the same item was only 508 msec. This result would seem to indicate that the pronounciation of a word is available 100 msec before the lexical entry for the word has been located, which would of course conflict with the previous interpretation.

This conflict is more apparent than real. What has been overlooked is the nature of the response selection systems involved. In the naming task, once the lexical entry has been located, the contents of the entry are used to determine the pronounciation, and the results of this computation are then routed to a speech-production system. In the lexical decision task, the contents of the entry presumably do not have to be examined (although they might), but before the correct decision can be made, a decision-making system must become aware of the *fact* that a lexical entry has been located and from this fact make the inference that the input item must be a word. It then remains to issue the appropriate command to the speech-production system. It should be evident that the latter sequence of steps could well take more time than the former. The speech-production system may have more rapid access to the contents of a lexical entry than does the decision maker; in addition, using the contents of an entry to compute the pronounciation of a word may well take less time than using the fact that an entry exists to make the inference that a word has been encountered.

A second example of the kind of interpretive problem that must be faced is taken from an experiment that was designed to distinguish between different levels of processing (Forster, 1974c). Two different tasks were used. The first task was designed to determine how rapidly lexical processing is completed when the input consists of a sentence. The subject was shown a sequence of words typed as in normal text (i.e., all words were presented simultaneously), and the subject merely had to decide whether or not all items in the input string were familiar words. Thus, the subject would respond "yes" to (1) and (2), but "no" to (3):

(1) The scouts annoyed the lady.
(2) The bicycle the calculated cognac.
(3) The plane gleashed the passengers.

The assumption behind this technique was that as soon as the lexical entries for each word had been located, a "yes" decision could be initiated, and the time for this decision would indicate how rapidly the necessary lexical processing could be completed.

The second task was intended to reflect the time required for sentential processing of the same material. In this case, the subject had to classify each input sequence according to whether or not it constituted a meaningful, grammatical sentence. Thus, the subject would respond "yes" to (1) and "no" to (2) and (3).

Restricting ourselves to just the "yes" responses in both tasks (i.e., occasions on which sentences were presented), a straightforward view might lead to the expectation that the lexical task should produce faster decision times than would the sentence task. For *both* tasks, the lexical status of each of the putative words in the sequence had to be established. But in the sentence task, considerably more analysis had to be carried out before the decision could be made, namely, a syntactic and semantic analysis of the properties of the input string.

However, this expectation also was not confirmed. The overall pattern of results showed no significant difference between decision times for the two tasks, and indeed for some types of sentences, the sentence task was slightly faster than the lexical task (although not significantly), which makes it seem unlikely that there really was a difference between the tasks that the experiment was not sufficiently sensitive to detect.

Careful analysis of the decision-making aspects of the tasks suggests a possible explanation for this strange result. In the sentence task, once the necessary structural analysis has occurred, it may be a relatively simple task to decide that a well-formed structure exists. Only one "object" (namely, a structural interpretation of the input) needs to be communicated to the decision maker, and only one "object" needs to be examined. However, in the lexical task, if there are N words and nonwords in the input, then the results of N different searches of the lexicon need to be *separately* communicated to the decision maker, and these N "objects" all need to be separately examined. Thus, N word–nonword decisions have to be made (less than N if any nonword actually occurs in the sequence), followed up by an inspection of *these* decisions to determine the "yes–no" decision.

Not very much is known about how such decisions are made, but it is generally felt that in terms of the time required, they are very expensive and consume a substantial proportion of the eventual decision latency. It is thus not at all unreasonable to raise the possibility that the time required to reach a "yes" decision in the lexical task may be *considerably* longer than in the sentence task.

We now have to solve a pair of simultaneous equations in which there are four unknowns. Although *processing* time is longer for the sentence task than for the lexical task, the *decision* time may be much shorter for the sentence task. Thus:

(4) $P(S) + D(S) = P(L) + D(L)$

where P stands for processing time, D stands for decision time, and S and L refer to sentence and lexical tasks, respectively, and where $P(S) > P(L)$, but $D(S) < D(L)$.

Obviously, we are not in a position to settle this issue, but we have at least provided a possible interpretation for the obtained results. In actual fact, it is even possible that:

(5) $P(S) + D(S) < P(L) + D(L)$

If this were the case, then for the sentences used in this experiment at least, the subjects could reach the conclusion that the input constituted a sentence *before* they could reach the conclusion that it consisted solely of words (this would not always be the case; syntactically complex structures such as doubly self-embedded sentences would very likely produce the reverse result).

But now we have raised the possibility that subjects in the lexical task may in fact have based their decision on the output of a sentential processor rather than a purely lexical processor (compare the assumptions outlined earlier).

Once the subjects realize that they are confronted with a sentence, they can infer that the input must have contained only words and can respond "yes" without directly examining the output from the lexical processor.

This theory explains the equality of the decision times for the two tasks in a more natural way than the theory embodied in (4), which must argue that the equality is essentially a coincidence. However, it does so at the price of forcing us to abandon the view that classification latencies reflect processing times in any simple way.

In what follows, I elaborate on this argument in a number of different settings. Before doing so, I should immediately note that this argument raises questions about the so-called "top-down" vs. "bottom-up" interpretations of existing experiments. For example, take the question of how rapidly subjects can monitor speech inputs for the existence of a target that is defined variously as a phonetic element, a syllable, or a word (e.g., Foss & Swinney, 1973; Rubin, Turvey, & Van Gelder, 1976; Savin & Bever, 1970). From the fact that the same input signal can be classified more rapidly when the target is specified as a syllable rather than as phonetic element, it has sometimes been inferred that the "primary" perceptual unit cannot be defined at a phonetic level. That is, the subject recognizes syllables (or words) and then infers the phonetic analysis from this analysis. Although this may in fact be the case, there are several alternative interpretations of the data. For example, recognition may still be "bottom-up" in the sense that the first level of analysis is phonetic, followed by a syllable or word level of processing, but the output of the phonetic level does not enable a decision to be reached rapidly enough to control the decision-making process. Much the same argument has recently been advanced by Blank and Foss (1977a). Or, it might be that processing proceeds independently at all three levels simultaneously, with the decision being controlled by varying levels, depending on the precise task conditions (see Healy & Cutting, 1976, and McNeill & Lindig, 1973, for further discussion of this issue).

Similar arguments may apply in other situations. For example, it has been reported that in a visual search task, subjects can determine whether a given symbol is a digit or a letter without having identified *which* symbol it is (Brand, 1971; Ingling, 1972; Jonides & Gleitman, 1972). This ability is apparently not based on simple physical differences between digits and letters and appears to be quite paradoxical, because the only reasonable view to take is that category membership cannot be perceived directly but must depend on prior identification. The argument developed here may serve to resolve this paradox; it may be that under special circumstances, category information is more accessible to the decision-making system than is identification information. Another problem concerns Posner's celebrated analysis of the same–different matching task in terms of processing at the so-called "physical" and "name" levels (Posner & Mitchell, 1967). In these experiments, subjects can recognize two visual forms to be instances of the same letter more rapidly when they are physically identical (e.g., AA) than when they are only nominally identical (e.g., Aa). This indicates that recognition and comparison can be carried out more rapidly at the lower level of visual features than at the higher level of identification. However, when the visual forms to be compared are orthographically regular letter sequences (e.g., THRIM THRIM) or words (e.g., DUST DUST), this conclusion is definitely false, because words are matched faster than regular letter sequences, which in turn are matched faster than letter strings (e.g., FTKL FTKL), even though the forms are physically identical and, hence, capable of being matched at the lowest level of analysis (Barron & Pittenger, 1974; Chambers & Forster, 1975). Once again, this apparent contradiction can be resolved by consideration of how the decision is made. In this case, pairs of mental objects produced at each level of analysis must be individually compared. When the forms are relatively simple (e.g., single letters), this comparison can be carried out quite rapidly, even for the lowest level of analysis; but when the forms are complex (e.g., words), the matching task becomes far more difficult to carry out at this level, so much so that higher levels of analysis have a chance to overtake the lower levels (even though they reach completion at a later time) and, hence, control the decision process. Thus, although the lower level representation may be made available for comparison before the higher level representation, the actual comparison process itself take far longer for the lower level representation, and, hence, decision times come to reflect the higher levels of analysis.

STRUCTURE OF THE LANGUAGE PROCESSOR

The broad outline of the proposed model of the language processor is depicted in Fig. 2.1. This is intended to capture only the perceptual aspect of the processor, and it is conceded that a quite different model would be necessary for a sentence-production system.

The model consists of four separate processing systems, three of which constitute the language processor proper, whereas the remaining system, the general problem solver (GPS), has no special role to play in the analysis of linguistic stimuli, but consists simply of a device for collecting information from the various subsystems of the language processor and acting upon that information. The GPS is the decision maker in the classification experiment but is incapable of interfering directly in the operation of any other system.

In digital computer terms, the GPS is to be thought of as a highly generalized and flexible central computing system, whereas the three components of the language processor are to be thought of as highly limited and totally dedicated microprocessors. That is, they are programmed to perform highly specific tasks in a quite inflexible manner, and they can do so quite

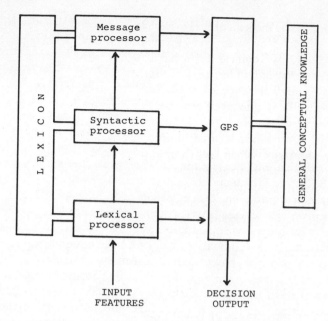

FIG. 2.1. Organization of language processor and GPS.

independently of any other system. They each have their own computational hardware and their own program. They each have access only to a language-oriented data storage (the lexicon), and no access at all to the general memory (general conceptual knowledge), which contains the person's general knowledge and beliefs about the real world. In turn, the GPS has no access to the lexicon but does have access to conceptual knowledge, and, in addition, the GPS has no information about the operation of the microprocessors, other than by observing their output.

The lexical processor accepts input from peripheral perceptual systems in the form of feature lists and attempts to segment this input and to access the entries in the lexicon that correspond to the lexical elements in the input string. This processor is assumed to consist of a number of access files that are organized to permit a search process to locate lexical entries under various different descriptions. One such file is organized according to orthographic properties (for reading), one according to phonetic properties (for listening), and a third is organized according to semantic and syntactic properties (for talking and writing). These access files are related to the lexicon in the same way as the card filing system of a library is related to the actual books in the library. The card file permits the same book to be located under a number of different descriptions (e.g., title, author, area) and the access file permits the same lexical entry to be located under varying descriptions (e.g., ortho-graphic, phonetic, semantic).

In recent years, the lexical processor has been extensively investigated (see Forster, 1976; Meyer & Schvaneveldt, 1976; Rubenstein, Lewis, & Rubenstein, 1971; Stanners & Forbach, 1973). For my present purposes, I note one property only: The final selection of the correct lexical entry involves a search through a range of candidates, the order of this search being controlled by the frequency of occurrence of the word corresponding to each candidate entry.

As lexical entries are located, pointers to these entries are passed to the syntactic processor, which is then able to extract from the lexical entry the information it requires to assign a syntactic structure to the sentence. As soon as a sufficient number of lexical entries have been located, syntactic processing commences. The final output of this device would be the surface structure of the sentence in the sense of Chomsky (1975), but this output can be relayed piecemeal to the next processor as viable syntactic constituents are identified (permitting interpretive work to be commenced before the final sentence structure has been determined).

The final processor contains a rather mixed set of procedures that convert a purely linguistic representation into a conceptual structure representing the intended message. Among its functions are: (a) identifying the referents of the referring expressions, (b) resolving ambiguities, (c) making inferences from the surface structure, and (d) supplying additional information from the lexicon that may be relevant to the interpretation of the sentence.

Each microprocessor outputs to the next highest microprocessor and to the GPS. Thus, the GPS is aware of the output of each level of analysis, but after a variable delay. Each microprocessor accepts input *only* from the next lowest level and from no other source. Thus, no microprocessor has any information at all about the operations of any higher level processor. This last assumption is most crucial: It implies total autonomy of processing. The lexical processor operates independently of both the syntactic and message-level processors, and the syntactic component operates independently of the message processor.

On the face of it, there are any number of facts that clearly refute this last assumption. But before I consider this issue, some comment should be made about the overall purpose of proposing such a model. What I have tried to do is to construct an account of sentence processing that makes strong and therefore interesting claims about the *structure* of the sentence processor. I have postulated a *linear chain* of processors, with each processor accepting input from one, and only one, other processor (excepting the GPS). This model makes a stronger claim than one in which, for example, there are any number of feedback loops, so that any one processor can be influenced by any higher level processor, including the GPS. Thus, the theory has far less room for maneuvering around obstacles, and this seems a highly desirable goal, provided, of course, that the theory still proves to be workable. The object of

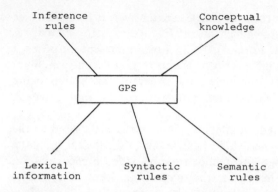

FIG. 2.2.   Language-processing system without language processor.

the exercise is to postulate a uniform system in which a given organizational principle applies across the board. By way of contrast, consider the model depicted in Fig. 2.2, in which minimal claims are made about the structure of the language processor. In this case, all the computational analysis is performed by the GPS, which is free to organize its processing in any way at all, moving as it sees fit from one level to another, even omitting some stages altogether. It seems to me that if we begin by postulating such a model, then there is very little hope of discovering interesting structural properties at all, and, consequently, we would be reduced to merely noting and cataloguing the kinds of problem-solving strategies that are (or can be) employed in various kinds of tasks. This may ultimately be the correct view to adopt, but it seems preferable to first thoroughly explore the alternatives to this view.

The essential feature of the current proposal is that the language processor and the general problem-solving system ought to be distinguished, although it must always be kept in mind that we can only gain access to the language processor through the GPS. That is, the language processor does not itself generate observable behavior. The kind of distinction envisaged is the same as that made by Schneider and Shiffrin (1977) between automatic and controlled information processing. They remark that:

> Automatic processing . . . is triggered by appropriate inputs, and then operates independently of the subject's control. An automatic sequence can contain components that control information flow, attract attention, or govern overt responses. Automatic sequences do not require attention, though they may attract it if training is appropriate, and they do not use up short-term capacity [p. 51].

These properties, I believe, characterize the language processor. Once a sequence of linguistic stimuli impinge on the appropriate receptors, the linear chain described earlier is automatically triggered, and operates totally independently of any other cognitive activity. The decision making of the GPS, on the other hand, involves controlled processing, which is, according to Schneider and Shiffrin (1977) "a temporary activation of nodes in a sequence that is not yet learned. It is relatively easy to set up, modify, and utilize in new situations. It requires attention, uses up short-term capacity, and is often serial in nature [pp. 51–52]."

As noted earlier, the concept of a linear chain of processing systems, in which each system accepts input from only one other system, implies total autonomy of each processing stage, and the absence of controlling feedback from higher to lower levels. Most of the discussion that follows is concerned with this issue in one form or another; we will either be concerned with the effects of semantic variables on syntactic processing, or the effects of semantic and syntactic context on lexical access. An essential requirement in this investigation is the design of experimental tasks that are sensitive to processing at each of the various levels. One task that shows considerable promise is the same–different matching task, which we will now consider in detail.

THE LOGIC OF THE SAME–DIFFERENT MATCHING TASK

In this task, which has been used so effectively by Posner and his colleagues (e.g., Posner & Mitchell, 1967), the subject is presented with two sequences of symbols and required to decide as quickly and accurately as possible whether they are the same or different. The two sequences can be either simultaneously or sequentially presented and can be either laterally or vertically opposed. One method of using this technique is to hold the stimuli constant and to vary the definition of "same" (e.g., nominal vs. physical identity); another method is to hold the definition of "same" constant and vary the nature of the stimuli. The latter method seems preferable, because it focuses more attention on the processing of the stimuli and less on the nature of the decision making, and in all the experiments to be discussed here, the "same" criterion is held constant at the level of physical identity.

Decision times in this task have these components: (a) the time required to develop a mental representation of each of the sequences, (b) the time required to compare these representations, and (c) the time required to evaluate the outcome of this comparison in terms of the task decision. This third component is necessary, because the time required to classify two stimuli as "different" will vary with their similarity; we assume that similarity has no effect on the comparison process itself but does affect the decision maker's interpretation of the results of the comparison.

Although this technique has not been used in the sentence-processing area, it has been applied very successfully to the problem of word recognition (e.g., Barron & Pittenger, 1974; Chambers & Forster, 1975; Egeth & Blecker, 1971; Henderson, 1974). In these experiments, the main concern has been to demonstrate a word-superiority effect, i.e., that words are somehow processed more efficiently than are other symbol strings. From the very first, the most intriguing puzzle in this task has been that "same" responses appear to behave very differently from "different" responses; so much so that it has even been suggested that different processing theories have to be applied, "same" decisions being controlled by one system and "different" decisions by another.

Chambers and Forster (1975) attempted to avoid this problem and to present a single theory that covered the facts for both types of responses. They postulated three levels of processing: a single-letter level, a letter-cluster level, and a word level. Sequences of symbols could be represented and compared at any or all of these levels simultaneously. A race model was adopted, and thus the decision would be controlled by whichever level of processing yielded a decisive comparison output first.

At each level, as soon as an element in one of the stimuli has been identified, it is compared with the corresponding element in the other stimulus (whether this element has to be identified or not is uncertain, but appears to be immaterial to the predictions). Thus, processing at the lowest level involves comparing pairs of letters, at the intermediate level it involves comparing pairs of letter combinations (perhaps syllables or possibly just familiar letter clusters, such as BL, ST), whereas at the highest level, processing involves comparing whole words.

No assumptions were made about the speed with which units were identified, but Chambers and Forster (1975) assumed that comparison time was critically dependent on the *number* of units involved in the three different types of mental representation.

Four types of stimuli were used: letter strings (e.g., CRTEH), orthographically legal nonwords (e.g., CLOST), low-frequency words (e.g., CREST) and high-frequency words (e.g., CLOTH). The letters were presented in uppercase, and the two strings were vertically aligned.

For "same" items, clear-cut results were obtained. High-frequency words were matched faster than were low-frequency words, and both of these were faster than were orthographically regular nonwords, which in turn were faster than were letter strings. These results can be interpreted in a straightforward way: although individual letters may take no longer to identify than do letter clusters, there are more of them to identify and compare, and, hence, the letter-cluster level produces decisive output faster than does the letter level. This accounts for the difference between letter strings and legal nonwords. Precisely the same relationship holds between the letter-cluster level and the word level. Because there are fewer pairs of units to identify and compare at the word level (i.e., one), this level is in turn faster than the letter-cluster level, which produces a faster decision time for words than for legal nonwords. The remaining difference between high and low frequency words presumably has nothing to do with *comparison* time, but simply reflects the faster identification time for high frequency words.

The situation changes dramatically for "different" items. When *all* letters were different (e.g., CHILD/BROWN, MOUNG/CLOOR, GTUMC/IKDTE), there were *no* differences between any of the conditions. This implies that the letter level (or perhaps some lower level than even this) was the first to detect the difference, and, hence, words would be handled in the same way as letter strings. This is because, no matter which letter pair is initially selected for analysis, a decisive output will be produced immediately; hence, only one pair needs to be compared. This contrasts with the "same" items, where *all* letter pairs had to be compared.

This argument suggests that legal words might be faster than would letter strings if more than one pair of letters had to be compared. This was indeed the case. When all letter pairs except one were the same (e.g., CHEER/CHEEK, THEAR/THEAK, EAOSR/EAOSK), legal nonwords were significantly faster than were letter strings. Despite considerable efforts, no significant difference was obtained between words and nonwords, although the difference increased steadily as the position of the different letter pair was moved to the right and eventually reached borderline significance when only the last letters differed.

This experiment suggests an extremely powerful analytical tool for studying the operation of different levels of processing. What is required is to find some task variable that has differential effects on speed of processing at the various levels, thereby enabling us to select out just one level for investigation. In the previous experiment, switching from "same" to "different" items has just such an effect. Processing time at the word level is relatively unaffected, because the number of units that have to be identified and compared is the same in both cases (although there may be a minor effect due to decision processes). However, for the lower levels this is not the case, because the number of comparison units is reduced for "different" items.

Applying this logic to sentence processing, it should be possible to manipulate the matching task so that any one of the previously postulated levels becomes the fastest. This would enable us to study levels in isolation, instead of having to study all levels simultaneously, as is the case in most current techniques.

Preliminary experiments conducted in our laboratory concentrated on "same" items and were designed merely to determine whether higher levels than the lexical (word) level were capable of controlling decision time. Four different types of items were used: (1) semantically plausible sentences, (2) semantically implausible sentences, (3) ungrammatical word strings, and (4) strings of legal nonwords with function words randomly interspersed. Word frequency was closely matched across all four conditions. Examples of these four types of items are given in (6) through (9).

(6) The workman repaired the factory slowly.
(7) The florist disguised the composer daily.
(8) Camper funeral the nearly the hardened.
(9) The fiddust devopered the epanter dombly.

Various methods of display were used, but we finally adopted the same procedure that had been used in the word studies, namely, vertically aligned strings in the same case. In all cases, the "different" items differed by only one word, the number of letters being kept constant. Examples of actual items are given below.

(10a) The young horse galloped quickly away.
(10b) The young house galloped quickly away.
(11a) Susan stroked the yellow bones quietly.
(11b) Susan stroked the yellow bones quickly.
(12a) Had heel finite replies Mary the.
(12b) Had peel finite replies Mary the.
(13a) The sen pantered his doother bune.
(13b) The sen pantered his beether bune.

The reports provided by our subjects were most encouraging for the multiple-level processing view. They reported two conflicting strategies: One method was to compare the two strings word for word; another was to read combinations of words in one string first, and then to make the comparison. The strategies conflict because the first was slower than the second, but apparently subjects could still perform both strategies simultaneously.

The results of the experiment were even more encouraging. There were marked and highly significant differences between all four types of items. Mean decision times in msec for the four conditions were: (1) plausible sentences: 2580, (2) implausible sentences: 2774, (3) ungrammatical word strings: 2960, (4) nonword strings: 3383.

The difference between conditions (4) and (3) shows that lexical processing of the material is faster than a comparison at the letter-cluster level. The difference between conditions (3) and (2) shows that higher level syntactically organized processing also improves efficiency, although we cannot tell from this result whether this is merely phrasal or whether the mental representations being compared are full surface structures. Finally, the difference between conditions (2) and (1) shows that some interpretive process at the message level of processing is also involved.

The finding that semantic plausibility affects efficiency of sentence processing is not novel (e.g., see Forster, 1974b; Forster & Olbrei, 1973; Forster & Ryder, 1971; Rosenberg & Jarvella, 1970; Watson, 1976), although it was nevertheless surprising to discover that in the same–different matching task, subjects were still attempting to interpret the input strings. We defined an implausible sentence to be one that refers to, describes, or presupposes events or properties that would be judged in our culture to have a low likelihood of occurrence. We referred to the processor that is affected by plausibility as a message processor rather than as a semantic processor simply to avoid confusion about the proper scope of the term *semantic*. Obviously, one goal of sentence processing is to determine the actual situation that is involved in the sentence, and this goal evidently takes longer to achieve when the situation is unusual or bizarre.

One interpretation of this result, then, is that the fastest level of processing is one that compares fully interpreted representations of the sentence, representations that are enriched by a specification of the situational context. However, this is not the only interpretation. It might be that subjects do not attempt to *compare* message-level representations; rather, it might be that message-level processing is designed merely to permit *lexical* processing to be enhanced. That is, words may be recognized faster in an appropriate semantic context. Another possibility is that *syntactic* processing is enhanced in plausible sentences. This would be expected if subjects used their knowledge of the likely interactions between objects in the real world to provide a kind of preliminary syntactic parsing of the sentence (e.g., Bever, 1970; Clark & Clark, 1977; Slobin, 1966). Of course, from the standpoint of the linear chain model represented in Fig. 2.1, these proposals are impossible, because each level of processing is fully autonomous.

Analysis of the "different" items in the sentence-matching task should yield information relevant to these issues. For example, suppose that lexical processing is facilitated by appropriate semantic and syntactic contexts. It would follow that it should be impossible to find a situation in which matching times were clearly sensitive to lexical processing (i.e., Condition 3 is faster than 4) but were not also sensitive to the syntactic and message levels (i.e., Conditions 1, 2, and 3 are equally fast). Similarly, suppose that syntactic processing is facilitated in plausible sentences. It should follow that no situation exists in which matching times are sensitive to syntactic effects (Condition 2 faster than 3) but are insensitive to plausibility effects (Conditions 1 and 2 equally fast).

The first intensive examination of the "different" items is currently being carried out by W. Murray. The research program is not yet complete, but the results so far are extremely encouraging (Murray & Forster, 1977). The first of these experiments was essentially the same as the experiment already described, except that the items were only five words in length, and the legal nonword condition was omitted. For the "same" items, exactly the same pattern of results emerged: a strong effect of grammaticality and a strong effect of plausibility. For the "different" items, however, all conditions produced equivalent matching times. This was the case whether the different pair of words occurred in the first or the second half (the point being that context may only exert an effect on words occurring in the second half of the string). A follow-up experiment used the same sequences, except that the difference between strings was made more obvious by making the words quite dissimilar (e.g., instead of the pair *shirts/shorts,* the pair *shirts/tables* was used). This had the desired effect of decreasing both "same" and "different" latencies, but the pattern of results for both types of items remained unchanged.

The implications of these results are clear. Meaning and syntax are highly relevant when the subject makes a "same" judgment, but not when a "different" judgment is being made. Provided we can be sure that the matching process was not being controlled by a sublexical level, we are led to the conclusion that lexical processing is unaffected by either syntactic or semantic context.

Because only borderline lexical effects were obtained in the Chambers and Forster (1975) experiment, this point ought to be established, although it seems highly unlikely that the fastest comparisons could have been made at a sublexical level. Fortunately, results of a separate study are available (Rice, Thorpe, & Gunn, 1977) in which the contrast between items such as (14) and (15) was examined:

(14a)   The girl wrote to the priest.
(14b)   The girl wrote to the office.
(15a)   The jolder gint to his gloob.
(15b)   The jolder gint to his quead.

In this experiment, a clear word superiority effect was obtained for "different" items, the mean matching time for items such as (14) being 1157 msec, whereas for items such as (15), the mean time was 1331 msec. Presumably, the reason that sentences produce a clear word-superiority effect for "different" items is simply that they are longer than words, and, hence, many more units need to be compared before the difference is detected. This conclusion is supported by the fact that a similar word superiority effect can be demonstrated for word pairs such as *quiet silent/quiet silver* compared with nonword pairs such as *queel sonnet/quell sanper* (Middleton, 1977).

These results show that speed of lexical processing is clearly relevant for both "same" and "different" items, and, hence, any variable that facilitates word recognition ought to have a decisive effect on both types of items. The absence of one of these two effects leads most naturally to the conclusion that semantic context is irrelevant to word recognition in *both* types of items. The only alternative is to postulate two types of word recognition; the first type is involved in "same" items, and is sensitive to contextual factors, whereas the second is involved in "different" items and is not sensitive to context.

At this point I would like to recall my earlier remark that it would always be possible to find a task that would refute any particular claim about sentence processing. We have here just such a case. Later, I return to this issue and attempt to reconcile this result with currently accepted views. For the moment, I merely point out that previous research has paid little or no attention to the problem of deciding which level of processing actually controls the response being made.

If the argument we have advanced so far is correct, then it ought to be possible to produce both semantic and syntactic effects with "different" items. This would then discourage any line of argument that postulates a special "difference" detector that is not subject to the same variables as the "sameness" detector. In two further experiments Murray (1978) appears to have demonstrated such effects.

To produce a syntactic effect, we need to slow down the lexical-comparison rate relative to the syntactic-comparison rate. One way to do this is to increase the length of the sentences, so that it is possible to include items in which a substantial number of words need to be compared before the difference is detected. In the first of these two experiments, "different" items of the following types were compared:

(16a) The dog growled fiercely at the p o s t m a n .
(16b) The dog growled fiercely at the t r a f f i c .
(17a) The lady belched bravely at the r a p i s t s .
(17b) The lady belched bravely at the w r i t e r s .
(18a) The at noisily the flapped box c a m p f i r e .
(18b) The at noisily the flapped box f a m i l i e s .

The position of the different word pair varied, but analysis was restricted only to those cases where the difference occurred at or near the end of the sequence. There were 20 examples of each type included, and 20 subjects were tested. For the "same" items in this experiment, the usual results were obtained: strong semantic and syntactic effects. For "different" items, however, the mean response times for the above types of items were 1974, 2035, and 2151 msec, respectively. The difference between plausible and implausible sentences was not significant (by both F_2 and *min F'*), but the difference between the sentences and the ungrammatical items *was* significant.

Thus, increasing the number of words to be compared at least brings the syntactic level into play, although the plausibility effect (61 msec) is very marginal, being significant by F_1 alone (this probably indicates that message level output is controlling the "different" decision for only a small proportion of the total set of items). Perhaps a further increase in length would have produced a significant effect for plausibility, but the sentences would then have been too long to be displayed on our equipment. Instead, a plausibility effect for "different" items was demonstrated quite unexpectedly in a repetition of the previous experiment using successive rather than simultaneous presentation. The first sequence was shown by itself for 3 sec, and then the second sequence appeared beneath the first. In our opinion, the opportunity to read the first sequence before the comparison begins vastly increased the speed of sentential processing relative to purely lexical processing. This was reflected by decreased matching times, and by the fact that a clear and significant plausibility effect now emerged, the mean times for the three conditions corresponding to (16), (17), and (18) being 1292, 1385, and 1573 msec, respectively.

These results show that difference detection is subject to the same influences as sameness detection, and, hence, the absence of syntactic or semantic influences for the shorter "different" items cannot be attributed to special properties of the difference detector, such as an insensitivity to familiarity, or linguistic properties. Thus, we can claim that an analysis of the "different" items shows two important effects: an effect of lexical-level processing in the absence of syntactic and message-level effects and an effect of syntactic processing in the absence of a message-level effect.

AUTONOMY OF SYNTACTIC PROCESSING

The claim that the syntactic processor is autonomous means that there is no higher level processor that is capable of directly intervening in and altering the operation of the syntactic processor. A given sequence of lexical units will be processed in exactly the same way, no matter what interpretation is assigned to the sequence. Assessing the validity of this claim is likely to be a highly intricate exercise, because there is no simple way to measure speed of syntactic processing directly.

I have already argued that if syntactic processing is not autonomous but is "guided" by an assessment of the plausible semantic relations that hold between the key lexical items, then there should be no task that is simultaneously sensitive to syntactic effects and insensitive to plausibility. The results obtained in the matching task disconfirm this prediction. As already mentioned, when five-word "different" items are presented simultaneously, there is a significant effect of grammaticality but no significant effect of plausibility. This ought to be impossible if the syntactic processor is guided by the presence of plausible relations between lexical items.

To my knowledge, this is the first time such an effect has been obtained. The literature abounds with examples of joint syntactic and semantic effects (e.g., Forster & Ryder, 1971; Martin, 1968; Miller & Isard, 1963), and in our experience at least, the only tasks for which plausibility effects disappear turn out to be also insensitive to syntactic effects (i.e., they are not sentential tasks). Evidently, it must be difficult to find just the right set of conditions to demonstrate this independence of syntactic and semantic effects (or else it would have been reported sooner), and no doubt the sentence-matching result was quite fortuitous. Hopefully, further research will enable us to say something about why the effect occurred in this situation and not in another and may even suggest other tasks that may have similar properties.

In the meantime, we can add this finding to the very meager list of positive indicators of autonomous syntactic processing. The only other member of that list is the fact that at least some of the perceptual consequences of syntactic structure are constant across wide variations in plausibility (Forster & Olbrei, 1973, Exp. I; Forster & Ryder, 1971). This evidence has already been discussed in the papers cited, and there is little point in repeating that discussion here.

There is one further finding that we may be able to add to this list. The results reported here are preliminary, and the technique requires improvement, but the initial results seem to be reasonably interesting.

In this experiment, I have used the so-called RSVP (rapid serial visual presentation) technique to measure sentence-processing time (Forster, 1970). The rationale for this technique is that the individual words in a sentence are presented visually, one at a time, at a rate so fast that they cannot be separately assimilated and remembered. However, if the subjects are able to impose a meaningful structure on the input sequence, or even just a part of it, then their ability to report the details of the input is enhanced. The more structure can be imposed, the more will be reported. Further, the more rapidly the correct structure can be discovered, then the more items should be reported. Of course, *some* of the words can be remembered even if there is no structure at all. These are being remembered as individual items in a list. The number of words remembered in this case represents a lower bound on performance.

In earlier experiments using RSVP, we had noticed that when, for example, two adjacent words were permuted, it was extremely difficult to detect this change in order, even with repeated viewings of the same sequence. Clearly, the perceptual system is somehow compensating for the order error. However, one would not expect this compensation to be cost-free, because if the processor takes the words in their presented order, computation must eventually block. This would force some kind of back-up procedure, and we would then be in the position of a garden-path sentence, where the sentence has to be reanalyzed . Thus, although we eventually perceive the sequence in a grammatical order, it has cost us something to gain this result.

Assuming for the moment that we can detect this cost factor, we now want to ask whether the cost would be the same for meaningful and anomalous items. That is, in the following set of sentences, would the performance difference between items (19) and (20) correspond to the difference between (21) and (22)?

(19) The speech was written carefully.
(20) The was speech written carefully.
(21) The dream was added relatively.
(22) The was dream added relatively.

If there *is* a constant effect of order error for the two kinds of sentences, then the most natural interpretation seems to be that the syntactic processor treats an anomalous sentence the same as any other sentence.

The experiment consisted of taking 24 quadruples of the above form and presenting the first and last versions to one group of 15 subjects, with the second and third versions being presented to another group of the same size. Although the subjects were required to write down as much as they could, we only scored the number of substantives (three in each sentence), regardless of the order in which they were reported. This procedure avoids the possibility that one condition would be better than another simply because the correct sequencing of the items was easier to reconstruct.

The order errors were either cases in which one word exchanged places with a neighbor, or moved two words away from its correct position, or where *two* words were moved. Examples of these items are as follows:

(23) The girl the surprised teacher.
(24) The attended the physicist seminar.
(25) The had restaurant food outstanding.

Performance on the meaningful sentences dropped from 61.3% of the key words being reported to 50.6% when order was changed, a difference of 10.6%. The corresponding drop for anomalous sentences was from 48.4% to 35.8%, a drop of 12.6%. The difference between 10.6 and 12.6 was nowhere near being statistically significant, although other effects were highly significant (such as the meaningful-anomalous comparison or the effect of order). Thus, it seems appropriate to conclude that the disruption caused by changing the word-order is the same for both meaningful and anomalous constructions.

By now, it should be apparent that this experiment is quite similar in design to the earlier experiment performed by Miller and Isard (1963). Basically, they found that although anomalous sentences were harder to perceive than meaningful sentences, they were still superior to totally scrambled word lists. The inference to be drawn from that experiment was that anomalous sentences are assigned a syntactic structure by the sentence processor, this structure somehow having beneficial effects on report. The experiments discussed here try to go further, to in fact establish that this structure is assigned by the same set of computational steps as would be involved in a meaningful sentence.

The latter point is important. If all we could show was that anomalous sentences received a syntactic analysis, we could say nothing about the design of the processing system. It could be done by analogy, i.e., finding a sentence with the same sequence of word types but not containing any anomalous constituents. Or it could be done by relaxing some of the constraints on lexical insertion into the underlying tree. But if we can claim that structure is assigned to anomalous sentences in a completely standard fashion, then I believe this fact places heavy constraints on the possible form of the grammar.

If the grammar (from which the processor is constructed) has lexical insertion rules that contain selectional restrictions, then the processor would be unable to assign a structure to anomalous sentences, no matter *how* the processor was constructed. It would have to adopt some special strategy of interpretation. But if we believe that there is nothing special about the way anomalous sentences are processed at the syntactic level, then it seems we have to assume that selection restrictions do not operate at the level of lexical insertion.

I now turn briefly to the evidence that appears to support quite different conclusions. This evidence consists of experiments demonstrating that semantic cues are regularly used to assist syntactic analysis. The prime example is the reversibility phenomenon reported by Slobin (1966). In this experiment, Slobin reported that the normal difference between actives and passives was found *only* when there were no semantic cues as to which NP was the logical subject. For example, *The flowers were watered by the girl* was no harder than its corresponding active, the assumption being that *flowers* is blocked by selectional restrictions from being the logical subject of *watered*.

The problem with this experiment is that it used a picture-verification technique. That is, after seeing the sentence, the subject is shown a picture and must say whether the sentence is a true description of the picture. Unfortunately, this technique appears to have little to do with on-line sentence processing, because the same results are obtained when the subject is given ample time to complete the processing of the sentence (Gough, 1966). In all probability, the cognitive operations involved in comparing sentences and pictures are far too complex to make this a useful procedure for making claims about speed of syntactic processing. In any event, we have tried hard to get reversibility effects using both RSVP and sentence classification and in several experiments have found no trace of the effect (Forster & Olbrei, 1973).

I have little doubt that there are many other sentence-processing tasks that will show effects of reversibility. For example, Herriot (1969) required subjects to state the logical subject and the logical object of the sentence and obtained the same result as did Slobin (1966). This appears to be a quite reasonable result, and I would not wish to claim that the results of experiments that show a reversibility effect are invalid. But I do want to raise one question: How should we interpret the absence of such an effect in, for example, the sentence-classification task? To reply that reversibility only applies in certain tasks is to avoid the central problem. If reversibility affects syntactic processing, then *all* tasks which reliably index speed of sentence processing should show such effects.

The only way to answer this argument is to try to argue that the sentence-classification task is somehow irrelevant. There are two possible lines of attack:

1. The sentence-classification task reflects only a very superficial processing of the sentence. Subjects do not need to understand the meaning of the sentence and, hence, do not use semantic strategies. This argument can be dismissed easily since semantic plausibility has a profound effect on performance in this task. But even if we accepted the argument, we should still need to know *how* superficial the processing could be. To recognize that (26) is grammatical and that (27) is not surely requires at least a syntactic analysis of the surface structure.

(26) The patient was cured by the doctor.
(27) The patient cured was by the doctor.

There is simply no other way in which this task can be accurately performed. From the point of view of a theory of the syntactic processor, this type of processing could scarcely be regarded as superficial.

2. The sentence-classification task is unnatural and artificial and discourages the subject from using "normal" semantically guided processing strategies. The first part of this criticism is irrelevant, but the second part may be correct. Any laboratory task will be artificial, but this artificiality does not count as a criticism. What is important is the degree to which the task requires the deployment of linguistic abilities while minimizing the influence of extralinguistic abilities. In this regard the classification task seems to me to be superior to tasks such as the verification task, the logical subject/logical object task, or even question–answering. Detection of ungrammaticality is, of course, a very "natural" task. When errors occur during sentence recognition (such as misreading words or making segmentation errors), then it is frequently the detection of ungrammaticality that signals the fact that an error has occurred. A particularly clear example is the reading of text in which a line has been omitted; what we appear to become aware of first is that the syntactic processor has totally failed to assign a structure to the input. The second part of this criticism is more relevant. It is possible that in this task,

subjects pay rather more attention to syntax than they would otherwise do. For example, the word-order error in (27) may well go totally unnoticed in connected text.

This may mean that reversibility only becomes relevant when the task deemphasizes careful attention to syntax. If this is the case, then it suggests that reversibility is having its effects at some level of processing other than the syntactic level. It certainly does not suggest that we should discard the sentence-classification task. Even if syntactic analysis were almost never required in normal situations (a nonsensical view in my opinion), one must still use a syntactic test if one wishes to claim that reversibility influences syntactic processing.

In conclusion then, the argument is as follows: The systematic failure to find reversibility effects with one bona fide syntactic task is enough to outweigh a number of positive findings on other tasks. Repeated demonstrations showing that other tasks show the predicted effects is beside the point unless the bona fides of the sentence-classification task can be challenged.

I should hasten to point out that the current evidence is scarcely convincing on either side of this debate. All I wish to claim is that the present evidence is not sufficient to rule out the principle of autonomous syntactic processing.

One possibility that should not be overlooked is that constructions other than the active–passive contrast may well give quite different results. It may be that reversibility is irrelevant only when the syntactic structure of the sentence is clearly and prominently marked. Steedman and Johnson-Laird (1976) have recently reported an experiment by J. G. Quinn that uses preposed indirect object constructions such as (28) and (29).

(28) The man took the girl the boy.
(29) The man took the girl the coat.

In (28), there are no semantic cues to the correct syntactic analysis because either *the girl* or *the boy* could be the indirect object. However, in (29) an implausible interpretation would result if the wrong syntactic assignment were made, and, hence, there is a strong semantic cue to the correct structural interpretation (the term *semantic* here really means nonsyntactic and covers cues based on both selection restrictions and purely pragmatic considerations).

The task in this experiment was deceptively simple. Subjects were asked to view a sentence and to press a button when they had understood it. The subject was then required to answer a question about the sentence such as *"who gave the coat?"* The measure of comprehension difficulty was defined as the initial viewing time.

The results of this experiment showed that preposing the indirect object produced a smaller increase in difficulty for semantically constrained sentences. That is, the difference between (28) and (30) was greater than the difference between (29) and (31).

    (30) The man took the boy to the girl.
    (31) The man took the coat to the girl.

This evidence clearly implies that the presence of the semantic cue altered the subjects' criterion for having understood the sentence. The task used in this experiment is not without its problems, however, because it is assumed that the subjects know how much time they actually require to understand a sentence. It seems likely that what the subjects were actually doing was viewing the sentence for long enough to make sure they could rapidly answer a question about it, and this may have involved rehearsal or even overt transformation of the preposed sentences into a more amenable form. As Steedman and Johnson-Laird themselves recognize, the latencies were exceptionally long for such short sentences, ranging from 2870 to 3400 msec.

If this effect proves to be clear-cut under other task conditions,[1] then it might be necessary to amend the argument to allow for effects of semantic constraints when syntactic processing is unusually difficult. It already seems clear that semantic constraints help young children to understand passives (Turner & Rommetveit, 1967), and they also help adults to understand doubly self-embedded sentences (Hall, 1969; Schlesinger, 1968). In both cases there are good grounds for arguing that the test sentences were well beyond the computational power of the syntactic processors involved. The preposed indirect object construction may fall into the same category (reading three or four examples of this construction one after the other seems to produce a rapid fatigue effect; so much so that a careful and almost conscious analysis of the sentence is required).

Assume for the moment that such semantic effects do exist. We now need to ask whether semantic constraints *also* assist the processing of quite simple constructions (although to a lesser degree). I imagine that the answer is likely to be that they do not.

If semantic constraints only assist in the comprehension of difficult structures, then a quite different argument emerges. It might be suggested that there is more than one way to "understand" a sentence. One way uses the output of the syntactic processor as a starting point. Another way uses perhaps just the key lexical items and makes "guesses" as to the likely message that the sentence is intended to convey. This latter method might, in fact, be

---

[1]A pilot investigation carried out in our laboratory by K. Fisher and L. McGregor-Carroll suggests that this may not be the case. They had subjects respond to sentences such as (28) and (29) or (30) and (31) in a sentence-classification task and found no effects of semantic cues either in the preposed or in the normal form.

mediated by the GPS and may be quite outside the activity of the language processor itself. For syntactically simple constructions, the GPS-mediated approach may well be slower than the syntax-based method, and, hence, semantic constraints are irrelevant. But for complex structures, the GPS system is faster, and, therefore, one obtains semantic effects.

If this argument can be independently supported, then the autonomy principle is preserved intact, because the site of the semantic effect is not the syntactic processor. The danger of making such an argument is that one can then be accused of inventing special processes whenever the autonomy principle is threatened; in more prosaic terms, it is a case of having one's cake and eating it.

But the theory is not totally protected. It clearly requires a reduction in semantic effects as syntactic complexity is decreased, eventually reaching a cut-off point below which no semantic effects at all can be observed. It also predicts that semantic effects should be eliminated entirely when the task cannot be performed accurately without syntactic analysis. For example, in the Quinn study (cited by Steedman & Johnson-Laird [1976]), this might be achieved by including sentences such as (32).

(32) The boy sold the newspaper the man.

In this case, a GPS strategy based on lexical items will return the wrong result, and, hence, the subject will be forced to rely on syntactic analysis to answer the question correctly.

Ratcliff (1975) has reported data that fit this analysis quite neatly. She compared sentence-classification times for 60 ungrammatical sequences such as (33) and (34).

(33) The musicians their played new songs.
(34) The musicians the shook new rifle.

In (33) there is a perfectly plausible sentence that can be formed by a permutation of two words, but in (34), there is no permutation that will produce a plausible interpretation. In these cases, the correct response was "no." Ratcliff asked whether the availability of a plausible rearrangement might interfere with the subject's ability to detect the ungrammaticality.

For correct rejections (i.e., the ungrammaticality was detected), there was virtually no difference in reaction time. The "plausible" items required 1216 msec, whereas the "implausible" items required 1224 msec (this difference was not significant). However, the error rate for the "plausible" items was 15.6%, which was significantly greater than the 7.8% error rate for "implausible" items.

Such a result makes sense if we assume that correct rejections were based exclusively on output from the syntactic processor; because semantic properties are irrelevant at this level, the correct rejection response latencies were unaffected by considerations of meaning. However, false acceptances are based on the GPS, where semantic properties are critical. Thus, on some relatively small proportion of trials, the output of the GPS was sufficiently fast (or the output of the syntactic processor was sufficiently slow) to enable the GPS to control decision making and to produce an error.

There are other ways of interpreting these results, but as Ratcliff (1975) pointed out, they do not cover both the latency and error data. For example, if we argue that there are two competing and independent methods of interpreting the input (one syntactic and one semantic), then they ought to produce conflict in the case of items such as (33), which would lead to longer rejection latencies. Alternatively, it might be suggested that the plausibility of the assigned meaning is used as a check on the accuracy of the syntactic analysis, which is not always error-free. When the meaning is found to be implausible, a reanalysis of the syntax is carried out. Hence, errors in syntactic processing are less likely to be detected when the assigned interpretation is highly plausible. This theory would explain the difference in error rates, but not the equivalence of rejection latencies, because some of the correct rejections of the "implausible" sequences should involve a reprocessing of the syntax and, hence, should have produced longer rejection times.

Postulating that the GPS is capable of some kind of rudimentary processing of linguistic material may be an unwelcome complication but appears unavoidable. There seems to be no doubt that word sequences such as (35) through (38) are capable of being understood in some sense, and it would be just as complicated to modify the theory of the sentence processor to allow it to process these sequences.

(35) dog man bite
(36) lemon sugar bitter sweet
(37) cure doctor patient
(38) the patient was by the cured doctor

That is, it would require a fundamental alteration of the nature of the syntactic processor to give it the power to discover that, for example, the words of (38) can be arranged to form sentence (39).

(39) The patient was cured by the doctor.

Such an increase in power would make it utterly hopeless to search for interesting relations between the grammar of the language and the form of the syntactic processor used by speakers of that language.[2] Hence, there seems to be no alternative but to postulate a general problem-solving system that can assign interpretations to word sequences. Of course, this system may still use such fragments of output that the syntactic processor may be able to provide (e.g., it might be easier to "guess" the meaning of *doctor patient cure* than the meaning of *patient doctor cure*; in the former case, the initial position of *doctor* may establish it as having the semantic function of actor). It may even use the sentence-production system to see whether a sentence that resembles the input sequence can be generated.

As a concrete example of the kinds of skills we must contemplate, consider the kind of processing that must be involved in constructing a sentence that *ends* in the sequence of words specified in (40).

(40) ... in that case on other fish which do.

Although our ability to solve such problems depends on interesting linguistic properties such as the tendency of the language to employ right- or left-branching constructions (Forster, 1974a), surely nobody would wish to claim that the language processor itself can solve such problems unaided. Rather, the ability to solve problems such as (40) should be seen as the product of the joint application of two separate information-processing systems, one being based on relatively inflexible language-processing routines, and the other comprising generalized problem-solving routines.

Returning to the main problem of the autonomy of the syntactic processor, there is one extremely interesting result Tyler and Marslen-Wilson (1977) found using a technique that is restricted to extremely fast, on-line processing capabilities. In this experiment, subjects were presented with a phonetically realized sequence of words followed by a visually presented word. They were simply required to pronounce this last word as rapidly as possible. Typical items were (41) and (42), where the visually presented word is given in uppercase letters.

(41) If you walk too near the runway, landing planes ARE...
(42) If you've been trained as a pilot, landing planes ARE...

The point of the experiment is that the phrase immediately prior to the word to be pronounced (i.e., *landing planes*) is structurally ambiguous. If the subject chose the wrong interpretation of this phrase (in these examples, a

---

[2]It seems most unlikely that the syntactic processor could be responsible for the reordering of (38) to form (39), because (38) is actually well formed as it stands, and, hence, there is no need for reordering at all.

verbal interpretation in which *planes* is the object of *landing*), then it was assumed that the time required to pronounce the next word would be affected. Given this assumption, one can then determine whether the meaning of the initial clause has affected the interpretation of the ambiguous segment. The data reported by Tyler and Marslen-Wilson are quite convincing and show that, for example, *are* takes longer to pronounce in items such as (42) than it does in items such as (41).

As the authors point out, however, the crucial question is whether the meaning of the first clause affects processing before or after the phrase *landing planes* has been analyzed. If the effect takes place before, then a clear violation of the autonomy principle is produced. However, this does not seem to be a very likely proposal. It would have to be argued that in (42) there is some property of the initial clause that would predispose the syntactic processor to treat *any* subsequent construction of the form V-ing N as being verbal in nature (i.e., the N being the object of V). Not only is it difficult to imagine what this property might be, it seems that such a predisposition would be inappropriate in many cases. For example, in (43) it is quite reasonable to suppose that a nominal interpretation is just as likely (i.e., N is subject of V).

(43) If you've been trained as a pilot, approaching storms...

These considerations suggest that the locus of the semantic context effect must be *after* the ambiguous phrase.

If this is the case, then it follows that the syntactic processor must treat the ambiguous phrase as ambiguous, and both structural possibilities are output to the message-level processor. What might happen next is difficult to judge. One possibility is that the message processor chooses one of these inputs and signals this fact to the syntactic processor, which then discards the relevant analysis. When the visual probe word turns out to be incompatible with the chosen analysis, syntactic reprocessing is required and pronunciation is delayed. This would definitely constitute a violation of the autonomy principle, although this would not be nearly as serious a violation. However, there is another possibility that should not be overlooked. The syntactic processor may be quite unaffected by the semantic context, as the autonomy principle requires. Two analyses of the ambiguous phrase are provided, and one is discarded when the subsequent disambiguating probe word is presented. As far as the syntactic processor is concerned, items (41) and (42) are indistinguishable. However, the message processor chooses one of the interpretations of the ambiguous phrase when the acoustic segment of the sentence terminates, only to discover that the *subsequent* output of the syntactic processor is incompatible with this choice.

With normal presentation of the sentence, we might not expect this effect to occur. Rather, the message processor might delay the choice between the two structural possibilities to see whether syntactic disambiguation will be possible. However, when the sentence actually terminates before the disambiguating word is presented (and some pause in the processing of the input stream is produced) and when the task obviously requires the subject to try to predict ahead, the message processor may commit itself to an interpretation immediately. This line of argument suggests an alternative experiment. Suppose that all words in the sentence are presented visually at a reasonably rapid rate (say, 500 msec a word), and the subject is required to pronounce *each* word (as in a shadowing task). In this situation, the message-level processor might not be so inclined to make a hasty decision, and, hence, the interference would not occur. More generally, we might expect that any task involving rapid and continuous presentation of the entire sentence would yield little evidence for an interference effect.

As I have remarked before, the degree of complexity and indeterminacy that such arguments as this inevitably introduce may strike some as totally unwarranted and downright subversive. I acknowledge this possibility and, like everyone else, earnestly hope that less tortuous arguments will win the day. But until this has been demonstrated, a more cautious approach is required. It seems to me that it is reasonable to ask which level of processing is actually responsible for the obtained experimental effects, and in the present case, there seems to be no compelling argument that it is the syntactic level that is responsible.

Thus, although we should acknowledge this possibility, we should also acknowledge that Tyler and Marslen-Wilson (1977) have drawn attention to a possible modification of the autonomy principle. The modification would be that higher levels of processing may affect the processing of lower levels by signalling which of several equally valued analyses is likely to be correct. Such a signal is produced *after* the lower level has completed its analysis of an ambiguous segment and not before.

Before leaving the question of syntactic processing, I would like to make one general remark about the possibility of semantic guidance of the syntactic processor. The whole point of a language having a syntax is to provide a clear and unmistakable indication of the correct interpretation of the sentence. Otherwise there would be no way to convey the meaning embodied in sentences such as the following:

(44) The patient cured the doctor.
(45) The boy sold the man to the newspaper.

Any move to allow the syntactic processor to be influenced by pragmatic factors works against the fundamental purpose of syntax. In fact, one might surmise that the evolution of syntax has been influenced by the degree to which it successfully guards against errors introduced by a consideration of pragmatic and semantic facts. Hence, it has always seemed strange to me that anyone should *expect* to find evidence for semantic influences on syntactic processing. To be sure, one might expect to find evidence that syntactic indicators are often overlooked or overridden when the appropriate semantic interpretation of the sentence seems obvious from context, or from a consideration of the lexical items used. In fact, we have already argued that the results obtained by Ratcliff (1975) should be interpreted in this way. But these effects are effects of pragmatic factors on *message* processing, not *syntactic* processing.

AUTONOMY OF LEXICAL PROCESSING

I would now like to consider the second half of the autonomy principle, the proposal that lexical processing is autonomous. This proposal makes two claims: that the process involved in locating the lexical entry of a word cannot be modified by processing at either the syntactic level or at the message level.

I begin by conceding that there are obvious *apparent* effects of both types of processing on the ease of word recognition, especially when the signal-to-noise ratio of the input signal is low, as it is in normal speech. What I hope to be able to show is that these effects are generally capable of more than one interpretation.

There are two major approaches to the problem of lexical access. The first approach utilizes the concept of a word detector (e.g., Meyer & Schvaneveldt, 1976; Morton, 1970). Corresponding to each word in the mental lexicon is a detector that is selectively tuned to the perceptual attributes of that word. Each detector has a threshold that is controlled by the frequency of occurrence of that word. When a test word is presented, the detectors for all words that have properties in common with the test word are activated, and whenever the level of activation of a given detector reaches threshold, the detector fires and makes available to other processing systems the information stored in lexical memory about that word.

In such a model, it is typically assumed that inputs to the detector system are not restricted to those arising from the presentation of the word itself. In addition, there are inputs arising from both the syntactic and semantic context in which the word occurs, so that in an environment where a noun has a high probability of occurring, the detectors for all nouns are activated to some degree. In effect, this lowers the threshold for all nouns, and this is assumed to facilitate lexical access. Thus, for detector models, the assumption is usually made that lexical processing is highly sensitive to both syntactic and message-level processing, and, hence, lexical processing is not autonomous.

The second approach to lexical access views word recognition as an active search process (e.g., Forster, 1976; Rubenstein et al., 1971; Stanners, Forbach, & Headley, 1971). When a word is presented, the perceptual attributes of the word are used to select a subset of the total set of lexical entries for intensive examination. These entries are then serially examined to determine whether the stored linguistic properties in each entry can be matched to the perceptual attributes of the test word. When a satisfactory match is found, the lexical-access process is completed, and the contents of the matching entry can be made available to other processing systems. The selection of the subset of entries to be searched implies that the entries are organized in some way according to the perceptual attributes of words. Once the subset has been selected, the order in which the entries are examined is controlled by frequency of occurrence (in order to maximize search efficiency), with the result that entries for high-frequency words are located before the entries for low-frequency words.

In the search model, the effects of syntactic and semantic context would have to be realized in the initial delimitation of the search set. Thus, if the syntactic context is such that a noun is likely to occur, then the search set could be delimited so that only nouns were included in the set. Similarly, if the semantic context were such that, for example, an animate noun were expected, then the search set could be further delimited to just the set of animate nouns. Because the speed of lexical access will depend on the size of the search set, context effects of this sort will produce a decrease in access time.

I have argued elsewhere (Forster, 1976) that this delimitation of the search set by both syntactic and semantic properties creates considerable problems. Consider the situation for an orthographically presented word occurring in the environment:

(46) The children were taught to regularly feed their _____.

The delimitation of the search set for such a word could be approximated by the tree structure shown in Fig. 2.3. The sentence environment is predictive of an animate noun, and pragmatic considerations would suggest that a domestic pet is the most likely category (thus *dog* would be recognized in this context faster than would *wolf*, which in turn would be recognized faster than, for example, would *ashtray*).

The selection of the appropriate subset (one of the boxes at the bottom of the tree) involves tracing through the tree using the known (or anticipated) syntactic and semantic properties. The final subclassification is according to orthographic properties of the actual test word, and in this case we are assuming that words are classified into four orthographic types, A, B, C, and

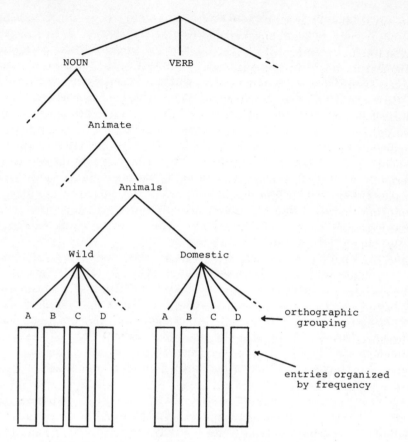

FIG. 2.3.   Access organized by function, form, and frequency.

D. At this point the orthographic properties of the target word itself would be examined to decide which of these four orthographic sets should be searched.

Apart from the enormous proliferation of categories, this system will work quite well when words are presented in context. But how would it operate when no context is presented, as in a lexical-decision experiment? In this case, all that is known is the orthographic coding of the word, but in the tree depicted in Fig. 2.3, there is no way of selecting the correct orthographic category. For example, if the word is Type A, then all the A categories will have to be searched in an essentially arbitrary sequence. We might, for example, have to search through all the A categories under the general heading of INANIMATE NOUN before we would get to the correct entry.

The fatal weakness in this account is that we would now have no mechanism to explain the effect of frequency on access time. That is, there is no way to search all the entries for words of Type A in order of their frequency of occurrence. Any attempt to construct such a method (e.g., by taking the most frequent members of all A categories first, and then taking the next most frequent members, and so on) is equivalent to constructing an *independent* access system that is organized just by orthographic category and frequency.

So the position is this. We either predict no frequency effect when words are presented out of context, or we construct another access system for such words. The first alternative is certainly wrong, because there are very strong frequency effects when no context is specified (e.g., Forster & Bednall, 1976; Forster & Chambers, 1973; Rubenstein et al., 1971). The second alternative is certainly possible but involves duplication of access mechanisms. It also makes the prediction that specifying a context should have the effect of reducing the magnitude of the frequency effect, because the search set in this case is smaller (a prediction that, as we shall see, has little to recommend it).[3]

What appears to be causing problems is the attempt to organize the lexicon in terms of both the form and the function of words. Given the problems, one might conclude that it would be simpler to organize lexical entries merely according to *form*. Because words have both a phonetic and an orthographic form, there will need to be two such organizations. As I have suggested earlier (Forster, 1976), it is perhaps more convenient to distinguish between data structures that represent what the speakers *know* about the words of their language (the lexicon proper) and the data structures that merely serve to gain efficient access to that knowledge. We thus postulate a lexicon, and two independent access files that permit rapid access to the lexicon from either a visual or an acoustic stimulus. The search and matching process takes place in the access files, not the lexicon. The entry for a word in either the orthographically or phonologically organized access file simply contains a pointer to the appropriate entry in the lexicon. This situation is depicted in Fig. 2.4.

Because the access files are organized purely according to form and frequency, there is no provision made for effects of a sentence context at all. That is, there is no way in which the lexical access system can utilize information from either syntactic or message-level processing. In short, lexical access is assumed to be autonomous.

The preceding argument gives some of the motivation for the claim of autonomy in lexical access and explains why one might wish to entertain this hypothesis despite the existence of evidence that appears to run counter to it. Some of this evidence is discussed later, and where context effects are clearly indicated, some additional mechanism will have to be invoked.

---

[3]A third possibility exists and that is to suggest that frequency has its effects after the entry has been located and does not affect the access process itself. For arguments against this proposal, see Forster and Bednall (1976), Taft and Forster (1976, Exp. II), Forster (1976).

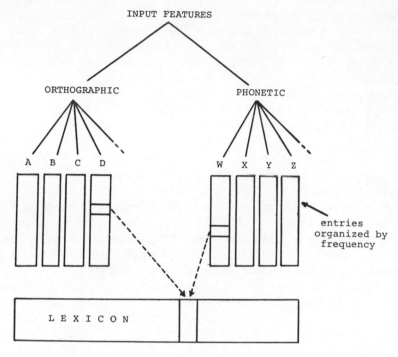

FIG. 2.4. Access organized by form and frequency.

LEXICAL ACCESS IN SENTENCES
AND LISTS

The most obvious method of studying lexical access in a sentence context is to use the lexical-decision task. Instead of presenting just single words, or word pairs, we present whole sentences and ask subjects to decide whether or not the input string consists entirely of words. This avoids the problems inherent in visual sentence-context experiments using tachistoscope exposure (e.g., Tulving & Gold, 1963) or in acoustic experiments using a low signal-to-noise ratio (e.g., Miller and Isard, 1963). These experiments use accuracy of report as the dependent variable and, hence, are forced to use a degraded input, which permits the subject to guess or reconstruct the input using the sentence context. Thus, the fact that fewer errors are made in recognizing words in a sentence context may mean that the context made lexical access more efficient, or it may mean only that context made it easier to guess what the target word must have been.

The experiment briefly discussed at the beginning of this paper (Forster, 1974c) used the lexical-decision task with samples of plausible sentences, implausible sentences, and ungrammatical strings. All items were five words in length. The distractors were either sentences or ungrammatical strings with an orthographically legal nonword replacing one of the words. The results of the experiment were very clear. Lexical decisions were faster for plausible sentences than for implausible sentences, which in turn were faster than for ungrammatical strings.

Superficially, these results provide a strong indication that both syntactic and message-level processing have increased the speed of lexical processing. However, the same items were also used in a sentence-classification task, and for the plausible sentences, similar results were obtained. In actual fact, for sentences there was no significant difference between the lexical-classification times and the sentence-classification times. As we remarked earlier, this raises the possibility that the lexical decisions were not based on the output of the lexical level, in which case the interpretation placed on the results changes. In Table 2.1, the results of the two experiments are summarized, together with the processing level assumed to be responsible in each case. For plausible sentences, the message level controls decisions in both tasks, producing equivalent times (the lexical time may actually be slightly longer, owing to the extra inferential step required). But for implausible sentences, the syntactic processor takes over for the lexical task but not for the sentence task, producing a significantly smaller effect of plausibility for the lexical task (179 msec) than for the sentence task (363 msec). For ungrammatical strings, the syntactic processor suffices for the sentence task but is inadequate for the lexical task, because the correct response here cannot be inferred from the syntactic output (ungrammatical sequences may consist of either words or nonwords), and, hence, a pronounced advantage for the sentence task is obtained.

This explanation covers the facts adequately, but we still need additional evidence before it can be accepted. Why, for example, should the sentence classification of an implausible sentence be based on the message level when the syntactic output is already available (as indicated by the lexical results)? Obviously, there are several other possibilities that could be suggested. For

TABLE 2.1
Mean Decision Times (in Msec) for Lexical and Sentence Classification
Tasks as a Function of Plausibility and Grammaticality

Task	Plausible	Implausible	Ungrammatical
Lexical			
Decision time	1347	1526	1701
Fastest level	Message	Syntactic	Lexical
Sentence			
Decision time	1258	1621	1513
Fastest level	Message	Message	Syntactic

example, in Table 2.1, the fastest levels for the lexical task could be message, lexical, lexical. This would explain the reduced effect of plausibility in the lexical task but would also indicate that grammaticality facilitates lexical processing (thereby violating the lexical autonomy principle). Similarly, the fastest levels for the sentence task could be message, syntactic, syntactic, which would indicate that syntactic processing was facilitated by plausibility (thereby violating the syntactic autonomy principle). Thus, the entries in Table 2.2 for the fastest levels are the only ones that permit the autonomy principle to be maintained.

I argued earlier that the decision phase of the lexical task would be very slow if only the lexical output was considered; this was attributed to the fact that a large number of output units would have to be considered by the GPS, and, hence, there would be an advantage to using a sentential output. If this is the correct interpretation, then decreasing the length of the sentence should increase the probability of the lexical output controlling the decision. Thus, if two-word sentences such as (47), (48), and (49) were compared, we might find that lexical-decision times are faster than sentence-classification times.

(47) Dogs growl.
(48) Dogs groan.
(49) Growl dogs.

If this result is obtained, then we could examine whether plausibility and grammaticality effects are still obtained when the lexical processor is more likely to be the fastest method of processing.

If they are not, then strong support for the autonomy argument will again be produced.[4] In the absence of such data (the appropriate experiments are currently underway), we must conclude that the lexical-decision task with longer sentences provides ambiguous data. It may simply be that lexical decisions for the plausible and implausible sentences were controlled by the message level, which would explain why both a plausibility and a grammaticality effect were observed.

Before we leave this experiment, it is perhaps worth reporting that the materials were designed to permit an examination of word-frequency effect. For half of the items, the major substantives of each sentence were relatively high-frequency words (above 40 per million), whereas the other half contained low-frequency words (below 40 per million). For both tasks, there was a highly significant effect of word frequency, and there was no evidence at

---

[4]Although we must consider the counter-argument that these sentences may be so short that there is insufficient context to exert any noticeable effect on the lexical processor. This claim itself can be countered by observing that in semantic priming experiments, a one-word context is quite sufficient to produce a context effect (e.g., Meyer & Schvaneveldt, 1971).

all to suggest that the plausible sentences produced a smaller effect than the implausible sentences. Thus, from the point of view of the search model, there is little evidence to support the view that the search subset is delimited by either syntactic or semantic categories.

More recently, Schuberth and Eimas (1977) have reported an effect of semantic context on lexical-decision times. In this experiment, no decisions were required for the context words, which were simply presented as an incomplete sentence for 1.5 sec under silent-reading instructions. The target word was then presented for lexical classification and was either a plausible or an implausible completion of the preceding incomplete sentence. Significant effects of plausibility were obtained, together with significant effects of target-word frequency, with no interaction between these factors (confirming the results of the previous experiment).

Because a decision was required for only one word, the decision phase of the subject's response would have been much shorter than in the previous experiment. Hence, there is less justification for arguing that the decision could have been controlled by a postlexical level. But the possibility is not ruled out, especially if we consider that the output of the message processor is probably far more accessible to the GPS than is any lower level (because the whole purpose of sentence processing is to convey a message interpretation to conscious awareness as rapidly as possible).

One feature of the results of this experiment was quite inexplicable. The sentence fragment *also* facilitated "no" decisions; i.e., nonwords were also processed faster when preceded by a sentence context (compared to no prior context). Moreover, the magnitude of this effect for legal nonwords (42 msec) was actually greater than for words (35 msec). This result suggests that whatever effect the sentence context had, it could not have been an effect on *word* recognition.

Postulating that the lexical decision was in fact controlled by a sentential level of processing may actually provide an explanation for this highly unexpected result. When a nonword is received, it will be marked as such by the lexical processor (after an exhaustive search has failed to find any entry). The syntactic processor will then fail and will mark the sequence as ungrammatical. If the output from the syntactic level reaches the GPS before output from the lexical level, then it might be expected that nonwords would be detected faster when presented in a sentence context.

So for nonwords, the syntactic level produces the fastest decision. But for words, there is the further possibility that the message level will produce even faster decisions, and, hence, a plausibility effect would also be expected. Thus, it is still possible to explain these results without assuming that lexical processing itself is affected by a sentence context. To provide this explanation, we need to assume that outputs from sentential levels of processing were still involved in this task, even though only one item had to be classified. There is one feature of the task situation that may have actually accentuated the importance of sentential representations: The subjects were required to recall the complete sentence after the lexical decision had been made. Obviously, the output of sentential processors would be far more effective for this aspect of the task than would the lexical processor, and this may have some kind of selective effect on the weight assigned by the GPS to the various output levels.[5]

But even if this interpretation were rejected, there are other factors to consider. For example, in this experiment, the target words *bone* or *hour* were presented in the context of (50). Is it possible that much the same effects would have been obtained with (51) as a context?

(50) The puppy chewed the _____
(51) chew puppy _____

If both (50) and (51) produced a similar context effect (the work of Meyer and Schvaneveldt [1971] suggests that they surely would), then we must seriously question whether the effect of (50) is really to be interpreted as a *sentence*-context effect. To demonstrate this point, we need to use sentence contexts that give reliably greater effects than simple word lists.

The most pressing problem, then, is to design a task in which the decision process is clearly controlled by the lexical level of processing. In an earlier paper (Forster, 1976), I described a preliminary series of experiments with a word-naming task that I felt ought to have qualified. The individual words of a sentence were exposed serially at varying rates, and the subject's task was to pronounce a designated target word from the sentence. The target word was printed in italics and occurred at unpredictable points in the sentence. In order to detect which word was in italics, all words had to be monitored; because we know from the Stroop phenomenon that it is impossible for the subject to avoid reading and interpreting words that are adequately registered in the visual system, we can guarantee that subjects were reading each word in the sentence.

The naming task has one advantage over lexical decision: There is no way the subject can infer the correct response from sentential properties of the input (as is possible in the lexical-decision task). Hence, naming times are more likely to reflect speed of lexical processing.

In these earlier experiments, no significant effects of plausibility were observed, although there was an effect of grammaticality. However, when the target item was degraded by a subsequently presented masking stimulus, there *was* a clear effect of plausibility.

---

[5]When several tasks must be performed simultaneously, it may be simpler for the GPS to use the one level of representation that is sufficient for all tasks, rather than to use different levels for each task. Thus, even if the lexical output were available to the GPS, it may be ignored.

These results were interpreted to mean that plausibility had no effect on lexical processing unless the stimulus was degraded. However, it should have been pointed out that there was an effect of grammaticality for nondegraded stimuli, and, hence, the autonomy assumption was violated, at least as far as the syntactic level was concerned.

Why should degrading the word produce a plausibility effect?

To explain this result, it was proposed that there are at least two fundamentally different methods of accessing words. The first of these is the system shown in Fig. 2.3, and we shall refer to this as the data-driven system. This system takes the *form* of the stimulus as its input. The second system could be described as context-driven, and it was proposed that this method of identifying words called upon an access system that would normally be used for sentence *production*. When we wish to talk or to write, we obviously need a system that can locate words having particular syntactic and semantic properties. In terms of the access model, we need a third access file that incorporates syntactic and semantic principles of organization. One possibility is that the lexicon itself is organized in this way, being some kind of network system in which lexical entries contain pointers to other words that are related to it. The access file may simply serve to map relatively diffuse conceptual intentions onto convenient starting points in the lexicon from which a search can commence for the precise word that will best serve the communicative purpose.

Trying to identify words using the production-access file is essentially equivalent to asking the following question: Given what we know about the situational context and the speaker, what sentence could we construct that has a similar form to the received input? That is, we use an extreme form of analysis-by-synthesis. We attempt to recognize an input by synthesizing a sentence that sounds (or looks) like the input sentence. Such a system is context-driven because the context is obviously important in developing hypotheses about the most likely sentence to synthesize.

When one word in a sentence is degraded, it can be suggested that the data-driven method either fails altogether to find a matching lexical entry or is slowed down considerably. In either case, it is now possible for a context-driven system to exert an influence on processing. Normally, this method is slower than the data-driven system, and, hence, we fail to find plausibility effects on word processing.

In effect, we are postulating a special processing mode to account for context effects. This is not entirely an ad hoc move, because the computational machinery is already required on independent grounds, namely, to permit the rapid location of suitable words for sentence-production purposes (it would hardly make sense to suggest that this search ought to involve a system organized by form, because form is seldom a relevant consideration, except in specialized situations such as poetic writing, alliteration). Usually, analysis-by-synthesis models are discounted on the grounds that the number of sentences that would have to be considered is so impossibly large. However, this problem may not be critical when the major details of the sentence structure have already been established by a pure analytic system. It is quite clear that speakers can rapidly reconstruct missing elements from sentences and are able to project ahead to provide a plausible completion of an unfinished sentence. Whether these abilities could play a role in sentence comprehension depends solely on whether there is sufficient time for them to be applied (data from speech-shadowing experiments indicate that this is quite likely to be the case, see, e.g., Marslen-Wilson, 1976).

These considerations suggest a reformulation of the context issue along the following lines. The central question is not simply whether context influences word recognition. Rather, what we need to explore is the range of conditions under which these effects can be observed and whether they have the characteristics that might be expected if they are produced by a sentence production system.[6] Most importantly, we need to know whether there are any conditions at all under which a context effect is *not* obtained.

If we can find such cases, then we will have justified the distinction between data- and context-driven methods of word recognition. If we cannot, then the distinction merely serves to protect the autonomy principle from disconfirmation.

Returning to the word-naming experiments discussed earlier, it has recently become clear that this experimental paradigm does not provide the clear evidence for autonomy that I had originally supposed. In a series of experiments using the same materials as my original experiments, R. E. O'Connor has obtained clear plausibility effects of about 30 to 40 msec on word-naming time. O'Connor argued that contextual effects depend on the subject knowing that a plausible sentence is being presented. Normally, plausible and implausible sentences would be mixed together in an unpredictable sequence. But if blocked presentation is used, we might well see a context effect. This proved to be incorrect, because plausibility effects were unexpectedly obtained for *both* blocked and mixed methods of presentation!

At the time of writing this chapter, no satisfactory explanation for these results is available. One possibility is that the later experiments involved more degraded stimuli than the earlier experiments (in the original method, typewritten words were photographed on 16 mm film and presented with a motion projector; the later experiments used a computer-controlled 5 × 7 dot matrix display), but in the absence of an adequate metric for stimulus quality, this line of argument cannot really be pursued. Another possibility is that the earlier experiments simply lacked sufficient power to detect the effect.

---

[6]For example, the effectiveness of certain types of context may be linked to the ability of subjects to construct completions for incomplete sentences.

Whatever the explanation, it would have to be conceded that these results are damaging to the autonomy principle. Whether they are fatal remains to be seen. To maintain autonomy, one would have to argue that performance on the word-naming experiment is not lexically controlled. One aspect of the performance of subjects in this task suggests that this may be the case. We had previously overlooked the fact that the target word often appeared to be pronounced with the intonation appropriate to a *sentence* rather than a list (because only one word is actually pronounced, it is difficult to establish this point convincingly). If this is in fact the case, then it is possible to argue that the correct pronunciation of the target word is recovered from a sentential representation of the input, not from a purely lexical representation. This is not at all a radical proposal, because the *normal* mode of control of the vocalization process would be through some sentential representation.

It may be, then, that we need to look further afield to find a task that is lexically controlled. Unfortunately, we are placed in an awkward position by not having any grounds other than the existence of context effects to decide which level is controlling decisions. This creates a circularity in the argument, because it is then true by definition that lexical processing is not affected by context.

It seems unlikely that this impasse can be avoided by using any of the currently available techniques. Most prominent among these is the phoneme-monitor task (Foss & Swinney, 1973), in which a subject monitors a spoken sentence for a word beginning with a designated target phoneme. Morton and Long (1976) have recently reported clear and strong effects of plausibility on monitor times; when the target phoneme was /b/, "probable" sentences such as (52) produced faster times than sentences such as (53).

(52) A sparrow sat on the *b*ranch whistling a few shrill notes to welcome the dawn.

(53) A sparrow sat on the *b*ed whistling a few shrill notes to welcome the dawn.

In evaluating these results, we need first to ask which level of processing controls the phoneme-monitor task. Blank and Foss (1977b) have presented evidence suggesting that this is variable; in some situations it may be controlled at a phonetic level and, hence, prior to lexical processing. In others, it is apparently postlexical. For our purposes, of course, we need to know whether subjects identify the target-bearing word by extracting it from a *sentential* (or possibly clausal) representation.[7] The second question to be

---

[7]It would be useful to determine whether plausibility effects can be obtained when the target word is not clause final. If message-level processing is delayed until a clause boundary is reached, then we may find a different pattern of results. The same comment applies to the word-naming experiments discussed earlier, where the target word was always clause (and sentence) final.

considered is the possibility of stimulus degradation. As we have argued, context-driven systems may be involved when subjects are uncertain that the input has been correctly processed. It seems likely that the speech signal is inherently a noisy signal, at least compared with a visual representation in a standard type face (but not compared with, for example, handwritten sentences).[8] At the moment, there is no way to settle this question. However, preliminary investigation in our laboratory suggests that there are important differences between acoustic and visual stimuli. In our experiments, we have employed a *letter*-monitoring task. Subjects were presented with typewritten sentences (simultaneous presentation of the entire sentence) and required to detect the presence of a word beginning with a certain letter. In this task, there were no traces at all of a plausibility effect. However, there were also no signs of *any* linguistic variables of interest being involved; subjects appeared to be able to perform the task at a very shallow level of processing, possibly prelexical.

Blank and Foss (1977b) argued that it is essential to consider the interaction between sentence comprehension itself and the tasks that are devised to measure this process, and the general tenor of my remarks here echo this concern. They point out, for example, that most phoneme-monitor experiments employ some procedure to guarantee that the subject is attempting to understand the sentence. Morton and Long (1976) required verbatim recall, whereas others have used a recognition test. Blank and Foss suggested that this difference may be critical. Our own practice is to avoid the use of such procedures altogether (the previously mentioned letter-monitor task is a case in point), mainly because they complicate the task and because they are manifestly unnecessary; the consistent presence of plausibility effects in tasks that do not require comprehension at all provides ample support for this claim.

In any event, the preliminary indications are that context effects can be demonstrated with the phoneme-monitor task, but we are no more certain of the correct interpretation of these results than we are in the case of the word-naming experiments.

Given these negative conclusions, it might be suggested that there is little point in persevering with the lexical autonomy principle. However, there are two lines of evidence that are promising and hold out some hope of reward.

First, recall that in several of the same–different matching experiments discussed earlier, there was no evidence for an effect of plausibility on "different" items, even though the processing involved was clearly sensitive to lexical properties. Unless these results are somehow shown to be artifactual,

---

[8]This can be shown by the fact that it would be a trivial task to design a machine that could read typewritten text, but to design a comparable device to recognize speech is difficult, to say the least.

there seems to be no way to escape the conclusion that word recognition in these experiments was unaffected by context. There are even good reasons for expecting such a result to appear in this task but not in others. The matching task appears to be the only one in which sensitivity to a given level of processing can be selectively tuned by adjusting the parameters of the task.

The second promising line of evidence concerns the effect of context on the processing of ambiguous words. In several experiments using the phoneme-monitor task, researchers have shown that monitoring latencies are longer for words that immediately follow an ambiguous word (Cairns & Kamerman, 1975; Foss, 1970; Foss & Jenkins, 1973). This effect has been attributed to the increased processing load involved in finding multiple lexical entries (but for opposing views, see Mehler, Segui, & Carey, 1978). On the assumption that this is indeed a lexical effect, one might expect that a prior disambiguating context would eliminate this difficulty, because the lexical search would be guided to the "correct" entry. Of course, the lexical autonomy model would specifically rule out this possibility. In a variety of tasks, investigators have shown that ambiguous words appear to be processed as ambiguous whether or not they are preceded by a disambiguating context (Conrad, 1974; Foss & Jenkins, 1973; Holmes, Arwas, & Garrett, 1977), and, hence, some support for the autonomy principle is provided. However, Swinney and Hakes (1976) have failed to repeat these findings using a set of highly biased contexts (e.g., the ambiguous word *bugs* occurring in the environment *spiders, roaches, and other* _____).

As will become clearer in the next section, it is important to distinguish between context effects that are mediated by sentential factors and effects that depend purely on the presence of particular lexical items. For example, in the Swinney and Hakes (1976) experiment, the meaning of the context phrase itself may be irrelevant; similar effects might have been obtained in simple word lists, such as *spiders roaches bugs*. In fact, Schvaneveldt, Meyer, and Becker (1976) have demonstrated just such a bias effect with the lexical-decision task. Thus, in order to show that the accessing of ambiguous words is altered by *message*-level processing per se, it would be necessary to control for the possible effects of the actual lexical items themselves.

The importance of the lexical ambiguity experiments for the present argument rests on the assumption that the ambiguity increases the time required for lexical processing. This is not the only interpretation that can be placed on the results. It may be that the effect stems from the increased time required by the message processor to decide which interpretation of the ambiguous item is intended. In the presence of a biasing context, this decision may be made more rapidly, and, hence, the ambiguity effect is lessened or eliminated entirely.

So far, we have restricted our attention to possible control of the lexical processor by the message processor. Garrett (1976b) has argued against this proposal but has also argued that a far stronger case may be possible for *syntactic* influences on lexical processing. In particular, Garrett has argued that open- and closed-class lexical items (roughly, content and function words, respectively) are computationally distinct; i.e., they are accessed by different procedures. Bradley (1977) has provided compelling evidence for this proposal in an experiment using an interference technique originally reported by Taft and Forster (1976). In this latter paper, Taft and Forster showed that in a lexical-decision task, correct rejections of nonwords took longer if the item contained a word in initial position. Thus, *footmilge* would take longer to reject than *cootmilge*. Evidently, words are parsed from left-to-right, and access is attempted with each parsing. The interference effect arises when the irrelevant entry for *foot* is located. Bradley sought to determine whether this would also occur when closed-case words were used; i.e., would *lessipen* take longer than *fessipen*? Bradley's results showed clearly that interference *only* arises for nonwords containing an open-class word. Thus, the left-to-right parsing of *lessipen* fails to ever access the entry for *less*.

Why should such a distinction be made? Garrett's argument is that the closed-class items are critically important to the syntactic processor, because a knowledge of the distribution of the closed-class items is often sufficient to assign form class to the remaining items, and in some cases will even indicate the correct syntactic analysis of the entire sentence, as in (54):

(54) The _____ will _____ to the _____.

Thus, it might be expected that closed-class items would be given special priority whenever syntactic processing is required. Garrett further suggested that when form class has been assigned to the open-class words, the lexical processor is directed to the appropriate segment of the lexicon, which is subclassified by form class, with the result that the efficiency of lexical search is substantially increased.

The latter part of this argument is as yet unsupported. If the lexicon *is* subclassified according to syntactic properties and if lexical search can be modified by a knowledge of likely form class, then it is clear that the lexical processor is not autonomous as far as the syntactic processor is concerned. To my knowledge, the only relevant evidence is inconsistent with this view. Forster and Bednall (1976) investigated lexical decisions for phrases such as *to push, the house, to year,* and *the panage* (the correct responses being "yes" to the first two items and "no" for the second two). They showed substantial interference effects for "no" responses when a lexical entry for the item existed but was of the wrong syntactic type (e.g., *to year* took longer than *to desp*). Moreover, *two* such entries created even more interference (e.g., *to pupil* took longer than *to year*), providing clear evidence that the noun entries were being accessed even when the context called for a verb. However, it is possible that assignment of form class in these very short phrases is not rapid enough to restrict the search. Or, it is possible that when the verb category has been exhausted, the search continues on to consider the noun category. Further research is required to examine these possibilities.

But Bradley's evidence is sufficient to indicate at least a subdivision according to open- and closed-class properties. Evidently, the search process that accesses *foot* does not also access *less*. If it did, then some time would be consumed while it was established that there was no compound word that could be formed from *less*. So it seems that there must be two types of search, one using a small list of closed-class items, the other using the full lexicon. What else may follow from this is unclear at the moment, but it seems likely that the activity of the lexical processor may well be modified in some way by syntactic factors. We shall return to this point again in the final section.

SEMANTIC PRIMING EFFECTS
IN LEXICAL ACCESS

We have so far only briefly alluded to the most powerful of all context effects, namely, the semantic priming effect discovered by Meyer and Schvaneveldt (1971). They showed that lexical-decision time for a word such as *nurse* was shorter when it was preceded by a semantically related word such as *doctor*. There can be no doubt at all about the reality of this effect, although its nature is a matter of some controversy.

There appear to be two alternative interpretations of the effect. According to the first, there is a passive spread of excitation from the detector for a recently accessed word to the detectors of semantically related words. This spread of activation increases the readiness of the related detectors to fire when the subsequent word is presented. According to the second interpretation, which is essentially equivalent to the dictionary-network model proposed by Loftus and Cole (1974), the lexicon is organized semantically, so that lexical entries for related words are linked together in a network of cross-references. Any word can be accessed in two ways: first its entry in the appropriate *access* file can be located, which then permits direct entry to the lexicon. Second, a search through the lexicon itself is possible, using the network of semantic cross-references. Thus, in the above example, *doctor* would be accessed in the orthographic access file; a search would then begin from the lexical entry for *doctor*, which would examine the set of entries for words related to *doctor*, eventually resulting in the accessing of *nurse* directly. Thus, the entry for *nurse* would not be located through the access file. For present purposes, these two accounts are essentially equivalent, but the latter explanation is more compatible with the model under discussion and, hence, is adopted without further discussion.

The most striking aspect of this effect is the clear demonstration that lexical access can be influenced profoundly by a prior semantic context. Surely this effect violates the assumption of autonomous lexical processing?

I see no reason to take this view. As we have described it, semantic priming is an intralexical effect, rather than an interlevel effect. That is, there is no evidence to suggest that priming involves levels of processing other than the lexical level. Once we have postulated a semantic network defined over lexical entries (which we have already suggested would be necessary for sentence production), we have given the lexical processor sufficient computational power to encompass the effect.

It would be quite a different matter if it could be argued that the priming effect was produced by the action of the message-level processor on the lexical processor, so that the context effect of a sentence fragment and the context effect of a single lexical item were seen as different manifestations of the same phenomenon.

What evidence we have on this point is largely negative. Watson (1976) investigated this point by comparing sentences such as (55), which contained a pair of associatively related nouns, with control sentences such as (56), which contained unrelated nouns. The design of such experiments is complicated by the fact that when the associative connection between the subject and object nouns is varied, the semantic plausibility of the sentence is also varied, as in (57) and (58).

(55) The teacher kissed the pupil.
(56) The teacher kissed the woman.
(57) The fireman put out the fire.
(58) The fireman put out the cat.

In order to avoid this confounding, it is necessary to select a verb that is itself relatively unrelated to the subject noun.[9]

Watson (1976) was unable to find any effect of associative connections when sentence-processing time was indexed by the sentence-classification task, which is normally highly sensitive to message-level effects. Bodi (1977) has also examined associative effects in visually presented word triples such as (59) to (62).

(59) Mice tree cheese.
(60) Horses tree cheese.
(61) Mice hate cheese.
(62) Horses hate cheese.

---

[9]There is no *necessary* connection between plausibility and associative relatedness. The sentences *Cows produce milk* and *Milk produces cows* vary greatly in plausibility, but not in the associative relatedness of the nouns.

In these cases, the associatively related pairs were always separated by only one word; the nature of this separating word was varied so that either a word list or a sentence was produced (once again, plausibility being held constant). In the first task used by Bodi, each word was separately named, and the words were sequentially presented with an interstimulus interval of 1400 msec. Significant priming effects on the naming of the last word in each triple were obtained for both lists and sentences (the naming times for the last word in the four conditions corresponding to (59) to (62) being 530, 546, 527, and 546 msec, respectively). However, sentences were responded to no faster than were lists, which suggests that performance was controlled purely by the lexical level.

The presentation rate in this task was extremely slow. Bodi (1977) sought to involve the higher processing levels by decreasing the interstimulus interval to just 500 msec, and by lengthening the sentence, producing items such as (63) and (64).

(63) After it decays mice hate cheese.
(64) After it decays horses hate cheese.

Because vocal responses take considerable time to complete, it was no longer possible to have subjects name each word. Instead they named a single target word (*cheese*) that was indicated by a visual cue.[10] The subjects were instructed to read and pronounce the remaining words subvocally. Under these circumstances, grammaticality effects were observed, which suggests that sentential-processing levels were now involved (the previously mentioned experiments by O'Connor obtained plausibility effects under exactly the same conditions). However, the associative effect was now totally absent, the mean vocalization onset times for sentences containing associated words being 511 msec, compared with 514 msec for the controls.

Although the interpretation of these results is no doubt complicated by task variables, there is little support for the notion that the priming effect is sentential in origin. What appears to be happening is that the associative effect becomes weaker when the rate at which input must be processed is increased.

The tentative conclusion, then, is that the associative effect occurs at the lexical level, and is produced by the network of cross-references defined over lexical entries. I should note that it is quite irrelevant to the present argument whether the effect is a product of automatic, involuntary processes, or consciously controlled strategies, or a mixture of the two, as suggested by

---

[10]The cue was a pair of "equals" signs on either side of the target word. Designating the target word by its initial letter (the visual analogue of the phoneme-monitor task) was avoided, because subjects could then use the cue to attempt to predict the target word prior to its actual occurrence. This appears to be a major weakness of the phoneme-monitor task.

Tweedy, Lapinski, and Schvaneveldt (1977). Whatever the final conclusion may be, it is still necessary to give an account of the information structures that could mediate the effect.

It is also necessary to consider what the purpose of such an information structure could possibly be. It might be that it has nothing to do with the problem of word recognition. This view is based on the conviction that sentences do not normally contain strongly associated pairs of words. For example, consider the pair *mirth–glee*. Is it conceivable that a sentence containing *mirth* is also likely to contain *glee*? Or that sentences containing *summer* have a high probability of including the word *winter*? Certainly one can find frequent examples of sentences that do contain such pairs (e.g., *Pass the pepper and salt*), but their frequency scarcely justifies an elaborate scanning of the associates of every word in a sentence in the hope that a pair of associatively related words will be present. Of course, the search cannot be restricted to just the frequent *associates* of a given word, because semantic priming occurs for words with extremely weak associative connections (Fischler, 1977b). Thus, the search would need to extend over entire semantic *fields*.

If we reject the view that associative priming is designed to make the task of word recognition easier, then what purpose could it have, except to assist in lexical-decision experiments? It may be that associative priming itself has no purpose at all but that the information structures it depends on do have a purpose, namely, to assist in locating words for the purpose of sentence production. When actually planning the lexical content of a sentence, it would make sense to execute a search that successively scanned *mirth* and *glee*, because these are both words that could be used in similar environments. In fact, there seems to be no other way to explain the semantically controlled word substitutions and blends that occur as speech errors (Garrett, 1975, 1976a). Thus, a person who says *melanade* has clearly accessed both *serenade* and *melody* as possible candidates for inclusion in the sentence. Moreover, such errors often involve associative connections (e.g., saying *write* instead of *read*) as well as other kinds of relations.

During sentence comprehension, this production system is available as a back-up word-recognition system, in case access based purely on form characteristics fails. Thus, if the input is actually (65), but the last word is too degraded to be recognized, then an attempt would be made to synthesize possible completions, using the production system.

(65) John's ridiculous behavior was greeted with glee.

In so doing, a search might encounter both *mirth* and *glee*, each of these words being compared with the decaying trace of the unrecognized word. The alternative that matches this trace best would then be selected.

When it comes to a lexical-decision task, the same production system may be employed, although now in a slightly different way. In this case, the starting point for a semantic search is not defined by sentential considerations, but merely by the lexical entry for the preceding word.

This view of the priming effect gains some support from the fact that the magnitude of the effect is increased when the stimulus is degraded (Meyer, Schvaneveldt, & Ruddy, 1975), because it is under these circumstances that the production system is most effective. However, it is not clear why subjects in a lexical-decision experiment would always use such a strategy. After it had been noticed that some of the words were related, it would be quite understandable that such a strategy might be used. However, the priming effect apparently occurs even when no previous pair of words has been related (Fischler, 1977a). Provided that this initial effect is not due to some post-access process (e.g., a bias to respond "yes" when two words are found to be related), we would be forced to argue that the semantic search is always executed. We would then need to explain what the normal function of this automatic search might be (the same goes for a spreading activation interpretation). Perhaps, after all, it does serve to assist the recognition of other words in the sentence. Because the search is not just limited to associates of the context word, but extends to an entire field of semantically related words (Fischler, 1977b), it may be possible to suggest that for any word in a normal sentence, there is a reasonably high probability of there being at least one other word that belongs to the same semantic field.

In conclusion, it has to be conceded that it is no easy matter to maintain the lexical autonomy principle. From the standpoint of a passive logogen model (Morton, 1970), the evidence discussed in this section presents no problems, because this model places no restrictions at all on the types of inputs that the logogen system can be sensitive to. But this ultimately may prove to be a weakness rather than a strength, because the interaction of the data and the theory do not generate new problems for investigation. On the other hand, the search model places heavy constraints on the types of interactions that can occur, and in adapting the theory to cover the facts, significant new issues seem to emerge. It may ultimately be necessary to abandon the lexical autonomy principle, but the evidence and arguments that eventually force this will have enriched our understanding of the language processor to a considerable degree.

PLAUSIBILITY AND THE MESSAGE PROCESSOR

Much of what has been said so far amounts to the claim that semantic plausibility has only one site of action, namely, the message processor. It is now necessary to consider how this effect occurs and what it tells us about the nature of the message processor.

It is clear that what we normally take to be a "full" understanding of the meaning of a sentence involves complex inferential processes. Some of these inferences are logical entailments, but others are not. For example, sentences (66) to (68) would each be interpreted in a fairly standard manner, but in each case a complex chain of inferences is involved that could not be regarded as logical entailments of the original sentences.

(66) John suggested aspirin for Harry's headache.
(67) Adrian wanted a present for his wife.
(68) Here are three easy problems.

Sentence (66) would normally be understood to mean that John attempted to persuade Harry that taking aspirin would ease the pain of his headache, yet this interpretation goes well beyond the specific information conveyed in the sentence. It is possible, although implausible, that John believed that aspirin would make Harry's headache worse. Similarly, most speakers of English would infer that (67) asserts that Adrian wanted to find a present to give his wife, but it is possible that Adrian's wife could have been giving the present to someone else, perhaps even Adrian himself. Again, in (68) we infer that the problems are easy to solve, but in fact they may be easy to read, or anything else that we might care to suggest (had *remarkable* replaced *easy*, then a different inference would have been made; i.e., we would not infer that the problems were remarkable to solve).

The precise meanings of these sentences could have been specified in the surface form, but in normal language use, a kind of shorthand form of expression is used when the intended interpretation is reasonably clear from context. Suppose for the moment that one of the functions of the message processor is to "expand" the interpretations of these sentences into their full form. The message processor would then be involved in using a fairly general store of conceptual (nonlinguistic) knowledge about the real world to find the necessary information to provide the correct set of inferences.

It seems likely that the effects of semantic plausibility (or rather, implausibility) arise during this expansion process. Thus, sentences (69) to (71) would involve extra computation compared with (66) to (68), simply because there is no information specified in the general concept system that will amplify the interpretation in a straightforward way.

(69) John suggested aspirin for Harry's marriage.
(70) Adrian wanted a mask for his wife.
(71) Here are three tasty problems.

In (69), for example, there is nothing stored in the lexical entries for *aspirin* or *marriage* that explains what the speaker had in mind nor does an examination of the general information stored about aspirin or marriages immediately reveal the answer. Eventually, *some* kind of an account can be given, but this takes extra time, and, hence, the output of the message processor would be delayed.

The view that full sentence comprehension involves some kind of inferential system that goes beyond logical entailments has been proposed before (e.g., Anderson & Ortony, 1975; Bransford & Franks, 1971; Frederickson, 1975), although the experimental demonstrations of this phenomenon have been restricted to memory experiments rather than on-line comprehension experiments. The importance of context in this process is considerable. Thus, when sentences (69) to (71) are actually used in an appropriate context, the effects of implausibility might be diminished or even eliminated entirely, suggesting that the message processor uses the context to constrain the search for the correct amplified interpretation. Although a diminished effect is possible, it seems unlikely that plausibility effects could ever be totally eliminated. Watson (1976) has found very persistent effects of plausibility, despite every attempt to provide as helpful a context as possible. Similarly, we still find an effect of plausibility on sentence-matching times (Murray & Forster, 1977), even when the first sentence is presented 3 sec before the second, presumably giving the message processor ample time to discover an interpretation of the first sentence.

If these proposals are correct, they raise serious problems for the model of sentence processing that is under discussion. They attribute to the message processor inferential capacities of a very general sort and imply that the message processor has access to nonlinguistic information stores. It is thus difficult to see how any useful distinction could be made between the activities of the message processor and general cognitive activity. In short, the message processor is indistinguishable from the GPS.

Fodor, Fodor, and Garrett (1975) make a sharp distinction between sentence comprehension and more general cognitive abilities. They propose that

> ... the distinction between processes that are involved in understanding a sentence and processes that are involved in drawing inferences from it corresponds to a distinction between mandatory, on-line psychological processes and optional long-term psychological processes. For, by hypothesis, the output of the sentence comprehension system is that representation of the sentence which must be recovered by anyone who understands it. But the application of principles of inference is presumably largely context-determined [p. 526].

Applying this principle would clearly suggest that the message processor should be assigned to the GPS and plays no role in the language *processor* at all.

However, there is one problem with this solution. It seems clear that the effects of plausibility *are* due to "mandatory, on-line psychological processes." For example, in the sentence-matching experiments, there is absolutely no requirement for the subject to take meaning or context into account, yet plausible sentences are still processed faster than are implausible sentences.

This argument can be put another way. In the sentence-classification task, we argue that the GPS can accept input either from the message level or the syntactic level. Because message-level outputs are more accessible to the GPS, they usually control the decision. But for implausible sentences, this output is delayed, and, hence, these sentences take longer to classify. This interpretation makes sense only if we distinguish between the message processor and the GPS. If the extra processing that implausible sentences require is in fact carried out by the GPS itself, then one could well ask why the GPS is unable to render a decision as soon as an output from the language processor is received.

One possible resolution of this problem is simply to dispense with the plausibility effect as some minor product of the subjects' desire to be absolutely sure of their decision. The sentences are, after all, implausible, and it is possible that the subjects recompute the analysis of the sentence to make sure that no error has occurred. More precisely, the GPS detects that an implausible reading for the sentence has been produced and issues a request to the language processor to reprocess the input (this much control over the language processor can safely be granted to the GPS). Such an interpretation is, of course, very difficult to test, because it is difficult to specify those conditions under which the GPS should be prepared to accept the initial output from the language processor. One might imagine that the delayed sentence-matching task should go close to providing the necessary conditions. During the initial 3 sec that the first sentence is displayed, there is ample time for any reprocessing to occur. All that remains is to test whether the second sentence is identical to the first, yet the implausibility of the second identical sentence still slows the matching process.

Ratcliff (1978) has recently reported an experiment that may shed some light on the issue. The purpose of this experiment was to determine whether the plausibility effect was influenced by the number of inferential steps required to provide a full interpretation.

Each sentence contained as subject a role term, such as *doctor, author,* or *nurse*. Sentence pairs were constructed that varied only in the role term used. One member of each pair was plausible, and the other implausible. There were three conditions. In the first condition, the inferences required to plausibly link the role term with the predicate were intended to be as simple as possible and to involve only information contained in the lexicon. For example, in (72), the information that tailors make clothes can be recovered from the lexicon, as can the fact that uniforms are a form of clothing. The plausibility of this sentence stems from the fact that if we substitute definitions for the nouns, we compute something like (74), i.e., the predication of the sentence asserts that the subject NP has a property that we have already established is typical of it. However, no such result is obtained in (73).

(72) The tailor made the uniforms.
(73) The usher made the uniforms.
(74) The person who makes clothes made the clothes.

In the second condition, this test for plausibility requires a more complex chain of inferences and also involves information that is unlikely to be specified in the lexicon.

(75) The carpenter bought the timber.
(76) The lecturer bought the timber.

For example, in (75), the connecton between *carpenter* and the predicate is established via the chain: Carpenters work with wood (timber) and to obtain it they usually buy it. The latter fact is nonlexical; i.e., the lexical entry of *carpenter* is not likely to contain the information that timber is usually bought by carpenters. In the third condition, the connection between the subject NP and the predicate is even more remote.

(77) The firemen sprayed the stadium.
(78) The gamblers sprayed the stadium.

To make the connection in (77), it is necessary to infer that the stadium in question is on fire (certainly not in the lexicon) and that spraying is a part of the normal activity or function of firemen in putting out fires.

In each condition, sentence-processing times were estimated for each sentence pair, using the sentence-classification task, with instructions emphasizing that the meanings of the sentences were irrelevant. The distractors were similar to the test items, except that one of the words was in the wrong position.

The results of the experiment showed a significant effect of plausibility (35 msec) in the first condition only. In the second and third conditions, the effects were in the expected direction (20 msec and 14 msec, respectively), but were totally unreliable (neither F_1 nor F_2 significant), despite the existence of a highly reliable *rated* plausibility difference in each condition. That is, although sentences such as (76) and (78) were reliably judged to be less plausible than (75) and (77), respectively, there was no significant effect of this plausibility difference on sentence-processing times.

The concept of the number of inferential steps required is obviously related to the notion of semantic distance in a Collins and Quillian (1972) network, except that Ratcliff attempted to distinguish between lexical and nonlexical information. How clearly this distinction can be made is very much open to question, because there is no adequate theory of the contents of the lexicon; hence, this approach can only be regarded as a very rough approximation. Similarly, we have no precise metric for measuring inference chains, and, hence, the adequacy of the experimental manipulation depends on purely intuitive evidence. However, the findings are quite suggestive and warrant further investigation.

The implication of these results is that the message processor only deals with certain types of inference, namely, lexically mediated inferences. It can thus be distinguished from the GPS, which can readily detect that (75) is more plausible than (76) and that (77) is more plausible than (78), as indicated by the ratings. Because GPS processing is assumed not to be involved in the plausibility effect but message processing is, we can explain why effects are obtained in the first condition but not in either of the other two conditions.

But if this interpretation is correct, it is no longer clear that the purpose of message-level processing is to amplify or enrich the meaning assigned to the sentence, because it is precisely in the second and third conditions where this type of processing is most relevant; i.e., sentence (74) can hardly be regarded as an enriched representation of the reading assigned to (72).

A further implication of this interpretation of the results is that sentences (75) and (77) have already reached the lowest point of implausibility as far as detectable effects on the sentence processor are concerned. But this is surely false, because it is almost certainly true that (79) would take longer to process than would (75).

(79) The carpenter bought the universe.

However, as Ratcliff (1975) has observed, we have now introduced a further factor, namely, the implausibility of the predicate itself; i.e., it is relatively implausible that *anyone* could buy the universe. Hence, we now have the option of arguing that (75) and (79) differ in that *timber* has the right lexical properties to be the object of the verb *buy*, but *universe* does not, and, hence, a plausibility effect is to be expected.[11]

The chief virtue of this line of argument is that it offers one way of distinguishing between the message processor and the GPS and also restricts the message processor so that it has access only to lexical information (although it could be argued that we have adopted a very liberal view of what might be in the lexicon). If this argument, or one like it, cannot be supported,

---

[11]The preceding argument could be construed as an argument for a lexical decomposition of sorts and, hence, is open to the objections raised by Fodor et al. (1975).

then we will have to face the possibility that the message processor does not really belong to the language processor at all. Otherwise, we are in danger of losing any distinction between the *language* processor and the GPS. We would than have adopted the model proposed by Fodor et al. (1975), who argued that language processing per se ceases once the surface structure (and possibly the logical form) of the sentence has been established.

Such a model would be strongly supported if it ultimately becomes clear that the lexical processor is not autonomous with respect to the syntactic level but is autonomous with respect to semantic and pragmatic factors. With the three-level system shown in Fig. 2.1, there would be no motivated way of explaining why the lexical level was independent of the message level, but not of the syntactic level. But with the message level removed altogether, one could simply abandon the subdivision of the language processor and postulate a single syntactic processor that can gain access to the lexicon either through form or syntactic function, or both.

In conclusion, I would like to emphasize again the aim of this paper. The aim has been to decompose sentence-processing activity into quasi-independent subsystems (to use Garrett's [1976a] phrasing), in which there is a correspondence between levels of processing and levels of linguistic description. The assumption of total autonomy (complete independence between levels), which has led to most of the problems, has been adopted for several reasons. It is a stronger and, therefore, more interesting claim. Further, marked interdependence between levels would tend to break down the distinctions between them and would make it that much more difficult to discern interesting structural properties. Finally, there is the promise that if independence can be maintained and supported, then powerful constraints are placed on the nature of the grammar from which the language processor has been constructed.

ACKNOWLEDGMENTS

I am deeply indebted to my close friend and colleague Merrill Garrett. This paper is a mere collection and extension of the arguments we have had over the past 14 years. Although he should not be blamed outright for the deficiencies of this paper, he cannot escape responsibility altogether, because he should have seen where I was headed. I would also like to record my indebtedness to Wayne Murray, Jan Ratcliff, Rod O'Connor, Liz Bednall, and Anna Bodi, who have also made direct contributions to this paper.

REFERENCES

Anderson, R. C., & Ortony, A. On putting apples into bottles—A problem of polysemy. *Cognitive Psychology,* 1975, *7,* 167–180.

Barron, R. W., & Pittenger, J. B. The effect of orthographic structure and lexical meaning on *same-different* judgments. *Quarterly Journal of Experimental Psychology*, 1974, *26*, 566–581.

Bever, T. G. The cognitive basis for linguistic structures. In J. R. Hayes (Ed.), *Cognition and the development of language*. New York: Wiley, 1970.

Blank, M. A., & Foss, D. J. *The role of context in the understanding of unambiguous sentences.* Paper presented at the annual meeting of the Midwestern Psychological Association, May 1977. (a)

Blank, M. A., & Foss, D. J. *Variable phoneme identification strategies can be employed during sentence processing.* Paper presented at the annual meeting of the Southwestern Psychological Association, Fort Worth, 1977. (b)

Bodi, A. *Semantic priming effects in sentences.* Unpublished honors thesis, Department of Psychology, Monash University, 1977.

Bradley, D. *Closed class items have privileged status in the lexicon: A demonstration experiment.* Unpublished manuscript, MIT, 1977.

Brand, J. Classification without identification in visual search. *Quarterly Journal of Experimental Psychology*, 1971, *23*, 178–186.

Bransford, J. D., & Franks, J. J. The abstraction of linguistic ideas. *Cognitive Psychology*, 1971, *2*, 331–350.

Cairns, H., & Kamerman, J. Lexical information processing during sentence comprehension. *Journal of Verbal Learning and Verbal Behavior*, 1975, *14*, 170–179.

Chambers, S. M., & Forster, K. I. Evidence for lexical access in a simultaneous matching task. *Memory & Cognition*, 1975, *3*, 549–559.

Chomsky, N. *Reflections on language.* New York: Pantheon, 1975.

Clark, H. H., & Clark, E. V. *Psychology and language.* New York: Harcourt, Brace, Jovanovich, 1977.

Collins, A. M., & Quillian, M. R. Experiments on semantic memory and language comprehension. In L. W. Gregg (Ed.), *Cognition in learning and memory*. New York: Wiley, 1972.

Conrad, C. Context effects in sentence comprehension: A study of the subjective lexicon. *Memory & Cognition*, 1974, *2*, 130–138.

Egeth, H., & Blecker, D. Differential effects of familiarity on judgments of sameness and difference. *Perception & Psychophysics*, 1971, *9*, 321–326.

Fischler, I. Associative facilitation without expectancy in a lexical decision task. *Journal of Experimental Psychology: Human Perception and Performance*, 1977, *3*, 18–26. (a)

Fischler, I. Semantic facilitation without association in a lexical decision task. *Memory & Cognition*, 1977, *5*, 335–339. (b)

Fodor, J. D., Fodor, J. A., & Garrett, M. F. The psychological unreality of semantic representations. *Linguistic Inquiry*, 1975, *6*, 515–531.

Forster, K. I. Visual perception of rapidly presented word sequences of varying complexity. *Perception & Psychophysics*, 1970, *8*, 215–221.

Forster, K. I. Linguistic structure and sentence production. In C. Cherry (Ed.), *Pragmatic aspects of human communication*. Dordrecht-Holland: Reidel, 1974. (a)

Forster, K. I. The role of semantic hypotheses in sentence processing. In F. Bresson & J. Mehler (Eds.), *Current problems in psycholinguistics*. Paris: Editions du CNRS, 1974. (b)

Forster, K. I. *Separation of the effects of meaning on word recognition and sentence processing.* Paper presented at the Experimental Psychology Conference, Monash University, 1974. (c)

Forster, K. I. Accessing the mental lexicon. In R. J. Wales & E. Walker (Eds.), *New approaches to language mechansims*. Amsterdam: North-Holland, 1976.

Forster, K. I., & Bednall, E. S. Terminating and exhaustive search in lexical access. *Memory & Cognition*, 1976, *4*, 53–61.

Forster, K. I., & Chambers, S. M. Lexical access and naming time. *Journal of Verbal Learning and Verbal Behavior*, 1973, *12*, 627–635.

Forster, K. I., & Olbrei, I. Semantic heuristics and syntactic analysis. *Cognition,* 1973, 2, 319–347.

Forster, K. I., & Ryder, L. A. Perceiving the structure and meaning of sentences. *Journal of Verbal Learning and Verbal Behavior,* 1971, *10,* 285–296.

Foss, D. J. Some effects of ambiguity upon sentence comprehension. *Journal of Verbal Learning and Verbal Behavior,* 1970, *9,* 699–706.

Foss, D. J., & Jenkins, C. Some effects of context on the comprehension of ambiguous sentences. *Journal of Verbal Learning and Verbal Behavior,* 1973, *12,* 577–589.

Foss, D. J., & Swinney, D. A. On the psychological reality of the phoneme: Perception, identification and consciousness. *Journal of Verbal Learning and Verbal Behavior,* 1973, *12,* 246–257.

Frederickson, C. F. Effects of context-induced processing operations on semantic information acquired from discourse. *Cognitive Psychology,* 1975, *7,* 139–166.

Garrett, M. F. The analysis of sentence production. In G. Bower (Ed.), *Psychology of learning and motivation* (Vol. 9). New York: Academic Press, 1975.

Garrett, M. F. Syntactic processes in sentence production. In R. J. Wales & E. Walker (Eds.), *New approaches to language mechanisms.* Amsterdam: North-Holland, 1976. (a)

Garrett, M. F. *Word perception in sentences.* Paper presented at the Convocation on Communications, MIT, April 1976. (b)

Gough, P. B. The verification of sentences: The effects of delay of evidence and sentence length. *Journal of Verbal Learning and Verbal Behavior,* 1966, *5,* 492–496.

Hall, L. C. *Semantic and syntactic analysis in language processing.* Unpublished honors thesis, Department of Psychology, Australian National University, 1969.

Healy, A. F., & Cutting, J. E. Units of speech perception: Phoneme and syllable. *Journal of Verbal Learning and Verbal Behavior,* 1976, *15,* 73–83.

Henderson, L. A word superiority effect without orthographic assistance. *Quarterly Journal of Experimental Psychology,* 1974, *26,* 301–311.

Herriot, P. The comprehension of active and passive sentences as a function of pragmatic expectations. *Journal of Verbal Learning and Verbal Behavior,* 1969, *8,* 166–169.

Holmes, V. M., Arwas, R., & Garrett, M. F. Prior context and the perception of lexically ambiguous sentences. *Memory & Cognition,* 1977, *5,* 103–110.

Ingling, N. W. Categorization: A mechanism for rapid information processing. *Journal of Experimental Psychology,* 1972, *94,* 239–243.

Jonides, J., & Gleitman, H. A conceptual category effect in visual search: O as letter or as a digit. *Perception & Psychophysics,* 1972, *12,* 457–460.

Loftus, E. F., & Cole, W. Retrieving attribute and name information from semantic memory. *Journal of Experimental Psychology,* 1974, *102,* 1116–1122.

Marslen-Wilson, W. Linguistic descriptions and psychological assumptions in the study of sentence perception. In R. J. Wales & E. Walker (Eds.), *New approaches to language mechanisms.* Amsterdam: North-Holland, 1976.

Martin, J. G. Temporal word spacing and the perception of ordinary, anomalous and scrambled strings. *Journal of Verbal Learning and Verbal Behavior,* 1968, *7,* 154–157.

McNeill, D., & Lindig, K. The perceptual reality of phonemes, syllables, words, and sentences. *Journal of Verbal Learning and Verbal Behavior,* 1973, *12,* 419–430.

Mehler, J., Segui, J., & Carey, P. W. Tails of words: Monitoring ambiguity. *Journal of Verbal Learning and Verbal Behavior,* 1978, *17,* 29–35.

Meyer, D. E., & Ellis, G. B. *Parallel processes in word recognition.* Paper presented at the annual meeting of the Psychonomic Society, San Antonio, 1970.

Meyer, D. E., & Schvaneveldt, R. W. Facilitation in recognizing pairs of words: Evidence for a dependence between retrieval operations. *Journal of Experimental Psychology,* 1971, *90,* 227–234.

Meyer, D. E., & Schvaneveldt, R. W. Meaning, memory structure and mental processes. *Science,* 1976, *192,* 27–33.

Meyer, D. E., Schvaneveldt, R. W., & Ruddy, M. G. Loci of context effects in visual word recognition. In P. Rabbit (Ed.), *Attention and performance V*. New York: Academic Press, 1975.

Middleton, D. *Effects of semantic relatedness on simultaneous word-pair matching*. Unpublished undergraduate research report, Department of Psychology, Monash University, 1977.

Miller, G. A., & Isard, S. Some perceptual consequences of linguistic rules. *Journal of Verbal Learning and Verbal Behavior*, 1963, *2*, 217–228.

Morton, J. A functional model of human memory. In D. A. Norman (Ed.), *Models of human memory*. New York: Academic Press, 1970.

Morton, J., & Long, J. Effect of word transitional probability on phoneme identification. *Journal of Verbal Learning and Verbal Behavior*, 1976, *15*, 43–51.

Murray, W. S. *Syntactic and semantic variables in sentence matching*. Paper presented at the Fifth Australian Experimental Psychology Conference, La Trobe University, May 1978.

Murray, W. S., & Forster, K. I. *Structure, meaning and the sentence matching task*. Paper presented at Language and Speech Conference, Melbourne University, 1977.

Posner, M. I., & Mitchell, R. F. Chronometric analysis of classification. *Psychological Review*, 1967, *74*, 392–409.

Ratcliff, J. *The plausibility effect*. Unpublished honors thesis, Department of Psychology, Monash University, 1975.

Ratcliff, J. *An investigation of the plausibility effect*. Paper presented at the Fifth Australian Experimental Psychology Conference, La Trobe University, May 1978.

Rice, L., Thorpe, G., & Gunn, P. *Processing levels in sentence recognition*. Unpublished undergraduate research report, Department of Psychology, Monash University, 1977.

Rosenberg, S., & Jarvella, R. J. Semantic integration as a variable in sentence perception, memory and production. In G. B. Flores d'Arcais & W. J. M. Levelt (Eds.), *Advances in psycholinguistics*. Amsterdam: North-Holland, 1970.

Rubenstein, H., Lewis, S. S., & Rubenstein, M. A. Evidence for phonemic recoding in visual word recognition. *Journal of Verbal Learning and Verbal Behavior*, 1971, *10*, 645–657.

Rubin, P., Turvey, M. T,, & Van Gelder, P. Initial phonemes are detected faster in spoken words than in spoken nonwords. *Perception & Psychophysics*, 1976, *19*, 394–398.

Savin, H. B., & Bever, T. G. The non-perceptual reality of the phoneme. *Journal of Verbal Learning and Verbal Behavior*, 1970, *9*, 295–302.

Schlesinger, I. M. *Sentence structure and the reading process*. The Hague: Mouton, 1968.

Schneider, W., & Shiffrin, R. M. Controlled and automatic human information processing: I. Detection, search and attention. *Psychological Review*, 1977, *84*, 1–66.

Schuberth, R. E., & Eimas, P. D. Effects of context on the classification of words and nonwords. *Journal of Experimental Psychology: Human Perception and Performance*, 1977, *3*, 27–36.

Schvaneveldt, R. W., Meyer, D. E., & Becker, C. A. Lexical ambiguity, semantic context, and visual word recognition. *Journal of Experimental Psychology: Human Perception and Performance*, 1976, *2*, 243–256.

Slobin, D. I. Grammatical transformations and sentence comprehension in childhood and adulthood. *Journal of Verbal Learning and Verbal Behavior*, 1966, *5*, 219–227.

Stanners, R. F., & Forbach, G. B. Analysis of letter strings in word recognition. *Journal of Experimental Psychology*, 1973, *98*, 31–35.

Stanners, R. F., Forbach, G. B., & Headley, D. B. Decision and search processes in word–nonword classification. *Journal of Experimental Psychology*, 1971, *90*, 45–50.

Steedman, M. J., & Johnson-Laird, P. N. *A programmatic theory of linguistic performance*. Paper presented at the Stirling Conference on Psycholinguistics, June 1976.

Swinney, D. A., & Hakes, D. T. Effects of prior context upon lexical access during sentence comprehension. *Journal of Verbal Learning and Verbal Behavior*, 1976, *15*, 681–689.

Taft, M., & Forster, K. I. Lexical storage and retrieval of polymorphemic and polysyllabic words. *Journal of Verbal Learning and Verbal Behavior,* 1976, *15,* 607–620.

Tulving, E., & Gold, C. Stimulus information and contextual information as determinants of tachistoscopic recognition of words. *Journal of Experimental Psychology,* 1963, *66,* 319–327.

Turner, E. A., & Rommetveit, R. The acquisition of sentence voice and reversibility. *Child Development,* 1967, *38,* 649–660.

Tweedy, J. R., Lapinski, R. H., & Schvaneveldt, R. W. Semantic context effects on word recognition: Influence of varying the proportion of items presented in an appropriate context. *Memory & Cognition,* 1977, *5,* 84–89.

Tyler, L. K., & Marslen-Wilson, W. D. The on-line effects of semantic context on syntactic processing. *Journal of Verbal Learning and Verbal Behavior,* 1977, *16,* 683–692.

Watson, I. J. *The processing of implausible sentences.* Unpublished doctoral dissertation, Monash University, 1976.

3 Time-Compressed Speech and the Study of Lexical and Syntactic Processing

Martin S. Chodorow
Hunter College of the City University of New York

One of the most salient characteristics of language comprehension is the great speed with which it is performed. At an average speaking rate, the listener receives a new word about every 300 msec. There is much to be done: The acoustic waveform must be segmented into lexical units, with each unit identified and its structural relationships established within some higher unit of the sentence. Whatever the nature of these processes, whether they are dependent upon one another or autonomous, parallel or serial, it is still the case that a new lexical item is presented to the language-processing system every third of a sec. In broadest terms, the problem involves limited resources on the one hand (e.g., restriction on short-term memory) and almost unlimited complexity on the other (i.e., the richness of the linguistic structures that must be recovered). Phenomenally, at least, language comprehension seems very much to be a real-time process. How, then, is it to be assessed experimentally?

Many of the paradigms used in psycholinguistic research are designed to measure the on-line cognitive load of sentence processing by interposing a competing task for listeners to perform as they comprehend test materials. This task typically involves detecting near-threshold tones, responding to suprathreshold clicks, monitoring for previously specified target phonemes, or remembering random word strings. Performance on the competing task is interpreted as an indirect indicator of the cognitive load produced by those processes that support comprehension. The logic and assumptions of interference paradigms have been much discussed (Foss, 1969; Norman & Bobrow, 1975). The underlying assumption is that the two tasks compete for cognitive resources drawn from a common pool. Language comprehension is usually viewed as primary, receiving higher priority in allocation of resources than does the competing task, which, consequently, shows greater effects of interference.

In this chapter, I discuss a different sort of interference paradigm, one in which the competing tasks are the same. Experiments have, of course, been performed using different messages presented simultaneously over two separate channels (Broadbent, 1958; Treisman, 1964). But in these experiments, the competing tasks are to avoid processing one channel while shadowing the message in the other. What might we expect when subjects are required to comprehend all the sentential material they are given, i.e., when the competition for resources comes from *within* a sentence?

In the sections that follow, time compression is discussed as an experimental manipulation for the study of language comprehension. The motivation for such a discussion can be expressed quite simply: If component processes in comprehension have different performance characteristics (e.g., resource requirements or maximal rates) then increasing the overall rate of input ought to affect them differentially. In this way, we might reasonably expect to pull apart otherwise quite entangled components.

The first section, *Component Processes,* contains a discussion of various processes that have been implicated as supporting comprehension. Two of these are examined in some detail. In the second section, I develop an experimental paradigm using time-compressed speech. On the basis of evidence about the relative time-courses of lexical and syntactic processing, some general predictions are made about their behavior under time compression. In the third section, the compressed speech paradigm is used to test the predictions, with lexical ambiguity and verb complexity serving as loads on lexical and syntactic processing. The fourth section is a comparison of three models of syntactic parsing and concludes with a suggestion for future research using compressed speech.

COMPONENT PROCESSES

It has often been suggested that language comprehension is supported by four main types of processing: phonetic, lexical, syntactic, and semantic. Phonetic processing, the segmentation of the acoustic waveform into phonemes, is not addressed in the discussion that follows. The goals of lexical processing are to identify a substring of phonemes as a word and to access certain basic information about the word, such as its part-of-speech and definition. Syntactic processing uses part-of-speech and other syntactic information to recover the grammatical relations expressed in the sentence. Semantic processing is responsible for construction of a representation of the sentence's meaning.

The relations between these four components have been the subject of much debate. Evidence from shadowing studies and word-monitoring experiments (Marslen-Wilson, 1975; Marslen-Wilson & Tyler, 1975) strongly suggests parallel computation in all four components, with full interaction among the processes. According to this parallel interactive model, decisions about word identification, for instance, are influenced by the semantic and syntactic processing performed up to the point of the word's occurrence in the sentence. Syntactic and semantic computations begin almost immediately in the course of analysis, so that the entire machinery of language comprehension can be brought to bear on each new item as it is encountered.

An alternative model restricts the relations between the components so that they are serial rather than parallel, with the outcome of processing at one level available only to the next. Although, in its strongest form, the serial model might have difficulty finding proponents, there are indications that some aspects of sentence processing fit the pattern. Fodor, Bever, and Garrett (1974) reviewed considerable evidence suggesting that the listener waits until a clause boundary is reached before performing a syntactic analysis based on information about part-of-speech, position, inflection, and verb subcategorization, i.e., information provided by prior lexical processing.

There are, of course, other possible language-comprehension models, ones that order some of the processes serially and arrange others in parallel (with or without interaction). Using the sentence-identification paradigm (i.e., asking "Do the items in this string constitute a sentence?"), Forster and Olbrei (1973) have produced evidence for the independence of syntactic processing from semantic processing. They found that the time required to analyze a given syntactic structure is approximately constant despite wide variations in the plausibility of a particular sentence having that structure. However, using the lexical-identification paradigm ("Are all the items in this string words?"), Forster (1974) was also able to demonstrate an effect of semantic plausibility. Here it appears that the speed with which the subject is able to identify each item as a word depends upon the plausibility of the sentence in which it is found. When considered jointly, these results are incompatible both with a fully interactive parallel model and with a strictly serial one.

The work discussed in the third section, *Experiments,* focuses on two of the components cited above, lexical processing and syntactic processing. Although we do not know the exact relationship between the components of sentence comprehension, we can still ask what effect increasing the load on one will have overall when other factors are held relatively constant.

Lexical Processing

In at least some respects, lexical processing within a sentence ought to resemble word processing in nonsentential contexts. In each case, the word must be located in the mental lexicon. When subjects are asked to indicate whether a given string of letters is a word, their time to do so is faster when the string constitutes a high-frequency word than when it forms a low-frequency one (Rubenstein, Garfield, & Millikan, 1970). Similar word-frequency effects are reported in sentence-processing tasks. For example, subjects respond faster to target phonemes that follow high-frequency adjectives in sentences than to the same targets following low-frequency adjectives (Cairns & Foss, 1971). When asked to indicate if a given string of words constitutes a sentence, subjects respond more quickly to strings consisting of high-frequency words (Forster, 1974).

There are, however, some notable differences between lexical processing in sentential and nonsentential contexts. When asked to indicate if a string of letters is a word, subjects respond faster to homographic items than to nonhomographic items, e.g., *bat* vs. *bird* (Rubenstein et al., 1970). It is presumed that at least some aspect of lexical access involves a random search, so that the existence of multiple entries (meanings) for the homograph increases the probability of one being located in a given amount of search time. In the lexical-identification task, finding one entry is sufficient for answering the question: Is it a word? But in sentence processing, the existence of multiple meanings for a word (i.e., lexical ambiguity) generally leads to longer response times. For example, phoneme-monitor latencies are greater for target phonemes immediately following an ambiguous item than for the same targets following matched unambiguous controls (Foss & Jenkins, 1973). In sentence processing, the lexical component must do more than just identify words; appropriate meanings must also be made available.

Foss and Jenkins (1973) have interpreted their results as evidence of greater processing load immediately following the ambiguous word, a load that reflects the presence of multiple readings for the ambiguous item. Support for this view comes from the work of Lackner and Garrett (1972), who reported that subjects' interpretation of a lexically ambiguous sentence can be biased toward either sense of the ambiguity by playing an appropriate context sentence to their "unattended" ear while they listen to the ambiguous sentence played in the "attended" ear. Lackner and Garrett argued that this ability to bias toward *either* of the meanings of the word can best be explained by assuming that both interpretations are available to the listener at the time of biasing. Additional evidence comes from Conrad (1974), who played test sentences to subjects and followed each with a visual probe word. The subject's task was to name the color of ink in which the probe was printed. Color-naming latency was greater if the probe word had been in the test sentence than if it had not. This increased latency is thought to reflect interference between the word and the color-naming response. For a sentence containing an ambiguous item, the color-naming latency was greater not only when the probe was the ambiguous item itself, but also when it was a word closely related to *either* sense of the ambiguity.

Indications of increased monitoring latency, plus evidence for the accessibility of multiple interpretations of the ambiguous word, suggest that lexical processing is really quite resource demanding; i.e., the addition of an extra meaning for an item delays response in a concurrent monitor task until the ambiguity can be resolved and resources freed from lexical processing. If this picture is correct, it would seem most desirable for such a resource-demanding process to be of brief duration. Cairns and Kamerman (1975) reported that phoneme-monitor latency is increased immediately subsequent to an ambiguous word but that no effect of the ambiguity is reflected in latency measures taken two syllables beyond. The experimenters interpreted their results as indicating that a resolution of the ambiguity occurs very shortly after it is encountered.

Also consistent with this interpretation are the conditions under which Conrad (1974) was able to produce a color-naming interference effect. Interference was produced by a probe word related to either interpretation of the ambiguous item only when the ambiguous item was the last word in the sentence, so that it was followed immediately by the probe. No effect was found when the ambiguous item was in a nonfinal position, separated from the probe by intervening words.

Finally, Holmes, Arwas, and Garrett (1977) reported that the rapid serial-visual presentation (RSVP) of test sentences produces a highly localized effect for lexical ambiguity. In their experiment, the overall recall of sentences containing ambiguous items did not differ from that of sentences with matched control words. However, the lexically ambiguous items *themselves* were recalled less reliably than their unambiguous controls.

Holmes et al.'s (1977) results are all the more remarkable because they are produced not only by instances of contextually biased ambiguity (e.g., *The ballplayers found a BAT in the basement*) but are also produced by ambiguity presented in neutral context (e.g., *The boys found a BAT in the basement*). It is not too surprising that the load associated with lexical ambiguity is short-lived in biased contexts (where preceding portions of the sentence strongly favor one of the senses of the ambiguous word), for here the listener has a basis for making a choice between the word senses. On the other hand, quick resolution of unbiased ambiguity raises an obvious question: Why don't listeners postpone their selection of an interpretation until they have had an opportunity to analyze the rest of the sentence, possibly choosing a reading on the basis of the context it may provide? The answer seems to be that lexical ambiguity imposes too heavy a burden, that it is too costly in terms of resources, to be maintained during subsequent sentence processing.

To summarize, when the sentence processor encounters a lexical ambiguity: (a) more than one meaning is accessed, (b) latency to perform a competing task is increased, but (c) the region of these effects is quite local. Lexical processing, it has been argued, closely accompanies in time the reception of each input word.

Syntactic Processing

By its very nature, syntactic processing ought to operate over a different time course than does lexical processing. Here we are no longer dealing with single words, but rather with groups to be organized into phrases of various kinds. Indeed, measurements generally reveal a more extended temporal effect for syntactic processing than for lexical processing; the former seems to be less closely tied to the input than does the latter. Bever and Hurtig (1975) reported that near-threshold tones are less reliably detected at the end of a clause than at its beginning. They view this as support for a model of sentence perception in which the listener accumulates input at the beginning of a clause and actively organizes it at the end. Considerable attention is required for this organizing; consequently, performance suffers on the competing task of tone detection. Foss and Cairns (1970) reported that when subjects are required to read two words aloud before repeating a right-branching or center-embedded sentence they have just heard, their repetitions are less accurate. Although this finding is open to a number of interpretations, the experimenters suggest that it may be the consequence of interrupting the structural processing that has continued beyond the termination of the acoustic signal.

Results such as those of Bever and Hurtig (1975) and Foss and Cairns (1970) support one view of the distribution of syntactic processing, i.e., that it tends to accumulate toward the ends of clauses. But the picture is by no means clear-cut; other studies have provided evidence for other distributions of the cognitive activity related to structuring input. For example, when Foss (1969) used phoneme monitoring to examine a variety of syntactic constructions, he found faster response times for late position targets than for early targets. Holmes and Forster (1970) reported a comparable pattern of reaction times in a click-monitor study. If monitoring time reflects processing load, then for many kinds of syntactic constructions, the load decreases as the listener moves through the sentence. However, Foss and Lynch (1969) reported that when the structure is made complex, as in the case of right-branching or self-embedded relative clauses, the load remains high throughout the sentence and may even increase toward the end. Perhaps some constructions facilitate processing by allowing the listeners to compute the formal properties of what they hear, as they hear it. Other constructions are either too weakly constrained (e.g., right-branching relatives) or too complex (e.g., self-embedded relatives) to be of immediate use, thus forcing processing to lag behind the input.

According to what I call the *structural determinacy hypothesis,* a listener's decisions about syntactic structure closely accompany the input in time or follow it at some delay, depending upon the listener's ability to determine its structure. The psychological significance of this difference can best be seen in the on-line character of the listener's task. Short-term memory is notoriously limited for unstructured items, but less so when structure is available for organizing what is to be stored (Miller, 1956). When the structural properties of the input are known, listeners have available an appropriate framework for organizing what they hear, as they hear it. If the syntactic structure of a sentence is known in advance, the sentence is perceived more accurately and verified more quickly (Mehler & Carey, 1967, 1968). However, when the structuring of the input must follow its arrival, material is accumulated before it is organized. In this latter condition, the limitations of short-term memory, for example, can be expected to make the processing more difficult.

Ideally, in order to test the structural determinacy hypothesis, we should manipulate structural information at a given point in a sentence and assess the listener's performance. The only requirement is that the information to be varied must be relevant for determining the structure of *subsequent* input. In a sentence, just this sort of information is carried by the verb: Individual verbs differ from one another in number of possible syntactic environments, e.g., the different kinds of verb phrase constructions in which they may appear as the head. In a generative–transformational model such as Chomsky's (1965), this notion of possible syntactic environment is captured by the subcategorization information associated with each verb: A syntactically simple verb such as *injure* has fewer constructions as possible environments than does a more complex verb like *believe*. *Injure* is restricted for the most part to transitive constructions (e.g., *Sally injured her elbow*), whereas *believe* can be followed either by a complement clause or by a nonsentential direct object (e.g., *The teacher believed the girl was sick. The teacher believed the girl.*).

Fodor, Garrett, and Bever (1968) reported that anagram and paraphrase tasks are easier with sentences containing simple transitive verbs than with sentences containing complement verbs followed by direct objects. A similar finding comes from work by Holmes and Forster (1972) with the RSVP paradigm. Both sets of experiments support the conclusion that processing complexity is greater for complement verbs than for simple transitive ones. This is precisely what we would predict on the basis of differences in determinacy of the verb-phrase structures of the two types of verbs.

By way of illustration, consider the following strings, which represent what a listener has heard at various points in time when given the sentence *The teacher believed the girl was sick.*

The teacher
The teacher believed
The teacher believed the girl
The teacher believed the girl was sick

When the listener has heard only the substring *the teacher believed,* the form of the verb phrase is undetermined; both the transitive and the complement possibilities remain open, as do several others (e.g., *The teacher believed in*...). After the noun phrase *the girl,* the verb phrase remains undetermined with respect to the transitive–complement distinction. Indeed, the listener cannot be certain of the structure until an indicator of the complement is encountered. Only after *was* is processed can an unambiguous assignment be made for *the girl,* as surface subject of the complement clause.

In single-clause constructions with simple objects (*The teacher believed the girl*), complement verbs are sources of processing complexity because a complement indicator (e.g., another tensed verb) is not present. However, when a simple transitive verb is used in the same construction (*The teacher injured the girl*), its environment is syntactically constrained, so that the choice of assignment for the noun phrase can be made without awaiting a subsequent cue. Structural indeterminacy, then, may be defined as temporary ambiguity in assigning a syntactic relation (e.g., direct object of verb, subject of complement clause, etc.) to a phrase of a given syntactic category (e.g., a noun phrase).

If this account of sentence processing is correct, then by reducing the indeterminacy, we should be able to reduce the difficulty of parsing. I have argued that the listener does not immediately impose an organization on the substring *believed the girl* because the relationship between the verb and the noun phrase is not determined. English, however, provides an optional cue to the structure of such sequences in the form of a complementizer, as shown below:

The teacher believed that the girl...

That introduces the complement clause and, thus, explicitly marks the relation between verb and noun phrase. We should, therefore, predict facilitation in the assignment of structure when the complementizer is present. Empirical support for this claim comes from Hakes (1972). He reported that, for a target in the noun phrase following a complement verb, phoneme-monitor times are faster when the complementizer is present. For example, subjects asked to monitor for /g/ responded more quickly to the target in Sentence (2) than in (1).

(1) The teacher believed the girl would improve her average.
(2) The teacher believed that the girl would improve her average.

If these latencies are measures of processing load, then the presence of the complementizer does indeed seem to reduce the load.

As defined above, structural indeterminacy must be present throughout most of the course of processing for almost every sentence. Rarely are listeners in an immediate position to uniquely organize all that they hear. One point of determinacy is at the end of an unambiguous sentence, where the completion of processing must result in a single structural description of the string. But this point is after the stimulus and, therefore, cannot be expected to contribute directly to the on-line organization of input. Are there sentence-internal loci from which a single structure can clearly be assigned to incoming elements? Likely candidates for such positions are syntactically simple verbs and more complex verbs that have been restricted, as, for example, by the presence of a complementizer.

To summarize, in contrast to lexical processing, which closely accompanies the reception of each word, syntactic processing generally must lag behind the input, primarily because structure is so often revealed only by an analysis of subsequent items. However, when syntactic determinacy is high, listeners should be able to impose organization more directly on what they hear, without the characteristic delay between input and processing.

TIME-COMPRESSED SPEECH

For several years, methods have been available to speed up the playback rate of recorded speech without drastically altering its pitch. Early investigations (Fairbanks, Guttman, & Miron, 1957) of time-compressed speech revealed that intelligibility of individual words spoken in isolation remains quite high even when the input is compressed to less than one-half its original duration. By contrast, *comprehension* of passages of connected text (e.g., paragraphs from novels) is very poor at such compression rates (cf. Foulke, 1969). These results mirror the subjective feeling often reported by listeners who experience a sensation of "falling behind" the input when they are given time-compressed passages of text. In this section, some empirical and theoretical underpinning is offered for this subjective experience.

Aaronson (1974) has reviewed much of the literature dealing with rate manipulation in the auditory presentation of list materials. She and her colleagues (Aaronson, 1968; Aaronson, Markowitz, & Shapiro, 1971) have examined the types of errors that subjects make in recalling random strings of digits when durations of items and interitem pauses are varied. Random digit strings, of course, differ from sentences, and, therefore, care must be taken in generalizing across such materials. But in some very general ways, list processing might be viewed as consisting of components that resemble the lexical and syntactic processes.

To recall a list, the individual items must be identified and, if it is ordered recall, the linear (precedence) structure of the list must be encoded. Performance can be analyzed in terms of two types of error: (a) a failure to recall an item (item error), and (b) a violation of the precedence structure of the sequence (order error). The two are at least partly dissociable. Aaronson

(1968) reduced the duration of interitem pauses and found that order errors increased more than item errors. When the duration of the items was reduced while the overall sequence length was held constant by increasing pause time, the result was a decrease in order errors and no changes in item errors. This pattern of results suggests that the interval following a stimulus item is crucial for its incorporation into a structural representation. Item identification, on the other hand, seems to be relatively unaffected by certain manipulations of stimulus duration and pause time. However, by varying the signal-to-noise ratio of the acoustic input, it is possible to produce a change in item errors without an accompanying change in order errors (Aaronson, 1968). Broadly speaking, then, there seem to be two sorts of activities taking place, one rapid and closely tied to the physical stimulus itself, the other occurring some time after the termination of the stimulus.

Aaronson (1968) provided additional evidence that the processing of order information lags behind the input. Reaction time to monitor for a predesignated target is longer when the subject must subsequently give an ordered repetition of the digit list. At fast presentation rates, this monitor-time difference between the repetition vs. no-repetition tasks is greater for late position targets than for early targets. The suggestion here is that the act of encoding order information lags behind input and, at high rates, its separation from the input becomes even greater toward the end of the string. Furthermore, there is evidence that even at slow rates processing outlasts the list itself. Aaronson and Sternberg (1963, cited in Aaronson, 1974) measured the time subjects took to indicate which of two lights had been turned on following a digit-list presentation. Response times were longer when the interval between the end of the list and the onset of the light was short. The experimenters interpret this as evidence of interference between postlist processing and the light-monitor task. They reasoned that with the longer interval between list and light, more of the processing is completed before the response is called for, and hence, reaction times are faster.

What implications can be drawn for the rapid presentation of sentence materials? First, with regard to an observation made at the beginning of this section, I might hypothesize that the comprehension difficulty encountered with compressed passages of text is the result of interference between lagging processing for one sentence and the reception of the next. If this is correct, then increasing the pause time following a sentence should allow more of its processing to be completed, thus improving performance. A second, corollary hypothesis is that a processing load that is not affected by manipulations of postsentence pause time must have a different (presumably, nonlagging) time-course.

Earlier, I argued that lexical processing is rapid and closely tied to the stimulus and that lexical ambiguity increases the load. If the digit-list studies can serve as a guide, what effects will accrue from speeding up the rate at which a sentence is input to the lexical component? (a) Even considerable increases in rate should produce little or no effect on normal lexical processing. (Rate manipulations had little effect on item errors in the digit-list studies.) However, (b) when the rate is fast and the words are ambiguous, demand might well exceed capacity. (Although there was no direct analog of lexical ambiguity in the digit-list experiments, I might wish to stretch a point somewhat by arguing that presentation in noise did introduce a kind of item ambiguity for the listener.) (c) Manifestations of this effect will be local and, in particular, should not be altered by manipulations of postsentence pause time.

The evidence of the first section, *Component Processes,* also indicates that syntactic processing becomes displaced from the stimulus as a result of structural indeterminacy. The digit-list experiments show that delays in structuring tend to accumulate more at fast presentation rates than at slow rates; but even for the latter, the activity of structuring can often outlast the stimulus itself. It is this kind of processing that ought to be most sensitive to the presentation rate and to the length of postsentence pause time. Specifically, (a) for fast presentation rates, when structural indeterminacy is increased and pause duration is held constant, performance should decline. Conversely, (b) when the degree of determinacy is held constant and pause time is increased, performance should improve. (c) Slowing the rate of sentence presentation ought to facilitate listeners' processing of the material by enabling them to avoid especially large accumulations of load at the end of the sentence, and beyond.

The Paradigm

Thus far, only passing reference has been made to assessing actual performance with time-compressed speech. Early studies with connected text and multiple-choice questions revealed comprehension difficulty for time-compressed material, but these experiments did not point to particular syntactic or processing variables as the source of the trouble. Any method that requires listeners to process many different sentences before making a response will be subject to a similar shortcoming; finding the locus of an effect is greatly complicated by the presence of many candidate loci.

A paradigm for studying processes of the kind discussed above must provide opportunities to vary both sentence speed and postsentence pause time and to measure the listener's performance "inside" and "outside" a given sentence. These requirements are met by the following presentation sequence (1, 2, 3) and response tasks (4, 5) adapted from a paradigm used by Savin and Perchonock (1965):

1. Present a test sentence at normal or compressed speed.
2. Introduce a silent pause interval of variable length.
3. Present a list of nonsentential words at fixed rate.

4. Ask subject to recall sentence.
5. Ask subject to recall words.

Steps 1 and 2 are the vehicles for manipulating rate and postsentence time. Steps 4 and 5 provide measurements of performance "inside" and "outside" the sentence.

In the experiments discussed in the next section, compressed sentences were reduced to one-half their original durations (i.e., 50% compressed). The postsentence pause interval was either 200-msec or 750-msec long. Presentation rate of the postsentence list (Step 3, above) was fixed at one word every three-quarter sec. The list itself consisted of eight semantic items, one drawn from each of eight categories, such as *furniture, weather, animals,* etc. Each category consisted of five members; e.g., for furniture, the members were *bed, chair, table, rug, sofa.* Before the experiment began, the subjects heard all the members of each list category. The presentation order of the categories was continuously in view throughout the experiment. Under these conditions, with the order given and the set of items known, the subject's task was to recall which one of the five possible members of each category had actually been presented.

If sentence processing lags behind the input and, in fact, continues beyond the physical termination of the sentence, then manipulation of pause time will effect the number of words recalled from the list. Specifically, when the pause is reduced from 750 msec to 200 msec, more of the displaced sentence processing will be competing with list input, and therefore list recall can be expected to suffer. Sentence recall should also show a decrement in this condition. But a more specific type of analysis can also be performed with the sentence data. For ambiguous materials, this means looking at recall of the ambiguous words themselves. Sentence data also provide an opportunity to compare recall of sentence substrings that differ with respect to a variable such as structural determinacy.

EXPERIMENTS

Lexical Ambiguity

Eight lexically ambiguous–unambiguous sentence pairs were used in the experiment. Members of each pair differed by only one element, the ambiguous word or its frequency-matched unambiguous control. Wherever possible, ambiguous and control words were also matched for number of syllables. (Mean lengths were 1.6 and 1.4 syllables, for ambiguous and control words, respectively.) An example pair is given below:

AMBIGUOUS: They knew that the large plant would be sold.
CONTROL: They knew that the large forest would be sold.

The ambiguities were previously assessed as relatively unbiased (i.e., .35 to .65 probability of the listener assigning one of the two word senses to the ambiguity). On separate tests, the ambiguous and control versions were rated as being equally "natural."

Three types of presentation condition were used: normal sentence speed (3.8 words per sec) and a 200-msec postsentence pause (Normal+200); compressed sentence speed (7.6 words per second) and a 200-msec postsentence pause (Compressed+200); compressed speed and a 750-msec pause (Compressed+750). Sixty subjects were divided into two response groups. One was required to recall the sentence verbatim before recalling the word list; the other had to paraphrase the sentence before recalling the list. Thus, each group produced the same kind of word-list data but different sentence data.

An analysis of variance for the list data revealed no significant main effect for the between-subjects factor of response group and no significant interactions of this factor with any others. The main effect for ambiguity was significant, $F(1, 58) = 6.64$, $p < .05$, by subjects; $F(1, 7) = 13.19$, $p < .01$, by sentences.

Figure 3.1 shows the ambiguous–unambiguous comparisons for the three presentation conditions. Orthogonal contrasts were used to test the three predictions made in the previous section. First, the effect of ambiguity was not significant at the normal presentation rate, $F < 1$, by subjects and sentences. Second, under compression, however, the effect due to ambiguity was significant, $F(1, 116) = 8.02$, $p < .05$, by subjects; $F(1, 14) = 4.48$, $p < .10$, by sentences. Third, changing the amount of pause time did not change this ambiguous–unambiguous difference ($F < 1$, by subjects and sentences).

The sentence data were examined separately for each response group. Using rather liberal criteria, an overwhelming majority of the paraphrases were judged acceptable. Of those that were unacceptable, no discernable pattern in their distribution implicated either the presentation or the ambiguity variables. When sentence data for the verbatim-recall group were analyzed, none of the main effects or interactions reached significance. However, an examination of recall for the ambiguous words and their matched controls was more revealing. At the normal presentation rate, there was no difference between the two; but under compression, the control word was recalled more often (by subjects, $p < .01$; by sentences, $p < .15$; both one-tailed sign tests).

As predicted, the effect of ambiguity was manifest at compressed but not at normal speed. This confirms the prediction of the model constructed in the first section of this chapter, according to which lexical processing is highly resource demanding and is temporally tied to the stimulus. At the normal input speed, there is sufficient time to resolve an ambiguity before the processing demands made by subsequent words become too great. At the 50%

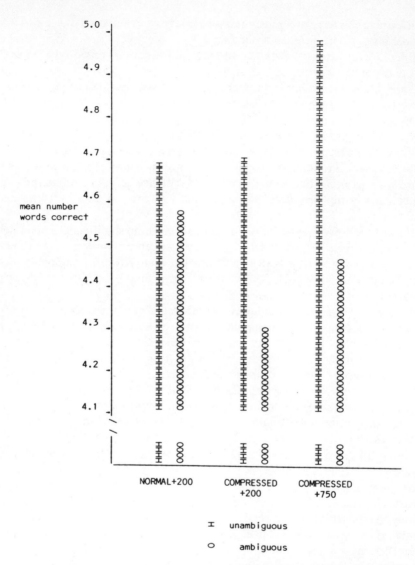

FIG. 3.1. Lexical ambiguity experiment: words recalled from list.

compressed rate, unambiguous words are also processed before subsequent demands become too pressing; but resolving an ambiguity requires too much time. The fact that there are no overall differences in sentence recall for the ambiguous and control materials but that differences do exist for the specific ambiguous and control words suggests that the effect is local, perhaps resulting from premature truncation of some ambiguity resolution procedure. Also consistent with this interpretation is the pattern found in the list data, where an effect of ambiguity can be seen at the compressed rate, yet the difference between ambiguous and control conditions is not diminished by addition postsentence time.

As a final note, it should be pointed out that postsentence time does seem to have an effect on list recall. For the unambiguous materials, the 750-msec pause resulted in somewhat better performance (though not statistically significant) than did the shorter interval at either of the input rates. Earlier it was suggested that, in general, syntactic processing outlasts the physical presentation of the sentence. Perhaps superior performance with the longer pause interval is a reflection of having completed this processing. With the short pause, the effect on list recall ought, then, to be indicative of the postsentence processing that remains to be done. Specifically, this lead to the prediction that, with the short pause, sentences that are structurally more indeterminate will produce a more sizable decrement on the list. This prediction is tested in the second experiment.

Verb Complexity

Twelve pairs of single-clause transitive sentences were used in the experiment. Members of each pair differed by only one element, the verb, that was either a simple transitive (TS) or a complement verb (TC). An example pair is given below:

TS: The physician studied some recent cases of the once-rare disease.
TC: The physician reported some recent cases of the once-rare disease.

The verbs of each pair were matched for frequency of occurrence, and the sentences themselves were judged to be equally natural on separate ratings tests.

Nine triples of complement sentences were also used in the experiment. Members of each triple differed in verb and/or complementizer. They were: noun-phrase complement verb followed by *that* (NPC-that), noun-phrase complement verb without *that* (NPC-0), verb-phrase complement verb (VPC). The three sentences that follow constitute one such triple:

NPC-that: The banker recalled that Joe had repaid the loan on time.
NPC-0: The banker recalled Joe had repaid the loan on time.
VPC: The banker trusted Joe to repay the loan on time.

Here too, the verbs were closely matched for frequency of occurrence. In naturalness ratings, VPC sentences were judged to be somewhat more natural than CNP-0.

Reasons for including the TS, TC, NPC-that, and NPC-0 materials were covered earlier. Transitive sentences with complement verbs (TC) are predicted to be of greater indeterminacy than matched sentences with simple transitive verbs (TS). The presence of the complementizer in NPC-that should reduce the indeterminacy that would otherwise exist, as in NPC-0. Added to these sentence types is the verb phrase complement sentence (VPC). Its inclusion serves an important purpose: VPC provides another verb + noun-phrase sequence for which the structural relation between verb and noun cannot be determined until subsequent input is processed. Although the noun in question (*Joe,* in the example sentence) can be assigned as object of the verb (*trust*), the possibility also exists that it will, in addition, be subject of an embedded complement (*Joe repay the loan on time*). This possibility is confirmed by the presence of the complementizer *to,* but unlike the complementizer in NPC-that sentences, *to* appears AFTER the noun phrase, not before it. In fact, *to* appears in the same position as the tensed verb (*had*) of the complement in NPC-0. According to the structural determinacy hypothesis, then, VPC ought to behave much like NPC-0; in each the structural cue is separated from the verb by a comparable distance.

Presentation conditions were the same as those in the lexical-ambiguity experiment: normal presentation speed (3.7 words per second) with a 200-msec postsentence pause (Normal+200), 50% compressed (7.4 words per second) with a 200-msec pause (Compressed+200), and compressed with a 750-msec pause (compressed+750). The paraphrase-response task was not used; all subjects were instructed to provide a verbatim repetition of the sentence before recalling the list. Briefly, the predictions are that presentation rate and pause length will affect both list recall and sentence recall and that performance with the more indeterminate materials will be more adversely affected by these manipulations.

Performance on the postsentence word list is presented graphically in Fig. 3.2. An analysis of variance for this data revealed no significant main effects for presentation condition, $F < 1$, or sentence type, $F < 1$. However, the predictions were confirmed concerning the effect of pause time on the processing of structurally indeterminate sentences. For these sentences (TC, NPC-0, and VPC), the shorter pause produced a significant decrement in list recall, $F(1, 280) = 4.47$, $p < .05$, by subjects; $F(1, 22) = 2.98$, $p < .10$, by single-clause sentences; $F(1, 32) = 3.07$, $p < .10$, by complement sentences. No such effect was observed for the more determinate structures, TS and NPC-that, $F < 1$, by subjects and sentences. As suggested previously, this pattern is consistent with a model in which processing lags farther behind input for the more indeterminate sentences, so that the shorter pause time is not sufficient for completion of processing before the list presentation begins. Curiously, compression alone seems to have little or no effect on list performance, at least when measured by the difference between the Normal+200 and Compressed+200 conditions. This is quite contrary to prediction and is a point to which I return later.

Figures 3.3a and 3.3b contain the sentence data (mean numbers of words recalled) for complement and single-clause sentences, respectively. Analyses

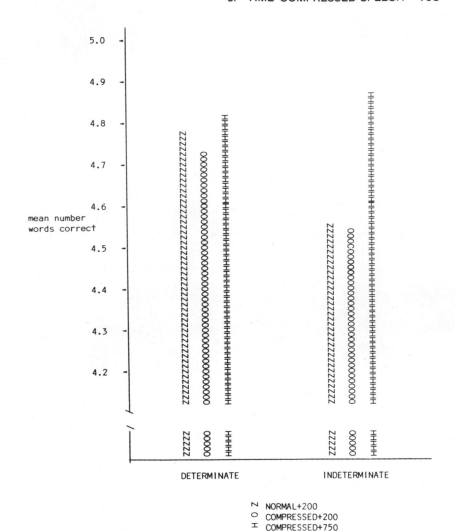

FIG. 3.2.   Verb complexity experiment: words recalled from list.

of variance revealed a significant main effect for presentation condition, $F(2, 70) = 13.24$, $p < .01$, by subjects; $F(2, 22) = 7.18$, $p < .01$, by single-clause sentences; $F(2, 16) = 9.20$, $p < .01$, by complement sentences. Performance at the normal presentation rate was superior to performance under compression. However, not all the sentences were affected in the same way by the two conditions involving compression. With additional pause time (i.e., Compressed+750), recall of the more determinate sentences (TS and NPC-that) improved significantly compared to their indeterminate versions (for TS, by subjects, $F(1, 280) = 3.23$, $p < .10$; by sentences, $F(1, 22) = 7.58$,

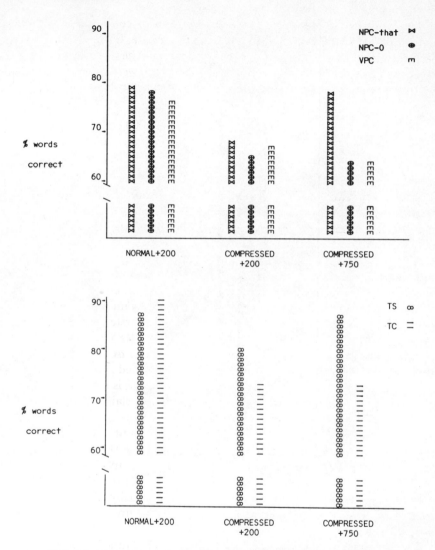

FIG. 3.3. Verb complexity experiment: words recalled from sentence.

$p < .05$; for NPC-that, by subjects, $F(1, 280) = 4.96, p < .05$; by sentences, $F(1, 32) = 7.09, p < .05$). Performance was equally poor for all sentences at the fast rate with the short pause, but with additional time, the more determinate sentences seem to have "recovered." This recovery might be interpreted as the completion of sentence processing; presumably, the indeterminate structures did not recover because the longer interval was still too short to accommodate all that remained to be done after the physical termination of those sentences.

The word-list results failed to show an effect of compression with the indeterminate sentences. In light of the sentence data, however, this failure seems somewhat less perplexing. The following schema indicates which response tasks (L for list recall, S for sentence recall) were adversely affected by the presentation conditions at each level of structural determinacy:

	Normal+200	Compressed+200	Compressed+750
determinate		S	
indeterminate	L	L, S	S

The indeterminate sentences were affected by the shorter pause time and the faster rate, but these effects were manifest in different measurements. The more determinate sentences were affected only by the combination of these manipulations (i.e., Compressed+200).

All of the sentence data discussed thus far have been based on measurements over entire sentences. In the lexical-ambiguity experiment, analysis of a particular sentence position revealed an effect of ambiguity. What might we expect from a more circumscribed examination of sentence data in the structural determinacy experiment? Forster (1970) provided evidence that under rapid serial visual presentation (RSVP) performance is directly dependent upon structuring the input items *as a sentence*. When subjects were given scrambled word strings, they recalled more of the words if they were able to restructure them into sentences. This is not too surprising; after all, there is plentiful evidence to support the claim that structuring facilitates storage. According to the structural determinacy hypothesis, under some conditions, syntactic processing lags behind input. When this occurs, input is accumulated before it is organized syntactically. Until it is structured, the string that has been accumulated should be more vulnerable to interference from other, temporally adjacent input and processing. In the case of compressed presentation, demands made by temproally adjacent input will be greater, and, therefore, holding a string of unstructured items will be more difficult.

To test the prediction, performance on structurally indeterminate substrings of NPC-0 and VPC sentences were compared under the Normal+200 and Compressed+750 conditions. In each case, the substring in question consisted of the matrix verb and its following noun. Figure 3.4 displays the results for four positions in the NPC-0 sentences. The left-most position is that of the noun preceding the matrix verb, whereas the right-most is the verb of the complement clause; these positions lie to either side of the indeterminate substring. The interaction between presentation condition and sentence position was significant, as was the decrement in recall of the indeterminate substring for Compressed+750, $F(1, 420) = 8.71$, $p < .05$, by subjects; $F(1, 96) = 7.74$, $p < .05$, by sentences.

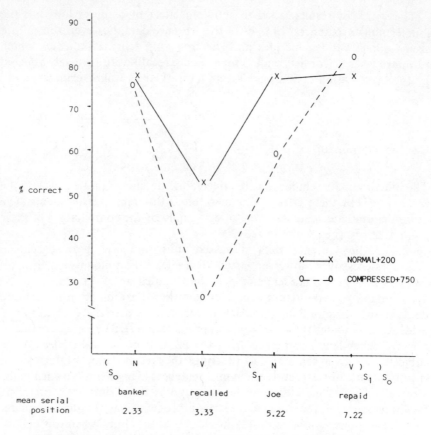

FIG. 3.4.   Recall of selected positions in NPC-0. Words along the abscissa are from the test sentence "The banker recalled Joe had repaid the loan."

Figure 3.5 contains the data for the VPC sentences. Here the right-most position is the verb following the complementizer *to*. The interaction between position and presentation condition was not significant, although there was a significant decrement for the indeterminate substring with Compressed+750, $F(1, 420) = 8.67, p < .05$, by subjects; $F(1, 96) = 7.69, p < .05$, by sentences.

MODELS OF PARSING

As noted at the beginning of this discussion, it is unclear just what relationships exist among the component processes in comprehension; nevertheless, it has been possible to study the time courses of individual components. Evidence from a number of sources suggests that lexical decisions are made quickly as each new word is received. Syntactic decisions

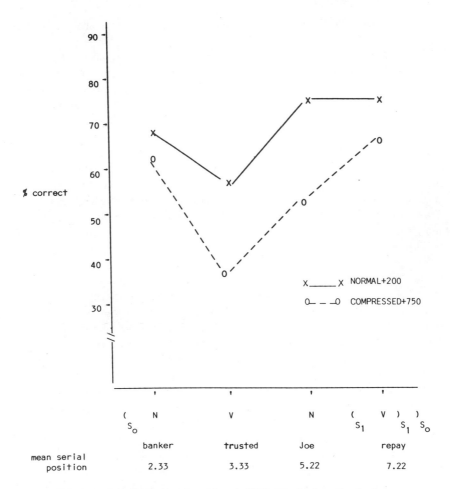

FIG. 3.5.   Recall of selected positions in VPC. Words along the abscissa are from the test sentence "The banker trusted Joe to repay the loan."

generally are not made in this fashion but instead often lag behind the input, as the parser builds up structure from accumulated items (i.e., performs bottom-up parsing). This pattern of syntactic processing differs markedly from that embodied in top-down serial parsing schemes (often represented by augmented transition networks; cf. Kaplan, 1972), where a single structural assignment must be made for each element as it is encountered in the input. At points of indeterminacy, the top-down serial parser chooses one of several possible "paths" to follow in making its subsequent structural assignments. For example, one path might represent a locative prepositional phrase; another, a direct object; still another, a complement clause. (Following a simple transitive verb, the complement clause path would not be available.)

When an error is made in path selection, a back-up procedure selects another path at the point of indeterminacy.

Consider how a top-down serial parsing model might account for the difference found for transitive sentences with simple and with complement verbs (TS and TC, respectively). The noun phrase following the simple verb in TS is parsed as a direct object because such an assignment is dictated by the only path open to an NP at that point. However, upon encountering the NP following the complement verb in TC, more than one path is available. Let us assume the complement path is taken by the parser, and the NP is assigned to be subject of the complement clause. When no verb is found in the remaining input, the parser must back-up and select the direct object path instead, an error correction that can be expected to consume both time and resources. Thus, the model accounts for generally poorer performance with TC sentences, as well as for the improvements produced by additional postsentence pause time (time in which the back-up and reparsing can occur).

The assumption that the complement path is selected first explains the results for transitive sentences, but it precludes a similar account for the complement sentences. If the complement path is taken with the noun phrase following the matrix verb in NPC-0 and VPC, then these sentences will require neither backup nor re-parsing and, therefore, should not differ from NPC-that, in which path selection has been correctly determined by the complementizer. In fact, in order to account for the difference among the complement sentences, we must assume that, in the absence of a complementizer, the complement path is *not* selected first. But this assumption is contrary to the one needed to explain the data for transitive sentences.

An alternative account might involve retaining the top-down parser but, rather than selecting one open path at a time, following instead all open paths simultaneously, i.e., in parallel. For example, as the noun phrase following the complement verb is picked up by the parser, it is parsed as direct object and as subject of the complement clause. If we assume an additional processing load is incurred by this parallel parsing, then the model can account for the difference between TS and TC. NPC-that sentences are less difficult than the other complement sentences because the complementizer enables the parser to select the complement path directly. Parallel parsing (and, therefore, increased processing load) should correspond to the indeterminate substrings of the sentences; this is consistent with the recall data given above.

What the top-down parallel model fails to explain is why the length of the postsentence pause affects performance. If parallel parsing follows the same time course as single-path parsing, this remains a mystery. However, the model can be saved with the added assumption that parallel parsing is not only more costly than single-path parsing but is also much slower. Results of the verb complexity experiment do not provide a basis for choosing between this modified top-down parallel parser and the bottom-up processor suggested by the structural determinacy hypothesis.

FUTURE RESEARCH: SOME SPECIFIC AND GENERAL APPLICATIONS

In the two compression studies, pause time was provided at the end of the test sentence. But what might we expect if, instead, the pause time were placed *inside* the compressed sentence? At some locations, where processing demand is low, the extra time ought to be of little value to the listener; at others, where processing load is high, it might well afford the listener an opportunity to "catch up." On the basis of the experiments, we can predict that pause time will be most effective (a) immediately after a lexically ambiguous word and (b) within the indeterminate substring following a complement verb. By examining the effects of additional time at various locations throughout a compressed sentence, it may be possible to map the entire course of its processing.

Finally, with regard to time-compressed speech as an experimental tool in psycholinguistic research, I should note that the same rate manipulation paradigm seems to have affected two components of sentence processing, the lexical and the syntactic. This suggests that time compression will be useful not only for exploring issues involving individual components, but also for addressing questions concerning the relationships between components (e.g., the interaction between syntactic and semantic processing).

ACKNOWLEDGMENTS

I am grateful to the following individuals for their helpful comments on earlier versions of this paper: John M. Carroll, William E. Cooper, John C. Thomas, and Edward Walker.

REFERENCES

Aaronson, D. Temporal course of perception in an immediate recall task. *Journal of Experimental Psychology,* 1968, *76,* 129–140.

Aaronson, D. Stimulus factors and listening strategies in auditory memory: A theoretical analysis. *Cognitive Psychology,* 1974, *6,* 108–132.

Aaronson, D., Markowitz, N., & Shapiro, H. Perception and immediate recall of normal and "compressed" auditory sequences. *Perception & Psychophysics,* 1971, *9,* 338–344.

Bever, T. G., & Hurtig, R. R. Detection of a nonlinguistic stimulus is poorest at the end of a clause. *Journal of Psycholinguistic Research,* 1975, *4,* 1–7.

Broadbent, D. E. *Perception and communication.* New York: Pergamon Press, 1958.

Cairns, H. S., & Foss, D. J. Falsification of the hypothesis that word frequency is a unified variable in sentence processing. *Journal of Verbal Learning and Verbal Behavior,* 1971, *10,* 41–43.

Cairns, H. S., & Kamerman, J. Lexical information processing during sentence comprehension. *Journal of Verbal Learning and Verbal Behavior,* 1975, *14,* 170–179.

Chomsky, N. *Aspects of the theory of syntax.* Cambridge: MIT Press, 1965.

Conrad, C. Context effects in sentence comprehension: A study of the subjective lexicon. *Memory & Cognition,* 1974, *2,* 130–138.

Fairbanks, G., Guttman, N., & Miron, M. S. Auditory comprehension in relation to listening rate and selective verbal redundancy. *Journal of Speech and Hearing Disorders,* 1957, *22,* 23–32.

Fodor, J. A., Bever, T. G., & Garrett, M. F. *The psychology of language.* New York: McGraw-Hill, 1974.

Fodor, J. A., Garrett, M. F., & Bever, T. G. Some syntactic determinants of sentential complexity. *Perception & Psychophysics,* 1968, *3,* 453–461.

Forster, K. I. Visual perception of rapidly presented word sequences of varying complexity. *Perception & Psychophysics,* 1970, *8,* 215–221.

Forster, K. I. *Separation of the effects of meaning on word recognition and sentence processing.* Paper presented at the first Experimental Psychology Conference, Monash University, 1974.

Forster, K. I., & Olbrei, I. Semantic heuristics and syntactic analysis. *Cognition,* 1973, *2,* 319–347.

Foss, D. J. Decision processes during sentence comprehension: Effects of lexical item difficulty and position upon decision times. *Journal of Verbal Learning and Verbal Behavior,* 1969, *8,* 457–462.

Foss, D. J., & Cairns, H. S. Some effects of memory limitation upon sentence comprehension and recall. *Journal of Verbal Learning and Verbal Behavior,* 1970, *9,* 541–547.

Foss, D. J., & Jenkins, C. Some effects of context on the comprehension of ambiguous sentences. *Journal of Verbal Learning and Verbal Behavior,* 1973, *12,* 577–589.

Foss, D. J., & Lynch, R. H., Jr. Decision processes during sentence comprehension: Effects of surface structure on decision times. *Perception & Psychophysics,* 1969, *5,* 145–148.

Foulke, E. The perception of time compressed speech. In D. L. Horton & J. Jenkins (Eds.), *Perception of language: Proceedings of a symposium of the learning research and development center,* University of Pittsburgh, 1969.

Hakes, D. T. Effects of reducing complement constructions on sentence comprehension. *Journal of Verbal Learning and Verbal Behavior,* 1972, *11,* 278–286.

Holmes, V. M., Arwas, R., & Garrett, M. F. Prior context and the perception of lexically ambiguous sentences. *Memory & Cognition,* 1977, *5,* 103–110.

Holmes, V. M., & Forster, K. I. Detection of extraneous signals during sentence recognition. *Perception & Psychophysics,* 1970, *7,* 297–301.

Holmes, V. M., & Forster, K. I. Perceptual complexity and underlying sentence structure. *Journal of Verbal Learning and Verbal Behavior,* 1972, *11,* 148–156.

Kaplan, R. M. Augmented transition networks as psychological models of sentence comprehension. *Artificial Intelligence,* 1972, *3,* 77–100.

Lackner, J. R., & Garrett, M. F. Resolving ambiguity: Effects of biasing context in the unattended ear. *Cognition,* 1972, *1,* 359–372.

Marslen-Wilson, W. Sentence processing as an interactive process. *Science,* 1975, *189,* 226–228.

Marslen-Wilson, W., & Tyler, L. K. Processing structure of sentence perception. *Nature (Lond.),* 1975, *257,* 522–523.

Mehler, J., & Carey, P. W. Role of surface and base structure in the perception of sentences. *Journal of Verbal Learning and Verbal Behavior,* 1967, *6,* 335–338.

Mehler, J., & Carey, P. The interaction of veracity and syntax in the processing of sentences. *Perception & Psychophysics,* 1968, *3,* 109–111.

Miller, G. A. The magical number seven plus or minus two, or, some limits on our capacity for processing information. *Psychological Review,* 1956, *63,* 81–96.

Norman, D. A., & Bobrow, D. G. On data-limited and resource-limited processes. *Cognitive Psychology,* 1975, *7,* 44–64.

Rubenstein, H., Garfield, L., & Millikan, M. A. Homographic entries in the internal lexicon. *Journal of Verbal Learning and Verbal Behavior,* 1970, *9,* 487–492.

Savin, H. B., & Perchonock, E. Grammatical structure and the immediate recall of English sentences. *Journal of Verbal Learning and Verbal Behavior,* 1965, *4,* 348–353.

Treisman, A. Verbal cues, language, and meaning in attention. *American Journal of Psychology,* 1964, *77,* 206–214.

4 Monitoring Sentence Comprehension

Anne Cutler
Dennis Norris
University of Sussex

INTRODUCTION

Psycholinguists have no way of directly observing the sentence-comprehension process. Therefore, they have on the one hand assessed the complexity of sentence processing by means of global measures of comprehension difficulty (paraphrasing, for instance, click location, sentence classification, or other tasks). On the other hand, they have devoted considerable ingenuity to inventing tasks that might be expected to reflect the operations of processing mechanisms during comprehension. The dependent variable in these latter tasks is reaction time (RT); as Pachella (1974) noted: "by default: there simply isn't much else that can be measured [p. 43]." If variations in response latency correlate with experimental manipulations of the sentences being understood, they are assumed to reflect variations in the complexity of processing.

Nearly all on-line studies of auditory comprehension have required subjects to monitor the sentence for a specified target. The targets are of three basic types: part of the sentence itself (a word or a sound), something *wrong* with the sentence (a mispronunciation), or an extraneous signal (e.g., a click) occurring during presentation of the sentence. By far the largest number of studies have involved monitoring for initial sounds of words. In this chapter we will discuss phoneme-monitoring in some detail, review word-monitoring, mispronunciation-monitoring, and tone/click-monitoring results, and conclude with a comparison and evaluation of the monitoring tasks.

MONITORING FOR PHONEMES

In a phoneme-monitoring experiment,[1] subjects listen for the occurrence of a word beginning with a specified sound in the sentence they are processing. Asked to listen for /b/ as in *boy* in the sentence "The punch barely affected the old man," for instance, they would be expected to press the response button as soon as they had become aware of the initial sound of the word *barely*. Comprehension is usually tested indirectly, by a short recognition test given at the end of the experiment. The technique was developed by Donald Foss.

Early Phoneme-Monitoring Work

Foss reported that RT was longer after the occurrence of a low-frequency as opposed to a high-frequency word (Foss, 1969), in structurally complex as opposed to structurally simple sentences (Foss & Lynch, 1969), and after a lexically ambiguous as opposed to an unambiguous word (Foss, 1970). Reaction time did not seem to be affected, however, by verb complexity, i.e. whether a verb can take sentence as well as noun phrase objects (Hakes, 1971).

Foss (1969) explained his results in terms of a limited-capacity central-processing mechanism, on which demands are made by all tasks a listener is concurrently performing. Thus, if comprehension is difficult, so that a relatively large amount of the finite processing capacity is taken up by some aspect or other of the comprehension process, such as syntactic analysis or lexical lookup, less capacity will be available for the performance of the phoneme-detection task; hence, this task will be performed relatively slowly. If comprehension is easy, more of the finite processing capacity is available for the detection task, which can then be performed relatively fast.

In the structural complexity experiment, for instance, Foss and Lynch (1969) assumed that the amount of processing necessary to assign the correct structural description to a sentence of relatively simple structure is less than that necessary to process a sentence of complex structure. They found that RT to the /b/ in the word *broke* was longer in the self-embedded sentence "The rioter who the whisky that the store sold intoxicated broke the window" than in the right-branching sentence "The store sold the whisky that intoxicated the rioter who broke the window." This result was confirmed for

---

[1]Strictly speaking, the term *phoneme-monitoring* may be a misnomer, because there is no indisputable evidence that subjects need to have identified the target at a level as abstract as the phonemic level in order to initiate a response. However, it is difficult to devise another name appropriate for a task in which subjects given the target specification /b/ as in *boy* can correctly detect the target in words as phonetically diverse as *big, badger,* or *blend.*

relative clauses by Hakes, Evans, and Brannon (1976). Other research (Hakes, 1972; Hakes & Cairns, 1970; Hakes & Foss, 1970) showed that if self-embedded or complement sentences contained relative pronouns (as in the example above), RT was faster than if they did not ("The rioter the whisky the store sold intoxicated broke the window"). Hakes and his colleagues concluded that the presence of relative pronouns facilitated the assignment of the appropriate structural description, thereby freeing more of the processing mechanism for performance of the monitoring task.

A similar interpretation was given for word frequency. Foss (1969) found that RT was lengthened when the word bearing the phoneme target was immediately preceded by a low-frequency word rather than a word of higher frequency (e.g., "itinerant bassoon player" vs. "travelling bassoon player"). Foss hypothesized that the accessing of a low-frequency word from the mental lexicon was an operation making greater demands on the finite processing capacity than the accessing of a more familiar word. Cairns and Foss (1971) subsequently presented evidence indicating that, under certain circumstances, sentential context can remove the frequency effect, although later work (reported in Foss, 1975) casts some doubt on these findings.

We discuss later the interpretation of these experiments. In the next section, however, we examine the fortunes of what was once held to be a basic fact: the effect of lexical ambiguity on phoneme-monitoring RT.

The Ambiguity Effect

Foss (1970) first reported that the presence of an ambiguous word immediately before the target-bearing item (as in the sentence "The punch barely affected the old man") led to longer RTs than those produced for the same sentence with the ambiguous word replaced by an unambiguous word ("The cocktail barely affected the old man"). Foss hypothesized that the entire set of readings of the ambiguous item is accessed from the mental lexicon, thus taking up more processing capacity. Further work (Cutler & Foss, 1974; Foss & Jenkins, 1973) showed that this effect did not disappear even if preceding sentential context was sufficient to determine which reading should be assigned to the ambiguous word, i.e., to disambiguate it (e.g., "The wine punch barely affected the old man"). Although common sense tells us that ambiguous lexical items are not recognized as ambiguous in context, phoneme-monitoring results appeared to show that contextual disambiguation does not remove the added complexity of processing resulting from the presence of an ambiguous word.

Cairns and Kamerman (1975) also found that lexical ambiguity produced an RT decrement that disappeared if the target-bearing word did not immediately follow the ambiguous word. Swinney and Hakes (1976) found that it was, after all, possible to construct contexts that would determine the choice between readings during rather than after lexical access; what was necessary was a context so strongly related to one reading of the ambiguous word that it virtually predicted it (e.g., *baseball* for *bat*).

These experiments have recently been called into question by the results of a study by Mehler, Segui, and Carey (1978), in which it was shown that longer words preceding the target-bearing word led to faster RTs than did shorter words. Mehler et al. explained this result as follows: long words generally require no more higher-level processing than do short words, but they take up more input time, thus delaying the arrival of the next item to be processed. At the end of a long word, therefore, processing has progressed further than at the end of a short word, so that more attentional capacity has been freed for phoneme detection.

In the five ambiguity experiments described above, the unambiguous control words were usually longer than the ambiguous words (e.g., *cocktail* as a control for *punch* in the example cited). Therefore, it is possible that all the supposed demonstrations of an ambiguity effect were in fact demonstrations of an effect of preceding word length. Indeed, Mehler et al. showed that ambiguous words paired with controls of the same length produced no RT decrement; ambiguous words that were longer than their control words actually produced faster RTs than did the controls.

Swinney (personal communication, 1976) has since claimed that those ambiguous words in the materials of Swinney and Hakes (1976) that are equal in length to their controls nevertheless exhibit the ambiguity effect; the same is said to be true of the materials used by Cairns and Kamerman (Cairns & Hsu, 1977). However, no new demonstration of an ambiguity effect with length controlled has yet been reported. A pilot study in our own laboratory, using ambiguous words very carefully matched for length and frequency with their controls, failed to show a significant difference due to ambiguity. It seems doubtful whether there ever was an ambiguity effect on phoneme-monitoring latencies.

Swinney (1976) has recently presented other evidence that, he claims indicates that the entire set of readings of an ambiguous word is accessed from the mental lexicon regardless of contextual disambiguation. Swinney required subjects to make a word–nonword judgment about a visually presented word while simultaneously listening to a sentence. When the sentence contained an ambiguous word (e.g., *bug*) that occurred immediately before the visual stimulus appeared, RT was faster to words connected with *both* readings of the ambiguity (*ant, spy*) than to control words, whereas when the sentence contained an unambiguous control word (e.g., *insect*), only the word related to that meaning was facilitated in comparison with the control. Furthermore, in the ambiguity case both related words were facilitated even with disambiguating prior sentence context.

This result may only indicate, however, an associative effect of accessing one lexical entry upon other entries: Occurrence of the word *bug* automatically primes the lexical entries of words associated with it, including both *ant* and *spy*, and this priming is reflected in faster word–nonword decision times. It does not necessarily show that both these interpretations of *bug* are read out of the lexical entry in the ordinary course of sentence comprehension.

Investigators have also claimed (Holmes, Arwas, & Garrett, 1977; Mistler-Lachman, 1975) that the time subjects take to classify a sentence as meaningful is increased by the presence of a lexical ambiguity. If this finding proves statistically reliable, it provides an interesting counterpoint to the failure to detect an increase in processing complexity due to lexical access of ambiguous words. It would indicate that the fact that a word has more than one lexical reading does not increase the time needed for lexical access, but may increase the time needed to comprehend the sentence. Whatever extra analysis is required to determine the appropriate reading of a sentence containing an ambiguous word need not have any local effect measurable with existing on-line techniques.

Characteristics of the Target-Bearing Word

Reaction time to targets on stressed syllables is faster than RT to targets on unstressed syllables (Shields, McHugh, & Martin, 1974). Stress on words also leads to faster RTs, and both open-class words (e.g., nouns and verbs) and closed-class words (e.g., conjunctions and prepositions) are similarly affected by stress (Cutler & Foss, 1977).

The acoustic correlates of stress are responsible for part of this effect, but not all of it, as is demonstrated by an experiment (Cutler, 1976) in which the target item in two conditions to be compared was acoustically identical and occurred in an invariant syntactic context in each condition; but the intonation contour imposed on the sequence preceding the target item was such that in one condition a high level of stress would be expected to occur at target position, whereas in the other condition the target would be expected to be relatively unstressed. Although the item was acoustically identical, RT in the first condition (high stress expected) was faster. This result indicates that the intonation contour of a sentence can direct attention during comprehension to the points at which high stress will fall. The value of this operation to the process of comprehension seems to be that the semantically most central (i.e. the focused) portions of the sentence are thereby located; in a further experiment, Cutler and Fodor (1979) showed that varying the focus of a sentence by means of preposed questions also resulted in focused targets consistently producing faster RTs than did nonfocused targets, despite the fact that the sentence containing the target remained acoustically constant, with only the preceding question being changed.

The nature of phoneme-monitoring targets was examined in detail in a series of experiments in which the materials were not sentences but lists of various kinds. Initially, the topic at issue seemed to be the "units of perception." Savin and Bever (1970) discovered that monitoring for an initial phoneme in a list of nonsense monosyllables produced RTs that were *longer* than those produced for the same list when the specified target was an entire syllable. On the basis of this result, they challenged Foss's (1969) explanation of phoneme-monitoring results in terms of a limited-capacity central-analyzing mechanism. Instead, they claimed, phoneme identification could only be performed after syllable identification, syllables being the primary units of perception. The slowing of phoneme-identification latencies around syntactically or lexically difficult portions of a sentence must be due to an increase in the time needed to perform operations that *necessarily precede* phoneme identification rather than an increase in the processing capacity required by *concurrent* operations.[2]

A reply to Savin and Bever's (1970) article was offered by Foss and Swinney (1973), who reported an experiment in which not only was syllable-monitoring RT faster than was phoneme-monitoring RT, but monitoring for words in a list of words produced even faster RTs than did monitoring for syllables in a list of syllables. Furthermore, Foss and Swinney drew attention to an experiment by Bever, Savin, and Hurtig (cited in Bever, 1970), in which they found that monitoring in a list of short sentences was performed faster if subjects knew the entire target sentence than if they knew just the initial word. By analogy to the Savin and Bever argument, then, the primary "unit of perception" should be the clause. Foss and Swinney proposed, however, a way out of this awkward situation: If a distinction were to be drawn between the perception of a linguistic unit and its identification, one could still hold that lower level units were perceived, as common sense would tell us, prior to higher level units, whereas the order in which units of the signal could be identified (i.e., brought to awareness) and, hence, responded to in a monitoring task, could be, up to a point, reversed; higher level units might be sooner accessed to consciousness.

A simpler explanation of these results, however, was offered by McNeill and Lindig (1973), who pointed out that in Savin and Bever's (1970) and Foss and Swinney's (1973) work, the fastest RTs had always been collected when

---

[2]Savin and Bever (1970) did not dispute the sensitivity of the phoneme-monitoring task to variables affecting comprehension difficulty, i.e., the usefulness of the task as a measure of comprehension difficulty, but merely Foss's (1969) explanation of this sensitivity. Moreover, their explanation of the effects of syntactic and lexical variables on monitoring RT was neither necessitated by their findings nor inapplicable to previous phoneme-monitoring findings.

the level of the target (phoneme, syllable, word) matched the level of the list in which the search was undertaken. McNeill and Lindig found that either upward (e.g., looking for a phoneme in a list of words) or downward (e.g., searching for a word in a list of syllables) mismatches produced longer latencies, and explained their result in terms of focus of attention: If the list contains syllables then the subject's attention will be focused at the syllabic level, and a syllable target will be easiest to respond to, and so on. In normal language use, they proposed, the focus of attention would be on the meaning of an utterance. Thus, the experiments on lists of items, which allow the focus of attention to be altered at will, tell us nothing about the "units of perception" in normal comprehension.

In a later experiment, Healy and Cutting (1976) found that a match between target and response item also facilitated RT when the search list was not homogeneous but was composed of some items that matched the level of the target and some which did not. This, result, therefore, cast doubt on McNeill and Lindig's (1973) focus explanation; Healy and Cutting preferred to conclude that simple physical identity of target and response item facilitated response latency, a known effect in visual tasks (cf. Posner & Mitchell, 1967). They also discovered that intrinsic ease of recognition of phonemes can determine whether phonemes or syllables are recognized faster when the matching variable is controlled; phonemes that produce faster naming latencies are recognized faster than are syllables, but syllables can generally be identified faster than can phonemes that produce slow naming latencies. This result would imply that phoneme identification is accomplished at a fairly low level of analysis.

Other findings from phoneme-monitoring in lists of items concern the linguistic naturalness of the material. Rubin, Turvey, and van Gelder (1976) found that RT to phoneme targets on words was faster than was RT to targets on nonwords. Cutler and Cooper (1978) reported that RT to targets embedded in lists that conformed to certain syllable-structure constraints of English was faster than was RT to targets in lists that defied these constraints.

None of the findings in this series of experiments reflected upon the usefulness of phoneme-monitoring as a measure of comprehension difficulty. In the typical phoneme-monitoring experiment, RT is compared to the *same* target under different conditions, preceded by different words, for instance, or different intonation contours. Thus, the relative difficulty of the particular target is controlled. Nevertheless, these studies concerned the level at which a phoneme can be identified, and recent work has indicated that the conclusions drawn from monitoring in lists may also hold for monitoring in sentences. Healy and Cutting's (1976) description of phoneme identification as a low-level prelexical process, in other words, may also be correct for sentence comprehension. The next section addresses this question in detail.

Phoneme-Monitoring and Lexical Access

Foss, Harwood, and Blank (Foss, personal communication, 1977) have recently demonstrated that although RT to a phoneme target is sensitive to the frequency of the immediately preceding word in the sentence, it is *not* sensitive to the frequency of the word bearing the target. Moreover, Foss and Blank (Blank, personal communication) have found that although RT to targets *following* nonwords is slower than is RT to targets following real words, there is no RT difference between targets beginning words and beginning nonwords.

On the basis of these results, Foss and his colleagues claim that phoneme targets can be detected before the word they are part of is looked up in the mental lexicon. Once the *preceding* word has been identified, only a low-level phonological analysis of the target-bearing word is necessary: If the target phoneme is in the first position in the string, it is in the required word-initial position and a response can be made. Phoneme monitoring responses, in other words, precede lexical access.

This claim is in conflict with other results. First, there is the experiment by Rubin, Turvey, and van Gelder (1976) referred to previously; in that experiment RT to targets *on words* was faster than was RT to targets on nonwords. On the surface, the only difference between Foss's word–nonword experiment (Blank, personal communication) and that of Rubin et al. was that in the former the materials were sentences; in the latter, lists: both lists of either words or nonwords alone and mixed lists consisting of both monosyllabic words and nonsense syllables.

Second, Morton and Long (1976) found that high contextual probability of the word bearing the target led to faster RTs than did low probability. They interpreted this result as a reflection of more rapid lexical access of more probable words. The phoneme-monitoring response was made, according to Morton and Long's account, *after* lexical access.

Current research on the relation of phoneme detection to lexical access seems, therefore, to be in disarray. On the one hand, Foss's results (Foss & Blank, personal communications) indicate that the detection response can be initiated before lexical access; on the other hand, Morton and Long's (1976) and Rubin et al.'s (1976) results indicate that the detection response is made after lexical access.

An initially appealing resolution of this contradiction invokes the precise task specifications. Because subjects in a phoneme-monitoring experiment are performing two concurrent tasks, detection and comprehension, some scope exists for altering the relative task payoffs. In the typical phoneme-monitoring experiment, subjects are aware that their comprehension—strictly speaking, their recall of the sentences—will be tested, but not until the end of the experiment. Meanwhile, the detection task must be performed on each new sentence, and a reminder of it is given in the form of the target specification preceding each sentence. Perhaps relatively more attention might be devoted to the detection than to the comprehension task, and the priority assigned to phoneme detection might encourage initiation of the response at the earliest possible moment. If the instructions emphasized the comprehension rather than the detection task, however, phoneme identification might be performed after lexical access simply because it had been assigned less attention than had the components of comprehension. In fact, Morton and Long (1976) required their subjects to recall each sentence verbatim immediately following its presentation.

This suggestion does not, however, provide a sufficient explanation of the contradictory results; high transitional probability of the target-bearing word leads to faster RTs even when comprehension is only tested afterwards by the usual brief recognition test (Foss, personal communication).

The apparent contradiction can be resolved, however, if one rejects the assumption that detection of the phoneme target must necessarily either precede or follow lexical access of the target-bearing word. Suppose, instead, that after an initial phonological analysis the two processes, looking up the phonologically analyzed string in the mental lexicon and determining whether the initial component of the string is the specified target, go on in parallel, and, other things being equal, the target identification process will be completed first. In this case, RT to the target will show no effect of lexical characteristics of the target-bearing word.

If lexical access is speeded up, however, it may be completed before the target-detection process has finished. In this case, the identification of the word may facilitate the monitoring process. There are two ways in which this may happen: on the one hand, it may be possible to respond on the basis of the phonological information in the lexical entry *instead of* awaiting completion of the target-detection process. On the other hand, lexical information may interact with the target-detection process to facilitate phoneme identification. Note that the effect of speeded lexical access can only be facilitative: Slower lexical access will simply not affect the target-identification process.

One factor that may speed up lexical access is preceding context that is highly predictive of a particular word. Another is intonation or context indicating that focal stress will fall on a certain word. Phoneme-monitoring RTs are sensitive to transitional probability of the target-bearing word (Morton & Long, 1976), to the prior occurrence of a related word (Rubin, 1975), and to cues to focus on the target-bearing word (Cutler, 1976; Cutler & Fodor, 1979).

Characteristics of the lexical entry of the target-bearing word will be unlikely to affect RT. Factors internal to the lexical entry of the *preceding* word, however (e.g., word frequency or simply whether the word is real) can affect RT.[3] In contrast to the effect of context, these effects can also be inhibitory. Words of low frequency and nonwords take longer to identify because the process of looking for them in the lexicon takes longer. To detect a *word-initial* target, it is necessary to have processed the preceding word; hence, slower target detection will be the result of slower lexical access of the previous word.

Of course, contextual effects that speed up lexical access should therefore facilitate RT to a target on the following word. They do, as was shown in an experiment by Blank and Foss (1977).

The effect of word length is interesting. As Mehler et al. (1978) showed, longer words are associated with faster detection of targets on the following word. The target-bearing word itself, however, should be associated with faster RTs when it is short.[4] This is because very short words may be retrieved quite quickly from the mental lexicon; the opportunity exists for lexical access to facilitate target detection. Long words, however, are often to a certain extent redundant and do not pose a proportionately greater identification problem than do short words. But because of the extra duration of a long word—at least the duration of one syllable, which in English averages 180 msec (Huggins, 1964)—more time is available for processing it. Thus, by the time the target on the following word arrives, processing has progressed further for a long word than for a short word. This reduction in processing *load* may itself lead to faster monitoring latencies, as Mehler et al. claim. However, it may also be the case that the result is due simply to the time at which the end of the word is identified. Because subjects are listening for word-initial targets only, a target cannot be detected until the end of the previous word has been identified. The end of a longer, more redundant, word may be identified as it occurs, whereas the decision that a short word has

---

[3]Lexical ambiguity does not appear to affect phoneme-monitoring RTs, as we have shown. However, the internal complexity of lexical entries may vary in other ways than in number of readings for the word. Kintsch (1974) reported finding no effect of derivational complexity on phoneme-monitoring RTs; but the materials he used differed in many ways other than in derivational complexity of the word preceding the target; in particular, the critical variables of word length and sentence length were quite uncontrolled.

[4]It might be expected that studies using predominantly monosyllabic target-bearing words would be more likely to find effects of characteristics of the target-bearing word itself, whereas studies in which the target-bearing words were predominantly polysyllabic would be more likely to find effects of the preceding word only. This is in fact the case. In Morton and Long's (1976) study, in which contextual plausibility of the target-bearing word led to faster RTs, approximately three-quarters of the target words were monosyllabic, one quarter polysyllabic. Studies from Foss's laboratory have, on the other hand, characteristically used more polysyllabic than monosyllabic target words. In the unpublished study by Blank and Foss (1977) referred to previously, in which word–nonword status was found to affect RT to targets on the following word but not to targets on the critically varied word, three-quarters of the target words were polysyllabic, one quarter monosyllabic.

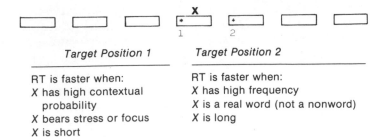

Target Position 1	Target Position 2
RT is faster when:	RT is faster when:
X has high contextual probability	X has high frequency
X bears stress or focus	X is a real word (not a nonword)
X is short	X is long

FIG. 4.1. A schematic representation of a sentence. X marks the word position in which the independent variable is manipulated; possible phoneme-monitoring positions with respect to X are represented by asterisks.

ended may not be arrived at until *after* it has ended, i.e., after the target has occurred; thus, the monitoring response would be delayed.

Figure 4.1 summarizes the effects that are crucial to our argument. We have claimed that there is a target detection process that neither precedes nor follows lexical access of the target-bearing word, but runs parallel to it. Target detection cannot be accomplished until the preceding word has been identified; therefore, the target-detection process is sensitive to lexical characteristics of the preceding word. Longer words allow more time for processing before arrival of the target; therefore, greater length of the preceding word results in faster target detection.

In unusual circumstances, lexical access of the target-bearing word can be speeded up to such an extent that target detection is facilitated by completed lexical access. Factors internal to the lexical entry of the target-bearing word do not have this effect, but contextual ("top-down") factors do: Cues to focus direct more attention to the focused word's lexical access; context that makes a particular word highly predictable has the effect of priming the lexical entry.[5] Also, very short words can be accessed more quickly.

Two concluding points remain to be made. First, our explanation of the effect on target-detection time of lexical characteristics of the preceding word assumes that target identification cannot succeed until the preceding word has been processed. This may only be true when subjects are monitoring for *word-initial* targets, as is usually the case in phoneme-monitoring experiments. Indeed, we would predict that subjects who were listening for *any* occurrence of the target sound would respond faster to the same word-initial targets than would subjects who were listening for initial sounds only.

Second, all that we have said in the foregoing discussion applies to sentences, but we would expect the same effects to show up in monitoring

---

[5]Very effective priming of the lexical entry is achieved by giving the word itself as target. This is one reason why word-monitoring times are faster than phoneme-monitoring times.

performed on lists of items,[6] with the obvious exception that context effects do not exist in lists. Rubin, Turvey, and van Gelder's (1976) finding that targets on words are detected faster than are targets on nonwords in mixed word–nonword lists seems to be a contradiction to this claim, because in sentences there is *no* RT difference between targets on words and nonwords. Closer inspection reveals, however, that this is not a counterexample at all. On the one hand, the stimuli in this experiment were all consonant-verb-consonant (CVC) syllables; we would expect such short words to be accessed extremely quickly and completed lexical access of the *words* to facilitate target detection. On the other hand, the monitoring task was disjunctive: The subjects were looking for one of two targets. Phoneme-monitoring RTs are slower if more than one target is being listened for both in lists (Foss & Dowell, 1971; Steinheiser & Burrows, 1973) and in sentences (Treisman & Squire, 1974). Therefore, if the target-identification process is slowed down by the added target, it is more likely that the lexical-access process will be completed first.

MONITORING FOR WORDS

Word targets can be detected faster than can lower level targets in lists of words (Foss & Swinney, 1973). This result was explained by McNeill and Lindig (1973) and Healy and Cutting (1976) as due to congruence of the target with the response item. Their explanation would hold as well for sentences as for lists of unrelated words, so that it comes as no surprise to find that detection of word targets is faster than is detection of phoneme targets in sentences also (Treisman & Squire, 1974).

Different types of word monitoring have been compared by Marslen-Wilson and Tyler (1975). In a normal sentence no difference was found between time to detect a word that rhymed with the specified target and time to detect a word belonging to the semantic category specified by the target. In anomalous or ungrammatical sentences, however, category monitoring produced longer RTs than did rhyme monitoring. Marslen-Wilson and Tyler claimed that this result indicated that during processing of a normal sentence construction of the semantic representation interacts with construction of representations at other levels in such a manner that the results of all levels of analysis are available in parallel. This interpretation, however, assumes that the results of different levels of analysis (phonological, lexical, semantic) are

---

[6]No direct investigation has been carried out of the effect of word frequency in lists. However, there is some evidence that frequency of the target-bearing word, which Foss, Harwood, and Blank (personal communication, 1977) found did not affect RT in sentences, also does not affect RT in lists. Results of a study in which the materials were lists of unrelated words showed no correlation between speed of response and frequency of the target-bearing word ($r_s = -.06$).

equally available as the basis for the monitoring response. But as we comprehend a sentence, we are not generally aware of the result of phonological analysis. Extra processing may well be needed before the output of such analysis can become accessible to the decision mechanism that makes the monitoring response. Therefore, a lack of RT difference between rhyme- and category-monitoring in normal prose may not directly reflect the temporal relation between processing stages. Normal processing may still proceeed serially, with phonological analysis being completed before higher level analysis.

More recently, Marslen-Wilson, Tyler, and Seidenberg (1978) have again used rhyme- and category-monitoring tasks to investigate the interaction of semantic and syntactic processes in comprehension. The targets in this experiment occurred either immediately before or immediately after clause boundaries. Response latencies were not determined solely by the position of the target relative to the syntactic boundary, however—as would be expected on a purely syntactic account of clausal structuring—but were also influenced by the "completeness' of the semantic representation of the clause; when semantic completeness was high, RTs were significantly faster before the boundary than after, but when the clause was less semantically complete, there was no significant difference between before-boundary and after-boundary monitoring times. Marslen-Wilson et al. interpreted this finding as further evidence that comprehension is an interactive process, in which the listener constructs a representation of the sentence word-by-word, drawing on both syntactic and semantic information in the input.

MONITORING FOR MISPRONUNCIATIONS

The technique of measuring latency to detect deliberate mispronunciations in a sentence was devised by Cole (1973), who found that changes in the later part of words produced faster detection latencies than did changes in initial sounds and that the more distinctive features had been altered the faster the alteration was detected; thus, a mispronunciation of /p/ as /b/, for example (a change involving only the feature voicing) produced longer detection times than did a mispronunciation of /p/ as /z/, a four-feature change. (Cole also reported that the fewer the features altered, the less likely the mispronunciation was to be detected at all, a finding corroborated by Marslen-Wilson and Welsh [1978]).

Recently, however, Cole has measured RT to detect mispronunciations during sentence comprehension and has found that large RT variations can be produced by manipulations of contextual factors. For instance, mispronunciation of the initial segment of the second syllable of *cargo* or *address* is detected faster if the preceding context determines that those two syllables comprise one word rather than two (*car go; a dress*). Similarly, if the mispronounced word has a high probability of occurrence in the context, is implied by the preceding context, or is closely connected with the main theme of the material being processed, reaction is speeded. (These experiments are summarized in Cole and Jakimik [in press]).

Monitoring for mispronunciations is, therefore, obviously a measure that is sensitive to many factors affecting sentence comprehension. Results from mispronunciation-monitoring experiments, however, although interesting in themselves, are not directly comparable with results from experiments in which the monitor target was part of an undegraded input signal. Cole and his coworkers are fairly scrupulous in constructing sentences that allow subjects only one option for an appropriate alternative to a nonsensical item, and their results indicate that subjects are locating this alternative, that is, not simply reacting with a positive detection response on encountering a nonword (a conceivable strategy in a mispronunciation-monitoring task), but are reacting to identification of the word *appropriate* for the sentence context, the word that has been mispronounced. Latency to detect a mispronunciation reflects, therefore, not simply word recognition but word *reconstruction*. Thus, it would necessarily be a more indirect measure of, for example, lexical access than is phoneme monitoring. For this reason, investigation of, for instance, the nature of lexical entries is less well served by the mispronunciation-monitoring task than by other monitoring techniques. Mispronunciation monitoring, on the other hand, lends itself well to the study of exactly *how* words can be reconstructed, i.e., the manner in which a "context" is created.

MONITORING FOR EXTRANEOUS SIGNALS

Lights, clicks, and tones have been employed as sentence-extraneous monitor targets. Monitoring for a visual signal, a flash of light, appears not to be sensitive to factors affecting complexity of sentence processing (Foss, personal communication). This may indicate that variations in comprehension difficulty are best reflected by tasks that involve the mechanisms engaged by the comprehension process; if the target is nonlinguistic, therefore, it should, in the case of auditory sentence comprehension, be auditory. Interestingly, Geers (1978) has shown that performance of deaf subjects on a flash-location task while lip-reading (i.e., while processing in the visual modality) is remarkably similar to the performance of hearing subjects on click-location during auditory comprehension.

Abrams and Bever (1969) and Holmes and Forster (1970) measured RT to detect the occurrence of a click as a function of processing load at various points in the syntactic structure of a sentence. Abrams and Bever found end-of-clause RT to be slower than beginning-of-clause RT, from which they concluded that processing load at the end of a clause was comparatively heavy. Both Abrams and Bever and Holmes and Forster found that RT declined across the sentence; however, Holmes and Forster reported RTs to clicks located in a major syntactic boundary to be faster than RTs to clicks not in a boundary, whereas Abrams and Bever found that this effect was obscured by the overall sentence-position effect.

Reaction time to a short tone was measured by Green (1977), who found that the task specifications strongly affected it: Those subjects who were required merely to memorize and repeat a sentence responded to the signal faster than did subjects who were required to provide an appropriate continuation for the same sentence.

Monitoring for a sentence-extraneous auditory signal possesses at least one technical advantage in comparison with monitoring for a target that forms part of the sentence being processed: Fewer constraints are imposed on the construction of experimental sentences. Materials for phoneme-monitoring studies, for example, have become increasingly more difficult to construct. Early studies used a variety of different initial sounds: obstruents, resonants, and vowels (see, e.g., Hakes, 1972). Researchers later noted, however, that RT varied as a function of the particular phoneme target, with stops, for example, producing generally faster RTs than did fricatives (Foss & Swinney, 1973; Morton & Long, 1976; Rubin et al., 1976; Savin & Bever, 1970). This result is probably due to the custom of aligning the signal that starts the timer in phoneme-monitoring experiments with the onset of the target phoneme, in conjunction with the longer intrinsic duration of fricatives in comparison with stops. Nonetheless, Rubin et al. (1976) found that their word–nonword difference held for the target /b/ but not for the target /s/. Most recent phoneme-monitoring research has used only stop consonants, which, although dependent upon the surrounding context for their unambiguous identification (Liberman, Cooper, Shankweiler, & Studdert-Kennedy, 1967), do not appear to introduce variation as a result of differing among themselves: A separate analysis of the results presented by Cutler (1976) revealed no effects due to differences between the three phoneme targets /b/, /d/, and /k/. Also, Martin (1977) reported that the six stop consonants do not appear to differ in detectability. No research has been carried out on whether RTs are affected by the number of different targets used in an experiment (a unique target is always specified in phoneme monitoring for each sentence); current practice usually involves three or four stop-consonant targets. Even given all six stop consonants as potential targets, however, the construction of phoneme-monitoring materials can be a formidable task, as any phoneme-monitoring researcher will testify. For instance, in an experiment in which the target is the initial phoneme of the critically varied word (e.g., Morton & Long, 1976) pairs of words must be selected that vary on the critical dimension under study but are both matched on such variables as length and word frequency *and* each begin with a stop consonant. Word-monitoring tasks, in which such factors as memorability of the target item might well play a role, can involve similar difficulties.

However, it appears that monitoring for sentence-extraneous signals does not reflect, or does not reflect in the same manner, the variables that affect monitoring for targets within the sentence. Three striking inconsistencies can be observed among results from the very few studies available using nonlinguistic auditory signals and results from phoneme-monitoring studies. The first difference concerns word frequency. Whereas the effect of increasing word frequency is to speed phoneme-monitoring RTs (Foss, 1969), Green (1977) reported that when subjects were required to provide a continuation for the experimental sentence, sentences containing noun phrases constructed of high-frequency words were associated with slower RTs to end-of-the-sentence tones than were sentences with low-frequency noun phrases. This difference was only evident when subjects were required to produce continuations from the experimental sentences. When the subjects' task was simply to memorize the experimental sentence for immediate recall, there was no significant effect of noun-phrase frequency. As Green pointed out, latencies in the continuation condition of his experiment may have reflected response variables (construction of the continuation) as well as processing variables, so that the increased RT in this instance could well be explained as a function of the difficulty of choosing between the larger number of possible continuations appropriate for a sentence containing high- as opposed to low-frequency words. Support for this conjecture is provided by MacKay's (1970) finding that sentence-completion times for sentence fragments containing lexical ambiguities are longer than are completion times for unambiguous fragments; there are presumably more possible continuations for ambiguous than for unambiguous fragments. Nevertheless, Green's failure to find any significant effect of word frequency in the noncontinuation condition of his experiment is clearly inconsistent with the phoneme-monitoring results.

The second inconsistency between monitoring for sentence-internal and for sentence-external targets concerns position in the sentence. Reaction time in phoneme-monitoring studies generally decreases across the sentence or clause (Cutler & Foss, 1977; Foss, 1969; Shields, McHugh & Martin, 1974), the only reported exception being the complex self-embedded sentences used by Foss and Lynch (1969). Word-monitoring RT also decreases across the clause (Marslen-Wilson et al., 1978). Reaction time to clicks, however, does not show such a consistent pattern. Holmes and Forster (1970) found that click-detection time decreased across the sentence and, to a small extent, across the clause. Abrams and Bever (1969) also found an RT decrease across the sentence. Analyzed with respect to clause boundaries, however, their results show that RTs at the end of the first clause are slower than are RTs at the beginning of the second clause. Finally, Bond (1972) found that RT to clicks became increasingly slower as the click occurred further into the phonological phrase ("any sequence that was demarcated by a clear intonation contour [p. 137]"), a finding in direct conflict with the phoneme-monitoring results.

The third inconsistency involves stress and again arises from the Bond study (1972). Whereas phoneme-monitoring RT is faster on stressed than on unstressed syllables (Cutler, 1976; Cutler & Foss, 1977; Shields et al., 1974), the reverse is true for click monitoring: Bond found that clicks in stressed syllables are detected slower than are clicks in unstressed syllables.

The lesson from these results appears to be that sentence processing affects RT to sentence-internal and sentence-external targets in different ways. With respect to stress, it appears plausible that this should be so. The faster phoneme-monitoring RT to targets on stressed words appears to reflect the direction of attention towards such items in order that the semantically more central items in the sentence might be identified (Cutler & Fodor, 1979). If attention is focused on the stressed word in this manner, then it could be considered to be as a consequence diverted from sentence-extraneous occurrences such as a click. Or, at a simpler level, the difference may simply result from competition between the input signals: The stressed syllables, being louder, mask the click more than do the unstressed syllables. Both these arguments can also be extended to the clause-position problem, because the highest stress in a clause tends to fall, ceteris paribus, at the end.

The failure of tone-monitoring RT to exhibit an effect of word frequency, however, indicates that lexical access processes may not affect RT to nonlinguistic signals either directly or indirectly. In any event, it seems that reaction to extraneous signals is a less direct measure of sentence comprehension than is reaction to sentence-internal targets. Before monitoring for nonlinguistic targets can be considered a useful measure, more information is required about exactly what processing operations it reflects and in what manner it reflects them. Comparative studies in which monitoring latencies for sentence-internal and sentence-external targets were collected and compared for the same materials would be particularly valuable.

CONCLUSION

Although not the only on-line measures of sentence comprehension,[7] monitoring tasks are certainly the most widely used. They are similar to each

---

[7]Other on-line tasks include word-by-word reading (Aaronson & Scarborough, 1976), shadowing latency (Marslen-Wilson & Welsh, 1978), lexical decision during comprehension (Swinney, 1976), naming latency during comprehension (Tyler & Marslen-Wilson, 1977). Postcomprehension RT measures, such as sentence-reading time (Garrod & Sanford, 1977; Haviland & Clark, 1974) sentence-classification time (e.g., Moore, 1972), or RT to a probe of various kinds (e.g., Green, 1975; Suci, Ammon, & Gamlin, 1967; Walker, 1976), which give a global index of the time required for completion of a large number of processes, necessarily obscure the individual contribution of each particular process. Therefore, they are of little value in investigating such topics as the role of lexical access in comprehension; but they can often provide a useful check on the persistence of observed on-line effects.

other in many important ways. First, they are all, technically speaking, divided attention tasks, because subjects are required to monitor for the target while at the same time comprehending the sentence. Thus, it is possible that one or both tasks could be performed less well under these conditions than in isolation. Indeed, it is likely that the target detection task is interfered with by concurrent sentence comprehension (Ball, Wood, & Smith, 1975; Martin, 1977). The subject of interest in monitoring experiments, however, is not the RT task per se, but how it can illuminate the sentence-comprehension process. Accordingly, a constant performance decrement due to concurrent comprehension should not confound the results. (The number of errors—missed targets—in phoneme-monitoring experiments is usually below 10%, few enough to leave adequate data if sufficient subjects and items are tested). The comprehension process itself seems unlikely to be adversely affected by the detection task;[8] overlearned tasks are generally resistant to interference from concurrent tasks (Moray, 1969), and sentence comprehension is about as overlearned a task as any that one could ask a subject to perform.

Second, all monitoring tasks are RT measures. Thus, they require a certain investment in equipment; they force the experimenter to consider such problems as the tradeoff between speed and accuracy of response; and the variability of baseline RT across subjects makes it very difficult to measure between-subjects variables. (For further discussion of these issues see Pachella [1974]).

In this paper, however, we have concentrated on the differences between the various forms of monitoring. We have suggested that the phoneme-monitoring task, for instance, is sensitive to contextual factors and to lexical factors, but in different ways. We have posited a target-identification process that goes on in parallel with the lexical-access process and that, other things being equal, will be finished before lexical access is completed. Top-down processing of predictive context or intonation can have the effect of speeding up lexical access so that it is completed before the target has been identified; this facilitates RT. Thus, the phoneme-monitoring task can be used as a measure of, for example, contextual predictability of the target-bearing word.

Factors internal to a word's lexical entry, however, affect RT to targets on the following word only; when lexical access is slowed down, the detection of a target on the next word is slowed down because a target in the specified word-initial position cannot be identified until the preceding word has been satisfactorily recognized. Thus, phoneme monitoring can also be used as a measure of lexical factors; in this case, manipulations of the independent variable would be effected in the word that preceded the target-bearing word. Of course, all the other factors that affect RT to phoneme targets must be

---

[8]However, Hakes and Foss (1970) found that paraphrasing was significantly less accurate when the monitor target occurred later in the sentence rather than earlier.

rigorously controlled, including word length. Phoneme-monitoring materials are not easy to construct. Nonetheless, there is probably considerable scope for future investigation of the internal characteristics of the mental lexicon using this task.

There is not, so far, sufficient evidence on which to base such detailed conclusions about the other monitoring tasks. We have suggested, however, that mispronunciation monitoring, because it requires subjects to reconstruct the mispronounced words, is suitable for the investigation of how effectively different types of context enable word reconstruction. Word monitoring of different kinds requires subjects to monitor for the target at different levels (e.g., the phonological level of a rhyme or the semantic level of category membership [Marslen-Wilson et al., 1978]) and is therefore suitable for investigating the speed with which decisions at various levels can be made. Monitoring for extraneous signals may, as we have pointed out, be sensitive to overall processing load due to comprehension at the time at which the target occurs; but because confounding acoustic factors have not been controlled in the very few relevant experiments, this is as yet far from certain.

Foss (1969) originally claimed that phoneme-monitoring RTs reflected total load on a limited-capacity processing mechanism shared by any and all tasks a listener might be performing. This conception has not proved correct. In fact, it may be the case that no monitoring task gives a global measure of total processing load at a particular point in sentence comprehension. However, what we have may be preferable: different tasks that measure different specific aspects of the comprehension process.

ACKNOWLEDGMENTS

During preparation of this paper, the first author was supported by a grant from the Science Research Council. Parts of the section on phoneme monitoring were reported by the first author at the International Congress of Psychology, Paris, July 1976, and by both authors at the fourth Salzburg International Linguistics Meeting, Salzburg, August 1977. We are grateful to Don Foss, Steve Riederer, and Ginny Valian for advice and discussion at earlier stages, and to Tony Ades and Phil Johnson-Laird for helpful criticism of the present paper. We also thank the many authors who provided us with papers and results that were unpublished at the time this paper was written (January 1978).

REFERENCES

Aaronson, D., & Scarborough, H. S. Performance theories for sentence coding: Some quantitative evidence. *Journal of Experimental Psychology: Human Perception and Performance,* 1976, *2,* 56–70.

Abrams, K., & Bever, T. G. Syntactic structure modifies attention during speech perception and recognition. *Quarterly Journal of Experimental Psychology,* 1969, *21,* 280–290.

Ball, F., Wood, C., & Smith, E. E. When are semantic targets detected faster than visual or acoustic ones? *Perception & Psychophysics,* 1975, *17,* 1–8.

Bever, T. G. The influence of speech performance on linguistic structure. In G. B. Flores d'Arcais & W. J. M. Levelt (Eds.), *Advances in psycholinguistics.* Amsterdam: North-Holland, 1970.

Blank, M., & Foss, D. J. *Context and the single sentence.* Unpublished manuscript, University of Texas at Austin, 1977.

Bond, Z. S. Phonological units in sentence perception. *Phonetica,* 1972, *25,* 129–139.

Cairns, H. S., & Foss, D. J. Falsification of the hypothesis that word frequency is a unified variable in sentence processing. *Journal of Verbal Learning and Verbal Behavior,* 1971, *10,* 41–43.

Cairns, H. S., & Hsu, J. R. *Effects of prior context upon lexical access during sentence comprehension: A replication and reinterpretation.* Unpublished manuscript, City University of New York, 1977.

Cairns, H. S., & Kamerman, J. Lexical information processing during sentence comprehension. *Journal of Verbal Learning and Verbal Behavior,* 1975, *14,* 170–179.

Cole, R. A. Listening for mispronunciations: A measure of what we hear during speech. *Perception & Psychophysics,* 1973, *1,* 153–156.

Cole, R. A., & Jakimik, J. Understanding speech: How words are heard. In G. Underwood (Ed.), *Strategies of information processing.* New York: Academic Press, in press.

Cutler, A. Phoneme-monitoring reaction time as a function of preceding intonation contour. *Perception & Psychophysics,* 1976, *20,* 55–60.

Cutler, A., & Cooper, W. E. Phoneme-monitoring in the context of different phonetic sequences. *Journal of Phonetics,* 1978, *6,* 221–225.

Cutler, A., & Fodor, J. A. Semantic focus and sentence comprehension. *Cognition,* 1979, in press.

Cutler, A., & Foss, D. J. *Comprehension of ambiguous sentences: The locus of context effects.* Paper presented at the annual meeting of the Midwestern Psychological Association, Chicago, 1974.

Cutler, A., & Foss, D. J. On the role of sentence stress in sentence processing. *Language and Speech,* 1977, *20,* 1–10.

Foss, D. J. Decision processes during sentence comprehension: Effects of lexical item difficulty and position upon decision times. *Journal of Verbal Learning and Verbal Behavior,* 1969, *8,* 457–462.

Foss, D. J. Some effects of ambiguity upon sentence comprehension. *Journal of Verbal Learning and Verbal Behavior,* 1970, *9,* 699–706.

Foss, D. J. On the time-course of sentence comprehension. In F. Bresson & J. Mehler (Eds.), *Current approaches to problems in psycholinguistics.* Paris: Centre National de la Recherche Scientifique, 1975.

Foss, D. J., & Dowell, B. E. High-speed memory retrieval with auditorily presented stimuli. *Perception & Psychophysics,* 1971, *9,* 465–468.

Foss, D. J., & Jenkins, C. M. Some effects of context on the comprehension of ambiguous sentences. *Journal of Verbal Learning and Verbal Behavior,* 1973, *12,* 577–589.

Foss, D. J., & Lynch, R. H., Jr. Decision processes during sentence comprehension: Effects of surface structure on decision times. *Perception & Psychophysics,* 1969, *5,* 145–148.

Foss, D. J., & Swinney, D. A. On the psychological reality of the phoneme: Perception, identification and consciousness. *Journal of Verbal Learning and Verbal Behavior,* 1973, *12,* 246–257.

Garrod, S., & Sanford, A. Interpreting anaphoric relations: The integration of semantic information while reading. *Journal of Verbal Learning and Verbal Behavior,* 1977, *16,* 77–90.

Geers, A. E. Intonation contour and syntactic structure as predictors of apparent segmentation. *Journal of Experimental Psychology: Human Perception and Performance,* 1978, *4,* 273–283.

Green, D. W. The effects of task on the representation of sentences. *Journal of Verbal Learning and Verbal Behavior,* 1975, *14,* 275–283.

Green, D. W. The immediate processing of sentences. *Quarterly Journal of Experimental Psychology,* 1977, *29,* 135–146.

Hakes, D. T. Does verb structure affect sentence comprehension? *Perception & Psychophysics,* 1971, *10,* 229–232.

Hakes, D. T. Effects of reducing complement constructions on sentence comprehension. *Journal of Verbal Learning and Verbal Behavior,* 1972, *11,* 278–286.

Hakes, D. T., & Cairns, H. S. Sentence comprehension and relative pronouns. *Perception & Psychophysics,* 1970, *8,* 5–8.

Hakes, D. T., Evans, J. S., & Brannon, L. L. Understanding sentences with relative clauses. *Memory & Cognition,* 1976, *4,* 283–290.

Hakes, D. T., & Foss, D. J. Decision processes during sentence comprehension: Effects of surface structure reconsidered. *Perception & Psychophysics,* 1970, *8,* 413–416.

Haviland, S. E., & Clark, H. H. What's new? Acquiring new information as a process in comprehension. *Journal of Verbal Learning and Verbal Behavior,* 1974, *13,* 512–521.

Healy, A. F., & Cutting, J. E. Units of speech perception: Phoneme and syllable. *Journal of Verbal Learning and Verbal Behavior,* 1976, *15,* 73–83.

Holmes, V. M., Arwas, R., & Garrett, M. F. Prior context and the perception of lexically ambiguous sentences. *Memory & Cognition,* 1977, *5,* 103–110.

Holmes, V. M., & Forster, K. I. Detection of extraneous signals during sentence recognition. *Perception & Psychophysics,* 1970, *7,* 297–301.

Huggins, A. W. F. Distortion of the temporal pattern of speech: Interruption and alternation. *Journal of the Acoustical Society of America,* 1964, *36,* 1055–1064.

Kintsch, W. *The representation of meaning in memory.* Hillsdale, N.J.: Lawrence Erlbaum Associates, 1974.

Liberman, A. M., Cooper, F. S., Shankweiler, D. P., & Studdert-Kennedy, M. Perception of the speech code. *Psychological Review,* 1967, *74,* 431–461.

MacKay, D. G. Mental diplopia. In G. B. Flores d'Arcais & W. J. M. Levelt (Eds.), *Advances in psycholinguistics.* Amsterdam: North-Holland, 1970.

Marslen-Wilson, W. D., & Tyler, L. K. Processing structure of sentence perception. *Nature,* 1975, *257,* 784–786.

Marslen-Wilson, W. D., Tyler, L. K., & Seidenberg, M. Sentence processing and the clause boundary. In W. J. M. Levelt & G. Flores d'Arcais (Eds.), *Studies in the perception of language.* London: Wiley, 1978.

Marslen-Wilson, W. D., & Welsh, A. Processing interactions and lexical access during word recognition in continuous speech. *Cognitive Psychology,* 1978, *10,* 29–63.

Martin, M. Reading while listening: A linear model of selective attention. *Journal of Verbal Learning and Verbal Behavior,* 1977, *16,* 453–463.

McNeill, D., & Lindig, K. The perceptual reality of phonemes, syllables, words and sentences. *Journal of Verbal Learning and Verbal Behavior,* 1973, *12,* 419–430.

Mehler, J., Segui, J., & Carey, P. W. Tails of words: Monitoring ambiguity. *Journal of Verbal Learning and Verbal Behavior,* 1978, *17,* 29–35.

Mistler-Lachman, J. L. Queer sentences, ambiguity, and levels of processing. *Memory & Cognition,* 1975, *3,* 395–400.

Moore, T. Speeded recognition of ungrammaticality. *Journal of Verbal Learning and Verbal Behavior,* 1972, *11,* 550–560.

Moray, N. *Attention: Selective processes in vision and hearing.* London: Hutchinson, 1969.

Morton, J., & Long, J. Effect of word transitional probability on phoneme identification. *Journal of Verbal Learning and Verbal Behavior,* 1976, *15,* 43–51.

Pachella, R. G. The interpretation of reaction time in information-processing research. In B. H. Kantowitz (Ed.), *Human information processing: Tutorials in performance and cognition.* Hillsdale, N.J.: Lawrence Erlbaum Associates, 1974.

Posner, M. I., & Mitchell, R. F. Chronometric analysis of classification. *Psychological Review,* 1967, *74,* 392–409.

Rubin, P. E. *Semantic influences on phonetic identification and lexical decison.* Unpublished doctoral dissertation, University of Connecticut, 1975.

Rubin, P. E., Turvey, M. T., & van Gelder, P. Initial phonemes are detected faster in spoken words than in spoken nonwords. *Perception & Psychophysics,* 1976, *19,* 394–398.

Savin, H. B., & Bever, T. G. The nonperceptual reality of the phoneme. *Journal of Verbal Learning and Verbal Behavior,* 1970, *9,* 295–302.

Shields, J. L., McHugh, A., & Martin, J. G. Reaction time to phoneme targets as a function of rhythmic cues in continuous speech. *Journal of Experimental Psychology,* 1974, *102,* 250–255.

Steinheiser, F. H., & Burrows, D. J. Chronometric analysis of speech perception. *Perception & Psychophysics,* 1973, *13,* 426–430.

Suci, G. J., Ammon, P., & Gamlin, P. The validity of the probe-latency technique for assessing structure in language. *Language and Speech,* 1967, *10,* 69–80.

Swinney, D. A. *Does context direct lexical access?* Paper presented at the annual meeting of the Midwestern Psychological Association, Chicago, 1976.

Swinney, D. A., & Hakes, D. T. Effects of prior context upon lexical access during sentence comprehension. *Journal of Verbal Learning and Verbal Behavior,* 1976, *15,* 681–689.

Treisman, A., & Squire, R. Listening to speech at two levels at once. *Quarterly Journal of Experimental Psychology,* 1974, *26,* 82–97.

Tyler, L. K., & Marslen-Wilson, W. D. The on-line effects of semantic context on syntactic processing. *Journal of Verbal Learning and Verbal Behavior,* 1977, *16,* 683–692.

Walker, E. C. T. Some grammatical relations among words. In R. J. Wales & E. C. T. Walker (Eds.), *New approaches to language mechanisms.* Amsterdam: North-Holland, 1976.

5 Intonation and Ambiguity

Roger Wales
Hugh Toner
University of Melbourne

INTRODUCTION

In psycholinguistics over the last 20 years or so, there has been a great deal of interest in both intonation and ambiguity. However, only recently has investigation begun on the question of whether, in everyday speech, intonation may be used as a cue for the selection of one of the meanings of an ambiguous utterance. As yet there is very little experimental evidence available, although, thanks to the work on the separate areas of intonation and of ambiguity it is not hard to find theories, sometimes conflicting, about the possible effects of intonation on ambiguities.

It seems to be widely true that when asked to consider the matter, the layman will almost always assume that intonation can indicate which meaning of an ambiguous sentence was intended by a speaker. Psycholinguists seem less ready to attribute such a *syntactic* function to intonation, although they do not deny that intonation can modify the meaning of a sentence at the affective level. Indirect support for this stance is provided by such widely cited studies as Garrett, Bever and Fodor (1966). In that study, the subjective displacement of an extraneous noise relative to an ambiguous segment of a sentence was found to be a function of syntactic rather than prosodic factors in processing the sentence (see also Stockwell, 1960). Lieberman (1967), in his discussion of intonation, specifically theorized about disambiguation by intonation. He stressed the idea of breath-groups that may mark off the constituent parts of the surface structure of a sentence. It follows that if different divisions (bracketings) of the surface structure produce differences in the meaning of the sentence (i.e., surface-structure ambiguities) then such differences in the meaning may well be indicated to hearers by the intonation that the speaker uses. Lieberman contended that it *is* possible for surface-structure (but not deep structure or lexical) ambiguities to be disambiguated by intonation cues. However, he also pointed out that in normal speech the context usually provides the necessary cues for the selection of the intended meaning of an ambiguous sentence, and he believes that if context is available, speakers will probably not take the trouble to use these intonation cues.

Although Lieberman's (1967) theory seems highly plausible, there is as yet little evidence of experimental investigation of these views. Not all theorists stress the grammatical function of intonation. Danes (cited in Magdics, 1963) sees three functions of intonation: it can indicate points of new information in the sentence; it can show whether a sentence is merely a statement or is one that invites some reaction; and it can convey the sentiments and emotions of the speaker. He denies that intonation has a grammatical function. This kind of view seems far from that of Lieberman (1967) who stressed the grammatical function of intonation, and said: "It is only when ambiguity arises that intonation becomes important [p. 110]."

Recently, some experimental work on this topic has been reported. Nash (1970), for example, used one sentence only with synthesized speech and found little support for Lieberman's (1967) view. Delbridge (1970) seemed to show that readers did not effectively use intonation to distinguish different interpretations of sentences, but that listeners seemed to be able to identify the correct intended meaning successfully. However, he gave results for just three dialogues, only one of which was a structural ambiguity (the others involved differences of emphasis). Scholes (1971) used 18 readings of a single ambiguous sentence and showed little clear support for one theoretical position rather than another.

The first experiment reported in this chapter was designed as an attempt to obtain some more general evidence that might elucidate the relative merits of the diverse theories. Specifically, it was aimed at examining the possibility that intonation has this grammatical function, i.e., whether it *can* be used to disambiguate sentences, taking into account Lieberman's (1967) contentions that it is only with surface structure ambiguities, probably only in the absence of disambiguating contexts, that disambiguation by intonation will be found.

In looking at this evidence, it is important to make some basic methodological moves clear. First, given that one reading of any ambiguous sentence may be more probable than the alternative, it would be no surprise to find speakers and hearers apparently able to select that intended interpretation. What is crucial for testing the hypothesis that intonation can be used to disambiguate is to see whether it can be used also to select for the hearer the unlikely interpretation. If this is not possible, then it seems sensible to assume that good performance on the more probable reading is simply a response bias to the preferred interpretation and may have nothing to do with intonation. So performance must be related to an independent measure of the bias of one reading as against the other for each ambiguous sentence. Our own hypothesis is that, in general, intonation cannot be used to reliably select both readings of ambiguous sentences. Given that we are effectively predicting the acceptance of the null hypothesis, we initially used less conservative statistical assumptions than those (properly) advocated by Clark (1973).

Second, the term *intonation* is used here in a very general sense. There does not seem to be yet an unequivocal physical measure (although fundamental frequency appears the best current candidate), and it is often difficult to distinguish the operations of intonation and stress (cf. Lehiste, 1970). The possible importance of the latter interaction is pointed out by Cutler's (1976) demonstration of the importance of prosody, especially stress, in processing such aspects of sentence structure as focus and presupposition. If the latter were always a viable manipulable effect, it would give greater credibility to the possibility of using prosody to select particular interpretations of ambiguous sentences, be they even lexical or deep structure ones. The generality of Cutler's argument would, of course, only be restricted if intonation cannot be used in this way.

Third, there is the question: If intonation cannot be reliably used to disambiguate, why do so many people believe that it can? One answer may lie with the response-bias effect mentioned above. Another may have to do with a strategy hearers might use that involves taking a variation from usual intonation as a signal to search for a/the unlikely reading. If this happens then the hearer might assume that an "unmarked" reading was "normal" and assign it the preferred reading. Such a strategy obviously assumes that the speaker is "marking" the unlikely reading in the sense that what is taken as an unusual intonation is used. However, this may not be the "right" intonation, in that perhaps there is no "right" intonation from a purely syntactic point of view. Thus, although we examine the possible existence of such a strategy and call it a *markedness strategy*, this is a term of convenience, because it is left as an open question whether there is a "normal" or "unmarked" intonation in any other linguistic sense than language users pragmatic behavior.

Fourth, many of the issues of analysis would be severely complicated if we were to consider whether the effect, or lack of it, was because of speakers rather than hearers, or vice versa. Thus, in principle, hearers might be good at interpreting intonation, but speakers not be competent at producing it correctly. Although this is a fascinating theoretical possibility, as far as real everyday communication is concerned, it would be of minor importance. Both speakers and hearers need to be competent (whether idealized or not) in order for communication to occur. Nevertheless, some attempt needs to be made to prevent such factors as dialect variation from seriously confounding the results. This was done here by varying the background of both speakers and hearers.

EXPERIMENT 1

Method

Subjects.   There were two experimental conditions, each using the same 48 subjects. Twelve of them werc Scottish females, 12 Scottish males, 12 English females, and 12 English males. All were students of various disciplines and at various academic stages. Our interest in the Scottish–English dimension was in controlling for the possibility that Scots and English might use intonation differently with regard to disambiguation of sentences; and for this reason our criteria for deciding "nationality" took into account the obvious accent differences. For example, we rejected from "Scottish" those who, though born and brought up in Scotland and of Scottish parents, had acquired an "English" (or other) accent (e.g., through private school education). On the other hand, we occasionally accepted as Scottish one who was born in England, of Scottish (or mixed) parents, but lived virtually all his/her life in Scotland in an environment that had produced an unmistakably Scottish accent. Mostly, however, the Scots (for example) were Scottish nationals born and brought up in Scotland and with Scottish accents. The counterpart of this was true of the English. These 48 subjects were the hearers in the experiments. There were also four readers: one Scottish female, one Scottish male, one English female, and one English male. These persons were selected as the best four from an original pool of eight readers. (For "English" read "South English," which is not to be confused with "RP", and for "Scottish' read "Central Southern—one east and one west coast.)

The bias-test condition involved 96 subjects, again, students of various academic years and studies. Twenty-four were Scottish females, 24 Scottish males, 24 English females and 24 English males. In addition, we ran another bias test (earlier), using different subjects: 30 males and 50 females, this time all second-year psychology students. All 228 subjects were undergraduates at St. Andrews University. The exact nature of the experiment was not made clear to readers or hearers, except that they would be reading on to tape or listening to tape recordings.

Materials.   Thirty ambiguous sentences were used. In 10 of them, the ambiguity was at the *lexical* level (e.g., "pupils": schoolchildren or center of eye); 10 had *surface-structure* ambiguity (e.g., "He hit the man with the stick") and 10 had *deep-structure* ambiguity (e.g., "The corrupt police can't stop drinking"). While these examples are quite clear instances of each kind of ambiguity, classification was not always so clear-cut. The distinctions between surface structure and deep structure, for instance, can be rather difficult to assess at times, because ambiguity of deep structure often results in alternatives in the surface structure. For example, "They are interesting farmers" has, obviously, deep-structure ambiguity in that the basic subject–object/complement relations are unclear. "They" may refer to the farmers who are interesting, or to the people or animals who capture the interest of the farmers. On the other hand, it can be argued that the surface structure is different for these two meanings: (a) (They) (are) (interesting farmers); or (b) (They) ((are) interesting)) (farmers).

Mehler, Bever, and Carey (1967) described sentences of this type as being both deep- and surface-structure ambiguities. Others might feel that the important ambiguity is the deep-structure one and that the surface-structure alternative is a less important manifestation of the ambiguity. In our categorization, we have tried to adhere simply to MacKay and Bever's (1967) definition of deep-structure ambiguities as the alteration of basic logical relations in the sentence: "An underlying structure ambiguity involves the basic subject–verb and/or verb–object relations between words in the main clause of the sentence [p. 199]." It is also possible to find disagreement on whether a sentence contains a lexical or a deep-structure ambiguity. For example, the sentence "The spy put out his torch as the signal to attack," which we originally had included as a lexical ambiguity ("extinguish..." vs. "extend the arm holding the..."), is given as an example of deep-structure ambiguity by Lackner and Garrett (1973). This sentence was eventually rejected from our final list of 30 sentences. (The sentence pairs used are listed in Appendix A.) The sentences were collected from various sources, including the psycholinguistic literature on ambiguity.

The 30 sentences (or rather pairs of sentences) were then incorporated unaltered into 60 short paragraphs composed such that the text of the paragraph disambiguated the sentence to one of the possible meanings, A or B (i.e., there were 30 A and 30 B context paragraphs). As and Bs were assigned arbitrarily but maintained throughout the experiments. Twenty further paragraphs were used that did not contain any ambiguous sentences. This approach was to minimize the likelihood of the reader becoming "set" for the ambiguity in every paragraph. These 80 paragraphs were typed on 80 index cards, the order of which was then randomized, so that the A and B occurrences of any one sentence never appeared consecutively.

Procedure. The readers were given written instructions to read the paragraphs in a natural and conversational voice and were asked to re-read the card if they made mistakes. Readers were not told about the ambiguity until after this part of the experiment was over. We pointed out that this was *not* a test of their reading ability, but that we just needed normal everyday speech on tape. They were aware that they were being recorded. The readers were then left in the room on their own as we assumed that the presence of the experimenter might be inhibiting. At the end of this task, most readers reported having noticed that "some" of the sentences had occurred twice, although in some way were different in the two appearances. Usually they agreed that they had seen the ambiguity sometimes (but not always), and some were surprised to know the sentences were ambiguous. The material for the second part of the experiment was then given to the readers. This consisted of a typed list in which each ambiguous sentence appeared, followed by two nonambiguous paraphrases: one the *A* meaning, and the other the *B*. Readers were instructed (again with written instructions) to study each sentence with its paraphrases and then to read the sentence to try to convey the *A* meaning and then again to give the *B* meaning. They were allowed to practice aloud or silently if they wished.

All readings for both parts of the experiment were recorded on magnetic tape at 7½ inches per sec, using a Revox 77 taperecorder. From these tapes, a master tape was recorded. The contexts surrounding the ambiguous sentences (in Part 1) were omitted, so that this second tape contained all the ambiguous sentences, both *A* and *B* meanings from Part 1 (in a second random order to eliminate possible effects of order of reading of sentence pairs) followed by the ambiguous sentences (*A* and *B* meanings) for Part 2 (in the reverse of the new order for Part 1 sentences). Thus, there were 120 sentences on tape, each read by all four readers. The utterances from the contextualized material could then be compared in the listening experiment with those uttered without contextual constraints. An analysis of the fundamental frequency of each sentence pair (from both contextual and noncontextual sets) showed them to be clearly different, although we could not see any consistent pattern in the differences. Of course, this does not mean that such patterns of consistent difference do not exist. A typescript was made of the 60 sentences of Part 1 in their order of appearance on tape, with each sentence followed by a typed paraphrase of the *A* meaning and of the *B* meaning. Duplicated copies of this script were used as the score in both experiments.

Experimental procedure. The subjects were told (in written instructions) that they would hear recordings of sentences, corresponding to the first of each group of 3 sentences on their sheets. They were then to judge which of the two typed paraphrases represented the meaning intended by the reader. We stressed that hearers were to base their judgment of which meaning the reader had intended *"solely on the basis of the way it is said,"* and not on whether the hearer thought one made more sense than the other. They were also told that the sentences would recur as they worked through the sheet, but not to let this matter to their interpretation: each sentence was to be judged on its own, according to the way it was said. They were not, however, told the number of occurrences (two in each part). Some thought there were three in all, instead of four, suggesting that they were not necessarily working on the basis of a two–two division of *A* and *B* meanings. When the hearers had decided which was the meaning, they were to tick the appropriate paraphrase. If they were unsure they could mark that they were guessing (G), but they still had to choose one of the meanings. It is theoretically possible that although they thought they were guessing, something (e.g., intonation) could be guiding their "guess." (This kind of response occurred insufficiently often to justify separate analysis.) Hearers were allowed to read each sentence and its two paraphrases before hearing it on tape. This was to eliminate the chance that the hearers might be biased towards one meaning to such an extent that they did not notice the other meaning and, therefore might possibly only "hear" the sentence in the way they imagined it. It was hoped that this experimental procedure would maximize the possibility of using intonation to disambiguate the sentences.

Each hearer listened to only one reader, such that each reader was heard by three Scottish males, three Scottish females, three English males, and three English females.

The response sheets were scored in terms of a comparison of the meaning assigned to each sentence by a hearer with the meaning the reader had intended (which was dictated by the context in the contextual and by the experimental instructions in the noncontextual sets. When the two matched, the hearer's response was judged correct.

Bias material. As indicated in the introduction, some ambiguous sentences are highly biased towards one meaning. Granted that this is so, it is evident that our experimental results for each sentence can only be meaningfully understood when compared with the "natural" bias of the sentence. It was, therefore, necessary to obtain an independent measure of the response bias for each sentence without drawing prior attention to the ambiguity. To this end, we asked 24 Scottish males, 24 Scottish females, 24 English males, and 24 English females to write a paraphrase under each of our 30 sentences, which were on a typed sheet. From the results of this, we obtained the percentage of *A* and of *B* responses—the response bias score.

Results

The scores for the experimental results were expressed as the percentage of total possible correct responses for all *A* and for all *B* meanings of each sentence. (Thus, it was theoretically possible to score 100% correct on *A* and also, independently, 100% correct on *B* meanings). The bias scores were also expressed as percentages; but the B meaning scores were, of course, not independent in this case. In the bias test, a number of responses could not be classified either as A or B (e.g., because the paraphrase itself was ambiguous), and we decided to exclude these responses. Our confidence in the reliability of our measure of the sentence bias (at least for St. Andrews students) was increased when these figures were compared with those of an earlier run of the same test (with 80 second-year psychology students). The two sets of data correlated highly: for lexical ambiguities, $r = .87$; for surface-structure ambiguities, $r = .95$; and for deep-structure ambiguities, $r = .985$. The overall correlation was $r = .924$. Three main analyses of variance were used: one on the results of the bias test (three-way: Nationality × Sex × Type of Ambiguity); two on the experimental results I (a six-way: Contextual Condition × Speaker Nationality × Hearer Nationality × Ambiguity Type × Degree of Bias × Preference) and experimental results II (a similar five-way analysis including a comparison with the bias effects in the context condition and excluding nationality of hearer as a factor). A fourth analysis of Scottish reader results was added, but as there were no differences in the significances of effects between this and overall analyses, this analysis is not reported further. In all of the analyses of variance, the results (in percentages) were arcsin transformed.

Bias test.   The analysis of variance showed that in the results of the bias test, there were no significant effects from the nationality (Scots–English) or sex variables. The only significant effect was from the type of ambiguity (lexical, surface, deep structure), $F(2, 18) = $, $p < .01$. Sentences with lexical ambiguity were, on the average, more heavily biased than surface-structure ambiguities, and these in turn were more biased than were the deep-structure ambiguities, where there was something nearer to a 50–50 (i.e., nonbiased) likelihood of any one meaning being selected. These differences between lexical, surface, and deep may be due to chance (i.e., it just happened that more biased sentences were chosen for lexical examples than for deep), or perhaps they may result from differences in processing of the different types of ambiguity by those who were tested. What is important to our study is not so much how the differences came about but that we take them into account when discussing the experimental results.

Experimental Results and Discussion

Analysis 1 found significant main effects for speaker nationality, type of ambiguity, and preferred vs. unlikely reading. No significant results were found for hearer nationality, contextual condition, and degree of bias. (The 10 sentences for each type of ambiguity were grouped into 5 highly biased (e.g., 70–30 preference towards one meaning) and 5 less-biased sentences ("unbiased"), i.e., where the likelihood of one meaning being chosen rather than the other was nearer to 50). No significant difference was found between the results of the two contextual conditions, nor did the nationality of the hearer (or the interaction between the nationality of the hearers and speakers) have any significant effect, although Scottish *speakers* elicited significantly higher results (i.e., correct hearer responses) than did the English speakers, $F(1, 4) = 11.9$, $p < .05$. Note that the Scottish–English dimension was included merely as a control, and because only four readers, two Scottish and two English, were used, it is not possible to infer from the results that this significance indicates a real Scottish–English difference rather than merely that two of our readers (who happened to be the Scottish ones) were in some sense significantly "better" readers than were the other two.

Another notable result from Analysis 1 is the ambiguity-type significance, $F(2, 8) = 13.5$, $p < .01$. What is interesting is that the lexical, surface, and deep-structure differences do *not* follow the order of those in the bias test. This time, results for surface were greater than for lexical and lexical greater than for deep structure (i.e., surface, lexical, deep structure as opposed to lexical, surface, deep structure in the bias test). It is not possible to assess the extent of this change of order (or whether it is caused by surface scores increasing or lexical decreasing in the experiment), until we compare the experimental results for each sentence with the bias-test results for that sentence. Analysis 2 was, therefore, performed incorporating the same factors as Analysis 1, with two exceptions: the Scottish–English hearer dimension was excluded, and a third level—the bias score—was added to the contextual factor. Most of the differences between Analyses 1 and 2, therefore, involve the contextual effect and that of contextual interactions. The contextual effect itself was significant in Analysis 2, $F(2, 18) = 8.4$, $p < .01$, indicating that at least one of the sets of experimental results (not significantly different from each other in Analysis 1) must be significantly different from the bias scores. In fact, scores for contextual and noncontextual sets were both *higher* than was the bias score, (109, 117, and 100, respectively). This contextual effect was significantly different for the high and low readings of the sentence pairs, i.e., experimental results for the unlikely reading of the sentence pair were much higher than were the bias scores, whereas with the preferred meaning, the difference between bias score and results was small, and the direction of this difference seems to be reversed (see Table 5.1).

This reversal, together with the smallness of the increase between bias scores and experimental results lead to the question of whether the contextual effect simply means that hearers can use the intonation cues to disambiguate the sentences. If the intonation gave no clue at all then we would expect either (a) that the hearers would score at the level of chance on both high and low readings (i.e., 50% each), if, as a result of experimental instructions, they were trying to avoid being biased by the "likelihood" of either meaning or (b) that

TABLE 5.1
Percentage Means by Preference, Condition, and Bias

	P^a	U^b	$P + U$
Bias	73	27	100
Condition C^c	69	40	109
Condition NC^d	65	52	117
"Marking" expected	73	50	123

[a]Preferred reading.
[b]Unlikely reading.
[c]Experiment in which sentences had been said in context.
[d]Experiment in which sentences were said alone without context.

hearers may follow the bias and assign a sentence the more likely meaning every time so that, on a 72–25 bias sentence, 75% of the readers would score 100% for the preferred reading and 0 for the unlikely reading, and 25% would score 100% for unlikely and 0 for preferred reading, i.e., if the hearers and the bias-test subjects are assumed to belong to the same population.

This description of option (b) is, of course, an oversimplification, and, in fact, it might be more likely that hearers would score somewhere between 75% and 50% on the preferred meaning and between 50% and 25% on the unlikely meaning (depending on the degree to which experimental task effect contested with bias effect). However, either way, we would expect a total of roughly 100 for the two meanings of the sentence pairs (where 200 is the maximum possible score). On the other hand, if intonation was a really effective aid to disambiguation, we would expect the total of scores for both meanings of sentences to approach 200, depending on how effective intonation was as a cue. But this increase would come from an increase in both scores from chance levels. The very small increase in experimental scores from bias scores suggests that intonation is at best, not every effective as a cue, and the decrease in preferred reading scores seems anomalous if intonation is effective. The evidence of intonation being used effectively in disambiguation is, to say the least, tenuous.

We must still, however, account for the small (but significant) rise in total experimental scores. One suggestion is that, in a sense, hearers are using a probabilistic strategy aided by the bias and some kind of "intonation" effect discussed in the introduction as the "marking" strategy. Using this strategy on a 72–25 bias sentence, 75% of the hearers would be 100% right on preferred readings and 25% would be 100% wrong; i.e., the preferred reading would be similar to the bias score. On the other hand, they would notice the marking of the unlikely reading. However, because the marking was not "right" (if it had been it would have indicated that this definitely *was* an unlikely meaning), the information from the marking would possibly only be enough to counteract the bias effect. That is, hearers would *not* automatically choose the bias reading when sentences were marked, but having no further information they would have to guess which meaning was intended so that scores for the unpreferred readings would be more like chance results. On this explanation, we would expect correct scores on our 75–25 example to be 75 (out of a possible 100) for the preferred reading, plus 50 out of 100 for the unlikely meaning, i.e. a total "marking" estimate of 125 out of 200.

Before proceeding to our discussion of the results in relation to this marking hypothesis, we must consider a basic assumption that underlies this estimate of the marking-hypothesis scores. The assumption is that the readers are leaving *all* the preferred meanings of the sentence pairs unmarked and are marking all the unlikely meanings. It is, of course, more than possible that the readers did not always find the meaning as defined by the bias test to be the more likely meaning as far as they were concerned. Indeed, it might be true that the probability of the readers concurring with the bias (in their selection of preferred meaning) is similar to the probability of anyone else preferring those meanings; i.e., readers might also be influenced by the degree of bias. This would result in our example in the marking prediction dropping to about 113 out of 200. However, given the communication constraints discussed in the introduction, it seems not unjustifiable to work on the assumption that readers are consistently interpreting preferred meanings (as established by our bias test) as the more likely, unmarked reading. (Some of the results on lexical and deep ambiguities might better fit the modified marking hypothesis).

To return now to the experimental results. In Table 5.2 (all readers), some interesting comparisons can be made between the pooled experimental results and the bias scores. First, it seems that the lowering in preferred-meaning scores noted earlier occurs with both lexical and deep-structure ambiguities but *not* with surface-structure ones. The total preferred and unlikely reading

TABLE 5.2

Percentage Means by Bias and Condition of the Three Types of Ambiguity

	Lexical			Surface			Deep		
	P^a	U^b	$P + U$	P	U	$P +U$	P	U	$P +U$
Bias	78	22	100	73	27	100	67	33	100
Conditions C & NC[c]	69	44	113	75	50	125	58	44	102
"Marking" expected[d]	78	50	128	73	50	123	67	50	117

[a]Preferred reading.

[b]Unlikely reading.

[c]Experiment in which sentences had been said in context and experiment in which sentences were said alone without context, respectively.

[d]Score predicted according to "marking" hypothesis.

result for lexical ambiguity (113, 116 Scottish readers) is somewhat lower than the marking hypothesis prediction of 128. In fact, it is about half way between the prediction according to chance and that according to the marking hypothesis. On the other hand, the results for deep structure are much clearer. The score of 102 (103 Scottish) is clearly evidence of guessing (chance) without any aid through marking. The surface-structure result (125) is almost identical with the marking score (123), but the Scottish reader result (139) seems to be somewhat higher than would be predicted on the marking hypothesis. Before making any suggestions about what factors are operating at this level, it would seem wise to consider the contextual and noncontextual set results separately, because although these two sets of results do *not* show up as significantly different (contextual effect in Analysis 1), there appears to be a definite trend to the effect that noncontextual scores (preferred and unlikely readings taken together) are always—in all the tables—higher than contextual results.

Table 5.3 shows that surface-structure results, over all readers, are very close to the marking predictions for both contextual and noncontextual (and also for the Scottish contextual condition). However, in noncontextual sets, with Scottish readers, the results (149) are noticeably higher than these predictions. This result is composed of an increase in both unlikely and preferred readings that suggests that when these Scottish readers read the sentence without any context to convey the meaning, they *can* disambiguate by use of intonation with a moderate degree of success. However, although this was the strongest effect of intonation found here, the result does not by any means approach the 200 mark, so it seems that either intonation is not in any sense a very powerful aid to disambiguation even of surface-structure ambiguities or that some of the 10 surface-structure sentences used were highly susceptible to intonation, whereas others were not. This possibility is discussed later.

TABLE 5.3
Percentage Means Separating Condition by Ambiguity Type

	Lexical			Surface			Deep		
	P^a	U^b	$P + U$	P	U	$P + U$	P	U	$P + U$
Bias	78	22	100	73	27	100	67	33	100
Condition C[c]	71	36	107	76	45	121	61	38	99
Conditions NC[d]	66	52	118	74	55	129	54	49	103
"Marking" expected	78	50	128	73	50	123	67	50	117

[a]Preferred reading.
[b]Unlikely reading.
[c]Experiment in which sentences had been said in context.
[d]Experiment in which sentences were said alone without context.

For lexical results, there were differences between contextual and noncontextual conditions. In the contextual condition scores were very close to the chance level (104, 107 Scottish), but in Experiment 2 they increased to something like the "marking" prediction of 128 (Scottish 128). Both overall (Scottish and English readers) and Scottish results, for *deep*-structure ambiguities, remained at chance level for both experimental conditions.

A curious result of the hearer's use of the probabilistic strategy according to marking effects can be seen from Table 5.4. When each of the lexical, surface, and deep-structure results is split into two groups of five sentences, a high-biased and low-biased group, it is clear that where it seems most certain that hearers are operating on the basis of marking strategies (e.g., lexical, noncontenxtual), they do slightly better than the marking hypothesis would predict on the low-bias group, an increase in scores that is caused by a rise in *unlikely*- meaning scores; i.e., although following the bias score for preferred meaning, they seem to realize that a *marked* sentence is more probably an unlikely meaning. This is presumably because the unlikely meaning is not so very unlikely with these less-biased sentences, so that it seems more plausible to them that for these low-bias sentences, both likely and unlikely meanings are included in the experiment. On the other hand, with the high-biased sentences, scores for the preferred meanings are *below* marking-theory predictions. It almost seems as if the extremely unusual unlikely meaning draws the hearers at times away from their strategies of assuming that an unmarked meaning is the preferred meaning, or perhaps it is rather that they are wary of putting too many eggs in one basket by taking the preferred meaning every time that they hear an unmarked reading of a 90–10 biased sentence.

Differences between contextual and noncontextual conditions have not yet been systematically discussed. Throughout all the tables, it can be seen that the total scores for sentences in all three kinds of ambiguity (regardless of whether the sentences belong to the high-biased or unbiased groups) were consistently higher in noncontextual than in contextual conditions, and, in turn, contextual results were consistently higher than were the bias scores (except in the case of deep-structure ambiguities). In the contextual condition, intonation seems to have no effect on lexical or deep-structure ambiguities (even with Scottish readers where intonation effects seem to be strongest), because results are very close to the chance level. With surface structure, however, it seems that there may be a marking effect, but not a real disambiguation by intonation. It is also clear (see Table 5.3) that lexical and deep-structure results generally are affected by the bias; i.e., although the hearers are guessing, they are placing more weight on the preferred reading than on the unlikely one.

In the noncontextual condition, the bias effect is not nearly so strongly reflected in the results. It would seem also that marking effects are now occurring with lexical ambiguities. That the effect of the bias seems to be

TABLE 5.4
Percentage Means by Bias, Condition, and Ambiguity Type and by High- and Low-Bias Groups of Sentence

| | Biased Groups | | | | | | | | | Unbiased Groups | | | | | | | | |
| | Lexical | | | Surface | | | Deep | | | Lexical | | | Surface | | | Deep | | |
	P[a]	U[b]	P+U	P	U	P+U	P	U	P+U	P	U	P+U	P	U	P+U	P	U	P+U
Bias	90	10	100	83	17	100	80	20	100	67	33	100	64	36	100	55	45	100
Condition C[c]	80	33	113	78	41	119	58	33	91	61	39	100	74	48	122	63	43	106
Condition NC[d]	69	51	120	80	51	131	48	49	97	63	54	117	68	58	126	59	49	108
"Marking" expected	90	50	140	83	50	133	80	50	130	67	50	117	64	50	114	55	50	105

[a]Preferred reading.
[b]Unlikely reading.
[c]Experiment in which sentences had been said in context.
[d]Experiment in which sentences were said alone without context.

reduced in noncontextual condition may be explained as a result of the exaggerated "marking" that is occurring in this condition. Perhaps too much marking is being given, in that some of the preferred readings may now also be marked to some extent (hence the small reduction in preferred reading scores for the noncontextual condition, and the hearers are also made more aware that there are differences in the intonation of the readings of any one sentence and, therefore, that both preferred and unlikely readings are occurring. Thus, they now respond as high as chance level on the low readings. The overall increase from contextual to noncontextual conditions is indeed due to the large rise in unlikely-meanings scores up to chance level or slightly above. With deep structure, the exaggerated "marking" in the noncontextual condition also had the effect of reducing the effect of bias, but scores remain at chance level expectations.

Surface-structure ambiguity scores, as already pointed out, do seem to increase with the increase in marking, from contextual to noncontextual conditions, and as this increase was for both preferred and unlikely meaning, and was a relatively substantial one, it can be assumed that to some extent there is a "correct marking" for each meaning or, in other words, a genuine disambiguating intonation cue. Two issues of interest arise with regard to the surface-structure effects. The first is that there would seem to be some doubt now concerning Lieberman's (1967) contention that intonation is not likely to be used to disambiguate as long as there is a context to do the job instead (i.e., our contextual condition). Although there is certainly less effect of intonation in the contextual than in the noncontextual condition, it does not seem true to say that there is no effect in the contextual condition. This point is more convincing in light of the next observation. This second point was mentioned earlier: The increase in surface-structure results is not so substantial that we can say unequivocally that intonation, in general, disambiguates surface-structure ambiguities. A reconsideration of the raw data shows that 4 of the 10 sentences with surface-structure ambiguity had high scores in the noncontextual condition (175 out of 200) and moderately high scores in the contextual condition (153 out of 200). There can be little doubt that for these four sentences, the intonation used by readers fairly reliably conveys the intended meaning when they are read with no disambiguating context. Even when read in such contexts, the intonation is still often used by the readers, although to a lesser extent. For the remaining six surface-structure sentences, scores are lower (108 out of 200, contextual; 133 out of 200, noncontextual). There does not seem to be even a marking effect in contextual results for these sentences, and in the noncontextual condition, the score of 133 is not so clearly above the marking-hypothesis prediction of 123 that it can definitely be said this is still a genuine (though weak) intonation effect rather than a marking-strategy technique.

The existence of the 4 sentences in which there seem to be some sign of effective disambiguation by intonation suggests that Lieberman's (1967) hypothesis may be true of a restricted subset of surface-structure ambiguities. Meanwhile, it seems clear that the general hypothesis that intonation can be used to disambiguate sentences is false.

The interesting next step is to try and construct hypotheses about why intonation may be used in disambiguating some surface-structure ambiguities but not others.

EXPERIMENT 2

From the broader point of view of general sentence-processing theory, it is interesting to note that the few cases where we can suggest that intonation has a syntactic disambiguating function are surface-structure ambiguities. The theory of sentence processing put forward by Fodor and Garrett (1967) on experimental grounds and Thorne, Bratley, and Dewar (1968) as a computational model suggested that processing of sentences can be facilitated by the presence of those cues in the surface structure of the sentence that indicate the deep-structure relations of the sentence. (For a general discussion see Garrett [1974] and Limber [1976]).

In as much as intonation does operate at all in disambiguating sentences, it seems to be only by cues in (or imposed on) the surface structure of the sentence, cues that indicate the deep-structure relations. This theory might also explain why intonation is not likely to work at the deep (or lexical) structure level of ambiguity. When the ambiguity is at the deep structure level the problem is that in general, *both* deep structures (i.e., both A and B meaning structures) have produced the same surface structure. The disambiguation can only be achieved by the generation of alternative surface structures for the two meanings (e.g., by paraphrase). This theoretical viewpoint is consistent with Lieberman's (1967), but none of these positions is adequate to the task of distinguishing those surface ambiguities where intonation is useful and those where it is not.

The hypothesis that we wish to propose is an extension of such theoretical approaches but modifies them in the light of considerations raised by the marking hypothesis. To introduce the hypothesis, remember that by definition surface-structure ambiguities involve (at least) two different surface bracketings: e.g., (1). (old men) (and women); (2). (old) (men and women). From the point of view of sentence processing, it is obvious that the relevant constituent boundary for (2) will be reached earlier than for (1). Our hypothesis is that when the preferred reading (in terms of bias) is associated with the first constituent boundary (i.e., the earlier, in processing terms) then intonation can be used reliably to disambiguate the sentence; i.e., both the interpretations can be reliably communicated and selected using intonation and no context. The rationale for this view is that it is going to be easier to mark the second boundary consistently as clearly different from the more natural—unmarked—first one. Given that the second, marked, boundary is associated with the unlikely reading, the hearer's use of the markedness strategy should be consistent and "correct." On syntactic grounds, the reason why it may be easier to mark the second boundary is because that one will typically also be associated with discontinuous constituents as far as the ambiguity is concerned.

The relevant experimental hypothesis is, then, to test whether surface-structure ambiguities that have an association between preferred reading and the earlier relevant constituent boundary (between continuous constituents) are reliably disambiguated, whereas surface ambiguities with the association the other are not.

Method and Materials

Twenty-six surface ambiguous sentences were given to 48 subjects (second-year undergraduates in psychology at University of Melbourne) to paraphrase and, thereby, give estimates on bias as in Experiment 1. From this set of sentences, 20 were selected, a group of 10 that had as the preferred interpretation the one where the relevant constituent boundary came first (Preferred 1) and a group of 10 where it came second (Unlikely 1). The sentences and their two separate interpretations (making 40 in all) were placed in random order. Then, a reader (Australian) selected for her reading ability, recorded the sentences as before in the noncontextual condition on a Revox 77 taperecorder. Only one sentence pair was juxtaposed in the list.

Half of the subjects heard the sentences in the first random order, the other half started with the second half of the list and finished with the first half. The instructions were the same as for the first experiment. We predicted for the Preferred 1 group of sentences that subjects would not differ significantly on the preferred and the unlikely readings in getting them correct. However, for the Unlikely 1 group of sentences, the prediction was that only on the preferred readings would the subjects get the intended reading, and on the unlikely version would perform at chance.

Results and Discussion

These are summarized in Table 5.5. Inspection of this table reveals support for the hypothesis. This is confirmed by the following comparisons: for Preferred 1, preferred vs. unlikely, $t = 1.6$, n.s.; for Unlikely 1, preferred vs. unlikely, $t = 5.15$, $p < .001$; for unlikely, Preferred 1 vs. Unlikely 1, $t = 5.85$, $p < .001$. Furthermore, if expected values for preferred and unlikely readings

TABLE 5.5
Results of Experiment 2

	Mean Correct Per Sentence[a]	SD	% Correct	Bias
Preferred 1[b]				
Preferred reading	42.4	3.89	88.3	82
Unlikely reading	39.6	4.07	82.5	18
Unlikely 1[c]				
Preferred reading	39.5	5.87	82.5	79
Unlikely reading	23.4	8.53	48.7	21

[a]A possible maximum of 48.

[b]Sentence type where the first relevant constituent boundary is that of the preferred reading.

[c]Sentence type where the first relevant constituent boundary is that of the unlikely reading.

are taken as 48 each, for Preferred 1, χ^2 = 2.15, n.s.; for Unlikely 1, χ^2 = 14.07, $p < .001$. Thus, it is clear that all the general predictions above are confirmed.

On close inspection of Table 5.5, it can be seen that none of the Preferred 1 sentences had a mean probability of correct of less than .75 even on the unlikely interpretation. Of the Unlikely 1 sentences, only 2 show any trend towards being correct on both preferred and unlikely readings, namely, "She told him not to be silly and give himself up" and "He gave it to the boy with a box of chocolates." For the former, the presence of the negative may be significant. For the latter, it may be relevant that the bias effect for this sentence usually goes the other way and is associated with the last noun phrase being definite. This may illustrate one instance where there was an important difference introduced by the written form of the bias test and the spoken form of the experimental test. Whether these points are simply special pleading, only further work will resolve. Another point worth illustrating is the difficulty that some sentences present in the expression of the different interpretations. With "They promised to appoint an officer to keep the peace" we first tried (a) "They would appoint a peace-officer," and (b) "The appointment was a political one to pacify people." There was a striking improvement in the judgments when (b) was changed to "The person appointed (to keep the peace) was an officer." Obviously, it would be ideal if the Preferred 1 and Unlikely 1 sentences were exactly matched for surface forms (and word frequency, word length, etc.). However, there is sufficient overlap to make such possibly confounding factors unlikely determinants of these results. The impossible takes a little longer.

Although intonation has been used in a rather wide sense here, it is worth also referring to three other studies on the perception of ambiguities: by Lehiste (1973), Lehiste, Olive, and Streeter (1976) and Levelt, Zwanenburg, and Ouweneel (1970). These studies involved acoustic analysis of the ambiguous sentences used, and many of these sentences could be disambiguated by the subjects. The study by Levelt et al. was on French, and they found a level of performance that corresponds closely to the overall results of Experiment 1 reported in this chapter. They also found some relation between the perceptual results and the pitch and amplitude analyses of the utterances used. Lehiste et al. worked on English. They found results remarkably consistent with the two studies reported here. Only surface-structure ambiguities showed reliable perceptual disambiguation. The acoustic analyses and experimental manipulation indicate that the basis for this was systematic differences in duration of words either side of the crucial syntactic boundary. It is perhaps worth noting that data collected by us on the relative biases of the Lehiste sentences showed only one of them not consistent with hypothesis of our Experiment 2. Nevertheless, this does strongly suggest a relationship between acoustic–phonetic parameters (perhaps especially duration) and the syntactic and pragmatic aspects of the perception of ambiguity studied here. It seems that acoustically controlled studies in both production and perception will be an important corollary to the studies reported in this chapter.

On the evidence of these results, it seems clear both when and why some surface ambiguities can be reliably disambiguated by the use of intonation. It is a result of being able to take both syntactic information (about the order of constituents) and pragmatic information (about preferred readings determined usually by real-life rather than linguistic expectations), and harnessing their interaction to prosodic means. What seems clear is that there is no direct interaction between syntax and intonation and that this particular effect results from a special case of what we have called the *marking strategy*.

ACKNOWLEDGMENTS

This work stems from pilot studies conducted some years ago with Gillian Brown. Experiment 1 was done while we were still at the University of St. Andrews. Aileen Williams helped with the recording of Experiment 2. Virginia Holmes and Ed Walker have provided critical comment at sundry times. Lynn Wales generated ambiguous sentences while dodging Melbourne's traffic. Ken Forster drove us to completion. Experiment 2 was done with the aid of a grant from the Australian Research Grants Commission. We are grateful to each for their help and support.

APPENDIX A

The following are sentences used in Experiments 1 and 2 (percentages refer to bias-test scores for each meaning). P = preferred reading, U = unlikely reading, * = sentences that showed definite effects of disambiguation by intonation.

Experiment 1

Lexical Ambiguities
1. The *pupils* seemed very small.
    P: Schoolchildren (70%)
    U: Pupil of eye (30%)
2. She couldn't even guess what *state* he was in.
    P: Mental or physical condition (96%)
    U: Part of USA (4%)
3. He was delighted with the new *pool*.
    P: Swimming pool (95%)
    U: Pool of players (5%)
4. It was a very good *ball*.
    P: A dance (61%)
    U: A spherical object (39%)
5. Isn't that what a *ruler* is for?
    P: A measuring instrument (71%)
    U: A head of government (29%)
6. He walked right past the *conductor*.
    P: Bus conductor (80%)
    U: Orchestral conductor (20%)
7. How important is his *appearance* to you?
    P: What he looks like (94%)
    U: The fact that he arrives (6%)
8. The soldiers took the *port* at night.
    P: Harbour town (71%)
    U: Wine (29%)
9. The *glasses* were broken.
    P: Spectacles (62%)
    U: Tumblers (38%)
10. He likes his new *position*.
    P: Job (83%)
    U: Posture (17%)

Surface-Structure Ambiguities
1. It was the tape-recorder with the foot-pedal that I bought yesterday.
    P: Bought tape-recorder with foot-pedal yesterday (96%)
    U: Bought pedal yesterday, for a tape-recorder already owned (4%)
*2. He carried nothing to indicate that he was one of the group.
    P: He did not carry anything that would have made him look like the
       group (89%)
    U: By not carrying he showed that he was one of the group (11%)
3. It is very easy to define the conditions which are essential for learning
    to develop.

P: ... essential for the development of learning (64%)
U: ... essential in learning to develop (36%)

4. We sighted the man with the binoculars.
P: The man had binoculars (58%)
U: We used the binoculars to see him (42%)

5. We never fought a bull with real courage.
P: It was we who lacked courage (55%)
U: It was the bull which lacked courage (45%)

6. He hit the man with the stick.
P: He used the stick to hit the man (75%)
U: The man was carrying the stick (25%)

7. They kept the car in the garage.
P: It was in the garage that they kept (86%)
U: It was the one in the garage that they retained (14%)

*8. He left with the dog he had found last Saturday.
P: He left (e.g., today) with a dog that he found last Saturday (79%)
U: He left last Saturday with a dog he found sometime (21%)

*9. He also searched military buildings for the Russian Agents.
P: He looked in buildings in order to find Russians (85%)
U: He was employed by Russians to search buildings for information (15%)

*10. The policeman's arrest was illegal.
P: It was illegal for the policeman to arrest the man (53%)
U: It was illegal for the policeman to be arrested (47%)

Deep-Structure Ambiguities

1. The corrupt police can't stop drinking.
P: Police cannot stop themselves from drinking (85%)
U: Police cannot stop others from drinking (15%)

2. He is quick to please.
P: He is ready to please others (54%)
U: He is easily pleased (46%)

3. Flying planes can be dangerous.
P: It is dangerous to fly planes (59%)
U: Planes which fly are dangerous (41%)

4. The shooting of the hunters was abominable.
P: The hunters were inexpert at shooting (54%)
U: It was atrocious that the hunters were shot (46%)

5. Visiting relatives can be very boring.
P: Going to visit relatives is boring (70%)
U: Relatives who come to visit are boring (30%)

6. The elephant is ready to lift.
P: The elephant is about to lift something (52%)
U: The elephant is about to be lifted (48%)

7.   He seemed nice to her.
      P: She thought that the man was nice (71%)
      U: (Someone) thought the man was kind to her (29%)
8.   He was delighted with her present.
      P: He liked the present that she bought him (88%)
      U: He liked the present which she had been given (12%)
9.   He gave it to the girl with the roses.
      P: It was to the girl who had roses that he gave it (68%)
      U: He gave both it and the roses to the girl (32%)
10.   He took the box with the pictures.
      P: He took the box which had pictures in/on it (65%)
      U: He took both the pictures and the (jewel) box (35%)

Experiment 2

Preferred 1 Sentences
1.   He left with the dog he had found last Saturday.
          (a) He found the dog last Saturday, and left (e.g., today). (79%)
          (b) He left last Saturday with a dog he found sometime. (21%)
2.   They promised to appoint an officer to keep the peace.
          (a) They would appoint a peace-officer. (87%)
          (b) The person they appointed (to keep th epeace) was an officer.
               (13%)
3.   They looked for a likely candidate with boundless energy.
          (a) They were very energetic in their search for a candidate.
               (20%)
          (b) They wanted a candidate who had boundless energy. (80%)
4.   He carried nothing to indicate that he was one of the group.
          (a) He did not carry anything that would have made him look
               like one of the group. (He was unidentifiable.) (89%)
          (b) By not carrying anything he showed that he *was* one of the
               group. (11%)
5.   She promised it to the man with the handkerchief.
          (a) Promised it and the handkerchief to the man. (8%)
          (b) Promised it to the man who had a handkerchief. (92%)
6.   She looked for a man in her mother's raincoat.
          (a) She was wearing the raincoat while she looked. (33%)
          (b) The man was wearing the raincoat. (66%)
7.   The race was for young boys and girls.
          (a) The race was for young boys and for girls (of any age). (6%)
          (b) The race was for young boys and for young girls. (94%)
8.   He likes going out with girls in pyjamas.
          (a) The girls he goes out with wear pyjamas. (68%)

(b) He wears pyjamas when he goes out with girls. (32%)
9. They are always asking me questions on aeroplanes.
    (a) They ask me questions when I'm on board aeroplanes. (17%)
    (b) They ask me questions about aeroplanes. (83%)
10. She asked me not to sing and drive.
    (a) She asked me not to sing while driving. (88%)
    (b) She asked me to stop singing, and instead, drive. (12%)

Unlikely 1 Sentences
1. She told him not to be silly and give himself up.
    (a) She advised him to give himself up. (86%)
    (b) She advised him *not* to give himself up. (14%)
2. He was given a cup for drinking four pints of beer.
    (a) He was given a cup which could hold four pints. (39%)
    (b) He was given a trophy after his drinking achievement. (61%)
3. They looked for the man under the bed.
    (a) They looked for the man who was under the bed. (16%)
    (b) They looked under the bed to see if the man was there. (84%)
4. He gave it to the boy with a box of chocolates.
    (a) He gave both it and the chocolates to the boy. (71%)
    (b) He gave it to the boy who had a box of chocolates. (29%)
5. It was the tape-recorder with the foot-pedal that I bought yesterday.
    (a) Yesterday I bought a tape-recorder with a foot-pedal. (98%)
    (b) I bought a foot-pedal yesterday, for a tape-recorder already belonging to me. (2%)
6. He bought a little potter's wheel.
    (a) He bought a small wheel. (94%)
    (b) He bought the wheel from a little potter. (6%)
7. He hit the man with the stick.
    (a) The man with the stick was hit (e.g., punched) by him. (25%)
    (b) He used the stick to hit the man. (75%)
8. They kept the car in the garage.
    (a) It was in the garage that they kept it. (100%)
    (b) It was the one in the garage that they had decided to keep. (0%)
9. It is very easy to define the conditions which are essential for learning to develop.
    (a) ... essential for the development of learning. (64%)
    (b) ... essential in learning to develop oneself. (36%)
10. He never fought a bull with real courage.
    (a) It was he who lacked courage in his fighting. (57%)
    (b) It was the bull who lacked courage. (43%)

REFERENCES

Clark, H. H. Language as fixed effect fallacy. *Journal of Verbal Learning and Verbal Behavior,* 1973.

Cutler, A. Beyond parsing and lexical look up: An enriched description of auditory comprehension. In R. J. Wales & E. C. T. Walker (Eds.), *New approaches to language mechanisms.* Amsterdam: North-Holland, 1976.

Delbridge, A. Intonation and ambiguity. *Kivung,* 1970, *3,* 112–119.

Fodor, J. A., & Garrett, M. F. Some syntactic determinants of sentential complexity. *Perception & Psychophysics,* 1967, *2,* 289–296.

Garrett, M. F. Experimental issues in sentence comprehension: Complexity and segmentation. In C. Cherry (Ed.), *Pragmatic aspects of human communication.* Dordrecht: Reidel, 1974.

Garrett, M. F., Bever, T. G., & Fodor, J. A. The active use of grammar in speech perception. *Perception & Psychophysics,* 1966, *1,* 30–32.

Lackner, J. R., & Garrett, M. F. Resolving ambiguity; Effects of biasing context in the unattended ear. *Cognition,* 1973, *3,* 359–372.

Lehiste, I. *Suprasegmentals.* Cambridge, Mass.: MIT Press, 1970.

Lehiste, I. Phonetic disambiguation of syntactic ambiguity. *Glossa,* 1973, *7,* 107–122.

Lehiste, I., Olive, J. P., & Streeter, L. A. Role of duration in disambiguating syntactically ambiguous sentences. *Journal of the Acoustical Society of America,* 1976, *60,* 1199–1202.

Levelt, W. J. M., Zwanenburg, W., & Ouweneel, G. R. E. Ambiguous surface structure and phonetic form in French. *Foundations of Language,* 1970, *6,* 260–273.

Lieberman, P. *Intonation, perception and language.* Cambridge, Mass.: MIT Press, 1967.

Limber, J. Syntax and sentence interpretation. In R. J. Wales & E. C. T. Walker (Eds.), *New approaches to language mechanisms.* Amsterdam: North-Holland, 1976.

MacKay, D. G., & Bever, T. G. In search of ambiguity. *Perception & Psychophysics,* 1967, *2,* 193–200.

MacKay, D. G., Bever, T. G., & Carey, P. W. What we look at when we read. *Perception & Psychophysics,* 1967, *2,* 213–218.

Magdics, K. Research of intonation in the past ten years. *Acta Linguistica Academicae Scientiarum Hungaricae,* 1963, *13,* 133–164.

Mehler, J., Bever, T. G., & Carey, P. W. What we look at when we read. *Perception & Psychophysics,* 1967, *2,* 213–218.

Nash, R. "John likes Mary more than Bill." An experiment in disambiguating using synthesized intonation contours. *Phonetics,* 1970, *22,* 170–188.

Scholes, R. J. On the spoken disambiguation of superficially ambiguous sentences. *Language and Speech,* 1971, *14,* 1–11.

Stockwell, R. P. The place of intonation in a generative grammar of English. *Language,* 1960, *36,* 360–367.

Thorne, J. P., Bratley, P., & Dewar, H. The syntactic analysis of English by machine. In D. Michie (Ed.), *Machine intelligence 3.* Edinburgh: Edinburgh University Press, 1968.

Wales, R. J., & Walker, E. C. T. (Eds.) *New approaches to language mechanisms.* Amsterdam: North-Holland, 1976.

6
Perceptual Mechanisms and Formal Properties of Main and Subordinate Clauses

Thomas G. Bever
Columbia University

David J. Townsend
Columbia University
and
Montclair State College

INTRODUCTION

Language displays an awesome number of systematic phenomena. This is what makes it a favorite topic of those interested in the human mind. Here we see encapsulated a capacity that is uniquely human (on Earth) and one that draws on aspects of persona sapiens, ranging from the most concrete to the most abstract. If we could advance our understanding of language, we would make a major advance in understanding ourselves. The richness of structures in language has prompted many thinkers to despair of explaining their presence except by appeal to specific innate mechanisms. In this view language is the way it is for the same kind of reason that we have five fingers on each hand (not four or six): We are simply "programmed" genetically to be that way. In this regard linguistic science can be viewed as exploring the universals of language in order to specify what it is that constitutes our innate endowment that is specifically grammatical.

To many, this view seems stultifying—to claim that a structure is "innate" seems to leave no further reason for study: If a mental property is in fact innate, what else is there to say about it? An opposing point of view is that linguistic structures arise because of the function that language serves or because of the way it operates. Scholars in this school attempt to argue that language is the way it is because it is shaped by other mental systems, which are presumed to be general properties of the world or mind, as opposed to specifically linguistic properties.

If we now turn to other biological sciences, we find that opposition between these points of view can be quite healthy. For example, it is a dual rallying cry

159

of evolutionary theory that form precedes function and that function guides form. With respect to any particular structure, the question becomes empirical rather than philosophical: Which aspects are directly evolved from previous structures, and which aspects evolved because of the function they could assume? In the case of language, it is imperative to know which aspects are innate sui generis and which exist because of the functions that govern it.

As an analogy, consider the description of a home-shop drill press. Many of its functions are attributable to the ways it is employed; e.g., it must be usable at different speeds, have a table to which objects-to-be-drilled can be clamped, and a convenient lever for lowering the drill that can be used by hand. Hence, many of its features are the way they are because of what the machine is for and who will use it. Other aspects, however, have no such direct explanation. For example, the pulley could be made out of many materials; the motor has an arbitrary number of windings; the drill chock a certain number of tightening holes: in fact all the *function* of a chock requires is that it grip the drill bit, *how* it does it is arbitrary and determined by current technology. Thus, a description of an actual drill press is partially independent of the functions it serves; certain aspects may be convincingly guided by those functions, and others will be due to the nature of machines in general or to specific historical accidents in the evolution of shop tools. The description is initially independent of such considerations.

We argue that this description is analogous to the current study of language. The description of what language is must proceed independently of particular functional explanations of why it is that way. At a practical level, we cannot know what to explain until we have isolated and described it. At a theoretical level, many aspects of language may indeed have become autonomous mental structures, whatever their original functional explanation might be. Specifically, we demonstrate in this chapter that certain universal aspects of the relation between main and subordinate clauses are explicable as a function of the way language is used. The structure of our argument is the following. First, we show that the universal restrictions on word order in subordinate clauses are interpretable as a reflection of the different perceptual heuristics that apply to main and subordinate clauses. Then, we demonstrate that the differentiation of the heuristics may be characteristic of other perceptual phenomena. In the course of these investigations, we show that the processing of subordinate clauses is influenced strongly by the semantic relation set up by the subordinating conjunction—a prediction that appears to be true. Thus, we have explained an existing phenomenon and correctly predicted new data, the best of all possible theoretical worlds.

There is a broader moral to our discussion than the descriptive status of main and subordinate clauses alone. In recent linguistic discussions, researchers have argued that the complexity of facts about language requires that semantic structures and syntactic structures be conflated: the so-called *generative semantics models* and their derivatives. The general argument underlying the specific research in this paper is that grammars that combine syntax and semantics strengthen the potential descriptive power of universal grammar and thereby weaken the psychological interest of any particular grammar. This paper serves as a case study in use of psychological theory and experimentation to relieve the grammar of formally powerful descriptive devices; if we can use experimental psychology in general for this purpose, we can maintain the study of syntax as distinct from semantics (and comprehension), thereby increasing the formal interest of universal grammar: The weaker it is descriptively (i.e., the more precise the distinction between what it could and could not describe), the greater the interest in it as the description of linguistic knowledge.

BRIEF HISTORY OF FUNCTIONAL EXPLANATIONS OF LANGUAGE

There have been two major kinds of attempts to explain linguistic structure as the result of speech functions. One we call the *behavioral context approach,* the other, the *interactionist approach.* The behavioral context approach argues that linguistic patterns exist because of general properties of the way language is used and general properties of the mind. The interactionist approach argues that particular mental mechanisms guide and form certain aspects of linguistic structure.

Behavioral Context Theories

Zipf (1949) offered one of the most noted attempts to explain language as a function of the context in which it is used. He proposed that language evolves so as best to serve the speaker and the listener in a communication situation. Both conversational participants set constraints so that conversations can proceed with the *least mental effort.* This proposal explains why frequently-used utterances become short (e.g., "television" becomes "TV"), and it led to the discovery of "Zipf's law": The frequency of a word in ordinary use is logarithmically related to its length. This striking observation was a focus for much concern until it was demonstrated that it would follow from the assumption that word boundaries are *randomly* assigned. That is, the law of least effort applied to the speaker/listener interaction does not constrain possible linguistic structures. Zipf's law turns out to be a demonstration that word length is not itself a function of linguistic structure: Some words are shorter than others for nonstructural reasons.

We are left with Zipf's (1949) plausible claim that one reason that frequent words are shortened is that this reduces the average effort needed by speakers and listeners. This observation is an acceptable hypothesis as far as it goes. However, it is not clear how to test it critically. A theory of least mental effort presupposes an independently motivated theory of mental function that can specify which utterances are relatively complex. The ultimate difficulty with the law of least effort is not that it is wrong. In a sense, it must always be circularly true if we discover which utterances are easy by looking for the ones that are uttered frequently. In Zipf's formulation, the "law" is too unconstrained to predict the particular linguistic structures that occur.

Zipf's (1949) considerations were rooted in the context of language being used by humans who actively apply a principle of least effort: Language is assumed to strike a balance between the functional needs of the listener (for the speaker to be explicit) and the speaker (to utter as little as possible to convey an idea). Martinet (1962) and his followers have offered a more abstract context in which to examine linguistic structure. The nature of each language unit is assessed in the context of the "functional information" that it conveys, relative to other language units. This view often focuses arguments on historical pressures to reduce the ambiguity of specific sounds or words. When a particular phonetic sequence carries too many potential meanings, its "functional load" is out of balance and provides pressure to change the language. This principle can apply to single sounds (e.g., in English the initial phoneme /t/ has a higher frequency and, hence, different functional load from the initial phoneme /dj/; this may result in a historical divergence of initial *t* into two separate phonemes if the functional load becomes too great, or a dropping of initial *dj* from the language if its functional load becomes too small). Martinet attempted to show that such pressures have determined the evolution of languages and, thereby, determine their apparent momentary structure.

The difficulty with this general proposal is that the notion of functional load *does not rest on a theory of speech function*; the only relevant facts are differences in abstracted frequencies in the units of a language and the notion that listeners and speakers pressure the language units so as to be uniformly "informative." Like Zipf's views, this notion may explain some of what speakers do with their language but not the structure of the language itself. As before, the difficulty remains that the functional theory does not constrain the possible language structures in a unique or motivated way.

The final attempt to explain language as a function of a general performance context is current in psychology and linguistics under the rubric of *computational models*. Because this development is just beginning, its inadequacies have not been fully displayed, although gloomy prognosis is clearly indicated. These models attempt to describe regularities in language behavior as a function of computationally adequate representations of language use (e.g., Lakoff & Thompson, 1974; Norman & Rumelhart, 1975;

Winograd, 1972). That is, language behavior is interpreted as arising in the context of a general set of computational mechanisms that can be used to simulate any behavior. In this view the goal of research on language is to provide an empirically adequate simulation of such behaviors as speech perception, production, question answering, and sentence-picture verification. Because such simulations can (in principle) represent data obtained in all language behavior, they can be taken as representing an exhaustive account of why language is the way it is.

This approach surely is a refinement over Zipf's (1949) behavioral principle of least effort and Martinet's (1962) notion of functional load. But it shares the same defect: a lack of a psychological theory of speech mechanisms. As in previous cases, there are no psychologically relevant constraints; rather, we must refer to general computational formalisms. Here too, the formalisms do not motivate any particular representation over many others. Different simulations are available to "account" for any pattern of results.

Therefore, one must be cautious not to condemn a priori all such computational models of speech behavior. It is certainly the case that such investigators might hit upon the correct behavioral model: Formal descriptive devices of general power must surely be able to describe the correct model as well as many incorrect ones. The point here is that isolation of the correct model would be a matter of descriptive luck, not a consequence of specific universal assumption.

One must also be cautious in claiming that, in principle, computational models lack explanatory force. After all, it certainly would be possible to represent a correct psycholinguistic theory in *some* computer program. Conversely, it might turn out to be the case that the elementary formal operations of a simulation program are just those of the universal psychology of grammar. Although possible, this is extremely unlikely in the present computational models, for several reasons. First, the current models are constrained by the characteristics of current computers and available programming languages: There is no reason to believe that the human mind is constrained in similar ways. Second, the computational models are directed at simulating aspects of human language performance, not at representing the mechanisms that carry out the performance. Finally, by focusing on performance, such models eschew formal constraints on language. Because behavioral simulations are doomed to represent only part of the data, they are in danger of representing even that part incorrectly.

Behavioral Context Theories: Summary

These theories share the same virtues and limitations: They purport to describe specific features of language by reference to the behavioral context in which language exists. One could hope that such investigations can clarify the extent to which grammatical properties of language are due to behavioral systems. However, the behavioral context theories are so general that they do not effectively predict specific properties of grammar. In any case, they characteristically do not consider grammar (e.g., Zipf, 1949), or they view synchronic grammar as nonexistent (e.g., Martinet, 1962), or they hold that "grammar" is a "convenient abstraction" (e.g., Lakoff & Thompson, 1964). In any of these views, there are no properties of language that are specifically "grammatical"; therefore, there is nothing to be accounted for by a functionalist explanation.

Interactionist Explanations

The previous models are reductionist in the sense that they seek to describe regularities of language behavior as a function of "lower-level" micro-structures and constraints. An alternative form of explanation is to refer to the mental systems that *use* language rather than elements out of which the language is constructed. These approaches assume that a grammar exists as a psychologically real structure; the quest is to show that certain aspects of grammar are due to the way it interacts with other mental systems. There have been three investigations of this type during the last few decades.

Osgood has claimed for many years that the hierarchical nature of many grammatical structures is due to the way that the mechanism of learning operates in general, rather than to innate grammatical structures. Expanding on Hull's studies of habit family hierarchies, Osgood (1963) argued that laws of learning in animals provide a direct precedent for the acquisition of hierarchies in humans. Consequently, phrase structure in language is not due to some specific linguistic property but is simply an extension of learning mechanisms that govern the acquisition of behavior in mammals. In this sense, phrase-structure hierarchies are not unique to language but are characteristic of the structure that the mechanism of learning imposes on all complex behavior.

As a student of Hull, and as a committed behaviorist, Osgood has been careful to maintain the empiricist position that all psychologically real "abstract" entities are rooted directly in observable behavior and stimuli; i.e., that abstractions are subsets of overtly describable events. Consequently, Osgood has attempted to reject any term (e.g., *space, time*) that cannot be shown to be grounded in observable data. This limits the possible grammars to those that are taxonomic. The specific theory of grammar that he chose to "explain" as a function of mechanisms of learning was essentially a phrase-structure model, a model that is inadequate in a number of ways. Thus, Osgood's enterprise was exactly correct: to explain aspects of grammatical structure as due to general psychological laws governing learning. However, he was working with a limited theory of learning and an incorrect theory of linguistic structure. Thus, the enterprise was correct but limited both by its theory of language and its theory of behavior.

A second specific model has been provided by Yngve (1960), who focused primarily on the influence of speech production on grammatical structure. His main hypothesis is that the needs of the speaker restrict the amount of phrase-structure left-branching. This, in turn, "motivates" the existence of rules that reduce the amount of left-branching in any given surface phrase structure. Transformations are such rules, because many transformations appear to reduce the amount of left-branching in the surface phrase-structure tree. Yngve suggested that (at least part of) the motivation for transformation is to reduce the psychological strain on the speaker. He argued that left-branching places an inordinate processing load on the speaker, for every initial constituent in a left-branching structure is related to what follows on at least two levels (see Fig. 6.1). That is, "a" is simultaneously the initial terminal member of (a,b) and of (AB). Thus, when uttering "a", the speaker must keep both "b" and "c" in mind, until they are uttered. This is not the case with a right-branching structure, as follows in Fig. 6.2. Thus, the needs of the speaker pressure the language to form right-branching structures, which, Yngve (1960) claimed is the overall function of transformations.

Yngve's (1960) proposals are intuitive and attractive, as far as they go. Their limitation is inherent to the fact that he was not clear as to whether they were intended as synchronic or historical explanations and whether transformations were to be viewed as current psychological structures or as psychologically motivated relics. Despite this obscurity, Yngve's proposals remain a landmark in the series of attempts to explain language as a function of specific properties of how it is used. Recently, Bever, Carroll, and Hurtig (1976) have used an extended theory of speech production to account for specific universals, in particular, the role of analogy and its behavioral basis as the source for linguistic neologisms.

TREE DIAGRAMS

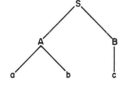

FIG. 6.1. Left-branching structure.

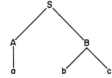

FIG. 6.2. Right-branching structure.

Yngve's (1960) proposals did not explain why left-branching does not *facilitate* sentence perception, although it increases the predictability of the latter parts of a sequence. This paradox directs the discussion to the third attempt to explain structures of language as a function of a mechanism for its use: by reference to speech perception. We discuss examples of this view in greater detail in the next section. The main features that have been explored so far involve the limitations on short-term memory: These limitations pressure listeners to segment incoming sentences into major syntactic units, which in turn, constrains the way in which certain sequences are interpreted and explains grammatical and behavioral restrictions that correspond to those constraints.

Interactionist Explanations: Summary

These models presuppose that grammar is a psychologically real entity. They attempt to explain certain properties of grammar as a function of one of the behavioral systems with which the grammar interacts. Taken together, the three specific interactionist proposals define the major systems of language behavior that could constrain grammatical structure: language learning (Osgood), speech production (Yngve) and speech perception (Bever). As these systems emerge in children, they constrain the kinds of speech neologisms and linguistic restructurings that the children will create. Thus, certain types of linguistic structures never appear, not because they are incompatible with *grammatical* universals, but because they are unusable or unlearnable. The importance of the interactionist program is that it allows us to state which observed facts about languages are due to behavioral systems and which are due to formal grammatical universals. This increase in predictive clarity makes the claims concerning innate linguistic structure more precise and, thereby, makes those claims more testable.

The Penthouse Principle

There are several formal differences between main and subordinate clauses (see Bever, 1974, 1975; Townsend & Bever, 1977a). First, Ross (1973, 1974) has noted that when there is a difference on constraints in the application of a syntactic rule that reorders words, the difference is always such that the rule applies less freely in subordinate clauses than in main clauses (see also Green, 1974; Hooper & Thompson, 1973). Differences in rule application are greater when the clause in question is the initial clause of the sentence:

(1a)　　*That tomorrow we will hire a new person is unlikely.

(1b)　　?It is unlikely that tomorrow we will hire a new person.

(1c)   Tomorrow we will hire a new person.
(2a)   *Though off went the alarm Bill kept sleeping.
(2b)   *Bill kept sleeping though off went the alarm.
(2c)   Off went the alarm.

These constraints on word order in subordinate clauses may exist because of a comprehension strategy to interpret a subordinate clause less deeply in the immediate processing of a sentence. The listener may do so because the main clause is "more important" and, hence, serves as the basis for integration of the two clauses. The use of such a strategy would entail that the subordinate clause be retained relatively longer in superficial form, which may be easier for clauses having canonical word order (e.g., Mehler, 1963; but see Bock, 1977).

Second, a subject pronoun in an initial main or coordinate clause cannot refer to a noun phrase in a following clause, but a subject pronoun in an initial subordinate clause can refer to a noun phrase in the following main clause (Chapin, 1970; Dik, 1968; Gleitman, 1965; Lakoff, 1968):

(3) $\begin{cases}\text{(a)*He} \\ \text{(b) John}\end{cases}$ will buy a car though $\begin{cases}\text{(a) John} \\ \text{(b) he}\end{cases}$ doesn't have enough money.

(4) $\begin{cases}\text{(a)*He} \\ \text{(b) John}\end{cases}$ will buy a car and $\begin{cases}\text{(a) John} \\ \text{(b) he}\end{cases}$ will get married.

Third, deletion of a coreferential verb-phase is permissable in an initial subordinate clause but not in an initial main clause (Lakoff, 1968):

(5a)   If Max does Sally will buy a car.
(5b)   *Sally will if Max buys a car.

The latter two types of syntactic constraints disallow "functionally incomplete" initial main clauses, but do allow functionally incomplete initial subordinate clauses (cf. Tanenhaus & Carroll, 1975). These differences in the form of main and subordinate clauses can also be attributed to the comprehension strategy of interpreting the main clause deeply during immediate processing, for if functionally incomplete initial main clauses did occur, the listener would not be able to obtain a complete propositional representation of the clause until after the following subordinate clause had been heard.

Why are main clauses processed more deeply in the initial phases of listening? We assumed above that the main clause contains more important information. Admittedly, this term is somewhat vague. It could be more useful to say that main clauses convey assertions or new information, and subordinate clauses convey presuppositions or old information.[1] Thus, we might say that listeners are sensitive to assertions and presuppositions in immediate processing and that it is this difference that accounts for the difference in syntactic constraints described above. However, it is clear that the information in a subordinate clause does not always carry a presupposition, as in, for example, *if* clauses and nonfactive complement clauses, and that a subordinate clause can convey assertions, as when a speaker reports an assertion that someone else made. It is noteworthy in this regard that D. W. Green (1975) and Hooper and Thompson (1973) have shown that word-order constraints in subordinate clauses are relaxed when the subordinate clause is emphasized or when it reports an assertion. Whether the difference in immediate processing of main and subordinate clauses is actually a difference in processing assertions (new) and presuppositions (given) is at present an open question, although this distinction does have psychological validity outside the context of clausal differences (see, e.g., Haviland & Clark, 1974; Hornby, 1972, 1974; Just & Clark, 1973).

SPEECH PERCEPTION

Before demonstrating how the interactionist model can explain such facts as those about main/subordinate clauses, it is necessary for us to review what is known about speech perception.

For several decades, psychologists have been investigating the problem of speech perception as defined by Miller in the early 1950s. Miller and his colleagues showed that listening to speech involves simultaneous reference to a number of linguistic levels, including the level of the sentence and meaning. A sample demonstration of this is the fact that a sequence of random words is harder to *hear* than the same words ordered into a sentence. The most striking aspect of this phenomenon is the fact that the words themselves seem to be acoustically clearer as a function of their role in the sentence, which suggests that the sentential structure is providing information that can guide the acoustic analysis of the signal. The question was, How does this kind of interaction in speech perception occur?

That question is with us today, still unanswered. However, it has stimulated a considerable body of research that has advanced our understanding of how to answer it. There are several principles guiding virtually every kind of

---

[1]The concept of presupposition has been given many names and definitions, and its linguistic usefulness has been questioned (see Garner, 1971; Harnish, 1976; Haviland & Clark, 1974; Kartunnen, 1973; Kempson, 1975; Wilson, 1972; and others.) We tentatively adopt the definition that the presupposition of a sentence retains its truth value when the sentence is negated, but that the assertion does not.

research program on speech perception. (a) The amount of information that can be stored in immediate memory in a single form is extremely limited. (b) The structure of language specifies a number of forms in which speech information can be simultaneously represented. These forms are structurally ordered in a hierarchy of levels. (c) The way to study the perception of a representation at a particular linguistic level is to vary the stimulus at another level and observe the changes in reports about the representation.

The linguistic levels applicable to an utterance include (at least) the following (ordered roughly according to a traditional and intuitive notion of increasing "abstractness"):

Psychoacoustics: a physiological specification of the speech waveform as transmitted by the ear.

Phonetics: a segmentation of the signal into discrete categories of speech sounds, using universal features.

Phonemes: a segmentation in terms of the categories of sounds and features used in the particular language.

Syllables: a segmentation of the sequence in terms of canonical acoustic forms that could be uttered in isolation (e.g., consonant-vowel-consonant [CVC], CV, VC).

Morphemes: a segmentation in terms of the (memorized) meaning-bearing units of the language.

Words: the minimal units, that could be uttered in isolation, in universal categories (noun [N], verb [V], etc.)

Phrases: hierarchical groupings of adjacent words into universal categories (noun phrase, verb phrase, . . .).

Clauses: Groupings of adjacent phrases in terms of the canonical external relations they bear to each other (e.g., subject, verb, object).

Sentoids: groupings of the phrases (not necessarily adjacent) in terms of the canonical internal grammatical relations they bear to each other (agent, action, object, modifier).

Semantics: interpretation (usually of a sentoid) in terms of relations to other utterances with which it is synonymous, contradictory, etc.

Speech act: analysis of the utterance in terms of the act it performs (promise, request, inform, etc.).

Intention: an analysis of what the utterance indicates to be the speaker's state of mind (often in universal terms: supportive, critical, assertive, submissive, etc.).

This list is by no means complete, nor is it the case that every school of linguistics claims that all of these levels are properly included within the domain of a formal grammar. The fact remains that we can analyze even the simplest utterance simultaneously in terms of a large number of different kinds of knowledge. For example, (5) can be represented in ways varying from an acoustic specification to a (possible) description of an act by a speaker who intends to indicate that he/she feels unwell.

(5)   Can you take out the garbage tonight dear?

In a logical sense, it might appear that each of the lower levels of representations *must* be present before the more abstract levels can be fully specified; e.g., how can one isolate the phonetic segments without first having fully analyzed the acoustic structure?

The answer is that *some* acoustic analysis must be available, but not necessarily a complete one, only one that renders those specific parameters that are criterial for phonetic analysis. Furthermore, the number of choices at a lower level are restricted by the representations at *higher* levels of analysis. For example, lexical and sentential information renders almost completely predictable the phonetic segment following the fragment in (6).

(6)   Can you take out the garba—

Almost *any* acoustic parameter of /ĵ/ will be sufficient for its perception at that point. Thus, perception at each level can facilitate the perception at the others. The availability of such a large number of interacting forms of simultaneous representation can reduce the limiting effect of immediate memory. In this view, speech perception is at least not magic; but how does it in fact occur?

This also raises an issue about the distinction between "top-down," "active," "bottom-up," and "passive" models of speech perception (cf. Marslen-Wilson, 1975). Obviously, perception must be passive, in part, or else it would be the equivalent of hallucination. As long as research is confined to individual clause perception, this issue can remain latent. Our present concern, however, is explicitly the perception of the relationship between clauses, which requires us to at least outline a theory of the way in which different levels of information can interact during speech perception.

Clausal Processing in Isolation

Much of the work on adult psycholinguistics has examined the processes the listener conducts while hearing a single sentence with minimal contextual cues. This research provides a useful framework for examining complex sentence processing.

The clausal-processing theory (Bever, 1970a; Fodor, Bever, & Garrett, 1974) maintains that the end of the first surface-structure clause in a complex sentence defines the major break in the structural description of the sentence.

The surface-structure clause functions as a unit during comprehension in at least three ways. (a) The listener determines the location of major surface-structure breaks during listening. This segmentation process is shown by experiments demonstrating that detection of a nonspeech noise is poorer when it occurs within a clause than when it occurs between clauses (Abrams & Bever, 1969; Fodor & Bever, 1965; Garrett, 1965; Garrett, Bever, & Fodor, 1966; Holmes, 1970; Holmes & Forster, 1970; see also Berry, 1970; Bever & Hurtig, 1975; Bever, Hurtig, & Handel, 1977; Bever, Lackner, & Kirk, 1969; Chapin, Smith, & Abrahamson, 1972; Dalrymple-Alford, 1976; Forster, 1970; Scholes, 1969; Seitz, 1972; Wingfield & Klein, 1971). (b) The listener applies perceptual mapping rules to assign the words of a clause to their semantic roles. Strategies for this mapping operation may include the use of semantic constraints that suggest the more plausible logical subject (Bever, 1970a; Slobin, 1966; Walker, Gough, & Wall, 1968; but see Forster & Olbrei, 1973; Glucksberg, Trabasso, & Wald, 1973, for instances where semantics is irrelevant), direct mapping of words onto underlying structure on the basis of the order of elements in underlying structure (Baird & Koslick, 1974; Bever & Mehler, 1967; Tanenhaus, 1977; Walker, 1969; Wanner & Maratsos, 1971; but see also Holmes & Watson, 1976; Sheldon, 1974, 1975), and mapping on the basis of syntactic properties of individual words occurring within the clause (Fodor & Garrett, 1967; Hakes & Cairns, 1970; Holmes & Forster, 1972). (c) As the listener determines a set of underlying logical relations within a clause and an interpretation for the clause, the exact word sequence of the clause fades. This process of "erasure" of words from immediate memory is shown by experiments that demonstrate abrupt shifts in verbatim recall and word-recognition performance at clause boundaries (Caplan, 1972; Jarvella, 1970; Jarvella & Herman, 1972; Marslen-Wilson & Tyler, 1976; Perfetti & Goldman, 1976). The process of deciding about an underlying structure for a clause and removal of the exact wording from immediate memory has typically been assumed to occur at the clause boundary (Bever, Garrett, & Hurtig, 1973).

Underlying Clauses as Units

The picture of sentence processing that emerges is that the listeners formulate hypotheses about underlying clauses as they hear the surface manifestations of them and make a decision about the intended underlying structure as they hear the last words of the clause, which suggests that it is the underlying clause, and not the surface clause, that is the unit of perception. Bever et al. (1969; see also Fodor, Fodor, Garrett, & Lackner, 1974) made the claim explicitly that the underlying clause functions as a better segmentation unit than does the surface clause and supported the claim by showing that click mislocations were greater into the position following the main verb when that position coincided with an underlying clause boundary. That is, the click effect was greater following *desired* in (7) than it was following *defied* in (8):

(7)   John desired Bill to resign.
(8)   John defied Bill to resign.

The conclusions of Bever et al. (1969) have been questioned, however, by Chapin et al. (1972), who presented evidence that clicks are subjectively misplaced towards major surface boundaries, in particular, the main subject–predicate break. The issue has not been resolved at present because of the difficulty of devising materials that adequately test the two positions and also because of problems with the click paradigm itself. (For a review of the issues involved in the interpretation of click effects, see Bever, 1973; Bever et al., 1969; Chapin et al., 1972; Carroll & Bever, 1976; Fodor et al., 1974; Freund, 1975; Johnson-Laird, 1974; Olson & Clark, 1976; Reber & Anderson, 1970; Wanner, 1973.)

It seems apparent, nevertheless, that the underlying clauses cannot always be segmentation units, because, for example, in conventional linguistic analyses *tall* in (9) is derived from the underlying clause S_2 in (10):

(9)   The tall lady requested a table for two.
(10)   (The lady (the lady is tall) requested a table for two.)
      S_1 S_2

If underlying clauses are segmentation units, segmentation should occur after *tall* in (9), and clicks should be attracted toward the boundary after *tall* in (9). For the present purposes, we can note that most of the evidence indicates that segmentation certainly occurs at those points where major surface structure breaks and underlying clause boundaries coincide.

With regard to the claim that the listener seeks to determine the underlying structure of sentences during listening, three additional areas of research are relevant and are considered briefly. These areas of research deal with the "cue-deletion" hypothesis, the effects of verb complexity, and the effects of underlying ambiguities.

Cue Deletion

The cue-deletion hypothesis states that a rule that deletes a cue to underlying structure increases complexity in sentence comprehension. Fodor and Garrett (1967) and Hakes and Cairns (1970) showed that sentences containing center-embedded relative clauses are easier to paraphrase when the relative pronouns are present, as in (11) than when the pronouns have been deleted, as in (12).

(11) The cow that the horse that the boy rode chased likes grass.
(12) The cow the horse the boy rode chased likes grass.

These results suggest that comprehension is easier when the underlying structure is more "transparent." Other studies have produced similar results with the phoneme-monitor task (Hakes, 1972; Hakes & Foss, 1970; Hakes & Cairns, 1970).

Verb Complexity

If listeners do entertain several hypotheses about underlying structure as they hear a surface clause, processing should be more difficult when there are more potential underlying structures. Fodor, Garrett, and Bever (1968) showed that paraphrasing a sentence containing a purely transitive verb, such as *slap*, is easier than paraphrasing one containing a verb that may take a simple direct object or a complement, such as *know*. This result was replicated by Hakes (1971), who also found, however, that phoneme-monitoring difficulty did not differ for sentences containing one or the other type of verb. On the other hand, Holmes and Forster (1972) found poorer performance for sentences containing complex verbs using the rapid serial-visual presentation task. For some tasks, at least, verbal complexity is related to processing difficulty, which suggests that listeners do compute several potential underlying structures when a complex verb is present.

Ambiguity

Research on the effect of ambiguities on sentence processing also suggests that listeners formulate hypotheses about underlying structure while hearing a clause and make a decision about the intended meaning at the clause boundary. Studies on ambiguities can be roughly divided into two groups: those finding that ambiguity increases processing difficulty and those finding no effect of ambiguity. Studies in the first group typically require the subjects to respond before they hear the end of the clause, i.e., before closure (Bever et al., 1973; Foss, 1970; Hurtig, 1978; Lackner & Garrett, 1973; MacKay, 1966), whereas those in the second group require the response after closure (Bever et al., 1973; Cairns, 1970; Carey, Mehler, & Bever, 1970; Foss, Bever, & Silver, 1968; Foss & Jenkins, 1973; Hurtig, 1978). The fact that ambiguity generally has its effect only before the hypothesized closure point strongly supports the clausal processing view. (We have not, however, considered here the effects of different types of ambiguity or the role of disambiguating context. See, for example, Bever, Garrett, & Hurtig, 1976; Cairns, 1971, 1973; Cairns & Kamerman, 1975; Conrad, 1974; Foss & Jenkins, 1973; Garcia, 1976; Holmes, Arwas, & Garrett, 1977; Hurtig, 1978; Tyler & Marslen-Wilson, 1977.)

Refinement of Clausal-Processing Theory

Although the clausal-processing theory outlined previously has an appealing simplicity, other considerations indicate that certain aspects of it cannot be correct even for single sentence processing. These considerations include the separability of the three major processes, surface properties of clauses, and underlying and semantic properties of clauses.

Separability of Processes

Marslen-Wilson and his colleagues (Marslen-Wilson, 1973, 1975; Marslen-Wilson & Tyler, 1975, 1976; Marslen-Wilson, Tyler, & Seidenberg, 1978; Tyler & Marslen-Wilson, 1977) have shown that listeners make lexical, syntactic, and semantic decisions about words within a clause while they hear the words of the clause. The view that listeners have available to them several sorts of representations of sentence information while hearing a clause is consistent with recent views of memory maintaining that immediate memory may include simultaneous analysis at several levels (Craik & Jacoby, 1975; Craik & Lockhart, 1972; Lockhart, Craik, & Jacoby, 1976) and that listeners can focus on one or another of these analyses or their products (Green, 1975). Such a view is inconsistent with the hypothesis that listeners passively accumulate lexical information during the early part of a clause, although it is not inconsistent with the hypothesis that a decision between alternative underlying structural hypotheses is made at the end of the clause.

The major evidence for the on-line interactive hypothesis is that rhyme and category-monitor times are a linear function of target position within a simple sentence. This evidence suggests that there is no discontinuity in the availability of lexical and semantic information within the sentence, a direct contradiction of the clausal-processing hypothesis, that the listener passively accumulates lexical information during a clause and determines the underlying structure at the end of the clause (Fodor et al., 1974). More recent work by Marslen-Wilson and his colleagues (Marslen-Wilson et al., 1978), however, has shown a discontinuity in rhyme-monitoring in some cases. The critical cases are the following:

(13a)   Even though they are quite small *cats*, they need a lot of space.
(13b)   Even though they are quite small, *cats* need a lot of space.
(14a)   Although Mary rarely cooks *trout*, when she does it is delicious.
(14b)   Although Mary rarely cooks, *trout* is one thing she prepares well.

The subject monitors the sentence for a word that rhymes with *bats* in sentence (13), or with *doubt* in sentence (14). Rhyme-monitor times were longer when the target occurred after the clause boundary in (14b) than when it occurred before the clause boundary in (14a), but there was no difference between (13a) and (13b). The presence of a clause-boundary effect in (14) suggests that information from the first clause is less accessible just after the clause boundary, so that it is not used as effectively to constrain the next word. The results for sentences like (14), then, appear to suggest a discontinuity in access to clausal information. But the results for sentences like (13) indicate that these initial clauses are relatively poor processing units and that segmentation and closure do not occur at the clause boundary.

Functional Clauses

A variety of surface properties of clauses may modify the processes of segmentation and erasure. One such property is the length of the clause (Carroll & Bever, 1976; Carroll, Tanenhaus, & Bever, 1977; Tanenhaus & Carroll, 1975). For example, it might be expected that segmentation and erasure would not be as compelling after a very short clause as compared to after a longer clause, because a very short clause would not make strong demands on processing capacity. A second surface property that may affect initial processing is the "completeness" of the clause. Tanenhaus and Carroll (1975) proposed a hierarchy of functional clauses that vary in their semantic explicitness, ranging from simple sentences and main clauses to nominalizations and showed that the more complete clauses serve as better segmentation units. For example, using a tone-location paradigm, they showed that tones are mislocated more often around the clause break (indicated by slash below) in sentences with adverbial subordinate clauses, as in (15), than they are around the clause break in sentences with headless nominalizations, as in (16):

(15)   The crook ran for safety/after he stole the young woman's bag.
(16)   Meeting the pretty young girl/was the highlight of Peter's trip.

In their view, this difference is due to the fact that the logical subject of the initial clause in (16) is not explicitly stated in the surface clause, making it difficult to represent as a complete proposition at the end of the clause. A further example of an incomplete clause is one containing a pronoun whose referent is unspecified, as in sentences such as (13).

Causal Relations

The clauses of a sentence may also differ in their underlying syntactic and semantic properties. To the extent that underlying structure and semantic properties are psychologically real in sentence processing, these differences can be expected to modify the processes described by the clausal-processing theory.

Main vs. Subordinate. A major difference in underlying structure between clauses is the main–subordinate distinction: A main clause dominates a subordinate clause in the structural description of a sentence. If part of the process of sentence comprehension involves reconstruction of the surface tree from the top-down and from left-to-right (Kimball, 1973; Kornfeld, 1973; Osgood, 1963; Yngve, 1960), comprehension would be quicker for clauses higher and to the left. Expressed in terms of the clausal processing theory, the dominant structure view would predict the segmentation and erasure processes to be more pronounced at the end of a main clause than at the end of a subordinate clause, all other factors constant.

A second formal difference between main and subordinate clauses that might suggest modification of the clausal-processing theory concerns their surface properties. There are generally greater constraints on the application of syntactic rules that reorder words when they are applied to subordinate clauses than when they are applied to main clauses (Ross, 1973, 1974, but see also Green, 1974; Hooper & Thompson, 1973), but constraints on the application of deletion rules and pronominalization are greater in main clauses than in subordinate clauses (Chapin, 1970; Dik, 1968; Gleitman, 1965; Lakoff, 1968). One interpretation of these formal differences is that they are a result of differences in the initial processing of main and subordinate clauses: word order in subordinate clauses is more like underlying word order because this word order is easier to retain for later integration with the meaning of the main clause (Bever, 1974; 1975),[2] and words may not be deleted as freely in main clauses because such deletions would prohibit a more complete interpretation while hearing the clause (Townsend & Bever, 1977a). According to this interpretation of the surface differences between main and subordinate clauses, the main clause is more readily interpreted.

There is considerable evidence that adults and children have better access to the meaning of a main clause, but better access to the verbatim form of a subordinate clause immediately or shortly after hearing a sentence (Amidon & Carey, 1972; Flores d'Arcais, 1978; Harris, 1976; Shedletsky, 1974; Singer, 1976b; Singer & Rosenberg, 1973; Smith & McMahon, 1970 in two of three experiments; Townsend, 1974; Townsend & Erb, 1975; Townsend, Ottaviano, & Bever, in press; but see Johnson, 1975, Kornfeld, 1973). The differential accessibility to different levels of representation follows directly from the hypothesis that main clauses are encoded more deeply during listening. In addition, several previous studies show that perception,

---

[2]Bock (1977, see also Bock & Brewer, 1974) has recently provided evidence that the use of alternate word order (e.g., use of passive, dative, particle movement) within a sentence depends on given–new relations, that reordering rules have the function of placing given information earlier in the sentence. How these functions of rules that are equally permissible in main and subordinate clauses interact with clause type has not been examined systematically.

comprehension, and long-term retention are easier with sentences with the main–subordinate order (Clark & Clark, 1968, for *before* sentences but not for *after* sentences; Foss & Lynch, 1969; Holmes, 1973; Hoosain, 1974), but immediate verbatim recall is easier with sentences with subordinate–main order (Jarvella & Herman, 1972). Finally, tone mislocations are more frequent at the end of a subordinate clause than at the end of a main clause (Carroll, Tanenhaus, & Bever, 1977, 1978; see also Flores d'Arcais, 1978). All of these differences are consistent with the view that a dominant strategy in sentence comprehension is an initially deeper interpretation of a main clause. Such a strategy would predict that main–subordinate sentences are easier to comprehend because the strategy can be applied to the first clause, which may result in deeper comprehension and, hence, better long-term retention of the main–subordinate sentence. An alternative interpretation of the long-term recall differences appeals to a preference for producing sentences with main–subordinate order, but even this presupposes that such a preference exists without explaining it.

All of these studies, however, tested performance after a complete sentence had been presented, and so they are subject to the criticism that the initial processing of main and subordinate clauses may not differ, but the organization of the two types in memory may. Following, we show that listeners had better access to the semantic form of main clauses than to that of subordinate clauses *while* they were hearing the sentences. This trend, however, varied considerably depending on the semantic role of the clause in the sentence.

Given vs. New.   Clauses differ in terms of level of emphasis. Some clauses convey information that is emphasized, and others convey information which is deemphasized. This property of clauses has been given many different labels. The deemphasized portion of a sentence has been called *given information, old information, presupposition, presumption, background, topic, psychological subject, theme,* etc., whereas the emphasized portion has been called *new information, focus, assertion, foreground, comment, psychological predicate,* and *theme* (Chafe, 1970; Halliday, 1967, 1970; Haviland & Clark, 1974; Hornby, 1972, 1974; Katz, 1972; Kuno, 1972, 1975). Although various authors make distinctions between some of these terms (e.g., Halliday), other authors use a single term in two different ways, and different authors use the same term for different properties. Kartunnen (1973), for example, has defined *presupposition* as information that the speaker assumes the listener already knows, which is the "speaker-based" or the "pragmatic" definition; and Katz (1972), for example, as a condition under which the proposition expressed by a sentence can make a statement. The status of these concepts is, at present, quite unclear, for some authors have questioned the usefulness of the concept of presupposition for semantic theory and whether presupposition is distinct from entailment (Boer & Lycan, 1976; Harnish, 1976; Kempson, 1975; Wilson, 1972; for further discussion of this issue see Garner, 1971; Hornby, 1972; Jackendoff, 1972; Kartunnen, 1971, 1973, 1974a, 1974b; Katz, 1972; Katz & Langendoen, 1976; Keenan, 1971; Lakoff, 1970; Morgan, 1969; Peters, 1975).

In any case, it appears that certain syntactically identifiable parts of sentences convey information that the listener is more likely to assume is true, to assume that the speaker believes to be true, or to assume that the speaker believes the listener already knows. Whether these parts of sentences are labeled *entailments* or *presuppositions* may be largely irrelevant for the purpose of studying sentence comprehension. The following examples contain some clauses whose validity the listener is less likely to question. The deemphasized clause is identified by applying the negation test that has typically been used to identify logical presupposition: The information in the underlined clause normally is taken to be true, even when "It is not the case that..." precedes the sentence, although the nonunderlined clause is normally taken to be false in this case.

(17a) Harry got sick although he ate the apple.

(17b) Harry got sick while he ate the apple.[3]

(17c) Harry got sick when he ate the apple.

(17d) Harry got sick before he ate the apple.

(17e) Harry got sick after he ate the apple.

(17f) John knows that Harry ate the apple.

(17g) John knows the man that ate the apple.

Applying the same test to the sentences with other types of clauses shows that neither clause is relatively deemphasized, as in:

(18a) Harry got sick because he ate the apple.[4]

(18b) Harry got sick if he ate the apple.

(18c) Harry ate the apple and John ate the orange.

(18d) Harry ate the apple but John ate the orange.

What seems to be denied when "It is not the case that..." precedes (18a through 18d) is the semantic relation between the clauses, not just one or the other clause.

---

[3]Stress pattern and clause position sometimes affect judgments of relative deemphasis.

[4]Some readers may feel that this sentence preceded by "It is not the case that..." tends to negate the event in the *because*-clause rather than that of the main clause.

The given–new (or emphasis vs. deemphasis) dimension may modify "normal" clausal processing in such a way that segmentation and erasure occur more readily at the end of an emphasized clause because the listener adopts the strategy of focusing greater attention on emphasized clauses. Another way of saying this is that emphasized clauses may be more deeply encoded while the listener hears them. Because of the correlation of the given–new dimension with the main–subordinate structural distinction, many of the studies in the previous section can be taken as support for the claim that emphasized clauses are more deeply encoded. Both Hornby (1974) and Just and Clark (1973) have suggested that presupposed information is less likely to be questioned than is asserted or implied information (see also Clark & Haviland, 1974, 1977; Harris, 1974a, 1974b; Haviland & Clark, 1974; Hupet & Le Bouedec, 1977; Offir, 1973; Singer, 1976b.)

Causal Relations. A complex sentence does not simply express a series of unrelated propositions. Rather, the propositions are related to one another in a variety of ways. To the extent that listeners are concerned with obtaining these higher order semantic relations between propositions while they hear sentences, it might be expected that clausal processing is modified (as Bever [1970a, 1970b] suggested might be the case for complex sentences). Many studies of memory show that higher order integration of propositions occurs beyond the simple grasp of propositional content (e.g., Bransford & Franks, 1971). This section describes some relations between clauses and how these relations might affect on-line processing. We deal here only marginally with implications and inferences of the sort studied by Bransford, Barclay, and Franks (1972), Just and Clark (1973), Clark and Lucy (1975), Brewer (1977), Johnson, Bransford, and Solomon (1973), Thorndyke (1976), and others, for at least some of these types of inferences are apparently derived after sentence closure (see Jenkins, 1972; Singer, 1976a).

Structurally, there are five major complex sentence types in English (Burt, 1971; Stockwell, Schachter, & Partee, 1973) containing coordinate clauses, complement clauses, adverbial clauses, relative clauses, and clefted clauses. The range of semantic relations between clauses, however, is much larger than this. Complement clauses bear a subject or object relation to the verb in the main clause, relative and clefted clauses generally have a modification, attribution, or identification relation to some element in the main clause, but coordinate and adverbial clauses express a variety of logical, causal, and temporal relations. A major concern of our research program is to examine the influence of the latter set of semantic relations on the on-line processing of clauses and sentences.

The nature of the semantic relation between clauses depends, to some extent, on the individual meanings of the clauses being related (see, e.g., Fillenbaum, 1971, 1974b, 1975, 1976; Johnson-Laird, 1969; Lakoff, 1971; Staal, 1968). Nevertheless, there is some regularity in the kinds of relations

TABLE 6.1
Some Semantic Relations Cued by Conjunctions

1. Cause: because, if, for, since, (after), (when)

	EFFECT	CAUSE
a.	the glass melted	because Floyd heated it
b.	the glass will melt	if Floyd heats it
c.	the glass melted	since Floyd heated it
d.	the glass melted	for Floyd heated it
(e.	the glass melted	after Floyd heated it)
(f.	the glass melted	when Floyd heated it)

2. + Prior: since, after (when), (and)

	– Prior	+ Prior
a.	Harry ate 12 apples	since Mary came home
b.	Harry ate 12 apples	after Mary came home
(c.	Harry filled the tank	when Mary ran out of gas)
(d.	Harry died	and he ate 12 apples)

3. Simultaneous: when, while, and

a.	Harry got sick	when he was eating the apple
b.	Harry got sick	while he was eating the apple
c.	Harry ate some cheese	and he ate an apple

4. – Prior: before, until, and, (so), (while)

	+ Prior	– Prior
a.	Harry was sick	before he ate the apple
b.	Harry was sick	until he ate the apple
c.	Harry threw the stick	and the dog retrieved it
(d.	Harry was sick	so he took some medicine)
(e.	Harry ate 12 apples	while Mary cleaned up the mess)

5. Effect: so, (before), (and), (while)

	CAUSE	EFFECT
a.	Floyd heated the glass	so it melted
(b.	Floyd heated the glass	before it melted)
(c.	Floyd heated the glass	and it melted)
(d.	Floyd ate 12 apples	while Mary cleaned up the mess)

6. Adversative: while, although, but, (and)

	CAUSE	UNEXPECTED EFFECT
a.	While Harry was sick	he ate an apple
b.	Although Harry was sick	he ate an apple
c.	Harry was sick	but he ate an apple
(d.	Harry was sick	and he ate an apple)

cued by different conjunctions. A partial list of the possible relations between the clause following the conjunction with respect to the other clause of the sentence includes the following: cause, + prior in time, simultaneous in time, – prior in time, effect, and adversative. Table 6.1 lists some examples of these relations. Sentences that seem to imply a given relation are parenthesized. The table ignores certain distinctions, for example, the specific cause–generic cause distinction and the distinction between evidentiary and causal relations (see Fillenbaum, 1975, 1976; Miller & Johnson-Laird, 1976), but these distinctions are not critical for the present purpose. (These semantic relations and various refinements are further discussed in Ballard, Conrad, and Longacre, 1971; Dakin, 1970; Dik, 1968; Gleitman, 1965; Heinamaki, 1972; Rips and Marcus, 1977; Simon and Rescher, 1966; Taplin and Staudenmeyer, 1973; and Wason and Johnson-Laird, 1972, as well as in the references cited previously in this paragraph.)

The relations illustrated in Table 6.1 can be summarized as follows. A subordinate clause (or coordinate clause in the case of *for*; cf. Dik, 1968) may express an event that causes the event described in the adjoined clause. The subordinate or coordinate clause may occur either *prior* in time to the adjoined clause, or late in time (– prior) than the adjoined clause. A clause may describe an event that is the *effect* of the event in the adjoined clause. Finally, the clauses of a sentence may be related in an *adverse* way: One clause may state an event that is unexpected based on the event in the adjoined clause. In Dakin's (1970) analysis, the causative and adversative relations are opposites. Both statements make two assertions, but the assertions in causative statements are compatible, whereas those in adversative statements are incompatible. For example, Sentence 1a of Table 6.1 asserts "the glass melted" and "the fact that Floyd heated the glass demanded that the glass melt," but Sentence 6b asserts "Harry ate an apple" and "the fact that Harry was sick demanded that Harry *not* eat an apple."

Several conjunctions take on two or more semantic relations. The relations that the various conjunctions listed in Table 6.1 can have are summarized in Table 6.2. What is striking about this table is the continuity of the meanings of the conjunctions. For example, a given conjunction may not express both a causal relation and a simultaneous relation unless it also expresses the + prior relation. The continuous meanings of the conjunctions suggest a single underlying dimension. An event that occurs prior in time to another event may be the cause of the later event, but not vice versa. Similarly an event that occurs later in time than another may be the effect of the earlier event, and not vice versa. In other words, causes are associated with earlier events and effects and adverse effects are generally associated with later events. Such an association is neither surprising nor newly discovered (see e.g., Miller & Johnson-Laird, 1976).

Another notable aspect of Tables 6.1 and 6.2 is that causes and prior events tend to occur in initial clause positions. For example, *so*-, *but*-, and *and*-clauses only occur in final position, and these may express some type of effect. Table 6.1 shows an *and*- clause expressing a prior event (Sentence 2d), but this sentence sounds strange. (This sentence may be interpreted as stating that the initial clause is an unexpected effect of the final clause; Fillenbaum [1971] has shown that such sentences are extremely hard to recall.) The only exception among coordinate clauses to the generalization of "cause and first event first, effect and second event second" is the *for*- clause.

TABLE 6.2
Semantic Relations Between Clauses

Conjunction	Cause	+ Prior	Simultaneous	− Prior	Effect	Unexpected Effect	Presuppositions in Conjoined Classes
Because	x						?
If	x						No[a]
For	x						?
Since	x	x					Yes
After	(x)	x					Yes
When	(x)	(x)					Yes
And			x	(x)	(x)	(x)	No
While			x	(x)	(x)	x	Yes
Until				x			Yes
Before				x	(x)		Yes
So				(x)	x		?
Although						x	Yes
But						x	No

[a] The "presuppositions" of an *if*-sentence interact with the mood of the verb in the *if*-clause (Morgan, 1969). *If*-sentences differ from other types of sentences in this respect.

Perceptual Implications.   What role do these semantic relations play in clausal processing, sentence integration, and recall? We can speculate that a semantic processing strategy exists that emphasizes early interpretation of underlying causes or potential causes. That is, a clause marked by a conjunction that signals a causal connection to another clause is more deeply processed during listening and more basic in the listener's postsentence organization. Table 6.2 ranks the various conjunctions according to their "causal efficiency": *because-* and *if-* clauses are the most causally efficient and *although-* and *but-* clauses are least causally efficient. We might further speculate that this strategy applies to clauses that could be causes by implication or inference. Thus, although *after* does not literally relate clauses in a causal way, the listener may, depending on the meanings of the clauses themselves, infer that the event in the *after-* clause is the cause of the event in the main clause, but not that the main clause event causes the *after-* clause event. The later inference is ruled out for the epistemological reasons noted earlier: An event cannot cause something to happen before the causal event occurs. The semantic processing strategy proposed here encompasses the order of mention strategy described previously (e.g., Bever, 1970b; Clark & Clark, 1968, 1977).

Most of the previous work dealing with conjunctions like those in Table 6.2 have been concerned with postsentence organization and memory, or with production, rather than on-line processing. To our knowledge, however, no work has examined the role of the more general causal-temporal dimension in either processing or memory. For example, Clark & Clark (1968; see also Smith & McMahon, 1970) showed that *before* and *after* sentences that present the events in their actual order of occurrence are easier to remember. Similarly, children perform better on acting out *before* and *after* sentences that present the events in their actual order of occurrence (Barrie-Blackley, 1973; Clark, 1971; Johnson, 1975), and such sentences appear relatively early in the child's speech (Clark, 1970; see also Osgood, 1971). The question "what happened first?" following a *before* or *after* sentence is answered more quickly than the question "what happened second?" (Smith & McMahon, 1970; see also Townsend & Ravelo, 1978). Other studies have considered the mental representation and use of *if* (Carpenter, 1973; Fillenbaum, 1975, 1976), *unless* (Clark & Lucy, 1975), and *or* (Fillenbaum, 1974a, 1974b; Springston & Clark, 1973), the inherent negativity of *but* with respect to *and* (Fillenbaum, 1971; Hoosain, 1973; Osgood & Richards, 1973), and the relative difficulty of *although* with respect to *because* and the preference for ordering events as "cause, effect" (Katz & Brent, 1968). Many of these studies provide data supporting the use of the causal-temporal dimension in organization and memory, but none has examined on-line processing of clauses nor have any examined a wide range of conjunctions.

EXPERIMENTS 1 AND 2—MEANING VS.
LITERAL REPRESENTATION

Both intuition and the studies cited suggest that main clauses are more immediately interpreted than subordinate clauses. Our first goal was to confirm this with a set of tasks that tap on-line perceptual processing, rather than short-term memory. In our tasks, the subjects hear only a fragment of a sentence, ending before either the last word of the initial clause or the last word of the final clause. The interrupted clause in either position is either main or subordinate (introduced by *if, since, when, while,* or *though*). After hearing the fragment, the subjects determine whether a visually-presented verb–object phrase is similar in meaning to what they have heard (Experiment 1) or they determine whether a probe-word had occurred in the fragment (Experiment 2). Reaction times (RTs) in the former task provide an index of the listeners' on-line accessibility to the meaning of the clause they had been hearing. In the latter task, we assume that the subjects have maintained the interrupted clause in more superficial form to the extent that their RTs are longer for target-words that had occurred later in the clause. This assumption is based on the view that a superficial representation is searched word-by-word from left-to-right, but that such a search process is impossible in an abstract representation, which, in the extreme case, does not contain information about word order, or even specific words. These tasks differ from those of many previous studies primarily in that they involve a test before the complete clause has been heard. Thus, any differences we find can be attributed to processing that occurs while the clause is being heard. The tasks provide a means of determining whether listeners process clauses with different properties in different ways. The properties under consideration here are the structural, presuppositional, and semantic roles of various clauses.

The conjunctions in this study display a variety of meanings on a causal–temporal dimension. The possible meanings of the conjunctions we used with respect to the causal–temporal dimension are excerpted from Table 6.1 in Table 6.3. Occupying one end of this dimension is the *if*-clause, which often states a cause for the event in the main clause, as shown in, "If Harry

TABLE 6.3
Semantic Relations Between Subordinate and Main Clauses

Conjunction	Cause	+ Prior	Simultaneous	– Prior	Adversative
If	X				
Since	X	X			
When	X	X	X		
While			X	X	X
Though					X

takes the arsenic, he'll die." At the other end of the causal–temporal dimension is a *though*-clause, which expresses an adversative relation, i.e., a denial of an expected cause–effect relation. A *though*-clause states an event that ordinarily would lead one to expect a certain effect, but it indicates that the expected effect did not occur (Dakin, 1970). For example, in "Though Harry took the arsenic, he didn't die," the speaker believes that taking arsenic ordinarily causes death.

Many conjunctions have meanings that fall between the causal and adversative extremes, and some conjunctions have multiple meanings. For example, in "Since Harry wrecked his car, he's been taking the bus," the *since*-clause may indicate an event that causes the main clause event, or it may simply indicate an event that occurs prior in time to the main clause event. *When*-clauses may have three meanings. A *when*-clause may indicate, by inference, a cause, as in "When Harry heated the glass, it melted," an event prior in time, as in "When Harry wrecked the car, Bill fixed it," or an event occurring simultaneously with the main clause event, as in "When Harry was raking the leaves, Bill was fixing the car." A *while*-clause also expresses several meanings; among these are a simultaneous event, as in "While Harry was raking the leaves, Bill was fixing the car," an event occurring later in time than the main clause event, as in "Harry threw the stick, while the dog retrieved it," or it may express an adversative relation, as in "While Harry did take the arsenic, he didn't die."

The particular meaning that is dominant depends on several factors, such as the meanings of the individual clauses, stress, and the order of the clauses. The meanings of the conjunctions, however, are orderly in that there are no discontinuities on the causal–temporal dimension, as shown in Table 6.1. Furthermore, causal and temporal meanings are associated: Those conjunctions that indicate prior events may, by inference, indicate causal events.

The question we address in these two experiments is whether listeners are sensitive to these differences in causal–temporal meanings during immediate processing. It is well known that postsentence performance is superior for temporal sentences that present the events in their actual order of occurrence and that questions about first events are answered more quickly than are questions about second events (Clark & Clark, 1968; Fillenbaum, 1971; Smith & McMahon, 1970; see also Katz & Brent, 1968). These results suggest that temporal sentences are organized in memory in terms of the temporal order of events. Experiment 1 was designed to determine whether listeners conduct this type of organization as they hear the sentence and whether the organization of temporally related events is part of a more general strategy of organizing causally related events. We refer to the prediction that causes and first events are more directly interpreted as the *causal–temporal hypothesis*.

Other types of relations between clauses may be the basis for modifying on-line processing. Structurally, main clauses dominate subordinate clauses in the surface-structure tree, and main clauses are more complete in that they can stand alone as a sentence. To the extent that listeners reconstruct the surface tree from the top-down (Kimball, 1973) or to the extent that more complete clauses serve as better processing units (Tanenhaus & Carroll, 1975), main clauses should be interpreted more directly than should subordinate clauses. We refer to this prediction as the *structural hypothesis*.

Main and subordinate clauses also differ in the types of information they convey. Main clauses often express an assertion, but subordinate clauses often express a presupposition (Keenan, 1971; but see also Boer & Lycan, 1976). For example, denying a sentence with a *though-*, *while-*, *when-* or *since*-clause appears to deny only the main clause and not the subordinate; hence, these subordinate clauses are said to convey a presupposition. The presuppositions of *if*-sentences, however, are more complex, and it is difficult to associate any simple presupposition with the *if*-clause (cf. Morgan, 1969). The presupposition–assertion distinction, at least for the clear cases, may serve as the listeners' basis for the organization of the two clauses of a sentence. That is, the assertion may be interpreted more directly, because it contains the "new" information, while the presupposition may simply be used to indicate where the new information is to be integrated into memory once it has been understood (cf. Haviland & Clark, 1974; Hornby, 1974). We refer to the prediction that presuppositions are less directly interpreted as they are being heard as the *presuppositional hypothesis*.

In Experiment 1, we examined the listeners' on-line accessibility to the semantic form of a clause. Subjects listened to two-clause sentences but were interrupted either before the last word of the first clause or the last word of the second clause. At the interruption point, they read and classified a verb–object phrase as being consistent or inconsistent with the meaning of what they had just heard. The interrupted clause varied in its causal–temporal, structural, and presuppositional role in the sentence. The causal–temporal hypothesis predicts that classification time is relatively faster for subordinate clauses that are more explicitly causal. The structural hypothesis predicts that classification time is faster for main clauses than for subordinate clauses. The presuppositional hypothesis predicts that classification time is faster for assertions than for presuppositions, more specifically, that times are faster for main clauses in *though-*, *while-*, *when-*, and *since*-sentences.

Experiment 1

Method

Procedure.   The subjects were tested individually, one subject for each of 16 lists. They were instructed to listen to a sentence fragment. Upon hearing a tone, a verb–object phrase in lowercase elite letters was projected onto a ground-glass screen. The subjects were instructed to read the phrase and decide whether it was similar in meaning to any part of the fragment. They were instructed to say, as quickly as possible, yes if they felt the phrase was consistent in meaning with the fragment, or no if they felt it was not consistent in meaning. The sentence fragments were presented with a Sony TC280 tape deck through headphones into the subject's right ear. The tone started a Hunter msec timer and simultaneously activated a shutter that allowed the phrase to be projected onto a screen. The subject's vocal response stopped the timer.

Sentence Fragments. Sentences for positive and negative trials were constructed with similar constraints. The actual form of each positive sentence varied across lists, but the form of negative sentences was constant across lists. There were 16 positive sentences (4 with *while* and 3 each with *if, since, when,* and *though*); and 12 negative sentences (3 with *when,* and 2 each with *if, since, while,* and *though*). Excluding the conjunction, one clause (the probed clause) contained 10 or 11 monosyllabic words, and the other contained 12 or 13 syllables. The probed clause contained a word that appeared in one of two positions without changing meaning (see Experiment 2). Across lists, each positive sentence appeared in eight forms, depending on the position of the movable word, the position of the probed clause, and the structural role of the probed clause. A complete set of eight versions of one sentence fragment is shown in (19a through d):

(19a) Initial Main: Good jobs are (now) quite scarce (now) in most large...

(19b) Initial Subordinate: Though good jobs are (now) quite scarce (now) in most large...

(19c) Final Main: Though there is little danger of a major depression, good jobs are (now) quite scarce (now) in most large...

(19d) Final Subordinate: There is little danger of a major depression though good jobs are (now) quite scarce (now) in most large...

The positive sentences were arranged into a single random order, as were the combinations of the independent variables (position of movable word, clause structure, clause position) within each block of eight sentences. Eight lists were generated by partially counterbalancing within blocks the combinations of variables across the single random order of positive sentences. Eight additional lists were generated by using the complement of clause position and clause structure for each positive sentence in the first list and again partially counterbalancing.

The 12 negative sentences were randomly placed among the 16 positive sentences and occupied the same relative position in each list. Half of the negative sentences had an initial main clause. Six practice sentences (3 with an initial main clause) were placed at the beginning of each list; half of these constituted positive trials.

A male speaker recorded the intact sentences with normal intonation. Fragments were produced by cutting out the last word of the initial clause and the remainder of the sentence for trials in which the initial clause was interrupted and by cutting out the last word of the final clause for trials in which the final clause was interrupted. A 50 msec, 500 Hz tone and blank tape were spliced onto the end of each fragment.

Phrases.   Phrases that were consistent with the meaning of one of the clauses of the sentences used for positive trials were obtained by administering a questionnaire to students in a psycholinguistics class at Montclair State College. The students were shown the 19 intact positive sentences as they appeared in one of the lists. In each sentence the probed clause was underlined. For some sentences the underlined clause was initial main; for some initial subordinate, etc. The students were asked to generate a 2- to 4-word verb–object phrase that was related to or consistent with the meaning of the underlined clause. They were instructed to produce phrases that did not repeat any of the content words in the sentence. From the pool of verb–object phrases obtained in this manner, the phrase generated most frequently for each sentence was selected for use in the experiment; for Sentence 1 through 4, for example, the phrase was *finding employment.* For negative trials verb–object phrases judged to be totally unrelated to the meaning of either clause were selected.

Subjects.   Sixteen undergraduate volunteers (8 males) at Montclair State College served in the experiment. All were right-handed native speakers of English.

Results

The error rate for trials in which the phrase was consistent with one of the clauses was 4.3%, whereas the error rate for trials in which the phrase was not consistent with either of the clauses was 7.8%. The percentage of errors and mean response times for correct responses in different clause types and positions are shown in Table 6.4. To simplify the statistical analysis of RT data, the RTs for positive trials on which errors were made were replaced by the mean RT for correct responses in the appropriate Clause Type × Clause Position × lexical content cell. For negative trials, error RTs were replaced by the means for correct responses in the appropriate Clause Type × Clause Position cell.

Positive Trials.   The initial statistical analysis of RTs for positive trials used analysis of variance with clause type, clause position, word order, block,

TABLE 6.4
Response Time (Msec) for Judgments of Consistency of Meaning
(Percentage of Errors in Parenthesis)

Type of Trial	Initial Clause		Final Clause	
	Main	Subordinate	Main	Subordinate
Positive trials[a]	1224(1.6)	1282(4.7)	1214(3.1)	1359(7.8)
Negative trial[b]	1224(8.3)	1306(12.5)	1302(6.3)	1295(4.2)
Overall	1224	1292	1252	1332

[a]The average standard error was 64.0 msec, ranging from 49.8 to 77.8.
[b]The average standard error was 68.1 msec, ranging from 56.7 to 81.9.

and lists as variables, the first four treated as within-subject variables. Because each subject was tested on a given lexical content with different combinations of independent variables, Lexical Contents × Treatments were nested within subjects. The analysis of variance, therefore, treats both subjects and lexical contents by treatments as random effects, and the statistical tests are generalizable to the larger population of subjects and materials (see Clark, 1973).

The means in Table 6.4 suggest that response times on positive trials were shorter when main clauses were interrupted. This conclusion was supported by the analysis of variance, $F(1, 16) = 4.58$, $p < .05$. The Clause Type × Clause Position interaction fell short of significance, $F(1, 16) = 3.14$, $p < .10$, and no other interactions approached significance, although there was a large effect of block, $F(1, 16) = 13.9$, $p < .01$, with the mean response time of Block 2 (1169 msec) much faster than that of Block 1 (1302 msec). Although there was a large practice effect, the major variable affecting overall response times was the type of interrupted clause: Subjects had much better access to the meaning of main clauses.

The relative effects of subordination did vary with conjunctions, however. Table 6.5 shows the difference in mean response time between subordinate and main clauses (mean RT for subordinate clauses minus mean RT for main clauses) for fragments using different conjunctions. The effect of subordination was opposite in initial *if-* and *though*-fragments: Response times were 136 msec faster on subordinate clauses in *if*-fragments, and 340 msec slower on subordinate clauses in *though*-fragments. Performance on initial clause fragments introduced by *since, when,* and *while* fell between these extremes, and followed the causal–temporal dimension illustrated in Table 6.1. On final clause fragments, there was also wide variation depending on the conjunction introducing the final clause; but in this case, response times were 295 msec slower on *if*-clauses than on the corresponding main clauses and response times for *though*-clauses and main clauses were about equal (a 21-msec difference).

TABLE 6.5

Effects of Clause Type on Judgments of Consistency of Meaning in Fragments with Various Conjunctions: (Response Time for Subordinate) – (Response Time for Main)

Conjunction	Initial Clause	Final Clause
If	−136	+295
Since	+9	+143
When	+19	+117
While	+68	+169
Though	+340	+21

Note. The critical difference ($p < .05$, df = 216) in (S-M) between conjunctions is 192. In initial clausees, relative response time for *though*-clauses differs from all other subordinate clauses, and *while* differs from *if.*

Negative Trials. For negative trials, Table 6.4 shows that response times were faster for main clauses when the initial clause was interrupted. Response times for negative trials were examined by analysis of variance with clause type, clause position, and blocks as variables. This analysis showed a trend toward an interaction between clause type and clause position, $F(1, 151) = 3.48$, $p < .10$. There were no other significant main effects or interactions in the analysis by subjects or by lexical contents. A comparison of main and subordinate response times for initial clauses indicated a marginal effect, $F(1, 121) = 2.92$, $p < .10$. A similar comparison for final clauses showed no difference between response times to main and subordinate clauses, $F' < 1$. Subjects were faster at deciding that a phrase was inconsistent with the meaning of an initial main clause than they were at doing so for initial subordinate clauses. However, they did not differ in the speed with which they decided that a phrase was inconsistent with the meaning of the sentence when final main or subordinate clauses were interrupted.

Discussion

Overall, on-line accessibility to meaning was faster in main clauses than in subordinate clauses. Although this result favors the structural hypothesis, the considerable variation in the size and even direction of subordinate–main differences across fragments using different conjunctions casts doubt on both the structural and presuppositional hypotheses as explanations for the data. The size of the subordinate–main differences in initial clause position, did, however, follow the causal–temporal dimension described in the introduction. The data suggest that initial clauses that are more explicitly marked as stating a cause for the event in the following clause are more directly interpreted and that initial *though*-clauses, which explicitly state that the event in the initial clause is *not* a cause for the following event, are less directly interpreted. An initial *though*-clause may be held in superficial form so that it can be interpreted in light of the meaning of the following main clause. The relative effects of *if*- and *though*-clauses in final clause position, however, were reversed. We return to this reversal in performance after considering whether the causal–temporal dimension is also related to the listener's accessibility to the literal form of a clause.

Experiment 2

In the second experiment, we presented subjects the same lists used in Experiment 1, but after each fragment we presented a probe word rather than a verb–object phrase. The subject's task was to say as quickly as possible whether or not the probe word was mentioned in the fragment. The critical variable was whether the target word occurred relatively early or relatively late in the interrupted clause. A notable aspect of our design was that the same word served as the target both early and late; such a design controls the effects of semantic and grammatical characteristics of the target words.

The central problem was whether the listeners search their representation of a clause differently depending on whether the representation is in relatively semantic form vs. relatively literal form. We suggest that semantic representations are searched by an essentially parallel process that is relatively insensitive to literal form, i.e., word order. That such a process operates on propositional representations is indirectly suggested, although not demanded by, several previous studies (Green, 1975; Kennedy & Wilkes, 1969, 1970). On the other hand, we suggest that literal representations are searched by a word-by-word, left-to-right scan that is sensitive to word order. Evidence for item-by-item scans has been found in previous studies that require retention of order information (Kennedy & Wilkes, 1969, 1970; Sternberg, 1967; see also Green, 1975).

This analysis suggests that target-position effects should be greater for those clauses that produced rather slow accessibility to meaning in Experiment 1. That is, target words occurring late in a subordinate clause should take longer to classify than target words occurring early in a subordinate clause, but there should be little difference between early and late targets in main clauses. Furthermore, the difference in response times between late targets and early targets in initial subordinate clauses, relative to main clauses, should decrease as the subordinate clause states more explicitly that it is a cause for the event in the main clause. This prediction follows from the results of Experiment 1, that the relative advantage of main clauses over subordinate clauses in accessibility to meaning decreased with the explicitness with which a subordinate clause states a causal relation.

Method

Procedure. The subjects were tested individually, one subject for each list. All subjects heard the sentences and probe words in the right ear. A tone signalled the end of the sentence fragment and activated a msec timer that was stopped by the subject's vocal response. Subjects were instructed to respond as quickly as possible to the word occurring after the tone, saying yes if the probe had occurred in the fragment and no if it had not. In order to induce comprehension of the fragments, subjects were instructed to generate a sentence that paraphrased the sentence fragment after they had responded to the probe. This requirement was effective in that all paraphrases were judged to be accurate.

Materials. The tape recordings used in Experiment 1 were modified for a word-probe experiment. For each fragment a monosyllabic target word was selected. For positive trials, which consisted of the same set of fragments used in positive trials in Experiment 1, the target was the movable word. Target words classified as early in the clause occurred 6 to 8 words from the end of the clause, with a mean of 7, whereas late targets occurred 3 to 5 words from the end, with a mean of 4. The early and late positions of a particular target word were separated by 2 to 5 words. The grammatical class of the target was distributed evenly across nouns, verbs, adverbs, and particles in positive trials as well as in negative and practice trials. The target word for negative trials did not occur in the fragments, nor was it similar in sound or meaning to any word occurring in the fragment. For half of the practice fragments, a word appearing in the fragment was selected as a target.

Tape recordings of the 34 probe words were made, and copies of these were spliced onto the tape containing the fragments. The probe was placed so that it began 333 msec after the end of the tone.

Subjects. Sixteen undergraduates (8 males) at Montclair State College were paid $2 for their participation. They were right-handed native speakers of English.

Results

The error rate was 0.4% when the target was in the sentence fragment and 3.1% when it was not. To simplify the statistical analysis, RTs for errors were replaced in a fashion similar to that used in Experiment 1.

Positive Trials. For positive trials overall, there was no RT difference between main and subordinate clauses, $F(1, 16) = 1.93$, $p > .05$, nor was

TABLE 6.6
Mean Response Time (Msec) for Recognition of Early and Late Target Words
(Percentage of Errors in Parenthesis)

| | Initial Clause | | | | Final Clause | | | |
| | Main | | Subordinate | | Main | | Subordinate | |
Type of Trial	Early	Late	Early	Late	Early	Late	Early	Late
Positive[a]	1098	1125	1085	1181	1117	1207	1157	1057
Mean positive	1112(0)		1134(1.6)		1162(0)		1107(0)	
Negative[b]	1157(4.2)		1280(2.1)		1352(2.1)		1342(4.2)	

[a]The average standard error was 53.3 msec, ranging from 33.8 to 65.3.
[b]The average standard error was 46.6 msec, ranging from 34.9 to 64.6.

there a difference between initial and final clauses, $F(1, 16) < 1$, as suggested by Table 6.6. That is, the average accessibility of the actual words did not differ by clause type or by clause position. The overall mean RTs by clause type, clause position, and target position, however, did vary. Target position had its strongest effects in subordinate clauses and its weakest effect in initial main clauses. Target position had opposite effects in initial and final subordinate clauses and larger effects in final main clauses than in initial main clauses. These conclusions were supported by a Clause Type × Clause Position × Target Position interaction, $F(1, 16) = 9.44$, $p < .01$. These variables together did not interact with list or block. Response times were slower for late targets than for early targets in initial subordinate clauses, $F(1, 16) = 6.35$, $p < .05$, and in final main clauses, $F(1, 16) = 5.58$, $p < .05$, but not in initial main clauses, $F(1, 16) < 1$, or in final subordinate clauses, which showed a large recency effect, $F(1, 16) = 6.89$, $p < .05$. The location of the target word had large effects on response time in all clauses except initial main clauses, where the position effects were negligible.

Table 6.7 presents the target position effects for fragments using different conjunctions. The table shows the effects of target position in subordinate clauses relative to its effect in the corresponding main clauses. That is, for each fragment we calculated the difference (mean RT late [L] minus mean RT early [E]) for the subordinate clause (S) and subtracted from that the difference (mean RT late minus mean RT early) for the main clause (M). The resulting score provides some control for differences between fragments in within-clause lexical items and structural complexity. The $(L–E)_S – (L–E)_M$ score is highly positive when response times are slower to late targets than to early targets in a subordinate clause but faster to late targets than to early targets in the corresonding main clause; a highly positive $(L–E)_S – (L–E)_M$ score indicates a "primacy" effect in subordinate clauses relative to main clauses.

TABLE 6.7

Effects of Clause Type on Word Recognition in
Sentences with Various Conjunctions: $(\bar{R}\bar{T}_L - \bar{R}\bar{T}_E)_S -$
$(\bar{R}\bar{T}_L - \bar{R}\bar{T}_E)_M{}^a$

Conjunction	Initial Clause[b]	Final Clause[b]
If	−159	+86
Since	−106	−329
When	−67	−125
While	+77	−34
Though	+399	−267

[a](Response times for late targets in subordinate clauses minus response times for early targets in subordinate clauses) − (response times for late targets in main clauses minus response times for early targets in main clauses).

[b]The critical difference ($p < .05$, $df = 216$) in derived scores between conjunctions is 143. In initial clauses relative target position effects in *though* and *while* differ from all other subordinate clauses.

The relative target-position effects varied widely depending on the conjunction in the fragment. In initial-clause position the relative primacy effects were strongest in *though*-clauses, and they became weaker as the subordinate clause became more causal. The primacy effect was actually weaker in initial *if*-clauses as compared to the corresponding main clauses. The relative primacy effects for other initial subordinate clauses fell between these extremes and followed the causal-temporal dimension of Table 6.3. In final-clause position the ordering of relative primacy effects was roughly opposite that in initial clause position: Subjects were most sensitive to the literal form of final *if*-clauses and (nearly) least sensitive to the literal form of final *though*-clauses.

Negative Trials. Those clause types that showed large overall effects of target position also showed a large difference between response times to positive and negative trials (see Table 6.6). The differences between positive and negative trials were assessed in a between-subject and between-lexical content analysis of variance with trial type, clause type, clause position, block, and list as variables. The type of trial interacted with the type and position of the interrupted clause, $F(1, 383) = 4.17$, $p < .05$. The slower response times for negative trials than for positive trials in initial subordinate clauses, $t(383) = 2.83$, $p < .01$, final subordinate clauses, $t(383) = 4.56$, $p < .01$, and final main clauses, $t(383) = 3.69$, $p < .01$, suggest that subjects examined every word of these fragments before responding only in the case of negative trials. On the other hand, the fact that response times for negative and positive trials did not differ in initial main clauses, $t(383) = 0.87$, $p > .10$, suggests either that subjects did not compare the probe with every word individually or that they did do so for both positive and negative trials. These comparisons of positive and negative trials are only suggestive however, because different sets of words were used in the two types of trials.

Discussion of Experiments 1 and 2

Overall, the target-position effects were much smaller in initial main clauses than in other types of clauses. This suggests that the literal form of an initial main clause is more quickly lost in immediate processing, supporting a structural or presuppositional hypothesis. However, the target-position effects were strongly influenced by the particular conjunction contained in the fragment. Among initial clauses, primacy effects in subordinate clauses were weakest in *if*-clauses, but these effects became progressively stronge in *since*-, *while*-, and *though*-clauses. These results indicate that on-line accessibility to superficial form in initial clauses increases in the order: *if*-clause, *since*-clause, *when*-clause, *while*-clause, and *though*-clause.

The results by conjunctions were quite similar in the two experiments. In initial clauses, the size of the subordinate–main differences were ordered identically in the two experiments; relative accessibility to meaning was poorest in *though*-clauses, but relative sensitivity to literal form was best in *though*-clauses. The results for final clauses were roughly opposite those for initial clauses in both experiments. The parallel results for conjunctions within clause positions strongly suggest that the underlying factor affecting performance is not the structural or presuppositional properties of the clauses but, instead, is the meanings of the conjunctions and the kinds of organizing strategies they elicit.

The two experiments also gave similar results across the 16 sentences from which the positive fragments were derived. For each of the 16 sentences, we calculated a total (subordinate–main) score as described previously, but now summed over initial and final clauses. These scores were highly correlated, $rs = +.57$, $t(14) = 2.59$, $p < .05$. This correlation indicates that those sentences that produced slower synonymy judgment times in subordinate clauses relative to main clauses also produced greater sensitivity to superficial form in subordinate clauses relative to main clauses. It follows that listeners' accessibility to semantic form is related to their word-recognition processes.

The first two experiments converge on the following conclusion: Listeners are sensitive to the possible semantic relations between clauses that are cued by conjunctions while they hear a two-clause sentence and modify their comprehension processes in terms of these semantic relations. Although the overall performance differences between main and subordinate clauses support structural and presuppositional hypotheses about clausal-processing differences, the variations in performance within different subordinate clauses do not support either of these hypotheses. Instead, the performance differences followed the causal–temporal dimension described in Table 6.3.

Initial subordinate clauses that more explicitly signalled a causal relation to the following clause were more deeply processed. Of the clauses studied here, the *if*-clause is most explicit in indicating a causal relation: It describes a generic set of conditions that either cause the main-clause event or constitute evidence for it. *Since* has a more specific causal sense than *if,* but it may also have the temporal sense of *after. When* may have, by inference, the causal or temporal meanings of *since,* but it more directly indicates an event occurring at the same time as the event in the main clause. *While* may have the temporal cooccurrence meaning of *when,* but it may also have an adversative reading of "contrary to the fact that the event in this clause would ordinarily cause, or lead one to expect, a certain event, some event other than the expected event has occurred." This contrary-to-expectation relation is strongest in *though,* where it is an explicit denial of the relation indicated by *if.*

Our results for initial clauses indicate that, relative to main clauses, more explicitly causal subordinate clauses are processed more deeply during listening, and less explicitly causal subordinate clauses are held in more literal form during listening. For example, listeners had easy access to the meaning of initial *if*-clauses. An initial *if*-clause is processed deeply as it is heard because it is important for evaluating the event in the final clause: an *if*-clause describes the conditions in which the event in the following clause will occur. On the other hand, initial *though*-clauses, indicating a denial of a causal relation, were held in very superficial form. This may be the case because, at the time listeners hear the initial *though*-clause, they cannot know which cause–effect relation the speaker is denying. For example, on hearing "Though Harry ate the apple...," listeners know that the speaker believes that "Harry ate an apple" would normally be a cause for some event or evidence for some belief, but listeners do not know what cause–effect or evidence–belief relationship the speaker has in mind. On hearing the main clause "... he got sick," the listeners now know that the speaker has denied the cause–effect relation of "eating an apple causes one to be healthy." But on hearing the main clause "... he wanted a steak," the listeners know that the speaker has denied the evidence–belief relation of "X ate an apple is evidence that X wanted to eat an apple." Listeners may hold initial *though*-clauses in relatively superficial form until they have interpreted the main clause so that they can determine which cause-expected effect relation has not been fulfilled.

The results for final clauses showed a strong reversal from the pattern found in initial clauses. In final-clause position, the meanings of *though*-clauses and of the corresponding main clauses were about equally accessible, but the meanings of *if*-clauses were much less accessible than the meanings of the corresponding main clauses. A similar shift occurred in relative sensitivity to literal form in word recognition. These shifts must be taken seriously, for the relative ordering of differences by conjunctions in final clause position were highly correlated ($rs = 0.7$) across the two experiments. The results, therefore, suggest that listeners do not process on-line for meaning in a final *if*-clause as much as they do for other clauses. This may be the case because the *if*-clause sets up a generic condition on the previously heard main clause. As such, the listener must interpret the final *if*-clause "as a whole" and perhaps reorganize the events of the sentence into their proper cause–effect relationship. Listeners may readily interpret a final *though*-clause because they can determine on-line the specific cause–effect relation that is being denied and because they already know the "unexpected effect" stated in the previous clause.

EXPERIMENT 3—WORD ORDER IN MAIN AND SUBORDINATE CLAUSES

Experiments 1 and 2 "converge" on the claim that the dominant representation of main clauses is immediately more meaning-based and less literal than that of subordinate clauses. We also showed that the size and direction of the difference in accessibility to meaning between main and subordinate clauses followed the causal-efficiency dimension. We interpreted these results to show that a subordinate clause that is less causally related to the main clause is less deeply interpreted in immediate processing. Thus, the previously observed differences in processing main and subordinate clauses may be due to the different causal and temporal roles that these clause types have in a sentence, rather than being due to structural or presuppositional differences.

In Experiment 3 we were concerned with the question of how listeners organize a two-clause sentence. We examined the effects of word order within main and subordinate clauses on listeners' accessibility to the words of a sentence immediately after they hear it. We used the identical word-probe task (see Caplan, 1972; Green, 1975; Kennedy & Wilkes, 1969; and others). We varied word order within clauses by using active vs. passive form, which occur without constraint in both types of clauses (e.g., Burt, 1971). The hypotheses that an initial main clause is interpreted more directly while hearing the sentence and that it serves as the basis for integration of the meanings of the two clauses, predict that word order within an initial main clause should have a smaller effect on word-recognition times than it has when varied within an initial subordiante clause. This prediction is based on the notion that once a clause or single sentence has been encoded, performance is generally less affected by the original form of the sentence (Anderson, 1974; Gough, 1966, but see Glucksberg, Trabasso, & Wald, 1973). We also examined word-order effects in sentences with different clausal relations: *since, when, while,* and *though.*

Method

Procedure

Subjects were tested individually. On each trial, they heard a sentence through the right channel of a set of headphones. Immediately after the sentence, they heard a 50 msec, 500 Hz blip in the left channel; and 333 msec later, a probe word in the right ear. Their instructions were to say as quickly as possible whether or not the probe word had occurred in the sentence. Response times were recorded by a Hunter msec timer. After responding to the probe, they turned over an index card and answered aloud a question that was printed on the card. Subjects received a total of 41 trials (25 positive).

Materials

Each subject heard 41 two-clause sentences. Twenty-four of these were used for critical trials in the current study; the remainder were filler sentences modified from a previous study (Townsend & Bever, 1977b). Of the 24 new sentences, 8 were used for negative trials for all subjects; these sentences had six to seven syllables in each clause in active voice (4 contained a passive clause) and contained either *since, when, while,* or *though* (two of each). The remaining 16 new sentences were used for positive trials. In half of these positive trials, the clauses contained six to seven syllables in active form, and in half they contained eight to nine syllables in active form, excluding subordinating conjunctions. Within each clause length, there were 2 sentences containing each of the conjunctions *since, when, while,* and *though.* Aside from these constraints on length and conjunction, the form of the critical positive sentences varied across eight groups of subjects. Each sentence appeared in different form for the eight groups, depending on whether the probed clause was active or passive, main or subordinate, initial or final. The eight forms of one sentence are as follows:

Initial, Main Active: The cat killed the parrot, when Sam left the house for a week.
Initial, Main Passive: The parrot was killed by the cat, when Sam left the house for a week.
Initial, Subordinate Active: When the cat killed the parrot, Sam left the house for a week.
Initial, Subordinate Passive: When the parrot was killed by the cat, Sam left the house for a week.
Final, Main Active: When Sam left the house for a week, the cat killed the parrot.
Final, Main Passive: When Sam left the house for a week, the parrot was killed by the cat.

Final, Subordinate Active: Sam left the house for a week, when the cat killed the parrot.

Final, Subordinate Passive: Sam left the house for a week, when the parrot was killed by the cat.

In all critical sentences, the target word was a verb (*killed* in the above sentences) having the same form in active and passive voice. The filler sentences were used to reduce bias toward verb targets.

Eight lists were prepared such that each list contained 2 critical positive sentences of each form (voice, clause type, clause positive). Counterbalancing ensured that each form appeared in all trial positions across the eight lists.

Subjects

Thirty-two right-handed undergraduate native English speakers at Columbia University and Montclair State College participated. Four subjects were assigned to each of the eight lists.

Results

The primary data were recognition times for trials on which correct responses were obtained for both recognition and the comprehension question following the word probe. On the 512 test trials, there were 16 word-recognition errors (3.1%) and 12 comprehension errors (2.3%). The distribution of word-recognition errors is shown in Table 6.8 and that of comprehension errors is shown in Fig. 6.3. For the statistical analysis, recognition times on error trials were replaced by the mean recognition times from the appropriate List × Length × Clause Type × Clause Position × Word-Order cell. The last four of these were within-subject variables in the statistical analysis; the last three were within-lexical content variables. Because different subjects received different combinations of clause type, clause position, and word order on a given lexical content, the statistical tests treat Subjects and Lexical Contents × Clause Type × Clause Position × Word Order as random effects (Clark, 1973). All statistical tests used a rejection level of .05.

TABLE 6.8
Percentage of Word-Recognition Errors in Experiment 3

	First Clause		Second Clause	
	Main	Subordinate	Main	Subordinate
Active	4.7	6.3	0	0
Passive	1.6	7.8	1.6	3.1

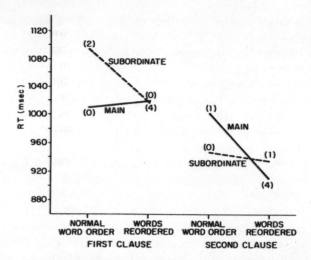

FIG. 6.3.   Recognition times to different clauses with normal and reordered word orders. Number of errors in parentheses.·

The major recognition-time results are shown in Fig. 6.3. This figure suggests (a) that recognition times were faster for words in final clauses than for words in initial clauses, (b) that recognition times were faster when the words of the probed clause were not in the normal active word order, (c) that word order had a larger effect on recognition times in initial subordinate clauses than in initial main clauses, and (d) that word order had a larger effect in final main clauses than in final subordinate clauses. Each of these impressions was confirmed by the statistical analysis. Recognition times were faster in final clauses than in initial clauses (means = 949 msec and 1035 msec, respectively, $F[1, 24] = 38.3$), faster in reordered clauses than in clauses with normal word order (means = 970 msec and 1014 msec, respectively, $F[1, 24] = 7.09$), and the clause type, clause position, and word-order variables interacted, $F(1, 24) = 8.23$. Further analysis of the three-way interaction showed that word order interacted with clause type in initial clause position, $F(1, 24) = 5.23$, and in final clause position, $F(1, 24) = 4.10$.

The overall results supported the prediction that word order within initial clauses has a relatively greater effect on accessibility to subordinate-clause information. For final clauses, however, the opposite result was obtained. One interpretation of the latter result is that a final subordinate clause can be interpreted directly because the basis for integrating the clauses has already been established. Processing a final main clause, however, is more difficult because the literal form of the preceding subordinate clause must be retained if it is to be interpreted in terms of the meaning of the main clause. Two additional results support the view that main–subordinate sentences are processed more directly than are subordinate–main sentences. First, of the 12 comprehension errors, 11 occurred on sentences with the subordinate–main order. Second, on negative trials response times were faster on main–subordinate sentences than subordinate–main sentences (means = 972 msec and 1038 msec, respectively, $F[1, 223] = 5.81$). On positive trials with comparable sentence length, however, mean response times were identical for main–subordinate and subordinate–main sentences (both means = 975 msec). These results suggest that the word-recognition process in subordinate–main sentences is a slower word-by-word scan based on a more literal representation of the sentence.

The main recognition times in active and passive clauses for positive trials, however, did vary in sentences with different conjunctions. The effects of word order in sentences containing *since, when, while,* or *though* are shown in Table 6.9. Because the various conjunctions were associated with different lexical items that may contribute to differences in absolute recognition times, and for the sake of brevity, this table simply presents the difference between mean recognition times in active and passive clauses (recognition time active minus recognition passive). The column headed "Sub–Main" presents the effect of word order in subordinate clauses relative to the effect in main clauses. It is clear that none of the sentence types shows the overall pattern of Fig. 6.3, because, for example, no sentence type showed a negligible effect of word order in initial main and faster times for passive than for active in initial subordinate. Thus, listeners do not organize sentences with different conjunctions in identical ways. In fact, for initial clauses there appear to be two groups of sentences: Three sentence types showed positive effects of passive in subordinate relative to main (i.e., passive is relatively faster in *since, when,* and *while* clauses), and one (*though*) showed a negative effect of passive in subordinate relative to main. For final clauses, there are also two groups: One sentence type (*since*) showed a positive or negligible effect of passive in subordinate relative to main, and three showed negative effects of passive in subordinate relative to main (*when, while,* and *though*). Thus, passive had positive effects in *since*-clauses in both positions, reversed its

TABLE 6.9
Effects of Word Order by Conjunction

	First Clause			Second Clause			
Conjunction	Main	Subordinate	Sub[a]–Main	Main	Subordinate	Sub[a]–Main	Total
Since	+91	+268	+177	+70	+95	+25	+202
When	−70	+10	+80	+138	+53	−85	−5
While	−69	+155	+224	+41	−95	−136	+88
Though	−33	−154	−121	+77	+7	−70	−257

Note. Entries are mean-active mean-passive scores.
[a]Subordinate.

TABLE 6.10
Word-Recognition Times (Msec) in Clauses of Different
Lengths

	First Clause		Second Clause	
Length	Main	Subordinate	Main	Subordinate
Long	1352	1406	1336	1276
Short	1342	1374	1243	1274

effects in *when-* and *while-*clauses in initial and final position, and had negative effects in *though-*clauses in both positions.

We also found that the length of the probed clause had an effect on recognition times. Recognition times were faster on short clauses than on long clauses (means = 975 msec and 1010 msec, respectively, $F[1, 24] = 9.44$). Table 6.10 shows the mean recognition times by length, clause type, and clause position. This interaction fell short of significance, $F(1, 24) = 2.7$, $p = .11$, but it is interesting to note that the direction of the differences between long and short clauses is parallel to that found with active and passive word order. In initial position, length had a larger effect in subordinate clauses than in main clauses; but in final position, length had a larger effect in main clauses. These near differences might suggest that the number of words in the original clause has little effect on recognition times when the clause is represented internally in abstract form.

Discussion

Over all sentence types in Experiment 3, word order had greater effects on accessibility to literal form in initial subordinate clauses than in initial main clauses. This pattern was reversed in final-clause position. Overall, there was evidence that sentences with initial subordinate clauses are represented in more literal form, confirming previous results obtained by Jarvella and Herman (1972) and Townsend, Ottaviano, and Bever (in press).

The word-order effects in main and subordinate clauses, however, varied considerably depending on the subordinating conjunction in the sentence. Word recognition in initial *though-*clauses was relatively longer in passive form than in active form, but in initial *since-, when-* and *while-*clauses, it was shorter in passive form than in active form. These patterns shifted when final clauses were tested, the *since-*clauses being the only ones that showed any tendency at all for passive form to produce relatively faster word-recognition times. It is apparent that sentences with different subordinating conjunctions are not processed and organized in identical ways.

The interpretation of these differences depends on the interpretation of the relation between active vs. passive form and word-recognition times. Overall, recognition times were faster for passive than for active clauses (see also Cairns & Blank, 1974). Yet, active sentences are usually found to be more quickly interpreted (e.g., Slobin, 1966), suggesting, in general, that the faster recognition times for passive clauses are due to rather shallow comprehension of the passive form. But in *though*-clauses, we found that recognition times were slower for passive than for active clauses. Such an outcome suggests that "normal" processing has not occurred. What kind of process would produce slower times for passive than for active? One possibility is that passives are more deeply comprehended than actives, but this seems unlikely, because it has almost never been obtained in previous work (but cf. Olson & Filby, 1972). A second possibility is that the literal form of the passive is simply harder to retrieve than is the literal form of the active, not because the passive has been represented more abstractly, but instead, because neither active nor passive has been actively attended to. The passive literal form is harder to retrieve because it does not correspond to the canonical underlying form. The latter explanation could account for the relatively longer recognition times for passive in initial *though*-clauses. In this interpretation, initial *though*-clauses are not analyzed for meaning, whereas all other initial clauses in this study do tend to be processed directly. This interpretation is consistent with the previous finding that relative accessibility to meaning is poorer for initial *though*-clauses than for other types of clauses (Townsend & Bever, 1977b).

As shown in Table 6.1, the semantic relations between the clauses of *since-*, *when-*, *while-*, and *though*-sentences differ. A *since*-clause may either state a cause or evidence for the main-clause event, or it may state an event prior in time to the main clause. *When* and *while* clauses also have a temporal sense, but *while,* like *though,* may have what has been called an adversative sense (Dik, 1968; Grimes, 1975). The adversative relation is opposite that of a causative relation. Both the causative and adversative relations involve two statements that are compatible in positive/negative value in the case of the causative, but incompatible in positive/negative value in the case of the adversative (Dakin, 1970). For example, "Since the lights were red John stopped" makes the statements "I state the fact that John stopped" and "I state that the fact that the lights were red demanded that John stop," both of which are positive in value. On the other hand, "Though John was late he stopped" makes the statements "I state the fact that John stopped" and "I state the fact that John was late demanded that he not stop," which are positive and negative in value, respectively. Thus, a *though*-clause is used to deny that an expected causal relation has been fulfilled, but a *since*-clause in its causative meaning asserts that the expected causal relation did occur. In their temporal senses, *when* and *while* differ from *though* in that they do not deny an expected event.

Our results suggest that listeners are aware of these differences in relations between clauses. Listeners hold an initial *though*-clause in relatively unanalyzed form while they hear it because they know that an opposite of the expected consequence of the subordinate event is going to be asserted in the following main clause. As a result, the effects of word order on word recognition differ in initial *though*-clauses as compared to other types of clauses.

Experiments 1, 2, and 3—General Discussion

These experiments suggest that subordinate clauses are held in relatively uninterpreted form, just insofar as their full interpretation depends on information within the main clause. Thus, in all three experiments *if*-clauses (or *since*-clauses in Experiment 3) tended to act most like independent clauses and *though*-clauses least like them. These results follow from the fact that the semantic material within an *if*-clause can be processed largely independently of the main clause; in *though*-clauses the adversative relation requires processing of the main-clause information in relation to the subordinate clause, in order to understand the respect in which the relation is "unexpected."

EXPERIMENT 4

Experiments 1 through 3 suggest that listeners can switch their mode of access of a clause on the basis of very quick decisions. However, some of this flexibility might be unique to language; indeed, it might be restricted to main vs. subordinate clauses because of the linguistic universals that differentiate them (i.e., the penthouse principle might cause the differentiation of the strategies rather than the reverse). To test for this possibility, we conducted an experiment using a standard nonlinguistic serial-search task to see if we could manipulate the kind of search strategies in ways that reflect the different approaches to main vs. subordinate clauses.

In the well-known Sternberg (1966, 1969) paradigm, a subject is presented with a memory set consisting of one to six digits, letters, or words. After seeing the memory set, the subject is shown a probe item from the same class as the items in the set and is instructed to indicate as quickly as possible whether the probe was contained in the set. Sternberg's results show that RT increases with the size of the memory set and that the slope of this RT function is similar for positive and negative trials. In addition, Sternberg reported that RT does not vary with the serial position of the target item within the memory set. The fact that RT increases with set size rules out a parallel scan, in which the subject simultaneously compares all memory-set items with the probe. The lack of serial-position effects, the similar slopes for positive and negative trials, and the equality of RTs to positive and negative trials all rule out a self-terminating scan, in which the subject compares the memory-set items with the probe one at a time and responds as soon as a match occurs. Instead, the data indicate that subjects conduct a serial exhaustive scan in which items are compared one at a time with the probe, but a response is not made until all items have been compared with the probe.

Although the exhaustive model has received broad support, several investigators have found reason to doubt the generality of the exhaustive model (see Sternberg [1975] for a review). One source of doubt is the frequent presence of serial-position effects in memory-scanning experiments. Recency effects have been found in several experiments (Baddeley & Ecob, 1973; Burrows & Okada, 1971; Clifton & Birenbaum, 1970; Corballis, 1967; Corballis, Kirby, & Miller, 1972; Corballis & Miller, 1973; Juola & Atkinson, 1971; Kennedy & Hamilton, 1969; Morin, DeRosa, & Stultz, 1967), although some of these effects could be explained in terms of a sensory store that retains the final items of the memory set. Even more problematical for the exhaustive model are those studies finding that RTs increase with the serial position of the target (Burrows & Okada, 1971; Corballis et al., 1972; Kennedy & Hamilton, 1969; Klatzky & Atkinson, 1970; Klatzky, Juola, & Atkinson, 1971; Sternberg, 1967). These increasing serial-position curves suggest a self-terminating scan and certainly cannot be explained in terms of a sensory store. In addition, two of these studies (Corballis et al., 1972; Klatzky & Atkinson, 1970) obtained greater slopes for negative trials than for positive trials, which also suggests the self-terminating scan.

A second source of doubt about the generality of the exhaustive model is evidence showing that scanning can be limited to a part of the memory set. Several studies (Clifton & Gutschera, 1971; Darley, Klatzky, & Atkinson, 1972; Naus, 1974; Naus, Glucksberg, & Ornstein, 1972; Williams, 1971) indicate that one portion of the memory set can be omitted from a subject's exhaustive scan. Other studies suggest that subjects use a self-terminating scan within sets of letters partitioned by a pause (Wilkes & Kennedy, 1970b) or within different constituents of a sentence (Kennedy & Wilkes, 1969; Shedletsky, 1974; Wilkes & Kennedy, 1969, 1970a). The evidence for the self-terminating scan in these studies is that RTs increase with the serial position of the target.

Experiment 4 is concerned with the question of whether a subject can use different scanning strategies, indicated by different serial-position effects and by different relations between RT for positive and negative trials, on different portions of a memory set. The studies reviewed in this section provide substantial evidence that the exhaustive and self-terminating scans can be used in different experimental situations and that scanning can be directed toward only one part of the memory set. However, only one study (Shedletsky, 1974), using a sentence as the memory set and testing only two serial positions within different portions of the set, found different serial-position effects in different portions of the memory set.

We examined the hypothesis that different scanning strategies can be used on different portions of a memory set by providing subjects with incentives for responding accurately to only one portion of the set. Although previous researchers (Banks, cited in Atkinson, Hermann, & Wescourt, 1974; Swanson & Briggs, 1969) have found that subjects do not use substantially different scanning strategies when given incentives for accuracy vs. speed on different memory sets, these studies have not shown the effect of incentives on scanning strategy within a memory set.

Method

Subjects

Eight undergraduates (four males, four females) at Columbia University were paid $3.50 to $4.50 for their participation. All subjects were right-handed.

Materials

Ninety 10-item sequences were generated. Half the sequences contained five letters followed by five digits, and half contained five digits followed by five letters. The letters were drawn from the first 10 letters of the alphabet; the digits were drawn from the 10 digits 0, 1, 2, ... 8, 9. Letters and digits were randomly assigned to sequences with the following constraints. Each letter and digit appeared approximately the same number of times within each block of 15 sequences. A single letter or digit never occurred in three consecutive sequences. Within a sequence there was never a run of three items in their normal order; e.g., a portion of a sequence never had "abc..." or "123..." Each item occurred approximately the same number of times in each position of the sequences.

Probe items were randomly assigned to the sequences such that each letter or digit appeared as a probe in approximately equal numbers in the 90 sequences and that, in each block of 15 sequences, there were approximately the same number of digit and letter probes. Each block contained 10 positive trials and 5 negative trials.

The sequences were tape recorded at a rate of 3½ items per second. A 50 msec, 500 Hz tone, a 333 msec blank tape, and the probe item were spliced onto the end of each sequence.

Procedure

The subjects were tested individually. They were randomly assigned to a letter-paid vs. digits-paid group such that each group contained two males. Subjects in the letters-paid group were told that they would be paid 10¢ for every letter probe they correctly recognized and nothing for correct recognition of digit probes. These instructions were reversed for the digits-paid group. Although the subjects were asked to respond to probes as quickly as possible, they were also encouraged to be as accurate as possible for both types of probes. Subjects were given feedback at the end of each block of 15 sequences and were paid the appropriate amount at the end of the experiment.

Sequences were presented to the subjects through binaural headphones. The tone signalled the end of a sequence and started a Hunter msec timer. The subjects stopped the timer by pressing one of two buttons, one on their right indicating a positive response and one on their left indicating a negative response.

Results

The hit rate for paid targets was 88.8%, whereas the false-alarm rate for paid targets was 10.0%. The unbiased measure of memory strength for paid targets was $d' = 2.51$ (Elliot, 1964). The hit rate for unpaid targets was somewhat lower, 77.9%, whereas the false-alarm rate for unpaid targets was higher, 15.8%. As a result, the estimate of memory strength for unpaid targets, $d' = 1.76$, was somewhat lower than for paid targets. The values of these measures of memory strength, however, suggest that subjects were not responding randomly for either paid or unpaid targets. The fact that the subjects' d's did not differ for paid vs. unpaid probes, $F(1, 7) = 1.01, p > .05$ (significance levels of .05 are used throughout this experiment), suggests that the average memory strengths of paid and unpaid items were not substantially different. The proposition of "new" responses was slightly higher to unpaid probes (.43) than to paid probes (.38), although this difference was not reliable, $F(1, 7) = 2.55$. Assuming that the proportion of new responses provides an estimate of the criterion the subject uses for deciding whether an item was in the set or not, subjects adopted a slightly higher criterion for unpaid probes.

The percentage of misses for each target position in paid and unpaid sequences is shown in the lower portion of Fig. 6.4. Misses were relatively stable in paid sequences, but, with the exception of the final target position, misses increased with target position in unpaid sequences. Analysis of variance on the frequency of misses indicated that subjects had more misses in unpaid sequences, $F(1, 7) = 6.76$, and that payoff condition interacted with target position, $F(4, 28) = 4.2$.

The statistical analysis of RTs includes only data for correct responses. The mean RTs for positive trials as a function of target position and payoff condition are shown in the upper portion of Fig. 6.4. Except for the relatively slow RT in the second target position, the RT curve for unpaid targets is flat. In contrast, the RT curve for paid targets increases with target position,

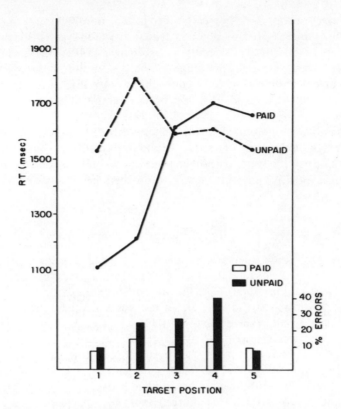

FIG. 6.4.   Recognition times by target position for paid and unpaid portions of the memory set.

except for a slight recency effect. The effect of target position in paid and unpaid sequences was assessed by analysis of variance with payoff condition, sequence position (target in the first five items vs. second five items), target position within a sequence, and blocks as variables. This analysis revealed a significant Payoff Condition × Target Position interaction, $F(4, 28) = 6.73$. These variables did not interact with either sequence position or blocks. Comparison of Target Positions 1 and 2 showed that RTs for paid items were faster than RTs for unpaid items, $F(1, 42) = 95.03$, whereas a comparison of Target Positions 4 and 5 showed that RTs for unpaid items were faster, $F(1, 42) = 4.49$.

Best-fitting straight lines were established by the least-squares method. This line for paid targets was RT = 1034 + 113.4(target position), whereas the line for unpaid targets was RT = 1630 − 13.6(target position). The relation between target position and RT was significant for paid targets, $F(1, 238) = 28.95$. The corresponding relation for unpaid targets was nonsignificant, $F(1, 238) < 1$. These results show that RT increases with target position in the paid portion but is unrelated to target position in unpaid sequences.

Reaction times for positive and negative trials were compared using payoff condition, trial type (positive vs. negative), sequence position, and block position as variables. This analysis showed a significant Payoff Condition × Trial Type interaction, $F(1, 694) = 6.11$, indicating different effects of trial type on RT to paid and unpaid probes. For paid probes mean RTs were longer for negative trials than for positive trials (1564 and 1388 msec respectively, $t[694] = 3.25$). For unpaid probes mean RTs were actually shorter for negative trials (1591 msec) than for positive trials (1591 and 1615 msec respectively), although this difference was nonsignificant, $t(694) = 0.44$. Thus, negative trials took longer than did positive trials for paid probes but did not differ from positive trials for unpaid probes.

Discussion

The RT results for serial position of target and for positive vs. negative trials suggest that different incentives for correct response can induce subjects to apply different memory-scanning strategies to different parts of a list. When subjects are motivated to respond accurately to a certain type of memory-set items they scan that portion of the stimulus in a self-terminating fashion. The evidence for this type of scan is the presence of serial-position effects in RT and differences in RT to positive and negative trials. When subjects are not provided monetary incentive for accurate responses to a certain category, their scan of items in that category is either parallel or serial exhaustive. The evidence for this second type of scan is the absence of serial position effects in RT and the absence of a difference in RT to positive and negative trials. In order to distinguish the serial exhaustive and parallel scans in the unpaid sequences, a minimal requirement would be to determine whether RT increased linearly or remained constant as the size of the unpaid set increased (but cf. Murdock, 1971; Theios, Smith, Haviland, Traupmann, & Moy, 1973; Townsend, 1971).

The overall error rate was much higher than that of previous scanning studies. This was true for both paid and unpaid sequences. The higher error rate can be partially attributed to the rapid rate of presentation of the memory-set items and to the relatively large size of the memory set. The high estimates of memory strength, however, suggest that there was substantial encoding of both types of sequences. Given the high degree of encoding and the fact that RT data were obtained only for correct responses, the RT data indicate that scanning procedures differ for the two types of sequences.

The implication of this study for scanning strategies requires further research, in particular to lower the error rate and to vary the set size. But the results do suggest that listeners can change their processing strategies outside of a linguistic context. The potential generalization that cuts across both the language and nonlanguage tasks is the following:

(20)   *"Easy" material is encoded (and/or accessed) in parallel. "Hard" material is encoded (and/or accessed) serially.*

In a recently completed master's thesis, Jeffra (1978) provided further general support for (20). In this study subjects listened to a sequence of 10 letters. Either the first 5 letters or the last 5 letters spelled a word; the remaining 5 letters were random. After hearing the 10 letters, subjects heard a probe letter, determined whether the probe was present in the sequence, and reported the word that had been spelled out within the 10-letter sequence. The serial-position effects for targets within word vs. nonword sequences differed radically: RTs increased sharply with ordinal position of the target in nonwords but decreased slightly with ordinal position of the target in words. These results suggest different modes of accessing words and nonwords for a specific letter.

These studies suggest that main clauses are treated like "unpaid" material (or "words") because their perceptual analysis is overdetermined; it is subordinate clauses that cause a processing load insofar as they must be held in memory for a time without a complete semantic analysis. We do not want to claim that listeners represent digit and letter information, or letters spelling words and nonwords, in just the same way as they represent sentence information. The results do, however, suggest that a recognition curve that increases with ordinal position of the target is due to a focus of attention on the literal form of memorized information. The results also suggest that different parts of both sentential and nonsentential stimuli can be represented in immediate memory in different ways and that the different types of representation lead to different memory search procedures.

THE NONLINGUISTIC BASIS OF
THE PENTHOUSE PRINCIPLE

The general allocation of different parts of a stimulus to different memory systems may be the basis for two types of differences in the form of main and subordinate clauses. In particular, the fact that subordinate-clause information is retained relatively longer in unanalyzed form in immediate memory provides an explanation for the observation that word order is more constrained in presupposed subordinate clauses than in asserted main clauses. We noted that other linguists (e.g., Hooper & Thompson, 1973) have pointed out that there is a difference in acceptability of sentences in which movement rules have applied in a subordinate clause, depending on whether the subordinate clause contains a reported assertion or a presupposition. For example, the rule that moves the verb phrase to the front of the first subordinate clause in "Sally plans for Gary to marry her and he vows that marry her he will" produces an unacceptable sentence when it is applied to a subordinate clause containing a presupposition as in "Sally plans for Gary to marry her and it bothers me that marry her he will."

The fact that the listener maintains the presupposed or less important information of subordinate clauses longer in unanalyzed verbatim form suggests that these differences in constraints on word order have a perceptual basis. Word order in a presupposed subordinate clause may be more like the canonical deep-structure order because this order is easier to retain in unanalyzed form. Word order is not as constrained in asserted clauses because these are interpreted as they are being heard and are not retained in unanalyzed form.

The fact that movement rules are more constrained in an initial subordinate clause than in a final subordinate clause is consistent with our results that initial subordinate clauses show the self-terminating memory search but final subordinate clauses do not. The listeners' dominant strategy is to postpone interpretation of an initial subordinate clause; the result of this is that word order is constrained in initial subordinate clauses. However, listeners interpret a final subordinate clause as they hear it because the main clause has already been interpreted and word order need not be as constrained.

A second type of difference in the form of main and subordinate clauses may be attributed to the listener's attempt to interpret as soon as possible the asserted information of the main clause. As we mentioned previously, Lakoff (1968) has noted that verb-phrase deletion is permissible in a sentence-final main clause as in "If Max buys a car Sally will" but is unacceptable in a sentence-initial main clause as in "Sally will if Max buys a car." On the other hand, verb-phrase deletion is equally acceptable in subordinate clauses in both positions. Lakoff has also noted that there are constraints on coreferential pronouns: A sentence with a final main clause containing a pronoun that refers to a noun in the preceding subordinate clause is acceptable, as in "Before John left town he ate supper," but a sentence with an initial main clause containing a pronoun that refers to a noun in the following subordinate clause is unacceptable, as in "*He ate supper before John left town." On the other hand, these constraints are not found with pronouns that occur in subordinate clauses.

The constraints on verb-phrase deletion and coreferential pronouns in initial main clauses follow directly from listeners' attempts to represent asserted main clauses in semantic form as quickly as possible. Application of these syntactic rules in initial main clauses would prevent the use of normal perceptual strategies because the new, important information of the initial main clause could not be recoded into semantic form until after the following subordinate clause had been interpreted. Verb-phrase deletion and coreferential pronouns in initial subordinate clauses, however, do not interfere with normal perceptual strategies because these strategies include postponing interpretation of the less important information of the initial subordinate clause until after the new information of the main clause has been interpreted.

These conclusions suggest that there may be different constraints on word order within different types of subordinate clauses, depending on how closely the main clause follows from the subordinate clause. The following examples indicate that there are subtle differences of this sort, noncanonical word order being somewhat more acceptable in more "causally efficient" clauses:

(21a)   Because tomorrow we are hiring a new person we're having a party.
(21b)   ?Since tomorrow we are hiring a new person we're having a party.
(21c)   *Though tomorrow we are hiring a new person we're having a party.
(22a)   It's time to get up because off went the alarm.
(22b)   ?It's time to get up since off went the alarm.
(22c)   *Bill kept sleeping though off went the alarm.

These differences may be due to differences in "assertiveness" of the various subordinate clauses, as suggested by G. M. Green (1974), but they may also be attributed to the listeners' strategies for interpreting and integrating sentences having different causal relations between clauses. Whether such differences are attributed to presuppositional or causal differences, they may be interpreted as the product of the processing mechanisms listeners use as they hear a sentence. Thus, our analysis of the behavioral basis of the penthouse principle predicts *new* facts, which a purely structural description could only "post-dict."

We started this chapter with the view that universal grammar is made more complex if it must account for phenomena that are actually due to behavioral systems of language use. The penthouse principle is a good case in point. It traditionally has two parts (23a, b):

(23a)   Reordering rules are more restricted in subordinate clauses.
(23b)   This effect is weaker when the surface order places the subordinate clause second.

We have added a third part:

(23c)   This effect is stronger for *though*-clauses than for *if*-clauses; in general, stronger for subordinate clauses whose interpretation depends on their main clause and is not a cause.

Even the first two parts are "global" constraints in the sense that they are not restrictions on possible transformations but, rather, are restrictions on the relative domain of transformations that result in certain types of deep-structure/surface-structure pairs. The third part is simply a description, extremely hard to interpret as part of universal grammar because it is, in fact, a statement about processing.

We are arguing that an independently motivated distinction in the way main and subordinate clauses are processed predicts the original penthouse principle; i.e., it predicts that if there is an asymmetry in the extent to which word order can be flexible, it will be in favor of main clauses. Furthermore, our interpretation brings to light a new set of predictions that were originally unnoticed. So not only is universal grammar relieved of this need for global rules, we can explain new facts as well.

INTERACTIONISM AND THE
POWER OF GRAMMARS

We have given examples in which a linguistic phenomenon is due to the way language is perceived and have intentionally addressed the discussions to a phenomenon that has been raised in the past decade as part of a reason to abandon transformational grammar in favor of a more powerful model. We have argued that independently motivated aspects of speech perception explain the phenomenon: This relieves the grammar of the descriptive responsibility and potentially reduces the descriptive power of grammatical universals.

There are several aspects of this research that are worth noting. First, our preoccupation with speech perception should not be taken as intended to exclude the interaction of language structure with other behavioral systems— most notably that of speech production. The role of perception has dominated our discussions because more is known about how perception operates; i.e., to some extent, we have an independently motivated perceptual theory. However, our general view is that there is a dynamic interaction between the grammar and both the systems of speech production and perception in children and adults.

Second, we have taken care to argue that each specific linguistic phenomenon is interpreted as due to independently motivated aspects of speech perception. We have attempted to avoid vague reference to properties such as "mental effort," "informativeness," "importance," "focus," "empathy," and so on. We do not mean that these terms are empty in principle; however, they are empty at the moment and, consequently, can have no clear explanatory force. This is a stolid, but necessary, methodological stance. Because of it, the rapidity of linguistic theorizing may often seem to outrun our behavioral explanations. But ultimate explanatory correctness requires that we base our claims on reasonably verified principles, not unconstrained theorizing. Remember the tortoise and the hare.

The final point concerns the claim that a grammar is psychologically real. For the past two decades, linguists have accepted that the goal of linguistic description is to account for a speaker's knowledge. This was in marked contrast with the position of linguists of the previous decades who emphasized that "regularities in linguistic data" are to be accounted for, leaving open the question of whether those regularities reflect knowledge. The claim that a grammar is a representation of knowledge is crucial to making linguistic science a contributer to the understanding of the human mind. Insofar as the grammatical descriptions are correct for adult speakers, they specify mental structures that underlie both linguistic behavior and linguistic knowledge. These structures, in turn, constrain our hypotheses about the structures in the infant's mind: clearly, structure that is possible in an adult language must either be learned by the child or must be innate. Hence, only if linguistic structures represent knowledge can we use linguistic science to increase our understanding of ourselves.

What is at issue in modern linguistics is the notion of the descriptive power of grammars. Confusion about this problem lies at the heart of many continuing controversies in the study of language. The term *descriptive power* refers to two kinds of questions concerning the status of grammar and the linguist's goal in constructing grammars: Are the formal devices in a grammar general or limited? Individual answers to these questions tend to coincide; i.e., those who argue that grammars are made up of an assemblage of specific descriptive devices also accept circumscribed goals for the domain of grammatical investigation.

The answers to the two questions are not logically linked even though they occur together; however, they are related methodologically. Consider first the generalist's view. We can feel impelled as scientists searching for general truths to find the most general formalisms to describe language. The reason for this is intuitively clear: The more general the mechanisms are, the less specific any given claim about their representation in the mind is and, therefore, the less radical appearing the claim that they are learned or innate. This goal would appear to accommodate the scientific method in the best sense: namely, to keep to a minimum the number of different kinds of formal devices that are postulated to exist, thereby increasing the plausibility and generality of the descriptions. Coupled with this is the desire to treat *all* systematic properties of language as due to the grammar; i.e., the domain of grammatical description is intended to be as broad as possible. This goal, too, appears to follow the requirements of good scientific practice: namely, it appeals to our desire to have one single theory account for many superficially different kinds of facts. We characterize this position as the "pan-theoretical" approach: the attempt to reduce all linguistic phenomena to a single theory that itself includes a single formal device.

We have noted that pan-theoretists tend also to be formal generalists. It is clear why the decisions to describe *all* linguistic phenomena in a grammar and to use a single formal device are mutually reinforcing. If every regular fact about language is ipso facto relevant to a grammar, then the researcher must try to find a common formal thread. Otherwise every new kind of fact forces a revision of the theory, thus reducing its significance. After all, to treat all linguistic phenomena within a "grammar" is of interest only insofar as it does not require a distinct theoretical mechanism for every kind of fact. Accordingly, the more kinds of facts about speech a grammar describes, the more pressure to find some common theoretical denominator. The danger is that such pressure impels theorists to resort to the common theoretical denominator that is *least*.

The pressures are bilateral: If one pretheoretically accepts the goal of using the smallest and most generally applicable number of formalisms, then one is under pressure to show that the formal devices have wide applicability; after all, to show that a single formal device is adequate to describe language is of interest only insofar as the notion of "language" is broad and superficially heterogeneous. Thus, the simpler the formal devices, the more pressure to find a wide variety of facts they describe. The danger here is that such pressure impels theorists to ignore real distinctions between different kinds of facts about language.

The individual cases discussed in this paper highlight the dangers of this dual dynamic for linguistic description. Too often, current linguistic practice appears to be at the mercy of this force, resorting to theoretically vacuous generalizations and obscuring the distinctions that must be maintained if we are to understand language at all. There are two kinds of pressures that make this position attractive, despite the fact that it stultifies theoretical understanding. First, the smaller the number of formal mechanisms is, the weaker appears the claim that such mechanisms are "innate" or "learned." That is, psychologists and philosophers who maintain that language (and all other mental faculties) are learned are comforted by the apparent formal simplicity of what there is to be learned. Those who view human beings in terms of "general purpose computational mechanisms" are charmed by the possibility that there may be only one elementary kind of mental operation involved in language.

This question comes into sharp focus over the need for "global rules" of the kind needed to state the penthouse principle, rules that are sensitive to nonadjacent trees in a derivation. Some researchers have argued that transformations are simply special cases of such general rules. The question now is, what is wrong with viewing all grammatical rules as different kinds of global rules and thereby reducing universal grammar to one formal structure? The answer lies in the descriptive power of a universal grammar that includes both "transformations" between adjacent trees and "derivational constraints" between nonadjacent trees. Such a universal grammar has more ways of describing any particular phenomenon than does a universal grammar consisting of only "transformations." The more powerful the formal mechanisms, the more solutions are available and theoretically plausible for any finite set of facts.

Such multiplicity of solutions quickly becomes a plethora. Recall that the goal of linguistic analysis is to use a set of universal formalisms that are adequate for the description of known language and, therefore, are candidates for psychologically innate or learned structures. However, this line of inquiry can proceed only if the grammatical solution for any set of linguistic facts *is reasonably* unique. If a variety of solutions is possible, the psychological pertinence of any particular solution is reduced: Whether it is empirically valid or not is of little interest because its nonuniqueness means its validity can neither uniquely confirm nor disconfirm the universal formalisms. The less unique a particular solution is, the less its validity confirms the explanatory power of the proposed universal formalisms. Finally, the less subject to confirmation the formal universals, the less of an empirical science is linguistics. For this reason, the invention of formal grammatical structures of increased descriptive power is to be avoided.

This argument highlights the complementary approach to linguistic research that ordinarily accompanies attempts to increase the formal power of universal grammar—the attempt to embrace all facts about language as necessarily "grammatical." Suppose that phenomena such as the penthouse principle are true. What makes them *grammatical* facts? Is their existence as generalizations only *truly* represented if they are represented within the grammar, among the many rules and structures that generate sentences? After all, (24) is a true generalization about language, but it is not ordinarily included as a grammatical universal.

(24)   Speech power 1 cm. from the mouth is louder than 5 db (ref. – dyne = 0 db) and softer than 150 db.

The reason for not including (24) as a universal of grammar is two-fold. First, to include acoustic sensitivity within grammar would introduce new formal power and conceivably multiply possible grammatical solutions for any data set (in this case, perhaps multiplying the possible solutions for stress phenomena). Second, there is a plausible, independently motivated explanation for (24) to be found in the mechanisms of speech perception and production. Less than 5 dB at the mouth would not be sufficient for ordinary listening, and the vocal system cannot produce more than 150 dB. Thus, the constraints of the mechanisms of perception and production predict that (24) is a true generalization about language, albeit an extra-grammatical one.

The question now concerns the facts about main and subordinate clauses. Are they grammatical or extra-grammatical phenomena? We have reviewed the theoretical disadvantages of admitting them as *grammatical* phenomena, but if there are no alternative solutions, then we must accept them. After all, the argument that transformations are needed beyond phrase structure rules involved increasing the formal mechanisms in a grammar and weakening the specificity of any grammatical solution. Transformations had to be accepted because there was no (known) way of accounting for the accepted facts with the existing formalisms (phrase structures). However, we argued that there are independently motivated descriptions for the phenomena; thus, we are not forced to accept the less constrained universal formalisms to describe those particular facts.

Of course, all such questions are empirical. It remains to be seen if all the phenomena that are referred to as motivating global constraints can be explained as due to independently motivated extra-grammatical mechanisms. It is our working hypothesis that all formalisms that constrain the structure of relations between basic and surface trees will be shown to be due to nongrammatical structures: If that turns out to be false, so be it. Our main motivation here is to explain why it is that such formalisms must be accepted reluctantly rather than apocalyptically embraced.

To put it briefly: If we can exclude such formalisms as global rules and maintain the notion of discrete grammaticality,

1. For any data set, the number of available grammatical solutions of equal complexity decreases.
2. This increases the uniqueness and power of a particular grammatical solution.
3. This in turn increases the interest of the possible grammatical universals underlying that grammatical solution.
4. Finally, this increases the precision and testability of claims about the human mind.

And, that is what the study of language is all about.

ACKNOWLEDGMENTS

Parts of this paper were originally presented at the Psychology of Language Conference, University of Stirling, Scotland in June 1976, and parts appear in Chicago Linguistic Society, Volume V, 1975, and in *Journal of Verbal Learning and Verbal Behavior,* in press. Preparation of the paper was supported by grants from the National Institute of Mental Health (No. 57352) and from the Montclair State College Faculty Research Released Time Committee to the second author, who is also affiliated with Montclair State College.

REFERENCES

Abrams, K., & Bever, T. G. Syntactic structure modifies attention during speech perception and recognition. *Quarterly Journal of Experimental Psychology,* 1969, *21,* 280–290.

Amidon, A., & Carey, P. W. Why five-year-olds cannot understand before and after. *Journal of Verbal Learning and Verbal Behavior,* 1972, *11,* 417–423.

Anderson, J. R. Verbatim and propositional representation of Ss in immediate and long-term memory. *Journal of Verbal Learning and Verbal Behavior,* 1974, *13,* 149–162.

Atkinson, R. C., Herrmann, D. J., & Wescourt, K. T. Search processes in recognition memory. In R. S. Solso (Ed.), *Theories in cognitive psychology: The Loyola symposium.* Potomac, Md.: Lawrence Erlbaum Associates, 1974.

Baddeley, A. D., & Ecob, J. R. Reaction time and short term memory: Implications of repetition effects for the high-speed exhaustive scan hypothesis. *Quarterly Journal of Experimental Psychology,* 1973, *2,* 229–240.

Baird, R., & Koslick, J. D. Recall of grammatical relations within clause containing sentences. *Journal of Psycholinguistic Research,* 1974, *3,* 165–171.

Ballard, D. L., Conrad, R. J., & Longacre, R. E. The deep and surface grammar of interclausal relations. *Foundations of Language,* 1971, *7,* 70–118.

Barrie-Blackley, S. Six-year-old children's understanding of Ss adjoined with time adverbs. *Journal of Psycholinguistic Research,* 1973, *2,* 153–165.

Berry, R. *A critical review of noise location during simultaneously presented sentences.* Unpublished doctoral dissertation, University of Illinois, 1970.

Bever, T. G. The cognitive basis for linguistic structures. In J. R. Hayes (Ed.), *Cognition and the development of language.* New York: Wiley, 1970. (a)

Bever, T. G. The comprehension and memory of sentences with temporal relations. In G. B. Flores d'Arcais & W. J. M. Levelt (Eds.), *Advances in psycholinguistics.* Amsterdam: North-Holland, 1970. (b)

Bever, T. G. Serial position and response biases do not account for the effect of syntactic structure on the location of brief noises during sentences. *Journal of Psycholinguistic Research,* 1973, *2,* 287–288.

Bever, T. G. The ascent of the specious, or There's a lot we don't know about mirrors. In D. Cohen (Ed.), *Explaining linguistic phenomena.* Washington, D.C.: Hemisphere Press, 1974.

Bever, T. G. Functional explanations require independently motivated functional theories. In R. E. Grossman, L. J. San, & T. J. Vance (Eds.), *Papers from the parasession on functionalism.* Chicago: Chicago Linguistic Society, 1975.

Bever, T. G., Carroll, J. M., & Hurtig, R. Speech production, perception, and the formalization of linguistic analogy. In T. G. Bever, J. J. Katz, & D. T. Langendoen (Eds.), *An integrated theory of linguistic ability.* New York: T. Y. Crowell Press, 1976.

Bever, T. G., Garrett, M. F., & Hurtig, R. The interaction of perceptual processes and ambiguous sentences. *Memory & Cognition,* 1973, *1,* 277–286.

Bever, T. G., Garrett, M. F., & Hurtig, R. Projection mechanisms in reading, or When the journal review process fails. *Journal of Psycholinguistic Research,* 1976, *5,* 215–226.

Bever, T. G., & Hurtig, R. R. Detection of a nonlinguistic stimulis is poorest at the end of a clause. *Journal of Psycholinguistic Research,* 1975, *4,* 1–7.

Bever, T. G., Hurtig, R. R., & Handel, A. *Response biases do not account for the effect of clause structure on the perception of nonlinguistic stimuli.* Manuscript submitted for publication, 1978.

Bever, T. G., Lackner, J. R., & Kirk, R. The underlying structures of sentences are the primary units of immediate speech processing. *Perception & Psychophysics,* 1969, *79,* 387–394.

Bever, T. G., & Mehler, J. *The coding hypothesis and short-term memory* (Air Force Technical Report). Cambridge: Harvard Center for Cognitive Studies, 1967.

Bock, J. K. The effect of a pragmatic presupposition on syntactic structure in question answering. *Journal of Verbal Learning and Verbal Behavior,* 1977, *16,* 723–734.

Bock, J. K., & Brewer, W. F. Reconstructive recall in sentences with alternative surface structures. *Journal of Experimental Psychology,* 1974, *103,* 837–843.

Boer, S. E., & Lycan, W. G. *The myth of semantic presupposition.* Indiana University Linguistics Club, 1976.

Bransford, J. D., Barclay, J. R., & Franks, J. J. Sentence memory: A constructive versus interpretive approach. *Cognitive Psychology,* 1972, *3,* 193–209.

Bransford, J. D., & Franks, J. J. The abstraction of linguistic ideas. *Cognitive Psychology,* 1971, *2,* 331–350.

Brewer, W. F. Memory for the pragmatic implications of sentences. *Memory & Cognition,* 1977, *5,* 673–678.

Burrows, D., & Okada, R. Serial position effects in high-speed memory search. *Perception & Psychophysics,* 1971, *10,* 305–308.

Burt, M. K. *From deep to surface structure.* New York: Harper & Row, 1971.

Cairns, H. S. *Ambiguous sentence processing.* Unpublished doctoral dissertation, University of Texas at Austin, 1970.

Cairns, H. S. *Ambiguous sentence processing.* Paper presented at the annual meeting of the Midwestern Psychological Association, Detroit, 1971.

Carins, H. S. Effects of bias on processing and reprocessing of lexically ambiguous sentences. *Journal of Experimental Psychology,* 1973, *97,* 337–343.

Cairns, H. S., & Blank, M. *Word recognition latency and the duration of clausal processing.* Unpublished manuscript, Queens College, 1974.

Cairns, H. S., & Kamerman, J. Lexical information processing during sentence comprehension. *Journal of Verbal Learning and Verbal Behavior,* 1975, *14,* 170–179.

Caplan, D. Clause boundaries and recognition latencies for words in sentences. *Perception & Psychophysics,* 1972, *12,* 73–76.

Carey, P. W., Mehler, J., & Bever, T. G. Judging the veracity of ambiguous sentences. *Journal of Verbal Learning and Verbal Behavior,* 1970, *9,* 243–254.

Carpenter, P. A. Extracting information from counterfactual clauses. *Journal of Verbal Learning and Verbal Behavior,* 1973, *12,* 512–521.

Carroll, J. M., & Bever, T. G. Sentence comprehension: A case study in the relation of knowledge and perception. *Handbook of perception, Vol. VII: Language and Speech.* New York: Academic Press, 1976.

Carroll, J. M., & Tanenhaus, M. K. Prolegomena to a functional theory of word formation. *Papers from The Chicago Linguistic Society,* 1975.

Carroll, J. M., Tanenhaus, M. K., & Bever, T. G. *The perception of relations: The interaction of structural, functional, and contextual factors in the segmentation of sentences.* IBM Research Report, 1977.

Carroll, J. M., Tanenhaus, M. K., & Bever, T. G. The perception of relations: Functional and contextual factors in the segmentation of speech. In W. J. M. Levelt & G. B. Flores d'Arcais (Eds.), *Studies in the perception of language.* London: Wiley, 1978.

Chafe, W. L. *Meaning and the structure of language.* Chicago: University of Chicago Press, 1970.

Chapin, P. G. Samoan pronominalization. *Language,* 1970, *46,* 366–378.

Chapin, P. G., Smith, T., & Abrahamson, A. Two factors in perceptual segmentation of speech. *Journal of Verbal Learning and Verbal Behavior,* 1972, *11,* 164–173.

Clark, E. V. How young children describe events in time. In G. B. Flores d'Arcais & W. J. M. Levelt (Eds.), *Advances in psycholinguistics.* Amsterdam: North-Holland, 1970.

Clark, E. V. On the acquisition of the meaning of *before* and *after. Journal of Verbal Learning and Verbal Behavior,* 1971, *10,* 266–275.

Clark, H. H. The language-as-fixed-effect fallacy: A critique of language statistics in psychological research. *Journal of Verbal Learning and Verbal Behavior,* 1973, *12,* 335–359.

Clark, H. H., & Clark, E. V. Semantic distinctions and memory for complex sentences. *Quarterly Journal of Experimental Psychology,* 1968, *20,* 129–138.

Clark, H. H., & Clark, E. V. *Psychology and language.* New York: Harcourt, Brace, & Jovanovich, 1977.

Clark, H. H., & Haviland, S. E. Psychological processes as linguistic explanation. In D. Cohen (Ed.), *Explaining linguistic phenomena*. Washington, D.C.: Hemisphere Press, 1974.

Clark, H. H., & Haviland, S. E. Comprehension and the given-new contract. In R. O. Freedle (Ed.), *Discourse production and comprehension* (Vol. I). Norwood, N.J.: Ablex Publishing Corp., 1977.

Clark, H. H., & Lucy, P. Understanding what is meant from what is said: A study in conversationally conveyed requests. *Journal of Verbal Learning and Verbal Behavior*, 1975, *14*, 56–72.

Clifton, C., & Birenbaum, S. Effects of serial position and delay of probe in a memory scan task. *Journal of Experimental Psychology*, 1970, *86*, 60–76.

Clifton, C., & Gutschera, K. D. Hierarchical search of two digit numbers in a recognition memory task. *Journal of Verbal Learning and Verbal Behavior*, 1971, *10*, 528–541.

Conrad, C. Context effects in sentence comprehension: A study of the subjective lexicon. *Memory & Cognition*, 1974, *2*, 130–138.

Corballis, M. C. Serial order in recognition and recall. *Journal of Experimental Psychology*, 1967, *74*, 99–105.

Corballis, M. C., Kirby, J., & Miller, A. Access to elements of a memorized list. *Journal of Experimental Psychology*, 1972, *94*, 185–190.

Corballis, M. C., & Miller, A. Scanning and decision processes in recognition memory. *Journal of Experimental Psychology*, 1973, *98*, 379–386.

Craik, F. I. M., & Jacoby, L. L. A process view of short-term retention. In F. Restle, R. M. Shiffrin, N. J. Castellan, H. R. Lindman, & D. B. Pisoni (Eds.), *Cognitive theory* (Vol. I). Hillsdale, N.J.: Lawrence Erlbaum Associates, 1975.

Craik, F. I. M., & Lockhart, R. S. Levels of processing: A framework for memory research. *Journal of Verbal Learning and Verbal Behavior*, 1972, *11*, 671–684.

Dakin, J. Explanations. *Journal of Linguistics*, 1970, *6*, 199–214.

Dalrymple-Alford, E. C. Response bias and judgments of the location of clicks in sentences. *Perception & Psychophysics*, 1976, *19*, 303–308.

Darley, C. F., Klatzky, R. L., & Atkinson, R. C. Effects of memory load on reaction time. *Journal of Experimental Psychology*, 1972, *96*, 232–234.

Dik, S. C. *Coordination: Its implications for the theory of general linguistics*. Amsterdam: North-Holland, 1968.

Elliot, P. B. Tables of *d'*. In J. A. Swets (Ed.), *Signal detection and recognition by human observers*. New York: Wiley, 1964.

Fillenbaum, S. On coping with ordered and unordered conjunctive sentences. *Journal of Experimental Psychology*, 1971, *87*, 93–98.

Fillenbaum, S. Or: Some uses. *Journal of Experimental Psychology*, 1974, *103*, 913–921. (a)

Fillenbaum, S. Pragmatic normalization: Further results for some conjunctive and disjunctive sentences. *Journal of Experimental Psychology*, 1974, *102*, 574–578. (b)

Fillenbaum, S. If: Some uses. *Psychological Research*, 1975, *37*, 245–260.

Fillenbaum, S. Inducements: On the phrasing and logic of conditional promises, threats, and warnings. *Psychological Research*, 1976, *38*, 231–250.

Flores d'Arcais, G. B. The perception of complex sentences. In W. J. M. Levelt & G. B. Flores d'Arcais (Eds.), *Studies in the perception of language*. London: Wiley, 1978.

Fodor, J. A., & Bever, T. G. The psychological reality of linguistic segments. *Journal of Verbal Learning and Verbal Behavior*, 1965, *4*, 414–420.

Fodor, J. A., Fodor, J. D., Garrett, M. F., & Lackner, J. R. Effects of surface and underlying clausal relations on click location. *Quarterly Progress Report No. 113*, Research Laboratory of Electronics, M.I.T., 1974.

Fodor, J. A., Bever, T. G., & Garrett, M. F. *The psychology of language: An introduction to psycholinguistics and generative grammar*. New York: McGraw-Hill, 1974.

Fodor, J. A., & Garrett, M. F. Some syntactic determinants of sentential complexity. *Perception & Psychophysics,* 1967, *2,* 289–296.

Fodor, J. A., Garrett, M. F., & Bever, T. G. Some syntactic determinants of sentential complexity, II: Verb structure. *Perception & Psychophysics,* 1968, *3,* 453–461.

Forster, K. I. Visual perception of rapidly presented word sequences of varying complexity. *Perception & Psychophysics,* 1970, *8,* 215–221.

Forster, K. I., & Olbrei, I. Semantic heuristics and syntactic analysis. *Cognition,* 1973, *2,* 319–347.

Foss, D. J. Some effects of ambiguity upon sentence comprehension. *Journal of Verbal Learning and Verbal Behavior,* 1970, *9,* 699–706.

Foss, D. J., Bever, T. G., & Silver, M. The comprehension and verification of ambiguous sentences. *Perception & Psychophysics,* 1968, *4,* 304–306.

Foss, D., & Jenkins, C. M. Some effects of context on the comprehension of ambiguous sentences. *Journal of Verbal Learning and Verbal Behavior,* 1973, *12,* 577–589.

Foss, D. J., & Lynch, R. H. Decision processes during sentence comprehension: Effects of surface structure on decision time. *Perception & Psychophysics,* 1969, *5,* 145–148.

Freund, A. Word and phrase recognition in speech processing. In D. W. Massaro (Ed.), *Understanding language.* New York: Academic press, 1975.

Garcia, E. Some remarks on "ambiguity" and "perceptual processes." *Journal of Psycholinguistic Research,* 1976, *5,* 195–213.

Garner, R. "Presupposition" in philosophy and linguistics. In C. J. Fillmore & D. T. Langendoen (Eds.), *Studies in linguistic semantics.* New York: Holt, Rinehart, & Winston, 1971.

Garrett, M. F. *Syntactic structures and judgments of auditory events.* Unpublished doctoral dissertation, University of Illinois, 1965.

Garrett, M. F., Bever, T. G., & Fodor, J. A. The active use of grammar in speech perception. *Perception & Psychophysics,* 1966, *1,* 30–32.

Gleitman, L. Coordinating conjunctions in English. *Language,* 1965, *41,* 260–293.

Glucksberg, S., Trabasso, T., & Wald, J. Linguistic structures and mental operations. *Cognitive Psychology,* 1973, *5,* 338–370.

Gough, P. Verification of Ss: The effects of delay of evidence and S length. *Journal of Verbal Learning and Verbal Behavior,* 1966, *5,* 492–496.

Green, D. W. The effects of tasks on the representation of sentences. *Journal of Verbal Learning and Verbal Behavior,* 1975, *14,* 275–283.

Green, G. M. The function of form and the form of function. *Papers from the 10th regional meeting of the Chicago Linguistic Society,* 1974.

Grimes, J. E. The thread of discourse. *Janua Linguarum Series Minor.* (The Hague: Mouton), 1975, *207,* 1–408.

Hakes, D. T. Does verb structure affect sentence comprehension? *Perception & Psychophysics,* 1971, *10,* 229–232.

Hakes, D. T. Effects of reducing complement constructions on sentence comprehension. *Journal of Verbal Learning and Verbal Behavior,* 1972, *11,* 278–286.

Hakes, D. T., & Cairns, H. Sentence comprehension and relative pronouns. *Perception & Psychophysics,* 1970, *8,* 5–8.

Hakes, D. T., & Foss, D. J. Decision processes during sentence comprehension: Effects of surface structure reconsidered. *Perception & Psychophysics,* 1970, *8,* 413–416.

Halliday, M. A. K. Notes on transitivity and theme in English: Part II. *Journal of Linguistics,* 1967, *3,* 177–274.

Halliday, M. A. K. Language structure and language function. In J. Lyons (Ed.), *New horizons in linguistics.* Baltimore: Penguin Books, 1970.

Harnish, R. M. Logical form and implicature. In T. G. Bever, J. J. Katz, & D. T. Langendoen (Eds.), *An integrated theory of linguistic ability.* New York: Thomas Crowell, 1976.

Harris, R. J. Memory and comprehension of implications and inferences of complex Ss. *Journal of Verbal Learning and Verbal Behavior*, 1974, *13*, 626–637. (a)

Harris, R. J. Memory for presuppositions and implications: A case study of 12 verbs of motion and inception-terminated. *Journal of Experimental Psychology*, 1974, *103*, 594–597. (b)

Harris, R. J. Memory for negation in coordination and complex Ss. *Journal of Experimental Psychology: Human Learning and Memory*, 1976, *2*, 308–314.

Haviland, S. E., & Clark, H. H. What's new? Acquiring new information as a process in comprehension. *Journal of Verbal Learning and Verbal Behavior*, 1974, *13*, 512–521.

Heinamaki, O. Before. In P. M. Peranteau, J. N. Leir, & G. C. Phares (Eds.), *Papers from the 8th Regional Meeting of the Chicago Linguistics Society*, 1972.

Holmes, V. M. *Some effects of syntactic structure on sentence recognition.* Unpublished doctoral dissertation, University of Melbourne, 1970.

Holmes, V. M. Order of main and subordinate clauses in sentence perception. *Journal of Verbal Learning and Verbal Behavior*, 1973, *12*, 285–293.

Holmes, V. M., Arwas, R., & Garrett, M. Prior context and the perception of lexically ambiguous sentences. *Memory & Cognition*, 1977, *5*, 103–110.

Holmes, V. M., & Forster, K. I. Detection of extraneous signals during sentence recognition. *Perception & Psychophysics*, 1970, *7*, 297–301.

Holmes, V. M., & Forster, K. I. Perceptual complexity and underlying sentence structure. *Journal of Verbal Learning and Verbal Behavior*, 1972, *11*, 148–156.

Holmes, V. M., & Watson, I. J. The role of surface order and surface deletion in sentence perception. *Quarterly Journal of Experimental Psychology*, 1976, *28*, 155–165.

Hooper, J. B., & Thompson, S. A. On the applicability of root transformations. *Linguistic Inquiry*, 1973, *4*, 465–497.

Hoosain, R. The processing of negation. *Journal of Verbal Learning and Verbal Behavior*, 1973, *12*, 618–626.

Hoosain, R. The processing and remembering of congruent and incongruent sentences. *Journal of Psycholinguistic Research*, 1974, *3*, 319–331.

Hornby, P. A. The psychological subject and predicate. *Cognitive Psychology*, 1972, *3*, 632–642.

Hornby, P. A. Surface structure and presupposition. *Journal of Verbal Learning and Verbal Behavior*, 1974, *13*, 530–538.

Hupet, M., & LeBouedec, B. The given–new contract and the constructive aspect of memory for ideas. *Journal of Verbal Learning and Verbal Behavior*, 1977, *16*, 69–75.

Hurtig, R. The validity of clausal processing strategies at the discourse level. *Discourse Processes: A Multidisciplinary Journal*, 1978, *1*, 195–202.

Jackendoff, R. S. *Semantic interpretation in generative grammar.* Cambridge, Mass.: MIT Press, 1972.

Jarvella, R. J. Effects of syntax on running memory span for connected discourse. *Psychonomic Science*, 1970, *19*, 235–236.

Jarvella, R., & Herman, S. Clause structure of sentences and speech processing. *Perception & Psychophysics*, 1972, *11*, 381–384.

Jeffra, C. *Scanning for letters in words vs. nonwords.* Unpublished master's thesis, Montclair State College, 1978.

Jenkins, C. M. Memory and linguistic information: A study of sentence memory, linguistic form, and inferred information. *Dissertation Abstracts International*, 1972, *33*, July (1-B), 463.

Johnson, H. L. The meaning of before and after for preschool children. *Journal of Experimental Child Psychology*, 1975, *19*, 88–99.

Johnson, M. K., Bransford, J. D., & Solomon, S. K. Memory for tacit implications of sentences. *Journal of Experimental Psychology*, 1973, *98*, 203–205.

Johnson-Laird, P. N. "&." *Journal of Linguistics*, 1969, *5*, 111–114.

Johnson-Laird, P. N. Experimental psycholinguistics. *Annual Review of Psychology*, 1974, *25*, 135–160.

Juola, J. F., & Atkinson, R. C. Memory scanning for words versus categories. *Journal of Verbal Learning and Verbal Behavior,* 1971, *10,* 522–527.

Just, M. A., & Clark, H. H. Drawing inferences from the presuppositions and implications of affirmative and negative sentences. *Journal of Verbal Learning and Verbal Behavior,* 1973, *12,* 21–31.

Kartunnen, L. Implicative verbs. *Language,* 1971, *47,* 340–358.

Kartunnen, L. Presuppositions of compound sentences. *Linguistic Inquiry,* 1973, *IV,* 169–193.

Kartunnen, L. Presuppositions and linguistic context. *Theoretical Linguistics,* 1974, *1.* (a)

Kartunnen, L. On pragmatic and semantic aspects of meaning. *Texas Linguistics Forum,* 1974, *1,* 51–64. (b)

Katz, E. W., & Brent, S. B. Understanding connectives. *Journal of Verbal Learning and Verbal Behavior,* 1968, *7,* 501–509.

Katz, J. *Semantic theory.* New York: Harper & Row, 1972.

Katz, J. J., & Langendoen, D. T. Pragmatics and presupposition. In T. G. Bever, J. J. Katz, & D. T. Langendoen (Eds.), *An integrated theory of linguistic ability.* New York: Crowell, 1976.

Keenan, E. Two kinds of presupposition in natural language. In C. Fillmore & D. Langendoen (Eds.), *Studies in linguistic semantics.* New York: Holt, Rinehart, & Winston, 1971.

Kempson, R. M. *Presupposition and the delimitation of semantics.* Cambridge: Cambridge University Press, 1975.

Kennedy, R. A., & Hamilton, D. Time to locate probe items in short lists of digits. *American Journal of Psychology,* 1969, *82,* 272–275.

Kennedy, R. A., & Wilkes, A. L. Analysis of storage and retrieval processes in memorizing simple sentences. *Journal of Experimental Psychology,* 1969, *80,* 396–398.

Kennedy, R. A., & Wilkes, A. L. A comparison of retrieval and location operations in active and passive sentences. *British Journal of Psychology,* 1970, *61,* 491–498.

Kimball, J. Seven principles of surface structure parsing in natural language. *Cognition,* 1973, *2,* 15–47.

Klatzky, R. L., & Atkinson, R. C. Memory scans based on alternative test stimulus representations. *Perception & Psychophysics,* 1970, *8,* 113–117.

Klatzky, R. L., Juola, J. F., & Atkinson, R. C. Test stimulus representation and experimental context effects in memory scanning. *Journal of Experimental Psychology,* 1971, *87,* 281–288.

Kornfeld, J. Syntactic structure and the perception of sentences: Some evidence for dominance effects. In C. Corum, T. C. Smith-Stark, & A. Weiser (Eds.), *You take the high node and I'll take the low node.* Chicago: Chicago Linguistic Society, 1973.

Kuno, S. Functional sentence perspective: A case study from Japanese and English. *Linguistic Inquiry,* 1972, *3,* 269–320.

Kuno, S. Three perspectives in the functional approach to syntax. *Papers from the parasession on functionalism.* Chicago: Chicago Linguistic Society, 1975.

Lackner, J. R., & Garrett, M. F. Resolving ambiguity: Effects of biasing context in the unattended ear. *Cognition,* 1973, *1,* 359–372.

Lakoff, G. *Pronouns and reference* (Parts I and II). Indiana University Linguistics Club, 1968.

Lakoff, G. Linguistics and natural logic. *Synthese,* 1970, *22,* 151–271.

Lakoff, G., & Thompson, W. Introducing cognitive grammar. *Proceedings of the Berkeley Linguistic Society,* 1974.

Lakoff, R. If's, and's, and but's about conjunction. In C. Fillmore & D. T. Langendoen (Eds.), *Studies in linguistic semantics.* New York: Holt, Rinehart, & Winston, 1971.

Lockhart, R. S., Craik, F. I. M., & Jacoby, L. Depth of processing recognition, and recall. In J. Brown (Ed.), *Recall and recognition.* London: Wiley, 1976.

MacKay, D. G. To end ambiguous sentences. *Perception & Psychophysics,* 1966, *1,* 426–436.

Marslen-Wilson, W. D. Linguistic structure and speech shadowing at very short latencies. *Nature,* 1973, *244,* 522–523.

Marslen-Wilson, W. D. Sentence perception as an interactive parallel process. *Science,* 1975, *189,* 226–228.

Marslen-Wilson, W. D., & Tyler, L. Processing structure of sentence perception. *Nature,* 1975, *257,* 784–786.

Marslen-Wilson, W. D., & Tyler, L. Memory and levels of processing in a psycholinguistic context. *Journal of Experimental Psychology: Human Learning and Memory,* 1976, *2,* 112–119.

Marslen-Wilson, W. D., Tyler, L., & Seidenberg, M. Sentence processing and the clause-boundary. In W. J. M. Levelt & G. Flores d'Arcais (Eds.), *Studies in the perception of language.* London: Wiley, 1978.

Martinet, A. *A functional view of language.* Oxford: Clarendice Press, 1962.

Mehler, J. Some effects of grammatical transformations on the recall of English sentences. *Journal of Verbal Learning and Verbal Behavior,* 1963, *2,* 346–351.

Miller, G. A., & Johnson-Laird, P. N. *Language and perception.* Cambridge, Mass.: Harvard University Press, 1976.

Morgan, J. L. On the treatment of presupposition in transformational grammar. In R. I. Binnich, A. Davison, G. M. Green, & J. L. Morgan (Eds.), *Papers from the 5th Regional Meeting.* Chicago Linguistic Society, 1969.

Morin, R., DeRosa, D., & Stultz, V. Recognition memory and reaction time. *Acta Psychologica,* 1967, *27,* 298–305.

Murdock, B. B. A parallel-scanning model for scanning. *Perception & Psychophysics,* 1971, *10,* 289–291.

Naus, M. J. Memory search of categorized lists: A consideration of alternative self-terminating search strategies. *Journal of Experimental Psychology,* 1974, *102,* 992–1000.

Naus, M. J., Glucksberg, S., & Ornstein, P. A. Taxonomic word categories and memory search. *Cognitive Psychology,* 1972, *3,* 643–654.

Norman, D., & Rumelhart, D. *Explorations in cognition.* San Francisco: W. H. Freeman, 1975.

Offir, C. E. Recognition memory for presuppositions of relative clause sentences. *Journal of Verbal Learning and Verbal Behavior,* 1973, *12,* 636–643.

Olson, D. R., & Filby, N. On the comprehension of active and passive sentences. *Cognitive Psychology,* 1972, *3,* 361–381.

Olson, G. M., & Clark, H. H. Research methods in psycholinguistics. In E. C. Carterette & M. P. Friedman (Eds.), *Handbook of perception, Vol. 7: Language and speech.* New York: Academic Press, 1976.

Osgood, C. On understanding and creating sentences. *American Psychologist,* 1963, *18,* 735–751.

Osgood, C. E. Where do sentences come from? In D. A. Steinberg & L. A. Jakobovits (Eds.), *Semantics: An interdisciplinary reader in philosophy, linguistics, and psychology.* Cambridge, England: Cambridge University Press, 1971.

Osgood, C. E., & Richards, M. M. From yang and yin to *and* or *but. Language,* 1973, *49,* 380–412.

Perfetti, C. A., & Goldman, S. R. Discourse memory and reading comprehension skill. *Journal of Verbal Learning and Verbal Behavior,* 1976, *15,* 33–42.

Peters, S. Presuppositions and conversation. *Texas Linguistic Forum,* 1975, *2,* 122–134.

Reber, A. A., & Anderson, J. R. The perception of clicks in linguistic and nonlinguistic messages. *Perception & Psychophysics,* 1970, *8,* 81–89.

Rips, L. J., & Marcus, S. L. Suppositions and the analysis of conditional sentences. In P. A. Carpenter & M. A. Just (Eds.), *Cognitive processes in comprehension.* Hillsdale, N.J.: Lawrence Erlbaum Associates, 1977.

Ross, J. R. The penthouse principle and the order of constituents. *You take the high node and I'll take the low node.* Chicago: Chicago Linguistic Society, 1973.

Ross, J. R. Three batons for cognitive psychology. In W. B. Weimer & D. S. Palermo (Eds.), *Cognition and the symbolic processes.* Hillsdale, N.J.: Lawrence Erlbaum Associates, 1974.

Scholes, R. J. Click location judgments. *Quarterly Report, Department of Speech, University of Florida,* 1969, *7,* 33–38.

Seitz, M. *AER and the perception of speech.* Unpublished doctoral dissertation, University of Washington, 1972.

Shedletsky, L. *Effects of some clause variables on memory-scanning.* Unpublished doctoral dissertation, University of Illinois, 1974.

Sheldon, A. The role of parallel function in the acquisition of relative clauses in English. *Journal of Verbal Learning and Verbal Behavior,* 1974, *13,* 272–281.

Sheldon, A. On strategies for processing relative clauses: A comparison of children and adults. *Minnesota working papers in linguistics and philosophy of language,* 1975, *2,* 188–200.

Simon, H. A., & Rescher, N. Cause and counterfactual. *Philosophy of Science,* 1966, *33,* 323–340).

Singer, M. Context inferences in the comprehension of sentences. *Canadian Journal of Psychology,* 1976, *30,* 39–46. (a)

Singer, M. Thematic structure and the integration of linguistic information. *Journal of Verbal Learning and Verbal Behavior,* 1976, *15,* 549–558. (b)

Singer, M., & Rosenberg, S. The role of grammatical relations in the abstraction of linguistic ideas. *Journal of Verbal Learning and Verbal Behavior,* 1973, *12,* 273–284.

Slobin, D. I. Grammatical transformations and sentence comprehension in childhood and adulthood. *Journal of Verbal Learning and Verbal Behavior,* 1966, *5,* 219–227.

Smith, K., & McMahon, L. Understanding order information in sentences: Some recent work at Bell Laboratories. In G. B. Flores d'Arcais & W. J. M. Levelt (Eds.), *Advances in psycholinguistics.* Amsterdam: North-Holland, 1970.

Springston, F. J., & Clark, H. H. *And* and *or,* or the comprehension of pseudoimperatives. *Journal of Verbal Learning and Verbal Behavior,* 1973, *12,* 258–272.

Staal, J. F. And. *Journal of linguistics,* 1968, *4,* 79–81.

Sternberg, S. High-speed scanning in human memory. *Science,* 1966, *153,* 652–654.

Sternberg, S. Retrieval of contextual information from memory. *Psychonomic Science,* 1967, *8,* 55–56.

Sternberg, S. Memory-scanning: Mental processes revealed by reaction-time experiments. *American Scientist,* 1969, *57,* 421–457.

Sternberg, S. Memory scanning: New findings and current controversies. *Quarterly Journal of Experimental Psychology,* 1975, *27,* 1–32.

Stockwell, R. P., Schachter, P., & Partee, B. H. *The major syntactic structures of English.* New York: Holt, Rinehart, & Winston, 1973.

Swanson, J. M., & Briggs, G. E. Information processing as a function of speed versus accuracy. *Journal of Experimental Psychology,* 1969, *81,* 223–229.

Tanenhaus, M. K. *Linguistic context and sentence perception.* Unpublished doctoral dissertation, Columbia University, 1977.

Tanenhaus, M. K., & Carroll, J. M. The clausal processing hierarchy ... and nouniness. In R. E. Grossman, L. J. San, & T. J. Vance (Eds.), *Papers from the parasession on functionalism.* Chicago: Chicago Linguistic Society, 1975.

Taplin, J., & Standenmeyer, H. Interpretation of abstract conditional sentences in deductive reasoning. *Journal of Verbal Learning and Verbal Behavior,* 1973, *12,* 530–542.

Theios, J., Smith, E. E., Haviland, S., Traupmann, J., & Moy, M. Memory scanning as a serial, self-terminating process. *Journal of Experimental Psychology,* 1973, *97,* 323–336.

Thorndyke, P. W. The role of inferences in discourse comprehension. *Journal of Verbal Learning and Verbal Behavior,* 1976, *15,* 437–446.

Townsend, D. J. Children's comprehension of comparative forms. *Journal of Experimental Child Psychology,* 1974, *18,* 293–303.

Townsend, D. J., & Bever, T. G. *Main and subordinate clauses: A study in figure and ground.* Indiana University Linguistics Club, 1977. (a)

Townsend, D. J., & Bever, T. G. *Semantic representation and word recognition while listening to main and subordinate clauses.* Paper presented at Psychonomic Society meetings, 1977. (b)

Townsend, D. J., & Erb, M. Children's strategies for interpreting complex comparative questions. *Journal of Child Language,* 1975, *2,* 1–7.

Townsend, D. J., Ottaviano, D., & Bever, T. G. Immediate memory for words from main and subordinate clauses at different age levels. *Journal of Psycholinguistic Research,* in press.

Townsend, D. J., & Ravelo, N. Immediate organization of sentences using *after, and,* and *before.* Paper presented at the annual meeting of the American Psychological Association, Toronto, 1978.

Townsend, J. T. A note on the identifiability of parallel and serial processes. *Perception & Psychophysics,* 1971, *10,* 161–163.

Tyler, L. K., & Marslen-Wilson, W. D. The on-line effects of semantic context on syntactic processing. *Journal of Verbal Learning and Verbal Behavior,* 1977, *16,* 683–692.

Walker, E. *Grammatical relations in sentence memory.* Unpublished doctoral dissertation, Indiana University, 1969.

Walker, E. C. T., Gough, P., & Wall, R. Grammatical relations and the search of sentences in immediate memory. *Proceedings of the Midwestern Psychological Association,* 1968.

Wanner, E. Do we understand sentences from the outside-in or from the inside-out? *Daedulus,* 1973, *102,* 163–164.

Wanner, E., & Maratsos, M. *On understanding relative clauses.* Unpublished manuscript, Harvard University, 1971.

Wason, P. C., & Johnson-Laird, P. N. *Psychology of reasoning.* London: B. T. Batsford, 1972.

Wilkes, A. L., & Kennedy, R. A. Relationship between pausing and retrieval latency in sentences of varying grammatical form. *Journal of Experimental Psychology,* 1969, *79,* 241–245.

Wilkes, A. L., & Kennedy, R. A. Response retrieval in active and passive sentences. *Quarterly Journal of Experimental Psychology,* 1970, *22,* 1–8. (a)

Wilkes, A. L., & Kennedy, R. A. The relative accessibility of list items within different pause-defined groups. *Journal of Verbal Learning and Verbal Behavior,* 1970, *9,* 197–201. (b)

Williams, J. D. Memory ensemble selection in human information processing. *Journal of Experimental Psychology,* 1971, *88,* 231–238.

Wilson, D. Presuppositions on factives. *Linguistic Inquiry,* 1972, *3,* 405–410.

Wingfield, A., & Klein, J. F. Syntactic structure and acoustic pattern in speech perception. *Perception & Psychophysics,* 1971, *9,* 23–25.

Winograd, T. *Understanding natural language.* New York: Academic Press, 1972.

Yngve, V. A model and a hypothesis for language structure. *Proceedings of the American Philosophical Society,* October 1960, *104,* 5.

Zipf, G. K. *Human behavior and the principle of least effort.* Cambridge, Mass.: Addison-Wesley, 1949.

7 Some Hypotheses About Syntactic Processing in Sentence Comprehension

V. M. Holmes
University of Melbourne

INTRODUCTION

Remarkably little can be said with any certainty about the role of syntax in normal verbal communication. Given the initial interest in syntax triggered by Chomsky's (1957, 1965) theories of language, it might seem somewhat surprising that psychologists have come up with so few lasting generalizations about this issue. One reason for this curious state of affairs is, however, well known. The idea espoused in the early 1960s, that operations for understanding and producing speech might be analogous to syntactic rules, proved to be far too simple a view of the relation between the grammar and psychological processes (Fodor & Garrett, 1966). Many researchers reacted to the failure of this theory by abandoning the study of syntactic processing altogether. One of the few attempts to tackle this problem was provided by Fodor and Garrett (1967) and Fodor, Garrett, and Bever (1968), who postulated instead that the listener utilizes strategies based on certain cues in the surface structure of a sentence to recover the underlying structure relations. However, reliable evidence for the existence of these strategies has been slow to accumulate.

This fact highlights another reason for the dearth of established principles in psycholinguistics. Much of the early research investigated sentences divorced from their basic communicative function and, consequently, did not increase knowledge of processes involved in actual comprehension and production situations. Thinking they could build a "performance model" based on any kind of linguistic performance at all, researchers employed tasks that called upon a multiplicity of unspecified cognitive processes. Rote learning of lists of sentences was required; subjects were asked to transform sentences from one structure to another; retrieval was probed for one word in a sentence given another. But tasks such as these tell us very little about what is likely to be happening in on-going communication. Even those tasks that seemed as though they might tap more relevant processes usually involved the construction or perception of single sentences isolated from any linguistic or nonlinguistic context. The feeling began to grow that any strategies used for dealing with syntax in these tasks would probably be radically altered if there were some form of background context. Perhaps syntax was, after all, some obscure arbitrary system invented by linguists and logicians, and it did not have the "psychological reality" that had originally been claimed for it.

This attitude was particularly reflected in views of sentence production current at the time. For example, Goldman-Eisler (1968) argued that speakers need time to plan the general semantic content of a sentence and the particular lexical items used but that no observable planning time is required for syntax. A ready-made syntactic schema is automatically selected, and while the sentence is being uttered, no further attention is paid to syntax. Syntactic sequencing was, therefore, thought to be run off as an entirely automatic skill. In production, it would be difficult to ascribe a more minimal role to syntax than that. After all, since people often do utter correctly structured sequences, the structure has to be decided upon in some way.

In comprehension, syntax has received even more cursory treatment, in that it has been suggested that the listener may often not have to process syntax at all in order to understand a sentence. The problem for comprehension is merely to try to decode a presented message by whatever means are available. Such a view has been advocated by Bever (1970), who argued that the crucial properties of sentences to which people normally attend are semantic rather than syntactic. Either prior context or the meanings of the major content words would often suggest probable semantic groupings, and the deep syntactic relations would be decided on this basis. Accordingly, Bever (1970) proposed that "most normal perceptual processing of sentences is probably carried out with little regard for actual sequence or structure [p. 297]." A similar view has recently been taken by many artificial-intelligence researchers. Schank (1973), for instance, has proposed that people do not necessarily have to complete syntactic analysis in order to understand a sentence. Instead, predictions about the syntax are made on the basis of prior context or the first few words of the sentence, and these predictions simplify or eliminate the need for further syntactic processing. An additional assertion that has often been made is that, even if superficial syntax is attended to during the construction of the basic meaning of the sentence, information about surface form is almost immediately forgotten (e.g., Carroll, 1972; Sachs, 1967).

In light of these claims, it is interesting to note a recent return to the idea that syntax does have a critical role in linguistic behavior. For example,

Garrett (1975, 1976a) has argued that a great many of the speech errors that occur in ordinary conversation must be a result of failures of planning at a syntactic level. Ford and Holmes (1978) have demonstrated that syntactic decisions do occur during the output phase in spontaneous speech production. A strong case has also recently been made for the centrality of syntax in sentence comprehension. Forster (1974) and Garrett (1976b) have proposed that the syntactic structure of a sentence is always computed, even if the meanings of the content words alone would have been sufficient to unambiguously specify the basic syntactic relations. On their argument, it is *not* the case that semantic processing is carried out prior to syntactic analysis. Rather, regardless of prior context or pragmatic knowledge, it is only after the entire surface- and deep-structure representation has been determined that the listener integrates the content-word meanings with the structure to obtain a semantic interpretation.

Even from this brief account, it is obvious that conflicting views currently exist about the part played by syntax in linguistic communication. It is either regarded as of primary importance in the production and comprehension of sentences or relegated to a subsidiary role besides contextual constraints and semantic processes. In this paper, I attempt to confront this theoretical dispute by examining evidence on several apparently diverse issues in sentence comprehension. On the basis of this evidence, some hypotheses about the way in which syntax is processed can be proposed.

ASSIGNING DEEP-STRUCTURE RELATIONS

Let us begin by contrasting the semantic and syntactic approaches to the problem of how deep-structure relations are determined. The semantic approach sees the listener as scanning the input for the major content words and putting these together in the most sensible way. Purely syntactic analysis, such as paying attention to the order of words, their inflections, and so on, is only necessary when this preliminary semantic analysis fails to come up with an unequivocal message. The syntactic approach, on the other hand, requires that the subject complete the syntactic analysis of at least a clause before semantic analysis can begin. Is there any evidence claiming to substantiate either approach?

Bever (1970) adduced support for his view from Slobin's (1966) findings using semantically reversible and nonreversible sentences. Although reversible active sentences like (1) were easier to verify than their passive counterparts, this (presumably syntactic) difference was not obtained when the sentences were nonreversible, for example, (2). Bever concurred with Slobin's conclusion that in the nonreversible sentences the meanings of the content words were used to make the correct assignment of deep-structure role, thereby avoiding in passives the extra syntactic complexity. A similar result, for sentences containing pragmatic rather than strictly semantic constraints, has been obtained by Herriot (1969). Unfortunately, a major problem with these experiments, and with the others cited by Bever, is that they used experimental tasks that were probably quite insensitive to effects that might occur in immediate comprehension. There is, however, a recent report of an experiment by Quinn (cited in Steedman & Johnson-Laird, 1977) that does not appear to be subject to this criticism. A difference in comprehension latencies was found between standard and preposed indirect-object constructions, for reversible but not nonreversible sentences. Thus, although there is some evidence that deep-structure relations can be assigned on the basis of word meanings, it is far from convincing.

(1)   The girl kicked the boy.
(2)   The girl watered the garden.

The most compelling support for the syntactic approach comes from experiments by Forster and Olbrei (1973), who obtained a constant active–passive difference in comprehension times for both reversible and nonreversible sentences. They explained the the apparent discrepancy between previous results and their own in terms of task differences, and they concluded that a complete syntactic analysis must be carried out prior to and independently of semantic processing. After all, if this were not true, why would nonreversible passives remain more difficult to comprehend than nonreversible actives?

Clearly, the evidence for either position is extremely limited and in no way enables one to favor one hypothesis over the other. In some recent experiments, I applied essentially the same logic as in those that have just been discussed (Holmes, 1978b). The first question posed was whether the presence of semantic constraints really could eliminate the problems encountered in difficult syntactic constructions. In order to assess this, it seemed inadvisable to confine oneself to a comparison of actives and passives. The additional lexical processing involved in the recognition of the extra two words in passives complicates enormously the interpretation of differences in comprehension time between the two structures. It was difficult to find any other suitable effects reported in the literature. However, in a preliminary experiment, I was able to establish a systematic difference in comprehension difficulty between different kinds of semantically neutral relative-clause sentences. Before this effect is explained more fully, the comprehension task will be described.

The experimental procedure was basically the same as one used by Forster and Olbrei (1973). People were asked to read an individual sentence on a screen, and their decision as to whether it was a completely meaningful sentence was timed. Relative-clause sentences containing an obvious selection-restriction violation in the final words were presented half the time as distractors. Other types of complex sentence were also included so that a variety of structures was encountered. The task taps the ability of subjects to read a sequence of words rapidly, and from it to try to construct a sentence meaning. By using visual presentation, one is limited to statements about what is happening during reading, but any problems associated with controlling for articulation, stress, and intonation are avoided.

In the situation described, sentences in which the relative pronoun was the subject of the relative clause (subject relatives) were found to be comprehended significantly faster than sentences in which the pronoun was the object (object relatives). (I use the term *significant* to mean significant at at least the .05 level by minimum F'.) To obtain this effect is hardly surprising, but, to my knowledge, it has not been reported. Presumably, the violation of the standard English subject–verb–object order in object relatives must be responsible for the increase in computational difficulty (Fodor, Bever, & Garrett, 1974). The effect was found for both center-embedded relatives, where the relative clause qualified the subject of the main clause, and right-branching relatives, where the relative clause qualified the object of the main clause. (There was no difference between center-embedded and right-branching relatives, suggesting that additional complexity due to embedding occurs only when there is more than one level of embedding, as was suggested by Holmes [1973]).

We are now in a position to consider the question of the possible influence of semantic constraints on deep-structure analysis. According to the syntactic approach, the difference between subject and object relatives should always be found, regardless of the presence of semantic cues. But the semantic approach predicts no subject–object difference for sentences where the deep-syntactic roles of the content words in the relative clause can be determined from the word meanings alone. That is, while in (3) and (4) the *a* sentences should be comprehended faster than the *b* sentences, in (5) and (6) the *a* and *b* versions should not differ.

(3a)   The lorry avoided the bus that crashed into the van.
(3b)   The lorry avoided the bus that the van crashed into.
(4a)   The bus that crashed into the van avoided the lorry.
(4b)   The bus that the van crashed into avoided the lorry.
(5a)   The actors ignored the noise that came from the audience.
(5b)   The actors ignored the noise that the audience was making.
(6a)   The noise that came from the audience irritated the actors.
(6b)   The noise that the audience was making irritated the actors.

As expected, for reversible sentences such as those in (3) and (4), there was a significant pronoun-function effect (3489 vs. 3597 msecs). For nonreversible relatives such as those in (5) and (6), the effect was still present, if anything somewhat larger (3228 vs. 3509 msecs). (In the analysis, the apparent interaction was far from significant.) Note that this subject–object difference must have arisen primarily from syntactic rather than semantic or lexical processing, insofar as these can be clearly distinguished. Within each sentence set, lexical-processing requirements were either identical, or corresponding words were equated in length and frequency. Some semantic equivalence was also guaranteed by obtaining pretest ratings of the plausibility of the sentence meanings, and these showed little systematic variation. At first glance, then, the results appear to provide overwhelming support for the idea that word meanings are not used to short-circuit syntactic processing.

The results of a subsequent experiment suggest, however, that this conclusion may not be warranted. The question asked in this experiment was whether prior context might provide a more effective way of allowing syntactic processing to be by-passed. Specifically, if people have to process a sentence containing a clause with basically the same meaning as a sentence they have just read, then they should be able to assign the deep-syntactic roles within the clause on the basis of the contextual information, with minimal analysis of the actual sequence and structure of the target sentence.

The relative-clause sentences that had been used before were now preceded for several seconds by a sentence that was basically the same as either the main or the relative clause. The nouns in the context sentence and the target clause were the same and retained the same deep-syntactic role; the verbs in the context were an extended paraphrase of those in the target. Nonmeaningful distractors with apparently relevant context sentences were also presented. The sentences in (7) were contexts specifying main-clause relations for (3) and (4), whereas those in (8) specified the relative clause relations. The sentences in (9) and (10) were contexts relevant to the main and relative clauses, respectively, for (5) and (6).

(7a)   The lorry narrowly missed hitting the bus.
(7b)   The bus narrowly missed hitting the lorry.
(8a)   The bus collided violently with the van.
(8b)   The van collided violently with the bus.
(9a)   The actors took no notice of the noise.
(9b)   The noise was disturbing to the actors.
(10a)   The noise emanated from the audience.
(10b)   The audience was producing the noise.

First of all, I established that the presence of the contexts actually did help the processing of the target sentences. Comprehension times, as evidenced by meaning classification responses, were substantially and significantly faster in this experiment than in the previous one. Main-clause and relative-clause contexts speeded up comprehension to the same extent. But context did not seem to assist in the assignment of deep-structure relations in the subsequent target sentences. Only the contexts specifying relative-clause relations could possibly help in the analysis of these roles in the relative clause of the target sentence. But for these items a significant pronoun-function effect was still obtained, whether the relative clause was reversible (2761 vs. 2925 msecs) or nonreversible (2657 vs. 2816 msecs). On the basis of these results, a significant subject–object difference would also be expected for sentences preceded by the irrelevant main-clause contexts. Although this was found to be true for nonreversible sentences (2706 vs. 2890 msecs), for reversible sentences the effect vanished (2851 vs. 2841 msecs).

How are these results to be explained? If the syntactic approach is correct, *all* conditions should produce a constant syntactic-complexity difference. On the other hand, if the contexts are used to predict deep-syntactic relations, the sentences preceded by relative-clause information should show no syntactic effect. Yet the results fit neither of these patterns. That the contexts were not simply being ignored is attested to by the fact that performance was facilitated in their presence. At least part of this facilitation must have come about through priming at a lexical level, because there were two identical nouns in each context and target pair. Given that the contexts were being processed, it remains to account for the apparently puzzling findings.

A plausible explanation can be found by considering the reversible and nonreversible sentences separately. First, taking the nonreversible sentences, the syntactic complexity effect was present whether or not there was advance knowledge of the relative-clause relations. Thus, subjects were not using contextual or semantic constraints to select automatically the correct deep-structure relations. The alternative assignment of the subject and object roles would, of course, be anomalous. It seems that these alternative potential "meanings" were sufficiently similar to the "meanings" of the anomalous distractors that subjects had to complete the syntactic analysis to avoid the possibility of falsely classifying these sentences as nonmeaningful. To say that the syntactic analysis had to be completed is not, however, to say at what point it is carried out. Surprisingly enough, the answer to this question comes from the results for the reversible sentences. Here, the syntactic relations of the relative clause only caused difficulty when these same relations had been specified in advance. This suggests the opposite of what might have been expected: Subjects may have been checking that the meaning of the target clause was the same as that of the context, rather than assuming that it would be. Further, the absence of a complexity effect when the main-clause relations were given in the context indicates that subjects realized that the relative clause was not directly relevant to the context, and so did not bother to complete its syntactic analysis. There would be no danger of misclassifying these sentences as nonmeaningful, because either noun could function meaningfully in the subject or object role of the clause. The implication to be drawn from this is critical. An analysis of the content-word meanings within the clause must have been made *before* any attempt to assign the deep-structure relations on the basis of syntactic properties. If this is true for some sentences, then it must be the case that for all the sentences the content-word meanings in a clause are accessed and combined together in some way, before a final allocation of the deep-structure relations is made.

In sum, the conclusion I draw from these experiments is that neither the syntactic nor the semantic approach is completely correct. The subject's initial hypothesis about the deep-structure relations of a clause is based on semantic cues provided by the content words. But this semantic analysis does not obviate the need for syntactic processing if the subject is to understand the sentence accurately. Therefore, it is usually followed by a check that the correct relational assignment has been made. This would be based on syntactic features that must have been recovered from the surface structure, such as word order and the distribution of function words and inflections. In these experiments the check was made when there was a possibility that an anomalous sentence might have been intended, or when the subject wanted to verify that the meaning of the clause was congruent with a prior context. However, the check was not carried out when the context was irrelevant, and both potential subject-object roles for the nouns were acceptable. In effect, the task was probably not forcing the subject to unambiguously determine the meaning of some of the sentences.

The syntactic effect obtained for reversible as well as nonreversible clauses when there was no context at all suggests that subjects *were* completing the syntactic analysis in this case, even though both interpretations of the clause would have been acceptable. It is not clear why the presence of context should change subjects' processing strategies in this way. Whatever the reason, the important point for the present argument is that subjects' failure to complete syntactic analysis in any such reversible sentences provides the insight that this aspect of syntactic analysis must have been taking place as a post-semantic check.

PROCESSING DEEP- AND SURFACE-STRUCTURE AMBIGUITIES

I have suggested that word meanings are accessed and integrated at some stage before deep-structure relations are finalized on the basis of syntactic properties; i.e., not all aspects of the syntax of a sentence are computed prior to a preliminary semantic analysis. Examining the comprehension of structurally ambiguous sentences allows an additional test of this proposal. The semantic approach would claim that the presence of alternative deep-structure interpretations of a sentence should have no impact on the comprehender, because the deep-structure roles would be uniquely determined by semantic probabilities. The syntactic approach, however, would assert that there is no way of knowing which meaning is more likely until the deep-structure relations have been computed. Thus, on this view, *all* permissible structures must be computed and semantically analyzed before a decision can be made as to which is the appropriate structure and meaning. Unless it is assumed that computing more than one structure can be performed just as rapidly as computing only one, the implication is that comprehension of ambiguous sentences should be more complicated than comprehension of unambiguous sentences. To obtain such a result would, then, conflict with my explanation of the findings so far.

Nothing has yet been said about how surface-structure relations are determined during comprehension. We can also learn something about this by studying ambiguous sentences. An approach assuming that surface details are not processed at all would, of course, predict no effect of surface-structure ambiguity. And even if surface structure is considered to be analyzed, one can argue that semantic probabilities could guide the analysis into a single structure that makes the most sense. But a syntactic approach would still expect a complexity effect, because all structures would have to be computed before any semantic reading could be assigned. Either outcome for surface ambiguities would be compatible with the conclusions that have been drawn so far.

The question of the possible complicating effect of ambiguity has received considerable attention in the literature, particularly following Garrett's (1970) analysis. It is probably fair to say that there have been more experiments claiming to support the idea that structural ambiguity does have perceptual consequences, than the opposing single-meaning view. But there are several reasons for doubting the validity of this conclusion. One is the tendency to discuss all kinds of ambiguity—lexical, deep, and surface— together, even though the results may not have been consistent for all types. Other reasons are methodological, such as the poor matching of control sentences or the failure to establish the generality of effects for items as well as for subjects. Of course, criticisms such as these apply to research in other areas as well. However, I believe that anyone reviewing all the research would agree that the question remains unresolved.

An unpublished study that I carried out recently with Katie Kirby investigated the processing of both deep- and surface-structure ambiguities. We constructed many examples of different kinds of structurally ambiguous sentences with two distinct meanings (6 sentences in each of 14 subtypes). Both meanings were made as natural and plausible as possible. Sentences such as (11a) were classified as being ambiguous at the deep-structure level, because the alternative structures involve different sets of subject–verb–

object relations. Others, such as (13a), were clearly ambiguous at a surface-bracketing level; the two structures did not differ in the basic deep-structure relations. The final set was classified as "mixed," because, although the ambiguity could be resolved by different surface bracketings, changes in deep structure relations also occurred. An example of such a mixed ambiguity is (12a).

(11a)   The baby lamb was too hot to eat.
(11b)   The baby lamb was too sick to eat.
(11c)   The baby lamb was too tough to eat.
(12a)   The woman knows that they are cooking apples.
(12b)   The woman knows that they are picking apples.
(12c)   The woman knows that they are ripe apples.
(13a)   The waiter knew the people had argued over dinner.
(13b)   The waiter knew the people had argued after dinner.
(13c)   The waiter knew the people had argued about dinner.

Examples of the unambiguous control sentences are given in the b and c versions. These were designed to correspond as closely as possible to the structure and meaning of the relevant interpretation. Wherever possible, the words were kept the same, or only a function word was changed. If a content word had to be substituted, it was approximately matched in length and frequency with the corresponding word in the ambiguous sentence. Comprehension of the sentences was assessed by means of the meaning-classification task, with the sentences being presented among appropriate nonmeaningful distractors.

The basic result can be summarized in one sentence: There was no effect of structural ambiguity at all. Comprehension times for the ambiguous and unambiguous sentences were 3304 vs. 3345 msecs for deep-structure ambiguities, 3189 vs. 3223 msecs for mixed ambiguities, and 3225 vs. 3174 msecs for surface-structure ambiguities. Dividing subjects into those who subsequently reported noticing that a substantial number of sentences had been ambiguous ($n = 17$) and those who did not notice any ambiguity ($n = 34$) produced virtually identical results. Clearly, our failure to find any difference between ambiguous and unambiguous sentences does not mean that the null hypothesis is proven. But, given the care with which the sentences were constructed, and the large number of items and subjects that were run, we feel that the results make it difficult to maintain that more than one structure of any kind of syntactically ambiguous sentence is usually processed.

If only one structure of a syntactically ambiguous sentence is perceived, what determines which structure is chosen? Sentence paraphrases were obtained, on the assumption that they would probably reflect the interpretations that had first occurred to the subjects. For each ambiguous sentence, the percentage of people reporting each reading was determined from the usable paraphrases, and an estimate of the bias towards a particular reading was given by the percentage value at or above 50. Plausibility ratings were also obtained for all of the sentences. We assumed that the plausibility ratings for the unambiguous sentences would provide a guide to the plausibilities of the two readings of the ambiguous sentence. Although we had attempted to construct sentences where both meanings were likely to be reported, there usually was a clear preference for one reading over the other. The average bias estimates were: 79% for both deep-structure and mixed ambiguities and 77% for surface ambiguities. Now, the semantic approach would expect that ambiguous sentences with a very high bias should be judged as describing highly plausible events, whereas ambiguous sentences with a low bias should have lower plausibility ratings. The approach would also expect that the unambiguous control sentences corresponding to the preferred reading would have higher plausibilities than the unambiguous sentences corresponding to the less-preferred reading, particularly for the highly biased items.

To test these two predictions, we classified the sentences of each major structural type as highly biased, slightly biased, or unbiased. The data showed neither of these relationships of plausibility and bias. The plausibility of the ambiguous sentences did not vary according to bias, and there were no differences in the plausibility of the unambiguous sentences corresponding to the more and less preferred readings. Thus, there was no evidence from this analysis that subjects use the probability or plausibility of events to help allocate either deep- or surface-syntactic relations.

Neither the semantic nor the syntactic approach has again provided an adequate explanation for the results. It is therefore necessary to explore a further alternative. Suppose that only one structure is assigned and that it is chosen, not on the basis of probable semantic groupings but on the basis of preferred analyses of syntactic properties; i.e., syntactic hypotheses could be constructed and tested in a fixed order. A particular structure may usually be assigned, and only if the resulting meaning turns out to be implausible or odd is the less preferred structure computed. Such an ordered allocation of readings has recently been suggested for lexical ambiguities (in terms of frequency of usage) by Holmes (1978a), among others. Evidence for the assignment of structures in a specific order would be found if the bias estimates of the ambiguous sentences of the same subtype tended to be consistently higher for one structure than for the other. The bias estimates were now averaged for the alternative *structures* of a given type. Even though individual sentences might be quite highly biased, if bias were unrelated to structure the average bias would be around 50%.

The results of this analysis were extremely interesting. Deep-structure ambiguities were only slightly and nonsignificantly more often biased to one structure rather than the other (60%). But there were significant biases according to structure for both mixed (71%) and surface (75%) ambiguities: One structure was perceived much more often than was the other. Some examples will help to make this finding clear. Deep-structure ambiguities of the type in (14) were, about half the time, primarily interpreted with the final noun as the subject of the "verbing" and about half the time as the object. For (14a) there was a strong bias towards the subject structure, whereas for (14b) the bias was strongly towards the object structure. By contrast, the majority of the mixed sentences exemplified in (15) were interpreted as in (15a), where the adverbial phrase was seen as modifying the verb rather than the preceding nominal. Only one sentence, (15b), completely reversed this bias. For surface ambiguities, the marked preference for one structure over another can be seen in (16). All sentences of this subtype were interpreted as having the adverb modifying the verb in the final clause rather than the relative clause. Sentence (16a) had a high bias towards this structure, whereas (16b) had a somewhat lower bias.

(14a)   We heard about the finding of the geologists.
(14b)   The spokesman confirmed the killing of the terrorists.
(15a)   The councillors discussed the difficulties with the mayor.
(15b)   The teachers arranged the discussion with the migrant parents.
(16a)   The judge who was presiding patiently questioned the witness.
(16b)   The girl who had watched the traffic nervously crossed the street.

It seems, then, that deep-structure ambiguities are not consistently interpreted according to a given structure. But neither did the bias estimates seem to coincide with the plausibility ratings. Because we had intended to construct sentences whose alternative readings were as plausible as possible, perhaps any differences in plausibility may have been too subtle to be detected by the plausibility rating scale used. In any event, in the absence of data to the contrary, it seems simplest to assume that deep-structure relations *are* assigned initially on the basis of semantic cues.

The picture presented for deep-structure ambiguities does not hold for ambiguous sentences that can be disambiguated by changes in surface bracketing, namely, surface and mixed ambiguities. These sentences appear to be initially interpreted according to preferred structural analyses. Presumably, only if the preferred analysis produces a fairly implausible meaning would the alternative less-preferred structure be computed. Fortunately, the plausibility data were consistent with this suggestion. For the small minority of surface- and mixed-ambiguous sentences where bias did *not* correspond with the preferred structure ($n = 8$), the plausibility ratings for the unambiguous sentences using the preferred structure were always substantially lower than those for the unambiguous sentences using the less-preferred structure. In addition, comprehension time for these ambiguous sentences having a nonstandard bias was significantly longer than for all the other ambiguous sentences of the same subtypes (3525 vs. 3214 msecs). These two results, albeit post hoc, indicate that the sentence may be reanalyzed into the less-preferred structure if the interpretation provided by the standard structure is implausible.

The results show that surface structure is not ignored by the comprehender nor is it first anlayzed in terms of likely semantic groupings. Instead, people apply unique structural analyses to the input, perhaps trying the most commonly encountered analyses first. They subsequently review and reanalyze the first hypotheses, if necessary. This conclusion is at odds not only with the semantic approach, but also with a syntactic approach that predicts that all structures must be computed for any structural ambiguity. As far as the computation of deep structure is concerned, the results are consistent with the idea that these relations are assigned on the basis of semantic cues, obtained both from the content words in the ambiguous segment and from the surrounding context. Compatible with this suggestion is a recent finding by Tyler and Marslen-Wilson (1977), who reported that prior context could immediately select one relevant interpretation of certain deep-structure ambiguities. The question remains as to how these two different forms of processing are to be related to one another. It would seem counterintuitive that surface analyses would be performed *after* semantic analyses. Rather, it seems more sensible to postulate that at least some surface analysis into constituents would occur before the content-word meanings within these constituents were adequately analyzed.

SURFACE STRUCTURE AND PRESUPPOSITION

The view that people try merely to establish the basic message of a sentence, paying little or no attention to superficial structure, seems certainly wrong. However, a less extreme semantic approach could still be maintained. It could be that once the surface structure has served its purpose in allowing the person to recover the deep-structure relations, it is immediately forgotten. In the experiments described in this section, I investigated how the meaning of a sentence is stored for immediate use. Is the representation stripped of its initial surface expression? Or can surface properties determine the form in which it is represented?

The function of certain surface structures to mark part of a sentence as asserted and part as presupposed provided a means of answering this question. This by now well-known distinction is illustrated by the sentences in (17), both of which express the basic proposition that the Frenchman took my chair. In (17a), it is presupposed that someone has taken my chair, and it is asserted that that someone is the Frenchman, whereas in (17b), it is presupposed that the Frenchman has taken something, and it is asserted that that something is my chair. The main clause conveys the assertion, and the subordinate clause conveys the presupposition. Sentences with such structures are often used to allow a fluent and natural link to a prior knowledge base: The presupposition usually contains information that is already known to the listener, whereas the assertion contains new, unknown information.

(17a)   It is the Frenchman who has taken my chair.
(17b)   It is my chair that the Frenchman has taken.

There is only indirect evidence that surface syntax is used to distinguish presuppositions and assertions in sentence comprehension. Haviland and Clark (1974) found that sentences with presuppositions that were fulfilled by a prior context were comprehended faster than sentences with unfulfilled presuppositions. These results are only suggestive, however, as they concerned lexically and not syntactically marked presuppositions. Perhaps the most directly relevant experiment is one by Hornby (1974), who found that sentences whose presuppositions were subsequently shown to be false in relation to a picture were verified incorrectly much more often than sentences whose assertions were shown to be false. Unfortunately, the experiment does not show unequivocally that syntax was causing the effect. The noun in the assertion was always given heavier stress than the other words, so the possibility that subjects searched the pictures for the stressed item first, regardless of the syntax, cannot be discounted. It should be noted that if people do analyze sentences into their asserted and presupposed parts, this would be unlikely to occur until after the whole sentence has been syntactically and semantically processed. Cutler (1976) has in fact suggested that such an analysis should be considered as part of a separate processing stage occurring after the literal interpretation has been recovered. Thus, in order to provide a fair test of the potential role of presupposition in comprehension, it is important to use an experimental task that appropriately taps this level of analysis.

In some experiments I carried out with Jenni Langford (Langford & Holmes, 1978), we investigated whether the surface structure of a sentence really can be used to recover the presuppositional or assertional status of the constituents. We first wanted to see whether this was true when sentences are comprehended in the light of a prior context. In the experiment, subjects were presented with a naturalistic context paragraph followed by a test sentence in which either the assertion or the presupposition was inconsistent with the context. Subjects read the paragraph at their own speed, then initiated the presentation of the test sentence, which they verified as quickly as possible.

True items were, of course, included. The context in (18) is inconsistent with the assertion in the sentences in (20), whereas the context in (19) is inconsistent with their presupposition. In addition to the cleft–pseudocleft structures of the sentences in (20), noun-phrase complements such as those in (21) were used. The *a* and *b* versions control for which constituent is mentioned first, the assertion or the presupposition, in case there was a simple strategy to always check the first-mentioned constituent first.

(18) Our guests last night were a rowdy lot. They dropped ash everywhere and spilt wine and coffee on our new carpet. The coffee came out easily, but nothing will budge the wine.

(19) Our guests last night were a rowdy lot. They dropped ash everywhere and spilt wine and coffee on our new sofa. The wine came out easily, but nothing will budge the coffee.

(20a) It was the coffee that ruined our carpet.

(20b) What ruined our carpet was the coffee.

(21a) Linda's teacher was delighted that she could solve the problem.

(21b) The fact that Linda could solve the problem delighted her teacher.

The verification times obtained showed that subjects were indeed analyzing the sentences into presupposition and assertion. Sentences whose presuppositions were false took significantly longer to verify than sentences whose assertions were false, both for cleft–pseudocleft structures (2624 vs. 3088 msecs) and for noun phrase complements (2632 vs. 2934 msecs). There was no sign of a strategy to check first the truth of the first-mentioned constituent. A possible objection to the experiment was that we might have represented more difficult facts in the presuppositions or that they were for some reason harder to compare with the contexts. To answer this, a control experiment was run, in which the test sentences were separated into two simple sentences such as those in (22). When these sentences were presented in the same conditions as previously, there was absolutely no difference between times to verify sentences that had formerly been presuppositions and those that had formerly been assertions.

(22a) Linda's teacher was delighted.

(22b) Linda could solve the problem.

We next asked whether subjects only treat assertions and presuppositions differently when there is some background context. In the absence of context, would the need to process and preserve surface-syntactic details disappear? This time we presented subjects with a sentence first and asked them to verify it in relation to a subsequently presented picture. A picture was used rather than a linguistic context to avoid too much verbal interference. Either the assertion or the presupposition was contradicted by the picture. For example, a simple line-drawing of a woman holding a picture with a boy standing next to her was preceded by one of the sentences in (23). The picture contradicts the agent of these sentences; in other items the object was contradicted. Exactly the same effect was found again. The times taken to classify the pictures were slower when presuppositions were false (1310 msecs) than when assertions were false (1157 msecs). This difference was found for all four structures and for contradictions of both the agent and the object.

(23a)   It's the boy who is holding the picture.
(23b)   It's the picture that the boy is holding.
(23c)   The one who is holding the picture is the boy.
(23d)   What the boy is holding is the picture.

In demonstrating that presuppositions and assertions are handled differently, we have shown that subjects must not only be processing the surface syntax, but also retaining the surface information in the representation of the sentence meaning. There is no way that the subject could respond differentially to presuppositions and assertions without having analyzed the sentence into main and subordinate clauses and without storing the clauses in some different way. The reason the presupposed information took longer to verify is not clear, however. Haviland and Clark (1974) explained their results by arguing that subjects search memory for antecedents for the presupposed or given information, and only afterwards process the asserted or new information. If this were true in the present study, one might expect faster rather than slower times for verifying false presuppositions. But they subsequently suggested that verifying sentences is like answering yes–no questions and that, therefore, a different strategy would be involved. Subjects would check the new information before the presupposed, the truth of the latter being assumed (Clark & Haviland, 1977).

The problem with this account is that it does little more than restate the question. Moreover, the results of the picture-verification experiment are difficult to explain merely in terms of the given–new distinction. Because all the information in the sentence was always new, the subject could not be assuming that the presupposed information could contain already known antecedents. It may be more fruitful to assume that the subject treats what is in the main clause as more salient than what is in the subordinate clause. After all, it is the function of syntactic subordination to present less important material, even when there are no presuppositions of the kind we have been discussing. Added to this is the fact that, in the absence of intonation, the main clause in these structures contains the semantic focus of the sentence. These structures make the semantic focus very prominent for subjects which in some way forces them to store the focused information in a special emphasized form.

The major point of these findings for our present concern is that subjects' mental representation of a sentence's meaning can be crucially determined by its superficial form, a point also recently made by Bock (1977). Subjects do not jettison the surface information once the basic message has been grasped. The surface structure of sentences comprehended both in context and in isolation is attended to and retained. It is interesting that in the picture-verification experiment, many subjects reported trying to translate the simple nonreversible propositions into a single statement. It seems that, despite these efforts, subjects were unable to prevent themselves from storing the meaning in a form dictated by the surface separation of the constituents into distinct clauses.

CONCLUSION

The evidence I have presented amply demonstrates that any model of sentence comprehension that minimizes the importance of syntax is misguided. Further, the results provide us with some clues as to exactly how syntax might be implicated in the comprehension process. It is clear that semantic processing is *not* postponed until the entire surface- and deep-structure representation of a clause is available. Final allocation of deep-structure relations does not occur until after the major content-word meanings have been accessed and tentatively combined. However, semantic analysis *is* preceded by a superficial analysis in which a unique surface-structure representation is imposed on the clause. It is also obvious that surface-structure information is not lost immediately; it can critically influence how the sentence meaning is represented for further processing. If these conclusions are correct, then a model of comprehension must include several stages during which the different kinds of decision are made.

First, there must be a stage at which a single surface structure is constructed for the sentence while the words are being identified. Among other things, this would involve classifying each word as a content or function word, analyzing inflections, deciding on the form class of content words, and extracting other syntactic properties of the content words. Clause boundaries would be located on the basis of the presence of relative pronouns, complementizers, and conjunctions (Fodor & Garrett, 1967) and from syntactic information contained in the verb (Fodor et al., 1968). Our ambiguity results suggest that there are many other structural decisions that have to be made *within* clauses, and this is an issue that deserves much more systematic investigation. For example, there was a predominant strategy to interpret sequences such as "old men and women" with the adjective referring to both nouns, and sequences such as "look over the fence" as verb-preposition rather than verb-particle. It would be interesting to know whether this is a reflection of a general preference in English for assigning right-branching structures or was specific to the sentences we used. Our results further suggest that the syntactic decisions that may be made independently of meanings concern the surface- and not the deep-structure relations. The facility with which we analyze sequences with nonsense content-words, but correct superficial structure, reinforces this idea. It is only after an initial surface analysis that meanings are taken into account.

Thus, a stage of semantic analysis must follow the superficial syntactic processing. The meanings of the content words must be accessed, temporarily stored if necessary, and when a large enough surface unit has been segmented, these meanings are put together in the most plausible way; i.e., a hypothesis as to the likely subject–verb–object roles is formed. The findings I have presented allow little more to be said about these operations. For instance, one fundamental question is the size of the unit over which the semantic analysis is defined. It is customary, and I think quite reasonable, to think of this as the clause, either at the surface- or the deep-structure level. But it may not have a consistent syntactic basis at all, depending on such factors as length and internal complexity (Tanenhaus & Carroll, 1975).

In the next stage, people check the accuracy of their preliminary hypothesis about the deep-structure relations, by integrating the word meanings and the results of the surface-structure analysis. This check allows subjects to discriminate between meaningful nonreversible sentences and semantically anomalous sequences. It would also be after this integration that subjects would modify their initial surface analysis if the meaning turned out to be too implausible. It is at this stage too that the consequences of obscure or complex deep-structure configurations would arise, such as the difficulty posed by object relatives. On the basis of the discussion of the relative-clause results, it seems clear that care has to be taken to ensure that experimental tasks really do require the subject to process the sentences to this level.

Although the computation at these three stages supplies the comprehender with the basic message of the sentence, there are many kinds of additional processing that could subsequently be carried out. One of these is the sorting of the sentential information into presupposed and asserted constituents. As we have shown, this can be based on how the elements in the basic message are allocated in relation to surface clause-structure. The fact that the surface form of the sentence continues to play a vital part even at this stage in the comprehension process has not previously been emphasized. It would be interesting to establish to what extent structures other than the ones we used involve this analysis.

Throughout this paper, I have maintained a distinction between surface- and deep-structure descriptions of a sentence. This contrasts with a recent view that the concept of deep structure should be completely abandoned as irrelevant to comprehension and production processes (Johnson-Laird, 1977, 1978). However, this attitude seems somewhat hasty, and certainly seems to be based on flimsier evidence than that which it discounts. The experiments I discussed initially indicate that processing the logical relations that deep structure describes, does form an important step in sentence comprehension. After all, why should object relatives be harder to comprehend than subject relatives? Because their *deep* structures are more difficult to determine, not their surface structures, and not the events they describe.

It may seem similarly old-fashioned to postulate separate stages of processing. Marslen-Wilson (1976) has recently suggested that sentence perception is an "on-line interactive" process, in which decisions at all levels of linguistic analysis take place simultaneously. Although it would be rash to argue that every stage is fully completed before the next one begins, there is the implication that the separate forms of analysis are, to a large extent, dependent on the results of prior analyses. Perhaps the difference between serial and interactive approaches is only terminological. One could, for example, suppose that all the types of decision that I have been discussing are initiated together, but that some take much longer than others to make. At present, there does not seem an easy way to decide between these formulations. Perhaps one resolution of the apparent conflict is that the stages of processing that I have proposed might be more applicable to reading than to listening. In contrast to rapid listening, in reading there is a much more permanent representation of the input available for relatively leisurely analysis and reanalysis.

ACKNOWLEDGMENTS

The research reported here was supported by a grant from the Australian Research Grants Committee.

REFERENCES

Bever, T. G. The cognitive basis for linguistic structures. In J. R. Hayes (Ed.), *Cognition and the development of language.* New York: Wiley, 1970.

Bock, J. K. The effect of pragmatic presupposition on syntactic structure in question-answering. *Journal of Verbal Learning and Verbal Behavior, 1977, 6,* 723–734.

Carroll, J. B. Defining language comprehension: Some speculations. In R. O. Freedle & J. B. Carroll (Eds.), *Language comprehension and the acquisition of knowledge.* New York: Wiley, 1972.

Chomsky, N. *Syntactic structures.* The Hague: Mouton, 1957.

Chomsky, N. *Aspects of the theory of syntax.* Cambridge, Mass.: MIT Press, 1965.

Clark, H. H., & Haviland, S. E. Comprehension and the given–new contract. In R. O. Freedle (Ed.), *Discourse production and comprehension.* Norwood, N.J.: Ablex Publishing, 1977.

Cutler, A. Beyond parsing and lexical look-up: An enriched description of auditory sentence comprehension. In R. J. Wales & E. Walker (Eds.), *New approaches to language mechanisms.* Amsterdam: North-Holland, 1976.

Fodor, J. A., Bever, T. G., & Garrett, M. F. *The psychology of language.* New York: McGraw-Hill, 1974.

Fodor, J. A., & Garrett, M. F. Some reflections on competence and performance. In J. Lyons & R. J. Wales (Eds.), *Psycholinguistic papers.* Edinburgh: Edinburgh University Press, 1966.

Fodor, J. A., & Garrett, M. F. Some determinants of sentential complexity. *Perception & Psychophysics,* 1967, *2,* 289–296.

Fodor, J. A., Garrett, M. F., & Bever, T. G. Some determinants of sentential complexity, II: Verb structure. *Perception & Psychophysics,* 1968, *3,* 453–461.

Ford, M., & Holmes, V. M. Planning units and syntax in sentence production. *Cognition,* 1978, *6,* 35–53.

Forster, K. I. The role of semantic hypotheses in sentence processing. In F. Bresson (Ed.), *Problèmes actuels en psycholinguistique.* Paris: Centre National de la Recherche Scientifique, 1974.

Forster, K. I., & Olbrei, I. Semantic heuristics and syntactic analysis. *Cognition,* 1973, *2,* 319–347.

Garrett, M. F. Does ambiguity complicate the perception of sentences? In G. B. Flores d'Arcais & W. Levelt (Eds.), *Advances in psycholinguistics.* Amsterdam: North-Holland, 1970.

Garrett, M. F. The analysis of sentence production. In G. Bower (Ed.), *Psychology of learning and motivation* (Vol. 9). New York: Academic Press, 1975.

Garrett, M. F. Sentence production. In R. J. Wales & E. Walker (Eds.), *New approaches to language mechanisms.* Amsterdam: North-Holland, 1976. (a)

Garrett, M. F. *Word and sentence perception.* Unpublished manuscript, MIT, 1976. (b)

Goldman-Eisler, F. *Psycholinguistics: Experiments in spontaneous speech.* London: Academic Press, 1968.

Haviland, S. E., & Clark, H. H. What's new? Acquiring new information as a process in comprehension. *Journal of Verbal Learning and Verbal Behavior,* 1974, *13,* 512–521.

Herriot, P. The comprehension of active and passive sentences as a function of pragmatic expectation. *Journal of Verbal Learning and Verbal Behavior,* 1969, *8,* 166–169.

Holmes, V. M. Order of main and subordinate clauses in sentence perception. *Journal of Verbal Learning and Verbal Behavior,* 1973, *12,* 285–293.

Holmes, V. M. *Accessing ambiguous words during sentence comprehension.* Unpublished manuscript, University of Melbourne, 1978. (a)

Holmes, V. M. *Semantic and contextual constraints on the assignment of deep structure relations.* Unpublished manuscript, University of Melbourne, 1978. (b)

Hornby, P. A. Surface structure and presupposition. *Journal of Verbal Learning and Verbal Behavior,* 1974, *13,* 530–538.

Johnson-Laird, P. N. Procedural semantics. *Cognition,* 1977, *5,* 189–214.

Johnson-Laird, P. N. Psycholinguistics without linguistics. In N. S. Sutherland (Ed.), *Tutorial essays in psychology* (Vol. 1). Hillsdale, N.J.: Lawrence Erlbaum Associates, 1978.

Langford, J., & Holmes, V. M. *Comprehending presuppositions in and out of context.* Unpublished manuscript, University of Melbourne, 1978.

Marslen-Wilson, W. D. Linguistic descriptions and psychological assumptions in the study of sentence perception. In R. J. Wales & E. Walker (Eds.), *New approaches to language mechanisms.* Amsterdam: North-Holland, 1976.

Sachs, J. S. Recognition memory for syntactic and semantic aspects of connected discourse. *Perception & Psychophysics,* 1967, *2,* 437–442.

Schank, R. C. Identification of conceptualizations underlying natural language. In R. C. Schank & K. M. Colby (Eds.), *Computer models of thought and language.* San Francisco: Freeman, 1973.

Slobin, D. Grammatical transformations and sentence comprehension in childhood and adulthood. *Journal of Verbal Learning and Verbal Behavior,* 1966, *5,* 219–227.

Steedman, M. J., & Johnson-Laird, P. N. A programmatic theory of linguistic performance. In P. Smith & R. Campbell (Eds.), *Proceedings of the Stirling Conference on Psycholinguistics.* London: Plenum, 1977.

Tanenhaus, M. K., & Carroll, J. M. The clausal processing hierarchy... and nouniness. In R. Grossman, L. J. San, & T. J. Vance (Eds.), *Papers from the Parasession on Functionalism.* Chicago: Chicago Linguistic Society, 1975.

Tyler, L. K., & Marslen-Wilson, W. D. The on-line effects of semantic context on syntactic processing. *Journal of Verbal Learning and Verbal Behavior,* 1977, *16,* 683–692.

8 Superstrategy

Janet Dean Fodor
University of Connecticut

INTRODUCTION

How does a listener or a reader parse a sentence that has been syntactically transformed? Superstrategy is offered as a general answer to this very general question. It asserts that the human parsing device processes a word sequence that is heard or read AS IF IT WERE THE TERMINAL STRING OF A WELL-FORMED DEEP STRUCTURE. Of course, this will rarely or never be the case; the word string will typically depart from deep structure well formedness at several points. It is claimed that such discrepancies are noted by the parser and are resolved on-line. In particular, a constituent that appears where it could not appear in a well-formed deep structure is tagged as a *filler*; and a position in which a constituent ought to appear in deep structure although none is present in the word string is tagged as a *gap*. Fillers and gaps are mated as they are encountered in the word string, in such a way that deep structure well formedness is restored.

The earliest psycholinguistic research based on generative grammar looked for direct processing analogs to syntactic transformations in the sequence of mental operations involved in the comprehension of sentences. But the optimism generated by the early sentence-matching and memory experiments (Clifton, Kurcz, & Jenkins, 1965; Miller & McKean, 1964) eventually proved to be unfounded. It is now widely accepted that the operations of the human sentence-parsing mechanism (hereafter, the parser) bear a rather indirect

249

relation to the formal operations defined by the grammar of a language.[1] In particular, it is generally assumed that the parser operates more or less 'from left to right', making decisions about the structure of the beginning of the word string before it has received the remainder of it. Natural languages are poorly designed from the point of view of a left-to-right parser. Phrase structure rules impose a hierarchical 'top-down' structure on sentences; and transformations create dependencies between widely separated constituents. This results in a considerable amount of temporary parsing ambiguity, i.e., cases where the correct analysis of part of a sentence cannot be determined until a later part of the sentence has been received and analyzed. It follows that a left-to-right parser must either engage in extensive parallel processing of all the candidate analyses until the disambiguating information is eventually received; or, as is usually assumed, it must use STRATEGIES to guide those of its decisions for which full information is not yet available.

A number of specific strategies have been delineated, usually by reference to examples in which they lead the parser to make the wrong decision, so that the sentence is difficult to parse correctly. As a result we now know something about the 'cue' function of grammatical morphemes, the preferences of the parser among right- and left-branching and center-embedded constructions, the use of subcategorization information about verbs, and so on. But it is noteworthy that a great deal of what has been discovered about the parser's analysis of sentence structure is neutral between deep and surface structure properties. For example, Kimball (1973), in reworking a number of strategies that had been proposed as a means of recovering the deep structures of sentences, could seriously present them as strategies for the recovery of surface structures. Even Fodor, Bever, and Garrett (1974), who argue that "listeners use heuristic strategies to make direct inductions about... aspects of base structure [p. 329]," gave little specific detail for those sentences in which deep structure and surface structure diverge.

Superstrategy is an attempt to fill this gap. It is not entirely a novel proposal; Jackendoff and Culicover (1973) invoked an informal version of it, and in a restricted form it is presupposed in the highly explicit augmented transition network (ATN) model of sentence parsing (see, for example, Wanner & Shiner, 1975, and references therein). I also don't regard it as a particularly controversial proposal, for there really seems to be no other plausible candidate once certain alternative approaches to sentence parsing

---

[1]The theory of Cognitive Grammar (Lakoff & Thompson, 1975a, 1975b) attempts to preserve the relation between parsing operations and grammatical rules by revising the form of grammatical rules. In the last section, A New Look at the Relation between Grammar and Parser, I suggest that this general project may succeed. But the arguments presented there and at the end of the section The Recovery of Deep Structure imply that the revisions that are needed are not those of Cognitive Grammar, but those of the Revised Extended Standard Theory (Chomsky, 1973, 1975, 1977, and elsewhere).

have been excluded. These exclusions can be incorporated into the question with which I began: How does a hearer or reader reconstruct the deep structure of a sentence which has been transformed, without first computing its surface structure, and without employing the standard syntactic transformations (or their inverses)? This question has three major presuppositions, which I will attempt to defend: (a) that the rules of a transformational grammar do not stand in any natural correspondence with the mental operations involved in sentence parsing; (b) that the parser does not reconstruct the surface structure of a sentence in the course of parsing it; and (c) that the parser does reconstruct the deep structure of the sentence.

I will take up each of these points in turn. For each one I will give a general argument first, and then some specific evidence concerning sentences that contain fillers and gaps. This evidence consists largely of intuitions about the relative parsing difficulty of various types of syntactic construction. It is fairly clear what sorts of experiments would be needed to assess the validity of these intuitions, but the judgments I shall present have been confirmed informally by a number of English speakers,[2] and I simply assume that they do reveal something about the operations of the parser.

THE NON-USE OF
SYNTACTIC TRANSFORMATIONS

Transformations could be employed by a parser in an analysis-by-synthesis (ABS) routine. Or, if they are inverted (i.e., their structural descriptions exchanged with their structural changes) and applied in reverse order, they could be used to 'detransform' surface structures into deep structures. Neither of these proposals is plausible. For one thing, they both imply that the operations by which deep structure is recovered are performed over the sentence as a whole, as in a grammatical derivation, i.e., that such processing does not begin until the whole lexical string has been received. It seems very much more likely that the human sentence-parsing device begins to compute deeper syntactic and even semantic representations of a sentence 'from left to right' while the lexical string is still being received. Without this assumption it is difficult to explain, for example, how people can understand the initial fragment of a sentence well enough to be able to supply a well-formed continuation for it.

Against ABS routines, there is the familiar objection that they are very wasteful of available information and of processing effort. The parser must pick a candidate deep structure, proceed through its syntactic derivation, and

---

[2]My informants were students and faculty at the University of Connecticut, the University of Pennsylvania , and Yale University, who heard presentations of this paper. My thanks to them for their valuable comments both about the data and about the conclusions to be drawn from them.

match the result with the lexical string received. If it picks its candidate deep structure at random, or on the basis of whatever superficial properties of the lexical string (e.g., length) are accessible prior to parsing, then it will very probably pick the wrong structure. It will then have to attempt another derivation, and typically a great many more such derivations, before it finds an acceptable match. The ABS hypothesis therefore makes the counter-to-fact prediction that people should be extremely slow at detecting that a given word string is UNgrammatical. It also fails to account for the fact, confirmed by a number of different experiments, that people are sensitive to specific aspects of the lexical string (such as the presence of complementizers, etc.) and draw structural inferences from them. If, for this reason, it is acknowledged that the parser's choice of a candidate deep structure is highly constrained by the properties of the lexical string, then the number of predicted false starts will be minimized, but the ABS routine will be correspondingly demoted to the status of little more than a final check on the validity of prior parsing operations which must themselves be of a quite different kind.

It may be less widely realized that 'detransformation' routines also involve extensive search through a set of candidate derivations. This is because the inverses of certain types of syntactic transformation are not well-defined. Fodor et al. (1974) discussed ungoverned deletion rules, such as the optional transformation which deletes relative pronouns in English. The inverse rule would INSERT a relative pronoun. But, unlike the deletion rule, the insertion rule must be contextually restricted (since a relative pronoun cannot appear just anywhere in a well-formed phrase marker), and its context would appear to be rather complex. I have argued elsewhere (Fodor, 1977) that the inverses of unbounded[3] movement rules cannot be formulated as local derivational operations at all, because their proper application depends on facts about later (i.e., deeper) phrase markers in the inverse derivation—facts about other transformational operations and about possible deep structures.

The inverse of the WH-Fronting transformation, for example, would have to be formulated sufficiently loosely to permit it to move a sentence-initial WH-constituent back into a variety of different positions in different

---

[3]The special properties of unbounded movement transformations, which may move a constituent across an indefinitely long stretch of a sentence, were first stressed by Ross (1967). More recently, Chomsky and others have proposed that a single application of a transformation may move a constituent only within its own clause or into an adjacent one. The appearance of unbounded movement is attributed to a succession of bounded movements of the same constituent. For my purposes this distinction is not important. I assume that for the parser the task is the same, whichever linguistic description is correct. (But see Footnote 10.) I shall therefore continue to refer to a transformation as unbounded just in case there is no limit on the distance between the deep structure position of a constituent and the surface position in which that constituent appears as a result of applying the transformation (once, or several times in succession).

sentences: into preverbal position in (1), postverbal position in (2), the position after the preposition in (3), and so on.

(1) **Who** did Sam say Δ was making a gift for Grandma? [Δ = gap]
(2) **What** did Sam say Joe was making Δ for Grandma?
(3) **Who** did Sam say Joe was making a gift for Δ?

These various effects of the inverse transformation cannot be incorporated as free options, for only one position is correct in each (unambiguous) sentence. But neither can the correct position be specified in the rule. It is determined by such facts as that every clause must have a subject, that a transitive verb such as *make* must be followed by a direct object, that a preposition must be followed by a noun phrase. But these are facts about DEEP structures; they do not necessarily hold at any more superficial stages of a derivation, such as the stage at which the inverse WH-Fronting rule must be applied by the parser. It follows that a detransformation parsing routine, which applies the inverse of WH-Fronting BEFORE establishing a deep structure for the sentence, could only hazard a guess as to the proper position for the WH-constituent. Depending on the length of the sentence, quite a number of inverse derivations based on different guesses would typically have to be pursued by the parser before a successful one is found. And for many sentences, the options for the WH-constituent would interact with other transformational operations and thus multiply further the number of blind alleys attempted on the way to finding a correct analysis.

Just as for ABS routines, a detransformation routine does not explain the ease with which hearers recognize ungrammatical sentences, such as (7a) below, which has a filler (the relative pronoun *whom*) but no gap for it to fit into. Comparisons between the other sentences in (4) through (7) also point toward an on-line gap-detection procedure that bears no relation to the syntactic transformation of WH-Fronting but is based instead on a running comparison between the word string as it is received and its candidate deep structures.

(4a) This is the picture **which** the teacher showed Δ to the children.
(4b) *This is the picture **which** the teacher showed Δ to the children with Δ.

(5a) This is the book **which** the teacher read (Δ) to the children.

(5b) This is the book **which** the teacher read (Δ) to the children from Δ.

(6a) This is the boy **whom** the teacher walked ((Δ)) to the office.

(6b) This is the boy **whom** the teacher walked ((Δ)) to the office with Δ.

(7a) *This is the boy **whom** the teacher went to the office.

(7b) This is the boy **whom** the teacher went to the office with Δ.

In all of the grammatical sentences here, WH-Fronting has applied to move a noun phrase to the beginning of the relative clause. In the *a* versions, it has moved the direct object of the verb; in the *b* versions, it has moved the noun phrase governed by the final preposition. The difference between the four sentence pairs concerns the possibility or necessity of a direct object noun phrase after the verb. In (4) the verb is *show*, which is obligatorily transitive, i.e., must have a direct object at the deep structure level. In (5) the verb is *read*, which is optionally transitive, i.e., may or may not have a direct object in deep structure.[4] The verb in (6) is *walk*, which is also optionally transitive, although it occurs much more often as an intransitive verb (e.g., *I walked to school*) than as a transitive verb (e.g., *I walked Albert to school*). Finally, in (7) the verb is *go*, which is obligatorily intransitive, i.e., never takes a direct object. Because no noun phrase follows the verb in the surface form of any of these sentences, there is a potential gap in postverbal position in each case. In (4) there is what I call a *doubtless gap,* i.e., a gap which MUST be filled, for it constitutes an undeniable mismatch between the surface string and any well-formed deep structure. In (5) and (6), the corresponding gap is a *doubtful* one, i.e., it may or may not need to be filled in order to arrive at a well-formed deep structure, and the deciding information is to be found only elsewhere in the sentence, in the presence or absence of another competing gap that must have the filler assigned to it. Finally, in (7) the potential postverbal gap is not really a potential gap at all, because no noun phrase is permitted in that position at the deep structure level.

The first conclusion to be drawn from these sentences is that doubtless gaps are readily detected by the parser. Sentence (4a) is easy to parse and shows no signs of 'garden pathing' the parser. And the ungrammaticality of (4b), which has two doubtless gaps but only one filler, is easy to detect. Similarly, it appears that 'impossible' gap positions, as after the verb *went* in the sentences of (7), are recognized as impossible by the parser. Sentence (7a) has an impossible gap after *went* and no gap elsewhere in the sentence, and it is easy to recognize as ungrammatical. And the correct analysis of (7b), in which the filler belongs after the preposition rather than after the verb, is also established with no apparent difficulty. These sentences do not garden path the parser, as they would if the impossible gap after *went* were mistakenly identified as a genuine candidate gap.

---

[4] I am assuming that the presence or absence of a direct object for a verb such as *read* is an option governed by the strict subcategorization features of the verb in just the same way as the optionality of a wide variety of prepositional phrases in the verb phrase. An alternative analysis would require *read* always to have an object in deep structure and would postulate an optional transformation that could delete it later. This analysis is not appealing because of the great variability among verbs in this respect. But even if it were correct, it would not materially affect my account of the parsing operations (although it would demand some rephrasing of it).

The claim that the parser is correctly distinguishing gaps from non-gaps in sentences for which there is no perceptible parsing difficulty is made more plausible by comparison with other sentences for which parsing proceeds less smoothly. For example, (6a) is apparently more difficult to parse than (6b) is. The hearer who has reached the end of sentence (6a) is typically surprised to discover that it IS the end; the expectation is that there will be further words, among which a gap will be present, as in (6b). The obvious explanation for this is that the parser overlooks the doubtful gap after *walked* in both sentences. In (6b) this creates no problem and may even save some processing effort, for the doubtful gap is not the true gap that the parser is looking for. But in (6a) this doubtful gap is the only gap in the sentence, and hence it must be the true gap. Because the parser ignores this gap on the first pass through the sentence, it misses the correct analysis and must then back up and try again.

Generalizing from the relative difficulty of (6a), we might suppose that all doubtful gaps are overlooked by the parser, i.e., that a potential gap is classed as a non-gap if there is any deep structure at all which is compatible with the word string as received up to that point. But it seems that the parser is not, in fact, as short-sighted as this suggests. Rather, it will recognize a gap in some position as long as there is some LIKELY deep structure that has a constituent in that position. Thus, the sentences of (5) contrast with those of (6). In (5) it is the *a* version which is easy to parse, and the *b* version which apparently garden paths the parser. The verb *read* very often takes a direct object at the deep structure level. Comparison of the word string with probable deep structures for the initial sentence fragment would therefore lead to the recognition of the doubtful postverbal gap. In (5a), which has no other gap for the filler, the doubtful gap is just the one that the parser needs, and so the correct analysis of the sentence is quickly established. But in (5b) the doubtful gap is NOT the true gap, and it 'decoys' the parser, leading to confusion when the doubtless gap after the preposition is subsequently encountered. This explanation is supported by a comparison of (5b) with (7b), which is closely matched in length and structure to (5b) but is easier to parse. The only structural difference between the two sentences to which this can be attributed is that (7b), with the verb *went*, has no doubtful postverbal gap which could mislead the parser. This comparison thus pinpoints the decoying effect of the doubtful gap in (5b), which demands the conclusion that at least probable doubtful gaps are detected by the parser.

The contrast between the *read* sentences and the *walk* sentences is quite unexplained by models of the parser in which the recovery of deep structure involves psychological processes corresponding to the syntactic transformations posited by linguists. There is no difference at all between *read* and *walk* with respect to the WH-Fronting transformation. If either of these verbs does have a direct object, then WH-Fronting may move that object; if either of them has no object, then WH-Fronting obviously cannot apply to it. The significant difference between the two verbs, which is a matter of HOW LIKELY each one is to have a direct object at the deep structure level, is not a difference that the syntactic transformation captures. The influence of this factor on parsing complexity can be explained only if the parser is forming hypotheses about possible gap locations not by reference to contextual restrictions on the applicability of the WH-Fronting transformation, but by reference to the plausibility of the deep structures that could correspond to the surface string. Furthermore, the parser is constructing these hypotheses on-line, as Superstrategy asserts, rather than postponing gap-location decisions until it has received the continuation of the word string. A postponement strategy applied to a sentence such as (5b) would reveal the true doubtless gap at the end of the sentence and thus protect the parser against the disrupting influence of the decoy gap after *read*. Comparison of the sentences in (8) with those of (5) also indicates that gaps are identified as they are encountered.

(8a)   This is the boy **whom** the teacher forced △ to go.

(8b)   This is the boy **whom** the teacher forced △ to leave (△).

In (8b) there is a false doubtful gap just as there is in (5b), but there is no obvious asymmetry in parsing difficulty between (8a) and (8b) as there is between (5a) and (5b). Assuming Superstrategy, this is simply explained, since the doubtful gap in (8b) FOLLOWS the unambiguous true gap and would therefore not be expected to decoy the parser.

THE NON-RECOVERY OF
SURFACE STRUCTURES

There is plenty of experimental evidence that the parser is sensitive to properties of a sentence more abstract than surface structure properties, and, indeed, that it constructs some kind of relatively abstract representation such as a deep structure phrase marker while parsing the sentence (see, e.g., Levelt, 1970; Wanner, 1968). There is also plenty of evidence that the parser makes use of surface information about the sentence in forming hypotheses about the properties of this deeper representation; except in a pure ABS model, there is really no other way in which it could proceed. What is less clear from the existing psycholinguistic literature is whether or not a full surface structure phrase marker for the sentence is constructed in the course of, and as an aid in, recovering the deep structure.

There is one very general reason for believing that this is not so, and this is that it could not be. That is, unless most of the syntactic research of the last 20 years has been fundamentally misguided, the well-formedness conditions on surface structures cannot be formulated directly but only indirectly, as an interaction between the well-formedness conditions on deep structures and the ordered transformations that apply to them.[5] I take this to mean that a parser which attempted to induce a surface structure phrase marker directly from the lexical string would be hampered by ignorance of the set of phrase markers from which it was permitted to choose. It might have access to principles defining an approximation to this set, either a superset or a subset of it. But in either case, the parser would be unable to use precise information about the set of possible surface structures to guide its search for a correct analysis of the sentence, or even to recognize an incorrect analysis as incorrect.

The consequences of this limitation on surface structure parsing are illustrated by sentences (9) through (13).

(9) It amused the young man *that Mary was going to marry.*   REL/ COMP

(10) Sam amused the young man *that Mary was going to marry.*   REL

(11) It took the young man *that Mary was going to marry* by surprise.   REL

(12) It amused Sam and he nudged the young man *that Mary was going to marry.*   REL

(13) It seemed to the young man *that Mary was going to marry.* COMP

A *that*-clause in English may be either a relative clause (REL) or a complement (COMP). Both interpretations are possible for (9), but the other sentences above are unambiguously interpreted as containing either a relative or a complement, as indicated. A parser which derived the surface structure of a sentence directly from the lexical string would have to decide for each of these sentences whether to represent the *that*-clause as a relative or as a complement in the surface phrase marker. But the properties relevant to the decision are not surface properties; they are deep structure and transformational regularities. For example, the complement analysis is incorrect for (10) because the verb *amuse* does not take an object complement and because there is no *it* earlier in the sentence from which the complement clause could have been moved by the Extraposition transformation. Of course, it would be a simple trick to build into a surface structure parser a device for counting occurrences of *it* in a sentence, and to permit the parser to analyze a *that*-clause as a complement only if an *it* is present. But this would not suffice to

---

[5]In the last section of this chapter, I consider the possibility that transformations play little or no role in the derivations of sentences. As indicated there, this would not invalidate my arguments for Superstrategy but would suggest an interesting reformulation of them.

protect the parser against the incorrect postulation of a complement clause in sentences such as (11) and (12). These sentences do contain an *it*, but the *it* is in the wrong position relative to the *that*-clause; i.e., the *it* and the *that*-clause are not related in a way that could have resulted from the operation of the Extraposition transformation. To establish the correct surface structure for such a sentence, the parser would therefore first have to consider whether there exist transformations by means of which the sentence might have been derived from a well-formed deep structure. Deep structure and transformational constraints are also crucial to the correct analysis of (13), in which the *that*-clause cannot be construed as a relative. This is because a complement clause analysis is obligatory, since *seem* (unlike *amuse*) MUST have a sentential subject at the deep structure level, and this subject complement must undergo Extraposition.[6]

My argument so far has been that there is no fail-safe way of determining the surface structure of a sentence prior to consideration of deeper structures in its derivation. Two alternatives now present themselves. One is that the parser, as implied by Superstrategy, induces the deep structure without first constructing a surface phrase marker. And this at least raises the possibility that it NEVER constructs a surface phrase marker; having found the deep structure, why should it bother? I will concede that it might do so in an ABS routine whose function is simply to check that no error crept in during the process of establishing the deep structure. But this would not contradict the claim I wish to defend, which is only that the surface phrase marker is not constructed first and used as a source for determining the deep structure. The other alternative is that the parser does first form a surface phrase marker even though it is bound to do so incorrectly for certain kinds of transformed sentence. After all, we know that the parser does make some tentative decisions without waiting to receive definitive support for them, and so there are no general grounds for denying that it does so in this respect as well. Arguments from parsing complexity differences may also be unreliable here. It is true that the surface-structure-first model of the parser predicts that errors of analysis will often be made, but these would only be temporary errors, corrected as soon as the parser does move to deeper levels of structure. So the fact that sentences such as (10) through (12) are not particularly difficult to parse, and apparently do not tempt the parser into an incorrect complement clause analysis, does not constitute compelling counterevidence against this model.

---

[6] I have argued elsewhere (Fodor, 1978) that the verb *seem* does not undergo Extraposition but has its complement clause in postverbal position at the deep structure level. If this is correct, my argument here would be better illustrated by other sentence types. But I think the general point is clear.

I will now give three arguments to the effect that the parser not only detects gaps but also fills them on-line. This amounts to saying that the parser reconstructs the deep structure of a sentence on-line, i.e., before the whole lexical string has been received, and hence before a full surface structure phrase marker could have been constructed. This does not entail that a surface phrase marker is not constructed by the parser at ANY stage in its operations. It is imaginable, for example, that a surface parsing unit sweeps through the lexical string just ahead of the deep parsing unit, and that phrase markers at BOTH levels are output at the end. But it does at least encourage a rather different picture, namely, that the parser assigns a surface analysis only locally to words as it receives them, and rearranges the surface constituents into their deep structure positions at the earliest point at which this is feasible. It is clear that SOME surface analysis must be performed. For example, to recognize that there is a noun phrase gap between a preposition and an adverb, the parser must at least recognize the preposition as the left daughter of a prepositional phrase that lacks a noun phrase as right daughter. But the assumption that ONLY small chunks of the surface phrase marker are ever constructed leads to a more efficient model of the parser. It would no longer have to squander its limited capacities on making surface structure decisions for which surface structure evidence is bound to be lacking. Its first and only (syntactic) priority would be to determine what deep structure analyses are compatible with the word string. And the resulting deep structure phrase marker, as it is developed, could, if necessary, be used to guide the analysis of words arriving later in the string.

My first argument for the on-line recovery of a deep structure representation is a very simple one, no more than an introspection about how one parses sentences such as (14) or (15).

(14)   In which of your books did you write that you would put the money?

(15)   To whom did Father say he would write?

In reading through (14), I (and many other native speakers I have consulted) first interpret the fronted phrase *in which of your books* as modifying the verb *write*. Then, as I read on into the second clause, this interpretation flips over, with much of the subjective effect of an ambiguous visual stimulus such as the duck-rabbit, into an interpretation of the fronted phrase as modifying the verb *put*. That is, the sentence first seems to be about writing in a book, and then turns out to be about putting money in a book. Sentence (15) is similar, except that since *write,* unlike *put,* does not DEMAND a locative modifier, both interpretations of the sentence remain acceptable throughout.

If these introspective impressions have any validity at all, they show that the parser not only notes the potential gap in the first clause of a sentence like

(14) but also fills it, before it has encountered the remainder of the sentence and recognized the more urgent claim of the later gap. Presumably, when it does find the later gap, it extracts the filler from the first gap and moves it into the later one. This assumption helps to make sense of a quite powerful, but otherwise mysterious, linguistic illusion. This is that a sentence such as (15) can be interpreted to imply that Father said to someone that he would write to THAT PERSON, i.e., that (15) can be derived by across-the-board WH-Fronting from the structure *Father said to whom$_i$ that he would write to whom$_i$*, rather than by a single WH-Fronting from either *Father said to whom that he would write* (which contains no overt indirect object for *write*) or *Father said he would write to whom* (which contains no overt indirect object for *said*). I call this an illusion despite the fact that many of my informants have insisted that this must indeed be a legitimate derivation which happens so far to have gone unnoticed by syntacticians. This is because sentences in which the first of the two gaps is doubtless are considerably more resistant to the across-the-board interpretation. For example, the ungrammaticality of (16) is detectable even to those who strongly favor a coreferential interpretation of (17).

(16)   **Who** did the policeman convince △ that he was going to arrest △?
(17)   **Who** did the policeman warn (△) that he was going to arrest △?

If across-the-board WH-Fronting were a legitimate syntactic process in such constructions, it should be equally legitimate in both (16) and (17). That its acceptability varies with the doubtful/doubtless status of the first gap suggests the following explanation. The parser inserts the filler into the first appropriate gap that it detects. It notes whether this gap is doubtful or doubtless, because a filler inserted into a doubtful gap may be extracted later if another gap should present itself, whereas a filler inserted into a doubtless gap must remain there. In the process of transferring a filler from an early doubtful gap into a later gap, the parser sometimes forgets to delete it from the early gap, so that in the resulting deep structure phrase marker it appears (illegitimately) in both positions simultaneously.

Sentences which have legitimate analyses which the parser does not recognize are well known in psycholinguistics (e.g., the triply center-embedded sentences, or *The horse raced past the barn fell*). Sentences such as (15) and (17) are, apparently, instances of a much rarer phenomenon: sentences for which the parser 'recognizes' an analysis that is not legitimate. But the moral to be drawn from these examples is that the parser does not wait until it has detected all the candidate gaps in a sentence before it begins the gap-filling operations involved in reconstructing the deep structure phrase marker.

My second argument for the on-line reconstruction of deep structure is more devious. It is that only this assumption permits the explanation of an otherwise quite arbitrary constraint on English sentences. It is possible, of course, that this constraint IS arbitrary. It might be due, like any other aspect of language, to some mere quirk in that part of the mind/brain which houses our knowledge of our language. Or it might have arisen as the accidental consequence of a series of language changes that have nothing in common and no discernible functional motivation. But it is at least interesting that the assumption of Superstratgey can account for both the existence and the direction of this constraint.

The constraint is what I have called the Nested Dependency Constraint (Fodor, 1978).

(18)   *The Nested Dependency Constraint (NDC)*
       When there are two or more gap-filler dependencies in a sentence, their scopes must either be disjoint or must be nested one within the other; they may not intersect.

The NDC applies to a wide variety of sentences that have been subjected to two gap-creating transformations. For example, the sentences (19) through (21) have the pattern F   F   G   G; i.e., they have two fillers preceding two gaps.

(19a)   **What sort of pot** is **pea soup** easy to cook △ in △?

(19b)   *****What sort of pot** is **pea soup** easy to cook △ in △?

(20a)   **What sort of soup** is **this pot** easy to cook △ in △?

(20b)   *****What sort of soup** is **this pot** easy to cook △ in △?

(21a)   What are boxes easy to store △ in △?

(21b)   *****What are boxes easy to store △ in △?

The *a* versions of these sentences have the nested dependency assignment F   F   G   G, and they are acceptable. That is, Sentence (19) can be interpreted coherently as about cooking soup in a pot; Sentence (20) has the pragmatically odd interpretation that the pot is to be cooked in the soup; and Sentence (21) has the interpretation that boxes are to be stored in something. The *b* versions have the intersecting dependency assignment F   F   G   G, and they are unacceptable. Sentence (19) does not have the pragmatically odd reading; (20) does not have the pragmatically plausible reading; and (21), which would be plausible on either reading, nevertheless cannot be construed as about storing things in boxes. Sentences (22) and (23) have two gaps preceding two fillers and show a similar contrast; the nested assignment G   G   F   F is acceptable, but the intersecting assignment G   G   F   F is not.

(22)   No-one (△) puts things (△) in the sink **that would   who wants**
block it   to go on
being a
friend of
mine.

(23)   *No-one (△) puts things (△) in the sink **who wants   that would**
to go on   block it.
being a
friend of mine

Sentences (24) and (25) show that where one filler precedes both gaps and another follows them, the disjoint assignment F̄ Ḡ G F is acceptable, but the intersecting assignment F̄ Ḡ G F is not.

(24)   **Who** do you think △ borrowed △ from the library **that old copy of Syntactic Structures?**

(25)   ***Which library** did you borrow △ from △ **that old copy of Syntactic Structures?**

Sentences with two gaps and two fillers obviously demand quite a lot of work from the parser. They are also potentially ambiguous. So it is perhaps not too surprising that there exists a constraint which rules out one of their potential analyses (even though, admittedly, there are many ambiguous constructions that are NOT so disambiguated by the syntax). But why should the constraint rule out the intersecting assignments of fillers to gaps and permit the nested assignments, rather than vice versa? Superstrategy provides an explanation as follows.

For the parser to find a filler and a gap (even a doubtless gap) in a sentence does not by itself warrant the assumption that the filler belongs in the gap in deep structure. The parser must also determine that that filler FITS in that gap, i.e., that replacing it in the gap results in a structure which is compatible with the well-formedness conditions on deep structures for the language. In most cases, the parser will be dealing with only the initial fragment of a sentence at the point at which it must make this grammaticality assessment. But it could at least test the well formedness of that portion of the deep structure phrase marker hypothesized so far to which the proposed filler-gap assignment is RELEVANT, i.e., that portion which includes the filler, the gap, and all intervening material.

In making a nested dependency assignment to a sentence with the pattern F F G G, the first assignment the parser will make is the one that relates the second filler to the first gap, and this assignment does pass the grammaticality test. In sentence (19a), for example, the relevant portion of the structure will be *it is easy to cook pea soup in...*, which can be part of a well-formed deep structure.[7] But if the parser were to attempt to assign the FIRST filler to the first gap—an assignment that would subsequently lead to intersecting dependencies, as in (19b)—the relevant portion of the structure would be *pea soup is easy to cook what sort of pot in...* This does not pass the grammaticality test because the effects of the Tough Movement transformation are still apparent within it; it contains the as yet unassigned filler *pea soup*. The parser will therefore conclude that this assignment is not a legitimate one, and will not develop this analysis of the sentence.

This convergence of the grammaticality test with the Nested Dependency Constraint holds quite generally. In an F F G G sentence, intersecting filler-gap assignments involve an assignment across an intervening unassigned filler. In a G G F F sentence or an F G G F sentence, intersecting assignments involve an assignment across an intervening unassigned gap. All the possible patterns are listed in (26) and it is clear that those which violate the NDC are just those for which, within the domain of the first filler-gap assignment, there is an unpaired filler or an unpaired gap which would make the resulting structure APPEAR to be incompatible with deep structure well-formedness conditions.

(26)

acceptable				unacceptable			
F	F	G	G	F	F	G	G
F	G	F	G				
F	G	F	G				
F	G	G	F	F	G	G	F
G	G	F	F	G	G	F	F
G	F	G	F				
G	F	G	F				
G	F	F	G	G	F	F	G

The suggestion, then, is that the Nested Dependency Constraint exists in English because hearers interpret sentences AS IF there were a Nested Dependency Constraint. Let us imagine a language exactly like English except that the NDC does not apply. A parser which assigns fillers to gaps on-

---

[7]To simplify the exposition here, I have ignored the possibility that the parser would simultaneously be 'undoing' the Extraposition transformation. I have also simply assumed that there is a Tough Movement transformation rather than a Tough Deletion transformation in English (but see Lasnik & Fiengo, 1974). As far as I can tell, neither of these matters substantially affects my general argument.

line must apply its grammaticality test on-line. It should avoid analyses in which the assignment of a filler to a gap leaves another filler or gap unpaired, because of the danger that this filler or gap will REMAIN unpaired when the analysis is complete and will thus invalidate it. The parser must therefore employ a criterion which is over-stringent and which happens also to exclude all intersecting dependency analyses even though these are (by hypothesis) perfectly well formed. But if the hearers of sentences in this hypothetical language do not recognize intersecting dependency analyses of sentences, there will be no intersecting dependence sentences in the effective data base for language learners, and they may then construct their grammar so that it rules out these sentences as ungrammatical. Their grammar would then be the grammar of English. Thus, although it is conceivable that the NDC has no connection at all with the problems of parsing transformed sentences, such an assumption would require us to acknowledge a remarkable coninicidence between those filler-gap assignments which are ungrammatical and those which the parser would, if it abides by Superstrategy, in any case reject.

My third argument for the on-line construction of the deep phrase marker is based on some other more familiar syntactic constraints. Ross (1967) argued that rightward movement rules are upward bounded, i.e., that a constituent which is moved to the right by a transformation may not move up into a higher clause of the sentence. Chomsky (1965, 1972) argued that there are no lowering rules, i.e., that a constituent which is moved by a transformation must either remain in the clause in which it originated or must move into a higher clause.[8] Together, these constraints have the effect of requiring a constituent that is moved to the right to remain in its clause, although a constituent moved to the left may move up into a higher clause and may even end up several clauses removed from its original deep structure position. Now a rightward movement rule creates a structure in which the gap precedes the filler; a leftward movement rule creates a structure in which the filler appears before the gap. In this respect, a rightward movement rule resembles a leftward deletion rule, and vice versa, for a leftward deletion rule creates a gap preceding its filler, and a rightward deletion rule creates a filler-first structure. And it is a very general fact about deletion that rightward (i.e., filler-first) deletion is very much more common and less constrained that

---

[8]In more recent work this constraint is imposed indirectly, as a consequence of the requirement that a moved constituent must be in an appropriate position to bind the trace which is left behind in its premovement position in the phrase marker (see last section of this chapter). This requirement will normally ensure that the moved constituent is no lower in the phrase marker after it is moved than it was before (see Fiengo, 1977). Conceivably, there will be some lowering operations that are not thereby excluded (e.g., *each*-Movement, which perhaps does not leave a trace); but other constraints (strict cycle, subjacency) would in any case severely limit their scope.

leftward (i.e., gap-first) deletion.[9] What we find, then, is a pervasive preference in natural languages for filler-first structures, particularly if the filler-gap dependency extends across a clause boundary. Once again, it may be misguided to look for a functional explanation of this fact. But once again, the Superstrategy model of the parser can make some sense of it.

First of all, the problems involved in LOCATING fillers and gaps would be decreased for a left-to-right parser if the more identifiable of the two appeared first in the sentence. And fillers are characteristically easier to identify than gaps are. After all, a filler is a something while a gap is a nothing. This means that there will, at most, be as many fillers in a sentence as there are constituents in it. But there can be as many gaps in a sentence as there are POSSIBLE constituents that MIGHT have been in it. Optionality is a deeply entrenched characteristic of natural languages. If we do not wish to specify, for example, the time, place, instrument, or manner of an action or the size, shape, color, or ownership of an object, the syntax does not force us to include semantically empty modifying phrases but permits us simply to omit them. Therefore, potential gaps abound in natural language. Another point is that a filler can carry information about which transformation created it, and this may help the parser by indicating where it should or should not look for the gap. Thus, a filler containing WH was rather obviously moved by the WH-Fronting transformation, a noun phrase filler without WH in presubject position must have been moved by Topicalization, a noun phrase filler in subject position before a *tough*-type predicate must have been created by Tough Movement, and so on. But a gap, being a nothing, cannot carry useful markers like WH, and at least in English its location is quite uninformative about what transformation created it and, hence, about where its filler should be. For example, a gap in object position in a clause may be due to WH-Fronting, Topicalization, Tough Movement or Heavy NP Shift.

Once fillers and gaps are located, they must be paired up. And this task would also be expected to show a strong preference for filler-first rules. If the

---

[9]Up to this point, my arguments have focused on movement rules, but I believe that the parser responds to deletion rules in a similar fashion. The filler would be the antecedent for the deletion, the gap would be the deletion site, and the only significant difference from movement rules would be that the parser must retain the filler in its surface position as well as entering it into the gap. Further research may, of course, show this generalization to be invalid. But I think it is significant that deletion rules (e.g., Too/Enough Deletion) obey the Nested Dependency Constraint, while pronominalization rules (which do not create gaps) do not (see Fodor, 1978, for details). The one exception I know of is the Gapping transformation, which obeys a different constraint (Hankamer, 1973). I have argued elsewhere (Fodor, 1974) that deletion rules such as Gapping, which delete variable material and leave specified constituents undeleted, should be formally distinguished (as 'remaindering rules') from rules which delete specified constituents and leave variable material undeleted. I conjecture that only rules of the latter class will be treated by the parser like movement rules, and that in the case of remaindering rules the parser seeks antecedents for the undeleted constituents rather than for the gaps.

parser finds a filler near the beginning of a sentence, it can note the filler and proceed to analyze the sentence while looking for the appropriate gap. Even if it has not found this gap by the time it reaches the end of the first clause of the sentence, it can continue into the next clause, retaining a representation both of the filler and of the first clause.[10] But if it is a gap that appears early in the sentence, the parser cannot form a representation of the first clause and of the gap; instead, its representation will be of an incomplete clause. In this case the task of pairing gap and filler will necessarily require the parser to return, later on, to this representation of the early part of the sentence in order to insert the filler once it has been found. In general, then, we would expect long distances between a gap and a subsequent filler to be disruptive for the parser, and considerably more so than long distances between a filler and a subsequent gap. And if, as Fodor et al. (1974) have argued, clauses are shunted, as soon as they have been analyzed, to a separate second-stage parsing unit, then the specific requirement that a gap preceding its filler must be in the same clause as its filler is also accounted for. For if well formedness of the clause is a precondition on shunting it, a gap unfilled by the end of its clause would block shunting and thereby overload the memory capacity of the first-stage parsing unit. And if, on the other hand, a clause may be shunted despite containing a gap, then it would have to be retrieved from the second-stage unit later on for its gap to be filled.

This sort of asymmetry between fillers and gaps is not explained on the assumption that parsing operations resemble standard syntactic transformations, nor on the assumption that the initial stage of parsing, as the sentence is being received, is devoted to the recovery of surface structure only.

THE RECOVERY OF DEEP STRUCTURE

In the preceding sections I have referred to the recovery of deep structure phrase markers for sentences, and what I have had in mind is deep structures of a rather traditional, *Aspects*-era, variety. Such deep structures are distinct not only from surface structures but also from semantic representations. That deep SYNTACTIC structures are implicated in sentence parsing is by no means self-evident. The only representation of a sentence that we can be sure a priori that the parser constructs is its semantic representation. And many of the experiments that have been taken to show the psychological reality of deep phrase markers in parsing (e.g., Wanner, 1968) do not clearly distinguish between deep structures and semantic representations. The importance of

---

[10]It would be of considerable interest to explore the relationship between this aspect of the parsing routine and the linguistic arguments for successive clause-by-clause movement of constituents by transformations like WH-Fronting (see Footnote 3).

deep syntactic structures may also be questioned on the basis of recent developments within syntactic theory. The Revised Extended Standard Theory (cf. Chomsky, 1973, 1975, 1977; Chomsky & Lasnik, 1977) assigns SURFACE structures the major role in determining the meanings of sentences. On this view of the grammar, it is no longer natural to think of deep structures as way-stations between surface structures and semantic representations. The arguments that follow are directed towards the claim that some nonsurface SYNTACTIC representation is computed by the parser before, and therefore presumably as an aid in, the construction of a semantic representation. The result is a model of sentence parsing based squarely on grammars of the standard theory variety. In the final section of this chapter, I consider how this model can be translated into Revised Extended Standard Theory terms, and discuss its implications for long-standing questions about the relation between the grammar and the parsing routines.

Let us assume at least temporarily, then, the validity of the standard level of deep structure. As I have argued previously (Fodor, 1977), the properties required of phrase markers at the deep structure level impose a 'wasp waist' or bottleneck on the class of derivations in a language. The class of surface structures is large and very varied, compared with the smaller and more regular set of syntactic deep structures. And so also is the class of semantic representations. It is more difficult to give a definitive argument here than in the case of surface structures, because at present we know so little about the formal properties that semantic representations must have. But one pretty solid claim is that the representation of the scope relations holding between quantifiers, negation, and similar operators must be fundamentally similar to their representation in the formulae of standard first order logic. Several specific variants have been proposed (e.g, Jackendoff, 1972; Lakoff, 1970), but what they have in common is that certain constituents (e.g., the quantifier itself, or the whole noun phrase) must appear in a position other than the deep structure position which represents its grammatical ('thematic') relations with other elements in the sentence and must bind a variable or comparable element which does appear in that position. To put it simply, a surface quantifier is represented at the semantic level by TWO elements, which appear in different and often widely separated positions. The dependencies between these two positions are not of the kind that can be captured by phrase structure rules, any more than are the dependencies found in surface structures. Rather, they are characteristic of transformationally derived structures.

In a standard grammar which derives semantic representations from deep structures, something formally comparable to a copying or movement transformation could take a noun phrase as input and create from it the semantic representation with its quantifier and bound variable. In a generative semantics grammar, whose derivations have semantic representations as their initial structures, the transformational properties of semantic representations must be captured, in a less obvious fashion, by means of filters. That is, the set of initial structures cannot be limited to just those that correspond to well-formed sentences, but must include some that contain illegitimate combinations of quantifiers and variables. These can be distinguished from legitimate dependencies only at a 'shallower' stage of the derivation at which quantifiers are 'lowered' onto the variables they bind, so that quantified noun phrases are no longer doubly represented, and all sentences can be required to meet very stringent phrase structure conditions. Thus, despite the apparent direction of derivations in such grammars, some of the conditions on well-formed semantic representations are in fact imposed in the form of conditions on structures nearer the 'middle' of derivations. Until the necessary filters have been formulated in detail, it is impossible to be sure, but general considerations suggest that they apply at a stage very like the deep structure level in standard grammars.

What I have been arguing is that, even if it has fallen into linguistic disrepute in recent years, there is a derivational level intermediate between the surface level and the semantic level, which imposes conditions on sentences that are both simpler and stronger than those at either 'end' of derivations. At this level, unlike the surface level, every sentence must consist of some number of complete clauses, each with its verb and a designated set of noun phrases or other complements. And at this level, unlike the semantic level, every quantifier must appear paired with a noun within a noun phrase.

We might speculate about the source of this 'deep structure bottleneck'. There are data compatible with the hypothesis that children learn their language 'from the middle out', beginning with a simple code in which neither surface structures nor semantic representations depart very far from the deep structures which mediate between them, and that the grammar is then elaborated outwards in both directions from this central core. It is even conceivable that language (or at least languages) itself evolved in this fashion. But whatever the origin of this design characteristic of human languages, it seems quite plausible to suppose that adult users of the language take advantage of it. The deep structure bottleneck constrains the possible pairings between the complex array of surface structures and the complex array of semantic representations. And the well-formedness conditions on deep structures, unlike those of the other levels, are relatively simple local conditions of the kind that can be captured by phrase structure rules. So we might very well expect that the parser would check its hypotheses against these deep structure conditions as an efficient way of avoiding certain misassignments of semantic representations to lexical strings.

Direct evidence for this proposal must rest on examples for which a clear distinction can be drawn between semantic hypotheses about sentences and deep syntactic hypotheses. In the present state of our knowledge, such examples are not easy to come by, but it turns out that this is what lies at the heart of the current controversy about the parsing of dative questions.

In a dative sentence such as (27), there are two noun phrases after the verb; the first is the indirect object, and the second is the direct object.

(27)   Sam gave his friend a sandwich.

The direct object (DO) may be fronted to form a question such as (28), or a relative clause as in (29).

(28)   **What** did Sam give his friend Δ?

(29)   The sandwich **which** Sam gave his friend Δ was scrumptious.

However, fronting of the indirect object (IO), as in (30) and (31), is generally agreed to be less than fully acceptable, and for some speakers is totally unacceptable.

(30)   ?***Who** did Sam give Δ a sandwich?

(31)   ?*The person **whom** Sam gave Δ a sandwich wasn't hungry.

Many people apparently construe these sentences along the lines of (28) and (29), and thus arrive at the pragmatically bizarre interpretation that Sam gave a sandwich someone, i.e., that Sam gave someone to a sandwich. Other people, following the dictates of the pragmatics, construe (30) as they would construe the coherent sentence *Who did Sam give a sandwich to?* and then balk at the lack of a final *to*. For a sentence such as (32), which would be pragmatically coherent whichever noun phrase was taken to be the direct object, there is also a strong preference for the fronted-DO analysis (32a).

(32a)   **Which doctor** did the nurse bring the patient Δ?

(32b)   ?***Which doctor** did the nurse bring Δ the patient?

The unacceptability of the fronted-IO analysis of dative questions and relative clauses does not fall naturally under any syntactic generalization in the grammar of English. It also seems to vary in degree from sentence to sentence and context to context as well as from speaker to speaker. For these reasons, it has often been suggested that both varieties of dative question should be generated by the grammar and that the unacceptability of the fronted-IO construction is to be attributed to the routines which people use for parsing these sentences. For some reason, the parser tends to overlook the fronted-IO analysis and detects only the fronted-DO analysis. Several different models of the parser have been appealed to in an attempt to account for this. I cannot do justice here to the intricacies of each one, but will focus on the difference between two general types of model.

Versions of what I call the Position Assignment Model have been proposed by Jackendoff and Culicover (1973) and by Wanner, Kaplan, and Shiner (1975), Wanner and Shiner (1975), and Wanner and Maratsos (1974). As will become clear, Superstrategy is also a version of this model. According to the Position Assignment Model, a constituent that has been moved by a transformation (i.e., a filler constituent) is first returned to the position in the lexical string from which it was moved, and its grammatical/semantic role in the sentence is then determined on the basis of the position that has been assigned to it.

The alternative model, which I call the Role Assignment Model, is represented in Langendoen, Kalish-Landon, and Dore (1974) and in the papers on Cognitive Grammar by Lakoff and Thompson (1975a, 1975b).[11] According to this model, a grammatical/semantic role is assigned to a moved constituent without first returning that constituent to its deep structure position. Langendoen et al. wrote: "We assume that the system of perceptual rules is designed to recover essentially the surface structures of sentences (as in Kimball, 1973) and 'annotations' of those surface structures that indicate the deep grammatical relations and perhaps certain other aspects of deep structure, where those are different from surface structure" (quote from Langendoen et al.'s [1974] Footnote 19). The grammatical roles or relations that are assigned include subject, direct object, indirect object, and presumably others such as instrument, location, etc.[12] Notice that the difference between the two models is not a matter of WHETHER such roles are

---

[11]Langendoen et al. (1974) and Lakoff and Thompson (1975a, 1975b) disagree over some of the details of the role-assignment parsing routines. They also make very different claims about the relation between grammatical rules and parsing operations. Cognitive Grammar claims that there is a very close correspondence between the two. But Lakoff and Thompson themselves admit that this is "absurd" in the case of unbounded rules such as WH-Fronting. The Role Assignment Model they propose is one attempt to bridge the gap, but they also sketch (Lakoff & Thompson, 1975b) what amounts to a Position Assignment account of the parsing of dative questions, in which they appeal to a constraint related to Klima's (1970) Constraint on Relational Ambiguity Principle. As they formulate it, this constraint is ad hoc and does not account for the full range of data I present below. But the important point is that both of these approaches to parsing involve mental computations that are not mirrored by the rules in a grammar of the kind that they advocate.

[12]Lakoff and Thompson (1975a) referred to the parser's hypotheses about grammatical relations as SEMANTIC hypotheses. They wrote: "The notion 'current semantic hypothesis' is basic to this conception of recognition grammar. . . . Essentially what rules of grammar do is make hypotheses about the grammatical relations borne by elements in the surface utterance as they are processed [pp. 296–297]." The particular relations they cited are not explicitly semantic; they include subject and direct object rather than agent, goal, theme, etc. (cf. Fillmore, 1968; Gruber, 1965). However, my arguments that these relations are not assigned without reference to the deep structure of the sentence should apply a fortiori to any model which assumes that fully explicit semantic representations are assigned without reference to deep structure.

assigned to constituents; both models agree that they are. And for constituents that have not been transformationally moved, they also agree on how such roles are assigned, i.e., by reference to the category of the constituent and its position (which will be the same in surface structure as in deep structure). The major difference between the models concerns the assignment of roles to MOVED constituents. Does the parser first replace a moved constituent in its original deep structure position before deciding on its grammatical role? Only if it does can we conclude that the parser makes crucial use of the deep structure phrase marker of a sentence in inducing its semantic representation from the surface lexical string.[13]

There is no general argument from economy of the parsing routines which would tip the balance in favor of one of these two models. The Position Assignment Model requires some gap finding and filling routines, but once the gaps have been filled the parser can assign roles to moved constituents by the same principles that it uses for non-moved constituents. The Role Assignment Model needs no gap finding and filling routines, but it assumes that there are some special routines for assigning roles to moved constituents. The only way to decide between the models, therefore, is on the basis of how well each can account for dative questions and other related constructions. I will argue that the Role Assignment Model can be made to predict the relative difficulty of the fronted-IO analysis of dative questions only on the basis of some completely ad hoc assumptions and at the cost of failure to capture a much broader generalization. The Position Assignment Model, by contrast, offers an EXPLANATION for the difficulty of the fronted-IO analysis.

The Position Assignment Model entails that the parser will detect the fronted-IO analysis for a sentence such as (32) only if it detects the first of the

---

To forestall a possible confusion, I should note that Lakoff and Thompson (1975b) used the term *semantic hypothesis* in a quite different sense, to refer to hypotheses BASED ON semantic properties of moved constituents (e.g., animacy of their referents). The parser's use of semantic hypotheses, in this sense, to supplement or shortcut parsing routines based on the syntactic properties of constituents is compatible with both the Position Assignment Model and the Role Assignment Model. (I note, however, that the preferred interpretation of a sentence such as (32) is exactly the opposite of what would be expected if the parser were relying heavily on the animacy of the fronted constituent as a clue that it is probably an indirect object.)

[13]There is another difference between the models, or at least between the versions of them that have been presented in the literature. Within a Position Assignment Model, it seems natural to assume that the parser makes its decision about the deep structure position of a fronted constituent only when it has reached that position in the sentence and has had a chance to examine what does or does not appear there. Within a Role Assignment Model, it seems more natural (for reasons which I do not fully understand) to suppose that the parser might make a guess about the role of the fronted constituent as soon as it encounters it in the sentence. In principle, however, both the waiting strategy and the guessing strategy are compatible with both models.

two potential gaps in the verb phrase. What needs to be shown, therefore, is that this gap is one of those that the parser is likely to overlook. Langendoen et al. (1974) have argued against the possibility of such an explanation, on the grounds that the parser can and does detect even doubtful gaps. As we saw in a previous section, The Non-Use of Syntactic Transformations, the parser will overlook a possible noun phrase gap only in positions where a noun phrase is relatively unlikely. But this is not true of the position following a dative verb; following *bring* there must be a noun phrase (cf. **I brought to the party*), and even *give* appears only rarely without one (as in *We gave to the United Fund*). These observations do not, however, invalidate the Position Assignment explanation of dative questions, for there is one special set of circumstances in which even an active and 'intelligent' gap-seeking routine would be expected to overlook a possible gap, and dative questions happen to provide just these circumstances.

In order to detect a gap, the parser must look at the next constituent in the lexical string. If a constituent of type X would be expected in that position and there is no X-type constituent present, the parser can identify a gap and resort to a fronted X-type constituent to fill it. But if the parser is expecting an X-type constituent and FINDS one in that position in the lexical string, the natural conclusion for it to draw (and the correct one in an overwhelming number of cases) is that there is no gap in the lexical string at that point. As Wanner and Shiner (1975) emphasize, it would be very wasteful of effort if the parser were to identify a possible gap after the verb *persuade* in a sentence such as *Who did Fred persuade Bill to speak to?* simply on the grounds that *persuade* must be followed by a noun phrase in deep structure. An efficient parser would first ascertain that *persuade* is already followed by a noun phrase in the surface string, and would conclude that there is no gap here for the WH-constituent. But now notice the consequences of this efficient parsing strategy for a sentence whose underlying structure originally contained two noun phrases in sequence. A dative question, for example, contains the sequence...V–NP–NP...before WH-Fronting applies. After WH-Fronting, it will have the form NP...V–NP regardless of which of the two noun phrases has been moved. And the parser will analyze this sequence in the same way in both cases. After it has processed the verb, it will be expecting a noun phrase to follow. It will then find a noun phrase, and its normally reliable strategy will lead it to conclude that this was the noun phrase it was expecting. It will therefore postulate no gap immediately following the verb. It will recognize a gap only at the next stage, when it discovers no second noun phrase in the surface string.[14] Thus a Position Assignment parser, even if it is

---

[14]I have oversimplified this last step in several ways. First, a verb such as *bring* permits either a noun phrase or a prepositional phrase to follow the postverbal noun phrase (cf. *I brought the baby a hacksaw, I brought the baby to Grandpa*). The parser might hypothesize a gap for either type of constituent; but only the hypothesis that there is a noun phrase gap will turn out to be successful, because the filler is a noun phrase.

generally very good at detecting gaps, will always assume that it is the second of two noun phrases that has been fronted.

If this is the correct explanation for the dative examples, we should be able to see its effects in other constructions too. Notice that the explanation does not depend on the fact that the moved constituent is a noun phrase, but only on the fact that it is a constituent of the same type as a constituent which is adjacent to it in the underlying structure. The dative examples should therefore be just one instance of the more general principle (33).

(33)   *The XX Extraction Principle*
       If at some point in its derivation a sentence contains a sequence of two constituents of the same formal type, movement of the second of these constituents will be more acceptable than movement of the first.

Hankamer (1973) quoted some French examples, from an unpublished paper by Ruwet (1973), in which the XX Extraction Principle applies to prepositional phrases. Ruwet noted that when a *de*-phrase precedes a *par*-phrase, as in (34a), it may be fronted to form the question (34b).

(34a)   J'ai vu le portrait d'Aristotle par Rembrandt.
(34b)   **De qui** as-tu vu le portrait Δ par Rembrandt?

However, when the *de*-phrase precedes another *de*-phrase, as in (35a), it may not be fronted; (35b) cannot be interpreted as diagrammed, but can only be

---

Second, *bring* does not REQUIRE any constituent at all to follow the postverbal noun phrase (cf. *I brought the beer*). However, the arguments in the section The Non-Use of Syntactic Transformations imply that the parser will nevertheless detect the gap in this position as long as it is LIKELY that a noun phrase should occur there. (Note that this is somewhat less likely in a sentence such as *The nurse found the patient some bandaids*. And the question *Which bandaids did the nurse find the patient?* seem correspondingly harder to parse, as if neither of its gaps is readily detectable.)

Finally, in order to simplify the exposition, I have assumed that the parser reconstructs the underlying sequence V–NP–NP for dative questions, although it is generally assumed that the deep structure contains the sequence V–NP–*to* NP, in which the direct object immediately follows the verb. But the same result is obtained on either assumption, although the argument is slightly more intricate in the latter case. If the parser is looking for the sequence V–NP–PP, it will be expecting a noun phrase after the verb. It will find one and conclude (as before) that there is no gap in this position. It will then be expecting a prepositional phrase. Finding none in the surface string, it will hypothesize a gap, but will discover that the fronted noun phrase is a legitimate filler for this prepositional phrase gap only on the assumption that the Dative transformation has applied. It will therefore 'undo' the Dative transformation, reversing the noun phrases and inserting *to*. As a result, the WH-constituent filler will end up immediately after the verb and before the newly created prepositional phrase, and it will therefore be interpreted as the direct object.

understood as if the second *de*-phrase had been moved, as in the acceptable (35c).

(35a) J'ai vu le portrait d'Aristotle de Rembrandt.
(35b) ***De qui** as-tu vu le portrait △ de Rembrandt?
(35c) **De qui** as-tu vu le portrait d'Aristotle △?

English prepositional phrases also show the predicted asymmetry, although in this case the parser's distaste for the early-gap analysis has apparently not been elevated to the status of a grammatical constraint.[15]

(36a) You aimed at the tree at the rock.
(36b) ?**At which tree** did you aim △ at the rock?
(36c) **At which rock** did you aim at the tree △?
(37a) Milly mowed the lawn for old Mr. Tomkins for Uncle Frank.
(37b) ?**For whom** did Milly mow the lawn △ for Uncle Frank?
(37c) **For whom** did Milly mow the lawn for old Mr. Tomkins △?

The fact that the second of the two possible gap positions is favored in all of these examples is exactly as predicted by the Position Assignment Model, but it is an embarrassment to the Role Assignment Model. The 'explanation' offered for dative questions on the Role Assignment Model turns out to be simply that the parser, when confronted with a moved noun phrase, favors the hypothesis that it is the direct object of the verb. This is an explanation only to the extent that it itself has an explanation, but so far none has been offered. No doubt it is true that direct objects are more common in sentences than are indirect objects. But at least Langendoen et al. (1974) cannot argue that the parser's preference is based on frequency considerations, because they claim that the parser formulates its hypothesis about the role of the fronted constituent AFTER it has identified the verb as a dative verb that takes indirect objects. The Role Assignment Model is unconvincing, therefore, because it could equally well have 'explained' a preference for the fronted-IO analysis

---

[15]In formulating the XX Extraction Principle, I have not specified the DEGREE of preference for the analysis with the later gap, since this seems to vary considerably. In French, if Ruwet is right, the parser's preference has been legitimized by the inclusion in the grammar of a constraint that prohibits extraction of the first X of an XX sequence. The same is true for NP–NP sequences for some English speakers, though not for all. This variability does not invalidate the explanation given, for sentences can be difficult to parse without being impossible to parse; the parser might have available some more elaborate routines designed to overcome its natural tendencies where these would lead it to overlook legitimate analyses of sentences. Counterevidence would consist of XX sentences in which the first gap was positively preferred over the second. Langendoen et al. (1974) claim to have found speakers for whom this is the case for dative questions (but see Footnote 16).

instead, merely by assuming a different ranking of the alternative analyses that the parser must consider.[16]

The major objection to the Role Assignment Model, however, is that it is incapable of explaining the XX Extraction Principle. The parser favors the direct object interpretation of a fronted noun phrase, the agentive interpretation of a fronted *de*-phrase, the locative interpretation of a fronted *at*-phrase, and the 'distant beneficiary' interpretation of a fronted *for*-phrase. In terms of grammatical ROLES, these various examples have nothing in common at all. A different role-assignment principle must be employed by the parser for each of these phrase types, and only an extraordinary coincidence could account for the fact that all of these principles happen to favor the second position of an underlying XX sequence.

My conclusion is that the Position Assignment Model is the correct one, i.e., that grammatical roles are assigned to transformationally moved constituents only after they have been returned to their deep structure positions. Deep structure representations do appear to mediate the recovery of sentence meanings, just as Superstrategy implies.

A NEW LOOK AT THE RELATION
BETWEEN GRAMMAR AND PARSER

My arguments about how the parser operates have been presented so far against the background of a theory of grammars that few linguists now take seriously. Among the more recent modifications of this theory, there is one, the Revised Extended Standard Theory, that is of particular interest in relation to Superstrategy.

---

[16]Langendoen et al. (1974) claim that in the metropolitan New York area there are speakers who prefer the fronted-IO analysis of dative questions to the fronted-DO analysis, and they consider it an asset of their model that it can accommodate this preference just as easily as the more usual one. But despite the questionnaires they administered, they have not clearly established the existence of genuine violations of the XX Extraction Principle. Only three of the sentences that they presented to informants in their Answer Form questionnaire were well-formed dative questions. Just under a quarter of the informants who answered appropriately preferred the fronted-IO interpretation for BOTH of the sentences "Who(m) did you show the woman?" and "Who(m) did you send the woman?" For each sentence individually the proportion was approximately one third. But for the sentence "Who(m) did you offer the man?" fewer than 10% of the informants favored the fronted-IO reading. The fact that lexical differences had such a large effect suggests that these informants were relying to some extent on semantic and pragmatic guesses rather than on syntactic parsing routines. Because it is natural to assume that a lower status person is shown, sent, or offered to a higher status person, it would take only a slight tendency towards male chauvinism in this population to account for the relatively high proportion of fronted-IO interpretations for the two *woman* sentences as compared to the *man* sentence.

In a number of recent papers, it has been argued that the transformational movement of a constituent leaves a TRACE in the original, pre-movement position (Chomsky, 1973, 1975, 1977; Chomsky & Lasnik, 1977). The moved constituent and its trace are co-indexed at the time of application of the movement rule. At the end of the transformational derivation, a trace that remains in the surface structure (i.e., which has not been substituted for by later transformations) may be construed as a variable bound by a logical operator derived from the moved constituent with which it is co-indexed. For example, from the surface structure (38), the construal rules would derive a representation of logical structure of the form (39).

(38) Who$_i$ did he say Mary kissed *trace$_i$*
(39) for which person x, he said Mary kissed x

The construal rules are subject to certain structural conditions, and it may happen that a trace has been generated in such a position that no construal rule can apply to it. In such cases, the surface structure is rejected as ill formed (uninterpretable). The construal rules thus function in part like filters, to winnow out derivations in which the free application of transformations has led to illegitimate results. Jenkins (1977) has argued that this filtering function of the construal rules undermines the traditional arguments for movement transformations. He proposed that deep structures can be generated with 'traces' (now a misnomer) already present. These traces will not be co-indexed with any other constituents at this stage, but the construal rules will subsequently determine which constituents may be co-indexed with which traces, as well as rejecting sentences that contain traces in illegitimate, unbindable positions. Jenkins' theory, though very new and as yet untested in detail, seems in some respects to be the natural end-point to Chomsky's progressive restriction of the power of the transformational rules in favor of construal rules. Although it may be premature to do so, I think it is of considerable interest to examine the implications of this new theory for the characterization of the parser's task.

Overlooking a great many details, we may say that, under this new theory, there are no transformations, and hence there is no distinction between the deep structure and the surface structure of a sentence. Each sentence has a single phrase marker, which may contain traces; and it has a semantic representation of some kind, which is derived from this phrase marker by the construal rules that relate the traces to other constituents. If we were to base a model of the parser on this theory of grammars, it would run roughly as follows. The parser receives a sequence of lexical items, which constitute the terminal string of the phrase marker for the sentence, except that there will be no overt phonological/orthographic realization for any traces that this terminal string contains.[17] The parser's goal is to determine the semantic representation of the sentence. It can achieve this by employing processing analogs of the construal rules, if it can first establish the positions of any traces within the lexical string. To identify trace positions, it will need to compare the lexical string with the well-formedness conditions on phrase markers, which specify where there must or may be a constituent of a given type. All three presuppositions of Superstrategy fall out quite naturally from this model.

First, the old tension between the existence of transformational rules in the grammar and their non-use by the parser simply dissolves away, for there ARE no such rules in grammars of the new kind.

Second, the fact that the parser does not form a representation of the surface phrase marker of the sentence follows from the fact that the grammar no longer provides any such representation. The one phrase marker that the grammar does define contains traces, i.e., represents gap positions. It is thus quite unlike the traditional surface structure phrase marker whose role in sentence parsing is denied by Superstrategy.

Finally, the claim that the semantic representation of a sentence is assigned on the basis of its deep structure phrase marker translates into the claim that the semantic representation is established by setting up binding relations between traces and other constituents in the phrase marker. In presenting

---

[17]King (1970) noted that contraction of the copula and of auxiliary verbs is not permitted before certain gaps, including gaps created by deletion as in (i), and gaps created by movement as in (ii).

(i) You'll need some and $\begin{cases} \text{I will} \\ *\text{I'll} \end{cases}$ $\triangle$ too.

(ii) Some day he'd like to be what $\begin{cases} \text{you are} \\ *\text{you're} \end{cases}$ $\triangle$ now.

Chomsky and Lasnik (1977) noted that liaison of *want to* to *wanna* is not permitted if a gap due to a movement rule intervenes, though it is compatible with a gap due to Equi.

(iiia) **Who** do you want $\triangle$ to go?

(iiib) ***Who** do you wan $\triangle$ na go?

(iva) **Who** do **you** want $\triangle$ to go with $\triangle$?

(ivb) **Who** do **you** wan $\triangle$ na go with $\triangle$?

These and other phonological effects at gap positions (see Cooper, 1976) may well provide the parser with useful clues about the location of gaps in the word string. It is interesting, however, that the UNambiguous forms are the reduced ones (*I'll, you're, wanna*) which signal that there is NO gap. The unreduced forms (*I will, you are, want to*) that occur when there is a gap are also compatible with no gap, at least in formal speech and written English. So it is clear that the parser could not be relying exclusively on such cues for locating gaps.

Superstrategy so far, I have implied that the parser MOVES CONSTITUENTS BACK into the positions they would fill in a traditional deep structure representation of the sentence. But it is now time to note that all of the arguments for Superstrategy are equally compatible with the assumption that the parser associates fillers with gaps/traces by means of co-indexing, mental arrows, or any other formally equivalent notational device.

This theory of grammars, in which construal rules rather than transformations do most of the work, thus meshes remarkably well with what we have been able to determine about the operations of the parser. The lexicon and the phrase structure rules must be appealed to in establishing the syntactic class of each word and determining the proper grouping of words into phrases. But, in addition to this, the parser's two main priorities are the finding of gaps (i.e., the identification of traces) and the filling of gaps (i.e., the binding of traces.).

This convergence between the grammar and the parser is all the more impressive because neither was developed with the other in mind. Chomsky (1977) has speculated on some possible functional motivations for the particular constraints that the construal rules obey; roughly, these constraints serve to narrow the domain within a sentence that the parser must search in order to locate the gap for a given type of filler. But the major arguments for trace theory have turned on descriptive and explanatory adequacy; it provides simpler descriptions of a variety of linguistic phenomena, and it permits the net around the class of possible grammars for human languages to be drawn more tightly. And the arguments given here for Superstrategy have quite explicitly not made any appeal to the assumption that parsing operations must parallel formal grammatical rules. It is all the more satisfying, therefore, to find signs that they do.

REFERENCES

Chomsky, N. *Aspects of the theory of syntax*. Cambridge, Mass.: MIT Press, 1965.

Chomsky, N. Some empirical issues in the theory of transformational grammar. In S. Peters (Ed.), *Goals of linguistic theory*. Englewood Cliffs, N.J.: Prentice-Hall, 1972.

Chomsky, N. Conditions on transformations. In S. Anderson & P. Kiparsky (Eds.), *A Festschrift for Morris Halle*. New York: Holt, Rinehart, & Winston, 1973.

Chomsky, N. *Reflections on language*. New York: Pantheon, 1975.

Chomsky, N. On *wh*-movement. In A. Akmajian, P. Culicover, & T. Wasow (Eds.), *Formal syntax*. New York: Academic Press, 1977.

Chomsky, N., & Lasnik, H. Filters and control. *Linguistic Inquiry*, 1977, *8*, 425–504.

Clifton, C., Kurcz, I., & Jenkins, J. Grammatical relations as determinants of sentence similarity. *Journal of Verbal Learning and Verbal Behavior*, 1965, *4*, 112–117.

Cooper, W. E. *Syntactic control of timing in speech production*. Unpublished doctoral dissertation, MIT, 1976.

Fiengo, R. On trace theory. *Linguistic Inquiry*, 1977, *8*, 35–62.

Fillmore, C. The case for case. In E. Bach & R. Harms (Eds.), *Universals in linguistic theory*. New York: Holt, Rinehart, & Winston, 1968.

Fodor, J. A., Bever, T., & Garrett, M. *The psychology of language.* New York: McGraw-Hill, 1974.

Fodor, J. D. *Gapping gapped.* Unpublished manuscript, University of Connecticut, 1974.

Fodor, J. D. *Semantics: Theories of meaning in generative grammar.* New York: T. Y. Crowell, 1977.

Fodor, J. D. Parsing strategies and constraints on transformations. *Linguistic Inquiry,* 1978, *9,* 427–473.

Gruber, J. *Studies in lexical relations.* Unpublished doctoral dissertation, MIT, 1965.

Hankamer, J. Unacceptable ambiguity. *Linguistic Inquiry,* 1973, *4,* 17–68.

Jackendoff, R. S. *Semantic interpretation in generative grammar.* Cambridge, Mass.: MIT Press, 1972.

Jackendoff, R. S., & Culicover, P. A reconsideration of dative movements. *Foundations of Language,* 1973, *7,* 397–412.

Jenkins, L. *On base generating trace.* Paper delivered at the eighth annual meeting of the North Eastern Linguistics Society, University of Massachusetts at Amherst, 1977.

Kimball, J. Seven principles of surface structure parsing in natural language. *Cognition,* 1973, *2,* 12–47.

King, H. V. On blocking the rules for contraction in English. *Linguistic Inquiry,* 1970, *1,* 134–136.

Klima, E. *Regulatory devices against functional ambiguity.* Unpublished manuscript, University of California at San Diego, 1970.

Lakoff, G. *Irregularity in syntax.* New York: Holt, Rinehart, & Winston, 1970.

Lakoff, G., & Thompson, H. Introducing cognitive grammar. In C. Cogen, H. Thompson, G. Thurgood, K. Whistler, & J. Wright (Eds.), *Proceedings of the first annual meeting of the Berkeley Linguistics Society.* Berkeley: Berkeley Linguistics Society, 1975. (a)

Lakoff, G., & Thompson, H. Dative questions in cognitive grammar. In R. Grossman, L. J. San, & T. Vance (Eds.), *Papers from the parasession on functionalism.* Chicago: Chicago Linguistic Society, 1975. (b)

Langendoen, D. T., Kalish-Landon, N., & Dore, J. Dative questions: A study in the relation of acceptability to grammaticality of an English sentence type. *Cognition,* 1974, *2,* 451–478.

Lasnik, H., & Fiengo, R. Complement object deletion. *Linguistic Inquiry,* 1974, *5,* 535–571.

Levelt, W. A. A scaling approach to the study of syntactic relations. In G. Flores d'Arcais & W. Levelt (Eds.), *Advances in psycholinguistics.* New York: American Elsevier, 1970.

Miller, G., & McKean, K. A chronometric study of some relations between sentences. *Quarterly Journal of Experimental Psychology,* 1964, *16,* 297–308.

Ross, J. *Constraints on variables in syntax.* Unpublished doctoral dissertation, MIT, 1967.

Ruwet, N. *How to deal with syntactic irregularities: Conditions on transformations or perceptual strategies?* Unpublished manuscript, Paris, 1973.

Wanner, E. *On remembering, forgetting and understanding sentences: A study of the deep structure hypothesis.* Unpublished doctoral dissertation, Harvard University, 1968.

Wanner, E., Kaplan, R. M., & Shiner, S. *Garden paths in relative clauses.* Unpublished manuscript, Harvard University, 1975.

Wanner, E., & Maratsos, M. *An augmented transition network model of relative clause comprehension.* Unpublished manuscript, Harvard University, 1974.

Wanner, E., & Shiner, S. *Ambiguities in relative clauses.* Unpublished manuscript, Harvard University, 1975.

9

Role of Efference Monitoring in the Detection of Self-Produced Speech Errors

James R. Lackner
Brandeis University
and
Massachusetts Institute of Technology

Betty H. Tuller
University of Connecticut, Storrs

COORDINATION OF THE VOCAL APPARATUS
DURING SPEECH PRODUCTION

The production of speech requires precise coordination of the many muscles that control the rate of airflow from the lungs and determine the moment-to-moment configuration of the vocal tract and articulatory apparatus; yet, little is known about how this regulation is achieved and accurately maintained. In recent years, the central and peripheral factors involved in the coordination of motor activities have received great attention, and the complexity of the afferent and efferent mechanisms involved in guiding head, trunk, and limb movements has been amply highlighted in many ingenious ways (cf. Evarts, Bizzi, Burke, DeLong, & Thach, 1971; Goodwin, McCloskey, & Matthews, 1972a, 1972b; Stein, 1974; Stein, Pearson, Smith, & Redford, 1973). One factor that has emerged with some clarity from such studies is the participation of internal motor feedback in the control of both extraocular and skeletal muscle (Higgens & Angel, 1970; Teuber, 1960; von Holst & Mittelstaedt, 1950). The observations to be described below indicate that such corollary-discharge information is also utilized during speech production.

In the course of natural speech, an utterance is sometimes produced that deviates from the intended one (Fromkin, 1971; Garrett, 1975; Lashley, 1951). Deviations can occur at levels of linguistic organization ranging from the phonetic to that of entire words and phrases (Fromkin, 1971). When an inappropriate sound sequence is produced (e.g., when the wrong word is spoken), speakers potentially could detect the error in several ways. They might recognize from auditory feedback that the possible phonetic representations of the produced sound are incompatible with the sound they intended. Or they might detect the error through recognition that the proprioceptive feedback accompanying the positional changes of the vocal apparatus had been incorrect. For example, spindle signals from the muscles of the jaw could contribute positional informatin about jaw angle, as could the joint receptors of the jaw. Spindle information from skeletal muscles has recently been shown to contribute to position sense of the limbs (Goodwin et al., 1972a, 1972b); moreover, Bowman and Combs (1968) have shown that spindle afferents in the tongue of the rhesus monkey potentially signal initiation, attainment, and release of position. Because the muscles of the tongue represent the vertical, lateral, and horizontal directions, spindles are present that potentially represent these directions and provide three-dimensional informaton about tongue position. Accordingly, refined proprioceptive information about the ongoing configuration of the tongue, jaw, and other parts of the vocal tract is present during articulation and could be used to monitor speech performance.

There is some evidence that production of a sound is accompanied by information about the efferent signal, as well as by proprioceptive and auditory feedback. For example, when a tape-recorded word (Warren & Gregory, 1958) or speech sound (Goldstein & Lackner, 1973; Lackner & Goldstein, 1975) is repeated over and over, listeners lose perceptual stability of the speech signal and make a variety of identification errors. By contrast, when the repeated speech sound is self-produced, perceptual stability is maintained under conditions that otherwise would result in loss of accurate phonetic resolution (Lackner, 1974). To account for the greater perceptual stability of self-produced sounds, Lackner proposed that corollary-discharge signals representing the intended speech sounds can be compared with the auditory and proprioceptive feedback resulting from the actual production of the intended sounds. If the auditory and proprioceptive properties of the produced speech sound are similar to those that would be characteristic of the intended sound, then the incoming sound is perceived as the intended sound. As a consequence, auditory adaptation or fatigue and minor distortions in articulation would fail to disrupt the accurate recognition of self-produced speech, whereas an error in production, an "unintended" utterance, would be readily detected.

This evaluative role of corollary-discharge signals is distinct from that of "cancellation" proposed by Sperry (1950), von Holst and Mittelstaedt (1950), and Teuber (1960) to account for the stability of visual direction during voluntary eye movement. As hypothesized here, the corollary-discharge signals associated with intended speech sounds are evaluated for goodness of fit, with the corollary-discharge representations of the efferent signals actually sent to innervate the articulatory apparatus, as well as with sensory signals, both auditory and proprioceptive, that are contingent on self-produced articulations. Such comparisons would enable speakers to determine whether an inappropriate sound sequence had been produced.

By this account, three sources of information, auditory, proprioceptive, and efferent, might be utilized singly or in combination in the detection of speech errors. We took it as given that auditory feedback could function in this manner; therefore, our approach was to determine whether corollary-discharge and proprioceptive signals could also be so utilized. To investigate the relative role of these factors in the production and control of speech sounds, we created a situation that enhanced the likelihood that speech errors would occur and then measured the ability of subjects to detect their own errors, both when auditory feedback was permitted and when it was masked by white noise. Because most natural speech errors involve segments of phonetic size (Fromkin, 1971) that are easy to characterize in terms of phonetic features, our experimental task was designed to elicit such errors.

EXPERIMENTAL EVALUATION OF THE USE OF COROLLARY DISCHARGE, AUDITORY, AND PROPRIOCEPTIVE INFORMATION DURING SPEECH PRODUCTION

The speech-production task required subjects to repeat sequences of phonetically similar stimuli at a rate of 4 syllables/sec for 30 sec. Each sequence consisted of either four consonant-vowel (CV) syllables (e.g., pi-di-ti-gi), four vowel (V) syllables (e.g., ae-i-o-u), or four alternated CV and V syllables (e.g., pi-ae-ti-o). The CV stimuli included the stop consonants /p/, /b/, /t/, /d/, /k/, /g/ in the vowel environment /i/; the V stimuli included /ae/, /e/, /i/, /o/, /u/.[1]

Normal auditory feedback was permitted during one session, whereas during the other, binaural white noise was presented over headphones at 100 dB. Following the auditory-masking session, the subject was questioned about the effectiveness of the white-noise mask in preventing auditory feedback; all subjects reported that the mask was effective. The subjects, who were all native speakers of English, were required to say one syllable of a stimulus sequence every time the indicator light on an interval timer turned on or off. The pace was set at four syllables/sec. The importance of not imposing

---

[1]As represented in the International Phonetic Alphabet, the stimuli are: (p) = (p^h); (t) = (t^h); (k) = (k^h); (b) = (b); (d) = (d); (g) = (g); (ae) = (ae); (e) = (ε); (i) = (ι); (u) = (u); (o) does not occur in English, it is a shorter version of the vowel in *boat*.

any rhythmic structure other than the pacing on the stimulus sequence and of saying each syllable as individually as possible was stressed when instructing the subjects because the imposition of such structure helps to reduce or prevent errors.

Subjects were told to press a telegraph key near their dominant hand whenever they made an error in the sequence being spoken. Depressing the key placed a signal tone on the second channel of the tape recorder and, thus, allowed a determination of the number of detected and undetected speech errors for each of the two experimental conditions. Prior to the start of a trial, the subjects were told the sequence for that trial and asked to repeat it once to insure that there was no confusion of identity or order of the four elements.

The number of false-positive responses was extremely small, averaging only 14 per subject across the entire experimental session. In addition, subjects detected a larger percentage of both CV and V errors in the masking condition when that condition was presented in the second experimental session rather than in the first, $p < .01$. Table 9.1 summarizes the accuracy of detecting production errors on CV syllables across subjects and across sequence types. The order of conditions was balanced across subjects; individual subjects received the same stimulus order during their two sessions. Data for the two conditions are presented separately, and the CV errors are categorized according to incorrect voicing, place of articulation, or both. When subjects were denied normal auditory feedback, their ability to detect place-of-articulation errors was slightly diminished, $F(1, 9) = 7.04$, $p < .05$, but the detection of voicing errors was extremely impaired, $F(1, 9) = 114.55$, $p < .001$, with subjects noticing only about 20% of all voicing errors. Errors involving both voicing and place-of-articulation were extremely rare, a total of 20 across all conditions, and no meaningful comparison of conditions was possible.

TABLE 9.1
Accuracy of Detecting Incorrectly Produced Consonant–Vowel (CV)
Syllables According to Condition, Session, and Phonetic Dimension(s) on
Which the Produced Syllable Deviated from the Target Syllable

	Auditory Feedback		Auditory Masking	
CV Error Type	Session 1	Session 2	Session 1	Session 2
Place of articulation	91% (66)	97% (32)	76% (78)	92% (38)
Voicing	61% (80)	82% (95)	11% (151)	27% (101)
Place and voicing	88% (8)	100% (1)	100% (10)	100% (1)

Note.   The entries in parentheses indicate the total numbers of errors in particular categories and the percentages indicate the total number of those errors that were detected.

TABLE 9.2

Accuracy of Detecting Incorrectly Produced Vowel Syllables According to
Condition, Session, and Whether the Target Vowel was Spoken as a
Different Vowel or as a Consonant

Vowel Syllable Spoken as	*Auditory Feedback*		*Auditory Masking*	
	Session 1	*Session 2*	*Session 1*	*Session 2*
Incorrect vowel	73% (124)	66% (136)	18% (144)	32% (205)
Consonant	79% (28)	95% (19)	69% (16)	62% (26)

Note.   Entries in parentheses represent the total numbers of errors, the percentages
indicate how many of those errors were detected.

The ability to detect errors on V syllables was also significantly affected by
masking of auditory feedback, $F(1, 9) = 10.4, p < .025$. Table 9.2 categorizes
errors for the V sequence syllables according to whether the sound produced
was vocalic or consonantal. It is apparent that in the absence of normal
auditory feedback, the ability to detect V syllable errors that result in the
production of a different vowel is significantly inferior to the ability to detect
those vowel errors that result in the production of a consonant, $F(1, 9)$
$= 28.67, p < .001$.

Errors for the V syllables that result in production of a different vowel are
summarized in Table 9.3 in terms of type of error and accuracy of error
detection. In general, the spoken vowel differs from the target vowel
minimally; e.g., /ae/ or /e/ is spoken instead of /i/. From Table 9.3 it can be
seen that certain vowel errors are easier to detect than others; e.g., /u/ spoken
instead of /e/ vs. /i/ spoken instead of /e/.

Latencies between the commission of an error and the key press indicating
the subject's awareness of the error are presented in Table 9.4. In interpreting
these latencies, it must be emphasized that the subjects were not instructed to
respond as rapidly as possible when they made an error, but only to respond;
i.e., no explicit premium was placed on speed of response. Even so, from
Table 9.4 it can be seen that some speech errors were detected with latencies
shorter than 50 msec (1.5% over all conditions), and more were reported with
latencies between 50 and 100 msec (2.6% over all conditions). When denied
auditory feedback, subjects detected a slightly larger percentage of their
speech errors with latencies between 0 and 100 msec than they did when
permitted auditory feedback (4.9% vs. 3.0%).

It is not surprising that without auditory feedback, errors on the voicing
dimension of CV syllables are more difficult to detect than place-of-
articulation errors. That small time differences would be more difficult to
capture than gross positional changes is not unnatural. The difference
between a voiced and an unvoiced consonant relates to the onset time of

TABLE 9.3
Classification of Vowel Errors According to Condition and Session in Terms of the Vowels that were Spoken for the Target Vowels

Condition/Target Vowel	Spoken Vowel				
	a	*e*	*i*	*o*	*u*
Auditory feedback					
Session 1					
a	—	12/16	2/2	2/2	1/1
e	6/14	—	3/7	8/8	1/1
i	1/1	3/11	—	1/1	7/7
o	0/0	4/4	1/1	—	23/32
u	1/1	2/2	2/2	11/11	—
Session 2					
a	—	4/12	0/0	2/2	0/0
e	10/16	—	2/6	2/2	3/13
i	1/1	3/6	—	2/2	6/6
o	1/1	2/2	1/1	—	38/63
u	3/3	0/0	0/0	10/10	—
Auditory masking					
Session 1					
a	—	2/13	0/0	0/0	0/0
e	2/27	—	0/14	3/6	0/0
i	2/5	2/23	—	0/1	5/5
o	1/1	4/6	0/0	—	3/29
u	0/0	0/0	0/0	1/14	—
Session 2					
a	—	0/27	0/0	1/1	0/0
e	9/27	—	1/15	0/1	1/2
i	1/1	4/24	—	3/3	6/7
o	2/4	3/4	1/1	—	24/68
u	1/1	1/2	1/1	7/17	—

Note. Accuracy of error detection is indicated as a fraction with the denominator specifying the total number of errors in a particular category, and the numerator the number that were detected.

TABLE 9.4
Distribution of Error-Detection Response Latencies (in Msec) According to Condition and Session

Condition/Session	Latency (Msec) for Detecting Production Error						
	0–50	51–100	101–150	151–200	201–250	251–300	301–
Auditory feedback							
Session 1	0.75	3.36	4.48	6.34	8.58	10.44	66.05
Session 2	0.00	1.65	3.85	4.40	7.14	9.89	73.07
Auditory masking							
Session 1	1.45	3.62	3.62	7.25	8.70	10.14	65.22
Session 2	3.10	1.55	4.65	3.10	3.90	9.30	74.40

Note. The entries represent the percentage of the total number of errors that were detected within the specified latency ranges in a particular condition and session. Latencies were measured from the offset of the error.

glottal vibration; in an unvoiced CV syllable, pulsation is about 100 msec later than in a voiced CV (Liberman, Cooper, Shankweiler, & Studdert-Kennedy, 1967). By contrast, place-of-articulation changes involve different gestures of the tongue and jaw. The latter also produce gross changes in the formant structure of the acoustic signal, whereas the former affect primarily the onset of the first formant; this consideration may account for subjects being more accurate in capturing place compared with voicing errors when permitted auditory feedback.

Error-detection rates on the V syllables can be understood in the same fashion. These errors involve positional changes in tongue or jaw, with resulting changes in the formant structure of the acoustic signal. In both the masking and auditory-feedback conditions, subjects were much less accurate in recognizing speech errors involving small positional changes, and accordingly small acoustic and proprioceptive changes, than recognizing errors involving more gross positional changes.

The short latencies (0 to 100 msec) of some of the error-detection responses suggest that the subjects were able to monitor corollary-discharge signals during speech production; choice reaction times (RTs) to both auditory and proprioceptive feedback are usually much longer, on the order of 300 to 400 msec (Woodworth & Schlosberg, 1954). Even though responses were obtained under experimental conditions that did not stress response speed, 5% of the errors in the masking condition were detected in less than 100 msec and 9% in less than 150 msec, compared with approximately 3% and 7%, respectively, in the auditory-feedback condition. To examine better the contribution of corollary-discharge signals to error detection, a second experiment was carried out that required responses to be as rapid as possible. This experiment included a control condition in which subjects were required to listen to repeated sequences of V or CV syllables that were comparable to those used in the speech-production task and to indicate as rapidly as possible by a key press whenever one of the sequence syllables was incorrect. The latencies of these responses provided a distribution of auditory reaction times for comparison with that obtained in the speech-production task.

For the speech-perception task, a stimulus tape was prepared consisting of repeated sequences of the V, CV, and alternated CV and V syllables described earlier. Sequences were constructed by splicing together four syllables in orders identical to the sequence orders to be used in the speech-production task. At three random points within each sequence, a syllable that was incorrect for the particular sequence was substituted for the correct syllable. For example, during the repeated presentation of the sequence /pi/, /ae/, /ti/, /o/, substitution of /di/ for /pi/ at some point would be a sequence "error." Three sec prior to the start of a sequence, a warning tone alerted the subjects. After 16 trials, the subjects were given a 5-min rest period. They were instructed that each sequence might contain an unspecified number of errors. As before, a telegraph key was positioned near the subjects' dominant hand,

and they were told to tap the key as quickly as possible upon hearing an incorrect syllable in a sequence.

Subjects were tested individually and participated in two experimental sessions, on one day receiving the perception task and on a different day, the production task. During the speech-production task, the subjects received binaural white noise at 100 dB over headphones. During both sessions, the experimenter frequently stressed the importance of responding to errors as rapidly as possible.

Latencies for the detection of an incorrect syllable presented during the perception task and latencies for the detection of a self-produced speech error

TABLE 9.5
Mean Latencies of Error-Detection Responses (in Msec)
for Subjects in the Tasks

Subject	Speech-Perception Task[a]	Speech-Production Task[b]
1	569	451
2	620	491
3	549	406
4	551	385
5	626	417
6	566	387
7	543	393
8	568	382

Note. Latencies are measured from error offset.
[a]Overall mean = 574 msec.
[b]Overall mean = 413 msec.

TABLE 9.6
Mean Latencies of Error-Detection Responses (in Msec)
for Subjects in the Tasks

Subject	Speech-Perception Task[a]	Speech-Production Task[b]
1	369	284
2	420	318
3	349	210
4	350	204
5	426	211
6	366	197
7	343	208
8	368	186

Note. Latencies are measured from error onset.
[a]Overall mean = 374 msec.
[b]Overall mean = 227 msec.

in the production task were measured in relation to both the onset and offset of each incorrect sound (see Tables 9.5 and 9.6, respectively). Using either measurement, we found significantly shorter response times for detecting a self-produced error than for detecting an error in a sequence to which the subjects simply listened ($p < .001$).

In the perception task, no subject responded to an error with a latency shorter than 150 msec, as measured from either the onset or the offset of the incorrect sound. From Tables 9.7 and 9.8, it can be seen that some self-produced speech errors were detected within 50 msec, measured either from the beginning (.9%) or the end (9.6%) of the incorrect sound; many more errors were captured with latencies between 50 and 100 msec (2.2% and 11.7%) and still more between 100 and 150 msec (2.8% and 13.8%).

TABLE 9.7
Distribution of Error-Detection Response Latencies (in Msec) for the Tasks

Task	0–50	51–100	101–150	151–200	201–250	251–300	301–
Speech perception	0	0	0	6.5	19.6	18.9	55.0
Speech production	9.6	11.7	13.8	14.1	11.2	11.3	28.3

Note. Latencies are measured from error offset. The entries represent the percentage of the total number of errors that were detected within the specified latency ranges in the two tasks.

TABLE 9.8
Distribution of Error-Detection Response Latencies (in Msec) for the Tasks

Task	0–50	51–100	101–150	151–200	201–250	251–300	301–
Speech perception	0	0	0	0	0	0	100.0
Speech production	.9	2.2	2.8	5.0	6.7	10.1	72.3

Note. Latencies are measured from error onset. The entries represent the percentage of the total number of errors that were detected within the specified latency ranges in the two tasks.

Errors made in the speech-production task were examined across subjects and sequence types. Table 9.9 shows the accuracy of detecting speech errors on CV syllables in terms of voicing and place-of-articulation errors. Table 9.10 summarizes the types of vocalic errors made on the vowel syllables and the accuracy of their detection. An examination of these tables indicates that the pattern of errors and error detection corresponds to that obtained in the masking condition of Experiment 1: In the absence of auditory feedback, errors involving small timing changes of the articulatory apparatus are more difficult to detect than errors involving positional changes of the articulators.

TABLE 9.9
Accuracy of Detecting Incorrectly Produced Consonant-Vowel (CV) Syllables in the Speech-Production Task According to Whether that Task was Presented in the First or Second Experimental Session

CV Error Type	Auditory Masking	
	Session 1	Session 2
Place of articulation	68% (63)	93% (100)
Voicing	57% (87)	52% (152)
Place and voicing	100% (27)	95% (21)

Note. The entries in parentheses indicate the total number of errors for which the produced syllables deviated from the target syllables on particular phonetic dimensions; the percentages indicate the total number of those errors that were detected.

TABLE 9.10
Classification of Vowel Errors According to Whether the Production Task was in the First or Second Experimental Session and in Terms of the Vowels that were Produced for the Target Vowels

Condition/Target Vowel	Spoken Vowel				
	a	e	i	o	u
Auditory masking					
Session 1					
a	—	2/8	2/4	4/4	3/3
e	11/27	—	0/4	1/1	3/3
i	1/1	7/13	—	1/1	4/7
o	0/0	2/2	4/4	—	14/25
u	1/1	0/1	0/1	5/14	—
Session 2					
a	—	2/8	2/2	1/5	1/2
e	9/23	—	5/22	4/5	3/4
i	0/1	5/15	—	0/0	5/7
o	2/2	3/4	1/1	—	14/30
u	1/1	3/4	2/4	13/21	—

Note. The denominator of each entry indicates the total number of errors in a particular category and the numerator, the number that were detected.

MULTIPLE LEVELS OF
COROLLARY-DISCHARGE REPRESENTATION
IN SPEECH PRODUCTION AND PERCEPTION

The experimental observations show that subjects can detect self-produced errors in a stimulus sequence much more rapidly than they can detect errors in a sequence to which they simply listen. That they can do so even when auditory feedback is masked implies that they must be making use of proprioceptive or corollary-discharge information to monitor their performance.

The extremely short latencies with which some self-produced speech errors can be detected provides evidence for an ability to determine whether the corollary-discharge signals associated with motor commands to the articulatory apparatus are appropriate for the intended speech sound. Detection of a production error must depend in part on an ability to compare representations of the actually occurring efferent signals with representations of the ones that should have been issued. Such a capacity means that some corollary-discharge signals issued during speech production convey information about the final output level of control of the articulatory apparatus. Utilization of corollary-discharge information in detecting motor errors is not restricted to speech production. Higgens and Angel (1970) measured error-correction latencies in an experiment in which subjects were required to amend their responses as rapidly as possible when they moved a joystick in the wrong direction. Some corrections could be initiated with latencies as short as 80 msec, a value well below proprioceptive or visual RTs; accordingly, Higgens and Angel concluded that their subjects were monitoring efferent signals, i.e., that they were utilizing corollary-discharge information.

Two final points deserve mention. In the first experiment, subjects who received the masking condition second made fewer errors than subjects who received it first. This finding is consistent with an observation reported by Lackner and Levine (1975), who found that when auditory feedback was eliminated, the duration of repetitions of memorized lists of words was more accurate. By contrast, Ringel and Steer (1963) earlier had found that both the duration and the rate of utterances were adversely affected when auditory feedback was masked while subjects were reading a script. Lackner and Levine (1975) argued that these different outcomes from masking auditory feedback are related to whether the subjects know the material they are going to speak; when the message is memorized and auditory feedback is eliminated, an improvement in accuracy is possible because the subject must attend to the fine details of articulation rather than to specifics of auditory feedback.

Because identical stimulus sequences were used during both experimental sessions, this same consideration would explain why fewer errors were made in the masking condition of our experiment when it comprised the second session: During the second session, the subjects were more familiar with the task and the material. Such a consideration may also explain why detection latencies tend to be somewhat shorter when auditory feedback is masked: Subjects cannot rely on auditory information and are forced to utilize proprioceptive and corollary-discharge information. Moreover, it is likely that emphasizing response speed forces speakers to attend more closely to proprioceptive and corollary-discharge information. For example, subjects in the second experiment were more accurate in detecting errors in voicing than were subjects in the auditory-masking condition of the first experiment, where speed was not stressed.

It is notable that our experiments provide evidence for more than one form of corollary-discharge signal. Detection of speech errors after extremely short latencies indicates that corollary-discharge representations of intended sounds can be compared with those actually issued. The evidence from our earlier work demonstrating the enhanced perceptual stability of self-produced speech sounds (Lackner, 1974) shows that not only does the aforementioned comparison occur, but that it must be possible to evaluate the status of the motor centers to which the actually issued efferent signals are being delivered so as to ascertain how these signals will drive the vocal apparatus. In other words, a final comparison is made in peripheral motor centers; and the resulting "low-level" corollary-discharge signal, when evaluated in relation to the issued motor commands, will indicate the articulatory configuration of the actually occurring speech sounds. Presumably, this latter information is available to perceptual mechanisms, thus making it possible for the speaker to maintain perceptual stability for self-produced speech sounds under conditions that otherwise would lead to perceptual transformations of the acoustic input.

Independent support for the existence of mechanisms like those we are proposing is provided by neurophysiological studies. Oscarsson (1967, 1968, 1973) and Miller and Oscarsson (1969) have shown that in the control of skeletal movements, multiple feedback pathways exist that make it possible to monitor activity in lower motor centers so that the consequences of descending motor commands can be determined without waiting for sensory feedback contingent on the forthcoming movement. Oscarsson has also provided detailed descriptions of how comparator functions can be carried out at brain stem, cortical, and cerebellar levels to determine the extent to which actual motor performance will correspond with intended motor performance. Hence, he has demonstrated for the control of skeletal movements the possible physiological bases for the kinds of monitoring and comparator functions that we consider to be an important aspect of human speech production and reception.

ACKNOWLEDGMENTS

We thank Edward C. T. Walker for his valuable comments and suggestions on this paper.

REFERENCES

Bowman, J. P., & Combs, C. M. Discharge patterns of lingual spindle afferent fibers in the hypoglossal nerve of the rhesus monkey. *Experimental Neurology,* 1968, *21,* 105–119.

Evarts, E. V., Bizzi, E., Burke, R. E., Delong, M., & Thach, W. T. Central control of movement. *Neurosciences Research Program Bulletin,* 1971, *9,* 1–170.

Fromkin, V. The non-anomalous nature of anomalous utterances. *Language,* 1971, *47,* 27–52.

Garrett, M. The analysis of sentence production. In G. Bower (Ed.), *The psychology of learning and motivation: Advances in research and theory* (Vol. 9). New York: Academic Press, 1975.

Goldstein, L., & Lackner, J. Alterations of the phonetic coding of speech sounds during repetition. *Cognition,* 1973, *2,* 279–297.

Goodwin, G. M., McCloskey, D. I., & Matthews, P. B. C. Proprioceptive illusions induced by muscle vibration: Contribution to perception by muscle spindles? *Science,* 1972, *175,* 1382–1384. (a)

Goodwin, G. M., McCloskey, D. I., & Matthews, P. B. C. The contribution of muscle afferents to kinesthesia shown by vibration induced illusions of movement and by the effect of paralyzing joint afferents. *Brain,* 1972, *95,* 705–748. (b)

Higgens, J., & Angel, R. Correction of tracking errors without sensory feedback. *Journal of Experimental Psychology,* 1970, *84,* 412–416.

Lackner, J. Speech production: Evidence for corollary-discharge stabilization of perceptual mechanisms. *Perceptual and Motor Skills,* 1974, *39,* 899–902.

Lackner, J., & Goldstein, L. The psychological representation of speech sounds. *Quarterly Journal of Experimental Psychology,* 1975, *27,* 173–185.

Lackner, J., & Levine, K. Speech production: Evidence for syntactically and phonologically determined units. *Perception & Psychophysics,* 1975, *17,* 107–113.

Lackner, J., Tuller, B., & Goldstein, L. Some aspects of the psychological representation of speech sounds. *Perceptual and Motor Skills,* 1977, *45,* 459–471.

Lashley, K. S. The problem of serial order in behavior. In L. A. Jeffress (Ed.), *Cerebral mechanisms in behavior.* New York: Wiley, 1951.

Liberman, A., Cooper, F., Shankweiler, D., & Studdert-Kennedy, M. Perception of the speech code. *Psychological Review,* 1967, *74,* 431–461.

Miller, S., & Oscarsson, O. Termination and functional organization of spinoolivocerebellar paths. In W. S. Fields & W. D. Willis (Eds.), *The cerebellum in health and disease.* St. Louis: Warren H. Green, Inc., 1969.

Oscarsson, O. Functional significance of information channels from the spinal cord to the cerebellum. In M. D. Yahr & D. P. Purpura (Eds.), *Neurophysiological basis of normal and abnormal motor activities.* New York: Raven Press, 1967.

Oscarsson, O. Termination and functional organization of the ventral spinoolivocerebellar path. *Journal of Physiology,* 1968, *196,* 453–478.

Oscarsson, O. Functional organization of spinocerebellar paths. In A. Iggo (Ed.), *Handbook of sensory physiology* (Vol. II). Berlin: Springer-Verlag, 1973.

Ringel, R. L., & Steer, M. D. Some effects of tactile and auditory alterations on speech output. *Journal of Speech and Hearing Research,* 1963, *6,* 369–378.

Sperry, R. Neural basis of the spontaneous optokinetic response produced by visual inversion. *Journal of Comparative and Physiological Psychology,* 1950, *43,* 482–490.

Stein, R. Peripheral control of movement. *Physiological Review,* 1974, *54,* 215–243.

Stein, R., Pearson, K. G., Smith, R., & Redford, J. *Control of posture and locomotion.* New York: Plenum Press, 1973.

Teuber, H.-L. Perception. In J. Field, H. Magon, & V. Hall (Eds.), *Handbook of physiology: Section I, Neurophysiology* (Vol. III). Washington, D.C.: American Physiological Society, 1960.

von Holst, E., & Mittelstaedt, H. Das Reafferenzprinzip (Wechselwirkungen zwischen Zentralnervensystem und Peripherie). *Naturwissenshaften,* 1950, *37,* 464–476. (Reprinted and translated in: von Holst, E. *The behavioural physiology of animals and man* (Vol. 1). Coral Gables: University of Miami Press, 1973.)

Warren, R. M., & Gregory, R. L. An auditory analogue of the visual reversible figure. *American Journal of Psychology,* 1958, *71,* 612–613.

Woodworth, R. S., & Schlosberg, H. *Experimental psychology* (2nd ed). New York: Holt, 1954.

10 Speech Errors as Evidence for a Serial-Ordering Mechanism in Sentence Production

Stefanie Shattuck-Hufnagel
Cornell University

INTRODUCTION

Errors made in spontaneous speech are not random, but are highly regular, as many studies over the past century have shown (Freud, 1901; Lashley, 1951; Merringer, 1908; also Foss & Fay, 1975; Fromkin, 1971; Garrett, 1975; MacKay, 1970). Speech-error regularities provide a valuable glimpse into the workings of the fluent sentence production mechanism, since the constraints they follow are presumably imposed by characteristics of the process by which normal, error-free speech is produced. For example, Fromkin (1971) has shown that the units that change and move in speech errors correspond remarkably well to the entities proposed by linguists for the statement of formal grammars: features, phonemes, morphemes, etc. She has suggested that these error units reflect the planning units in terms of which utterances are processed for production. Other investigators have found support in error patterns for further aspects of linguistic theory, such as an autonomous syntactic component (Garrett, 1975, 1976) and even the psychological validity of specific syntactic transformations in the derivation of sentences (Fay, 1978; Foss & Fay, 1975).

In the studies just cited, error data were used to test predictions based on linguistic theory. Lashley (1951) used error data in a slightly different way. He argued that the simple fact that anticipatory errors occur at all reveals an important aspect of the speaking process. Errors such as

A *street* on Eddy *House*   (house on Eddy Street)
They put their *lips* through their *teeth*.   (teeth through their lips)
There's no word *in* it *for* English.   (for it in English)

show that the speaker must have access to a representation that spans more than the next word of the utterance: Otherwise, how could the word from later in each utterance appear earlier than it should? Models of normal sentence production that do not have this characteristic (e.g., word-by-word stimulus–response models) can be ruled out simply by examining the logical implications of anticipatory errors. The purpose of this paper is to expand on Lashley's general claim that errors show the sentence-production process involves planning beyond the next word, by spelling out as completely as possible the characteristics that any production model must have if it is to account for speech errors. The position being taken here is that these characteristics are specified in such detail by error patterns that they dictate a model of the normal production process explicit enough to generate testable predictions.

The proposed model of sentence production is discussed in two sections. In the first section, an inventory of the forms of errors in the Massachusetts Institute of Technology (MIT)–Cornell University (CU) corpus of more than 6000 spontaneous speech errors provides the basis for inferences about the underlying mechanism of production. The constraints on these errors are summarized in a model of the process by which the planning units of speech are arranged into their appropriate serial order for a given utterance. This section is concerned with issues of general psycholinguistic interest. In the second section, problems are examined that arise from using error data in both this and other studies; this section will be of interest to practicing errataphiles.

A MODEL OF THE PROCESS OF SERIAL ORDERING IN SPEECH PRODUCTION

The range of error types is introduced here with a brief description of the MIT–CU speech-error corpus, the way it was collected, and the classification of error types based on their surface form. This is followed by a discussion of the implications of constraints on errors for a production model, a description of the proposed model, and some supporting distributional evidence from the MIT–CU corpus.

Collection and Classification

The errors analyzed in the present study were collected by two listeners, Merrill Garrett (MIT) and the author (CU), over a period of more than 6 years. Errors heard in ordinary conversation, in public presentations, or in the observer's own speech were written down immediately, usually within 30 seconds or the time it took to find a pencil. The MIT–CU corpus collected in this way contains about 6000 errors at the time of writing and is still growing. A brief discussion of the advantages and problems inherent in error data from natural settings is included in the second section.

In discussing speech errors, researchers commonly use three terms that have not yet been rigorously defined: *target* segment, *intrusion* segment, and *source* segment. The target is the segment that is changed, moved, or omitted in an error. The intrusion is the segment that appears in place of a target or is added to the target sequence. The source is a nearby segment that is identical to the intrusion segment. For example, consider the phoneme-substitution error "about four or *p*ive pages" (five). In this error, the *target* segment is the (presumably) intended initial /f/ in *five*, the *intrusion* segment is the /p/ that appeared instead, and the *source* is the nearby /p/ in *pages*. Difficulties of definition arise because it is not clear in what sense the speaker ever intended to utter the /f/ in *five*. The fact that the listener and the speaker agree that an /f/ belongs there reveals nothing about the nature of the speaker's actual representation of the word during the planning process.

Additional problems arise because it is uncertain what criterion should be used to decide that a nearby segment is the source of an intrusion. For example, if the error is one of phoneme substitution, must the source phoneme be in a word position similar to that of the target? In a word adjacent to the target word? If the target utterance in the example above had been "Make up about four or five pages," could the final /p/ in *up* have been the source?

In spite of these difficulties, a presumed target, an observed intrusion, and an apparent source have been noted for each error in the corpus where it is possible to do so. The terms are used freely here as classificatory devices, but the implied claims about the underlying mechanism (e.g., that the intrusion provided by the source replaced the planned target segment during production) are taken as hypotheses to be explored, rather than as assumptions.

The definition of error used here is likewise a workable but not yet formalized one. Errors are those parts of utterances that do not correspond to what the speaker intended to say. Excluded by this definition are utterances that are ill-formed to the listener but perfectly correct according to the grammar of the speaker (e.g., "You ought to have done"), changes of plan in midsentence (e.g., "We went——on Thursday we took the bus to New York"), heavily slurred speech in which the slurring is according to the speaker's own rules (e.g., "Doncha" for "Don't you?"), intentional distortions and spoonerisms (e.g., "Speech errors moggle my bind"), and mispronunciations such as "nukular" for "nuclear" if they are part of the speaker's dialect. Precisely what is meant by the phrase "what the speaker intended to say" in this definition has not been specified. Evidence that an utterance failed to correspond with what the speakers meant to say included self-correction, speakers' acknowledgment (by chuckle, pause, or facial twitch) that something had gone wrong in an utterance, speakers' surprise when confronted by a repetition of what they said, or (in some obvious cases) the observer's intuitions.

Once detected and written down (in English orthography except where broad phonetic transcription is necessary to avoid ambiguity), errors are classified along three dimensions: (a) error units, or the nature of the target and intrusion segments (phoneme, morpheme, word, etc.), (b) error types, or the fate of the target and intrusion segments (change in identity, location, etc.), and (c) the direction of influence from presumed source to target location (backward or forward in the utterance). Each of these dimensions offers insights into the production process that are discussed later in this section; problems of classification are discussed in the next section.

Error Units

Error patterns in the MIT–CU corpus generally confirm Fromkin's (1971) finding that error segments correspond to the units that a linguistic grammar predicts as processing units. The elements that change in errors include features, phonemes, morphemes (both bound and free), words, and sentence constituents. In particular, two points can be made. First, error segments usually correspond to linguistically motivated units. Second, exceptions fall into a small number of categories that can be accounted for in other ways (see the next section for further discussion.)

Error Types

At first glance it appears that anything that is logically possible can happen to a planning segment in a speech error. In fact, Roche-Lecours and L'Hermitte (1969), examining the errors of French-speaking aphasics, describe all errors in terms of two events: either something fails to appear where it should and/or something appears where it should not. Like the General Confession, however, the claim that "we have done those things which we ought not to have done, and we have left undone those things which we ought to have done" leaves out the most interesting details. More useful error evidence comes from a fine-grained analysis of what does and does not occur.

There are five major classes along the dimension of error type: *substitution* errors (in which the identity of a target segment is changed but the number of target segments remains the same), *exhange* and *shift* errors (in which one or more target segments are moved but no segments are added or deleted), and *addition* and *omission* errors (in which a target is omitted or an intrusion added). In the following examples of each major error class, only single phoneme errors are cited so that comparisons will be clear. However, each of the five types occurs for words, morphemes, and sentence constituents as well. Examples of a wider range of error segments across error types are shown in Appendix A drawn from the MIT–CU corpus, and further published examples from the UCLA corpus can be found in Fromkin (1973).

Substitution: A target segment is replaced by an intrusion segment, which may or may not have an apparent source within the utterance.
1. It's a shallower *t*est—chest, but broad.
2. because my *f*and—my hand
3. Any*m*ay, I think   (anyway)
4. is a*b*ung our panelists tonight   (among)
5. These lovely twining vi*m*es are   (vines)

Exchange: Two target segments change places in the target sequence, each serving as the other's intrusion segment.
1. p*lor*iferation   (proliferation)
2. e*men*y   (enemy)
3. guinea *k*ig *p*age   (pig cage)
4. It's *p*ast *f*assing—fast passing by.
5. because all the *m*ax—mmm—
    *w*elts—ah!   (wax melts)

Shift: A target segment disappears from its appropriate location and appears at another location in the target sequence.
1. State-*l*owned _and—owned-land   (state-owned land)
2. bad high*v*way dri_ing   (highway driving)
3. most c*l*audal s_ide   (caudal slide)
4. I did it my*n* ow_ way.   (my own way)
5. in a b_ack b*l*o—black box

Addition: An extra segment is added to the target sequence; this intrusion may or may not have an apparent source within the utterance.
1. either the p*l*ublicity would be bad   (publicity)
2. complete and un*j*in—uninterrupted "Circe"
3. measures of *s*public speaking anxiety (public speaking)
4. *n*lon-linguistic   (non-linguistic)
5. they bring ab*r*out—about a

Omission: A target segment is dropped from the target sequence; there may or may not be a similar sequence elsewhere in the utterance.
1. high sequentially-probable ph_ase   (phrase)
2. piano sonata _umber ten   (number)
3. the d_ug—the drugs
4. If this is too mentali_tic for you   (mentalistic)
5. all on the same matri_s?   (matrix)

Direction of Influence

The third dimension of error categorization is the sequential relationship between the target and the presumed source segment in the utterance. As defined previously, the source is a nearby segment that is identical to the intrusion. If this candidate source is later in the sentence, so that the error precedes it, the error is classified as *anticipatory*. Anticipatory errors are found in the class of substitutions:

1. You have such a nice pa*m*orama
   of village life.   (panorama)
2. one, *th*oo and three   (two)
3. if you can change the *p*irst part   (first)
4. I tightened my bel*ch* two notches   (belt)
5. pre*t*eding material   (preceding)

in the class of additions:

1. you can p*l*ass planes through space   (pass)
2. white sidewall *tr*ires   (tires)
3. These *tr*ue traditions   (two)
4. ver*l*y early   (very)
5. when the story*ng* started appearing   (story)

in the class of omissions:

1. p_ays—plays an important role   (Note /p/, without /l/, in "important")
2. for cam_ing—camping this summer   (Note /m/ without /p/ in "summer")
3. might he_p set   (Note /ɛ/ without /l/ in "set")

and in the class of shifts:

1. *s*tree_—trees
2. the displacement of a patt*n*er_—pattern
3. That was Eys*n*e_ck, right?   (Eysenck)
4. lying just we*ts*_—west of
5. a *m*eating _arathon   (eating marathon)

In all of these cases, the influence of the presumed source on the error is anticipatory, from later in the sentence to earlier. In contrast, if the candidate source is earlier in the sentence, so that the error follows it, the error is classified as *perseveratory*. Perseveratory errors are found in the same four classes of error types as are anticipatory errors: substitutions, additions, omission, and shifts. Not all error types can be classified as to direction of influence. Because exchange errors have both an anticipatory and a perseveratory component, they are not classified along this third dimension, but only by error segment and type. Likewise, a substitution, addition, or omission that has no discernible source in the fragment of context preserved with it in the corpus cannot be classified as either anticipatory or perseveratory. It is labeled a simple or "no-source" substitution, addition, or omission. To summarize, some additions, omissions and substitutions are anticipatory or perseveratory (i.e., those with a source). Others appear to have no source among the planning segments of the utterance and are so labeled. All shifts are either anticipatory or perseveratory (because each has an identifiable source). Exchanges are not classified as either anticipatory or perseveratory, because they involve a component of each direction of influence from source to error.

This brief summary of the three surface-classification dimensions for speech errors that are found in the MIT–CU corpus has served to introduce the range of possible errors and suggest some of their similarities and differences. Note that the surface classes may not correspond to underlying error mechanisms. For example, apparent phoneme additions such as "t*r*ake" for "take" may actually arise from the substitution of one abstract initial consonantal element (the cluster /tr/) for another (the single consonant /t/). Classification issues are discussed in the second section. For present purposes, the surface categories serve to group similar errors together so that their distributional regularities can be observed. In addition, categorization makes it easier to see what types of errors do not occur in the MIT–CU corpus; such constraints, and their implications for a production model, are discussed next.

Constraints and Their Implications

A number of arguments can be made about the nature of the error-producing process, based on the patterns into which errors consistently fall. Strictly speaking, these arguments apply only to the process by which errors occur. However, it is assumed here that this process can best be described as a minor malfunction in the process by which correct utterances are produced. Thus, constraints on error patterns are a function of both the normal process of sentence production and the nature of possible malfunctions. In the following discussion, I argue that one basic way in which the process can go wrong is by misselection among available planning segments. That is, the wrong segment is selected for a particular slot or location in a separately computed utterance framework. First, however, let us examine the constraints observed by other investigators to govern the type and distribution of errors, and what those constraints reveal about the normal process of computing utterances for articulation.

At least four constraints have been thoroughly substantiated in earlier error studies. They are basically confirmed in the MIT–CU corpus. Exceptions and qualifications are discussed in greater detail, along with some questions they raise, in the next section of this paper. In this section, these constraints are assumed:

Constraint 1:   Error segments may appear several words earlier in an utterance than they belong.
  Implication for a model: The span of sentence processing must be greater than a single word (Lashley, 1951).

Constraint 2:   Errors often (although not invariably) involve the units and devices of linguistic grammars: phonemes, morphemes, words, and sentence constituents.
  Implication for a model: These entities are part of the psychological representation during normal sentence processing for production. Moreover, the moved/changed segments must have been represented independent of their target slots or locations (Fromkin, 1971; Fry, 1969; Garrett, 1975; Shattuck, 1975).

Constraint 3:   A target and its intrusion can be described as single segments at the same level of description: in general, a phoneme substitutes for another phoneme, a word for a word, etc.
  Implication for a model: Some aspect of the planning mechanism permits malfunctions which result in substitutions of elements within a level of description, but not across levels (Shattuck, 1975).

Constraint 4:   A target-intrusion pair almost always shares linguistically relevant characteristics: phoneme pairs share distinctive features; morphemes share syntactic category; words share phonological, syntactic, and/or semantic characteristics; sentence constituents share syntactic structure; etc.
  Implication for a model: These dimensions are part of the psychological representation of utterances during planning for production (Fromkin, 1971, 1973; Garrett, 1975, 1976; Goldstein, 1977; MacKay, 1970; Nooteboom, 1969; Shattuck-Hufnagel & Klatt, 1975, 1977).

Assuming the first four constraints, I have focused this section on a discussion of four further constraints derived from analysis of the MIT–CU corpus:

Constraint 5:   When a planning segment moves to a new location in an error, that movement is limited to a small set of possible slots or locations, which are predictable on the basis of either other error changes in the sentence or its underlying structure.

Implication for a model: These "slots" or locations must be predefined in some way during the planning process, independent of the segments they are to contain.

Constraint 6:   Anticipatory and perseveratory errors often involve the "double use" of a target segment, once in its appropriate location and once as an intrusion.

Implication for a model: The production process must include a step that, when it goes wrong, permits a planning segment to be used more often than it should be in a given utterance.

Constraint 7:   Errors often appear in utterances that contain sequences of similar segments or repeated instances of a particular unit.

Implication for a model: The production process must include a mechanism by which similar or repeated sequences facilitate errors.

Constraint 8:   Errors of all five basic types (exchanges, substitutions, additions, omissions, and shifts) occur for each error segment observed (phoneme, morpheme, word, and sentence constituent), although constraints vary from one error or segment type to another.

Implication for a model: The most parsimonious model, and the one that should provide a point of departure, is one in which a single underlying mechanism accounts for all error types across all segment types. Differences in constraints arise from the fact that the mechanism operates at several different levels of representation, with access to different kinds of information.

In the remainder of this section, the evidence for these four constraints and their implications are discussed in greater detail.

Constraint 5: Slot Limitations and Influences. The implication of this constraint is that slots in an utterance are represented in some way during the production process independent of their segmental contents. Evidence to support this suggestion is of two major kinds. First, there are constraints on the locations to which segments can be moved in an error. Second, there is evidence for similarity between the "slot" of a target segment and the "slot" of its intrusion source. Each of these lines of evidence is examined separately.

Both kinds of errors that involve movement of planning segments, exchanges and shifts, exhibit constraints on movement that provide evidence for independently represented slots. The evidence derives its persuasiveness from the fact that each of these kinds of error has two parts that are almost certainly related to each other. For example, in word exchanges such as "If the *rough* is *ride* . . ." (ride is rough), it is difficult to believe that the two word substitutions occurred independently. A more tenable view is that the later target word *rough* was available to the planning mechanism well before the occurrence of the word it should have followed in the utterance (*is*) and that it served as the source of the first intrusion in the exchange. If this is so, then for at least some sentences, planning must involve representation of later sections at an earlier point in the planning process than one would expect in a word-by-word association model. This was essentially Lashley's (1951) point, and he viewed all anticipatory errors as providing this kind of evidence. Notice, however, that some anticipatory errors provide much weaker evidence than exchanges on this issue. For example, in anticipatory substitution errors, such as "It's the mynah *v*ird vocal apparatus" (bird), it is conceivable that the substitution of /v/ for /b/ in *bird* occurred independently of the later /v/ in *vocal*. For anticipatory errors involving morphemes and words, where the set of possible items is much larger (approximately 500,000 words as opposed to 24 consonantal phonemes in English), the possibility that the error is not related to its apparent source is correspondingly less likely, but still remains as a remote chance. Exchanges, however, leave almost no room for such an explanation. The probability that a pair of symmetrical substitutions would happen by chance in the same utterance must be vanishingly small. Thus, exchange errors point convincingly to the conclusion that the production process involves a representation that includes the downstream target segment well before its preceding word is articulated.

Similarly, anticipatory shift errors such as "tri̯mb‿el" (timbrel) have two parts that are unlikely to have occurred independently of each other. In Roche-Lecours and L'Hermitte's (1969) terms, the two parts are the appearance of an /r/ in *trim-* and the disappearance of /r/ from *-bel*. Shifts provide further evidence that the source segment is represented in the speaker's head well before its target location is reached in articulation.

Exchange errors not only suggest a representation of segments independent of slots, but also argue for the complementary claim. Slots are represented independent of segments; i.e., in an exchange error, the downstream slot where the first source segment should have appeared must be represented independently of its segment. Evidence for the claim that the slot is represented separately from its segment comes from the lacunae that appear in the set of anticipatory error structures found in the MIT–CU corpus. To describe the lacunae, it is necessary to review the kinds of anticipatory errors that do occur in the corpus.

Consider four pieces of information about an error with an anticipatory component, i.e., one in which the direction of influence from the presumed source toward the target is anticipatory, because the error precedes the source in the utterance. First, the error location A, at which the intrusion segment appears; second, the fate of the target segment A, which was displaced by the intrusion; third, the later source location B; and fourth, the segment that appears at location B. For example, in the anticipatory substitution error "If you can change the *p*irst part" (first), the error location A is the initial slot in *first*, the displaced target segment A is the target /f/ for that slot, and the source location is the initial slot in *part* that has the target segment /p/. In all errors with an anticipatory component, the target segment from location B appears at the error location A as an intrusion: that is the definition of an anticipation. What are the possibilities for the displaced target segment A and the source location B? If A can appear *anywhere* in the utterance, then there is no need for a mechanism to define possible slots for it to be displaced into. Similarly, if slot B disappears when it loses its target segment to another location, then there is no need for a mechanism to preserve the slots independent of their segments. On the other hand, if segment A can appear only in one of a limited set of slots and slot B does not disappear when bereft of its segment, then such a slot-defining mechanism is required.

The set of logically possible anticipatory-error structures is given in Table 10.1. One of these structures (labeled *exchanges*) requires a mechanism in the production process to maintain the downstream source slot B and to ensure that the displaced target segment A appears there. Otherwise, this neatly symmetrical type of error must be ascribed to chance, which seems highly unlikely given the number of other locations in the sentence where the displaced target could appear. Another structure (labeled *anticipatory*

TABLE 10.1
Possible Anticipatory Error Structures

Structure	*Error Type*
Location A gets intrusion segment B	
No target segment A existed	
Location B gets target segment B	(1) Anticipatory additions (e.g., will p*l*ose little danger)
Location B remains empty	(2) Anticipatory shifts (e.g., displacement of a patt*n*er [pattern])
Target segment A does not appear	
Location B gets target segment B	(3) Anticipatory substitutions (e.g., change the *p*irst part)
Location B remains empty	(4) Does not occur
Target segment A appears elsewhere in the utterance but not at location B	
Location B gets target segment B	(5) Does not occur
Location B remains empty	(6) Does not occur
Target segment A appears at location B	(7) Exchanges (e.g., do it by *p*utting and *c*asting)

substitutions) is compatible with an independent slot representation but does not require it, because the displaced target segment A does not appear in these errors. Two more structures (labeled *anticipatory additions* and *anticipatory shifts*) are neutral on the question of slot B, because there is no target segment to be displaced from slot A into slot B and reveal the presence of a slot independent of its segment. (Note, however, that additions and shifts do require a representation of slot location A. This issue is discussed later.) The other three logically possible anticipatory structures either require the source slot B to disappear (labeled 4), require the displaced target segment to appear somewhere other than location B (labeled 5) or require both (labeled 6). *None of these three kinds of errors appear in the MIT–CU corpus.* In other words, if a displaced target A reappears in the utterance, it goes into slot B. Otherwise, target segment B goes into slot B. In summary, slot B only disappears if there is no displaced target segment A to fill it. Furthermore, a displaced target segment A never appears in a random location, but only in slot B.

Thus, among the logically possible anticipatory-error structures, the only ones found in the MIT–CU corpus are those which either require a separate slot representation for B (exchanges) or are compatible with one (substitutions, additions and shifts). The error structures that are not compatible with such a representation fail to appear in the corpus. Similar structural lacunae appear for errors with a perseveratory component.

Exchange errors provide the strongest evidence for a slot representation, because their anticipatory and perseveratory nature is least in doubt. Shift errors provide a second kind of evidence for a slot representation independent of the segmental contents. When shifts of a single phoneme occur, the movement of the target segment is always to a location that is permissible by the phonotactic rules for English. For example, no /tl/ or /ŋ/ sequences move into the initial position of a word as the result of a phoneme-shift error. The fact that shift errors move phonemes into permissible slots but not into nonpermissible ones suggests a representation in which such slots are not only represented but also marked in some way that shows the segments that could legally appear there in an English word. That is, such slots exist even if there are no target segments for them in a particular utterance. The question of word and morpheme shifts is more complex. Evidence suggests that words and morphemes can be moved only into locations that are defined by an underlying structural representation, but further investigation of the limits on movement of large units is necessary to establish this claim conclusively (Fay, 1977; Garrett 1975).

We have discussed movement constraints on the locations to which errors can move segments as evidence for a representation of those locations independent of their target segments. A second kind of evidence for such slots is the similarity between target and source location in many errors. The hypothesis is that similarity between the intended slots of two target segments in an utterance increases the possibility that they will become the target and source segment in an error. That is, "extrinsic similarity" of segments (e.g., similar location in their respective structures) can influence the pattern of segmental errors, just as "intrinsic similarity" (e.g., shared segmental features) can. One line of evidence to support this claim concerns the relation between target and source slots and a second concerns the relation between the target slot and that of a newly defined segment, the *trigger*.

Source/target slot similarities take three forms in the MIT–CU corpus. First, exchange errors at the phoneme level take place between phonemes that are in comparable syllable positions. Second, when substitutions, additions, and omissions have an apparent source in the utterance, the source usually appears in the same position as the error. Third, shifts move segments into locations that are similar to their target locations.

The position constraint is clear in the present MIT–CU corpus of 211 between word phoneme-exchange errors: of these all but 4 take place between phonemes in similar positions in their respective syllables. Thus, the evidence clearly indicates a constraint on slot similarity between exchanged phonemes. The constraint cannot be described in terms of absolute syllable position, because of errors such as "*k*otalled the *s*tore" (totalled the score). A strict syllable-initial constraint would predict errors of the form "**sotalled** the *t*kore," which do not occur, and would fail to predict the form above. Instead, the constraint appears to be based on the structural possibilities of English morphemes or syllables. Exchanges can take place between target phonemes whose locations in these structures are similar.

Like exchanges, other errors show a similarity between the location of the target and the location of the presumed source, although this evidence is weaker than the exchange evidence because the source is not as certain. Anticipatory and perseveratory errors that support the slot-similarity argument include substitutions, additions, omissions, and shifts. Anticipatory phoneme errors, for example, have their target and candidate source in similar syllable position in 70% of the cases in the MIT–CU corpus, and a parallel pattern emerges for perseveratory errors. Because so many of the phoneme errors in the corpus occur in initial position in monosyllabic, monomorphemic words, the position constraint can also be formulated in terms of word or morpheme position, but the syllable constraint captures the most regularity.

The position constraint on anticipatory and perseveratory phoneme shifts is not merely a reflection of the phonotactic constraints of English: If this were the case, then phonemes could shift into phonotactically permissible locations that were quite different in syllable position from their original target location. For example, the /s/ in "sometime" might shift into the medial position in "mechanical" to form "*me*s*chanical*," or into the pre-final position in "wreck" to form "*wre*s*k*." Because these kinds of shifts do not occur (except in a very few cases of within-morpheme shifts), it appears that the same position constraint that governs target/source slot similarity for other errors influences shift errors as well.

A second line of evidence for the role of slot similarity, and thus indirectly for an independent slot representation, is the relationship between a target segment and a new category of error segment not previously defined: the *trigger*. Recall that the source segment in an error was defined as a nearby segment that is identical to the intrusion. For example, in the error "Well, they're *r*ell rid of her, anyway" (well), the target segment is the /w/ in *well rid*, and the presumed source of the intrusion segment /r/ is the target segment /r/ in *rid*. The *trigger* segment in this error is the /w/ in the first *well*. This segment is identical to the target, but remains unchanged in the error. Such a segment appears in a surprising number of cases and may play a role in the generation of some errors (see the following discussion of Constraint 7). Examples of errors with trigger segments include

had no good words for the *M*est (West)	(trigger is /w/ in "words")
He answered quite a few /k_s/—questions	(trigger is /w/ in "quite")
the sort of blanket Training G_ant (Grant)	(trigger is /r/ in "Training")
ba*n*oon are a little childish (balloons)	(trigger is /l/ in "little")
awfully few *f*ars—cars coming through	(trigger is /k/ in "coming")

The trigger segment is related to Roche-Lecours and L'Hermitte's (1969) concept of "pair-destroying errors," introduced to describe a similar phenomenon in the phoneme substitutions of certain kinds of French-speaking aphasics. It is also illustrated in MacKay's (1970) observation that in Merringer and Meyers (1895) corpus of German speech errors, phoneme exchanges appear in utterances that contain another occurrence of one of the exchanged segments more often than would be expected by chance. MacNeilage and MacNeilage (1973) also cites the "triggering role" of a phoneme identical to the target phoneme.

Numerical analysis is under way to test the significance of the informal observation that error utterances in the MIT–CU corpus often contain such trigger segments. If their apparent tendency to appear in positions similar to those of the error targets is confirmed, the role of slot similarity will be further supported.

Thus, two kinds of error constraints suggest independent representations of the segments in an utterance and of the slots or locations where the segments will appear: segment movement constraints and slot similarity constraints. In both cases, exchange errors provide the most compelling evidence, because one can be reasonably sure of the target, source, and intrusion segments. Besides suggesting independent slot and segment representations, exchange errors also require a mechanism to locate the displaced target segment from the first part of the error in the precise slot where the first intrusion should have appeared as the target, i.e., to insert the displaced target segment A into source slot B and nowhere else. This consideration is relevant to the next constraint.

Constraint 6: Double Use of Target Segments. In the discussion of Constraint 5 on slot restrictions, it appeared that the production mechanism must include some device for inserting the displaced target segment from the first part of an exchange error into the location where the first intrusion segment should have appeared. A mechanism that would accomplish this is suggested by a different aspect of speech errors; i.e., a given planning segment often has an extra occurrence in an utterance. For example, consider perseveratory errors such as "between word-clustering and picture-*p*luh—clustering" or "and a cray*f*rish" (crayfish). The first is a perseveratory substitution of /p/ for the target /k/ in *clustering*, and the second is a perseveratory addition of /r/ to *fish*. Evidently, the intrusion segment /p/ in the first error has its source in the initial /p/ in *picture*, and the intrusion segment /r/ in the second error has its source in the post-initial /r/ in *cray-*. If the production process involves inserting the planning segments directly into their slots, it is difficult to account for the fact that the intrusion segment can appear a second time to form each of these errors. It should have been "used up" by its earlier occurrence in the source location.

The answer to this problem proposed here is a scan-and-copy mechanism. When this mechanism operates correctly, it scans the set of planning segments for the appropriate item to copy into each slot in a separately represented "slot framework." In the first example above, the scan-copier correctly copies the target segment /p/ into its slot in *picture*, but also copies it mistakenly into the initial slot in *clustering* to form the error.

A scan-copy mechanism will account for the fact that the intrusion segments in perseveratory errors (/p/ and /r/ in the previous examples) are available to the processor even though they have already appeared in their appropriate target locations in *picture* and *cray-*. A parallel line of evidence that suggests a scan-copier comes from anticipatory errors such as "I want to buy some *f*lant food—plant food." A production model must account for the fact that the intrusion segment /f/ is available to appear in its proper location in *food*, even after it has already appeared as the error in *f*lant. A scan-copier can transfer information into the appropriate slot without destroying it and so can account for the double use of a planning segment in anticipatory errors as well as perseveratory ones.

Finally, in exchange errors, the scan-copier provides the necessary mechanism for locating the displaced target segment A in the source slot B: It simply copies segment A into slot B by the usual copying mechanism. But why copy segment A into slot B, forming an exchange, instead of copying the appropriate target segment B? Segment B is still available, even though it has already appeared as an intrusion in the earlier slot A, because it was copied from the planning set rather than transferred. Why not copy it again, this time into its appropriate slot? An answer to this question is suggested by the next constraint.

Constraint 7: Two Kinds of Evidence for Monitors. Constraint 6, the common double-use of a planning segment in an error, necessitated a copying mechanism in the production process. This addition, along with several other lines of evidence from the MIT–CU corpus, necessitates a further addition to the model: a monitor. First, there is the suggestion from exchange errors, noted above, that when the second part of an exchange is reached, the appropriate target segment (formerly the source segment B) is no longer available to the scan-copier, so it must settle for the displaced target segment from the earlier slot A. (Segmental similarities between the two targets, and slot similarities between the two locations, facilitate the misselections; further discussion follows in the next section. Why is the original target segment for slot B no longer available to the processor? A reasonable hypothesis is that this target segment has been marked in some way as already used. When a segment that has been copied from the planning set is marked as "used," it then becomes unavailable to the scan-copier. A used segment is marked even if it has been erroneously copied as an intrusion. How does this fit with the claim made in the previous discussion of Constraint 6 that planning segments must sometimes be available for "double use" in errors? The two claims fit together in the following way. When the scan-copier and the checkoff device operate properly, no errors occur. Thus the scan-copier selects a planning segment for a slot, and the checkoff monitor operates properly to mark it as used: that segment will not be available for later use. However, if both the scan-copier and the checkoff device misfire on the same segment, so that a misselected segment also fails to be marked as used, then it is available to be copied again and can appear twice. The details of generation of the error types in the corpus by these devices are discussed later.

Exchange errors, then, suggest a monitor that marks or deletes planning segments as they are copied into their slots. A second line of evidence suggests a monitoring mechanism with slightly different characteristics. It was noted above that many error utterances contain a trigger segment identical to the target segment of the error. Many different kinds of partial repetitions of sequences in the target utterance seem to be associated with errors. Examples include omission of the second of two consecutive occurrences of the same element ("That would be __having [behaving]), errors in a word that is used several times in an utterance, paragraph or conversation ("down over the hip and over the *hip* of the *k*—curve of the hip", and "an element moves from state C to s__ate—state T"), and errors that arise from the re-use of a phrase or part of a sentence in another phrase or sentence ("two extra steps, one extra __tep—

step"). Merringer (1908) described a similar error involving repetition in German: at an inn, the speaker ordered "ein Achtel Weisswein" and when the waiter did not immediately respond, called out "ein *Weiss*el *Acht*wein."

Another line of evidence comes from the set of errors in which a trigger is associated with an omission, as in "enclosed p_ease find" (please), where the earlier occurrence of a prevocalic /l/ in *enclosed* may have caused the monitor to edit out the later target /l/ in *please*.

Each of these error circumstances suggests that the production mechanism is capable of keeping track of the segments that have appeared and will appear in an utterance. A production processor is susceptible to segmental errors of the types described above needs a monitor that is sensitive to just this aspect of sentences. A scan-copier and checkoff monitor system, when it misfires, will sometimes result in double use of planning segments, and these must be detected and edited out. Because the task of monitoring for suspiciously repetitious sequences from errors is not equivalent to the task of marking off used planning segments in the target set, the two monitor functions are kept separate in the model proposed here, as the checkoff monitor and the error monitor.

The existence of an error monitor that scans a planned utterance for repetitions and suspiciously similar sequences would explain a puzzling aspect of error patterns: the tendency of speakers to change perfectly correct utterances into errors. The MIT–CU corpus contains a number of examples such as "An item goes into state C and stay—s_ays in state T" (stays). In addition, speakers sometimes repeat correct utterances in a puzzled tone, reporting that they thought they might have made an error. These occurrences should be collected and analyzed to see how often they involve the repetitious use of segments.

An error monitor may also explan how trigger segments participate in the error process in other ways than by causing an omission. If the second of two occurrences of a segment is detected as an error, it may be edited out (causing an omission), or it may be edited into something else (causing a substitution with no apparent source). For example, in the error "Papageno and *Tam*—Pameno," the second /p/ may have been edited into a /t/ because it was too much like the earlier /p/ in *Papageno*." This might explain some of the substitution errors in the corpus that have no apparent source.

One final useful aspect of an error monitor is its ability to account for the phenomenon of "errors heard in the head." Speakers sometimes report that they know what the second part of a two-part error was going to be even though they only uttered the first part or report an error that they made in their inner speech that never got articulated at all. These errors appear to be of the same type as those spoken aloud, i.e., changes in the number, identity, or location of planning segments, e.g., "for pay-*stub checks*" (pay-check stubs). In-the-head detection of speech errors would be a natural result of an error monitor. Extensive discussion of this issue appears in Laver (1977), where a model of production is proposed in which monitoring plays a critical role at several different points.

In summary, error patterns suggest that the production process includes two monitoring functions. Each planning segment is marked as it is used, and repetitious appearances of segments that are likely to have arisen from the kinds of errors the system is prone to are detected and edited out. These two functions may or may not be performed by the same mechanism, but there is no question that the production process is sensitive to repeated occurrences of a planning segment at many levels of description, from the phoneme to the sentence constituent. A production model must account for this fact.

Constraint 8: Basic Error Types Occur at All Segment Levels from the Phoneme to the Sentence Constituent.   It is a reasonable guess that the same five error types arise across segment types because the errors are caused by the same kinds of malfunction in the normal production process at many different levels. The malfunction proposed here is misselection, among similar available planning segments, of a segment to be copied into a particular slot. As an initial hypothesis, this is a very attractive proposal for several reasons. First, it permits the explanation of most errors (see the next section for exceptions) in terms of a mechanism that is needed on independent grounds in a production model, i.e., a serial-ordering mechanism. Garrett (1975) has pointed out that the production mechanism is a means of translating ideas into sequences of well-integrated articulatory gestures that occur in a particular order. Because that order is not inherent in the intent to voice a given thought, it must be imposed during the psychological process by which sentences are planned for articulation. How is this to be accomplished? For example, if words are not retrieved one at a time from the lexicon in the order in which they are spoken, as anticipatory errors suggest they are not, then how are they arranged into the appropriate sequence? The slot-segment representation, scan-copier, and monitor mechanisms described above amount to just such a serial-ordering mechanism for speech; no special error mechanisms are required to generate errors.

The most persuasive argument for the single-basic-malfunction hypothesis, however, is that it suggests a model that will (a) account for the production of error-free utterances, (b) account for all of the error types observed and (C) make testable predictions about the distributional facts in an error corpus. The remainder of this section deals with these three issues.

A Production Model

The serial-ordering model proposed here is derived from the inferences suggested by eight constraints on speech errors. It has three parts: (a) a dual representation, consisting of serially ordered slots and an equal number of independently represented target segments, at least at the word level and at the sound level; (b) a scan-copier that selects the appropriate segment from the set of available planning segments and copies it into each slot; and (c) two monitors, including a checkoff monitor, which marks or deletes segments as they are copied into their target slots, and an error monitor, which detects and deletes or otherwise edits error-like sequences in a planned utterance. How would the three-part mechanism impose the correct serial order on the planning segments of an error-free utterance?

Consider the level of word ordering, for the sentence "Pigs eat acorns." In some way not yet specified, an ordered framework of three word slots is generated, and a corresponding set of three target lexical items is retrieved from the lexicon, and stored in a short-term buffer. The scan-copier then scans the set of target lexical items in the buffer for the one that belongs in the first of the ordered slots. In this case, it is reasonable to suspect that the lexical item is *pig* rather than *pigs* and that some representation of its plural nature forms part of the slot description (Garrett, 1975).

When the morpheme *pig* is found, it is copied into the first slot and the checkoff monitor marks it as "used" in the target set or deletes it from the set. The scan-copier moves to the second of the ordered slots and scans the target set for the appropriate lexical item, copies it, marks it, etc. At the phoneme level, the same kind of ordering mechanism works with phoneme-sized target segments and ordered sequences of phoneme-sized slots. For example, the set of target phonemes /pIg/, /it/, /ekɔrn/ is scanned first for the segment that belongs in the initial slot of *pig*. When the /p/ is found it is copied and then marked while the scanner searches for a match for the second slot, etc. It is easy to see how two similar segments that belong in two similar slots could be exchanged by this mechanism.

A question arises immediately. Once the words have been copied into their appropriately ordered slots, why is it necessary to re-order their component phonemes by the serial-ordering mechanism proposed here? This question highlights one of the most interesting paradoxes revealed by speech errors. Theories of the mental lexicon almost always postulate that lexical items are stored with their component phonological segments in the appropriate surface order. Debates rage over the completeness of each form (vs. minimal storage with later expansion of the skeletal forms via redundancy rules), over the completeness of the inventory (as opposed to storage of base forms only, with other forms being derived as needed, using word-formation rules), and over the abstractness of the phonological units involved, but not over the serial order of those units. Yet, speech errors show clearly that single sound units can become misordered during the production process. The strong implication of this fact is that, counter to one's intuitions, the production process includes a serial-ordering mechanism for phoneme-sized segments.

One proposal that suggests the storage of lexical items as sets of unordered segments is Wickelgren's (1966) context-sensitive phoneme theory. He proposed that, for example, the lexical item for *pig* would consist of the three segments $/_\phi\mathrm{p}_I, {}_p\mathrm{I}_g, {}_I\mathrm{g}_\phi/$ in any order. These segments are then processed into the only order in which they will fit together during production. This proposal, however, flies in the face of considerable evidence that shows that the initial parts of lexical items are important markers in the lexical retrieval process (e.g., Brown and McNeill, 1966). In addition how are such context-sensitive segments to be smoothly integrated into their new phonetic environment after an error has occurred?

The alternative view maintained in this paper is that items are stored in the lexicon with their phonological segments in the proper order and retrieved from the lexicon in that form, but that at some point during the production process these segments must be copied one-by-one into waiting ordered slots that have been computed independently. The precise manner in which this occurs is not yet clear, but a reasonable suggestion is that the lexical items are entered in a short-term storage buffer as they are retrieved, perhaps with initial, medial, and final elements lined up for the syllables of the target lexical items, as in:

$$/\# \; \mathrm{p} \; \mathrm{I} \; \mathrm{g} \; \#/$$
$$/\# \; {}_\phi \; \mathrm{i} \; \mathrm{t}\#/$$
$$/\# \; {}_\phi \; \mathrm{e} \; {}_\phi \; \mathrm{k} \; \mathrm{\scriptstyle\supset} \; \mathrm{r} \; \mathrm{n}\#/$$

The slots might then be separately derived from a rule of canonical syllable structure in English and the stress patterns of the words. If the scan-copier then scans this positionally organized buffer for a particular word-initial target segment, the most likely error (should one occur) is the misselection of a similar word-initial target to copy. This would explain the position constraint described previously (pp. 303–312).

The question of why phoneme-sized units must be actively arranged into their surface sequence after their words have already been ordered correctly is just one of the interesting issues raised by the model in its present form. Others include the size of the greater-than-one-word span over which segments and slots are computed, possible variation in the span at different levels of computation, the form in which the segments are represented, and the form in which the slots are represented. At present, the only sure claim is that there must be a good enough match between target and slot descriptions so that a correct selection is made in almost all cases. A discussion of these issues will appear in forthcoming publications.

Generation of Observed Error Types

A more prosaic question, which can be dealt with in the confines of this chapter, concerns the way in which the proposed model generates the error types observed in the MIT–CU corpus. Possible malfunctions in the three-part serial ordering mechanism include (a) misselection of a target by the scan-copier, (b) premature checkoff of a target segment by the checkoff monitor, and (c) delayed or failed checkoff by the checkoff monitor. These three malfunctions, alone and in combination, result in each of the five major error types. In all five cases, at least one active misselection is involved. *Exchanges* arise in the following way. The slot and segment specifications are generated for some span of the utterance. For example, for the error "*p*utting and *c*asting" (cutting and pasting), the span must include both the target segments $/p/$ and $/k/$. The scan-copier selects appropriate segments and copies them into the waiting slots while the checkoff monitor checks off each copied segment in the planning set, until the first error location is reached. Then, instead of selecting the target $/k/$, it selects a target segment that belongs in a later slot, the intrusion segment $/p/$. This intrusion segment may be misselected for a number of reasons. For example, it is in a similar location in its target word (initial), it precedes a similarly stressed vowel, and it shares the features *stop* and *voiceless* with the target $/k/$.

The checkoff monitor correctly marks the misselected planning segment $/p/$ as used, and the scan-copier proceeds through the ordered slots, selecting and copying segments correctly, until the second error slot (in *pasting*) is reached. The target segment for this initial slot, $/p/$, has already been removed from the available set of planning segments, so it is not available to be copied. There is, however, an unused consonantal target segment $/k/$ that is represented as appropriate to word-initial and pre-stressed-vowel position and that shares many distinctive features with the unavailable target $/p/$, so that it fits the slot description fairly well. The scan-copier selects this $/k/$ as the best possible match among the available planning segments, copies it into the word-initial slot in *pasting*, and the checkoff monitor correctly marks it as used. The scan-copier proceeds on to the next slot, finishing up the rest of the utterance correctly.

The sequence of malfunctions in the serial-ordering mechanism that could cause an exchange error has been described at the single phoneme level, and most of the following discussion also concerns examples at that level. It is not difficult to imagine, however, the same mechanism at work at other levels. For example, a word exchange could occur when a similar misselection is made among the planning set of words. It would also not be surprising if the span over which the processor was operating were different in the case of words and if other differences between word exchanges and phoneme exchanges were found. Certainly it must be the case that the set of slots and segments are generated differently for words and for phonemes, and it is very likely that the kinds of information the processor has access to is quite different for the two kinds of errors. Garrett (1975) has argued persuasively from error data that such differences do exist. Nonetheless, in the model proposed here the basic serial-ordering mechanism goes wrong in the same way to cause both word and phoneme exchanges. Differences between the two types arise from differences in the representation of the utterance at the point during the production process when each type characteristically occurs.

One particularly interesting aspect of this account of exchange errors is that they are the result of a single mismatch: the first misslection of the first intrusion segment by the scan-copier. Once that initial mismatch has taken place and the wrongly chosen segment copied and marked, then the second part of the error results from the scan-copier doing the best it can with what is left. The matching process may well be somewhat cursory under normal conditions of production anyway, because many utterances do not contain confusable segments in similar slots and a sloppy scan will often suffice to select the correct target segment. In some utterances, however, the available planning segments are similar enough that an incomplete match will select the wrong one. Errors should be particularly common in such utterances. In addition, errors should occur in other circumstances where an incomplete match might be expected, such as conditions of stress, time pressure, distraction, or fatigue. These predictions offer a way to put the proposed model to experimental test, which will be pursued in further studies.

The scan-copier model also provides an account of the four other error types besides exchanges. Substitutions, both anticipatory and perseveratory, also involve an intrusion segment with a candidate source in the utterance. As in exchanges, the intrusion segment displaces a target segment. Thus, the malfunction that causes substitution errors might be expected to have much in common with the one underlying exchanges, and this is indeed the case. Like exchanges, substitutions can be modelled as the result of a malfunction in the mechanisms of the normal serial-ordering process. For example, an anticipatory substitution such as "that much ca*ss* for six glasses of wine" (cash) would arise from two such mistakes. First, the scan-copier misselects the intrusion segment /s/ instead of the target /š/ for the last slot in *cash,* perhaps partly because they follow the same vowel, /æ/. Second, the checkoff monitor fails to mark the /s/ after it is copied. As a result, the /s/ is still available in the planning set, and when the scan-copier reaches the medial slot in *glasses,* there is no difficulty in finding a match. The target /s/ is correctly copied into this slot, the checkoff monitor marks it and anticipatory substitution has occurred.

An error of this kind involves two separate misfirings of the ordering mechanism: a scan-copier misselection and a separate failure by the checkoff monitor to mark the mistakenly selected segment after it has been copied. Perseveratory substitution errors arise from the same two kinds of misfirings but in the opposite order. For example, the error "dining room *d*ox" (box) would arise because the segment /d/ was not checked off in the planning set after it was copied into the initial slot in *dining,* and so was still available when the scan-copier reached the initial slot in *box.* If the correct planning segment

/ b/ were then selected for this slot, no observable error would occur despite the checkoff failure. But the misselection of the intrusion segment /d/ from the planning set results in the perseveratory substitution "*dox.*"

A third kind of substitution error, the no-source substitution, appears at first to be an exception to the implication drawn from Constraint 8. That is, there is no evidence that no-source substitutions arise because two similar planning segments were simultaneously available to a processor that selected the wrong one. Since they do not have a candidate source, how are they to be accounted for? A number of possible explanations are compatible with the present model. For example, the source of the intrusion segment may lie in the part of the utterance that was not recorded with the error. Many errors were written down with very little of their sentential context, particularly in the early stages of collecting, and there is a good chance that if the whole utterance had been transcribed it would contain a candidate source.

A second possible account of apparent no-source substitution errors is that they arise from copying errors (in which the information specifying a target segment is incompletely or incorrectly transferred to the slot location), or even from an error in the original generation of the slot and segment representation. For example, the error "composed of *j*epartment—department chairpeople" may have occurred when the string of segments in the lexical item *department* was retrieved from the lexicon, or in the representation of the initial slot or target segment, or when the segment specification was incorrectly copied from the target segment to its slot. (This particular error illustrates still another possibility for some apparent no-source phoneme substitutions: There may have been some contamination from the affrication feature in the later initial segment of *chairpeople*.)

A third possible account is that apparent no-source substitutions have a source for their intrusion segments in a word that found its way into the set of planning segments by mistake. In fact, there must be some mechanism that permits this, because of the existence of Freudian slips. In such errors (e.g., "Just leave the key under the *mattress*" [doormat]), an utterance contains an intrusive word or phrase that does not belong there, but that is associated with the target word or phrase in the mind of the speaker (Freud, 1901/1958). In addition, some errors involve the substitution of words that have apparently entered the planning set because the speaker was listening to them while planning to speak or perceiving something that led to their retrieval from the lexicon. Examples of the latter kind include "Where's *Diane*?", said while looking at Diane and trying to ascertain the whereabouts of Sarah, and "We'll have to get a new *refrigerator*," said while standing in the kitchen looking at the refrigerator but discussing the wisdom of purchasing a new washing machine. It should be pointed out that the present model makes it easy to account for such errors by simply allowing the source of the intrusion to enter the set of target segments and become available for misselection. Because some such mechanism is required for independent reasons, it can be invoked as a possible source of the intrusions in no-source errors.

It is possible that all three of these accounts, as well as other explanations in terms of articulatory errors that have nothing to do with the planning process will be necessary in order to account for every case of substitution without apparent source. Presently available data do not distinguish between them, but it is important to note that all of these alternative explanations are compatible with the model being proposed for the generation of errors that do have a candidate source in the immediate sentence context.

Additions and omissions at the level of the single phoneme look like a change in the number of planning segments in an utterance, but they are actually ambiguous in this respect. As pointed out above, the apparent addition of a segment (as in "has s*l*ides sloping in" [sides]) may reflect the substitution of one planning unit for another at the level of initial consonantal sequence (e.g., the /sl/ from *slope* may be the source of the intrusion entity /sl/ in *slides*). Hockett (1967) has proposed such a level of linguistic analysis on the basis of other facts about errors (see the next section for discussion). If initial consonant sequences are cohesive units at some level of description, then many apparent phoneme addition and omission errors may actually be substitutions at the level of this larger unit. This is particularly convincing in the case of errors where there is a candidate source for the intrusion cluster in the utterance, such as the previous example "*sl*ides slope." Note also the possibility of accounting for this particular error as a semantically-related word substitution ("slides" for "sides" in the context of "slope"). This common occurrence of multiple explanations raises problems for the classification system which are discussed in the next section.

Even if errors like "*sl*ides slope" are reclassified as substitutions of one element for another at the cluster level, the MIT–CU corpus still contains a substantial number of errors that have no apparent source at this level, but do have a candidate source at the single phoneme level. For example, the anticipatory addition "G*l*od bless you" (God) had a candidate source in the /l/ of *bless*, but no candidate source for a /gl/ substitution. How would the present model account for such errors if they take place at the single phoneme level?

An anticipatory phoneme addition would arise from a misselection followed by a checkoff error, just as an anticipatory substitution does. In this case, however, the misselection is not of one target segment for another, but of a target segment for a slot that should be empty. This raises an interesting question: How does the location where the intrusion segment is added come to have its slot? Is it represented as a slot, albeit an empty one, or does the scan-copier simply fit an extra segment between two correct planning slots? This question is considered further in later discussion in this section.

A perseveratory phoneme addition also arises from the combination of a misselection and a checkoff error, but in the reverse order. First, a target phoneme is correctly selected for its slot and copied, but the checkoff monitor fails to mark it. Thus, when a similar but untargeted slot is reached later in the sentence, the unmarked segment is available and through a second error is misselected even though that slot should remain empty, resulting in errors such as "next seme*x*ter" where a perseveratory /k/ has been added. Again, the question arises of how that slot came to be available (see following).

Omission errors are a little tricky to define as anticipatory or perseveratory, although they often seem to have such a flavor. The problem arises because of the difficulty of specifying the intrusion segment. In some sense the intrusion in an omission error is the null segment ϕ, i.e., the absence of a segment. What could the source of the null intrusion segment be? In the context of the present model, the source of the null intrusion segment is a nearby slot that has a position similar to the target slot, but that contains the null segment as its target. Thus, an anticipatory omission error such as "Dr. _inclair has emphasized" (Sinclair) arises from two malfunctions in the serial-order process. First, the null segment is misselected by the scan-copier for the initial slot in *Sinclair*. The null segment is available in the planning set because it is the target segment for the first slot in *emphasized*. Second, the checkoff monitor fails to mark the copied null segment, so that when the scan-copier reaches the first slot in *emphasized*, it can correctly select the null target segment for the initial consonant element, for an anticipatory omission.

Perseveratory omission errors such as "The cup was c_umsily dropped" (clumsily) arise because the target null segment was correctly selected for the second slot in *cup* but it was not checked off after copying so was available to be misselected later for the second slot in *clumsily*, instead of the target segment /l/.

Omission errors in the context of a nearby null segment are thus a special case of substitution errors. Like anticipatory and perseveratory substitutions, they arise from two malfunctions (one a misselection and one a checkoff error), and the displaced target segment does not appear. In omissions, however, the source of the intrusion segment is a null target segment from elsewhere in the sentence, rather than a real target segment.

A second kind of omission error also has an apparent perseveratory or anticipatory component. These are omission errors that have an apparent trigger segment earlier or later in the sentence. Recall that the trigger is defined as a segment identical to the (displaced) target in an error. For example, in the error "He's probably _till telling the story" (still), it is possible that the target /st/ in *still* was edited out by the error monitor under the influence of the later /st/ in *story*. (The possible source of an intrusion segment /t/ in *telling* only complicates the issue and illustrates the ambiguities and multiple explanations at many levels that are common in speech errors. It will be ignored here for the purposes of discussion.)

If the trigger plays a role in omission errors just as the null-segment source does, how would the model account for it? In the case of anticipatory triggering such as this one, the error monitor scans the utterance for similar sequences, registers the twin examples of /st/, and edits the upstream example into something else, in this case a /t/. In the case of perseveratory triggered omissions such as "piano sonata _umber 10" (number), the error monitor edits out the downstream /n/ instead.

Like omission errors, addition errors sometimes have a trigger, in the form of a segment similar to the target segment in a similar sequence somewhere else in the utterance. Since the target segment for an addition slot is the null segment, what would its trigger look like? It is a sequence similar to the target sequence, which also has a null target in the same position. The trigger has either an anticipatory or a perseveratory influence, as in "He had his bank maintain interest-free bralances" (balances), where the earlier sequence /bæ/ in *bank* may have triggered a change of the later sequence /bæ/ in *balances* to /bræ/. As noted in the discussion of triggers above, it is not yet clearly established that such segments appear in error sequences more often than would be expected by chance, but if they do, the model can account for them.

Like substitutions, additions and omissions sometimes fail to show either an apparent source or an apparent trigger in the fragment of sentential and conversational context recorded in the corpus. These are classified as no-source additions and omissions. For example, "related _amphlets— pamphlets will be of help" and "when I go to the /kʲup/every Saturday morning" (Coop). The alternative mechanisms proposed for no-source substitutions could also account for no-source additions and omissions.

Finally, shift errors are caused by the same malfunctions as the other four major types, but in a different combination. Shifts involve the apparent movement of a target segment from its target location to another location in the utterance with no loss or gain of any segment. How could such an error occur in the present model? The first thing to notice is that shift errors move single phonemes into phonotactically permissible slots, as exchange and addition errors do. How is this limitation to be explained?

There must be some aspect of the production process that marks the slot representation of an utterance for locations into which phonemes could fit without violating the morpheme structure rules of English. For example, in the error "Walter C_onkrite" (Cronkite), the slot representation of the word *Cronkite* must have been of such form as to permit the insertion of an /r/ between the /k/ and the /ai/ of -*kite*, but not after the final /t/.

It is barely possible, of course, that the disappearance of the /r/ from *C_on*- and the appearance of the same segment in *krite* are two unrelated events. In that case, the error could simply be regarded as two separate substitutions (initial /k/ for /kr/ and medial /kr/ for /k/), and it would not be necessary to postulate a mechanism that specifies where in the utterance the /r/ can appear if it moves. But the independence of these two events is so unlikely that it almost forces the model to include such a mechanism. Although less compelling because the source and intrusion are not so tightly linked by probability, the evidence from anticipatory and perseveratory addition errors points in the same direction. All of these lines of evidence suggest the existence of markers in the planning slot sequence that specify where moved and added segments can go. Because it is extremely unlikely that such markers are there only to constrain errors, it makes sense to include them in a model of the normal production process. One logically simple although representationally expensive way to do this is to generate a slot sequence that corresponds to the canonical structure of English syllables, with many of the slots empty, for each morpheme in an utterance. The same hypothesis was advanced previously to account for the representation of slots independent of their segments.

This suggestion is intuitively unsatisfying, but if it is rejected, then another mechanism for restricting the locations to which segments can move in errors must be found. In addition, the possibility of explaining some errors as the substitution of a null target segment from the planning set would be lost, and the observation that many omission errors occur in contexts that include such a null segment to serve as a target would be unaccounted for. Further discussion of these issues will appear in Garrett and Shattuck-Hufnagel (in preparation).

If null target segments are part of the representation of sentences for production, then shift errors can be accounted for as a special case of substitution. That is, they arise from two malfunctions in the serial-ordering mechanism: a misselection of a segment for a null slot and a misselection of a null segment for a slot that should receive a real segment. For example, an anticipatory shift like Fromkin's (1971) "Frish G_otto" (Fish Grotto) would arise from the misselection of the /r/ for the post-initial slot in *fish* that should have remained empty but is phonotactically capable of accepting an /r/, and the subsequent misselection of the available null target segment for the post-initial slot in *grotto* that should have received the /r/. (In contrast, if the checkoff monitor had failed to mark the mistakenly selected /r/ after its use in *fish*, than /r/ would have been available in the planning set to be selected for its later correct target slot. The resulting error would have been an anticipatory addition rather than a shift: "frish grotto.") Perseveratory shifts such as "using ch_omat*r*ic stimuli" (chromatic) arise when the same two malfunctions occur in the opposite order: first, misselection of a null segment for a targeted slot, followed by misselection of a target for null slot.

The set of shift errors is the only one of the five basic error types that involves two full misselections. Moreover, both misselections occur between a null segment and a real target segment. No other errors require such a sharp departure from the normal process of serial ordering. Exchanges arise from a single misselection plus a compromise on a similar and simultaneously available planning segment, probably the closest match among the available segments in the planning set. Substitutions arise from a misselection plus a checkoff error. Additions and omissions require a misselection plus a checkoff error involving a null segment. Only shifts require two full misselection errors, in each case between a real segment and a null segment. Under this analysis, shifts should be a rare occurrence in the MIT–CU corpus (see later discussion).

In summary, each of the five error types that occur at all levels in the MIT–CU corpus can be accounted for as some variation on the basic mechanism of a malfunction in the segment-selection process described in the model. Copying and checkoff errors combine with this basic malfunction in different ways to cause the range of error types observed in the corpus. It must be admitted, however, that the account of errors given above is only one of many possible accounts that could be formulated. For example, one might imagine a model in which the set of target segments is made up of one instance of each of the phonemes of English, and the scan-copier selects among the entire inventory for each slot. The evidence against such an alternative model is the pervasive presence of source and trigger segments; if the set of available target segments is not limited to those that are specified by the lexical items in the utterance, then why do these segments so often appear as intrusions and triggers? This evidence will become even more convincing if it can be shown that a source and/or a trigger plays a role in almost every error that occurs. Such a demonstration will require a method of recording errors as they occur that is not limited by the immediate memory of the listener, so that more of the context can be included. So far, the evidence in the MIT–CU corpus points strongly in this direction, but further numerical analyses and experimental tests will be necessary to resolve the issue. Meanwhile, several independent lines of evidence from the corpus offer support for the proposed model.

Further Evidence From the Corpus

Any model of the speech-production process will have to account for the fact that intrinsically unordered items are arranged in a specific order, and that segments of the utterance can change or move in speech errors. In addition, a model must account for the eight constraints described in the early part of this paper. The model proposed here not only accounts for the constraints, but also accounts for the generation of each of the five basic error types as the result of a few minor malfunctions in the normal process of serial ordering in sentence production.

Further support for the model is found in three separate lines of evidence from the MIT–CU corpus:

1. A sixth kind of error, which occurs only in free morphemes, words, and sentence constituents, occurs just where the model predicts it should.

2. There is evidence that exchange errors are more common than substitutions, which are in turn more common than shift errors, as the model predicts.
3. Distributional evidence from the phoneme confusion matrix generated from the phoneme errors in the corpus supports the model's prediction about the symmetry of substitution between any two given phonemes.

Blend Errors

The sixth major type of error in the MIT–CU corpus is the blend. A blend occurs when portions of two free morphemes, words, or phrases are combined in a single form. There are two kinds of blends. One involves the merging of two more-or-less synonymous candidate units for the same slot, as in "prubble" (problem + trouble), "symblem" (symbol + emblem), and "kype" (kind + type). These are called synonymous blends. The second kind is called a sequential blend, because it involves the merging of two items that belong in different locations in the surface form of an utterance. The intervening sequence is left out, as in "Tennedy" (Ted Kennedy).

How are blends to be accounted for in the present model? In both cases, the scanner must jump from the slot-and-segment representation of the first word or phrase to the slot-and-segment representation of the second one. In synonymous blends the two units are two different candidate lexical items or phrases for the same slot. Recall that a mechanism for permitting extraneous candidates to enter the set of planning segments has already been motivated independently by Freudian slips and substitutions from immediate perceptual context. Now a third category of error requiring the presence of extra candidate words in the planning set has been found.

In sequential blends, the two units that merge are lexical items belonging in different slots in the utterance. In both kinds of blend, however, the model predicts that the jump from one set of slots to the other should occur at a point where the two sequences are similar. When the scan-copier is searching for target segments under their slot descriptions and copying them into their appropriate locations, the presence of two slot sequences with a point of strong similarity should increase the chances of slippage from one set to the other.

This prediction finds considerable confirmation in the blends in the MIT corpus. Lacking experimental evidence that the presence of such similar slot sequences will result in a higher rate of errors, the best evidence is a higher-than-expected proportion of blend errors that satisfy the condition. Although it is difficult to quantify slot or segment similarity without committing one's self to a particular feature system, two kinds of qualitative evidence offer support. First, blends such as "*troubloblem" (trouble + problem) have not been found. That is, when the blend occurs, it happens where the two units are structurally similar, so that the discarded portion of the second candidate is much like the articulated portion of the first candidate. The dimensions of similarity seem to include stress pattern, number of syllables, and sequential location in the syllable structure. Thus, the discarded first portion of *trouble* and the articulated first portion of *problem* have much in common, and the blend occurs at a point of similarity.

Second, a surprising number of word blends occur at a point where the two words actually share a phoneme. For example, (trouble + problem) blend at the common /r/ to give "troblem", (symbol + emblem) blend at the common /b/ to give "symblem", and (kind + type) blend at the common /ai/ to give "kype." Thus, in at least two ways, blend errors confirm the prediction that merging will take place at points of similarity, where a leap from one slot sequence to another during scanning or copying could easily take place. (Sequential blends also have this property.)

Blend errors support the model in another and quite unexpected way. Occasionally when blends are corrected, the result is a second error that is extremely informative about the speaker's mental representation. For example, consider the errors "There's a *back* on my desk" (batch + pack), "the *larden*" (lawn + garden), and "I *bess* you"(bet + guess). In the first error, the model predicts that the planning segments for the blend slot included /b, æ, č/ from *batch* and /p, æ, k/ from *pack*. After the blend error /bæk/, the planning segments /b, æ, k/ will have been marked by the checkoff monitor as used, but the leftover planning segments /p, æ, č/ will still be available because they were never copied. In the second error, /g, ɔ, n/ should be left over, and in the third error, /g, ɛ, t/. When the speaker attempted to correct each of these errors, the result was a second error consisting of just those unused segments: "patch on my desk", "gawn" and "I get you." This is convincing evidence that in at least some cases the serial-ordering mechanism behaves in exactly the way the model predicts. Examples of correction attempts using leftover fragments even extend to the level of blends between whole phrases: "I don't *matter*—I mean, *it doesn't* mind," and "There might be *able*—*we might be* ways—to do a kind of bifocal search."

Frequency of Occurrence

The model predicts that exchange errors, which involve only a single misselection (with a later compromise on the best available planning segment), will be more common than shifts, which involve two separate wrong choices between a null segment and a real segment. This prediction is confirmed in the 1974 count of the MIT–CU corpus, which contained 259 complete phoneme exchanges and only 31 phoneme shifts. In fact, the prediction may be even more strongly supported than these numbers imply. A category of errors called *incomplete errors* was developed for the many instances in the corpus that could have been either exchange errors or anticipatory substitutions, but that were caught by the speaker after the first intrusion and corrected. For example, "Can you tell me when the next *m*us to—bus to Monticello leaves?" might have been completed as "next *m*us to Monticello" (an anticipatory substitution of /m/ for /b/), or it might have been "next *m*us to *B*onticello" (an exchange of /m/ and /b/); the articulated portion of the error leaves both possibilities open. Recent analysis of the incomplete phoneme errors in the 1977 count of the MIT–CU corpus suggests that feature constraints on exchanges and substitutions are quite different and that incompletes are indistinguishable from exchanges but significantly different from substitutions in their feature constraints (Shattuck-Hufnagel & Klatt, in preparation). If additional evidence can be found that lumps the incomplete errors in the corpus with exchanges, rather than with substitutions as has been traditional, then the proportion of exchanges in the phoneme-error corpus, including both complete and incomplete instances is greater than 30%, whereas shift errors make up less than 1%.

Distributional Evidence in the Phoneme Confusion Matrix

The model predicts that for any segment x, the number of errors in which that segment appears as a target will be approximately equal to the number of errors in which that same segment appears as an intrusion. This is because errors arise from misselection among available planning segments on the basis of slot and/or segmental similarity. Thus, substituted segments should be similar, and for any pair of segments, either direction of substitution should be equally likely. Other models, in which a set of "strong" segments systematically displaces a weaker set, predict that for certain phoneme pairs there should be large asymmetries in the direction of substitution: The strong member should displace the weak one more often than vice versa.

When the prediction of symmetry in direction of substitution was tested in the 1977 count of the MIT–CU corpus, it had to be rejected, ($p < .001$.) However, almost all of the significant asymmetry was found in the interaction of the apical voiceless stop and fricative (/t/ and /s/) with their palatalized counterparts (/č/ and /š/). In particular, there was a significant tendency for these sounds to palatalize (in errors such as /t/ → /č/ and /s/ → /š/) more often than the palatal targets "unpalatalize" to /t/ and /s/.

The fact that the significant asymmetry in target-intrusion rates is confined to fewer than 1% of the possible phoneme pairs in the corpus suggests that, in general, the prediction of symmetry is confirmed. Furthermore, the direction of the observed limited asymmetry is not what a "strong displaces weak" model would predict: /t/ and /s/ are more frequent in English, later acquired and less highly marked than /č/ and /š/. This suggests that there are two different error mechanisms at work. The most important one, misselection during the serial ordering process, results in a basic pattern of target-intrusion symmetry for most of the 24 consonantal segments in the corpus. The second and less important mechanism superimposes a palatalizing influence on this symmetry for the apical consonants /s/ and /t/ and is responsible for the disproportionately large number of palatalizing errors such as "*Sh*imon and Schuster" (Simon) and "school cla*sh*rooms" (classrooms). When these excess errors are removed from the matrix, there is no significant difference between target and intrusion rates for any of the 24 consonantal segments. These results have been confirmed in a corpus of 1367 consonantal errors collected by Fromkin (Goldstein, 1977) at UCLA (Shattuck-Hufnagel & Klatt, 1978).

Conclusion

The model proposed here for the serial ordering of planning segments in sentence production leaves a number of important questions unanswered. To cite just two important examples, it does not specify how the proposed slots get their labels or what form the labels take, and it says almost nothing about the interaction of the proposed slot-and-segment representations with other components of the production process such as lexical retrieval, derivation of syntactic structure, and manipulation of derivational and syntactic bound morphemes. At the other end of the scale, it does not deal with errors that result from execution rather than planning: presumably in the case of a bad cold "id duh doze" there is nothing wrong with the serial-order mechanism, and these errors must also be accounted for. What the model does do is to embody the constraints derived from analysis of a large corpus of speech errors in such a way as to permit all observed error types to be generated as the result of a small number of minor malfunctions in the normal production mechanism. Some of its quantitative predictions have been confirmed in the MIT–CU corpus, but these represent only the beginning of the work of testing the model. Some of its premises are challenged by work showing that the same type of error follows quite different constraints at the word and sound level (Garrett, 1975, 1976). It remains to be seen whether the initial hypothesis that error types are similar enough to be reflections of a single basic mechanism can be maintained (see Garrett & Shattuck-Hufnagel, in preparation).

In this paper the aim has been to press the single-error-mechanism hypothesis as far as it would go, to see if it could be made to account for all error types and constraints, and if it provided insights into the psychological process of planning and producing speech. In fact there are several related activities that might benefit from analysis from the same point of view. Typing and writing, for example, both produce some errors that are constrained by the particular physical activity they involve (finger control, for example) and other errors that are apparently constrained by factors similar to those that constrain speech errors. For example, a common typing error involves omitting the second of two consecutive occurrences of the same letter, as in "change nough" for "change *e*nough" and "its even" for "its *s*even." Errors like this are similar to spoken omission errors such as "that would be __having" (be behaving) and could be accounted for if the proposed serial-ordering mechanism were used in typing as well. Each kind of activity requiring that abstract planning segments be reflected in a particular order in a sequence of behavior can be expected to show influences in its error patterns that are specific to that activity, but may also exhibit regularities that arise from the proposed serial-ordering mechanism.

There are many human activites that have this characteristic, ranging from speaking, writing, and typing to playing music, singing, dancing, etc. Some kind of planning mechanism must exist for imposing the correct order on the units that are selected from long-term storage, and anticipatory errors (among other things) show that this mechanism cannot be the simple one of retrieving them one at a time as needed. Perhaps this examination of speech-error patterns has given us a glimpse of a mental tool that plays a role in many activities. It is certainly not unusual for the human organism to use a single mechanism in many different behaviors. Consider the muscular mechanism for opening the jaw, which is used in a number of different activities, including eating, smiling, yawning, whistling, and singing. Is it to be supposed that a mental mechanism is any less flexible?

Such rank speculation is clearly beyond the scope of this paper. In the next section, some details of error analyses are examined that bear on Constraints 1 through 4, discussed previously. These four constraints were assumed in broad outline for the purposes of discussion, but they require some qualification on the basis of error data from the MIT–CU corpus.

A CLOSER LOOK AT CONSTRAINTS 1 THROUGH 4

A detailed study of the entire range of errors in the MIT–CU corpus suggests that some of the claims in the preceding section, while accurate in broad outline, require amplification. Because these details may have implications for the set of possible models of the speech production process, they are discussed here even when the questions they raise have not been resolved. Several problems in the collection and classification of errors are described, and the first four constraints from the preceding section are scrutinized.

Collection and Classification

The advantage of collecting spontaneous speech errors is that they are very readily at hand, and one can be reasonably sure that they occurred during the normal speaking process. A few hours of concentrated listening will convince the reader that speech errors of the kind defined in this study are easily

SHATTUCK-HUFNAGEL

extracted from everyday speaking situations. The difficulty lies not in hearing the errors but in remembering them. So adept is the average speech decoder at determining that an error has occurred, identifying it, and dismissing it from further consideration, that a real effort is necessary to hold an error in mind long enough to write it down.

A second problem is the notorious unreliability of the human auditory system as recording device. No one would question the fact that a listener tends to distort what is heard in the direction of a comprehensible message and to ignore aspects of the wave form that do not make a difference. In addition, it would not be surprising if certain kinds of errors were easier to hear and remember than others. These factors raise the question of how accurately the distribution in a speech-error corpus represents the population of errors that actually occur. Are there some types of errors that do not get recorded? Are there systematic distortions in the forms of the errors that do get recorded?

The similarity among corpora collected in different places by different observers (e.g., the MIT–CU corpus collected in Boston and Ithaca, and the UCLA corpus collected in Los Angeles by Fromkin [1971, 1973]) is comforting, as is their similarity to small tape-recorded corpora (e.g., Boomer & Laver, 1968) and the inclusion of errors made by the observers themselves who presumably can keep track of what their articulatory apparatus has done. But none of these guarantees that a corpus will be free of the distorting influences of human perception and memory processes.

However, it is possible to minimize the dangers by giving some thought to the kinds of distortion that might be expected. For example, in many error studies investigators have remarked that phoneme errors do not result in the articulation of sounds that are not part of the phonemic repertoire of the speaker, that substitution errors do not create "illegal" sequences of phonemes (such as initial /sr-/ in English), and that sound substitutions result in real English words unexpectedly often. Each of these constraints *might* be at least partially the result of a tendency for the listener to distort what is heard in the direction of a sensible message.

In fact, the MIT–CU corpus contains several exceptions to the constraint on illegal sequences of phonemes. One set of examples involves initial clusters such as /št/ and /šk/. These sequences are acceptable in some dialects of American English, and it is possible that only the speakers of those dialects make such errors. Another small set of errors creates the unacceptable syllable-initial cluster /vr/.

In contrast to constraints that might be at least partially predicted on the basis of a listening bias, other constraints on the corpus would be difficult to account for as the result of perceptual or memory distortion. For example, Shattuck-Hufnagel and Klatt's (1978) finding that a given phoneme appears about equally often as a target and as an intrusion segment in errors would require that an uneven distribution in occurrence be exactly matched by the opposite uneven bias in listening, which would be extremely surprising. Similarly, Garrett's (1975) findings that the span across which word exchanges take place is different from that for sound exchanges, and that word exchanges and sound exchanges obey different form-class constraints, are not the kinds of differences one would predict from listener bias.

Resolution of these difficulties will only be possible with a large sample recorded under perfectly natural speaking conditions. A taped sample would also give a more reliable estimate of the rate at which errors occur and determine whether different types of errors occur at different rates. Deese (1978) has recently published a partial analysis of such a taped sample, in which he notes that errors occur at an average rate of 1 per 100 utterances. Until the errors in such a sample are fully analyzed, reasonable care should be exercised in drawing firm conclusions based on the assumption that the range and distribution of error types in a corpus are reliable indicators of the total population of errors in spontaneous speech. As Garrett (1975) pointed out, error results are best used as a source of hypotheses to be tested in other ways. Convergent evidence from several different aspects of an error corpus for a single theoretical claim is, of course, more convincing.

Constraint 1:   Error segments may appear several words earlier in an utterance than they belong.

Implication: The planning span for an utterance is greater than a single word.

As every error analyst notes, Lashley (1951) made this point in his discussion of word-anticipation errors such as "and the *class* will be an in-class exam" (the exam will be an in-class exam). The caveat here is that this claim raises more questions than it answers. For example, what is the size of the greater-than-one word span? Garrett (1975) suggested the clause, while admitting that sound exchanges seldom span more than a few words. Does the size of the span change during the planning process; e.g., is it longer when syntactic structure is being computed, shorter when phonological details are being worked out? Is it the same for all speakers in all circumstances? Compare dictating an original manuscript, reciting a memorized poem, reading aloud, and greeting people in a receiving line.

A second question concerns the representation that can be inferred from the fact that the planning unit must encompass the two exchanged words (and, according to the model proposed here, their slots as well). That is, what was the representation of the part of the utterance *between* the two target items when the error occurred? For example, in the "exam/class" error cited above, it seems reasonable to hypothesize that the intervening morphemes *will be an in-* were represented in the same form as the targets *exam* and *class* were, when the exchange occurred. But this is not necessarily so. In fact, evidence that certain classes of morphemes do not interact with others suggests that they are represented differently at the point during production when errors occur. Garrett (1975) has made such a claim about closed-class and open-class morphemes. Thus, caution should be exercised in leaping from claims about the representation of error segments to claims about the representation of the rest of an utterance.

In short, Constraint 1 raises a number of interesting questions about the representation of the planning span during production, which can only be answered by a much more detailed model than is presently available.

Constraint 2:   Errors often (although not invariably) involve the units and devices of linguistic grammars: phonemes, morphemes, words, and sentence constituents.

Implication: These units are part of the psychological representation of utterances during planning; moreover, they must be represented independently of their locations or slots.

The difficulty with this constraint lies in determining the strength of the claim that can be made about the equivalence of planning units and linguistic entities. The claim that error segments are planning segments for normal speech seems a reasonable one: Fromkin (1973) has pointed out that it would be very surprising to find that error segments corresponded to linguistic entities if normal processing segments did not. But how strong is the equivalence? Is it the case that all and only linguistically motivated entities appear as segments that are moved or change in speech errors? There are two classes of evidence showing at least that not all linguistic entities are planning segments in the sense described here and that not all error units correspond to traditional linguistic "chunks."

The error evidence for the independent representation of phonemes, morphemes, words, and sentence constituents is clear. Further evidence suggests that distinctive features and syllables also play a role in the production process, but not as independently represented planning segments. Traditional error arguments for the psychological validity of the syllable have been of two kinds. First, syllables move and change as units, as in the error "at Camper Unli__ted" (Camper Unlimited), where the syllable -mi- is omitted. Second, syllable position constraints govern phoneme errors, as in "a rotorcycle ride" where the presumed source is in the same syllable position as the target. The first line of evidence, that syllables move as units, must be reevaluated in light of the fact that in the MIT–CU corpus, other sequences of phonemes move and change in errors much more often than syllables do. This is a surprising result, if the level of representation intermediate between phoneme and morpheme is the syllable. Only 10% of the phoneme-sequence errors in the corpus involve a syllabic unit as a whole, even under the most generous definition of the syllable. Consider the following examples:

borrow a *sho*w-*sno*vel   (snow shovel)
got their *fre*st—first fresh
each of op*ula*—operations
*h*ever _ardly   (hardly ever)
*ca*ssy *pu*t   (pussy cat)
the Patriot's number one draft *Plunk*—heh, heh,—number one draft pick, Jim Plunket

Errors such as these involve changes in submorphemic sequences of phonemes that sometimes correspond to syllables but more often do not. Errors involving nonsyllabic sequences pose a problem for any theory claiming that planning units correspond to linguistic entities, at least, if one accepts the view that error units correspond to normal planning units in all cases. How are they to be handled in the model proposed here?

There are two possible responses to the dilemma. One can give up the claim that all error units reflect planning units and hypothesize that in some ways the planning process permits random sequences of phonemes within a morpheme to be run off wrong. Or, one can look for constraints on the kinds of phoneme sequences that show up as error units, to see if they might be motivated by the grammar.

Several lines of evidence suggest that the latter course might meet with success. First, there are some clearly recognizable linguistic entities in the set of phoneme-sequence errors. Consonant cluster error units, for example, are limited to those within a single morpheme and do not include cases such as /kb/ in "blackboard." Another plausible unit is the sequence left behind when word-initial consonants and clusters move or change in an error: the rest of the word. In errors such as "*pan caints*" (paint cans) and "you b*ind* while I gr*one*" (you bone while I grind), in fact, "the rest of the word" appears to be a moveable unit on its own. A level of linguistic analysis consisting of [initial consonant sequence] followed by [rest of the word] was proposed by Hockett (1967) for English monosyllables, on the basis of both errors and patterns of change in Pig Latin (where speakers change words such as *street* to *eet-stray*, suggesting that the initial consonant cluster is represented as a cohesive unit). Word blend errors should be examined for evidence to support this hypothesis, but the facts in the MIT–CU corpus are obscured by the number of cases that blend at a shared phoneme (e.g., "prubble" for [problem + trouble]), making it impossible to determine whether the blended portions correspond to the initial consonant sequence and the rest of the word or not.

In summary, evidence for planning segments larger than a single phoneme and smaller than a morpheme exists, but the degree of correspondence between those error units and lingustic entities needs further study. Specification of the constraints on sequences that can serve as error units will help to resolve the problem. For example, the MIT–CU corpus apparently contains no errors in which a stop-liquid cluster followed by a vowel changes both the liquid and vowel, while leaving the stop intact (e.g., *"plea"* for "pry"). The lack of such errors is predicted by an analysis in terms of initial consonant sequence as one unit, followed by the rest of the word as another.

Although evidence for the syllable as a moveable planning segment is weak, the evidence that it serves as a kind of framework for phoneme location is strong. As noted in the preceding section, there is a powerful position constraint on the locations that phonemes can move into and also on the relationship between an error target and its source (perhaps its trigger as well). Phonemes move into permissible syllable positions, and they influence each other primarily from similar syllable positions.

The distinctive feature is a second linguistic entity that evidently plays a different role in the planning process than that of a discrete, moveable, independently represented planning segment. There is no question that feature-exchange errors do occur (e.g., *"ponato"* (tomato), Dennis Klatt, personal communication, 1976) where the features defining place of articulation have evidently been exchanged). At first this seemed to suggest a separate mechanism for processing features independent of the phonemes they specify, even though these errors are extremely rare: There are only two in the entire MIT–CU corpus that must be accounted for as feature exchanges. There are many phoneme substitution errors in which the target and intrusion segments differ by only a single feature, but these can be accounted for as phoneme errors under a feature-similarity constraint and do not require a mechanism for ordering individual features one by one. In fact, Shattuck-Hufnagel and Klatt (1978) have pointed out that the number of unambiguous single-feature errors in the MIT–CU corpus is much smaller than would be expected if the feature were the unit that changed to cause apparent phoneme substitution. Thus, like syllables, distinctive features are supported by the error data as psychologically real but not as independently represented planning segments that must be serially ordered one-at-a-time for production. In the present model, features and syllables may play a role in defining the slots that planning segments are copied into, in some way that needs further specification.

Constraint 3:   A target and its intrusion can be described as single units at the same level of description.
Implication: Some aspect of the planning process permits confusions between segments of the same type, but prevents confusions across segment types.

This simple observation, so obvious that it almost escapes notice, tempts one to ascribe a separate processing level to each error segment type, although as can be seen in the case of features, discussed previously, the data do not dictate such a step. The constraint forms the basis of the three-way classification system used in the MIT–CU corpus. It actually involves several claims, each of which needs qualification in light of the errors in the corpus: first, that all errors involve segmental changes; second, that the level of segment involved can be identified in every case (i.e., error segment); third, that the nature of the change can be determined (i.e., error type); and fourth, that the direction of influence from source to target can always be distinguished. None of these claims is quite true as it stands.

First, do all errors involve segmental changes? The majority of errors in the 1974 count of the MIT–CU corpus, 96%, do consist of a recognizable change in or movement of a linguistically motivated segment in the utterance. There are a few errors, however, that do not quite fit this description, and although they do not change the theoretical import of Constraint 3, they should be mentioned for the sake of completeness.

Complex errors are not exceptions to the claim that errors consist of changes in planning segments; they are emphatic cases in which two or more apparently unrelated segmental changes occur in the same utterance. For example, "*pruranism*" (pluralism) and "the frequencies w*rich*—with which." Complex errors make up less than 1% of the MIT–CU corpus.

Syntactic errors are an exception to the principle of segmental substitution but not, apparently, to the principle that errors occur when some part of the normal production process misfires. Examples such as the following are classed as syntactic:

and what we're all called on by our constitution is to
The lives of 6600 Americans does not appear to be in danger.
That's the kind of joke which I never know if it's funny or not.
A newspaper is planned to be started.

Fay (1977) has argued that some syntactic errors can be accounted for as the misapplication of a syntactic transformation during the derivation of a sentence. Others appear to be violations of selection restrictions. This interesting and informative class of errors, which deserves further study, makes up about 5% of the MIT–CU corpus.

Finally, *stress errors*, which do not conform in any simple way to the pattern of misselection among available planning segments, again confirm the principle that errors involve a malfunction in the normal production process. A common stress error, for example, is the assignment of word-stress to the wrong vowel, as in "investigátors" and "lingúists." Cutler (1977) has pointed out that in each of these cases another form of that same root exists in the lexicon with the stress pattern of the error (e.g., "investigátion" and "lingúistics," for the examples above.) This constraint also governs the stress errors in the MIT–CU corpus, which make up less than 1% of the total number of errors.

The second claim behind Constraint 3 is that the appropriate level of segmental description can be determined for each error unit. This is rendered almost impossible by the hierarchical nature of linguistic descriptions. For example, in the error "the age s*k*an" (age span), what is the error unit? Is it the feature for place of articulation? the phoneme /k/? the consonant cluster /sk/? the word *scan*? the noun phrase "the age scan"? Almost all target and intrusion segments share this problem to some degree; i.e., they can be described as segments at more than one level. This may merely reflect the nested nature of language constituents, or it may be because the likelihood that an error will reach the stage of being articulated increases with the number of segmental descriptions at different levels it satisfies. For the purposes of error studies such as this one, the problem is that in order to group errors of a similar kind together, one needs to know what kind of segment was involved in each error.

A possible solution to this problem is to classify every error in as many categories as it will fit into. By this rule, the "age s*k*an" error above would be filed under all five segment levels. This solution is cumbersome and may obscure important regularities. In classifying errors in the MIT–CU corpus, we follow a simple though somewhat arbitrary principle instead. If there is a level of description at which target, intrusion, and presumed source (and even possible trigger) can all be regarded as single segments, then the error is categorized at that level. The error "meas*u*res of *sp*ublic speaking anxiety" (public), then, is classed as the substition of the intrusion sequence /sp/ for the target sequence /p/, because of the candidate source in *speaking*. But the error "G*l*od bless you!" (God) is indexed as the addition of the phoneme /l/, because there is no candidate source for the sequence /gl/.

This method of triangulation is useful in disambiguating two problematical kinds of errors in which the target and intrusion segments appear to be of different levels. The first of the two is the set of errors in which both error units are complete entities, but they seem to be of different levels. This includes target/intrusion pairs consisting of a single consonant and a cluster, a monomorphemic word and a polymorphemic word, or a one-word phrase and a phrase made up of several words. Such errors are classified as consonant sequence errors (such as "*st*and-hamped" [hand-stamped]), where one of the sequences happens to contain only one element; as whole-word errors (like "Let me run my *hair* through your *fingers*" [fingers through your hair] or "in front of the *cushions* on the *fire*" [fire on the cushions]) where one of the words happens to contain only one morpheme, and as whole-phrase errors (such as "Can you call me *last night?*" [tonight]) where one of the phrases happens to contain just a single word.

The second class of errors with an apparent target-intrusion segment level difference consists of substitutions where one of the segments is a complete unit but the other seems to break up a larger unit. This group includes errors that break up a consonant cluster (as in "I *p*eel like *f*laying" [feel like playing]), which break up polymorphemic words (as in "They used to make *hand*s by *violin*" [violins by hand] or "get the *gum rugg*ed up" [rug gummed up]), or which break up multi-word phrases (such as "is like the *experiment* in *situation* two" [situation in experiment two]). Errors such as these are classified at the level of the smaller of the two units (single C, morpheme and word), because that is the level of description at which both target and intrusion can be regarded as a single segment.

Where the principle of triangulation does not yield an unambiguous classification of error-segment type, the error is classified as the smallest possible segment unless there is good reason to do otherwise. An example of a good reason to do otherwise is Garrett's (1975) observation that the constraints on movement for the phoneme /s/ are different when it represents the plural morpheme or the third person marker than when it does not, which suggests that the error should be classified differently when the moved /s/ represents a morpheme.

The third claim behind Constraint 3, concerned with another dimension of classification, is that the error type can always be determined. As noted previously, when a two-part error is detected by the speaker and corrected before the second part occurs, it is impossible to be sure which error type it would have been. For example, as noted previously (p. 325) the incomplete error "Can you tell me when the next *m*us to—bus to Monticello leaves?" could have been either the anticipatory substitution "*m*us to Monticello," or the exchange "*m*us to *B*onticello." Similarly, the incomplete error "You either have to give *h*up—give up headroom or" might have been either the anticipatory addition "give *h*up headroom" or the anticipatory shift "give *h*up _eadroom." Speakers' intuitions about what they were going to say next provide a hint but cannot be relied on absolutely. Another source of evidence as to the type of an error is the discovery that exchanges and substitutions as classes of errors have quite different characteristics. For example, Shattuck-Hufnagel and Klatt (in preparation) have found that phoneme exchanges are significantly less tightly constrained by feature similarity than are phoneme substitutions. They report that the incomplete phoneme errors in the MIT–CU corpus are indistinguishable from exchanges along this dimension, but significantly different from substitutions, suggesting that the class of incompletes is largely made up of aborted exchanges.

The fourth issue in Constraint 3 is the direction of influence from presumed source to error target segment. There are several types of source-direction ambiguity. First, except for exchange and shift errors whose two-part nature makes their source almost certain, most presumed sources are no more than reasonable candidates: In reality, they may have nothing to do with the intrusion error. Second, some errors have a candidate source both before and after the error (as in "the friction on a *br*ank reel" (blank), where the intrusion /r/ may be related to either the /r/ in *friction* or the /r/ in *reel* or both). Third, there may be a candidate source on one side of the error and a candidate trigger on the other (as in "prior to any *bub*—publication of any book" where the source is the /b/ in *book* or in *publication* and the trigger is the /p/ in *prior,* or "I can't just /pʌt/ and—cut and paste," where the source is the /p/ in *paste* and the trigger is the /k/ in *can't*). The two-source cases are simply called anticipatory–perseveratory, because the presence of two candidate sources may turn out to be important. Cases where source and trigger candidates bracket the error are filed according to the direction of influence from the source, since the role of the trigger mechanism has not been conclusively demonstrated.

Thus, Constraint 3 conceals several classification problems and, in fact, sometimes serves as the principle for resolving those problems.

Constraint 4:   A target and its intrusion segment are similar along linguistic dimensions.
Implication: These dimensions are part of the psychological representation of utterances during the production process.

The import of this constraint is that the processing system has access to the kinds of grammatical information embodied in linguistic dimensions: Elements that are similar to a linguist are similar to the processor. Beyond the level similarity of Constraint 3, claims about target-intrusion similarity fall into two groups. First, an error target and its intrusion segment are members of the same major category at their level of segmental description. For example, at the phrase level, noun phrases interact with noun phrases but not with verb phrases. At the word level, the major categories of content words and noncontent words very seldom if ever interact as target and intrusion segments. Garrett (1975) has pointed out that the set of open-class morphemes (approximately nouns, verbs, and adjectives; the classes of words to which new items can easily be added) do not interact in errors with the set of closed-class morphemes (approximately adverbs, pronouns, prepositions, and both derivational and inflectional affixes; the classes that do not easily admit new members). At the phoneme level, consonants interact with other consonants but almost never with vowels, and vice versa. The representations used for processing must capture these constraints on noninteracting segments.

Second, a target and its intrusion segment share the features that distinguish individual items at their level of description, unexpectedly often. For example, a target word and its intrusion can share semantic features (e.g., are antonyms, synonyms, parallel constructions, or members of the same general class as in "*month*" [day] and "*sister*" [cousin]), and/or phonological form (e.g., specific phonemes, number of syllables, stress pattern). These casual observations raise interesting questions about the information available to the processor at the point when word and morpheme errors occur. Further analysis is badly needed here (see Garrett & Shattuck-Hufnagel, in preparation).

At the level of the phoneme, quantitative information about feature similarity between target and intrusion segments is available. The claim that target/intrusion pairs share distinctive features seemed at first to be disconfirmed in a study by Boomer and Laver (1968). In a small corpus of fewer than 200 errors in English, they found no evidence to support feature similarity. On the other hand, MacKay's (1970) study of 100 phoneme exchanges in German (collected by Merringer and Meyer, 1895) provided evidence for the features nasal and voicing, but no evidence for the features defining place of articulation. Furthermore, Nooteboom (1969) reported that in a corpus of more than 700 phoneme substitutions in Dutch, feature similarity between target and intrusion was significantly greater than chance.

Shattuck (1975) using a method of analysis developed by Klatt (1968) for the study of phoneme confusion matrices, found that in a matrix of 1180 consonant substitutions from the 1974 count of the MIT–CU matrix, target segments shared distinctive features with their intrusion significantly more often than chance. A separate matrix of 215 vowel substitutions also showed feature constraints. Goldstein (1977) has found similar evidence for features in Fromkin's UCLA corpus of 1367 consonant errors. Finally, Blumstein (1973) and Keller (1978) have found that the phoneme-substitution errors made by certain kinds of English-speaking aphasics also follow feature constraints.

Subject to the warning that errors are filtered through the human auditory system, it seems clear that target and intrusion phonemes are similar along the dimensions captured by distinctive features. This general conclusion raises several further questions: (a) Which of the several feature systems proposed by linguists best describes the similarity of target and intrusion segments? (b) Do all types of errors show the same degree of feature similarity between target and intrusion segments? e.g., are exchanges different from substitutions? (c) Is there convincing evidence for binary features as opposed to multi-valued dimensions of similarity? (d) Is there evidence for a hierarchy of features? i.e., are some features more resistant to change in errors than others? Some of these issues are dealt with in Shattuck-Hufnagel and Klatt (in preparation).

Conclusion

Although detailed analysis of the MIT–CU corpus has generally confirmed Constraints 1 through 4, it has also suggested qualifications that are embodied in the following reformulations.

Constraint 1: Errors that span more than a single word require a planning span greater than one word, but the precise nature of its representation is unclear. The size of the span, the representation of the nonerror elements within it, and the degree of variation across speakers and speaking situations need further investigation.

Constraint 2: Linguistic entities that move and change independently in speech errors include at least phonemes, morphemes, words, and sentence constituents. Other linguistic entities (such as features and syllables) participate in errors differently, and this difference suggests that they play a different role in the planning process. Errors can also involve within-morpheme sequences of phonemes whose formal grammatical significance remains to be worked out.

Constraint 3: Target and intrusion segments seem without exception to be single units at the same level of description. Apparent exceptions to this principle can be resolved by assuming that "smaller" units are actually larger units with one or more empty slots in their representation.

Constraint 4: Speech error target and intrusion segments share linguistic characteristics to a significant degree. Often, a target/intrusion pair share characteristics of many different types: e.g., a phoneme target may share distinctive features as well as word or syllable position and phonetic context with its intrusion and presumed source; a word target may share phonological as well as syntactic and semantic characteristics with its intrusion. It is important to note that the shared characteristics need not all be taken account of in the same representation or level of processing in production planning.

The model that has been proposed here for the serial ordering of planning units in speech is far from complete, but it accounts for many of the significant regularities and constraints in the MIT–CU corpus. Perhaps its most puzzling aspect is the question of why a mechanism is proposed for the one-at-a-time serial ordering of phonemes when their order is already specified in the lexicon. The fact is, however, that speech errors commonly involve the misordering of single phonemes, so some such mechanism must be included in a production model. It is likely that the description of the scan-copier given here conceals a much more significant mechanism which performs a critical role in normal error-free speaking, and only incidentally functions as a scan-copier. One suggestion has been voiced by MacNeilage and MacNeilage (1973), who postulated that the mechanism that removes planning segments serially from the buffer also provides timing information that would be useful in the later specification of articulatory targets. If flow charts and verbal descriptions of production models based on speech-error data can be expanded and made more precise than present formulations, they may permit us to derive a detailed model of the steps in the psychological process of planning and producing sentences. Such a model, with powerful implications for the understanding of many kinds of behavior, would more than repay the hundreds of speakers who have been momentarily aggravated by the excessive attention paid to their mistakes by their psycholinguistic friends.

APPENDIX A

The five basic error types occur at all levels of segmental description. The error types are: exchange (E), substitution (S), addition (A), omission (O), shift (Sh). A sixth type, blend, which is discussed in the text, is also illustrated.

Phonemes
1. I *s*ould be *sh*eeing him soon (should be seeing) (E)
2. *r*ode of *N*anvier (node of Ranvier) (E)
3. a *b*ut-gusting meal (gut-busting) (E)
4. no good words for the *m*est—western nations when he spoke. (S)
5. The Globe, the Heral*b* and the New York Times (Herald) (S)
6. I didn't explain this *c*larefully enough. (carefully) (A)
7. but not *n*engma—engma (A)
8. the sort of blanket training g_ant (grant) (O)
9. salu_a—salutations (O)
10. Do you want to feed *H*andrew _ot dogs (Andrew hot dogs) (Sh or E)

Phoneme sequence
1. do you think we should get a pap*el* tow*er*? (paper towel) (E)
2. I haven't done any word tod*all* at *ay* (today at all) (E)
3. It's a mail *ow*der—order house. (S, incomplete)
4. *sears yih*—six years ago (E)
5. playing *guit*orders and *rec*ars (recorders and guitars/guitars and recorders) (E)
6. all the political philosoph*ic*ies (philosophies) (A)
7. anterior*or*ity (anteriority) (A)
8. keeps you comp__y (company) (O)
9. Carneigie Mell*i*gan men (Mellon) (A)
10. *gui*tune my __tar (tune my guitar) (Sh)

Morphemes: affixes
1. When Mon*ny* isn't sun*day* (Monday isn't sunny) (E)
2. lots of moisture and protec*ture* (protection) (S)
3. People read the backs*es* of boxes (backs) (A)
4. calling for complete*ment* of (completion) (S)
5. They needed to be mad*ed* (made) (A)
6. Who could __form at a—perform at a higher level (O)
7. by Miller, Nice*er*—Nicely and others (S)
8. should *under be* taken only in extraordinary circumstances (be undertaken) (Sh or E)
9. *inspeech* pediment (speech impediment) (Sh or E)
10. You lose significant*s* amount_ of heat (significant amounts) (Sh)

Morphemes: roots
1. *nam*ing a *wear* tag (wearing a name tag) (E)
2. Your *match*es don't even *voice* (voices don't even match) (E)
3. I had to give my *time* a little *self* (myself a little time) (E)
4. I hate *rain*ing on a *hitch*y day (hitching on a rainy day) (E)
5. They may not be *give you*-ing any fruits, but they sure do grow (giving you) (Sh or E)

6. of the way the *shape* is *spac*ed (space is shaped) (E)
7. I used my time last night to *birth* a—birth a bakeday cake! (bake a birthday) (E, incomplete)
8. the salesman was a *slick*y—a city slicker (E, incomplete)
9. As soon as Barbara goes, the *lock*'s—the *lock*'s doored! (E, incomplete)
10. I'm not so sure he was objec*tion*ing—objecting (A)

Words

1. Any *guys* you *time* (time you guys) (E)
2. I used to sit in her *read* and *room* (room and read) (E)
3. No, here, keep the *bottom*—keep the top. (S)
4. The crazy *idea* who had a good idea but doesn't have a grant (guy) (S)
5. The other thing that's different is the way perceptually *similar*—simpler (S)
6. Agnes Moffit, *tenor,* did I say tenor? I meant contralto. (S)
7. That tends to keep the *dull* off them (shine) (S)
8. I heard it over the *radiator* (radio) (S)
9. I want to clear __ one point (clear up) (O)
10. We really do have to __ something (to do) (O)

Sentence constituent

1. They won't stay "prestigious" unless they *mean it* (have a right to say it) (S)
2. No, *I'm don't* (I'm not/I don't) (Blend)
3. *Bless you* (Come in) (S)
4. You'd be *out in left base* (out in left field/way off base) (Blend)

Stress errors

1. cognitive devélopmental
2. for the attorney general's investigátors
3. for a psychó—psycholinguist

Syntactic errors

1. anything more deeper than phonology (deeper than)
2. She hang up. She hungs up. (She hung up)
3. The sentence that takes more transformations will be *later to learn* (learned later)
4. It will be helped by what's in the key punches, won't *they*? (won't it)
5. You can reach the dwarf variety without a ladder, *aren't they*? I mean, can't you?

Complex errors

1. synchro*size* the *phones* (synchronize the watches)
2. I went on to a *rotor my*cle ride (motor cycle)
3. high *loise*—high energy, low noise
4. I think I'm gonna might haveta drive but I can't haveta be asleep.

REFERENCES

Blumstein, S. *A phonological investigation of aphasic speech.* The Hague: Mouton, 1973.
Boomer, D. S., & Laver, J. D. M. Slips of the tongue. *British Journal of Disorders of Communication,* 1968, *3,* 2–12.
Brown, R., & McNeill, D. The "tip of the tongue" phenomenon. *Journal of Verbal Learning and Verbal Behavior,* 1966, *5,* 325–337.

Culter, A. *Queering the pitch: Errors of stress and intonation.* Paper prepared for the working group on slips of the tongue. (V. Fromkin, Chairperson), XII International Congress of Linguists, Vienna, Austria, September 1977.

Deese, J. Thought into speech. *American Scientist,* 1978, *66,* 314–321.

Fay, D. *Transformational errors.* Paper prepared for the working group on slips of the tongue (V. Fronkim, Chairperson), XII International Congress of Linguists, Vienna, Austria, September 1977.

Foss, D., & Fay, D. Linguistic theory and performance models. In J. Wirth & D. Cohen (Eds.), *Testing linguistic hypotheses.* New York: Hemisphere Press, 1975.

Freud, S. *The psychopathology of everyday life* (A. A. Brill, trans.). New York: New American Library, 1958. (Originally published, 1901).

Fromkin, V. A. The non-anomalous nature of anomalous utterances. *Language,* 1971, *47,* 27–52.

Fromkin, V. A. Introduction. In V. A. Fromkin (Ed.), *Speech errors as linguistic evidence.* The Hague: Mouton, 1973.

Fry, D. B. The linguistic evidence of speech errors. *Brno studies in English,* 1969, *8.*

Garrett, M. F. The analysis of sentence production. In G. Bower (Ed.), *The psychology of learning and motivation* (Vol. 9). New York: Academic Press, 1975.

Garrett, M. F. Syntactic processes in sentence production. In R. Wales & E. C. T. Walker (Eds.), *New approaches to language mechanisms.* Amsterdam: New Holland, 1976.

Garrett, M. F., & Shattuck-Hufnagel, S. Speech errors and a sentence production model. (Manuscript in preparation.)

Goldstein, L. *Categorial features in speech perception and production.* Paper prepared for the working group on slips of the tongue (V. Fromkin, Chairperson), XII International Congress of Linguists, Vienna, Austria, September 1977.

Hockett, C. F. Where the tongue slips, there slip I. In *To honor Roman Jakobson* (Vol. 2). The Hague: Mouton, 1967.

Keller, E. Parameters for vowel substitutions in Broca's aphasia. *Brain and Language,* 1978, *5,* 265–285.

Klatt, D. H. The structure of confusions in short term memory between English consonants. *Journal of the Acoustical Society of America,* 1968, *44,* 401–407.

Lashley, K. S. The problem of serial order in behavior. In L. A. Jeffress (Ed.), *Cerebral mechanisms in behavior (the Hixon symposium).* New York: Wiley, 1951.

Laver, J. D. M. *A model of the speech production process.* Paper prepared for the working group on slips of the tongue (V. Fromkin, Chairperson), XII Congress of Linguists, Vienna, Austria, September 1977.

MacKay, D. G. Spoonerisms: The structure of errors in the serial order of speech. *Neuropsychologia,* 1970, *8,* 323–350.

MacNeilage, P. F., & MacNeilage, L. A. Central processes controlling speech production during sleep and waking. In F. H. McGuigan & R. A. Schoonover (Eds.), *The psychophysiology of thinking.* New York: Academic Press, 1973.

Merringer, R. *Aus Dem Leben der Sprache.* Berlin: Verlag, 1908.

Merringer, R., & Meyer, C. *Versprechen und Verlesen.* Berlin: Verlag, 1895.

Nooteboom, S. G. The tongue slips into patterns. In A. G. Sciarone (Ed.), *Nomen: Leyden studies in linguistics and phonetics.* The Hague: Mouton, 1969.

Roche-Lecours, A., & L'Hermitte, F. Phonemic paraphasias: Linguistic structures and tentative hyptheses. *Cortex,* 1969, *5,* 193–228.

Shattuck, S. R. *Speech errors and sentence production.* Unpublished doctoral dissertation, MIT, 1975.

Shattuck-Hufnagel, S., & Klatt, D. H. *An analysis of 1500 phonetic errors.* Paper presented at the 90th annual meeting of the Acoustical Society of America, San Francisco, November 1975.

Shattuck-Hufnagel, S., & Klatt, D. H. *Phonetic speech errors rule out three models of sentence production.* Paper prepared for the working group on slips of the tongue (V. Fromkin, Chairperson), XII International Congress of Linguists, Vienna, Austria, September 1977.

Shattuck-Hufnagel, S., & Klatt, D. H. The limited use of distinctive features and markedness in speech production: Evidence from speech error data. *Journal of Verbal Learning and Verbal Behavior,* 1978, in press.

Shattuck-Hufnagel, S., & Klatt, D. H. *Feature constraints on different types of phonetic speech errors.* (Manuscript in preparation).

Wickelgren, W. A. Distinctive features and errors in short-term memory for English consonants. *Journal of the Acoustical Society of America,* 1966, *39,* 388–398.

11 *Like* Syntax

John Robert Ross
Massachusetts Institute of Technology

William E. Cooper
Harvard University

In developing a theory of ongoing speech production, researchers have typically assumed that important clues may be provided by studying factors that occur in casual speech but not in writing. This assumption serves as a basis for investigating speech errors (e.g., Fromkin, 1971; Garrett, 1975; Shattuck-Hufnagel, Chapter 10 of this volume), hesitation pauses (e.g., Boomer, 1965; Goldman-Eisler, 1968; Martin, 1971), and various phonological reductions (Baker, 1972; King, 1970; Stampe, 1972; Zwicky, 1970). Here, we invoke the assumption as a rationale for studying restrictions on the occurrence of the word *like* as a filler, meaning roughly *for example* or *approximately*, as in (1).

(1a) John is like the best baseball player in town.
(1b) We intended to leave Chicago at like 9 o'clock.

The precise meaning of *like* as a filler varies in different sentences (a matter we will return to later). Our primary concern, however, lies not with these shades of meaning but with restrictions on *like*'s occurrence.

In many sentences, including (1), *like* can occur in casual speech without an accompanying pause. In this respect, *like*'s behavior can be distinguished from interjections (e.g., *oh, well, say*) studied by James (1973). In other contexts, as in (2), a bordering pause is required:

(2a) Bob's like *(,) father would not leave town without us.
(2b) We should leave town *(,) like.

In (2) and throughout this paper, we denote a pause by a comma. An asterisk is placed outside the parenthesized comma to signify that the sentence is ungrammatical when the comma is not present.

Initially, we confine our remarks to *like* as it occurs in contexts that do not require a pause. We then consider pause-bounded *like* and relate *like*'s behavior to adverbial intensifiers such as *even, only, also,* and *just.* The analysis of *like* and intensifiers provides consequences for the analysis of English auxiliaries and other issues. Finally, we discuss implications for a theory of sentence processing.

PAUSELESS *LIKE*

Let us examine a typical example of the kind of puzzle that *like* poses to any researcher. Consider (3):

(3) $_\lambda$Why$_\lambda$don't$^1_\lambda$we$_\lambda$call$_\lambda$both$_\lambda$Harriet$_\lambda$and$_\lambda$Suzie$_\lambda$up
    ?*   *   *   *   ?*   *

    $_\lambda$this$_\lambda$afternoon$_\lambda$?
     *   *

The results of inserting one or more *like*s in the various niches between the words of (3) are given by what appears under the lambdas in (3): if nothing is there, we would find grammatical a sentence appearing with *like* in the position of the lambda. On the other hand, if an asterisk or some other index of less than perfect grammaticality is under a lambda, *like* in that place will produce a sentence that is ungrammatical to that extent.

A number of factors can be isolated that predict such arrays of asterisks as appear in (2) and (3). Let us briefly examine some.

First, as Bill Cantrall has pointed out to us (personal communication, 1977), because *like* often means something close to "approximately," it will be semantically odd if it precedes any element about which the speaker must be certain [examples due to Cantrall]:

(4a)   Give 'em hell, (*like) Harry!   (Speakers know to whom they are speaking.)
(4b)   What's (*like) that?   (out when *like* is not a preposition)
(4c)   May I introduce you to (*like) my mother?   (out as a bona fide introduction)

---

[1]When the pronoun receives emphatic stress, however, *like* is permitted. This observation is accounted for in the following discussion by reference to *like*'s association with focus.

Although these examples argue strongly that one component in a description of *like* must be a semantic one, there are equally strong arguments to the effect that phonology must play a role.[2] This appears most clearly in cases involving two synonymous expressions, one of which is longer than the other, such as *submarine* and *sub*, or full names and nicknames.

(5a) They photographed two like submarines.

(5b) ?They photographed two like subs.

(6a) Did they invite like Isadore?

(6b) ?*Did they invite like IZ?

Of course, the short and long expressions also differ in their degree of formality, but *like*'s preference for casual speech would predict, if anything, that (5b) and (6b) would be better than (5a) and (6a), contrary to fact. It seems probable to us that the reason for these contrasts is phonetically determined; i.e., after *like,* an elaborate fundamental frequency gesture must be executed and that with a short closed syllable, there is not enough time to perform this gesture.

The occurrence of *like* is also influenced by overall speaking rate, with greater acceptability at faster rates. Thus, *like* can only appear in sentences spoken at a fairly rapid rate of speech, e.g., (7a), and not in the same sentence read with exaggerated slowness, as in (7b).

(7a) I was (like) very disappointed in you.

(7b) I . . . was . . . (*like) . . . very . . . disappointed . . . in . . . you.

It appears that *like* is often used in fast speech because of the speaker's need to buy processing time.

To demonstrate that a full description of the behavior of *like* will have to be sensitive to both semantic and phonological parameters, we examine cases of

---

[2]Dennis Peacock (personal communication, 1977) has suggested that the preferred position of *like* is at the first +juncture to the left of a stress increase. Such an account would correctly block *like* before the head noun of an NP. In addition, according to Peacock, the juncture account would block *like* from occurring between two words not separated by a +juncture, as in (ib) below, where *want to* is not separated by a +juncture and is reducible to *wanna.*

(ia) He wants like to do it alone. (Peacock's judgments)

(ib) *I want like to do it alone.

In our speech, however, (ia) and (ib) are equally acceptable. Also, the +juncture account fails to predict the acceptability of cases such as the following, where *like* can be inserted at a location where no +juncture exists, as evidenced by the reductions possible when *like* is omitted:

(iia) I got like your message. (*got your→gotcha*)

(iib) Let's aid like your mother. (*aid your* d→j̈ palatalization)

constituent structure ambiguity. Consider (8a), in which the prepositional phrase *to Kennedy* either can be the indirect object of *send*, on which reading (8a) and (8b) are synonymous, or can be an object of the adjective *insulting*, on which reading it is (roughly) synonymous with (8c).

(8a)   The pranksters sent the letters that were insulting to Kennedy.
(8b)   The pranksters sent Kennedy the letters that were insulting.
(8c)   The letters that were insulting to Kennedy were sent by the pranksters.

Note that *like* is often associated with elements that bear emphatic stress, as *Kennedy* would, in (8a), if it were used to answer (9).

(9)   To whom did the pranksters send the letters that were insulting?

What is of interest here is that, although *like* could precede *to Kennedy* in an answer to (9), it could not precede *insulting:* thus, (10a) can answer (9), but (10b) cannot.

(10a)   The pranksters sent the letters that were insulting like to Kénnedy.
(10b)   *The pranksters sent the letters that were like insulting to Kénnedy.

On the other hand, there are contexts in which (10b) could be used; e.g., as an answer to (11).

(11)   What kind of letters did the pranksters send?

In an answer to (11), *insulting to Kennedy* would be a constituent, whereas it would not be one in an answer to (9). This type of syntactic difference is the kind that we, rather arbitrarily, single out as a starting point for our examination of the behavior of *like*.

Pauseless *like* is typically prohibited before certain grammatical categories, including head nouns, tensed auxiliaries, and pronouns, as in (12):

(12a)   *Bob's like bank is closed on Fridays.
(12b)   *We saw a red like helicopter at the state fair.
(12c)   *Ed like is working nights.
(12d)   *It like has been raining for two days.
(12e)   *We gave like her a birthday party.
(12f)   *Did like you have a good round?

However, a moment's reflection serves to indicate that describing constraints in terms of grammatical categories per se is the wrong tree to bark up. Each of the sentences in (12) becomes acceptable when the word following *like* is emphatically stressed, as in (13):

(13a) Bob's like BANK is closed on Fridays.
(13b) We saw a red like HELICOPTER at the state fair.
(13c) Ed like IS working nights.
(13d) It like HAS been raining for two days.
(13e) We gave like HER a birthday party.
(13f) Did like YOU have a good round?

Thus, we seem to be driven to the conclusion in (14):

(14) Pauseless *like* precedes and is associated with focused elements.

By *focus*, we mean new information contained in an utterance that is not assumed by the speaker to be previously shared by both speaker and hearer (following Chomsky, 1971; Jackendoff, 1972). Although it is not always clear exactly which element in a sentence contains focus, it is generally agreed that, in question-answer cases, the focus is associated with that part of the answer that corresponds to the *wh* word of the question, as in (15) through (17).

(15a) *Who* is sending eggs to Marie?
       Focus
(15b) *They* are sending eggs to Marie.
       Focus
(16a) *What* are they sending to Marie?
       Focus
(16b) They are sending *eggs* to Marie.
           Focus
(17a) *Who* are they sending eggs to?
       Focus
(17b) They are sending eggs to *Marie*.
            Focus

As Chomsky (1971) has noted, the focused element need not correspond to a constituent in deep structure. Thus, *like* can be associated with the focused phrase "certain to lose" in the following sentence in reply to the question "Is John certain to win?"

(18) No, John is like certain to lose.

In this case, the approximate deep structure is:

(19) [$_s$John win]$_s$ is certain. = Chomsky's [57]

In the *a* sentences of (15) through (17), it is clear that the *wh*-words can be preceded by *like*:

(20a)   Like who is sending eggs to Marie?
(20b)   Like what are they sending to Marie?
(20c)   Like who are they sending eggs to?

The claim made by (14) is that in the *b* sentences *like* can only modify the focused elements. That it *can* modify these elements can be seen in (21); that it cannot modify other elements can be seen from the ungrammaticality of the sentences in (22), when these are understood as answers to (15a) through (17a).

(21a)   Like THEY are sending eggs to Marie.
(21b)   They are sending like EGGS to Marie.
(21c)   They are sending eggs to like MARIE.
(22a)   %THEY are like sending eggs to Marie.
(22b)   *THEY are sending like eggs to Marie.
(22c)   *THEY are sending eggs like to Marie.
(22d)   *THEY are sending eggs to like Marie.

We have prefixed (22a) with the percentage sign to indicate our belief that there is a good deal of variation in judgments of acceptability for this type of sentence. Whereas (22a) is dubious for us, there are speakers who accept it. In addition, there are some sentences that do not differ from (22a) in any significant respect, as far as we can see, in which a *like* following the focused element is acceptable for us. One such example is (23b).

(23a)   What sort of thing might appear, if we say this spell?
(23b)   A DEMON might like appear.

As far as we know, pauseless *like* can follow the focused element in this specific context only: The focus is on the subject noun phrase (NP), and *like* follows the tensed auxiliary. When *like* is further away from the subject, as in (22b) through (22d), we know of no speakers who accept the sentences.

Let us now turn to a consideration of the positions in which *like* can appear in sentences such as (16) and (17), where the focused NP is not a subject. The relevant facts appear in (24) and (25), respectively.

(24a)   Like they are sending EGGS to Marie.
(24b)   *They like are sending EGGS to Marie.
(24c)   They are like sending EGGS to Marie.
(24d)   They are sending like EGGS to Marie.
(24e)   *They are sending EGGS like to Marie.

(24f)   *They are sending EGGS to like Marie.
(24g)   *They are sending EGGS to Marie like.
(25a)   Like they are sending eggs to MARIE.
(25b)   *They like are sending eggs to MARIE.
(25c)   They are like sending eggs to MARIE.
(25d)   *They are sending like eggs to MARIE.
(25e)   They are sending eggs like to MARIE.
(25f)   They are sending eggs to like MARIE.
(25g)   *They are sending eggs to MARIE like.

Initially, this distribution of asterisks is puzzling, but we believe the basic principles are fairly simple. First, the ungrammaticality of (24e), (24f), (24g), and (25g) is due to the subpart of principle (14) which states that *like* must precede the focus. We formulate this law as in (26).

(26)   *"Like" First* (LF)
Pauseless *like* must precede the element it modifies (except that for some speakers, *like* may follow a tensed auxiliary, yet be modifying a focused subject).

However, if *like* could appear anywhere to the left of the focused element, the sentences (24b), (25b), and (25d) would all be well formed. We believe that the reason for their ill-formation is a stronger law, given in (27).

(27)   *The "Like" as a Left-Bracket Condition* (LLBC)
Pauseless *like* must open a constituent that dominates the focused element.

Condition (27) will explain the ungrammaticality of (24b) and (25b), under the assumption that sentences with auxiliaries are ternary branching, as suggested in (28), which is presented in Fig. 11.1.

It is immaterial to our analysis whether there is a node auxiliary (Aux) that is distinct from verb (V), whether there is a node verb phrase (VP) or not. All that is required for the LLBC to explain why *like* can follow but not precede *are* is a structure that assigns constituency to the string of words from *sending* to *MARIE* and does not assign such status to the string of words from *are* to *MARIE*. Because this last node, NP_3, is the focused element (we have circled it for dramatic effect), the LLBC will allow *like* to open NP_3 itself, or S_2 or S_1. Because V_1 is not one of these, *like* cannot precede it, cf. *(24b) and *(25b), and the same is true of NP_2, which explains the badness of *(25d).

A fairly clear argument for the correctness of Condition (27) is provided by the structures of (29a) and (29b):

(29a)   red and white and blue
(29b)   red, white, and blue.

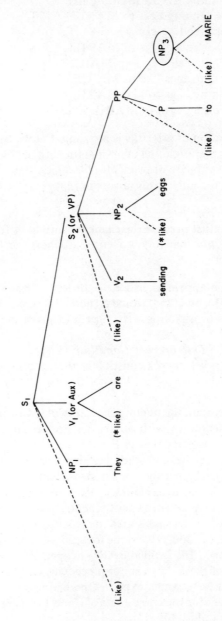

FIG. 11.1. Example (28)

We assume that (29a) can be assigned the coordinate, ternary-branching structure shown in (30), which is demonstrated in Fig. 11.2, as well as the two binary-branching structures shown in (31), presented in Figs. 11.3 and 11.4. This claim of a three-way structural ambiguity for (29a) is uncontroversial, as far as we know, as is the claim, embodied in (32), that only the first of these structures, (30), can lose its first *and* by the operation of *Conjunction Deletion*.

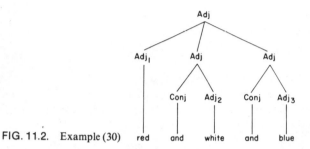

FIG. 11.2. Example (30)

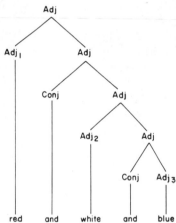

FIG. 11.3. Example (31a)

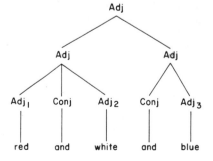

FIG. 11.4. Example (31b)

(32)   *Conjunction Deletion*
When *n* elements of a coordinate structure, $n \geq 3$, are separated by
$n - 1$ occurrences of coordinating conjunctions, such as *and* or *or*,
the first $n - 2$ of these may be deleted and replaced by a (sometimes
optional?) "comma intonation."

Supposing, now, we focus on *blue* in (29), by forming the echo questions
shown in (33).

(33a)   red and white and WHAT?
(33b)   red white and WHAT?

We assume that although the first of these is still three-ways structurally
ambiguous, the second has only the coordinate structure corresponding to
that in (30). Under this assumption, the differential behavior of *like* in (33) can
be explained: cf. (34).

(34a)   (like) red and (like) white and (like) WHAT?
(34b)   (like) red, (*like) white and (like) WHAT?

The LLBC will only allow a *like* before *white* if *white and WHAT* is a
constituent, as is the case in a structure such as (31a). However, in order for
Conjunction Deletion to be able to remove the first *and* of (33), its structure
must have been like (30), and in this structure, a *like* before *white* could not
open a constituent that dominates *WHAT*. Thus, it appears that the LLBC
properly characterizes a major constraint on *like*'s occurrence.

PAUSE-BOUNDED *LIKE*

In summary, pauseless *like* precedes the focused element and opens the
constituent containing this element. Let us turn now to *like* as it occurs with
an accompanying pause. Recall that in sentences (24) and (25), the focused
elements could be immediately preceded, but not followed, by pauseless *like*.
In sentence (35), however, we see that the same focused elements can be
followed, but not preceded, by pause-bounded *like*:

(35a)   THEY, like, are sending eggs to Marie.
(35b)   They are sending EGGS, like, to Marie.
(35c)   They are sending eggs to MARIE, like.

In general, whenever pauseless *like* can immediately precede the focused
element, we can find a synonymous grammatical sentence in which pause-

bounded *like* immediately follows the focused element. To account for this highly systematic distribution, we propose the following transformational rule:

(36) *"Like" Hopping*

	X	*like*	A	Y	
Structural					OPTIONAL
Description	1	2	3	4	$\Longrightarrow$
Structural					
Change	1	0	3+, +2+, 4		

Condition: A is a constituent that contains the focused element (as determined by the LLBC)

For a clear demonstration that hopped *like* must follow the focused element, reconsider sentence (25d), reproduced below:

(25d) They are sending like eggs to MARIE.

Now note that if *like* is hopped around *eggs,* the sentence is still ungrammatical: cf. (37).

(37) *They are sending eggs, like, to MARIE.

Contrast (37) with (25e), which we have repeated for convenience as (38).

(38) They are sending eggs like to MARIE.

Despite the fact that (37) and (38) contain the same sequence of words, we see that they differ in grammaticality because, although the pauseless *like* of (38) can only be associated with a following focused element, the pause-bounded *like* of (37) can only be associated with a preceding focused element, and in (37) *MARIE* follows pause-bounded *like*.

The same point can be made another way: In (39b), we give the sentence that would result if we applied *"Like"-Hopping* to (24d), which we repeat as (39a).

(39a) They are sending like EGGS to Marie.
(39b) They are sending EGGS, like, to Marie.

In *(40), we have repeated the ungrammatical *(24e), which is identical to (39b), except that there are no commas bounding *like*.

(40) *They are sending EGGS like to Marie.

The generalization that emerges from these two pairs of string-identical sentences (actually, all four are identical if we disregard intonational factors) is stated in (41).

(41)   Pauseless *like* must precede the focused element it is associated with; pause-bounded *like* must follow it.

Condition (41) predicts that *like* must be pauseless when it appears in sentence-initial position, whereas it must be bounded by a pause in sentence-final position. The prediction for sentence-final position is confirmed by (42).

(42)   George and I are leaving tomorrow* (,) like.

the prediction for sentence-initial position fails, however, as shown in (43).

(43)   Like (,) George and I are leaving tomorrow.

We suspect that the pause allowable in (43) is a hesitation pause, distinguishable from the pause normally accompanying *like* when it is hopped, although we cannot at present provide any support for such a distinction. We believe that the pause in (43) would be empirically distinguishable by its longer duration, compared with the duration of pauses that accompany hopped *like*.

Thus, it appears that, in general, pause-bounded *like* must directly follow the constituent that contains the focused element: This is the only kind of situation that our hopping rule (36) allows. Thus, (36) will account for the badness of *(44d).

(44a)   Who is working on Greek?
(44b)   Like BOB is working on Greek.
(44c)   BOB, like, is working on Greek. (from [40b], via *"Like" Hopping)*
(44d)   *BOB is, like, working on Greek.

Note, however, that (44a) can be answered by (45).

(45)   BOB is working on Greek, like.

If *like BOB* is a constituent, an NP, in (44b), *"Like" Hopping* will be unable to apply to produce (45). Suppose, however, that *like* is not attached to BOB, but merely opens the sentence, as shown in (46), shown in Fig. 11.5.

The LLBC, (27), would allow *like* to be associated with *BOB*, in this case, yet *"Like" Hopping* would still be unable to produce (45). The only way to generate (45) by (36), while preserving the LLBC, would be to postulate that

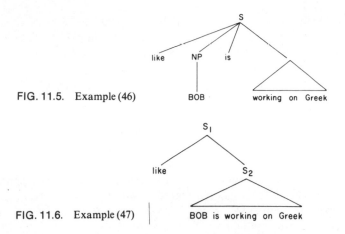

FIG. 11.5. Example (46)

FIG. 11.6. Example (47)

"BOB is working on Greek" can be a constituent in (44b), presumably in some structure such as (47), shown in Fig. 11.6.

The conclusion that an immediately self-dominating structure is necessary to allow *"Like" Hopping* to operate correctly can be supported by simpler cases of hopped *like*. Consider (48b), the hopped version of (48a), which is an alternate answer to (44a).

(48a)   Like THE LINEBACKER is working on Greek.
(48b)   The LINEBACKER, like, is working on Greek.

Again, if the formulation in (36) is correct, the subject of (48a) must have a structure such as that shown in (49b); (49a) would not provide a constituent for *like* to hop over (see Fig. 11.7).

Let us return now to the prediction implicit in our formulation of *"Like" Hopping*: That a pause-bounded *like* must immediately follow a focus-containing constituent. This prediction correctly excluded *(44d), and, similarly, it can explain why (50c) cannot be used as a *like*-hopped version of (50b), in replying to (50a).

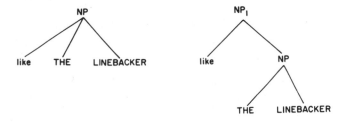

FIG. 11.7.   Example (49a) left and (49b) right

(50a)   How should we get the onions to my sister?
(50b)   Why don't we like MAIL your sister the onions?
(50c)   *Why don't we MAIL your sister, like, the onions?

Similarly, (51c) is not a possible *like*-hopped version of (51b):

(51a)   How can I get my aunt off of the dock?
(51b)   Why don't you like PUSH your aunt off?
(51c)   *Why don't you PUSH your aunt, like, off?

Nonetheless, the prediction seems to be too strong, in some cases. Sentence (50a) can be replied to by (52a), and it seems to us as if (52b), which contains a pause-bounded *like*, can also be used, despite the fact that the focused element, *MAIL*, is not immediately followed by the pause-bounded *like*.

(52a)   Why don't we like MAIL the onions to your sister?
(52b)   Why don't we MAIL the onions, like, to your sister?

We have not found any satisfactory account of the difference between *(44d), *(50c), and *(51c), on the one hand, and the unexpectedly acceptable (52b), on the other.

There is one final factor that influences the operation of *"Like"-Hopping*. Consider the (b) versions of (53) through (56), which are answers to the (a) versions. From all that we have said to date, we should expect *like*-hopped variants to exist. Nonetheless, the predicted (c) versions are all blemished, to a greater or lesser extent.

(53a)   Whose wallet is this?
(53b)   That's like BOB's wallet.
(53c)   *That's BOB's, like, wallet.[3]
(54a)   How heavy was that wallet?
(54b)   It was like UNEXPECTEDLY heavy.
(54c)   *It was UNEXPECTEDLY, like, heavy.
(55a)   How should we position the microphones with respect to the bridge?
(55b)   Why don't you put them like UNDER the bridge.
(55c)   ?*Why don't you put them UNDER, like, the bridge.

---

[3]We have asterisked (53c) only as a *like*-hopped answer to (53a). There are circumstances under which the same string of words as (53c) can be used, with a pause after *like*, but not before, to suggest that the speaker is not sure whether *wallet* is the correct word to use to describe the odd steel and sandstone device that he knows Bob carries around his money in. We might punctuate this sentence as in (i), "That's Bob's like—wallet." We believe this type of "hesitation-*like*," to give it a name, to have different properties from hopped *like*, but we have not studied this question in any detail.

(56a)   How should we get the onions to my sister? [=50a]
(56b)   Why don't you like MAIL the onions to your sister. [=50b]
(56c)   ??Why don't you MAIL, like, the onions to your sister.

Note that the focused elements in these sentences are all on left branches.

It is, thus, almost generally true that *like* may not be hopped over a constituent, if the constituent that is hopped over opens a larger constituent. We have qualified with "almost" because, for reasons we do not understand, *like* can hop over a subject NP, despite the fact that the subject is on a left branch.

Another case where *like* seems not to be able to hop over a left branch is in coordinate structures:

(57a)   Who is similar to you?
(57b)   Like TOM and I are similar.
(57c)   ??TOM, like, and I are similar.

To account for (54) through (57), we introduce the following restriction.

(58)   *The Left-Branch Hopping Ban: "Like"-Hopping* is blocked if term 3 of (36) is a left branch of any node type other than S.

Armed with the observations concerning hopped *like*s, let us return to the LLBC. If we are correct in our claim that *like* can only hop over constituents, then it is most probable that when *like* precedes a constituent, it forms a structure such as that of (59) (see Fig. 11.8), to which *"Like"-Hopping* will always be able to apply, unless A_1 is a left branch. After it has applied, the resulting structure will be as shown in (60) (see Fig. 11.9). In this formulation, we assume arbitrarily that such "nodes" as COMMA (which signal the rules that assign intonation contours to produce high F_o on both sides of *like*) are sisters of *like*.

Now we see that another way of formulating the relationship between *like* and the elements it is associated with is to use the relationship of C-command (Constituent command), introduced and argued for by Reinhart (1976). Node

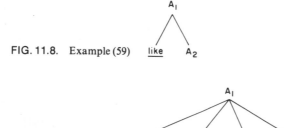

FIG. 11.8.   Example (59)

FIG. 11.9.   Example (60)

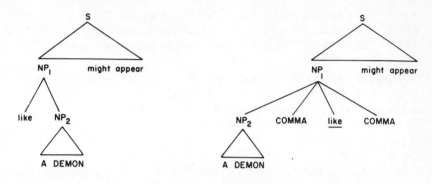

FIG. 11.10.   Example (63a) left and (63b) right

A C-commands node B in tree T if the next node up from A dominates B.[4] Given this notion, we can replace (26) and (27) by (61).

(61)   *The "Like" as a C-commander Condition* (LCC)
Like must be adjacent to a constituent that C-commands the focused element.

To give an example of the LCC, it would allow either (62b) or (62c) to be used as answers to (21a), which is repeated for convenience as (62a).

(62a)   What sort of thing might appear, if we say this spell?
(62b)   Like A DEMON might appear.
(62c)   A DEMON, like, might appear.

If (62b) has the structure shown in (63a), *"Like"-Hopping* will convert it into (63b) (see Fig. 11.10).

Note, however, that the LCC would also allow (64), see Fig. 11.11, to be the structure of (62b).

Like C-commands NP_1 in (64), because S_1 dominates NP_1. And (64) would appear to be necessary, in order for *"Like"-Hopping* to be able to apply to produce (65), which is also a grammatical reply to (62a).

(65)   A DEMON might appear, like.

It may even be possible to argue on intonational grounds for associating both (63a) and (64) with (62b): Note the possibility of pausing after *like* in (66).

---

[4]This relationship is, thus, the inverse of Klima's (1964) relationship *in construction with.*

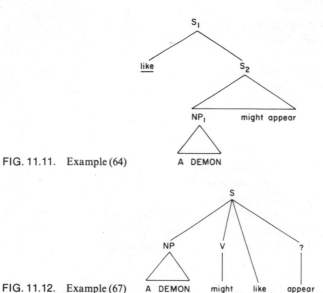

FIG. 11.11.   Example (64)

FIG. 11.12.   Example (67)

(66)   Like, A DEMON might appear.

It may be that arguments can be found that this sentence has only structure (64), and the pauseless structure of (62b) has only (63a). We will leave this question open. For the present, note that if sentence (23b) has the structure of (67), see Fig. 11.12, the LCC would not correctly characterize it as a possible reply to (23a).

We noted earlier in (12a) that *like* cannot immediately precede the head noun of an NP. If we are to retain the LLC and yet prohibit *like* from occurring just before the head noun, we must add an ad hoc restriction prohibiting *like* in this environment.[5] We note that the restriction is particular to NPs, because *like* can occur in other situations between a modifier and its head, as in (68).

---

[5]Another ad hoc restriction on *like*'s occurrence may be needed to prohibit *like* before sentency complements, as in

(i)   *We won't report like that you're sick.
(ii)   ??I'll arrange like for James to sleep upstairs.
(iii) We tried like $\left\{ \begin{array}{l} \text{??to get} \\ \text{getting} \end{array} \right\}$ back early, but we were delayed.
(iv)   I wonder like $\left\{ \begin{array}{l} \text{whether} \\ \text{when} \\ \text{where} \end{array} \right\}$ I'll get another chance.

(68a) His proposal was almost like laughable.

(68b) I nearly like strangled him.

Although we remain puzzled by the within-NP constraint on *like*, it is possible that this restriction may be understood in terms of speaking rate. We noted earlier that the occurrence of *like* is partly dependent on moderate to fast speech rates, and it might reasonably be argued that *like* is prohibited within an NP because NPs represent constituents that speakers typically utter as integral (cases of hesitation represent a clear departure from this generality) rhythmic units. The insertion of *like* within the NP would break up the normal moderate-to-fast rate at which the NP could be uttered, accounting for the otherwise ad hoc restriction.

The prohibiting of *like* within simple NPs has a consequence for the analysis of prepositional phrases. Note that *like* can occur between a preposition and its head, as in (69), as well as before the entire prepositional phrase.

(69) I studied architecture $_\lambda$in $_\lambda$Chicago.

If prepositional phrases are analyzed as PP → P + NP (see Jackendoff, 1973), than *like*'s occurrence between preposition and head requires no modification of the constraint prohibiting *like* within simple NPs. However, if prepositional phrases are viewed as NPs analyzed as NP→P + NP, then the restriction on *like* would need to be modified to prohibit *like* only within NPs that do not dominate NP.

LIKE AND ITS NEIGHBORS

Even

When one examines a wider range of lexical items in English, to try to find parallels to the behavior of *like, even* immediately presents itself. This obstreperous word has been the subject of scrutiny in a number of syntactic and semantic studies, among them Kuroda (1965), Horn (1969), Anderson (1972), Fauconnier (1975), Fraser (1971), and Jackendoff (1972).

Pauseless "Even". Possibly the most salient parallel to *like* is the fact that *even* can only be associated with a focused element. Thus, because the pronoun *it* cannot ever be stressed,[6] it cannot be preceded by *even*:

---

[6]Except, for some reason, when *it* appears as a first conjunct:

(i) The table tipped over, but $\left\{ \begin{array}{l} \text{it and the vase} \\ \text{?the vase and it} \end{array} \right\}$ both survived the fall.

(70)   We could wash even $\left\{\begin{array}{l}\text{*it}\\\text{that}\end{array}\right\}$.

Thus, when we return to the three questions of (15a) through (17a), which are repeated for convenience as (71a), (71b), and (71c), respectively,

(71a)   Who is sending eggs to Marie?
(71b)   What are they sending to Marie?
(71c)   Who are they sending eggs to?

we find that by replacing *like* by *even* in (21), which contains three possible answers to (15), (16), and (17), grammaticality is preserved: cf. (72).

(72a)   Even THEY are sending eggs to Marie.
(72b)   They are sending even EGGS to Marie.
(72c)   They are sending eggs to even MARIE.

In (22), we showed the results of repositioning *like* in (21a): in (73), we see an almost identical pattern of grammaticalities for the reorderings of the *even* in (72a).

(73a)   THEY are even sending eggs to Marie.
(73b)   *THEY are sending even eggs to Marie.
(73c)   *THEY are sending eggs even to Marie.
(73d)   *THEY are sending eggs to even Marie.

The one puzzling disparity is in the contrast between the fully grammatical (73a) and the controversial (22a): Although not all speakers always allow post-auxiliary *like* to be associated with a focused subject, this never seems to be objectionable in the case of *even*.

Proceeding with our comparison of *like* and *even*, we find that just as the unstarred sentences of (24) can serve as answers to question (16a) [= (71b)], so can the unstarred sentences of (74), which exhibit the results of systematically repositioning the *even* in (72b).

(74a)   *Even they are sending EGGS to Marie.
(74b)   They even are sending EGGS to Marie.
(74c)   They are even sending EGGS to Marie.
(74d)   They are sending even EGGS to Marie. [= (72b)]
(74e)   *They are sending EGGS even to Marie.[7]
(74f)   *They are sending EGGS to even Marie.
(74g)   *They are sending EGGS to Marie even.[7]

---

[7]These examples are to be read with pauseless *evens*. The behavior of pause-bounded *even* will be discussed later.

Finally, just as (74) parallels (24), (75) parallels (25): if one repositions *even* in (72c), the following results:

(75a)   *Even they are sending eggs to MARIE.
(75b)   They even are sending eggs to MARIE.
(75c)   They are even sending eggs to MARIE.
(75d)   *They are sending even eggs to MARIE.
(75e)   They are sending eggs even to MARIE.
(75f)   They are sending eggs to even MARIE. [= (72c)]
(75g)   They are sending eggs to MARIE even.[7]

The only important differences between (24) and (74), and (25) and (75), are in the (a) and (b) versions: Although *like* is good before subjects and bad after them, *even* shows the opposite behavior. This complementary behavior can be described well by either of the following transformational rules:

(76)   *"Even" In*
$$X - [even [NP - V Y]] - Z$$
           s   s   s s
       1   2   3   4   5   OBL
       1   0   3 + 2   4   5   ⇒
(77)   *"Like" Out*
$$X - [NP - like - V Y] - Z$$
          s   s
       1   2   3   4   5   OBL
       1 3# [2   0   4] 5   ⇒
              s   5

The question that confronts us here is: Which one of these candidates for transformationhood is the correct rule for English? Should we start out by generating both *like* and *even* sentence-initially, and then move *even*, rightwards, as in (76), or should we instead say that *like* and *even* start out to the right of subjects, with *like* being moved obligatorily to the left, as in (77)?

There is some evidence that favors the adoption of an *"Even" In* analysis, but as it is complex, involving the structure of the auxiliary, we will defer its presentation until the section *The Constituent Structure of the English Auxiliary*.

Having argued for the conclusion that *like* and *even* are identical in distribution, except for the difference produced by one of the rules in (76) and (77), let us now attack this conclusion, for in fact, there are many cases where *like* is possible, but *even* is not. Some are cited in (78) through (86).

(78)   *Before postnominal modifiers, full or reduced:*

(78a) The kids $\left\{\begin{matrix} \text{like} \\ \text{*even} \end{matrix}\right\}$ who were in THE LIVING ROOM were quiet.

(78b) The kids $\left\{\begin{matrix} \text{like} \\ \text{?even} \end{matrix}\right\}$ in THE LIVING ROOM were quiet.

(78c) Somebody who was $\left\{\begin{matrix} \text{like} \\ \text{even} \end{matrix}\right\}$ INSANE must have attacked this lemon meringue pie.

(78d) Somebody $\left\{\begin{matrix} \text{like} \\ \text{*even} \end{matrix}\right\}$ who was INSANE must have attacked this lemon meringue pie.

(78e) Somebody $\left\{\begin{matrix} \text{like} \\ \text{*even} \end{matrix}\right\}$ INSANE must have attacked this lemon meringue pie.[8]

(79)   *One "even" per surface clause, multiple likes:*[9]

(79a) [Only hard-core male supremacists would stoop to reading girlie mags. But there appear to be some sexist pigs even among the most intelligent members of our group. Bob, whose IQ is 120, reads even *Hustler*. And Tony's IQ is higher: 159.]
       *And even Tony reads even *Hustler*.

(79b) Q: What kind of bike was Hobo ridin', man?
       A: Like he was like riding like a huge BSA, like.

(80)   *Before contrastively stressed auxiliary complexes:*

(80a) It $\left\{\begin{matrix} \text{like} \\ \text{%even}^{10} \end{matrix}\right\}$ IS possible that we'll win.

(80b) James Bond $\left\{\begin{matrix} \text{like} \\ \text{*even} \end{matrix}\right\}$ was NOT working for Smersh.

(81)   *Before the focus of a cleft or pseudo-cleft sentence*:

(81a) It was $\left\{\begin{matrix} \text{like} \\ \text{*even} \end{matrix}\right\}$ PETER that I meant.

(81b) (The one) who I meant was $\left\{\begin{matrix} \text{like} \\ \text{*even} \end{matrix}\right\}$ PETER.

(82)   *Before universally quantified NPs:*

---

[8]Note that whereas the ungrammaticality of (78a) and (78d) could be attributed to a failure to undergo the obligatory rule of *"Even" In,* no such account can explain the "?" of (78b) and the * of (78e).

[9]This important observation, which is due to Kuroda (1965), is also discussed insightfully by Anderson (1972).

[10]One of the authors does not have this contrast in his (sloppy) speech.

(82a)   We are fingerprinting $\begin{Bmatrix} \text{like} \\ \text{*even} \end{Bmatrix}$ $\begin{Bmatrix} \text{EACH} \\ \text{EVERY STUDENT} \\ \text{ANY STUDENT(S)} \\ \text{NO STUDENTS} \\ \text{ALL STUDENTS} \end{Bmatrix}$.

(82b) $\begin{Bmatrix} \text{Like} \\ \text{*Even} \end{Bmatrix}$ when were you in East Berlin?

(83)   *After degree modifiers:*

(83a)   Jefferson was $\begin{Bmatrix} \text{like} \\ \text{even} \end{Bmatrix}$ AFRAID of the mouse.

(83b)   Jefferson was $\begin{Bmatrix} \text{very} \\ \text{extremely} \\ \text{somewhat} \\ \text{quite} \\ \text{etc.} \end{Bmatrix}$ $\begin{Bmatrix} \text{like} \\ \text{*even} \end{Bmatrix}$ AFRAID of the mouse.

(84)   *Before (most ? all?) indefinite quantifiers:*

(84a)   The Feds nabbed SOME protesters, and the local cops busted $\begin{Bmatrix} \text{like} \\ \text{*even} \end{Bmatrix}$ $\begin{Bmatrix} \text{SEVERAL} \\ \text{MANY} \end{Bmatrix}$.

(84b)   We don't subscribe to MANY magazines, but we do subscribe to $\begin{Bmatrix} \text{like} \\ \text{*even} \end{Bmatrix}$ SOME.

(85)   *Before sentence adverbs:*

(85a)   It is $\begin{Bmatrix} \text{like} \\ \text{even} \end{Bmatrix}$ POSSIBLE that he'll be back at 5.

(85b) · $\begin{Bmatrix} \text{Like} \\ \text{*Even} \end{Bmatrix}$ POSSIBLY, he'll be back at 5.

(86)   *Before adverbs that do not end in -ly:*

(86a)   Sarah picked me $\begin{Bmatrix} \text{like} \\ \text{*even} \end{Bmatrix}$ RIGHT UP.

(86b)   They have been working $\begin{Bmatrix} \begin{Bmatrix} \text{like} \\ \text{even} \end{Bmatrix} \text{STRENUOUSLY} \\ \begin{Bmatrix} \text{like} \\ \text{?*even} \end{Bmatrix} \text{HARD} \end{Bmatrix}$.

(86c)   He might show up here $\begin{Bmatrix} \begin{Bmatrix} \text{like} \\ \text{even} \end{Bmatrix} \text{FREQUENTLY} \\ \begin{Bmatrix} \text{like} \\ \text{?*even} \end{Bmatrix} \text{OFTEN} \end{Bmatrix}$

With this impressive array of differences (most, as far as we know, unexplained by previous analyses of *even*), one might be tempted to generalize as in (87).

(87)   Wherever *even* is possible, *like* is, but not the converse.

But (87) is also incorrect, as shown by (88).

(88a)   He realized $\left\{\begin{array}{c}?*\text{like}\\\text{even}\end{array}\right\}$ that HE was unpopular.

(88b)   The mail $\left\{\begin{array}{c}*\text{like}\\?\text{even}\end{array}\right\}$ Jimmy CARTER gets is opened.

(88c)   TOM must have gone by now, and JANE may $\left\{\begin{array}{c}*\text{like}\\\text{even}\end{array}\right\}$ have, too.

At present, we must be content to state that, while (87) cannot be maintained, *like* is generally freer than *even*.

Pause-Bounded "Even". In the immediately preceding section, we showed how pauseless *even* exhibits strong parallels to pauseless *like*, with respect to the structural configurations in which an *even* can appear when it is not adjacent to the focused element. Interestingly, the behavior of pause-bounded *even* also shows an exact parallel to the behavior of pause-bounded *like*. This parallel can be accounted for by the account of *even* provided by Anderson (1972), (see later discussion), which has the same empirical consequences as our LCC restriction for *like*.

The sentences in (35) were the *like*-hopped variants of the sentences in (21). The sentences in (72), which are the result of replacing the *like*s in (21) by *even*s, can also undergo hopping, with the sentences in (89) being the result.

(89a)   THEY, even, are sending eggs to Marie.
(89b)   They are sending EGGS, even, to Marie.
(89c)   They are sending eggs to MARIE, even.

Just as we argued that pause-bounded *like* must immediately follow a constituent containing the focused element, so we argue for pause-bounded *even*. Above, in *(44d), this condition was violated for pause-bounded *like*; in *(90d), a corresponding ungrammaticality has arisen.

(90a)   Was EVERYBODY working on Greek?
(90b)   Yeah—even BOB was working on Greek.

(90c)   Yeah—BOB, even, was working on Greek.
(90d)   *Yeah—BOB was, even, working on Greek.

And just as pause-bounded *like* can appear sentence-finally, in (45), so we find a final pause-bounded *even* in (91).

(91)   Yeah—BOB was working on Greek, even.

And just as hopping *like* around left branches of constituents other than S produces varyingly unhappy results (such as *[53c], *[54c], ?*[55c] and ??[56c]), so does hopping *even* in similar sentences: cf. (92c) through (95c) below.

(92a)   Did they weigh EVERYBODY'S wallet?
(92b)   Yeah—they weighed even BOB'S wallet.
(92c)   *Yeah—they weighed BOB'S, even, wallet.
(93a)   Was the wallet VERY heavy?
(93b)   Yeah—it was even ALARMINGLY heavy.
(93c)   *Yeah—it was ALARMINGLY, even, heavy.
(94a)   Should we put microphones EVERYWHERE—ALL AROUND the bridge?
(94b)   Yeah—why don't you put them even UNDER the bridge.
(94c)   ?*Yeah—why don't you put them UNDER, even, the bridge.
(95a)   Should we use ANY MEANS to get the onions to my sister?
(95b)   Yeah—you might even MAIL the onions to your sister.
(95c)   ??Yeah—you might MAIL, even, the onions to your sister.

It, thus, seems fairly clear to us that our rule (36) is stated too narrowly: It must be generalized to apply to *even* as well as to *like*. However, we are not much nearer to understanding *like*-Hopping merely because we can show that one other similar item hops. Indeed, if being associated with the focused element is the only criterion of similarity, then we might expect any element that shares this property with *like* and *even* to hop similarly. Not so. Let us widen our field of view and examine the behavior of some other focus-linked items: *only* and *just*, on the one hand, and *also* and *too* on the other.

"Only" and "Just."   The words *only* and *just* parallel the behavior of *like* and *even* in many ways, as can be seen by comparing (96), used as an answer to (71), with (72).

(96a) $\left\{\begin{array}{l}\text{Only}\\\text{Just}\end{array}\right\}$THEY are sending eggs to Marie.

(96b)   They are sending $\left\{\begin{array}{l}\text{only}\\\text{just}\end{array}\right\}$EGGS to Marie.

(96c)   They are sending eggs to $\left\{ \begin{matrix} \text{only} \\ \text{??just} \end{matrix} \right\}$ MARIE.

And just as we can find *even* to the left of MARIE in (75), so we also find *only* and *just* in the same kinds of environments: cf. (86).

(97a)   * $\left\{ \begin{matrix} \text{Only} \\ \text{Just} \end{matrix} \right\}$ they are sending eggs to MARIE.

(97b)   They $\left\{ \begin{matrix} \text{only} \\ \text{just} \end{matrix} \right\}$ are sending eggs to MARIE.

(97c)   They are $\left\{ \begin{matrix} \text{only} \\ \text{just} \end{matrix} \right\}$ sending eggs to MARIE.

(97d)   *They are sending $\left\{ \begin{matrix} \text{only} \\ \text{just} \end{matrix} \right\}$ eggs to MARIE.

(97e)   They are sending eggs $\left\{ \begin{matrix} \text{only} \\ \text{just} \end{matrix} \right\}$ to MARIE.

However, when we try to hop these words, we find radically different patterns from those we encountered with *like* and *even*. First of all, it appears that there are no contexts whatsoever in which *just* can hop: compare *(97), as answers to (71), with (96).

(98ai)   *THEY (,) just (,) are sending eggs to Marie.
(98aii) *THEY are just sending eggs to Marie.
(98b)   *They are sending EGGS (,) just (,) to Marie.
(98c)   *They are sending eggs to MARIE (,) just.

A further indication that *just* never hops is the fact that it never occurs sentence-finally.

(99)   *THEY are sending eggs to Marie, just.

In general (and for reasons we do not understand) *just* is much more limited in its distribution than *only*, as was already apparent in (96c). A further point of difference is the fact that there are contexts in which a pause-bounded *only* can appear sentence-initially, with roughly the sense of "There's only one thing: X."

(100) $\left\{ \begin{matrix} \text{Only} \\ \text{*Just} \end{matrix} \right\}$, $\left\{ \begin{matrix} \text{he wasn't in his room last night.} \\ \text{be careful where you put the } H_2SO_4. \\ \text{where can we get some Kool-aid to mix with it?} \end{matrix} \right\}$

As is evident from the asterisk in (100), this is another case where *only* but not *just* can appear. The following generalization seems to obtain:

(101) Wherever *just* can appear with the sense of *only* that is described in Horn (1969), *only* can also appear.

An exception to (101) appears in (102), which shows that only *just* can appear before imperatives, although not with the most common meaning of *only* as described in Horn (1969).

(102) $\left\{\begin{array}{l}\text{*Only}\\\text{Just}\end{array}\right\} \left\{\begin{array}{l}\text{get lost}\\\text{be quick about it}\\\text{give me that}\end{array}\right\}$!

Let us turn now to an examination of the hopping behavior of *only*. First of all, the most typical intonation for a post-focus *only* has no pauses, as can be seen in (103), which corresponds to (96).

(103a) $\left\{\begin{array}{cc}2 & 1\\\text{THEY} & \text{ONLY}\\1 & 1\\\text{??THEY,} & \text{ONLY,}\end{array}\right\}$ are sending eggs to Marie.

(103b) They are sending $\left\{\begin{array}{cc}2 & 1\\\text{EGGS} & \text{ONLY}\\1 & 1\\\text{??EGGS,} & \text{ONLY,}\end{array}\right\}$ to Marie.

(103c) They are sending eggs to $\left\{\begin{array}{cc}2 & 1\\\text{MARIE} & \text{ONLY}\\1 & 1\\\text{??MARIE,} & \text{ONLY}\end{array}\right\}$.

That is, the standard hopped *only* is pauseless. This may be connected with the fact that hopping *only* around a left branch always produces solid stars, whereas *like* and *even* hop around some left branches without totally destroying the sentence. Thus, compare the (c) versions of (104) through (107) below with the (c) versions of (92) through (95).

(104a) Did they weigh EVERYBODY'S wallet?
(104b) No, they weighed only BOB'S wallet.
(104c) *No, they weighed BOB'S only wallet.
(105a) Was the wallet VERY heavy?
(105b) No, it was only SOMEWHAT heavy.
(105c) *No, it was SOMEWHAT only heavy.

(106a)   Should we put microphones EVERYWHERE—ALL AROUND the bridge?

(106b)   No—why don't you put them only UNDER the bridge.

(106c)   *No—why don't you put them UNDER only the bridge.

(107a)   Should we use ANY MEANS to get the onions to my sister?

(107b)   No—why don't you only MAIL the onions to your sister.

(107c)   *No—why don't you MAIL only the onions to your sister.

Also and *Too*

Having compared the hopping behavior of *like* and *even* with that of *only* and *just*, let us turn to the focus-bound elements *also* and *too*. When these words are associated with subjects, as in answers to a question such as (108), their syntactic behavior is as shown in (109).[11]

(108)   Were only THE DOBBASES sending eggs to Marie?
                    2   1
(109ai)   No, ALSO THE PILLINGS were sending eggs to Marie.
                      1   2
(109aii)   *No, THE PILLINGS ALSO were sending eggs to Marie.
                    2   1
(109aiii)   No, THE PILLINGS ALSO were sending eggs to Marie.
                    2   1
(109aiv)   No, THE PILLINGS were ALSO sending eggs to Marie.
                    2   1
(109av)   *No, THE PILLINGS were sending ALSO eggs to Marie.
                    2   1
(109avi)   No, THE PILLINGS were sending eggs to Marie ALSO.
(109bi)   **No, TOO THE PILLINGS were sending eggs to Marie.
                      1   2
(109bii)   *No, THE PILLINGS TOO were sending eggs to Marie.
                      1   1
(109biii)   ?No, THE PILLINGS TOO were sending eggs to Marie.
(109biv)   *No, THE PILLINGS were TOO sending eggs to Marie.
(109bv)   **No, THE PILLINGS were sending TOO eggs to Marie.
                    2   1
(109bvi)   No, THE PILLINGS were sending eggs to Marie TOO.

The salient points about *also* and *too* include the following.

---

[11]We mark the location of primary and secondary sentence stress in some of the following examples with a superscripted "1" and "2" above the appropriate syllables. This notation is, thus, in the spirit of the notation of Chomsky and Halle (1968).

(110a)   In contrast with *like, even, just* and *also, too* may never precede the focused element. [cf. *(109bi)]

(110b)   In contrast with *like* and *even*, post-focus *only* and post-focus *also* and *too* must carry main sentence stress. [cf. the contrasts in *(109aii) and (109aiii) and *(109bii) and (109biii).]

(110c)   *Also* can appear adjacent to the focused element, in post-tensed-auxiliary position or sentence-finally. *Too* can appear only immediately after the focused element, or sentence-finally.

When we extend our investigation to answers to questions such as (111) and (112), in which the focused constituents are direct and indirect objects, respectively, it appears that the generalizations stated in (110) stand. Sentence (113) answers (111), and (114) answers (112).

(111)   Were they sending only EGGS to Marie?

(112)   Were they sending eggs to only MARIE?

            2   1

(113ai)   ?No, ALSO they were sending BANANAS to Marie.

            2   1

(113aii)   No, they ALSO were sending BANANAS to Marie.

              2   1

(113aiii)   No, they were ALSO sending BANANAS to Marie.

                  2   1

(113aiv)   ?No, they were sending ALSO BANANAS to Marie.

                   1   2

(113av)   *No, they were sending BANANAS ALSO to Marie.

                 2   1

(113avi)   ?No, they were sending BANANAS ALSO to Marie.

                 2   1

(113avii)   No, they were sending BANANAS to Marie ALSO.

(113bi)   **No, TOO they were sending BANANAS to Marie.

(113bii)   **No, they TOO were sending BANANAS to Marie.

(113biii)   **No, they were sending TOO BANANAS to Marie.

                  2   1

(113biv)   No, they were sending BANANAS TOO to Marie.

                  2   1

(113bv)   No, they were sending BANANAS to Marie TOO.

            2   1

(114ai)   ?No, ALSO they were sending eggs to MARIE.

            2   1

(114aii)   No, they ALSO were sending eggs to MARIE.

              2   1

(114aiii)   No, they were ALSO sending eggs to MARIE.

$$\overset{2}{}\qquad\qquad\overset{1}{}$$

(114aiv) *No, they were sending ALSO eggs to MARIE.

$$\overset{2}{}\qquad\qquad\overset{1}{}$$

(114av) No, they were sending eggs ALSO to MARIE.

$$\overset{2}{}\qquad\qquad\overset{1}{}$$

(114avi) ??No, they were sending eggs to ALSO MARIE.

$$\overset{1}{}\quad\overset{2}{}$$

(114avii) *No, they were sending eggs to MARIE ALSO.

$$\overset{2}{}\quad\overset{1}{}$$

(114aviii) No, they were sending eggs to MARIE ALSO.

(114bi) **No, TOO they were sending eggs to MARIE.

(114bii) **No, they TOO were sending eggs to MARIE.

(114biii) **No, they were TOO sending eggs to MARIE.

(114biv) **No, they were sending TOO eggs to MARIE.

(114bv) **No, they were sending eggs TOO to Marie.

(114bvi) **No, they were sending eggs to TOO Marie.

$$\overset{1}{}\quad\overset{2}{}$$

(114bvii) *No, they were sending eggs to MARIE TOO.

$$\overset{2}{}\quad\overset{1}{}$$

(114bviii) No, they were sending eggs to MARIE TOO.

A few additional comments about (109), (113), and (114) are in order here. First, the ungrammaticality of *(109av), **(109bv), and *(114aiv) shows that *also* (and *too*) are similar to *like* and *even* in obeying the LCC. Furthermore, the ungrammaticality of *(97d) shows that *only* and *just* are also subject to this constraint. As far as we know, therefore, the generalization stated in (115) can be maintained.

(115) All focus-linked elements obey the LCC.

Second, we note from examples such as ?(113ai) and ?(114ai) that, in contrast with *only* and *just*, sentence-initial *also* is not totally excluded. Because *only* and *just* must, like *even*, be ruled out in sentence-initial position [cf. *(97a)], we will have to generalize our rule of *"Even" In* so that *only* and *just* will also be moved obligatorily to post-subject position, and a condition will need to be added that specifies that such a repositioning rightwards is preferable for *also*, although not mandatory.[12]

Third, for reasons that remain opaque to us, of all the focus-linked elements that can ever precede the focus, *also* most strongly resists being inserted between a preposition and an NP [cf. ??(114avi) and (116)].

---

[12]Alternatively, we can generalize *"Like" Out* so that it applies obligatorily to *like* and half-heartedly to *also*. Both solutions look messy. We find it hard to invest much in either.

$$(116) \quad \text{I was talking to} \left\{ \begin{array}{l} \text{like} \\ \text{even} \\ \text{only} \\ \text{?just} \\ \text{?*also} \end{array} \right\} \text{MORGAN about that.}$$

Let us return now to the issue of the stress on *also*. Examining the (a) versions of (109), (113), and (114), a clear pattern emerges:

(117)   Regardless of the relative order of *also* and the focused element, the rightmost of these two bears the primary sentence stress, with the leftmost bearing the second highest stress in the sentence.

This is a particularly interesting generalization, for it is unstatable as a phonological rule in any framework that we know of. Therefore, rather than trying to construct a totally new type of phonological rule, we tentatively propose a syntactic solution.

We assume that the stress dependence of *also* and the focused element is an indication that they once were members of the same phrase. If they are reordered by a generalized rule of *Intensifier-Hopping*, which is ordered before the Nuclear Stress Rule,[13] then the rightmost element will receive the highest stress.

So far, we have succeeded only in accounting for the stress differences of (109ai)/(109aiii), ?(113aiv)/(113avi), and ??(114avi)/(114aviii). But what about the fact that in (113ai), *also* has [2 Stress], while it bears [1 Stress] in (113avii)? These sentences are synonymous, as indeed all sentences in (113) are. What we propose to do is to account for this synonymy by deriving the sentences in (113) in which *also* precedes *bananas* from (113aiv), and (113avii), in which it follows *bananas*, from (113avi), by the following rule:

(118)   *"Also" Climb*

$$W - [_B X - [\,also - A\,] - Y_B] - Z$$

$$1 \quad\quad 2 \quad\quad 3 \quad\quad 4 \quad\quad 5 \quad\quad 6 \quad\quad \text{OPT}$$
$$\Rightarrow$$
$$1\ 3\# \ [_B 2 \quad\quad 0 \quad\quad 4 \quad\quad 5_B] \quad 6$$

This rule will Chomsky-adjoin an *also* which precedes its focus to the left of any higher node.[14] The rule must follow the two rules of *Intensifier-Hopping* and the *Nuclear Stress Rule*, as shown in (119).

---

[13]For a description of this process, see Chomsky and Halle (1968). The suggestion that this rule should precede certain syntactic operations appeared first in Bresnan (1971).

[14]Obviously, this is only half of the required rule, which must also raise *also*s that follow their focus and adjoin them to the *right* of any higher node. That is, rule (102) should be rewritten as a mirror-image rule (cf. Langacker [1969] for discussion).

(119) *Rule ordering*
    A. *Intensifier-Hopping* (OPT)
    B. *Nuclear Stress Rule*
    C. *"Also" Climb* (OPT)

Given this system, (113aiii) and (113avii) will be derived as in (120) and (121), respectively.[15]

                                    1   1

(120a) No, they were [sending ALSO BANANAS to Marie]   *NSR*
                                   2   1   ⇒

(120b) No, they were [sending ALSO BANANAS to Marie]   *"Also"*
                                                   Climb
                          2   1   ⇒

(120c) No, they were [ALSO [sending BANANAS to Marie]]
                                  1   1   *Intensifier-*

(121a) No, [they were sending ALSO BANANAS to Marie] *Hopping*
        S   S   ⇒
                                1   1   *NSR*

(121b) No, [they were sending BANANAS ALSO to Marie]   ⇒
                                    2   1   *"Also"*

(121c) No, [they were sending BANANAS ALSO to Marie] *Climb*
                                                  1   ⇒

(121d) No, [[they were sending BANANAS to Marie] ALSO]

The other derivations in (109), (113) and (114) will proceed similarly.

We return to the rules in (119) below in subsection *Conclusions on "Like" and Intensifiers*, where we propose extending them to handle much of the distribution of intensifiers. First, however, let us examine the behavior of *also* when it is hopped around left branches.

Sentences (122) through (126) show that hopping *also* around left branches results in sentences that are totally unacceptable, as was the case with *only*.

    (122a) Did they weigh only ZEKE'S wallet?
    (122b) No, they weighed also BOB'S wallet.
    (122c) *No, they weighed BOB'S also wallet.
    (123a) Do you mug only EXPENSIVELY dressed men?
    (123b) No, I mug also POORLY dressed men.
    (123c) *No, I mug POORLY also dressed men.
    (124a) Should we put microphones only ON the bridge?

---

[15]We have drawn in the brackets surrounding the constituent to which *also* attaches, although we have not labeled them, for the issue as to whether they should be called Ss or VPs is irrelevant here.

(124b)   No—why don't you put them also UNDER the bridge.
(124c)   *No—why don't you put them UNDER also the bridge.
(125a)   Should we only CARRY the onions to my sister?
(125b)   No, why don't you also MAIL the onions to your sister.

(125c)   ?*No, why don't you $\begin{Bmatrix} \overset{2}{\text{MAIL}} \ \overset{1}{\text{ALSO}} \\ \underset{}{\text{MAIL}} \ \text{ALSO} \\ \overset{1}{\text{MAIL}} \ \overset{2}{\text{ALSO}} \end{Bmatrix}$ the onions to your sister.

Summary of rules for intensifiers.   Let us summarize the discussion of the section *"Like" and its Neighbors* up to this point. We have found the following similarities in the behavior of intensifiers, i.e., of focus-linked items:

(126a)   All obey the LCC.
(126b)   All (except *just*) can appear to the right of the focused element (*too* can only appear there).
(126c)   All obey the LBHB.

We noted in (117) a generalization about the interaction of *also* and the location of primary sentence stress, suggesting that a syntactic treatment, involving the ordering of the Nuclear Stress Rule before a syntactic rule of *"Also" Climb*, was preferable to the creation of a new type of phonological rule. This leaves us in a rather redundant situation with respect to the LCC for the following reason. The rule of *"Also" Climb* makes it unnecessary to state the LCC for *also*, for the output of any sentence with a climbed *also* will necessarily obey the LCC. Thus, for *also*, the LCC can be dispensed with, in favor of the rule of *"Also" Climb*.

The trading relationship between the LCC and *"Also" Climb* in the case of *also* immediately suggests that the same type of relationship may obtain in the case of the other intensifiers, given their widespread similarities in distribution. That is, for the other intensifiers, we are naturally led to look to see if there is any independent reason to choose the LCC over a solution that would involve climbing intensifiers other than *also*.

As far as we have been able to ascertain, no such evidence exists. And because the stress facts noted in (117) above can be accounted for, given a climbing solution, but cannot be accounted for merely by the LCC, we conclude that the LCC can be dispensed with entirely, in favor of the following rule, which should also be construed as a mirror-image rule, as discussed in Footnote 14.

(127)   *Intensifier Climb*

$$W - [_B X - [_A \text{ Intensifier} - \acute{A}_A] Y -] Z$$

1		2	3	4	5	6	OPT
1	3# $[_B$	2	0	4	$5_B]$	6	$\Rightarrow$

Condition: If 3 + 4 is the NP object of a preposition, the rule is obligatory if 3 = *also*, and is preferred if 3 = *just*. [Cf. (116)]

The variables in this rule deserve much more study than we have been able to carry out. Such questions as the following arise:

(128a)   Is *Intensifier Climb* a bounded rule? That is, can intensifiers climb out of clauses?

(128b)   Is *Intensifier Climb* subject to constraints on movement rules, such as those proposed by Ross (1967)?

(128c)   Are there asymmetries in the climbing behavior of intensifiers that are on left branches vis-à-vis those that are on right branches?

Our answer to the first question is a blunt "yes and no." Intensifiers seem to be able to climb out of all (?) nonfinite complements and out of some tensed clauses: the (b) and (c) versions of (129) through (131) are synonymous answers to the (a) versions:

(129a)   Did he $\left\{ \begin{array}{l} \text{want} \\ \text{begin} \\ \text{hope} \\ \text{etc.} \end{array} \right\}$ to translate anything else into French?

(129b)   Yeah, he $\left\{ \begin{array}{l} \text{wanted} \\ \text{began} \\ \text{hoped} \\ \text{etc.} \end{array} \right\}$ to translate even YOUR LETTERS into French.

(129c)   Yeah, he even $\left\{ \begin{array}{l} \text{wanted} \\ \text{began} \\ \text{hoped} \\ \text{etc.} \end{array} \right\}$ to translate YOUR LETTERS into French.

(130a)   Did they $\left\{ \begin{array}{l} \text{avoid} \\ \text{stop} \\ \text{plan on} \\ \text{etc.} \end{array} \right\}$ kicking only MORTON?

(130b)   No, they $\left\{ \begin{array}{l} \text{avoided} \\ \text{stopped} \\ \text{planned on} \\ \text{etc.} \end{array} \right\}$ kicking also YOUR UNCLE.

(130c)   No, they also $\left\{ \begin{array}{l} \text{avoided} \\ \text{stopped} \\ \text{planned on} \\ \text{etc.} \end{array} \right\}$ kicking YOUR UNCLE.

(131a)   Do the bosses $\begin{Bmatrix} \text{think} \\ \text{believe} \\ \text{hope} \\ \text{say} \end{Bmatrix}$ that only ZACK was at the rally?

(131b)   No, they $\begin{Bmatrix} \text{think} \\ \text{believe} \\ \text{hope} \\ \text{say} \end{Bmatrix}$ that $\begin{Bmatrix} \text{?also OSCAR} \\ \text{OSCAR also} \end{Bmatrix}$ was at the rally.

(131c)   No, they also $\begin{Bmatrix} \text{think} \\ \text{believe} \\ \text{hope} \\ \text{say} \end{Bmatrix}$ that OSCAR was at the rally.

However, it does not seem possible to climb intensifiers out of factive clauses, with strong factives like *surprised* blocking such a putative reordering more clearly than do weak factives like *know*. Thus, whereas (132a) and (132b) are *probably* impossible to read as synonymous, (133a) and (133b) seem to us to *definitely* not be synonymous.

(132a)   Do the police know that Dr. Hunger also IRRADIATES us?
(132b)   Do the police also know that Dr. Hunger IRRADIATES US?
        ?
         [$\neq$ (132a)]
(133a)   Are the police surprised that Dr. Hunger also IRRADIATES us?
(133b)   Are the police also surprised that Dr. Hunger IRRADIATES us? [$\neq$ (112a)]

Thus, it appears to us that *Intensifier Climb* will have to be made subject to the type of nondiscrete constraints on variables that are discussed in Ross (1975), where a number of other processes are cited that behave differentially with respect to complements of verbs such as *think* as opposed to complements of verbs such as *surprise*.

The answer to the second question in (123) appears to us to be extremely unclear at present, despite the fact that Anderson (1972) cited such Complex-NP-constraint violating cases as (134) [= Anderson's (9a)], (135) [= Anderson's (17a)], and (135) [= Anderson's (10)]

(134)   You can do a lot of things with Skrunkies: I even know a guy who SMOKES them.
(135)   I even included a problem that FRESHMEN could solve.
(136a) John even has the idea that HE is tall for a Watusi.
(136b) John even has the idea that he is tall for a WATUSI.

and such cases as (137) [= Anderson's (12)], for which *even* would have to climb out of a sentential subject.

(137a) Jones' wife considers him absolutely honest; I imagine his even THINKING such a thing would amaze her.

(137b) Jones' wife considers him completely honest; I even imagine his THINKING such a thing would amaze her.

Although we agree in general with Anderson's (1972) grammaticality judgments here (although we find (137b) more dubious than he does), we note that *have the idea that* does not make very strong islands: whereas questioning out of a following S is difficult (cf. (138a)), relativizing often seems acceptable [cf. (138)]:

(138a) ?What does John have the idea that he should build?

(138b) The problems that John has the the idea that he can solve are all exceedingly trivial anyway.

Thus, (136) does not provide solid evidence that the Complex NP Constraint should be viewed as having been violated. Nonetheless, *even* cannot climb out of a sentential subject, in (139b), (which corresponds to (139a), except that the *even* has made a similar climb), as the Sentential Subject Constraint would predict.

(139a) It's likely that there will be pictures of lots of planets; I'd say that there being a picture of even PLUTO is possible.

(139b) ?*It's likely that there will be pictures of lots of planets; I'd even say that there being a picture of PLUTO is possible.

Anderson's (1972) strongest cases, then, are (134) and (135). We agree that, if *even* leaves the relative clauses in these cases, via *Intensifier Climb*, it will be violating the Complex NP Constraint. Our feeling, however, is that (134) and (135) may be atypical, for note that the (b) versions of sentences below should all be variants of the corresponding (a) versions, if the Complex NP Constraint is never involved in the relationship between *even* and its focus.

(140a) He ridiculed your hypothesis that we could even DETECT this radiation.

(140b) He even ridiculed your hypothesis that we could DETECT this radiation. [a ≠ b]

(141a) This compound dissolved the plastic that even THE AQUA REGIS left unblemished.

(141b) This compound even dissolved the plastic that THE AQUA
?
REGIS left unblemished [a ≠ b].

Thus, we have not been able to ascertain whether *even* can or cannot generally climb out of complex NPs. It does, however, seem to obey the Coordinate Structure Constraint wholeheartedly:

(142a)   I'll invite both Beth and Marge, and even TOMMY, to the party.
(142b)   *I'll even invite both Beth and Marge, and TOMMY, to the party.

In sum, then, the rule of *Intensifier Climb* presents a mixed picture with respect to constraints on variables. Our present belief is that the theory advanced by Ross (1967), which sought, basically, to develop only constraints that all rules of all languages would abide by, is too inflexible. Rather, there appear to be stronger and weaker constraints and stronger and weaker rules. The Complex NP Constraint is a weaker constraint than the Coordinate Structure Constraint; and the rule of *Question Formation* is a weaker rule than the rule of *Relative Clause Formation* (which accounts for the contrast in (117) above).[16] The rule of *Intensifier Climb* appears to be even stronger than the rule of *Relative Clause Formation*, but not so strong as to be absolutely constraintless, as Anderson (1972) seems to suggest.

Turning briefly to the third question in (128), we can see immediately that, although it is possible for intensifiers to move leftwards across nonfinite clause boundaries [cf. (129c) and (130c), and maybe (137b)], they appear not to be able to move across right-clause boundaries: Thus, (143a) cannot become (143b).

(143a)   Your even SUGGESTING it to Doris was stupid.
(143b)   Your SUGGESTING it to Doris was stupid, even.

Thus, although it is not clear what sort of constraints should be imposed on the variable in Term 2 of rule (127), it does seem that this rule obeys the Right Roof Constraint that was proposed by Ross (1967): An intensifier that climbs from a right branch must command any nodes it is to climb over.

THE CONSTITUENT STRUCTURE OF
THE ENGLISH AUXILIARY

"Even" In vs. *"Like" Out*

Let us now examine the consequences of our rule of *Intensifier Climb* for the analysis of auxiliary verbs. Consider (144a), a question that has a maximally complex auxiliary, and a possible answer, (144b):

---

[16]For some discussion of a nondiscrete treatment of constraints on variables, see Ross (1975).

(144a)   Could Fay Wray have been being gripped by only RODAN?
(144b)   No, she could have been being gripped by even KONG.

If we now try to climb *even* in (144b), we find that it can attach to the prepositional phrase *by KONG*, and also that it can appear to the left of *gripped*, or to the left of any of the preceding auxiliaries,

(145a)   She even could have been being gripped by KONG.
(145b)   She could even have been being gripped by KONG.
(145c)   She could have even been being gripped by KONG.
(145d)   She could have been even being gripped by KONG.
(145e)   She could have been being even gripped by KONG.
(145f)   She could have been being gripped even by KONG.

If the rule of *Intensifier Climb* is correct, these facts require that auxiliaries be assigned a right-branching structure such as that shown in (146), Fig. 11.13.

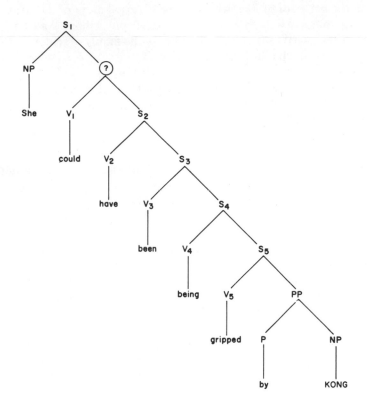

FIG. 11.13.   Example (146)

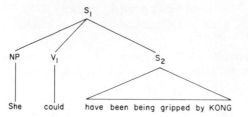

FIG. 11.14.   Example (147)

We need not be overly concerned with certain details yet. In particular, the *Intensifier Climb* analysis is compatible with a structure with the nest of right-branching nodes all being sentences, as in (146), or with them all being VPs.[17]

We have designated the right sister of the subject NP in (146) with the cryptic emblem "?", because we wish to argue that, in fact, there should be no node dominating the sub-string starting with *could* and ending with *KONG*. Rather, we wish to maintain a ternary-branching analysis of S_1, as in (147), Fig. 11.14.

The reason that we find this preferable to the binary analysis of (146) has to do with the behavior of *like*, which seems to reveal more of the structure of auxiliaries than does the behavior of the other intensifiers. And we find, as possible answers to (148a), a large number of the family of sentences that are abbreviated by the parentheses in (148b):

(148a)   Who could Fay Wray have been being gripped by?
(148b)   (Like) she (*like) could (like) have (like) been (like) being (like) gripped (like) by (like) KONG.

The fact that *like* is only impossible before *could* in (148b) would follow from our formulation of *Intensifier Climb*, if (148b) had the structure shown in (149), Fig. 11.15.

We do not wish to claim that all of these *like*s must have originated from a copying process that would proliferate a single *like* that is adjacent to *KONG* in remote structure. This could be the case here, but is arguably not the case in other multiple-*like* sentences. For the present discussion, let us restrict our attention to the variants of (148b) that have only one *like,* which we will assume to have been moved, by *Intensifier Climb,* from being under its source node, the circled NP′ of (149), to being Chomsky-adjoined to any of the six higher nodes, as shown in (149).

Note that if there were some node dominating the whole string from *could* to *KONG,* namely, the node "?" of (124), we would predict that *like* could also attach to "?", which would yield the asterisked variant of (148b).

_____

[17]For previous treatments of auxiliaries in which they are analyzed as right-branching constructions, see Ross (1969) and Keyser and Postal (1976).

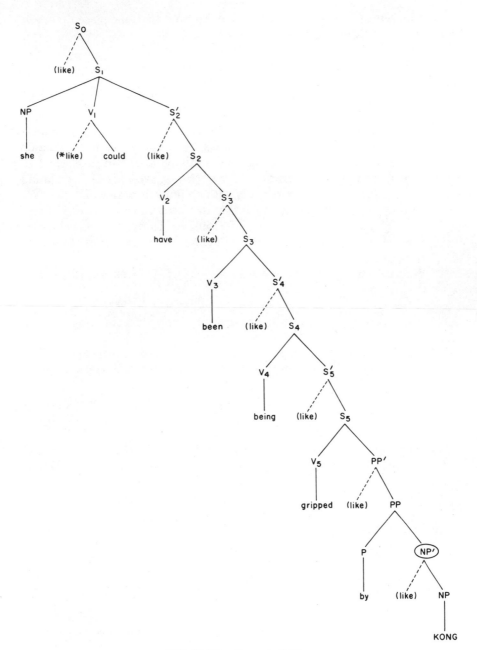

FIG. 11.15.   Example (149)

Let us return to (144b) for a moment, to note that one place that *even* cannot appear is to left of the whole sentence:

(150)   *Even she could have been being gripped by KONG.

Thus, although *like* can precede subjects, but not follow them, *even* (and the other intensifiers) have the opposite restriction.

We noted earlier in the subsection *Pauseless "Even"* that this situation could be accounted for in either of two ways: by postulating that the situation with *even* was basic, positioning *like* initially after the subject, and obligatorily moving it leftwards (by *"Like" Out*) analysis, or by postulating that the situation with *like* was basic, with an obligatory rule of *"Even" In*.

The following puzzle suggests to us that this latter course is correct; What, in a *"like" Out* analysis, would rule out *(150)? Evidently, it would have to be some condition on Intensifier Climb, something to the effect of (151).

(151)   Condition: if $2 + 3 + 4 + 5 = S$, and if $3 = even, only, just$ and (weakly) *also*, the rule blocks.

That is, *even, only, just,* etc. would have to be prevented from being attached to S.

There are, however, sentences that seem to indicate clearly that (151) is too strong and that *even* must be able to be attached to S. Consider (152).

(152)   It is possible even that she could have been being gripped by KONG.

Disregarding the question at issue at present, namely, what the structure of the complement of (152) is, the structure of the matrix clause is generally agreed to be representable as in (153a) or (153b), Fig. 11.16 (where the issue as to whether S_2 is part of the VP of S_1 is not germane to the present discussion). That is, it is agreed that what follows *possible* in (152) is a sentence, but not an NP.[18]

But, if (152) shows that *even* can indeed be *Intensifier Climb*ed to be Chomsky-adjoined to S, then what explains the difference between (152) and the ungrammatical *(150)? Our hypothesis is that the complementizer is responsible. Note that if *that* is deleted in (152), as is generally permitted with

----

[18]The only theory of complementation with which we are familiar that would claim that the *that*-clause of (152) retains its NP status is the theory of relational grammar that is presently under development by Perlmutter and Postal (1978). In this theory, it would be claimed that the *that*-clause is an NP, a chômeur, that has been produced by the insertion of the dummy *it* in subject position. Until we are more familiar with the details of this theory, in particular with the evidence for the claim that extraposed clauses must retain their NP status, we continue in the familiar assumption that extraposed clauses are only dominated by S.

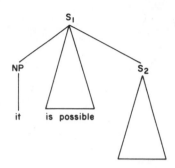

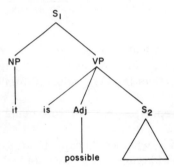

FIG. 11.16. Example (153a) top
and (153b) bottom

adjectives such as *possible, afraid, sure, lucky, likely,* etc. [see (154)], the result
is ungrammatical [cf. *(155a)], unless *even* is moved after the subject, as in
(155b).

(154) $\begin{cases} \text{It's possible} \\ \text{I'm afraid} \\ \text{We're sure} \\ \text{It's lucky} \\ \text{It isn't likely} \end{cases}$ (that) you'll survive a week in Las Vegas.

(155a) *It is possible even she could have been being gripped by KONG.
(155b) It is possible she even could have been being gripped by KONG.

A related case shows the importance of complementizers for the formal
statement of the rule that moves *even* rightward. Consider the following
sentences, which indicate that the direct object NP of *report* can be modified
by *even*, as we would expect:

(156a) She reported even HER PRIVATE INCOME.
(156b) She reported even THERE HAVING BEEN A BROWN-OUT.
(156c) She reported even THAT SHE COULD HAVE BEEN BEING
GRIPPED BY KONG.

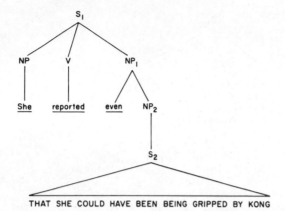

THAT SHE COULD HAVE BEEN BEING GRIPPED BY KONG   FIG. 11.17.   Example (157)

We will assume that in these cases, the *even* is Chomsky-adjoined to the direct object NP of *reported*, as in (157), Fig. 11.17.

Like the adjectives in (132), *report* allows deletion of *that*.

(158)   She reported (that) we were being followed by a sasquatch.

The question is, what would happen if the rule of *"That"-Deletion* were to delete the *that* which introduces S_2 in (157)? The result would be *(159).

(159)   *She reported [even [[SHE COULD HAVE BEEN
                        NP_1 NP_2 S_2
BEING GRIPPED BY KONG]   ]   ]
                        S_2 NP_2 NP_1

It might be thought that this could be saved by repositioning the *even* to the right of *she*. However, although the result, (160), is grammatical, it does not seem to us to have the same meaning as (156c); i.e., although (156c) can be used as an answer to (161), (160) cannot, in the same sense.

(160)   She reported she even could have been being gripped by Kong.
(161)   Did she report anything else?

It would seem that there are only two ways of avoiding *(159): The first would be to make the rule of *Intensifier Climb* obligatory here, and the second would be to block the rule of *"That" Deletion*, if there is a preceding *even*. The first "solution" has nothing to recommend it. The second, although it initially sounds dreadfully ad hoc, may be on the right track, for note that it is often impossible to delete *that* unless the *that*-clause immediately follows the predicate of which it is the complement [cf. (162) and (163) below].

(162a)   It was reported (that) they had found a solution.

(162b)   It was reported $\left\{\begin{matrix} \text{in } \textit{The Times} \\ \text{by Harold} \end{matrix}\right\}$ *(that) they had found a solution.

(163a)   I believe (that) we will win from the bottom of my heart.

(163b)   I believe from the bottom of my heart *(that) we will win.

(164a)   I believe (that) we will win, and you believe (that) we will lose. *Gapping*
⇒

(164b)   I believe (that) we will win, and you *(that) we will lose.

 (165)   What I believe is *(that) Horton may have a point.

So although there are some cases of constituents that can intervene between a verb and a deleting *that* [cf. the underlined elements of (166)], the asterisked sentences in (162) through (165) provide some independent motivation for an adjacency-to-matrix-predicate condition that might be appealed to in order to prevent (157) from becoming (159).

(166a)   He told *us* (that) we were fools.

(166b)   It seemed *to us* (that) you were wrong.

(166c)   I figured *out* ?(that) my phone was bugged.

Note, however, that if *that* cannot delete after *even* in (157), it will also be blocked from being deleted in (152), at least by the simplest statement of the rule. Thus, our earlier assertion that (152) can be converted into (155a), and later, by *"Even" In*, to (155b), turns out, upon inspection, to require qualification.

What (152) shows is that *even* can be attached to the node S. The fact that (152) is synonymous with (155b) will, thus, have to be accounted for by a rule that moves intensifiers to post-subject position, over an optional complementizer. If the complementizer is present, the rule is optional; if nothing intervenes between the intensifier and the subject, the rule is obligatory. The rule that has this effect is formulated in (167).

(167)   *Intensifier In*

$$X - [\begin{Bmatrix} \text{just} \\ \text{only} \\ \text{even} \\ \text{also} \end{Bmatrix} - [(\begin{Bmatrix} \text{that} \\ \text{for} \end{Bmatrix}) - NP - V\ Y]] - Z$$

1	2	3	4	5	6	OPT ⇒
1	0	3	4+2	5	6	

Condition: If Term 3 is null, the rule is obligatory for all intensifiers except *also*, for which it is preferred, and *like,* for which it blocks (in our idiolects).

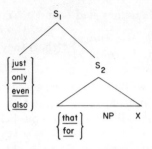

FIG. 11.18. Example (168)

It appears necessary to require that intensifiers only move inward when in such structures as (168), see Fig. 11.18, (i.e., when they are immediately dominated by an S-node that immediately dominates another S-node), for otherwise, *even* would be able to move after *she* in (157), producing a sentence, (169), that is grammatical, but which, like (160) above, does not have the same meaning as (156c).

(169)   She reported that she even could have been being gripped by Kong.

Let us recapitulate the points we have made, for they are complex. We have argued that all intensifiers must be allowed to be Chomsky-adjoined to S, on the basis of sentences such as (152), and that all intensifiers except *like* must subsequently be allowed to be moved to the post-subject position, by rule (167). Thus, we have rejected *"Like" Out*, and adopted (essentially) *"Even" In* (see subsection *Pauseless "Even"*) concluding, therefore, that the behavior of *like* is more indicative of the base structure of sentences than is the behavior of the other intensifiers. And *like* suggests that sentences must be ternary branching at the highest node, not binary (thus, we reject (146) in favor of (147)), and right-branching thereafter. We believe the structure of the maximally complex auxiliary, therefore, to be as it is diagrammed in (149).

Previous Analyses of *Even*

Jackendoff's Analysis.   We now treat two of the previously proposed accounts of the distribution of *even* bearing most directly on the issue of the structure of the auxiliary.

Jackendoff (1972) proposed the following condition (p. 249):

(170)   If *even* is directly dominated by a node X, X and all nodes dominates by X are in the range of *even*. [= Jackendoff's (6.93)]

Jackendoff cited the following type of case in support of this principle. In (171), the noun *BICYCLE* is not in the range of *even*, so the sentence is ungrammatical.

(171) *John gave even his daughter a new BICYCLE. [in Jackendoff's
(6.91)]

Jackendoff observed that if *even* is dominated by the NP that dominates *his
daughter*, his principle, (170), accounts for this ungramamticality, for *even*
would not C-command *BICYCLE*.

We find one difficulty with Jackendoff's proposal, namely, if *even* were not
attached to *his daughter* in (171), but instead were directly dominated by VP,
as in (172), see Fig. 11.19, then sentence (171) would incorrectly be ruled
acceptable. The question is, can structures such as (172), in which *even* is a
daughter of VP, be excluded in principle?

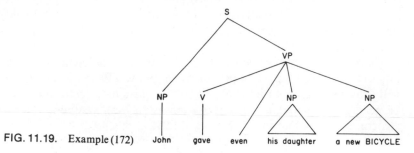

FIG. 11.19.   Example (172)   John   gave   even   his daughter   a new BICYCLE

Jackendoff (1972) was not very explicit about where *even* is to be
introduced in remote structure; the only comment he made on this topic was:

(173)   These words [i.e., *even, only,* and *just*—JRR&WEC] can occur
before NPs and in the auxiliary. (p. 247).

However, one of the sentences that he cited allows us to infer that there
must be some *even*s that are immediately dominated by VP. The sentence,
Jackendoff's (6.97), is repeated in (174);

(174)   John will have even given his DAUGHTER a new bicycle.

Jackendoff remarked in connection with (174): "The following examples bear
this out: *even* after the second auxiliary is unacceptable with subject focus,
although other foci are possible [p. 251]."

We agree with Jackendoff (1972) that *even* is linked to *DAUGHTER* in
(174), but note that, although it might be true for some theories of the English
auxiliary (e.g., in the classical analysis of Chomsky's *Syntactic Structures*, in
which the node Aux is expanded as in (175),

(175)   Aux → C (M) (have-en) (be-ing) (be-en)

that *even* in (174) is occurring "in the auxiliary"), this is not the case for the analysis of the auxiliary that Jackendoff adopted in his chapter on adverbs. There, on p. 76, he proposed the following rules:

(176a)   S → NP – Aux – VP [Jackendoff's (3.122)]
(176b)   Aux → Tense – (Modal) [Jackendoff's (3.123)]
(176c)   VP → (have – en) (be – ing) V – (NP)...[Jackendoff's (3.124)]

There is one more rule that affects the structure of the auxiliary: Jackendoff's rule of *"Have-Be" Raising* [Jackendoff's (3.127)], which has the effect of putting either *have* or *be* under the node Aux, if that node does not contain a modal and consists entirely of Tense.

Because there is a modal (*will*) in (174), however, *"Have-Be" Raising* will not be relevant, and the remote structure of (174) would have to be as shown in (177), Fig. 11.20.

The question now arises as to how (173) is to be amended in such a way as to allow (177). If we simply add the words "or in the VP" to the end of (177), we will provide an account for (177), but we will also incorrectly allow *(171) to be generated, as well as a sentence such as *(178a), assuming that it has a structure such as that in (178b), Fig. 11.21.

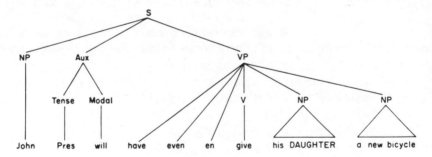

FIG. 11.20.   Example (177)

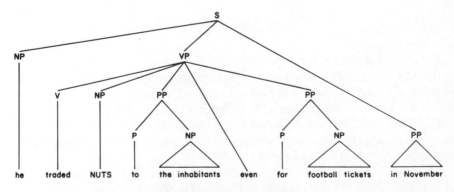

FIG. 11.21.   Example (178b)

(178a)   *He traded NUTS to the inhabitants even for football tickets in November.

The alternative would seem to be to replace (173) by a very unsatisfying disjunctive list of categories, such as that in (179):

(179)   The words *even, only* and *just* can occur either before [i.e., as left daughters of ?] NP or before [i.e., as left sisters of]:

–en	[cf. (177)]
–ing[19]	
V	[cf. (95b) above]
VP	[for sentences such as "Jim may even have been eating GRAPES"]
Aux	[for sentences such as "Jim even may have been eating GRAPES"]
Adj	[for sentences such as "Tex may be even ANGRY at me"]
Adv	[cf. (93)]
P	[cf. (94b)]
PP	[cf. (75e)]
Complementizer [cf. (152)]	

Possibly some other less disjunctive alternative can be devised that stays within the spirit of Jackendoff's (1972) analysis. We will not search for one here, but rather sketch an approach to the distribution of *even* that seems to be more fruitful to us.

Our basic disagreement with Jackendoff (1972) lies in the fact that such statements as (173), or the more exhaustive (179), are too close to the surface. We propose to replace these with a characterization such as that in (180), which is essentially semantic.

(180)   *Even* can modify any semantic predicate or argument.

This characterization will have the effect of allowing *even* in remote structure to modify any lexical category, namely, nouns, verbs, adjectives, or (meaningful) prepositions, as well as NPs. But it will lead to some surface problems: although (181) is a possible remote structure (because *window* is a noun), it is a bad surface structure.

(181)   *They may fingerprint Ben's even WINDOW.

---

[19]This would be necessary in order to generate sentences such as (i), whose remote structures are parallel to (177) in all relevant respects: (i) "John may be even giving his DAUGHTER a new bicycle."

We propose to make the rule of *Intensifier Climb* obligatory in such cases: *Even* must be adjoined either to the direct object NP of *fingerprint* or to the constituent following *may* in (181), which we would analyze as a clausal remnant, following Ross (1969), not as a VP. The result would be either (182a) or (182b).[20]

(182a)   They may fingerprint even Ben's WINDOW.
(182b)   They may even fingerprint Ben's WINDOW.

That is, in our view, the surface positions of *even* are most effectively accounted for by adopting a highly restricted semantic characterization of the remote elements that it may modify and then by letting the rule of *Intensifier Climb* (and the subequent rule of *Intensifier In*) produce surface results that may not reflect the underlying semantic regularities in any direct way.

The most salient problem for this analysis of *even* is the fact, noted by Anderson (1972), that *even* can be associated with surface structure constituents that are not elements of semantic representation. An example is (183).

(183)   Our new boss is a dream; he's pleasant, he doesn't make you take shorthand, he gives half-hour coffee breaks, and he's even easy to get a raise out of, if you wear short enough skirts. [Anderson's (7)]

Under the *"Tough" Movement* analysis, which we assume to be correct (but any rule making derived subjects would have the same force), *easy to get a raise out of* corresponds to no piece of semantic representation, as Anderson pointed out.

One possible solution within the framework advocated here is to say that the relevant sentence in (183) has a history like that shown in (184).

(184a)   Approximate remote structure: even (for one to get a raise out of him) is easy for one ⇒ (*via* Equi, Deletion of *for one* after *easy* and *"Tough" Movement*)   *Intensifier Climb*
(184b)   He is easy even to get a raise out of.   ⇒
(184c)   He is even easy to get a raise out of.

It is extremely unclear to us at present exactly how the difference in meaning between (184a) and (184c) (which is subtle but real, we feel), is to be represented in a formal semantic representation. The latter sentence seems to predicate something of *he*, whereas the former one does not. But how is

---

[20]Note that *Intensifier Climb* must be made obligatory in other contexts as well: neither *also* nor *just* can comfortably precede an NP that is the object of a preposition [cf. (96c) and (114avi)].

"predication" reflected structurally? If there were some extra semantic primitive, presumably an empty predicate, in the semantic representation of (184c) [something that is not in the representation of (184a)], then possibly *even* could, within the confines of (180), be said to modify this element. Or possibly *even* modifies the complement of *easy* underlyingly, as suggested by the representation in (184a), with the rule of *Intensifier Climb* being globally constrained not to change (184b) into (184c) except in the presence of whatever semantic structure is relevant to producing this predication interpretation. Our present understanding of this area is too limited.

Let us recapitulate our remarks on Jackendoff's (1972) analysis. We have argued that Jackendoff's statement (173) is inadequate to account for the location of *even* in (174) and that there is no simple way to modify (173) in such a way as to account for (174) without also generating (171). And any such list as (179) should be avoided if at all possible. Our suggestion is to adopt the right-branching analysis of the auxiliary that is implicit in (149) and to allow the rule of *Intensifier Climb* to apply to position intensifiers to the left of any auxiliary except the first.

Anderson's Analysis.   The basic condition on *even* that Anderson (1972) stated is cited in (185):

(185)   We could accordingly restrict the scope of *even* to constituents that are either directly adjacent to *even*, or dominated by a node that is [p. 899].

Using the notion of C-command introduced by Reinhart (1976), we can recast Jackendoff's (1972) definition [(170)] and Anderson's (1972) as in (186a) and (186b), respectively, which will more clearly bring out their differences.

(186a)   Jackendoff: *even* C-commands any focused element with which it is associated.

(186b)   Anderson: *even* C-commands any focused element with which it is associated, and it must be adjacent to either the focused element, or to some node that dominates the focused element.

Why did Jackendoff, whose work followed Anderson's, adopt a less restrictive condition on *even*? The reason, we believe, is that Anderson did not consider sentences such as (187).

(187)   JOHN will even have given his daughter a new bicycle. [≅ Jackendoff (6.96)]

This sentence is clear evidence against Anderson's adjacency clause in (186b).

On the other hand, such sentences as *(171), "*John gave even his daughter a new BICYCLE," which are equivalent in all respects to sentences such as (188), are what impelled Anderson (1972) to argue for the adjacency clause. As we have seen, Jackendoff (1972) can apparently only avoid generating sentences such as (171) and (188) by assuming that the *even*s in them are attached to the following NP. However, sentences such as (174) suggest the need for postulating VP-dominated *even*s in Jackendoff's system, and an unwieldy disjunctive specification soon heaves into view.

(188)   *Jones eats even Skrunkies for BREAKFAST. [Anderson's (13c)]

The way we propose to resolve this conflict is basically in keeping with Anderson's (1972) condition, for notice that any intensifier that has undergone *Intensifier Climb* will be in an output configuration that will satisfy Anderson's condition. Because the stress facts with *also* provide independent support for *Intensifier Climb*, we assume that sentence (187) must be accounted for by another rule, because it cannot be produced by *Intensifier Climb* from (189), which we assume to underlie it.

(189)   [Even JOHN] will have given his daughter a new bicycle.
        NP

If *Intensifier Hop* applies to (189), (190a) will result, and the only place that *even* could climb to is the S node, which would produce (190b).

(190a)   [JOHN, even,] will have given his daughter a new bicycle.
         NP
(190b)   JOHN will have given his daughter a new bicycle, even.

Alternatively, we could apply *Intensifier Climb* directly to (189), producing (191a), to which *Intensifier In* would obligatorily apply to produce (191b).

(191a)   [Even [John will have given his daughter a new bicycle]]
         S   S   S S
(191b)   JOHN even will have given his daughter a new bicycle.

But no rules yet given can produce the desired (187).

Before we turn to proposing a rule that will, let us take issue with Jackendoff (1972) on a grammaticality judgment. Jackendoff asterisked (187) if the *even* follows *have*. He remarked:

(192)   This analysis provides confirmation of the theory of the auxiliary presented in section 3.8, in which it was argued that, in the surface

structure, the first auxiliary is dominated by S and the other auxiliaries are dominated by VP. This analysis predicts that the subject is within the range of *even* only if *even* comes before the second auxiliary, since otherwise *even* would be dominated by VP, not S [pp. 250–251].

However, although we can agree with Jackendoff (1972) in finding *even* after *have* in (187) slightly less acceptable than before *have* [cf. (193)], we would not rate it fully ungrammatical, as he does. Its awkwardness seems to us not to have to do with *even* so much as with *will*: with some other modals, as in (194), the sentence is unexceptionable, to our ears.

(193)   ?JOHN will have even give his daughter a new bicycle.

(194)   JOHN $\begin{Bmatrix} \text{should (?n't)} \\ \text{could (n't)} \\ \text{may} \\ \text{might (n't)} \end{Bmatrix}$ have even given his daughter a new bicycle.

Other examples confirm this intuition:

(195a)   Were OTHER STUDENTS eligible for the grant?
(195b)   Yeah, SOPHOMORES could have even applied for it.
(196a)   Could only TEX have gotten to see the princess?
(196b)   No, SULLY might have even been able to do it.

It seems, then, as if the full set of facts pertaining to *even*s that follow a focused subject are in conflict with even the weaker condition imposed by Jackendoff (1972), for *even* in (194) through (196) will not C-command the subjects, either under Jackendoff's analysis of the auxiliary or under our right-branching account. Thus, some new rule is needed.

The rule must move not only *even*, but also *also*: cf. (197).

(197a)   Could anyone else be indicted?
(197b)   Yeah—also PROFESSOR BEEBE could be indicted.
(197c)   Yeah—PROFESSOR BEEBE could also be indicted.

However, *only* is not affected by the rule [thus (198a) cannot become (198b)], and neither is *like*, for us usually [cf. the previous discussion of (22) and (23)]. Thus, the rule is highly ad hoc: we formulate it as in (199).

(198a)   Only HAROLD can get us out of this.
(198b)   *HAROLD can only get us out of this.

(199) *Intensifier Post Tense*

$$\left[\left\{\begin{matrix}even\\also\end{matrix}\right\} - NP\right] - \left[\begin{matrix}+\,Aux\\+\,Tense\end{matrix}\right] - X$$

$$NPOPT$$

1	2	3	4	⇒
0	2	3 + 1	4	

Note that this rule produces structures such as (187), which would be forbidden by Anderson's (1972) condition, though not by Jackendoff's (1972). However, as it stands, it will not generate (194) through (196), which would also be blocked by Jackendoff's condition. Thus, it will have to be amended in some way to produce these sentences. As Jackendoff noted, *even* and *also* are barred from being three auxiliaries away from a focused subject (to say nothing of four):

(200a) Could anyone else have been being shadowed?

(200b) *Yeah—JESSICA could have been $\left\{\begin{matrix}even\\also\end{matrix}\right\}$ being shadowed.

(200c) **Yeah—JESSICA could have been being $\left\{\begin{matrix}even\\also\end{matrix}\right\}$ shadowed.

It appears, however, that what is involved here is not just a simple counting of auxiliaries, for note that *even* and *also* refuse to follow the bare stem *be*, or the gerund *being* [cf. (201) and (202)].

(201a) Could anyone else be being shadowed?

(201b) *Yeah—JESSICA could be $\left\{\begin{matrix}even\\also\end{matrix}\right\}$ being shadowed.

(202a) Is anyone else being shadowed?

(202b) **Yeah—JESSICA is being $\left\{\begin{matrix}even\\also\end{matrix}\right\}$ shadowed.

In fact, they do not even like it very much after *been*:

(203a) Has anyone else been $\left\{\begin{matrix}\text{working hard}\\\text{in that room}\\\text{sick}\\\text{a nuisance}\end{matrix}\right\}$?

(203b)   Yeah—JESSICA has been $\left\{\begin{array}{l}\text{even}\\\text{also}\end{array}\right\}$ $\left\{\begin{array}{l}\text{??working hard}\\\text{*in that room}\\\text{*sick}\\\text{*a nuisance}\end{array}\right\}$.

Rather than "ad hoc"-ening rule (199) even more, by inserting an optional (*have*) at the end of Term 3 (which would generate (193) through (196), but would predict that (203b) is totally bad, even with *working hard*, which it is not), we will briefly cite some parallel facts involving quantifiers, which suggest to us that the solution to the problem of what auxiliaries *even* can follow lies elsewhere than in making amendments to (199).

There is a process known as *Quantifier Floating*, which has the effect of converting (204a) into (204b).

(204a) $\left\{\begin{array}{l}\text{All}\\\text{Both}\end{array}\right\}$ of them are snoring.

(204b)   They $\left\{\begin{array}{l}\text{all}\\\text{both}\end{array}\right\}$ are snoring.

We would agree with Postal's (1974b) assessment of the way this is effected: *Quantifier Floating* works by ascending the object NP of *of* to make this NP the derived subject of *are snoring*.[21]

We also find *all* and *both* after *are*, and, in fact, after any tensed auxiliary verb:

(205)   They are $\left\{\begin{array}{l}\text{all}\\\text{both}\end{array}\right\}$ snoring.

(206a)   They could $\left\{\begin{array}{l}\text{all}\\\text{both}\end{array}\right\}$ be snoring.

(206b)   They have $\left\{\begin{array}{l}\text{all}\\\text{both}\end{array}\right\}$ $\left\{\begin{array}{l}\text{taken Benzedrine}\\\text{*work to get done}[22]\end{array}\right\}$.

(206c)   They don't $\left\{\begin{array}{l}\text{all}\\\text{both}\end{array}\right\}$ snore.

If the second auxiliary is *have*, we find floated *all* and *both* to its right:

---

[21]The fairly extensive treatment of *Quantifier Floating* by Postal (1974b) is challenged by Fiengo and Lasnik (1976). See also Maling (1976) for some important related points.

[22]This is bad because when *work to be done* follows *have, have* is a main verb, not an auxiliary.

(207) They $\begin{Bmatrix} \text{can't} \\ \text{must} \\ \text{should} \\ \text{way} \\ \text{etc.} \end{Bmatrix}$ have $\begin{Bmatrix} \text{all} \\ \text{both} \end{Bmatrix}$ been lucky.

However, if the second auxiliary is the bare stem *be*, or the gerund *being*, the quantifiers cannot follow it:

(208a) *They $\begin{Bmatrix} \text{will} \\ \text{must} \\ \text{should} \\ \text{may} \\ \text{etc.} \end{Bmatrix}$ be $\begin{Bmatrix} \text{all} \\ \text{both} \end{Bmatrix}$ spies.[23]

(208b) **They are being $\begin{Bmatrix} \text{all} \\ \text{both} \end{Bmatrix}$ pests.

With quantifiers, the position after *been* is bad, even if a progressive follows:

(209) *They have been $\begin{Bmatrix} \text{all} \\ \text{both} \end{Bmatrix}$ $\begin{Bmatrix} \text{working hard} \\ \text{in that room} \\ \text{Turkish} \\ \text{nuisances} \end{Bmatrix}$.[24]

---

[23]For some reason, after *can't be* and *couldn't be*, things are often looser than with other modals, with *all* being freer to float to the right of *be* than is *both*. Thus, for us, the following contrasts obtain:

(i) They $\begin{Bmatrix} \text{?can't} \\ \text{?couldn't} \\ \text{?*could} \end{Bmatrix}$ be all spies.

(ii) They $\begin{Bmatrix} \text{??can't} \\ \text{??couldn't} \\ \text{*could} \end{Bmatrix}$ be both spies.

We have no explanation for this differential behavior of *can* and *could*.

[24]For reasons we do not understand, however, some of the sentences in (209) sound better with modals and *all*:

(i) They $\begin{Bmatrix} \text{must} \\ \text{could} \\ \text{should} \\ \text{may} \end{Bmatrix}$ have been all $\begin{Bmatrix} \text{working hard} \\ \text{in that room} \\ \text{??Turkish} \\ \text{*nuisances} \end{Bmatrix}$.

(ii) They $\begin{Bmatrix} \text{must} \\ \text{could} \\ \text{should} \\ \text{may} \end{Bmatrix}$ have been both $\begin{Bmatrix} \text{?working hard} \\ \text{??in that room} \\ \text{??Turkish} \\ \text{*nuisances} \end{Bmatrix}$.

These facts leave us with mouths agape.

The parallels between (201) through (203) and (207) through (209) appear to us to be more important than the differences. Accordingly, we would like to give intensifiers and quantifiers highly similar analyses. In the case of quantifiers, Postal (1974a) has argued that *Quantifier Floating* is a cyclic rule. The motivation for this claim arises from variants of sentences such as (210).

(210)   It is likely that it will appear to you that $\begin{Bmatrix} \text{all} \\ \text{both} \end{Bmatrix}$ of them are snoring.

Assuming that this sentence is underlain by a remote structure along the lines of (211), see Fig. 11.22, we note that since both *appear* and *(be) likely* are *Subject Raising (A-Raising)* triggers,[25] NP_3 can be raised once, to become the superficial subject of *appear*, as in (212), or twice to become the superficial subject of *(be) likely*, as in (213):

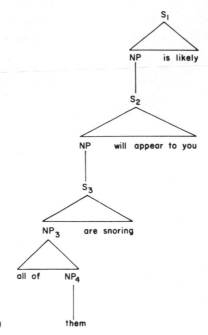

FIG. 11.22.   Example (211)

(212)   It is likely that $\begin{Bmatrix} \text{all} \\ \text{both} \end{Bmatrix}$ of them will appear to you to be snoring.

(213) $\begin{Bmatrix} \text{All} \\ \text{Both} \end{Bmatrix}$ of them are likely to appear to you to be snoring.

---

[25]For an extensive treatment of the process of *A-Raising,* cf. Postal (1974a).

Now if we assume that *Quantifier Floating*, which converts (204a) to (204b) by ascending *them* to become the superficial subject of (*be*) *snoring*, is an optional cyclic process, then we would expect to find that *all* and *both* could show up before (*be*) *snoring* (whose deep subject they were part of) or *appear* [because the quantified NP can be raised once, to become *appear*'s subject, as in (212)], or before (*be*) *likely* [because the quantified NP can be raised again, as in (213)]. All of these predictions are in fact attested: cf. (214).

(214a)   It is likely that it will appear to you that they all are snoring.
(214b)   It is likely that they all will appear to you to be snoring.
(214c)   They all are likely to appear to you to be snoring.

In fact, although the quantified NP has been raised twice in (214c), there is no necessary correlation between the number of applicatons of *A-Raising* and the position of *all* in surface structure. If *Quantifier Floating* applies on the first cycle, with *they* subsequently being raised twice, (215a) will ensue, and if *all of them* is raised once before the quantifier is floated, with *they* subsequently being raised once more, (215b) will result.

(215a)   They are likely to appear all to be snoring.
(215b)   They are likely all to appear to be snoring.

Postal (1974a) notes (p. 158, Footnote 18) that, given an analysis of auxiliaries in which each auxiliary is a main verb that undergoes *A-Raising,* the cyclical *Quantifier Floating* analysis would predict that quantifiers should be able to precede any auxiliary. The sentences he cited in (i) of Footnote 18 are reproduced in (216).

(216a)   All of the rockets will have been decaying for some time.
(216b)   The rockets will have been (probably) all decaying for some time.
(216c)   The rockets will have all been decaying for some time.
(216d)   The rockets will all have been decaying for some time.
(216e)   The rockets all will have been decaying for some time.

He observed: "(ib) [= (216b)] without *probably* is bad for many speakers because of an output condition blocking intensed *be* directly before a Q, that is:

$$*\text{be} \left(\left\{ \begin{matrix} \text{ing} \\ \text{en} \end{matrix} \right\} \right) \text{Q}"$$

We find ourselves in general agreement with the proposed output condition, with the exception that the three conditions abbreviated in Postal's condition are different in strength. No one we know of tolerates quantifiers after *being*, with the bare stem *be* being only slightly less impossible, perhaps [cf. (208)]. The situation with *been* is non-uniform: Compare (209) with the sentences in Footnote 24.

Although we know of nothing that would completely explain these differences in strength, the following observations may be of some relevance. The passive auxiliary *be* allows its complement, the passive participle, to be deleted by *VP Deletion*, except after *being*.

(217a) John was arrested, but Christina was not (arrested).
(217b) John has been arrested, but Christina has not been (arrested).
(217c) John will be arrested but Christina will not be (arrested).
(217d) John is being arrested, but Christina is not being *(arrested).

The same paradigm obtains for predicate nouns and adjectives:

(218a) John was $\begin{Bmatrix} \text{polite} \\ \text{a pest} \end{Bmatrix}$, but Christina was not ($\begin{Bmatrix} \text{polite} \\ \text{a pest} \end{Bmatrix}$).

(218b) John has been $\begin{Bmatrix} \text{polite} \\ \text{a pest} \end{Bmatrix}$, but Christina has not been ($\begin{Bmatrix} \text{polite} \\ \text{a pest} \end{Bmatrix}$).

(218c) John will be $\begin{Bmatrix} \text{polite} \\ \text{a pest} \end{Bmatrix}$, but Christina will not be ($\begin{Bmatrix} \text{polite} \\ \text{a pest} \end{Bmatrix}$).

(218d) John is being $\begin{Bmatrix} \text{polite} \\ \text{a pest} \end{Bmatrix}$, but Christina is not being *($\begin{Bmatrix} \text{polite} \\ \text{a pest} \end{Bmatrix}$).

This does not seem to be a property only of *being* when it follows the progressive auxiliary: In (219), we find parallel facts when the *-ing* on *be* is induced by the matrix predicate *continue*.

(219) Tim was polite at first, but he has not continued $\begin{Bmatrix} \text{to be} \\ \text{*being} \end{Bmatrix}$.

We note that the tight bond between *being* and its object cannot be sundered by ripping rules, either. Note the sentential *which*-clauses related to the sentences in (217).

(220a) John was arrested, which Christina was not.
(220b) John has been arrested, which Christina has not been.
(220c) John will be arrested, which Christina will not be.
(220d) *John is being arrested, which Christina is not being.

We might propose the following positive output condition:

(221) *The Great Chain of "Being"*
If an instance of the verb *be* appears with the suffix *-ing*, whatever immediately follows this *be* in remote structure must immediately follow it in surface structure.

This constraint will not only block deletions such as those in (217) through (219), and choppings, such as that in (220), from taking place but also such "insertions" as **(200c), *(202b), and **(208b).[26]

In addition, the constraint may shed new light on the tag question construction, which, despite a 20-year history of investigation within generative grammar, still presents many mysteries [cf. (222)].

(222a) Hank might have been being bluffed, mightn't he?
(222b) Hank might have been being bluffed, mightn't he have?
(222c) ?Hank might have been being bluffed, mightn't he have been?
(222d) *Hank might have been being bluffed, mightn't he have been being?

It is too early to tell, but it may well be the case that there are conditions on *be* and *been* which are similar to (221), but weaker. If there is in addition an interacting hierarchy of rule strengths, with deletion rules, such as *VP Deletion* being "stronger" (i.e., able to apply in more environments) than chopping rules, such as the one that forms the *which*-clauses of (220), and with chopping rules being in general stronger than insertions, then such differences in acceptability as (217c) or (220c), on the one hand, and (208a), on the other, may find an explanation. The situation, thus, would parallel the general state of affairs in island constraints; in both areas, nondiscrete treatments would be necessary.

However, to pursue these matters further here would take us too far from the task at hand, namely, accounting for the positions in which *even* and *also* can appear in the auxiliary. What makes floating quantifiers relevant to the distribution of *even* and *also* are the parallels between (193) through (196) and (207), or between *(201b) and *(208a), or between *(202b) and **(208b). These sentences show that *even* and *also* can appear roughly where *all* and *both* can.

We must say "roughly," because the parallelism is not perfect: Quantifiers seem to be able to follow *been* slightly better than do intensifiers. Compare

---

[26]We have placed quotation marks around *insertions*, because, in line with our acceptance of Perlmutter and Postal's (1978) ascension analysis of floated quantifiers, constraints on surface order of auxiliaries and quantifiers will either have to be expressed as output conditions, as Postal did, or as constraints on *Raising to Subject Position*. For the present, this point of detail is irrelevant, and we continue to speak of "inserting" quantifiers after auxiliaries and other verbs.

(200b) and the sentences in Footnote 24 above. Furthermore, when we examine the behavior of *even* and *also* in nests of Subject-Raising constructions, like (211), we find that quantifiers can be separated by a longer string of Subject-Raising triggers from the subject NP they quantify over than can *even* and *also* be separated from a focused subject with which they are associated. Thus, although (223a) and (224a) can be answered with (223b) and (224b), respectively, for all speakers, and by (223c) and (224c) in many dialects, we know of no speakers who would allow (223d) or (224d).

(223a) Is EVERYBODY likely to appear to me to be snoring?

(223b) Yeah—PRESIDENT HUGHES $\begin{Bmatrix} \text{even is} \\ \text{is even} \end{Bmatrix}$ likely to appear to you to be snoring.

(223c) %Yeah—PRESIDENT HUGHES is likely $\begin{Bmatrix} \text{even to} \\ \text{to even} \end{Bmatrix}$ appear to you to be snoring.

(223d) *Yeah—PRESIDENT HUGHES is likely to appear to you $\begin{Bmatrix} \text{even to} \\ \text{to even} \end{Bmatrix}$ be snoring.

(224a) Is only MRS HUGHES likely to appear to me to be snoring?

(224b) No, PRESIDENT HUGHES $\begin{Bmatrix} \text{also is} \\ \text{is also} \end{Bmatrix}$ likely to appear to you to be snoring.

(224c) %No, PRESIDENT HUGHES is likely $\begin{Bmatrix} \text{also to} \\ \text{to also} \end{Bmatrix}$ appear to you to be snoring.

(224d) *No, PRESIDENT HUGHES is likely to appear to you $\begin{Bmatrix} \text{also to} \\ \text{to also} \end{Bmatrix}$ be snoring.

The (d) versions of the sentences here are to be compared with (215a) and the (c) versions with (215b).

There are, then, two cases that seem to show that the general parallelism between quantifiers and intensifiers is overlaid by a tendency for quantifiers to occur in more environments than intensifiers.

Let us now turn to a detailed examination of (223c) and (224c), for these sentences have an important bearing on the analysis of *even* and *also: they show that neither Jackendoff's (1972) nor Anderson's (1972) condition on "even" can be true of surface structure.* Rather, the range of *even* (and *also*) seems to have to be determined cyclically. We propose the derivation for (223c) shown in Figs. 11.23 through 11.26.

The only problem that is posed by our cyclical analysis of *even* and *also* is the ungrammaticality of (223d) and (224d). The first of these could arise, for instance, if the optional rule of *Intensifer Climb* were allowed to apply on the S_3 cycle of (225a). *Intensifer In*, an obligatory rule, would then have to apply, and *even* would remain as a constituent of S_3.

At present, the only remedy we can suggest is a global filter, which would mark as ungrammatical any surface structure containing a focused surface subject and an *even* or *also* that is more than one clause down from this subject, if the main verb of the clause in question is not an auxiliary verb.

This is an extremely ad hoc restriction, but the (c) versions of (223) and (224) seem to force a cyclical treatment, and we know of no alternative

(225a)   Approximate remote structure

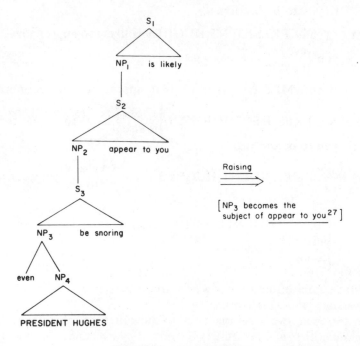

FIG. 11.23.   Example (225a)

---

[27]When the subject of the complement of *appear* ascends to become the derived subject of *appear*, the remnant of the old complement (*to be snoring*) becomes a chômeur, which we indicate in (225b) by the notation $\widehat{NP_2}$. See Perlmutter and Postal (1978) for more details.

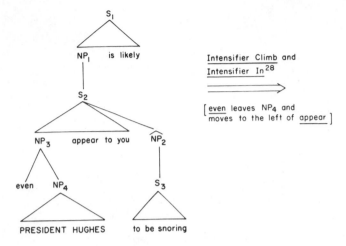

FIG. 11.24. Example (225b)

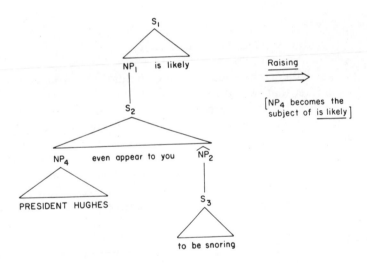

FIG. 11.25. Example (225c)

[28]It might be thought that it is possible to achieve the effect of the two rules of *Intensifier Climb* and *Intensifier In* by allowing NP$_4$ to undergo the type of NP-ascension that underlies *Quantifier Floating*. This would convert *even* into a chômeur, and it (and *also*) could be assigned the same position in the linear ordering as *all* and *both*. However, we are dubious. On the one hand, *Intensifier Climb* is needed in objects, independently of what happens in subject position: See the sentences in (74), (75), (97), (113a), and (114a). Furthermore, on the basis of sentences such as (152), we have argued that *even* must be able to be climbed to attach to higher S nodes. This being the case, *Intensifier In* will be necessary to repair sentences such as (150). Thus, we see no advantage to postulating that the conversion of (225b) into (225c) is accomplished by *Quantifier Floating*.

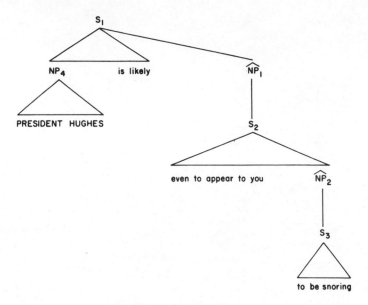

FIG. 11.26.   Example (225d)

account in which there is no equally ad hoc condition that would correspond to the global filter that we have adumbrated above.

Some sugar coating for the bitter pill of the global filter is available, however: The cyclical analysis of *even* and *also* obviates the need for the rule of *Intensifier Post Tense* [(199)]. Recall that this rule was postulated in order to account for sentences such as (187), "JOHN will even have given his daughter a new bicycle," because the *even* here violates Anderson's (1972) adjacency clause, which otherwise seems desirable. But if auxiliaries are treated as main verbs, then this sentence will derive from a remote structure such as (226), Fig. 11.27.

This cyclical analysis of nonadjacent subject-linked intensifiers thus kills two birds with one stone: No rule (199) is necessary at all, let alone an ad hoc optional *have* in Term 3 of that rule. Both sentences such as (187), which violates Anderson's adjacency condition, and sentences such as (193) and (194) through (196), which even violate Jackendoff's (1972) weaker C-command condition, drop out of the analysis as a consequence of a main-verb analysis of auxiliaries, coupled with the principle of the transformational cycle.

Further Parallels Between Intensifiers and Quantifiers

Before concluding our discussion of the English auxiliary, which has been based in part on some similarities between intensifiers and floated quantifiers,

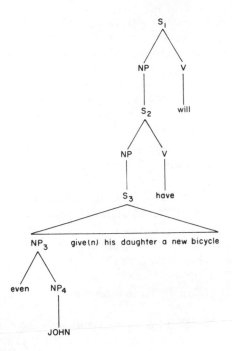

FIG. 11.27. Example (226)

let us draw attention to an additional point of similarity between these two classes of words.[29]

As we have seen above, *Intensifier Climb* can move *only* from its original location in (204), adjacent to *PLAYBOY,* to Chomsky-adjoin it to any higher constituent.

(227)   They could [have [read only *PLAYBOY*]].

Thus, *Intensifier Climb* can by itself produce either (228a) or (228b) from (227), and if *only* is first climbed to be adjoined to the highest S node and subsequently moved to the post-subject position by *Intensifier In*, (229) will result.

(228a)   They could [have [only [read *PLAYBOY*]]].
(228b)   They could [only [have [read *PLAYBOY*]]].
 (229)   They only could have read *PLAYBOY*.

---

[29]We assume here that the rule that has the effect of moving *even* and *also* rightward from focused subjects can be identified with *Quantifier Floating*, despite the fact that quantifiers are more flexible than intensifiers, as we have noted. Nothing in the discussion rests on this assumption, however.

Thus, in a sentence with an object-linked intensifier, there are usually three positions to the left of that object in which the intensifier can appear.

Let us now consider a sentence with a subject-linked intensifier, such as (230).

(230)   Even THE NEPTUNIANS could have read it.

This sentence derives from a structure similar to that in (226): If *Quantifier Floating* applies on the lowest cycle, (231a) will be generated, and if it applies on the next lowest, (231b) will result.

(231a)   %THE NEPTUNIANS could have even read it.[30]
(231b)   THE NEPTUNIANS could even have read it.

And if *Intensifier Climb* applies to the remote structure of (230), *Intensifier In* will obligatorily produce (232).

(232)   THE NEPTUNIANS even could have read it.

Thus, we see that there are usually also three places to the right of a focused subject in which a subject-linked intensifier can appear.

Consider the situation in which there are *two* intensifiers, one associated with the subject and one with the object. The restriction operative in such cases seems to be as follows: If we imagine crêpe-paper bands running from an intensifier to the focused NP with which it is associated, then such bands may not cross. To see this crossing restriction at work, imagine the possible responses to (233a), all of which are variants of the answer in (233b).

(233a)   Could ANY OTHER OUTWORLDERS have been reading only *PLAYBOY*?
(233b)   Yeah—even THE NEPTUNIANS could have been reading only *PLAYBOY*.

If *even* remains to the left of *THE NEPTUNIANS, only* can appear in the normal three places, as is indicated by the three lines from its prenominal location to the carets in (234), Fig. 11.28.

If *even* has undergone *Intensifier Climb* and *Intensifier In*, then there are only two possible locations for *only* (Fig. 11.29).

Note that the variant of (235) in which *only* precedes *even* could be excluded by the proposed constraint, for the crêpe-paper bands from *THE*

---

[30]This type of sentence is untarnished for us, but we have prefixed it with a percentage sign to indicate our belief that this is a controversial judgment.

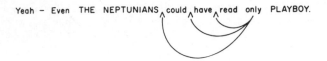

FIG. 11.28. Example (234)

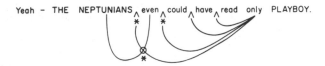

FIG. 11.29. Example (235)

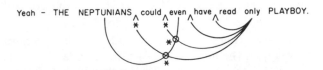

FIG. 11.30. Example (236)

NEPTUNIANS to *even* and from *PLAYBOY* to *only* would have to cross, and such a crossing would be prohibited by the informally stated constraint given above. However, we are inclined to think that this sentence should instead be blocked by some form of "one-per-slot" constraint, because it is also impossible for *only* to immediately follow *even* in (235), despite the fact that no crossing bands can be found. Thus, in what follows, we point out the various occurrences of the one-per-slot constraint as they arise, although we do not propose a formal constraint, because our investigation of its range is at present far too preliminary.[31]

A clearer instance of a band-crossing violation can be seen in (236) (Fig. 11.30), where *even* has quantifier-floated on the second cycle, as in (231b). Here, the reason that *only* cannot precede *could*, as it generally can, is that the *even*-band and the *only*-band[32] cross at the *-ed circle.

Some final cases of a band-crossing violation can be seen in (237) (Fig. 11.31), where *even* has been floated on the lowest cycle, as in (231a).

It is worth pointing out that it is not enough for the linear order of the intensifiers to be the opposite of that of the focused elements with which they are associated. This point can be seen on the basis of the sentences in (238b), which are versions of (233b) that would have arisen by applying *Intensifier*

---

[31]Note, for instance, that whereas *only* cannot precede *even* in (236), it can follow it, yet presumably both are in the "same slot."

[32]Here we are considering the band from *even* to *THE NEPTUNIANS* and the band from *only* to *PLAYBOY*, respectively.

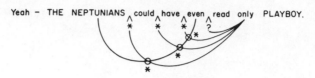

FIG. 11.31.   Example (237)

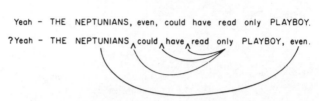

FIG. 11.32.   Examples (238a) top and (238b) bottom

Hop to (233b), producing (238a) (Fig. 11.32), to which *Intensifier Climb* would apply to adjoin the hopped *even* to the S node.

These sentences are certainly awkward, but they are not unintelligible. This fact shows that bands, or their functional equivalents, are necessary for any formulation of the restrictions on multiple intensifiers: One could not say anything like (239).

(239)   If there are *n* foci in a sentence, and *n* intensifiers associated with these foci, the sentence will be ungrammatical if there is any difference in order between any two foci and their corresponding intensifiers.

The reason that (239) is inadequate is apparent. There are differences in order of the kind mentioned in (239) both in (236) and (237) and in (238), but only those of the former type produce violations. What distinguishes the two types is the notion of *bands,* and of *crossing*, both of which we conclude are essential.

We will now show how the band-crossing constraint interacts with the floating of *all* and *both*. Consider the sentences in (240).

(240a)   Both (of) the Neptunians could have read only *PLAYBOY*.
(240b)   The Neptunians both could have read only *PLAYBOY*.
(240c)   The Neptunians could both have read only *PLAYBOY*.
(240d)   The Neptunians could have both read only *PLAYBOY*.

These sentences show the widest set of environments for floated quantifiers. However, as was the case with a subject-linked *even* that was not adjacent to the subject, we find that if *only* undergoes *Intensifier Climb, both* cannot freely float to its right. This restriction is documented in sentences

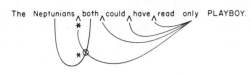

FIG. 11.33.   Example (241)

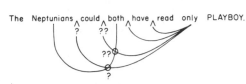

FIG. 11.34.   Example (242)

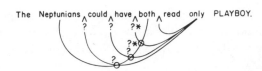

FIG. 11.35.   Example (243)

(241) through (243), Fig. 11.33, 11.34, and 11.35, where the designated circles again denote band-crossing violations of the type encountered above.

What is immediately apparent here is that although quantifiers and intensifiers can produce band-crossing violations, they are much milder than those produced by two intensifiers.

One might be tempted to conclude that this is a transderivational fact; after all, although (244b) is ungrammatical when read as a band-crossing variant of (244a) (see Fig. 11.36), it is fine as a variant of (245).

(245)   Only BILLY was writing even FRENCH poems.

And it could be pointed out that although in English, nonadjacent quantifiers can show up to the right of the NP they modify, they cannot show up to its left[33] (see Fig. 11.37). Thus, it might be said, since *both* in (241) through (243) can only be linked to *The Neptunians,* no ambiguity can arise, so the sentences are all uniformly better than intensifier-crossed examples like (236) and (237). That is, it might be held that band-crossing violations are essentially a kind of no-ambiguity constraint.[34]

---

[33]There is no general prohibition against such a situation arising. In French, (i) can become (ii), via the rule of *L-Tous* (cf. Kayne, 1975).

(i)	Henri	a voulu	lire	tous	d'eux.
	Henry	has wanted	to read	all	of them.
		[=wanted]			
(ii)	Henri	a tous	voulu	les	lire.
	Henry	has all	wanted	them	to read.

[34]See Hankamer (1973) for discussion bearing on the avoidance of ambiguity.

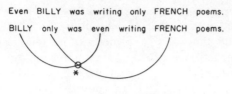

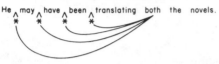

FIG. 11.36.   Example (244a) top and (244b) bottom

FIG. 11.37.   Example (246)

However, such a conclusion would be hasty. For if we recall that *only* cannot undergo *Quantifier Floating* [thus (247a) cannot become (247b)], we can see that there is a version of (237) that has no reading at all. It is given in (248).

(247a)   Only WIDENER is opposite from Schoenhof's.
(247b)   *WIDENER is only opposite from Schoenhof's.
(248)   *THE NEPTUNIANS could only have even read *PLAYBOY*.

Here, although *even* could be linked to *PLAYBOY, only* could not have been floated away from *THE NEPTUNIANS,* as *(247b) shows. Thus, *(248) is not starred on a band-crossing reading merely because of the existence of a stronger reading that would not entail band-crossing; (248) is ungrammatical on all readings.

Our conclusion, then, is not that (241) through (243) are better than (236) and (237) for transderivational reasons, but rather that quantifiers are less subject than intensifiers to band-crossing constraints, which is due to the fact that quantifiers are more flexible than are intensifiers, as regards being separated by raising from a subject to which they are linked. This difference in flexibility we have noted already, in connection with examples (223) and (224).

The point of this section lies in the (less than perfect) parallelism between (236) and (237) and (241) through (243). The fact that both intensifiers and quantifiers can give rise to band-crossing violations is an indirect piece of evidence for our analysis of *even* and *also*, which we argue come to be nonadjacent to, and to the right of, focused subjects by the same processes that have this effect in the case of quantifiers.

Summary Remarks on Auxiliaries

Our conclusion is that the distribution of intensifiers with respect to auxiliary verbs is best accounted for if auxiliaries are analyzed as main verbs that trigger *A-Raising*. Our assessment of previous work on intensifiers suggests that Anderson's (1972) more restrictive adjacency condition (186b) is to be preferred to the less restrictive C-command condition proposed by Jackendoff (1972) (186a), but that neither condition is adequate, if formulated in terms of surface structure. Rather, based on the grammaticality of such sentences as (193) through (196) and (224c), we argued for a cyclic analysis of *even* and *also*, in which these words are moved rightward from focused subjects by an expanded rule of *Quantifier Floating*. The rules in question are stated in the following section.

Conclusions on *Like* and Intensifiers

We can summarize the discussion of *like* and its neighbors by observing that the similarities in behavior among *like, even, also, only, just,* and *too* far outweigh the differences. In fact, a very large amount of otherwise inexplicable data can be handled by the ordered application of the following general rules:

(249) 1. *Intensifier Hopping*

X	Intensifier	A	Y	
1	2	3	4	OPT
1	0	3+,+2+,4		⇒

   Conditions: (a) blocked if A is on a left branch of some other constituent than S.
   (b) obligatory for *too*
   (c) blocks for *just*
   (d) A is a constituent that contains the focused element

(249) 2. *Nuclear Stress Rule*
   Vowel → [1 stress] / [##[$\overline{1\ \text{stress}}$] Y##
   Condition: Y ≠ [1 stress]

(249) 3. *Quantifier Floating* (optional and cyclic): In subject position, a NP that is "modified by" *all, both, each, even,* or *also* can ascend to become the derived subject, with the former modifiers being attached to the verb.[35]

(249) 4. *Intensifier Climb*
   A. W – [X – [Intensifier – A] – Y] – Z

	B	A		A	B	
1	2	3		4	5	6	OPT
13#[2		0		4	5]	6	⇒

---

[35]This rule is stated in words, rather than as a transformation, because it is intended as an approximation to a relational ascension rule. For the formal apparatus for stating relation-changing laws, see Perlmutter and Postal (1978).

B. W – [X – [A – Intensifier] – Y] – Z
   B A   A B
  1 2 3 4 5 6 OPT
  1 [2 3 0   5]#4 6 ⇒

Conditions: (a) obligatory for *just* and *also* in PPs
      (b) obligatory for all intensifiers if 3 + 4 = N
      (c) Rule 4B cannot apply if term 4 = *only*

(249) 5. *Intensifier In*
   X – [Intensifier [NP – V Y]] – Z
    S   S   S S
    1   2 3 4 5
    1   0 3 +2 4 5 ⇒

Conditions: (a) obligatory for *even* and *only*
      (b) blocks for *like*
      (c) preferred for *also*

The ordering relations that obtain among these rules are shown by the lines drawn in (250):

(250) ⎧1.
   ⎨2.
   ⎩3.
   ⎧4.
   ⎩5.

where a line between two rules means than the two rules must apply in the order given in (250), and where no line means that the rules can apply in either order. Rules 1 and 4 and 4 and 5 are intrinsically ordered, but it appears that Rules 1 and 2 must be extrinsically ordered.

We wish to extend the claim in (180) about the remote structure location of *even* to all intensifiers except *like*:

(251) The intensifiers *even, also/too,* and *only/just* can modify any semantic predicate or argument.

The reason for excluding *like* is that it appears to be able to modify in remote structure an even wider class of items than can the other intensifiers [cf. (252)].

(252) Jenny picked it $\begin{Bmatrix} \text{like} \\ \text{*even} \\ \text{*also} \\ \text{*only} \end{Bmatrix}$ *(right) up.[36]

---

[36]We note in passing that verbal particles such as *up, away, out, in, along,* etc. can only be modified by *like* if they are preceded by *right.* We have no explanation for this puzzling fact.

In addition, although we assume that tenses are to be represented in semantic structure as predicates and should thus be modifiable by all intensifiers, some are worse than others:

$$(253) \quad \text{Helen} \left\{ \begin{array}{l} \text{like} \\ \text{only} \\ \text{?just} \\ \text{??also} \\ \text{??even} \end{array} \right\} \text{WAS a spy.}$$

The general tendency seems to be for *like* to be able to occur in all environments where the other intensifiers can and in some others as well. In particular, it appears that *like* is freer than other intensifiers, in that it can be associated with any type of constituent, including NP, VP, N, V, Adj, Adv, Prep, Det, and Aux. Some of the more exotic of *like*'s associations follow.

(254a) He's not only A bass player, he's like THE bass player.
(254b) Jill's not ABOVE the car, she's like UNDER it.
(254c) Tom gambled yesterday, and he like WILL gamble tomorrow.

Other intensifiers can be associated with most types of constituents, but not the full range exemplified by *like*, as shown below:

$$(255) \quad \text{Bob's} \left\{ \begin{array}{l} \text{like} \\ *\text{even} \\ *\text{also} \\ *\text{only} \end{array} \right\} \begin{array}{l} \text{FATHER went to Chicago with us.} \\ \text{(association with N)} \end{array}$$

We noted at the outset of this paper that *like* can sometimes take the meaning of *approximately*, as in (256).

(256) I left at like nine o'clock.

Thus, *approximately* or *about* could replace *like* in (255) without a change in meaning. *Approximately* and *about* are more restricted than is *like*, however, in that they cannot modify a relational term, as in (257).

$$(257) \quad \text{I left} \left\{ \begin{array}{l} \text{like} \\ *\text{approximately} \\ *\text{about} \end{array} \right\} \text{early.}$$

On the other hand, fillers having similar meaning such as *kinda, sorta,* and *really* require a relational term.

(258a)   I left $\left\{\begin{matrix}\text{kinda}\\\text{sorta}\end{matrix}\right\}$ early.

(258b)   *I left at $\left\{\begin{matrix}\text{kinda}\\\text{sorta}\end{matrix}\right\}$ nine o'clock.

It, thus, appears that *like* as a filler meaning *approximately* is less restricted than other words having the same meaning. This parallels the less restricted behavior of *like* as an intensifier as compared with *even, only, just, also,* and *too*.[37]

LIKE AND MOVEMENT RULES

If *like* is associated with focus, as argued here, then its behavior should provide a litmus test for focus assignment in cases for which such assignment is debatable. In most of our examples to this point, we have relied on question–answer sentences where the focus is generally agreed upon. Now, however, we wish to extend the analysis of *like* to cases in which the location of the primary focus is less clear.

Langacker (1974), among others has claimed that fronting and backing rules serve complementary functions. Whereas fronting rules place focus on the moved constituent, backing rules reduce focus. Based on the prior discussion of *like*'s association with focus, we predict that pauseless *like* should be allowed to precede moved constituents when fronted, but not when backed. This prediction is confirmed below in the case of left- vs. right-dislocation.

(259a)   Like John's stereo, it really bothers me.
(259b)   *It really bothers me, like John's stereo.

Also consider topicalization (fronting) vs. heavy noun-phrase shift (backing).

(260a)   Like these trivial points I'd never bring to Morgan's attention.
(260b)   ??I'd never bring to Morgan's attention like these trivial points.

A preference for *like* with fronted constituents is also observed for some adverbs, as shown below; but, for reasons that we do not understand, *like* can occur equally well with fronted vs. nonfronted prepositional phrases:

---

[37]It seems particularly difficult to distinguish *only* and *just* semantically, yet we have observed striking differences in their behavior. If a relevant semantic difference cannot be found, we must turn to phonology for an explanation of their different behavior. In this regard, note that hopped *like* and *even* require pauses, whereas hopped *also, only,* and *too* do not. The members of the latter group each terminate in an open syllable, unlike members of the former. We do not dare, however, suggest that the phonological distinction between open and closed syllables will lead to an account of why only some hopped intensifiers, in fact, require pauses.

(261a) Like maybe we should leave tomorrow.
(261b) *We should leave tomorrow like maybe.
(262a) Like in Chicago I'll attend the hardware convention.
(262b) I'll attend the hardware convention like in Chicago.

Using *like* as a means of ascribing focus has thus produced support (although not unanimous) for Langacker's claim about the functional distinction between fronting and backing rules.

SPEECH PROCESSING

At the outset, we hoped that the study of *like*, occurring as a filler in casual speech, would shed light on the nature of the speaker's code. Our findings suggest that this code contains an intricate syntactic component, similar to one required for intensifiers found in both speech and writing.

From the standpoint of speech production, the salient feature of this study is the systematic relation between *like*'s position and the presence or absence of pausing. This finding, also generalized to intensifiers, raises the question: "Why is *like* accompanied by pausing when it follows the focused element but not when *like* precedes?" We have not been able to arrive at a satisfactory answer, although an account of this highly systematic relation must surely be included in any comprehensive theory of speech production. One possibility is that the pausing that accompanies hopped *like* and most intensifiers is produced as a consequence of the speaker's programming a relatively low fundamental frequency for these hopped words. Typically, the focused element carries a relatively high fundamental frequency (F_o), bearing stress, and the speaker might need to insert a short pause in order to make the laryngeal adjustments required for a subsequent low F_o (for a review of these laryngeal adjustments, see Halle & Stevens, 1971). In order for this account to hold, it must also explain why *like* is not accompanied by pauses in most circumstances when it precedes the focused element. To handle this fact, it would be necessary to motivate a principle stating that abrupt F_o lowering (of the kind that accompanies hopped *like*) requires more time to make laryngeal adjustments than the gradual F_o raising that accompanies pauseless *like*. No strong motivation is apparent, however, and, even if it were obtained, the account would leave unexplained why a pause also occurs just after *like* when it follows the focused element.

The pauses that occur both before and after hopped *like* seem related to the pauses that accompany parentheticals. As with *like*, parenthetical expressions such as "I guess" are bounded by pauses when such expressions follow the constituent they are associated with, as in (263b).

(263a) I guess HARRY flunked the writing exam.

(263b)   HARRY, I guess, flunked the writing exam.
(263c)   Harry is I guess FLUNKING the writing exam.
(263d)   Harry is FLUNKING, I guess, the writing exam.

In short, it seems like a principled account of why pausing accompanies hopped *like* and intensifiers should also be capable of handling the pausing that accompanies "hopped" parentheticals (Cooper, in press; Emonds, 1976).

The present study also appears to have implications for speech perception. In some circumstances, *like* may be inserted by speakers as an aid to listeners, signalling focus. *Like*'s occurrence in such instances might produce a momentary heightening of attention in listeners, enabling them to process the focused element more efficiently (whether this element has just entered the perceptual system, as with hopped *like*, or is about to be entered, as with pauseless *like*). The listeners' heightened attention might be revealed experimentally during the performance of perceptual tasks such as phoneme-monitoring (Foss, 1969) or listening for mispronunciations (Cole, 1973). It is also possible that *like*'s insertion, especially during very fast speech, serves as an aid to listeners by allowing them an extra fraction of a second to catch up in processing the input, as might be revealed in performance on tasks such as those utilized by Chodorow (Chapter 3, this volume).

Finally, speakers themselves might be more likely to insert *like* when they are speaking to listeners who appear generally inattentive. With some stalwart *like* users, this possibility does not hold. For them, *like* is inserted during fast speech regardless of how the speaker perceives the listener's inattentiveness (in some cases, the speaker may not even be aware of the listener's state). But for those speakers who use *like* less frequently and who are sensitive to their listeners' attentiveness, *like* may be inserted as an attention-getting device. This possibility can be tested experimentally by examining conversations in which the listener's attentiveness is systematically varied.

In summary, this chapter has raised a number of questions about speech processing, and certain of these questions have been sufficiently well defined to permit subjecting them to empirical test. An ongoing interplay between armchair and laboratory seems to be the most promising way of continuing this study of casual speech. And so the moment has arrived for us to don our laboratory whites.

REFERENCES

Anderson, S. R. How to get *even*. *Language,* 1972, *48*, 893–906.
Baker, C. L. Stress level and auxiliary behavior in English. *Linguistic Inquiry*, 1972, *2*, 167–181.
Boomer, D. S. Hesitation and grammatical encoding. *Language and Speech,* 1965, *8*, 148–158.
Bresnan, J. W. Sentence stress and syntactic transformations. *Language,* 1971, *47*, 257–281.

Chodorow, M. S. Time compressed speech and the study of lexical and syntactic processing. In W. E. Cooper & E. C. T. Walker (Eds.), *Sentence processing: Psycholinguistic studies presented to Merrill Garrett*. Hillsdale, N.J.: Lawrence Erlbaum Associates, 1979.

Chomsky, N. Deep structure, surface structure, and semantic interpretation. In D. Steinberg & L. Jakobovitz (Eds.), *Semantics: An interdisciplinary reader in philosophy, linguistics, and psychology*. New York: Cambridge University Press, 1971.

Chomsky, N., & Halle, M. *The sound pattern of English*. New York: Harper & Row, 1968.

Cole, R. A. Listening for mispronunciations. *Perception & Psychophysics*, 1973, *14*, 153–156.

Cooper, W. E. Syntactic-to-phonetic coding. In B. Butterworth (Ed.), *Language production*. New York: Academic Press, in press.

Emonds, J. E. *A transformational approach to English syntax*. New York: Academic Press, 1976.

Fauconnier, G. Do quantifiers branch? *Linguistic Inquiry*, 1975, *6*, 555–567.

Fiengo, R. W., & Lasnik, H. Some issues in the theory of transformations. *Linguistic Inquiry*, 1976, *7*, 182–191.

Foss, D. J. Decision processes during sentence comprehension: Effects of lexical item difficulty and position upon decision times. *Journal of Verbal Learning and Verbal Behavior*, 1969, *8*, 457–462.

Fraser, B. J. An analysis of 'even' in English. In C. Fillmore & D. T. Langendoen (Eds.), *Studies in linguistic semantics*. New York: Holt, Rinehart, & Winston, 1971.

Fromkin, V. A. The non-anomalous nature of anomalous utterances. *Language*, 1971, *47*, 27–52.

Garrett, M. F. The analysis of sentence production. In G. Bower (Ed.), *Advances in learning theory and motivation* (Vol. 9). New York: Academic Press, 1975.

Goldman-Eisler, F. *Psycholinguistics: Experiments in spontaneous speech*. New York: Academic Press, 1968.

Halle, M., & Stevens, K. N. A note on laryngeal features. *Quarterly Progress Report of the M.I.T. Research Laboratory of Electronics*, 1971, *101*, 198–213.

Hankamer, J. Unacceptable ambiguity. *Linguistic Inquiry*, 1973, *4*, 17–68.

Horn, L. R. A presuppositional analysis of *only* and *even*. In R. I. Binnick, A. Davidson, G. Green, & J. Morgan (Eds.), *Papers from the fifth regional meeting of the Chicago Linguistic Society*. Chicago: Chicago Linguistic Society, 1969.

Jackendoff, R. S. *Semantic interpretation in generative grammar*. Cambridge, Mass.: MIT Press, 1972.

James, D. *The syntax and semantics of interjections in English*. Unpublished doctoral dissertation, University of Michigan, Ann Arbor, 1973.

Kayne, R. *French syntax: The transformational cycle*. Cambridge, Mass.: MIT Press, 1975.

Keyser, S. J., & Postal, P. M. *Beginning English grammar*. New York: Harper & Row, 1976.

King, H. V. On blocking the rules for contraction in English. *Linguistic Inquiry*, 1970, *1*, 134–136.

Klima, E. S. Negation in English. In J. A. Fodor & J. J. Katz (Eds.), *The structure of language: Readings in the philosophy of language*. Englewood Cliffs, N.J.: Prentice-Hall, 1964.

Kuroda, S-Y. *Generative grammatical studies in the Japanese language*. Unpublished doctoral dissertation, MIT, 1965.

Langacker, R. W. Mirror image rules I: Syntax. *Language*, 1969, *45*, 575–598.

Langacker, R. W. Movement rules in functional perspective. *Language*, 1974, *50*, 630–664.

Maling, J. Notes on quantifier-postposing. *Linguistic Inquiry*, 1976, *7*, 708–718.

Martin, J. G. Some acoustic and grammatical features of spontaneous speech. In D. J. Horton & J. J. Jenkins (Eds.), *The perception of language*. Columbus, Ohio: C. E. Merrill, 1971.

Perlmutter, D. M., & Postal, P. M. *Relational grammar*. Book in preparation, 1978.

Postal, P. M. *On raising: One rule of English grammar and its theoretical implications*. Cambridge, Mass.: MIT Press, 1974. (a)

Postal, P. M. On certain ambiguities. *Linguistic Inquiry,* 1974, *5,* 367–424. (b)

Reinhart, T. *The syntactic domain of anaphora.* Unpublished doctoral dissertation, MIT, 1976.

Ross, J. R. *Constraints on variables in syntax.* Unpublished doctoral dissertation, MIT, 1967.

Ross, J. R. Auxiliaries as main verbs. In W. Todd (Ed.), *Studies in philosophical linguistics—Series one.* Evanston, Ill.: Great Expectations, 1969.

Ross, J. R. Clausematiness. In E. L. Keenan (Ed.), *Formal semantics of natural language.* New York: Cambridge University Press, 1975.

Shattuck-Hufnagel, S. Remarks on an aspect of a sentence production model based on speech-error patterns. In W. E. Cooper & E. C. T. Walker (Eds.), *Sentence processing: Psycholinguistic studies presented to Merrill Garrett.* Hillsdale, N.J.: Lawrence Erlbaum Associates, 1979.

Stampe, D. *How I spent my summer vacation.* Unpublished doctoral dissertation, University of Chicago, 1972.

Zwicky, A. M. Auxiliary reduction in English. *Linguistic Inquiry,* 1970, *1,* 323–336.

12

Three Cheers for Propositional Attitudes (Some Reflections on D. C. Dennett's "Intentional Systems")

J. A. Fodor
Massachusetts Institute of Technology

The belief that P has fallen upon hard times.[1] Here is how it came about. Many respectable philosophers used to think that substitution instances of the scheme *y believes tht P* (*=S*), together with their friends and logical relations, are eliminable from English *salva* the expressive power of the language. Roughly, each sentence generated by substitution in *S* was to be replaced by some (logically equivalent, perhaps synonymous) sentence in which the predicate expresses a form of behavior or a disposition to behave. Insouciance prevailed; nobody actually provided the analyses, and there were those who seemed to glory in not providing them. So, Ryle (if I read him right) held both that talking about propositional attitudes is just a way of talking about behavior or behavioral dispositions *and* that nothing that can be (finitely) said about behavior or behavioral dispositions can, in the general case, exhaust the content of the ascription of a propositional attitude. A darkish doctrine, no doubt, but those were darkish times.

At their very worst, however, the *facticity* of such ascriptions went unimpugned. If, after all, claims about the belief that P are claims about the

---

[1] I use 'believe' as my paradigm of a verb of propositional attitude, but sometimes vary the verb to break the tedium. What I assume that all such verbs have in common (insofar as they engage the topic of this paper) is their tendency to establish opaque (specifically, intentional) contexts. Opaque contexts are, for example, those in which the substitution of coreferring expressions fails to preserve truth. That is a miserably imprecise characterization of the class of cases at issue, but no more precision is needed for the purposes at hand.

A note on orthography: I use 'inten*s*ional' to mean, in effect, *opaque,* and I use 'inten*t*ional' to mean *opaque and psychological.* Some intensional contexts are thus nonintentional in this usage: whereas, all intentional contexts are ipso facto intensional.

behaviors of organisms, then surely they are at ontological par with other things that we say about the doings of middle-sized objects. Even if the analysis of such ascriptions should exhibit them as intractably dispositional, it is arguably a fact that salt is soluble: Why should it not be as good a fact that P-believers are disposed to P-behave (disposed, for instance, to utter tokens of 'I believe that P')?

We all know now that this will not work. Not, of course, that it is impossible to find some formula logically equivalent to "x believes that P" in which 'believes' does not occur: there are expressions in French that would do for that. The point is, rather, that any such expression is itself bound to contain intentional idioms, so if what one had in mind was not so much doing without 'believes' but eliminating intentionality at large, it looks as though the behaviorist program just cannot be carried out. Take uttering "I believe that P." Doing that is not (as one used to say) "criterial" for believing that P unless producing the utterance at least constitutes the making of a statement. But statements are utterances intentionally (in the other sense, namely, willfully) uttered: mere random giving voice will not do. And, of course, 'intentional' is intentional. So, by one or the other route, the verbs of propositional attitude bend back upon themselves: they are, perhaps, interdefinable, but there appears to be no way out of the circle of intentional idioms.

"So be it," some philosophers have said, "and so much the worse for the circle of intentional idioms. If believers won't behave, we won't have any." Hence, the view is now widely current among philosophers that the refutation of *logical* behaviorism was tantamount to a demonstration of the *un*facticity of ascriptions of propositional attitudes and, thus, to the establishment of a sort of *eliminative* behaviorism. Strictly speaking, according to this new account, there is no question of truth of falsity about what a man believes, hopes, intends, supposes, etc. Strictly speaking, we could encounter all the facts there are and not encounter any facts like these. So, it is all right if we *cannot* express in our purely extensional (or, anyhow, purely nonintentional) language—the language we reserve for such solemnities as formalizing physics—what we *can* express by reference to intentions. Physics is, perhaps, committed to saying all there is to say that is strictly true; but there is nothing strictly true that can be said about propositional attitudes. What can't be said can't be said, and it can't be reduced to physics either.

It is worth emphasizing the difference between this reaction and the one that has been typical among psychologists. The psychologists have reasoned: statements about mental states and processes are not translatable into statement about behavior. Hence there must be facts about mental states and processes. Hence, behaviorism is false. Whereas, the philosophers have reasoned: statements about mental states and processes are not translatable into statements about behavior. Hence there must not be facts about mental states or processes. Hence behaviorism is true. Clearly, one or the other of these lines of reasoning must be unsound. This paper is about which one.

To begin with, if there are no facts about mental states and processes, that is *very* surprising. For, the simple facticity of at least *some* ascriptions of propositional attitudes had seemed to be among life's little certainties. So, prior to philosophical instruction, one might have thought it straightout true not only that, say, Carter's name begins with *C,* but also that one *believes* that Carter's name begins with *C.* And, one might have thought, there is not much to choose between these truths. After all, Carter's name does begin with *C,* and one knows, more or less, how to spell. So why on Earth should one *not* have the belief when all the evidence conspires to tempt one to it? The burden of argument lies, surely, upon those who say that it is not the case that one believes even what one is strongly disposed to believe that one believes.

Moreover, nobody supposes that the failure of logical behaviorism literally *entails* the unfacticity of propositional attitude ascriptions. "Behaviorism or nothing" will strike the sophisticated as not self-evidently true. If, in short, the burden of argument is to be taken up, supporting considerations will need to be adduced. Such considerations have recently been proposed on several hands. I want to look at some of them in this paper. In particular, I want to consider in detail D. C. Dennett's (1971) account of the role of intentional ascriptions in explanations of behavior. Dennett's theory, if true, would make it clear why it is unreasonable to expect such ascriptions to be more than just heuristic. Whereas I am inclined to think that, so far at least, the case against propositional attitudes rests unproven. For all that anyone has thus far shown, ascriptions of beliefs, when true at all, are literal.[2]

Dennett recommends that we "Consider the case of a chess-playing computer, and the different strategies or stances one might adopt as its opponent in trying to predict its moves [p. 87]." It may not, at first, be clear why we should *want* to consider a chess-playing computer in the course of considering what underlies our ascriptions of intentional properties to intentional systems: prima facie, a computer is a shaky example of such a system, and it is not beyond doubt that ascriptions of intentional properties to machines rest on relatively dubious analogies to solid paradigms like us. Still, marginal cases can have their philosophical uses, and I suppose that Dennett's strategy is this: In deciding what to say about a marginal case, we shall have to trot out reasons and that should help clarify what kinds of reasons can, in principle, be alleged in favor of intentional ascriptions.

Moreover, as Dennett sees very clearly, the example serves to illustrate the involvement of intentional ascription in the prediction and explanation of

---

[2]I take it that this conclusion is important if correct. After all, if there are no facts about mental states and processes, then there is, quite literally, nothing for psychology to be about. In this respect, the methodological implications of the new, eliminative behaviorism are even *more* radical than those of the old, reductive behaviorism. On the latter view psychology at least had a subject matter: the organization of behavior.

To put it brutally, the choice used to be between mentalism and tedium. It is now between mentalism and unemployment.

behavior: Our interest in intentional ascriptions is—at least for the present case—part and parcel of our interest in figuring out what the machine is likely to *do*. Dennett (says:

> A man's best hope of defeating such a machine in a chess match is to predict its responses by figuring out as best he can what the best or most rational move would be given the rules and goals of chess. That is, one assumes not only (1) that the machine will function as designed, but (2) that the design is optimal as well, that the computer will 'choose' the most rational move [p. 89].

Now, it is notable, according to Dennett, that the recourse to intentional ascription is not the *only* way that we could, in principle, go about predicting the machine's moves. For, on the one hand, the moves could be predicted from a knowledge of the physical construction of the machine (assuming, as we may for present purposes, that the machine's physical construction determines its moves) and, on the other, the moves could also be predicted by reference to the machine's teleological or functional structure. Dennett says that, in making predictions in the first way, we are adopting a "physical stance" towards the machine and that in making predictions in the second way we are adopting a "design stance." "The essential feature of the design stance is that we make predictions solely from knowledge of assumptions about the system's functional design, irrespective of the physical constitution of the innards of the particular object [p. 88]." Design-stance predictions are riskier than are physical-stance predictions, for, presumably, if we have an inference whose premises are physical laws and a specification of the physical state of the machine at t, and whose conclusion is that the machine will do such-and-such at t', then that prediction can go wrongly only insofar as the physics of the machine is not deterministic. Whereas, consider a corresponding inference whose premises are true generalizations about the functional design of the system (e.g., its program) and a specification of its functional state at t. Such an argument will be reliable only when the machine functions as it is designed to function: when, for example, it does not break down, blow out, strip a gear, etc. Failures-to-function yield exceptions to design-stance predictions but not to physical-stance predictions.

The intentional stance is like the others in that we adopt it insofar (perhaps *only* insofar; Dennett does not say) as we are interested in the prediction of behavior. And, like the design stance, it is prone to kinds of fallibility that the physical stance is immune to. When we assume the intentional stance, we figure out what the system will do by figuring out what it would be *rational* to do and then predicting that the system will do *that*. Now, supposing that the system *is* rational, it will still be true that intentional-stance predictions will typically go astray insofar as the system misfunctions, so intentional stance predictions inherit the kinds of fallibility that design-stance predictions are prone to. But, moreover, they have problems of their own since, even if the system does not misfunction—even if no gear strips—it may fail to do the rational thing because it failed to be designed to be rational. Where the, as it were, program of the device is less than optimal, the intentional-stance prediction will be correspondingly less than reliable.

Why, then, resort to the intentional stance at all? For two reasons (both of them, notice, *purely* epistemological). First, because we may know what it would be rational for the system to do even if we do not know what the physical constitution or the program of the system is, so we may be in a position to predict behavior from the intentional stance even when we are not in a position to predict it from the physical or design stances. Second, even if we *do* know what the physics is, or what the functional analysis is, predictions based upon either may become unfeasible in practice when the system is sufficiently complicated. In either case, then, it is essentially practical considerations that force us to intentional ascriptions: in particular, it is *not* considerations of *truth*. Dennett says: "The decision to adopt the strategy is pragmatic and is not intrinsically right or wrong. One can always refuse to adopt the intentional stance, . . . one can switch stances at will . . . etc. [p. 91]." We, as it were, adopt the intentional stance towards a system because of facts about *us,* not because of facts about *it.*

So, Dennett's analysis takes us where it was supposed to; it explains the utility (and hence, presumably, the prevalence) of the intentional idiom without assuming that there are facts that intentional ascriptions correspond to. If the analysis is right, then the least hypothesis is, surely, that there are no such facts and that appears to be the conclusion Dennett wants us to endorse.

What, then, can be said in favor of the analysis? Dennett gives two kinds of arguments, and we will want to look at them in turn. The first argument goes like this: Since intentional stance predictions will work only insofar as we are dealing with rational systems, an assumption of rationality is implicit in every such prediction. But such assumptions are ours to make or to withhold: i.e., they are themselves heuristic idealizations, justifiable only insofar as they lead, by and large, to true intentional stance predictions. So, we can conclude the unfacticity of propositional attitude ascriptions from the unfacticity of rationality assumptions that they presuppose. Second, Dennett holds that intentional stance predictions are, in a sense to be explored, inherently question-begging. Why Dennett thinks that will take some unpacking later in the paper, but the rough idea is something like this: Intentional stance explanations typically advert to one or another form of problem-solving activity that the agent is presumed to have performed: We may explain an action, for example, by referring to the beliefs and utilities of the agent and to some principle of reasoning that we assume the agent has applied. However, applying principles of reasoning is itself a form of intelligent activity; Dennett puts it that, insofar as intentional explanations postulate such processes, they "take out a loan of intelligence [p. 96]." But, "In the end, we want to be able to explain the intelligence of man . . . so whenever we stop in our explanations at the intentional level we have left an unexplained instance of rationality [p. 96]."

I do not think either of these arguments is very convincing either in the condensed form in which I have just sketched them or in the unpacked versions in which Dennett gives them. Let us now have a look at the details.

ARGUMENT 1: THE POSTULATE OF RATIONALITY

Dennett needs to show (a) that some assumption of rationality is implicit in any attempt to predict the behavior of an organism from its intentional states and (b) that such assumptions are somehow just heuristic. I am going to focus on (a) for the moment; given the purposes that Dennett has in mind for it, if (a) cannot be sustained, it does not matter much what the case is for (b).

Let us start with some softening-up arguments.

First, it just is not true that "A man's best hope of defeating a machine in a chess match is to predict its responses by figuring out as best he can what the best or most rational move would be" and predicting that move for the machine. Indeed, the hope one cherishes in playing chess with a machine (or with, for that matter, some better instance of an intentional system—say, a Russian) is that (s)he/it *won't* make the best, most rational, optimal (etc.) move, but will, instead, make the very move that falls for one's little ruses, springs one's little traps, and, in general, exhibits levels of intellectual functioning gratifyingly inferior to one's own. Trap-baiting is itself rational only in the light of such hopes and predictions.

I am not quibbling. Dennett's case is supposed to show us straight-off that our predictions from the intentional stance depend upon postulates of optimal functioning. Whereas, it is precisely from the intentional stance that we hope and fondly expect that our opponent will not *notice* our traps, or that if our traps are noticed they will not be *understood,* or, if they are understood, no way out of them will be *seen, remembered,* or otherwise *conjured up.* These, surely, are intentional idioms par excellence, so it is precisely here that we would expect postulates of optimality to be deployed. For all that, we do not play chess on the assumption that our opponent will make the optimal move; indeed (a small point) in any game much more complicated than, say, tick-tack-toe, one is unlikely to have a clue as to what the optimal move is, or even, indeed, whether one exists. The intentionality of one's opponent's propositional attitudes in not thereby impugned.

These observations point in two directions, and I want to look both ways. First, there is something odd about a theory of intentional ascription which does not explain why intentional idioms have the characteristic properties they do: namely, the property that inferences warranted in transparent contexts *fail* when the context is opaque. Second, it seems clear that intentional explanation works in all sorts of cases where it is precisely *lapses* from optimal rationality that are at issue. These points in order.

1. A theory of intentional ascription ought to explain why intentional predicates are intensional (with-an-'s'), and the theory that assumptions of rationality are at the core of intentional ascriptions does not do so. On the contrary; quite generally, the more rational a system is assumed to be, the more justified we are in substituting in the (syntactic) objects of statements about its propositional attitudes: i.e., in reading such statements *transparently* rather than opaquely. Consider God. God is, I suppose, *fully* rational in the sense of rationality that Dennett explicitly has in mind. That is, God believes the entailments of his beliefs, so that, from 'God believes P' and 'P entails Q', we have the right to infer 'God believes Q'. Whereas, though God's beliefs are closed under the entailment relation, ours very notably are not. It is part and parcel of the opacity of *our* propositional attitudes that the inference from 'we believe P' and 'P entails Q' to 'we believe Q' is not, in general, valid. Suppose, now, that God is not merely rational but also omniscient. Then we have the full transparancy of all belief contexts for God; i.e., we have not only the closure of God's beliefs under entailment, but also under material implication; and we have their closure under substitution of coreferring expressions. So, if God believes that Cicero denounced Catiline, and if Cicero = Tully, then God believes that Tully denounced Catiline. Similarly, mutatis mutandis, for God's views about Bernard Ortcutt and the man in the brown hat.

So, the more rational the system, the less opaque its belief contexts. The *more* we assume "optimality of functioning," the *less* intentionality, opacity, etc., we have to deal with.[3] How, one is inclined rhetorically to demand, could it then be that an assumption of rationality and optimality of functioning is somehow built into our ascriptions of intentional predicates?

It may be worth reemphasizing that what holds for God *in excelsis* holds for chess playing machines only *in moderation*. Suppose I have moved my knight to KB4, and suppose that my knight's being at KB4 = my knight's threatening Black's queen. We assume that Black knows the general principles of chess, whatever those may be. So then, by hypothesis, it follows from what Black knows and notices that the positioning of my knight = (hence entails) the threatening of Black's Queen. The principle of rationality is, inter alia, the

---

[3]It is worth noting (as Dennett and others have pointed out to me) that the closure of *belief* under entailment does *not* imply the transparency of such *other* propositional attitudes as, for example, remembering. Assume: *a remembers that P* and *a believes that P→a believes that Q*. It does not follow from these premises that *a remembers* that Q. Roughly, to get transparency of a propositional attitude, you need closure (under the relevant consequence relation) of *that very attitude*.

principle that noticings are closed under their entailments. So, if I am assuming Black's rationality, I am assuming, inter alia, that Black notices the threat.

Whereas, what I hope and predict is precisely that the threat will go unmarked. Nor, in so predicting, have I abandoned the intentional stance. On the contrary, I may rationally predict Black's lapse precisely *because* of what I know or believe about Black's intentional states: in particular, about what he is and is not likely to notice. I have, let's suppose, a mini-theory about Black's noticings. Put vulgarly, the theory might be that Black is a sucker for a knight fork. I get my prediction from this theory, and the postulates of the theory reek of intentionality. Where is the assumption of rationality? If to be rational is to believe the consequences of one's beliefs, and if the opacity of propositional attitudes is the failure of closure under the consequence relation, then to ascribe an intentional predicate to a system will often involve postulating its *ir*rationality if the predicate is opaquely construed. Or, to put the moral of the example slightly differently, it is not postulates of rationality that license intentional stance predictions: it is (mini- or maxi-, formal or informal) theories about who is likely to have which propositional attitude when, and what behavioral consequences are likely to ensue.[4]

2. This brings us to the second point, which is precisely that intentional explanations run rampant just where they should not if the postulate of rationality story were true: namely, in the psychology of one or another *dis*function. What I have in mind is not so much the exotic specimens that get retailed in psychoanalytic paperbacks, but rather the psychology of such mundane propositional attitudes as, say, forgetting and misunderstanding. Much of our most respectable cognitive psychology operates in this area, and it operates essentially with intentional predicates. Quite a lot is known, for example, about the kinds of mistakes that people make in deductive reasoning. So, to come to cases, it is known that one does worse with arguments that contain negative premises than with matched arguments in the affirmative mode (for a review, see Wason & Johnson-Laird, 1972). You will do better, that is to say, with the information that P is true than with the information that not-P is false, and the difference remains when banal variables are controlled away. But, of course, 'information' must be opaquely

---

[4]Of course, to say that intentional stance prediction often rests upon assumptions of less than optimal functioning is not to say that they rest on the assumption that the system will act at random or go nuts. What *is* assumed, if anything is, is that the system will, by and large, behave in ways that are intelligible in light of its beliefs and utilities. But there is no methodological moral to be drawn from *that* assumption, since it is just a solemn way of saying that we do not offer intentional ascriptions unless we assume the phenomena under investigation to be susceptible of *some intentional explanation or other*. And that, of course, is not a deep insight into the notion of intentionality; it is just a truism. It is admirable about Dennett's paper—and essential to an understanding of what he is up to—that it is something much stronger than this truism that Dennett is arguing for.

construed if this generalization is to be so much as stated. The information that P is the information that not-P $\supset$ F on the transparent construal. And equally, of course, it is all One to God whether P or not (not P), since belief is closed under entailment for a perfectly rational Being functioning optimally.

Such cases are legion, but I will not provide more here. What I take it that they all come to for our purposes is that ascriptions of intentionality and postulates of optimality are largely independent in precisely the area where it is most important that intentional idioms should be available; namely, in the (formal and informal) psychology of cognition. What *is* characteristic of this area—what I believe *does* explain the opacity of typical psychological idioms—is the relativization of our descriptions of the intentional states of a system to the way that the system represents the objects of its propositional attitudes. That is, however, a very long story, and one that I have tried to tell elsewhere (Fodor, 1975, 1979). Suffice it to say here that much of our psychology is the psychology of lapses from rationality, and its typical idioms are opaque all the same.

These were, as I remarked, softening-up arguments. I suspect that, for Dennett's purposes, they could all be met by a judicious pulling in of horns. Suppose, then, that we limit the discussion (not to intentional explanations at large, but) just to the cases where the behavior of a system is explained/predicated by reference to its beliefs and utilities. I imagine that these are the cases Dennett has most in mind and, surely, if postulates of rationality are somewhere in the offing, it is here that we are likely to find them. In what I take to be a key passage, Dennett argues as follows:

> The assumption that something is an intentional system is the assumption that is is rational; that is, one gets nowhere with the assumption that an entity x has beliefs p, q, r unless one also supposes that x believes what follows from p, q, r ... otherwise there is no way of ruling out the prediction that x will, in the face of its beliefs ... do something utterly stupid, and if we cannot rule out *that* prediction, we have acquired no predictive power at all [p. 95].

So, I take it that Dennett's view is this: A typical prediction from the intentional stance rests on (what I call) an *intentional argument*. An intentional argument has the form F:

Premise 1: In situation S, a rational agent performs action A. (I will suppose, for convenience, that situation S is specified entirely by reference to the beliefs and utilities of the agent).
Premise 2: x is in situation S.
Premise 3: x is a rational agent.
Conclusion/prediction: x performs (will perform) action A.

Dennett's point is two-fold; first, that our 'intentional stance' theories license (only) generalizations such as Premise 1 (as we have seen, Dennett holds that to adopt the intentional stance is to argue from what the system *would* do if it were rational). But, second, if this is right, then premises such as 3 figure essentially in intentional arguments. Knowledge of what a rational agent would do in situation *S,* and knowledge that x is in *S,* licenses predictions about what x will do in *S* only insofar as we assume x's rationality. So we appear to have precisely what we wanted: the essential involvement of a rationality premise in any warranted intentional stance prediction.

Now, this much is surely true: If the general premises of intentional arguments are essentially concerned with the behavior of rational agents qua rational agents, then Dennett's case is made. Patently, Premise 3 occurs essentially in *F.* So, if I am going to make an argument to the contrary, it will have to be that intentional arguments are not (or anyhow, need not be) of form F. In particular, I will argue that we need not advert to the rationality of agents in the general premises of intentional arguments and, hence, that rationality premises such as 3 contribute nothing essential to intentional stance predictions.

First, however, I want to consider briefly a methodological issue that is lurking in the background. Arguments of the form *F* look to be special cases of kinds of argument quite familiar from areas of science other than psychology: namely, arguments from idealized models to predicted observations. So, to cite a familiar example, we argue from the known functional relation between the temperature and pressure of an ideal gas to the predicted relation between the temperature and pressure of a laboratory sample. In this case, as in Dennett's, the generalizations that the theory licenses are stated, prima facie, for ideal objects. So, prima facie, we need some sort of argument analogous to *F* to mediate the relation between what the theory talks about and what the laboratory scientist applies the theory to. In particular (still prima facie), we need something analogous to Premise 3 if we are to use the theory to grind out predictions. For, on the one hand, the theory applies to the sample only insofar as the latter satisfies such predicates as the generalizations of the theory deploy; and, on the other hand, 'is an ideal gas' figures largely among such predicates. It looks as though we will need a premise such as 'the sample is an ideal gas' if we are to predict the behavior of the sample from the generalizations of the theory.

And this, in turn, can look very paradoxical. For, after all, we want not only that our scientific theories should figure in the making of true predictions, but also that they should do so via sound arguments. Only a silly philosophy of science is content *just* to save the appearances. Yet we seem to have here a case where a premise that figures essentially in an argument from theory to prediction is, and is known to be, patently false. For, of course, our laboratory samples are not ideal gasses within the meaning of the theory, nor are the containers in which we keep them ideally impervious, etc.

There is a temptation to panic at this point. So, one might say not just of intentional stance theories, but also of the theory of gasses, that it is after all, 'not intrinsically right or wrong', 'heuristic', a mere 'stance' that we can 'switch at will', etc. It is, in short, easy to get into a frame of mind where one treats the rationality assumption in intentional arguments as analogous to standard cases of scientific idealization and then infers the unfacticity of the rationality assumption from a conventionalist account of idealization at large. I do not know if this is actually what happened in Dennett's case. But whether or not it did, I think that the assimilation of intentional arguments to idealized arguments is pretty clearly ill advised.

Paradigm cases of scientific idealization (the thermodynamics of ideal gasses, the chemistry of literally pure samples, the mechanics of frictionalless planes, etc.) involve a very special kind of relation between the parameter values the theory predicts and the ones that experimentation derives: namely, the latter *approximate* the former. The indispensability of idealization lies, at least in part, in the fact that it is only 'in the limit' that we obtain parameter values that precisely satisfy the laws. Which is to say that, strictly speaking (and barring accidents), we do not obtain them at all. At best the observations tend to converge upon the ideal values, and we need the idealization because it is only at the point of convergence that the lawful relations that the theory postulates are strictly satisfied. Unless the ideal objects yield the predicted parameter values, nothing does.

Whereas, the rationality case is quite different. Here the problem is not that our behavior tends towards rationality *in the limit*. It is rather that our behavior is only rational *some of the time*: namely, barring the exceptions. We get, as it were, the parameter values that the rationality premise predicts, but we also get counter cases due to lapses of attention, weakness of the flesh, and, for that matter, sheer bull-headedness. Now, my point is this: It may well be that predictive power depends upon idealization in the approximation-to-the-limit cases, for as we have seen, in such cases it is only at the limit that the predictions of the theory are ever true. But it is quite unclear that idealization contributes to predictive power in the barring-the-exceptions cases. In particular, it is quite unclear that it buys us predictive power in the case of intentional arguments. So, to return to cases: suppose we recast argument F as follows:

F':
Premise 1: Being in situation S causes agents to perform action A.[5]

---

[5]For present purposes we could, if we wished, settle for something less tendentious, along the lines of 'agents in situation S perform action A'. I have chosen the causal version because (a) it seems to me overwhelmingly plausible that the relation between the beliefs and utilities of the agent on the one hand, and his actions on the other, *is* causal, and if it is, why not say so? (b) I want to emphasize that I am taking premise 1 of *F* to be a *contingent* generalization; that the contingency of such premises is not impugned by the consideration that action A may be the rational, reasonable, logical, etc., thing for an agent in S to do.

Premise 2: x is in situation S.

Premise 3: x is an agent.

Conclusion/prediction: x performs (will perform) action A.

Now, the first thing to notice about F' is this: insofar as Premise 1 holds only for rational agents, it will fail to subsume x when x is *ir*rational. It follows that cases of irrational *x*s will be cases for which the argument is unsound, hence cases for which the conclusion of the argument is unreliable. So, it may seem that we have, after all, lost predictive power in going from F to F', just as Dennett warned us that we would.

But, of course, we have not, since *the cases where irrationality makes x a counter-instance to Premise 1 of argument F' will also be the case where irrationality makes x a counter-instance to Premise 3 of argument F*. If, in short, irrational agents are not covered by intentional stance theories, then they are not covered. We cannot, as it were, make the theory better by a mere exercise of charity to *x*s. All we can do that way is to transfer the locus of unsoundness from Premise 1 to Premise 3. But an argument with a false premise is an unsound argument, and a prediction derived by an unsound argument is an unwarranted prediction. It does not matter which shell we put the pea under.

So, just as one might have supposed, one does not have a case where we increase the power of a theory to make *warranted* predictions by adding false statements to the theory; and who cares about increasing the power of a theory to make *un*warranted predictions? In short, the rationality premise of F has brought us nothing that we could not have had without it via F'.

One further point. Arguments such as F can never be made exceptionless: Organisms will always be fallible, so Premise 3 will always be susceptible to counter-example. Whereas, precisely because arguments of the form F' *are not* committed to rationality premises, there is some chance that, as our psychology gets better, we may approach the formulation of general premises that will make such arguments strictly sound. That is, arguments such as F' should be preferred to arguments such as F even if it were not independently desirable to eliminate the worrying postulate of rationality. Premise 1 of F' is not, after all, noticeably worse than, for example, "matches light when struck": the counter-examples can be enumerated insofar as they are systematic and ignored insofar as they are not.

Thus far I have been reading Dennett as holding, in effect, that intentional arguments are heuristic because their predictive power depends essentially on a rationality premise. I have tried to meet that argument by suggesting that such premises can always be replaced by corresponding causal premises and that making the switch yields no loss of warranted predictive power. It may be, however, that the argument I have attacked is not the one that Dennett is proposing. It may be that Dennett's point is just that intentional arguments rest on intentional theories and such theories are per se inherently heuristic, take it or leave it. Dennett sometimes writes in ways that make one inclined to think that he thinks that, but there is no place where he straight-out says it. What he *does* say is that, though he assumes that there are intentional systems, "the definition of Intentional systems I have given does not say that Intentional systems *really* have beliefs and desires, but that one can explain and predict their behavior by ascribing beliefs and desires to them [p. 91]." But we have all been here before. People used to say (I suppose some still do) that we do not have to accept electrons; only that the world behaves in such fashion that one can predict and explain by ascribing electrons to it. To which there is a standard and decisive reply: It's a good hunch that the reason the world behaves in such fashion as to allow us to predict by ascribing electrons to it is that the world is made of electrons. Indeed, that would seem to be the only hunch in town. Similarly, of course, for ascriptions of beliefs and desires. It is, to put it mildy, an odd sort of argument for the *un*facticity of P that we cannot get our science off the ground unless we assume that P. Note, however, that if we are going to play the hunch that the reason our theories work is that they are true, then we shall be ontologically committed to the intentional properties our theories talk about. There is, in ontology, no such thing as a free hunch (wherein ontology recapitulates ecology).

One more point, and then I can turn briefly to the second major line of argument that Dennett gives for the heuristic character of intentional ascriptions.

I have been saying, in effect, that insofar as we want to make predictions of the form *agent x believes Q* on the grounds that *agent x believes P, P entails Q,* and *x is rational,* we might as well drop these premises and make our predictions on the grounds: *agent x believes P* and *the belief that P causes the belief that Q.* But it might be said that there is something peculiar here all the same. For, very often we will be able to predict that the belief that P causes the belief that Q *just* from the knowledge that P entails Q: and does that not show that what we are really doing here is not empirical psychology but logic disguised as empirical psychology? Does it not show that the general premises of intentional arguments are not really empirical truths at all? Dennett uses (what appears to be) this argument (circa p. 97) and seems to take it to heart.

But, so far as I can see, there is not much in it beyond what we already knew: that typically, in intentional-stance arguments, we take the agent's beliefs to be among the causes of his actions. If I have suitably motivated (and suitably literate) subjects, then I can predict with some accuracy what they will do when asked, say, to finish the line "Break break, break on thy cold..." It is perfectly true that, to make the prediction, I have to assume that the subjects have the appropriate beliefs about the rest of the line and that such beliefs contribute (presumably causally) to determine the subject's behavior in the test situation. Now, there are many ways in which I might come to have beliefs about what the subject believes about the line. In the present case, the most likely way is that (a) I know how the line continues, and (b) I have reason to believe that the subject knows approximately what I know. So, I use what I know about a bit of English literature to construct an intentional argument that runs from the subject's beliefs to his behavior; psychology recapitulates anthology. Does *that* show that there's something wrong with the predictions? For example, that its premises are somehow English lit premises and not honest-to-goodness empirical psychological premises? To suppose so would be to confuse *what the premises state* (that the subject probably knows that the line continues so-and-so) with *the reasons one has for taking the premises to be true* (the line does continue so-and-so, and I know that it does).

Similarly, mutatis mutandis, with the entailment case. In simple, nonpathological examples where P entails Q, it will be safe to assume the existence of a causal chain that runs from the subject's belief that P to his belief that Q (and that runs, often enough, via his belief that Q is entailed by P). The reason that this assumption is safe is that, as Dennett himself points out, Darwinian selection guarantees that organisms either know the elementary entailments or become dead.[6] You can get by with no Tennyson at all, but a smattering of logic is sine qua non.

ARGUMENT 2: THE VACUITY OF INTENTIONAL EXPLANATIONS

Well, then, forget about the postulate of rationality. Are intentional explanations not question-begging all the same? Dennett says this:

> Any time a theory builder proposes to call any event ... a *signal* or *message* or command (or otherwise endows it with content) he *takes out a loan of intelligence.* He implicitly posits along with his signals, messages or commands, something that can serve as a signal-*reader,* a message *understander,* or *commander* (else his "signals" will be for naught, will decay unreceived, uncomprehended.) This loan must be repaid eventually ... The intentionality of all such talk of signals and commands reminds us that rationality is being taken for granted, and in this way shows us where a theory is incomplete [p. 96, Dennett's italics].

Sometimes, however, the charge is worse than incompleteness: "whenever a theory relies on a formulation bearing the logical marks of Intentionality, there a little man is concealed [p. 96]," and, four pages later, "Intentional theory is *vacuous* in psychology, in virtue of its assumption of rationality

---

[6]It is slightly odd that Dennett *should* point this out. One would have thought that, if there is no fact of the matter about our beliefs, it could not be a consequence of an *empirical* theory that some of our beliefs are rational.

(though it's not necessarily) vacuous from all points of view [p. 100, my italics]."

Now, first, not all intentional explanations *do* advert to "signals, messages, and commands." Consider, for example, such typical examples of the species as "he said it because he believed it" and "he did it because he wanted to." I know of no reason not to regard such statements, when true, as schematic (but literal) accounts of the causal chain that runs from intentional states to behaviors. Perhaps, on closest examination, they will prove to bear the imprint of the little man who lives in the head. But Dennett's arguments give no reason to suppose that they do, and I, for one, do not believe it for a minute.

Still, some intentional explanations do operate with the sorts of constructs that Dennett has in mind: e.g., the computational explanations that machine-minded psychologists often give. Let us, therefore, consider what it might be about such explanations that would relegate them to the status of the merely heuristic. I can think of two considerations that point, prima facie, in that direction.

1. Typically, computational explanations specify the psychological process that terminates in some theoretically interesting psychological state. So, for example, computational explanations might seek to tell us how generalizations are learned from their instances, or how sentences are understood, or how chess problems are solved, etc. Typically, too, computational explanations work by specifying a sequence of subprocesses of which the macroprocess is alleged to be composed. So, it might be claimed that understanding a sentence (token) crucially involves determining where the phrase boundaries in the sentence are; or that the perceptual integration of visual arrays crucially involves determining which color discontinuities are object boundaries, and so forth. Now, to come to the point, it is often true that the same sort of *how*-questions that can be asked (and answered) about the macroprocesses can also be asked (and answered) about the constituent microprocesses. *How* does one find the phrase boundaries in a sentence? *How* does one determine whether a color discontinuity is an object boundary? Similarly, mutatis mutandis, *how* does the putative decoder in the brain 'read' the putative messages in the neural code?

There are several different kinds of things that can happen at this point. In one kind of case, we may say: "I don't know how; leave it for further research." This really *is* a case of incomplete explanation, though not, of course, a case of *vacuous* explanation. It is, after all, *something* to be told that you cannot make an omelete without breaking eggs; that is worth knowing even if you do not know, and have not been told, how to break eggs. Or again, we can imagine that the explanation may have gone as far as it *can* go, and we have to say "explanation has to stop somewhere; this explanation stops here." It is this second case, if any, that will reveal the vacuity of computational explanation, so let us consider it for a moment. I propose to make up a psycholinguistic theory and use it to show how computational explanations run out, and what happens when they do. The theory itself is puerile, as made-up psychology so often is. Philosopher's license.

—How do we understand sentence inscriptions?
—Well, say, by identifying the sequence of words of which they are composed.
—How do we identify a word?
—Well, say, by identifying the sequence of letters of which it is composed.
—How do we identify a letter?
—(Warming) Well, actually, that is *quite* an interesting question. It appears that it is done by identifying the set of features that determine the letter. By a feature I have in mind such properties of the letter as, e.g., whether it is straight or curved, whether and where the segments cross, whether there is a bit that runs below the line and, if there is, whether *that* bit is straight or curved, and so on. It is likely that there is a fixed, finite set of such features involved in letter identification, but psychologists disagree about which they are. If you are really interested, cf....
—Never mind about that. What I want to know is: how do you identify a feature?
—Well, in no *way* at all; you just *do*.
—Uh huh.

I suppose that any explanation of the sort Dennett has in mind runs out, eventually, in this fashion. We mark the points where it does so as 'elementary' or 'basic' computational processes (either absolutely basic or basic relative to the macroprocess under analysis). In recent papers, Dennett suggests that to get down to elementary computational processes *is* to repay the 'loan of intelligence' that intentional explanations take out. But I think, in fact, that this line is ill-advised (as was my endorsement of a similar view in Fodor, 1968). For, after all, basic processes may (usually will) *also* require to be intentionally described. In the present case, one identifies a feature *as the feature F;* one does not, ever, recognize it under every true description that it satisfies. So either taking out a loan of intelligence is not *intrinsic* to intentional explanation, or, if it is, getting down to elementary processes does not, in general, constitute the repayment of the loan.[7] What we have, then, is

---

[7]What prompts the confusion, I think, is that, at least in computers, getting down to elementary operations is often also getting to a level where computational descriptions of machine processes match up with engineering descriptions in a relatively simple way. In the easiest case, there is one and only one (type of) mechanism for each of the elementary computational operations. It is thus easy to fall into the habit of speaking of what is in fact merely a reduction from complex to elementary computational processes *as though* it somehow constituted a reduction to mechanisms. Hence, the suggestion that computational microanalysis pays back the loan of intelligence, avoids intentional ascriptions, and so forth.

This muddle is very nearly ubiquitous in discussions of the relation between 'hardware' and 'software' during the last decade or so. It is thus worth emphasizing that the principled relation between programs and machines is that the former instantiate the latter, and this holds *both* for macro-processes *and* micro-processes. The only difference is that, for some sorts of machines, instantiation is a one–one relation at (and only at) the level of elementary processes.

this: intentionalistic explanations eventually run out. Does this show that they are ultimately just heuristic? And, if not, why not?

First, all explanations, including physical stance explanations, eventually run out. You cannot go higher than the highest covering law, and you cannot go deeper than the deepest 'hidden power'. (If there is no highest covering law or deepest hidden power, then the charge against physical explanations is that, though they do not run out, they do not get 'completed' either). At its best, then, the present line of argument will not show that there is something *specially* wrong with computational explanations. But, moreover, to say that computational explanations run out is not to say that they leave us with a mystery. We have the option of characterizing the basic computational operations in terms of the notion of causal sufficiency.

So, in the example above, we can say something like this: There is no *way* in which one identifies a feature. Rather, the organism is so constructed (or so conditioned, or both, depending upon the example) that exposure to a certain sort of stimulus configuration (i.e., exposure to a token of feature F) is causally sufficient for the organism coming to be in a certain intentional state (i.e., the state of taking the token to be a token of feature F). It is no objection to this move that we could have made it earlier, e.g., that we could have avoided the computational explanation entirely by saying that the answer to "how do you identify a sentence inscription" is "exposure to a token of the *sentence* is causally sufficient for the organism coming to be in a certain intentional state (i.e., the state of taking the token to be a token of that sentence)." For, if the computational theory is true, this latter causal generalization will hold only when (and only because) the causal chain that the computational theory specifies intervenes between the presentation of the sentence stimulus and its identification, namely, only when (and only because) the subject identifies the words, letters, and features that constitute the inscription. Surely, we want our science to record this fact. Or, to put the same point another way, there is (by assumption) no answer to the *how-question about features, but there is* an answer to the *how*-questions about sentences and, presumably, we want our science to answer all the *how*-questions it can. To make the move to causal sufficiency *earlier* than elementary operations is to explain less than we can explain. Why should we want to do that?

2. I can think of one other respect in which computational explanations might be held intrinsically unsatisfactory: namely, in that they fail to specify *mechanisms* for the processes that they postulate. Dennett seems sometimes to have just this in mind: "In seeking knowledge of internal design our most promising tactic is to take out intelligence-loans, endow peripheral and internal events with content, and then look for mechanisms that will function appropriately with such 'messages' so we can pay back the loans [p. 99]." Now, agreed, it would be nice to know something about the (say) neural mechanisms that execute intentional processes, but it surely is not a charge

against the *facticity* of intentional ascriptions that there exist such mechanisms. What sort of conjunction is: 'the lifting of the tumbler is the mechanism whereby the key opens the lock *and* there is no such thing as the key opening the lock'? There cannot surely, be facts about how intentional processes are executed unless there are facts about intentional processes.

Note, by the way, that it is not obvious that this goes the other way around: i.e., that there is a conceptual requirement upon intentional explanations that there should *be* a mechanism whereby the processes they postulate are carried out. I suppose that there could be angels and that, if there were, they would satisfy intentional ascriptions. But, in that possible Heaven, intentional ascription is as far as you go; the cognitive processes of angels are mediated by no mechanisms at all, so limpid are their propositional attitudes.

So to sum up (1) and (2): sure, there are limits to what computational explanations can do; but (a) not all intentional explanations *are* computational; (b) there are limits to what *any* explanation can do, and (c) it is an odd charge against the facticity of P that there are facts other than the one that makes P true. It seems to me that the case for the vacuity of intentional explanations cannot be made along the lines that Dennett is pursuing.

Still, are there propositional attitudes after all? Isn't *three* cheers going it a bit? I am not inclined to take the burden of defense much further, but there is this much that can be said briefly. No one has over developed a serious theory in cognitive psychology that was other than intentionalist through-and-through, and common-sense psychological explanation cannot get started without intentional ascription. So what we have in favor of the belief that P is both the available science and the evidence of our day-to-day experience. Sicitur ad astra; I mean: what better kinds of reasons have we for believing there are stars?

REFERENCES

Dennett, D. C. Intentional systems. *Journal of Philosophy,* 1971, *68*(4), 87–106.

Fodor, J. A. The appeal to tacit knowledge in psychological explanation. *Journal of Philosophy,* 1968, *65,* 627–640.

Fodor, J. A. The language of thought. New York: Crowell, 1975.

Fodor, J. A. Propositional attitudes. *The Monist,* 1979, in press.

Wason, P. C., & Johnson-Laird, P. N. *Psychology of reasoning: Structure and content.* Cambridge: Harvard University Press, 1972.

Author Index

Numbers in italics refer to the pages on which the complete references are listed.

Subject Index